TRADING SYSTEMS AND METHODS

Third Edition

WILEY TRADING ADVANTAGE

TRADING SYSTEMS AND METHODS

Third Edition

PERRY J. KAUFMAN

John Wiley & Sons

New York • Chichester • Weinheim • Brisbane • Singapore • Toronto

TradeStation® is a registered trademark of Omega Research, Inc.

Library of Congress Cataloging-in-Publication Data:

Kaufman, Perry J.
    Trading systems and methods / Perry J. Kaufman.—3rd ed.
        p.   cm.—(Wiley trading advantage)
    Rev. ed. of: The new commodity trading systems and methods. 1987.
    Includes bibliographical references and index.
    ISBN 0-471-14879-2 (cloth : alk. paper)
    1. Commodity exchanges—Statistical methods. I. Kaufman, Perry
J. New commodity trading systems and methods. II. Title.
III. Series.
HG6046.K34 1998
332.64'4—dc21   98-24482

Printed in the United States of America.

10 9 8 7 6 5 4 3 2 1

To Barbara, for providing dauntless support

*If you have a minute, I'll tell you how to make money in stocks.
Buy low and sell high—Now if you have five or ten years,
I'll tell you how to tell when stocks are low and high.*

JRL June, 1966

Contents

Preface to the Third Edition

CLOSING THE GAP BETWEEN EXPECTATIONS AND REALITY

It has been a remarkable 11 years since I wrote the last edition of this book. The changes that have occurred during that time are staggering, and they are reflected in new chapters, the expansion of many topics, and a thorough updating of most other areas. The ideas are no longer limited to futures markets, but are equally applicable to equities, index markets, interest rates, and foreign exchange.

Technology has had an immense impact on every phase of the financial markets, from the broadest scope of economic globalization to the most specific tools that we use when we make a trading decision. We see electronic exchanges in many countries, electronic headphones on the trading floors, Internet, and handheld quote machines. It's a tremendous leap forward since I wrote the second edition of this book; at that time, no one was sure what role the computer or technical analysis would play in the future. Now it seems certain that, to be competitive, you need to be automated in every aspect of trading.

You can't underestimate the effect of the computer on our lives. Investors, traders, analysts, and the markets themselves are in the process of change; and although these changes have come quickly, they seem natural. Many of us have adjusted to a new way of operating without actually being conscious of it happening. We now expect to receive instant price quotes from around the world; we don't expect our data feeds or our computers to fail; we find it very normal to view the price charts of the long-term interest rates in the United States, Europe, and Asia on the same screen. We can watch how a Bundesbank announcement of lower interest rates impacts the German stock market and almost instantly affects the S&P 500 and Eurodollars. These changes create ideas and opinions on how these markets interact and how we might profit from those relationships. It is much easier to see a chart of the impact of one market on another than to intellectualize the cause-and-effect situations or study the economic theory.

The greatest change of all has been in the expectations of traders and market analysts. When you look at an historic price chart it is impossible to ignore seeing how profits could have been made. Once you have seen the long trend in bond prices in the early 1990s, it is easy to believe that those profits could have been yours. If you add the new trading tools, especially the variety of testing software and intelligent quote machines, you have the ability to combine and manipulate price data, find intermarket relationships, test and monitor trading strategies, create buy and sell orders, and even execute them electronically. With all these tools and hindsight we form expectations that surpass reality.

High expectations put pressure on us to perform better. We may have missed the gold move that began in 1977 and lasted until January 1980 (which would have returned $60,000 on a $2,000 investment), but we don't expect to miss the next one. History is full of sustained trends, price shocks, and languishing periods of meandering sideways price patterns. Had we purchased crude oil during the Gulf War, the investment would have returned 1,200% during a few months. The dilemma is that these situations are only clear in retrospect; we would never have made those decisions correctly at the right time. As a consequence, investors torture themselves because they are certain that those profits were really within their reach.

Because the investor can see past opportunities and believe them to be attainable, brokerage firms and investment managers, along with the investors themselves, try to create strategies that will profit from similar situations in the future. But the big profits of the past, just as ones that will come in the future, are spectacular and unusual; they are exceptions to normal market activity. To focus on those events would be to ignore the day-to-day trading needed to yield steady returns. In the long run, if you can't trade profitably each day, or each week, you would never survive the period in between these events. You cannot compete against a perfect, imaginary adversary.

The key idea in a successful trading program is robustness, not a few large profits. An investment program must work on a broad sampling of markets, under many different conditions. This requires extensive testing using many years of historic data. There will be periods when the strategy is not successful, but a part of the problems can be corrected with diversification and asset allocation. If you concentrate on fixing a bad performance period in one market, you will have worse results in another market or at another time. Fiddling with individual profits and losses undermines the effort.

Technology, in the form of faster computers and strategy development software, gives us the ability to look at the big picture, to compare one method with another, one market with another, all test results and many years at one time. Robustness is found in the big picture, not under the microscope. The robust solution is not perfect, but it will bring success.

Just a few last words about what I have included and not included in this edition. The choices were not always easy because a lot has been written in the past 11 years. Mostly, I have expanded on the different trading systems and techniques, as you would expect. I have included many computer programs and spreadsheet code to make it easier for you to transfer these to any computer and begin your own work.

A large number of new topics have been added and all of the traditional ones have been expanded. You'll find a chapter on adaptive techniques and another on volume; seasonal methods and cycles have their own chapters; there is a short chapter on multiple time frames, and much more on advanced techniques, testing, and behavior. All the chapters have been rewritten because there have been so many changes in technology. Where applicable, system studies have been retested using current data and the computer programs used for testing have been included so that you may continue on your own. For better or worse, many of the studies and all of the opinions and conclusions in this book are entirely my own. These methods have been applied to the broader group of cash, derivatives, and equity markets.

There are some new tools, such as neural networks, that have become an entire study of their own, and there are many books devoted to that subject. Instead, you will find a general discussion and examples of how neural networks, fuzzy logic, and genetic algorithms work, and how they might help the development of a trading strategy. In some cases you can adapt your current tools to produce the same results, perhaps without the elegance of these new techniques.

Lastly, I have left some of the references to older technical works, along with their charts and examples. Not only do these valuable writings hold important information in very simple form, but they are a part of our Industry's history. Many successful techniques have strong roots in the past.

We are very fortunate that today's world markets make this an exciting time to be an investment decision maker. I hope this new edition provides a lasting resource to help you achieve greater success.

Perry J. Kaufman

Chicago
1998

Introduction

Quantitative methods for evaluating price movement and making trading decisions have become a dominant part of market analysis. At one time, the only acceptable manner of trading was by understanding the factors that make prices move, and determining the extent or potential of future movement. The market now supports dozens of major funds and managed programs, which account for a sizable part of futures market open interest and operate primarily by decisions based on "technical analysis." Stock selection, which can require sorting through thousands of individual world equities each day, has become a problem in data reduction—finding specific patterns that offer the best expectations of profit. Many commercial participants in the markets, who once restricted research to supply and demand, or institutions once only interested in earnings and debt, now include various technical methods for the purpose of "timing" or confirming price direction.

In many ways, there is no conflict between fundamental and technical analysis. The decisions that result from economic or policy changes are far-reaching; these actions may cause a long-term change in the direction of prices and may not be reflected immediately. Actions based on long-term forecasts may involve considerable risk and often can be an ineffective way to manage a position. Integrated with a technical method of known risk, which determines price trends over shorter intervals, investors at all levels have gained practical solutions to their trading problems.

Leverage in the futures markets has a strong influence on the methods of trading. With margin deposits ranging from 5 to 10% of the contract value (the balance does not have to be borrowed as in stocks), a small movement in the underlying price can result in large profits and losses based on the invested margin. Because high leverage is available, it is nearly always used. Methods of analysis will therefore concentrate on short-term price fluctuations and trends, in which the profit potential is reduced, so that the risk is often smaller than the required margin. Futures market systems can be characterized as emphasizing price moves of less than 20% of the contract value. Trading requires conservation of capital, and the management of investment risk becomes essential.

Even with the distinction forced by high leverage, many of the basic systems covered in this book were first used in the stock market. Compared with securities, the relatively small number of futures markets offer great diversification and liquidity. The relative lack of liquidity in a single stock lends itself to index analysis, whereas the "commodity" index, now tradeable as the CRB index, has never become very popular.

TECHNICAL VERSUS FUNDAMENTAL

Two basic approaches to trading futures are the same as in trading equities: fundamental and technical analysis. In futures, a fundamental study may be a composite of supply-and-demand elements: statistical reports on production, expected use, political ramifications, labor influences, price support programs, industrial development—everything that makes prices what they are. The result of a fundamental analysis is a price forecast, a prediction of where prices will be at some time in the future.

Technical analysis is a study of patterns and movement. Its elements are normally limited to price, volume, and open interest. It is considered to be the study of the market itself. The results of technical analysis may be a short- or long-term forecast based on recurring patterns; however, technical methods often limit their goals to the statement that today's prices are moving up or down. Some systems will go as far as saying the direction is indeterminate.

Due to the rapid growth of computers, technical systems now use tools previously reserved for fundamental analysis. Regression and cycle (seasonal) analysis are built into most spreadsheet programs and allow these more complex studies, which were once reserved for serious fundamental analysts, to be performed by everyone. Because they are computerized, many technicians now consider them in their own domain. There will always be purists on either side, rigid fundamentalists and technicians, but a great number of professionals combine the two techniques. This book draws on some of the more popular, automated fundamental trading approaches.

One advantage of technical analysis is that it is completely self-contained. The accuracy of the data is certain. One of the first great advocates of price analysis, Charles Dow, said:

> The market reflects all the jobber knows about the condition of the textile trade; all the banker knows about the money market; all that the best-informed president knows of his own business, together with his knowledge of all other businesses; it sees the general condition of transportation in a way that the president of no single railroad can ever see; it is better informed on crops than the farmer or even the Department of Agriculture. In fact, the market reduces to a bloodless verdict all knowledge bearing on finance, both domestic and foreign.

Much of the price movement reflected in commodity cash and futures markets is anticipatory; the expectations of the effects of economic developments. It is subject to change without notice. For example, a hurricane bound for the Philippines will send sugar prices higher, but if the storm turns off course, prices will drop back to prior levels. Major scheduled crop reports cause a multitude of professional guessing, which may correctly or incorrectly move prices just before the actual report is released. By the time the public is ready to act, the news is already reflected in the price.

PROFESSIONAL AND AMATEUR

Beginning traders often find a system or technique that seems extremely simple and convenient to follow, one that they think has been overlooked by the professionals. Sometimes they are right, but most often that method doesn't work. Reasons for not using a technique could be the inability to get a good execution, the risk/reward ratio, or the number of consecutive losses that occur. Speculation is a difficult business, not one to be taken casually. As Wyckoff said, "Most men make money in their own business and lose it in some other fellow's."

To compete with a professional speculator, you must be more accurate in anticipating the next move or in predicting prices from current news—not the article printed in today's newspaper ("Government Buys Beef for School Lunch Program"), which was discounted weeks ago, and not the one on the wire service ("15% Fewer Soybeans and 10% More Fishmeal"), which went into the market two days ago. You must act on news that has not yet been printed. To anticipate changes, you must draw a single conclusion for the many contingencies possible from fundamental data, or

1. Recognize recurring patterns in price movement and determine the most likely results of such patterns.
2. Determine the *trend* of the market by isolating the basic direction of prices over a selected time interval.

The bar chart, discussed in Chapter 9 ("Charting"), is the simplest representation of the market. These patterns are the same as those recognized by Livermore on the ticker tape. Because they are interpretive, more precise methods such as point-and-figure charting are also used, which add a level of exactness to charting. Point-and-figure charts are popular because they offer specific trading rules and show formations similar to both bar charting and ticker-tape trading.

Mathematical modeling, using traditional regression or discrete analysis, has become a popular technique for anticipating price direction. Most modeling methods are modifications of developments in econometrics, basic probability, and statistical theory. They are precise because they are based entirely on numerical data.

The proper assessment of the price trend is critical to most commodity trading systems. Countertrend trading is just as dependent on knowing the trend as a trend-following technique. Large sections of this book are devoted to the various ways to isolate the trend, although it would be an injustice to leave the reader with the idea that a *price trend* is a universally accepted concept. There have been many studies published claiming that trends, with respect to price movement, do not exist. The most authoritative papers on this topic are collected in Cootner, *The Random Character of Stock Market Prices* (MIT Press); more recent and readable discussions can often be found in *The Financial Analysts Journal,* an excellent resource.

Personal financial management has gained an enormous number of tools during this period of computerized expansion. The major spreadsheet providers include linear regression and correlation analysis; there is inexpensive software to perform spectral analysis and apply advanced statistical techniques; and development software, such as *TradeStation* and *MetaStock,* have provided trading platforms and greatly reduced the effort needed to program your ideas. The professional maintains the advantage of having all of their time to concentrate on the investment problems; however, the nonprofessional is no longer at a disadvantage because of the tools.

RANDOM WALK

It has been the position of many fundamental and economic analysis advocates that there is no sequential correlation between the direction of price movement from one day to the next. Their position is that prices will seek a level that will balance the supply-demand factors, but that this level will be reached in an unpredictable manner as prices move in an irregular response to the latest available information or news release.

If the random walk theory is correct, many well-defined trading methods based on mathematics and pattern recognition will fail. The problem is not a simple one, but one that should be resolved by each system developer, because it will influence the type of systematic approaches that will be studied. The strongest argument against the random movement supporters is one of price anticipation. One can argue academically that all participants (*the market*) know exactly where prices should move following the release of news. However practical or unlikely this is, it is not as important as market movement based on anticipation of further movement. For example, if the prime rate was raised twice in two months, would you expect it to be increased in the third month? Do you think that others will have mixed opinions, or that they assess the likelihood of another increase at different levels (i.e., one might see a 25% chance of an increase and another see a 60% chance). Unless the whole market view expectations the same way, then the price will move to reflect the majority opinion. As news alters that opinion the market will fluctuate. Is this random movement? No. Can this appear similar to random movement? Yes.

Excluding anticipation, the apparent random movement of prices depends on both the time interval and the frequency of data used. When a long time span is used, from 1 to

20 years, and the data averaged to increase the smoothing process, the trending character-istics will change, along with seasonal and cyclic variations. Technical methods, such as moving averages, are often used to isolate these price characteristics. The averaging of data into quarterly prices smooths out the irregular daily movements and results in noticeably positive correlations between successive prices. The use of daily data over a long time interval introduces noise and obscures uniform patterns.

In the long run, most futures prices find a level of equilibrium (with the exception of the stock index, which has had an upward bias) and, over some time period, show the characteristics of being *mean reverting* (returning to a local average price); however, short-term price movement can be very different from a random series of numbers. It often contains two unique properties: exceptionally long *runs* of price in a single direction, and *asymmetry*, the unequal size of moves in different directions. These are the qualities that allow traders to profit. Although the long-term trends that reflect economic policy, easily seen in the quarterly data, are not of great interest to futures traders, short-term price movements—caused by anticipation rather than actual events, extreme volatility, prices that are seen as far from value, countertrend systems that rely on mean reversion, and those that attempt to capture trends of less duration—have been successful.

It is always worthwhile to understand the theoretical aspects of price movement, because it does paint a picture of the way prices move. Many traders have been challenged by trying to identify the difference between an actual daily price chart and one created by a random number generator. There are differences, but they will seem more subtle than you would expect. The ability to identify those differences is the same as finding a way to profit from actual price movements. A trading program seeks to find ways to operate within the theoretical framework, looking for exceptions, selecting a different time frame and capture profits—and all without ignoring the fact that the theory accounts for most of the price movements.

BACKGROUND MATERIAL

The contents of this book assume an understanding of speculative markets, particularly the futures markets. Ideally the reader should have read one or more of the available trading guides, and understand the workings of a buy or sell order and the specifications of con-tracts. Experience in actual trading would be helpful. A professional trader, a broker, or a purchasing agent will already possess all the qualifications necessary. A farmer or rancher with some hedging experience will be well qualified to understand the risks involved. So is any investor who manages his or her own stock portfolio.

Literature on markets and trading systems has greatly expanded in the 11 years since the last edition of this book. During that time the most comprehensive and excellent work has been Jack Schwager's two-volume set, *Schwager on Futures* (Wiley, 1995), which includes one volume on fundamental analysis and the other on technical analysis. John Murphey's *Technical Analysis of the Futures Markets* (New York Institute of Finance, 1986) and *Intermarket Technical Analysis* (Wiley, 1991) are highly recommended. Ralph Vince published a popular work, *Portfolio Management Formulas* (Wiley, 1990), and there is Peter L. Bernstein's *The Portable MBA in Investment* (Wiley, 1995), which again provides valuable background material in readable form. There have been quite a few books on spe-cific systems and some on the development of computerized trading methods. The one comprehensive book of studies that stands out is *The Encyclopedia of Technical Market Indicators* by Robert W. Colby and Thomas A. Meyers (Dow Jones-Irwin, 1988), which offers an intelligent description of the calculation and trading performance of most market indicators oriented toward equities traders. Comparing the results of different indicators, side by side, can give you valuable insight into the practical differences in these techniques.

The basic reference book for general contract information has always been the *Commodity Trading Manual* (Chicago Board of Trade), but each year *Futures* magazine publishes a *Reference Guide*, which gives the current futures and options markets traded around the world. No doubt, all of this information will be available through Internet. For beginning or reviewing the basics, there is Todd Lofton's *Getting Started in Futures* (Wiley, 1989); Little and Rhodes, *Understanding Wall Street, Third Edition* (McGraw-Hill, 1991); and *The Stock Market, 6th Edition* by Teweles, Bradley, and Teweles (Wiley, 1992). The introductory material is not repeated here.

A good understanding of the most popular charting method requires reading the classic by Edwards and Magee, *Technical Analysis of Stock Trends* (John Magee), a comprehensive study of bar charting. Writings on other technical methods are more difficult to find. The magazine *Technical Analysis of Stocks & Commodities* stands out as the best source of regular information; *Futures* magazine has fewer technical articles, but many of value and many other commodity books express only a specific technical approach. Current analysis of many market phenomena and relationships can be found in *The Financial Analysts Journal.*

On general market lore, and to provide motivation when trading is not going as well as expected, the one book that stands out is Lefèvre's *Reminiscences of a Stock Operator* (originally published by Doran, reprinted by Wiley in 1994). Wyckoff mixes humor and philosophy in most of his books, but *Wall Street Ventures and Adventures Through Forty Years* (Harper & Brothers) may be of general interest. More recently, Jack Schwager's *Market Wizards* (New York Institute of Finance, 1989) has been very popular.

A reader with a good background in high school mathematics can follow most of this book, except in its more complex parts. An elementary course in statistics is ideal, but a knowledge of the type of probability found in Thorp's *Beat the Dealer* (Vintage) is adequate. Fortunately, computer spreadsheet programs, such as *Excel* and *Quattro,* allow anyone to use statistical techniques immediately, and most of the formulas in this book are presented in such a way that they can be easily adapted to spreadsheets. Having a computer with trading software (such as Omega's *SuperCharts, MetaStock,* or any number of products), or having a data feed (such as *Telerate* or *CQG*), which offers technical studies, you are well equipped to continue.

RESEARCH SKILLS

Before starting, a few guidelines may help make the task easier. They have been set down to help those who will use this book to develop a trading system.

1. *Know what you want to do.* Base your trading on a solid theory or observation, and keep it in focus throughout development and testing. This is called the *underlying premise* of your program.
2. *State your hypothesis or question in its simplest form.* The more complex it is, the more difficult it will be to evaluate the answer.
3. *Do not assume anything.* Many projects fail on basic assumptions that were incorrect.
4. *Do the simplest things first.* Do not combine systems before each element of each system is proven to work independently.
5. *Build one step at a time.* Go on to the next step only after the previous ones have been tested successfully. If you start with too many complex steps and fail, you will have to simplify to find out what went wrong.
6. *Be careful of errors of omission.* The most difficult part of research is identifying the components to be selected and tested. Simply because all the questions asked were satisfactorily answered does not mean that all the right questions were asked. The most important may be missing.

7. *Do not take shortcuts.* It is sometimes convenient to use the work of others to speed up the research. Check their work carefully; do not use it if it cannot be verified. Check your spreadsheet calculations manually. Remember that your answer is only as good as its weakest point.

8. *Start at the end.* Define your goal and work backward to find the required input. In this manner, you only work with information relevant to the results; otherwise, you might spend a great deal of time on irrelevant items.

OBJECTIVES OF THIS BOOK

This book is intended to give you a complete understanding of the tools and techniques needed to develop or choose a trading program that has a good chance of being successful. Execution skill and market psychology are not considered, but only the development of a system that has been carefully thought out and tested. This itself is an achievement of no small magnitude.

Not everything can be covered in a single book; therefore, some guidelines were needed to control the material included here. Most important are techniques that are common to most markets, such as trend and countertrend techniques, indicators, and testing methods. Popular analytic techniques, such as charting, are only covered to the degree that various patterns can be used in a computerized program to help identify support and resistance, channels, and so forth. There has been no attempt to provide a comprehensive text on charting. Various formations may offer very realistic profit objectives or provide reliable entry filters, even though they are not included.

Some popular areas, such as options, are not covered at all. There are many good books on options strategies, and to include them here would be a duplication of effort. Also, those strategies that use statistics, such as price/earnings ratios, specific to equities, have not been included, although indicators that use volume, even the number of advancing and declining issues, you will find in the section on volume because they fit into a bigger picture. This remains a book on trading futures markets, yet it recognizes that many methods can be used elsewhere.

This book will not attempt to prove that one system is better than another, because it is not possible to know what will happen in the future. It will try to evaluate the conditions under which certain methods are likely to do better and situations that will be harmful to specific approaches. Most helpful should be the groupings of systems and techniques, which allow a comparison of features and possible results. Seeing how analysts have modified existing ideas can help you decide how to proceed, and why you might choose one path over another. By seeing a more complete picture, it is hoped that common sense will prevail, rather than computing power.

PROFILE OF A TRADING SYSTEM

There are quite a few steps to be considered when developing a trading program. Some of these are simply choices in style that must be made, while others are essential to the success of the results. They have been listed here and discussed briefly as items to bear in mind as you continue the process of creating a trading system.

Changing Markets and System Longevity

Markets are not static. They evolve because the world changes. Among those items that have changed during the past 10 years are the market participants, the tools used to watch the market, the tools used to develop trading models, the economies of countries such as Japan, the union of European countries, the globalization of markets, and the risk of participation. Under this changing situation, a trading system that works today might not work far into the future. We must carefully consider how each feature of a trading program is affected by change and try to create a method that is as robust as possible to increase its longevity.

The Choice of Data

System decisions are limited by the data used in the analysis. Although price and volume for the specific market may be the definitive criteria, there is a multitude of other valid statistical information that might also be used. Some of this data is easily included, such as price data from related markets; other statistical data, including the U.S. economic reports and weekly energy inventories, may add a level of robustness to the results but are less convenient to obtain.

Diversification

Not all traders are interested in diversification, which tends to reduce returns at the same time that it limits risk. Concentrating all of your resources on a single market that you understand may produce a specialized approach and much better results than using a more general technique over more markets. Diversification may be gained by trading more than one method in addition to a broad set of markets, provided the programs are unique in style. Proper diversification reduces risk more than returns.

Time Frame

The time frame of the data impacts both the type of system and the nature of the results. Using 5-minute bars introduces considerable noise to your program, making it difficult to find the trend, while using only weekly data puts so much emphasis on the trend such that your trading style is already determined. A shorter time may guarantee faster response to price changes, but it does not assure better results. Each technique must be applied properly to the right data and time frame.

Choosing a Method of Analysis

Some methods of analyzing the market are more complex than others. This in itself has no bearing on the final success. All good trading methods begin with a sound premise. You must first know what you are trying to extract from the market before you select a technique. If you want to capitalize on long interest rate trends or on the result of government policy, then a weekly moving average or trend system will be the place to start. If you see false breakouts whenever price penetrates the high of the day in the second half of the trading session, you'll want to look at a momentum indicator based on 5-, 10-, or 15-minute data. First the idea, then the tool.

Trade Selection

Although a trading system produces signals regularly, it is not necessary to enter all of them. Selecting one over another can be done by a method of filtering. This can vary from a confirmation by another technique or system, a limitation on the amount of risk that can be accepted on any one trade, the use of outside information, or the current volume. Many of these add a touch of reality to an automated process. You may find, however, that too many filters result in no trading.

Testing

There has been a lot of emphasis on testing, and there is a complete discussion in this book; however, testing is most important to confirm, or validate, your ideas. It fails when you use broad tests to find successful techniques. The purpose of testing is to show robustness, that the method works over a wide range of situations in a similar manner. A robust solution will not appear to be as good as the optimal result, but performed properly, it will be a more realistic assessment of expectations.

Risk Control

Every system must control its risk, and most analysts believe that nearly any system can be profitable with proper risk management. This also means that any system can lead to ruin without risk controls. Risk can be managed from the trade level, with individual stop-losses, to asset allocation, by varying the size of the position traded, and by leveraging and deleveraging. Some form of management is necessary.

Order Entry

A system that performs well on paper may be dismal when actually traded. Part of a trading program is to know the method of entering and exiting the market and the cost of each trade. Style and cost will have a greater impact on short-term systems, which have a smaller profit per trade and are, therefore, more sensitive to transaction costs. There is equal damage in overestimating costs as there is in underestimating them. By burdening a system with unrealistic fees, it may show a loss when it should be a successful trading method.

Performance Monitoring and Feedback

A system is not done when you begin trading, it is only in a new phase. Actual trading results must be carefully monitored and compared with expectations to know if it is performing properly. It is very likely that slippage will result in some changes to the system rules or to the size of the position traded. Performance monitoring provides the essential feedback needed to be successful. Even a well thought-out and tested program may start out badly, but proper monitoring can put it on track.

A WORD ON NOTATION USED IN THIS BOOK

In attempting to make the contents of this book more practical for many readers, there are three types of notation that can be found mixed together. Of course, the standard mathematical formulas for most methods appear as they had in the previous editions. Added to that are spreadsheet examples, using Corel's *Quattro* code, which is very similar to Microsoft's *Excel*. Readers should have no trouble transferring the examples found here to their own choice of spreadsheet.

Finally there is extensive program code with examples in Omega's *Easy Language*. Although these programs have been entered and tested on *TradeStation*, there are occasional errors introduced during final editing and in transferring the code into this book. Readers are advised to check over the code and test it thoroughly before using it. In addition, there are times when only a single line of code is shown along with the standard mathematical formula to help the reader translate the technique into a more practical form. Because of the many different forms of formulas, you may find that the standard deviation function takes the spreadsheet form of *@std* rather than the *Easy Language* notation *@stddev*, or that *@avg* appears instead of *@average*. Please check these formulas for notation consistent with your needs.

2

Basic Concepts

. . . economics is not an exact science: it consists merely of Laws of Probability. The most prudent investor, therefore, is one who pursues only a general course of action which is "normally" right and who avoids acts and policies which are "normally" wrong.

L.L.B. Angas

There will come a time when we no longer will know how to do the calculation for long division, because miniature voice-activated computers will be everywhere. We might not even need to be able to add; it will all be done for us. We will just assume that it is correct, because computers don't make mistakes. In a small way this is happening now. Not everyone checks their more complicated spreadsheet calculations by hand to be certain they are correct before going further. Nor does everyone print the intermediate results of computer calculations to verify their accuracy. Computers don't make mistakes, but people do.

With computer software rapidly making technical analysis easier, we no longer think of the steps involved in a moving average or linear regression. A few years ago we used correlations only when absolutely necessary, because they were too complicated and time-consuming to calculate. It would even be difficult to know if you had made a mistake without having someone else repeat the same calculations. Now we face a different problem—if the computer does it all, we lose our understanding of *why* a moving average trendline differs from a linear regression. Without looking at the data, we don't see an erroneous outlier. By not reviewing each hypothetical trade, we miss seeing that the slippage can turn a profit into a loss.

To avoid losing the edge needed to create a profitable trading strategy, the basic tools of the trade are explained in this chapter. Those of you already familiar with these methods may skip over it; others should consider it essential that they be able to perform these calculations manually.

ABOUT DATA AND AVERAGING

The Law of Averages

The *law of averages* is a greatly misunderstood and misquoted principle. It's most often referred to when an abnormally long series of losses is expected to be offset by an equal and opposite run of profits. It is equally wrong to expect a market that is currently overbought to next become oversold. That is not what is meant by the law of averages. Over a large sample, the bulk of events will be scattered close to the average in such a way as to overwhelm an abnormal set of events and cause them to be insignificant.

This principle is illustrated in Figure 2-1, where the addition of a small abnormal grouping to one side of a balanced group of near-normal data does not affect the balance. A long run of profits, losses, or price movement is simply abnormal and will be offset over time by the large number of normal events. Further discussion can be found in "The Theory of Runs" (Chapter 22).

Bias in Data

When sampling is used to obtain data, it is common to divide entire subsets of data into discrete parts and attempt a representative sampling of each portion. These samples are then weighted to reflect the perceived impact of each part on the whole. Such a weighting will magnify or reduce the errors in each of the discrete sections. The result of such weighting may cause an *error in bias*. Even large numbers within a sample cannot overcome intentional bias introduced by weighting one or more parts.

Price analysis and trading techniques often introduce bias in both implicit and explicit ways. A *weighted average* is an overt way of adding a positive bias (positive because it is intentional). On the other hand, the use of two analytic methods acting together may unknowingly rely doubly on one statistical aspect of the data; at the same time, other data may be used only once or may be eliminated by offsetting use. The daily high and low used in one part of a program and the daily range (high to low) in another section would introduce bias.

How Much Data Is Enough?

Technical analysis is fortunate to be based on a perfect set of data. Each price that is recorded by the exchange is exact and reflects the netting out of all information at that moment. Most other statistical data, although it might appear to be very specific, are normally an *average* value, which can represent a broad range of numbers, all of them either larger or smaller. The average price received by all farmers for corn on the 15th of the month cannot be the exact number. The price of Eurodollars at 10:05 in Chicago is the exact and only price.

When an average is used, it is necessary to collect enough data to make that average accurate. Because much statistical data is gathered by sampling, particular care is given to accumulating a sufficient amount of representative data. This will hold true with prices as well. Averaging a few prices, or analyzing small market moves, will show more erratic results. It is difficult to draw an accurate picture from a very small sample.

When using small, incomplete, or representative sets of data, the approximate error, or accuracy, of the sample should be known. This can be found by using the standard deviation as discussed in the previous section. A large standard deviation means an extremely scattered set of points, which in turn makes the average less representative of the data. This process is called the *testing of significance*. The most basic of these tests is the error resulting from a small amount of data. Accuracy usually increases as the number of items becomes larger, and the measurement of deviation or error will become proportionately smaller.

$$\text{Error} = \frac{1}{\sqrt{\text{number of items sampled}}} = \frac{1}{\sqrt{N}} \text{ or } 1/@sqrt(N)$$

FIGURE 2-1   The law of averages. The normal cases overwhelm the unusual ones. It is not necessary for the extreme cases to alternate—one higher, then the other lower—to create a balance.

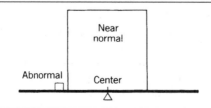

Therefore, using only one item has an error factor of 100%; with four items, the error is 50%. The size of the error is important to the reliability of any trading system. If a system has had only 4 trades, whether profits or losses, it is very difficult to draw any conclusions about performance expectations. There must be sufficient trades to assure a comfortably small error factor. To reduce the error to 5%, there must be 400 trades, which presents a dilemma for a very slow trend-following method that may only generate 2 or 3 trades each year. To compensate for this, the identical method can be applied to many markets and the sample of trades used collectively. By keeping the sample error small, the risk of trading can be better understood.

ON THE AVERAGE

In discussing numbers, it is often necessary to use representative values. The *range of values* or the *average* may be substituted to change a single price into a general characteristic to solve a problem. The average (*arithmetic mean*) of many values can be a preferable substitute for any one value. For example, the average retail price of one pound of coffee in the northeast is more meaningful to a cost-of-living calculation than the price at any one store. However, not all data can be combined or averaged and still have meaning. The average of all futures prices taken on the same day would not say anything about an individual market that was part of the average. The price changes in copper, corn, and the German DAX index, for example, would have little to do with one another. The average of a group of values must meaningfully represent the individual items.

The average can be misleading in other ways. Consider coffee, which rose from 40¢ to $2.00 per pound in one year. The average price of this product may appear to be $1.40; however, this would not account for the time that coffee spent at various price levels. Table 2-1 divides the coffee move into four equal price intervals, then shows that the time intervals spent at these levels were uniformly opposite to the price rise. That is, price remained at lower levels longer, and at higher levels for shorter time periods, which is very normal price behavior.

When the time spent at each price level is included, it can be seen that the average price should be lower than $1.40. One way to calculate this, knowing the specific number of days in each interval, is by using a weighted average of the price and its respective interval

$$W = \frac{a_1 d_1 + a_2 d_2 + a_3 d_3 + a_4 d_4}{d_1 + d_2 + d_3 + d_4}$$

$$W = 105$$

$$W = \frac{6000 + 8000 + 8400 + 7200}{280}$$

TABLE 2-1   Weighting an Average

Prices Go		Average	Total Days		
From	To	during Interval	for Interval	Weighted	1/a
40	80	$a_1 = 60$	$d_1 = 100$	6,000	.01666
80	120	$a_2 = 100$	$d_2 = 80$	8,000	.01000
120	160	$a_3 = 140$	$d_3 = 60$	8,400	.00714
160	200	$a_4 = 180$	$d_4 = 40$	7,200	.00555

Although this is not exact because of the use of average prices for intervals, it does closely represent the *average price relative to time*. There are two other averages for which time is an important element—the *geometric* and *harmonic means*.

Geometric Mean

The geometric mean represents a growth function in which a price change from 50 to 100 is as important as a change from 100 to 200.

$$G = (a_1 \times a_2 \times a_3 \times \cdots \times a_n)^{(1/n)} \text{ or @mult(list)} \char`\^ \text{ (1/length of list)}$$

To solve this mathematically, rather than using a spreadsheet, the preceding equation can be changed to either of two forms:

$$\ln G = \frac{\ln a_1 + \ln a_2 + \cdots + \ln a_n}{n}$$

or

$$\ln G = \frac{\ln (a_1 \times a_2 \times a_3 \times \cdots \times a_n)}{n}$$

The two solutions are equivalent. Using the price levels in Table 2-1, disregarding the time intervals, and substituting into the first equation:

$$\ln G = \frac{\ln 40 + \ln 80 + \ln 120 + \ln 160 + \ln 200}{5}$$

Had one of the periods been a loss, that value would simply be negative. We now perform the arithmetic to solve the equation:

$$\ln G = \frac{3.689 + 4.382 + 4.787 + 5.075 + 5.298}{5}$$

$$\ln G = 4.6462$$

$$G = 104.19$$

The geometric mean has advantages in application to economics and prices. A classic example is to compare a tenfold rise in price from 100 to 1,000 with a fall to one-tenth from 100 to 10. An arithmetic mean of 10 and 1,000 is 505, while the geometric mean gives

$$G = (10 \times 1000)^{(1/2)} = 100$$

which shows the relative distribution as a function of comparable growth. Due to this property, the geometric mean is the best choice when averaging ratios that can be either fractions or percentages.

Quadratic Mean

The quadratic mean is as calculated:

$$Q = \sqrt{\frac{\sum a^2}{N}} \text{ or @sqrt(@sum(list of } a^2\text{)/length of list)}$$

The square root of the mean of the square of the items (root-mean-square) is most well known as the basis for the *standard deviation*. This will be discussed later, in the section "Dispersion and Skewness."

Harmonic Mean

The harmonic mean is more of a time-weighted average, not biased toward higher or lower values as in the geometric mean. A simple example is to consider the average speed of a car that travels 4 miles at 20 mph, then 4 miles at 30 mph. An arithmetic mean would result in 25 mph, without considering that 12 minutes were spent at 20 mph and 8 minutes at 30 mph. The weighted average would give

$$W = \frac{(12 \times 20) + (8 \times 30)}{12 + 8} = 24$$

The harmonic mean is

$$\frac{1}{H} = \frac{\dfrac{1}{a_1} + \dfrac{1}{a_2} + \cdots + \dfrac{1}{a_n}}{n}$$

which can also be expressed as

$$H = n/\sum_{1}^{n} \left(\frac{1}{a_i}\right) \text{ or length of list/@sum(list of } 1/a)$$

For two or three elements, the simpler forms can be used:

$$H_2 = \frac{2ab}{a + b} \qquad H_3 = \frac{3abc}{ab + ac + bc}$$

This allows the solution pattern to be seen. For the 20 and 30 mph rates of speed, the solution is

$$H_2 = \frac{2 \times 20 \times 30}{20 + 30} = 24$$

which is the same answer as the weighted average. Considering the original set of numbers again, the basic form of harmonic mean can be applied:

$$\frac{1}{H} = \frac{\dfrac{1}{40} + \dfrac{1}{80} + \dfrac{1}{120} + \dfrac{1}{160} + \dfrac{1}{200}}{5}$$

$$= \frac{.05708}{5} = .01142$$

$$H = 87.59$$

We might apply the harmonic mean to price swings, in which the first swing moved 20 points over 12 days, and the second swing moved 30 points over 8 days.

DISTRIBUTION

The measurement of distribution is very important because it tells you generally what to expect. We cannot know what tomorrow's S&P trading range will be, but we have a high level of confidence that it will fall between 300 and 800 points. We have a slightly lower confidence that it will vary from 400 to 600 points. We have virtually no chance of picking the exact range. The following measurements of distribution allow you to put a value on the chance of an event occurring.

Frequency Distributions

The *frequency distribution* can give a good picture of the characteristics of the data. To know how often sugar prices were at different price levels, divide prices into 10 increments (e.g., 5.01 to 6.00, 6.01 to 7.00, etc.), and count the number of times that prices fall into each interval. The result will be a distribution of prices as shown in Figure 2-2. It should be expected that the distribution of prices for a physical commodity, interest rates (yield), or index markets, will be *skewed* toward the left-hand side (lower prices or yields) and have a *long* tail toward higher prices on the right-hand side. This is because prices remain at higher levels for only a short time relative to their long-term characteristics. Commodity prices tend to be bounded on the lower end, limited in their downside movement, by production costs and resistance of the suppliers to sell at prices that represent a loss. On the higher end, there is not such a clear point of limitation; therefore, prices move much further up during periods of extreme shortage relative to demand.

The measures of *central tendency* discussed in the previous section are used to qualify the shape and extremes of price movement shown in the frequency distribution. The general relationship between the results when using the three principal means is

arithmetic mean > geometric mean > harmonic mean

Median and Mode

Two other measurements, the *median* and the *mode,* are often used to define distribution. The median, or middle item, is helpful for establishing the center of the data; it halves the number of data items. The median has the advantage of discounting extreme values, which might distort the arithmetic mean. The mode is the *most commonly occurring value.* In Figure 2-3 the mode is the highest point.

In a normally distributed price series, the mean, median, and mode will all occur at the same value; however, as the data become skewed, these values will move farther apart. The general relationship is:

FIGURE 2-2   Hypothetical price-frequency distribution.

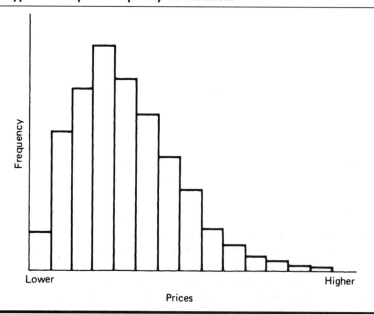

FIGURE 2-3   **Hypothetical price distribution skewed to the right, showing the relationship of the mode, median, and mean.**

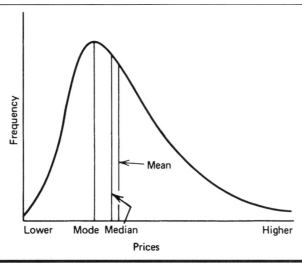

mean > median > mode

The mean, median, and mode help to tell whether data is normally distributed or skewed. A normal distribution is commonly called a bell curve, and values fall equally on both sides of the mean. For much of the work done with price and performance data, the distributions tend to extend out toward the right (positive values) and be more cut off on the left (negative values). If you were to chart a distribution of trading profits and losses based on a trend system with a fixed stop-loss, you would get profits that could range from zero to very large values, while the losses would be theoretically limited to the size of the stop. Skewed distributions will be important when we try to measure the probabilities later in this chapter.

Characteristics of the Principal Averages

Each averaging method has its unique meaning and usefulness. The following summary points out their principal characteristics:

The *arithmetic mean* is affected by each data element equally, but it has a tendency to emphasize extreme values more than other methods. It is easily calculated and is subject to algebraic manipulation.

The *geometric mean* gives less weight to extreme variations than the arithmetic mean and is most important when using data representing ratios or rates of change. It cannot always be used for a combination of positive and negative numbers and is also subject to algebraic manipulation.

The *harmonic mean* is most applicable to time changes and, along with the geometric mean, has been used in economics for price analysis. The added complications of computation have caused this to be less popular than either of the other averages, although it is also capable of algebraic manipulation.

The *mode* is not affected by the size of the variations from the average, only the distribution. It is the location of greatest concentration and indicates a typical value for a reasonably large sample. With an unordered set of data, the mode is time consuming to locate and is not capable of algebraic manipulation.

The *median* is most useful when the center of an incomplete set is needed. It is not affected by extreme variations and is simple to find if the number of data points are known. Although it has some arithmetic properties, it is not readily adaptable to computational methods.

DISPERSION AND SKEWNESS

The center or central tendency of a data series is not a sufficient description for price analysis. The manner in which it is scattered about a given point, its *dispersion* and *skewness*, are necessary to describe the data. The *mean deviation* is a basic method for measuring distribution and may be calculated about any measure of central location, for example, the arithmetic mean. It is found by computing

$$MD = \frac{\sum \left| price_i - \sum \frac{price_j}{n} \right|}{n} \qquad \text{or} \qquad @Avg(@AbsValue(price - @Avg(price,n)),n)$$

where *MD* is the mean deviation, the average of the differences between each price and the arithmetic mean of the prices, or other measure of central location, with *signs ignored*.

The *standard deviation* is a special form of measuring average deviation from the mean, which uses the root-mean-square

$$\text{Standard deviation} = \sqrt{\frac{\sum \left(price_i - \sum \frac{price_j}{n} \right)^2}{n}} \qquad \text{or}$$

$$= @Sqrt(@Avg((price - @Avg(price,n))^2,n))$$

where the differences between the individual prices and the mean are squared to emphasize the significance of extreme values, and then total final value is scaled back using the square root function. This popular measure, found throughout this book, is available in all spreadsheets and software programs as @Std or @Stdev. For *n* prices, the standard deviation is simply @Std(price,n).

The standard deviation is the most popular way of measuring the degree of dispersion of the data. The value of one standard deviation about the mean represents a clustering of about 68% of the data, two standard deviations from the mean include 95.5% of all data, and three standard deviations encompass 99.7%, nearly all the data. These values represent the groupings of a perfectly *normal* set of data, shown in Figure 2-4.

Probability of Achieving a Return

If we look at Figure 2-4 as the annual returns for the stock market over the past 50 years, then the mean is about 8% and one standard deviation is 16%. In any one year we can expect the compounded rate of return to be 8%; however, there is a 32% chance that it will be either greater than 24% (mean plus one standard deviation) or less than −8% (the mean minus one standard deviation). If you would like to know the probability of a return of 20% or greater, you must first rescale the values,

$$\text{Probability of reaching objective} = \frac{\text{objective} - \text{mean}}{\text{standard deviation}}$$

If your objective is 20%, we calculate

$$\text{Probability} = \frac{20\% - 8\%}{16\%} = .75$$

FIGURE 2-4 Normal distribution showing the percentage area included within one standard deviation about the arithmetic mean.

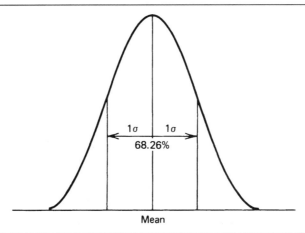

We look in Appendix A1 under the probability for normal curves, and find that a standard deviation of .75 gives 27.34%, a grouping of 54.68% of the data. That leaves one-half of the remaining data, or 22.66%, above the target of 20%.

Skewness

Most price data, however, are not normally distributed. For physical commodities, such as gold, grains, and interest rates (yield), prices tend to spend more time at low levels and much less time at extreme highs; while gold peaked at $800 per ounce for one day, it has remained between $375 and $400 per ounce for most of the past 10 years. The possibility of falling below $400 by the same amount as its rise to $800 is impossible, unless you believe that gold can go to zero. This relationship of price versus time, in which markets spend more time at lower levels, can be measured as *skewness*—the amount of distortion from a symmetric shape that makes the curve appear to be short on one side and extended on the other. In a perfectly normal distribution, the median and mode coincide. As prices become extremely high, which often happens for short intervals of time, the *mean* will show the greatest change and the *mode* will show the least. The difference between the mean and the mode, adjusted for dispersion using the standard deviation of the distribution, gives a good measure of skewness

$$(\text{Skewness}) \ S_K = \frac{\text{mean} - \text{mode}}{\text{standard deviation}}$$

Because the distance between the mean and the mode, in a moderately skewed distribution, is three times the distance between the mean and the median, the relationship can also be written as:

$$(\text{Skewness}) \ S_K = \frac{3 \times (\text{mean} - \text{median})}{\text{standard deviation}}$$

This last formula may be more practical for computer applications, because the mode requires dividing the data into groups and counting the number of occurrences in each bar. When interpreting the value of S_K, the distribution leans to the right when S_K is positive (the mean is greater than the median), and it is skewed left when S_K is negative.

Kurtosis

One last measurement, that of *kurtosis,* should be familiar to analysts. Kurtosis is the "peakedness" of a distribution, the analysis of "central tendency." For most cases a smaller standard deviation means that prices are clustered closer together; however, this does not always describe the distribution clearly. Because so much of identifying a trend comes down to deciding whether a price change is normal or likely to be a leading indicator of a new direction, deciding whether prices are closely grouped or broadly distributed may be useful. Kurtosis measures the height of the distribution.

Transformations

The skewness of a data series can sometimes be corrected using a *transformation* on the data. Price data may be skewed in a specific pattern. For example, if there are ¼ of the occurrences at twice the price and ⅑ of the occurrences at three times the price, the original data can be transformed into a normal distribution by taking the square root of each data item. The characteristics of price data often show a logarithmic, power, or square-root relationship.

Skewness in Price Distributions

Because the lower price levels of most commodities are determined by production costs, price distributions show a clear boundary of resistance in that direction. At the high levels, prices can have a very long tail of low frequency. Figure 2-5 shows the change in the distribution of prices as the mean price (over shorter intervals) changes. This pattern indicates that a normal distribution is not appropriate for commodity prices, and that a log distribution would only apply to overall long-term distributions.

Choosing between Frequency Distribution and Standard Deviation

You should note that it is more likely that unreliable probabilities will result from using too little data than from the choice of method. For example, we might choose to look at the distribution of one month of daily data, about 23 days; however, it is not much of a sample. The price or equity changes being measured might be completely different during the next month. Even the most recent five years of S&P data will not show a drop as large as October 1987.

FIGURE 2-5   Changing distribution at different price levels. A, B, and C are increasing mean values of three shorter-term distributions.

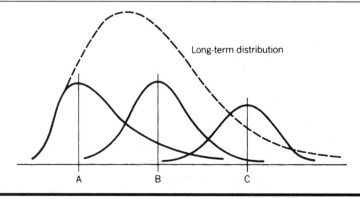

Although we can identify and measure skewness, it is difficult to get meaningful probabilities using a standard deviation taken on very distorted distributions. It is simpler to use a frequency distribution for data with long tails on one side and truncated results on the other. To find the likelihood of returns using a trend system with a stop-loss, you can simply sort the data in ascending order using a spreadsheet, then count from each end to find the extremes. You will notice that the largest 10% of the profits cover a wide range, while the largest 10% of the losses is clustered together.

A standard deviation is very helpful for giving some indication that a price move, larger than any we have seen in the data, is possible. Because it assumes a normally shaped curve, a large clustering of data toward one end will force the curve to extend further. Although the usefulness of the exact probabilities is questionable, there is no doubt that, given enough time, we will see price moves, profits, and losses that are larger than we have seen in the past.

Student t-test

Throughout the development and testing of a trading system, we will want to know if the results we are seeing are as expected. The answer will keep referring back to the size of the sample and the amount of variance that is typical of the data during this period. Readers are encouraged to refer to other sections in the book on *sample error* and *chi-square test*. Another popular method for measuring whether the average price of the data is significantly different from zero, that is, if there is an underlying trend bias or if the pattern exhibits random qualities, is the *student t-test*,

$$t = \frac{\text{average of price changes}}{\text{standard deviation of price changes}} \times \sqrt{\text{No. of data items}}$$

and where *degrees of freedom = number of data items* − 1. The more trades in the sample, the more reliable the results. The values of *t* needed to be *significant* can be found in Appendix 1, Table A1.2, "*T*-Distribution." The column headed ".10" gives the 90% confidence level, ".05" is 95%, and ".005" is 99.5% confidence.

If we separate data into two periods and compare the average of the two periods for consistency, we can decide whether the data has changed significantly. This is done with a 2-sample *t*-test:

$$t = \frac{\overline{x}_1 - \overline{x}_2}{\sqrt{\dfrac{v_1^2}{n_1} + \dfrac{v_2^2}{n_2}}}$$

where $\overline{x}_1$ and $\overline{x}_2$ are the averages of data periods 1 and 2, v_1 and v_2 are the variances of periods 1 and 2, and n_1 and n_2 are the number of data items in periods 1 and 2. The degrees of freedom, *df*, needed to find the confidence levels in Table A1-2, can be calculated as:

$$df = \frac{\left(\dfrac{s_1^2}{n_1} + \dfrac{s_2^2}{n_2}\right)^2}{\dfrac{\left(\dfrac{s_1^2}{n_1}\right)^2}{(n_1 - n_2)} + \dfrac{\left(\dfrac{s_2^2}{n_2}\right)^2}{(n_2 - n_1)}}$$

The student *t*-test can also be used to compare the profits and losses generated by a trading system to show that the underlying system process is sound. Simply replace the data items by the average profit or loss of the system, the number of data items by the number of trades, and calculate all other values using the profit/loss to get the student t-test value for the trading performance.

STANDARDIZING RETURNS AND RISK

To compare one trading method with another, it is necessary to standardize both the tests and the measurements used for evaluation. If one system has total returns of 50% and the other of 250%, we cannot decide which is best unless we know the duration of the test. If the 50% return was over 1 year and the 250% return over 10 years, then the first one is best. Similarly, the return relative to the risk is crucial to performance as will be discussed in Chapter 21 ("Testing"). For now it is only important that returns and risk be annualized or standardized to make comparisons valid.

Calculating Returns

The calculation of *rate of return* is essential for assessing performance as well as for many arbitrage situations. In its simplest form, the *one-period rate of return R,* or the *holding period rate of return* is

$$\text{Return} = \frac{\text{Ending value} - \text{Starting value}}{\text{Starting value}} = \frac{\text{Ending value}}{\text{Starting value}} - 1$$

$$R = \frac{P_1 - P_0}{P_0} = \frac{P_1}{P_0} - 1$$

where P_0 is the initial investment or starting value, and P_1 is the value of the investment after one period. In most cases, it is desirable to standardize the returns by *annualizing.* This is particularly helpful when comparing two sets of test results, in which each covers a different time period. Although calculations on government instruments use a 360-day rate (based on 90-day quarters), a 365-day rate is common for most other purposes. The following formulas show 365 days; however, 360 may be substituted.

The *annualized rate of return on a simple-interest basis* for an investment over n days is

$$R_{\text{simple}} = \frac{P_1 - P_0}{P_0} \times \frac{365}{n}$$

The *annualized compounded rate of return* is

$$R_{\text{compounded}} = \left(1 + \frac{P_n - P_0}{P_0}\right)^{(365/n)}$$

The geometric mean is the basis for the compounded growth associated with interest rates. If the initial investment is \$1,000 (P_0) and the ending value is \$1,600 (P_y) after 12 years ($y = 12$), there has been an increase of 60%. The simple rate of return is 5%, but the compounded growth shows

Ending value = Starting value $\times$ (1 + Compounded return)^y

$$P_y = P_0 \times (1 + R)^y$$

or

$$R = \left(\frac{P_y}{P_0}\right)^{(1/y)} - 1$$

$$R = \left(\frac{1600}{1000}\right)^{(1/12)} - 1$$

$$R = .0398 \text{ or about } 4.0\%$$

The use of the standard deviation and compounded rate of return are combined to find the probability of a return objective. In the following calculation,[1] the arithmetic mean of continuous returns is $\ln(1 + R_g)$, and it is assumed that the returns are normally distributed.

$$z = \frac{\ln\left(\dfrac{T}{B}\right) - \ln(1 + R_g)n}{\sqrt{s \times n}}$$

where z = standardized variable (can be looked up in Appendix A1)
  T = target value or rate-of-return objective
  B = beginning investment value
  R_g = geometric average of periodic returns
  n = number of periods
  s = standard deviation of the logarithms of the quantities 1 plus the periodic returns

Indexing Returns

The Federal Government has defined standards for calculating returns in the Futures Industry Commodity Trading Advisors (CTAs). This is simply an indexing of returns based on the current period percentage change in equity. It is the same process as creating any index, and it allows trading returns to be compared with, for example, the S&P Index or the Lehman Brothers Treasury Index, on equal footing. Readers should refer to the section later in this chapter, "Constructing an Index."

Calculating Risk

Although we would always like to think about returns, it is even more important to be able to assess risk. With that in mind, there are two types of risk that are important for very different reasons. The first is catastrophic risk, which will cause fatal losses or ruin. This is a complicated type of risk, because it may be the result of a single price shock or a steady deterioration of equity by being overleveraged. This form of risk will be discussed in detail later in the book.

Standard risk measurements are useful for comparing the performance of two systems and for understanding how someone else might evaluate your own equity profile. The simplest estimate of risk is the variance of equity over a time interval commonly used by most investment managers. To calculate the variance, it is first necessary to find the mean return, or the expected return, on an investment:

$$E(R) = p_1 R_1 + p_2 R_2 + \cdots + p_n R_n$$

The most common measure of risk is *variance,* calculated by squaring the deviation of each return from the mean, then multiplying each value by its associated probability.

$$\text{variance} = \sum_{i=1}^{n} p_i R_i$$

The sum of these values is called the variance, and the square root of the variance is called the standard deviation. This was given in another form in the early section "Dispersion and Skewness."

$$\text{standard deviation} = \sqrt{p_1[R_1 - E(R)]^2 + p_2[R_2 - E(R)]^2 + \cdots + p_n[R_n - E(R)]^2}$$

$$= \sqrt{\sum_{i=1}^{n} p_i[R_i - E(R)]^2}$$

[1] This and other very clear explanations of returns can be found in Peter L. Bernstein's *The Portable MBA in Investment* (John Wiley & Sons, New York, 1995).

The greater the standard deviation of returns, the greater the risk. In the securities industry, annual returns are most common, but monthly returns may be used if there are not enough years of data. There is no clear way to infer annual returns from monthly returns.

Downside Risk

Downside equity movements are often more important than profit patterns. It seems sensible that, if you want to know the probability of a loss, then you should study the history of equity drawdowns. The use of only the equity losses is called *lower partial moments,* in which *lower* refers to the downside risk and *partial* means that only one side of the return distribution is used. A set of relative lower partial moments (RLPMs) is the expected value of the tracking error (equity drawdowns, the difference between the actual equity and the annualized returns) raised to the power of *n:*

$$\text{RLPM}_n = E[(R - B)^n], \qquad \text{over the range where } R < B$$
$$= 0, \qquad \text{over the range where } R \geq B$$

where R = return on investment
B = benchmark or corresponding regression return at that point in time
E = expected or mean return (described at the beginning of this section)

Therefore, the elements of the probability have only losses or zeros. The value n represents the order or ranking of the RLPMs. When $n = 0$, RLPM is the probability of a shortfall, Probability $(R < B)$; when $n = 1$, RLPM is equal to the expected shortfall, $E[R - B]$; and when $n = 2$, RLPM is equal to the relative lower partial variance.

One concern about using only the drawdowns to predict other drawdowns is that it limits the number of cases and discards the likelihood that higher than normal profits can be related to higher overall risk. In situations where there are limited amounts of test data, both the gains and losses will offer needed information.

THE INDEX

The purpose of an average is to transform individuality into classification. When done properly, there is useful information to be gained. Indices have gained popularity in the futures markets recently; the stock market indices are now second to the financial markets in trading volume. These contracts allow both individual and institutional participants to invest in the overall market movement rather than take the higher risk of selecting individual securities. Furthermore, investors can hedge their current market position by taking a short position in the futures market against a long position in the stock market.

A less general index, the Dow Jones Industrials, or a grain or livestock index can help the trader take advantage of a more specific price without having to decide which products are more likely to do best. An index simplifies the decision-making process for trading. If an index does not exist, it can be constructed to satisfy most purposes.

Constructing an Index

An index is traditionally used to determine relative value and normally expresses change as a percentage. Most indices have a starting value of 100 or 1,000 on a specific date. The index itself is a ratio of the current or composite values to those values during the base year. The selection of the base year is often chosen for convenience, but usually is far enough back to show a representative, stable price period. The base year for U.S. productivity and for unemployment is 1982, consumer confidence is 1985, and the composite of leading indicators is 1987. For example, for one market, the index for a specific year is

$$\text{Index (year } t) = \frac{\text{current price (year } t)}{\text{starting price (base year)}} \times 100$$

If the value of the index is less than 100, the current value (year t) is lower than during the base year. The actual index value represents the percentage change.

For each year after the base year, the index value is the sum of the previous index value and the percentage change in price over the same period,

$$\text{current index value} = \text{previous index value} + \frac{\text{current price}}{\text{previous price}} - 1$$

It is very convenient to create an index for two markets that trade in different units because they cannot be otherwise compared. For example, if you wanted to show the spread between gold and the U.S. Dollar Index, you could index them both beginning at the same date. The new indices would both be in the same units, percent, and would be easy to compare.

Most often, an index combines a number of related markets into a single number. A *simple aggregate index* is the ratio of unweighted sums of market prices in a specific year to the same markets in the base year. Most of the popular indices, such as the New York Stock Exchange Composite Index, fall into this class. A *weighted aggregate index* biases certain markets by weighting them to increase or decrease their effect on the composite value. The index is then calculated as in the simple aggregate index. When combining markets into a single index value, the total of all the weighting normally totals to the value one, although you may also divide the composite value by the total of all the individual weights.

U.S. Dollar Index

A practical example of a weighted index is the U.S. Dollar Index, traded on the New York Futures Exchange. In order of greatest weighting, the 10 currency components are the Deutschemark 20.8%, Japanese yen 13.6%, French franc 13.1%, British pound 11.9%, Canadian dollar 9.1%, Italian lira 9.0%, Netherlands guilder 8.3%, Belgian franc 6.4%, Swedish kroner 4.2%, and the Swiss franc 3.6%. This puts a total weight of 75.5% in European currencies with only the Japanese yen representing Asia, not a practical mix for a world economy that has become dependent on Far Eastern trade. Within Europe, however, allocations seem to be proportional to the relative size of the economies.

The Dollar Index rises when the U.S. dollar rises. Quotes are in foreign exchange notation, where there are 1.25 Swiss francs per U.S. dollar, instead of .80 dollars per franc as quoted on the Chicago Mercantile Exchange's IMM. For example, when the Swiss franc moves from 1.25 to 1.30 per dollar, there are more Swiss francs per dollar; therefore, each Swiss franc is worth less.

In the daily calculation of the Dollar Index, each price change is represented as a percent. If, in our previous example, the Swiss franc rises .05 points, the change is 5/125 = .04; this is multiplied by its weighting factor .208 and contributes +.00832 to the Index.

PROBABILITY

Calculation must measure the incalculable.

Dixon G. Watts

Change is a term that causes great anxiety. However, the effects and likelihood of a chance occurrence can be measured, although not predicted. The area of study that deals with uncertainty is *probability*. Everyone uses probability in daily thinking and actions. When you tell someone that you will be there in 30 minutes, you are assuming:

Your car will start.

You will not have a breakdown.

You will have no unnecessary delays.

You will drive at a predictable speed.

You will have the normal number of green lights.

All these circumstances are extremely probabilistic, and yet everyone makes the same assumptions. Actually, the 30-minute arrival is intended only as an estimate of the average time it should take for the trip. If the arrival time were critical, you would extend your estimate to 40 or 45 minutes, to account for unexpected events. In statistics, this is called *increasing the confidence interval.* You would not raise the time to 2 hours, because the likelihood of such a delay would be too remote. Estimates imply an allowable variation, all of which is considered normal.

Probability is the measuring of the uncertainty surrounding an average value. Probabilities are measured in percent of likelihood. For example, if M numbers from a total of N are expected to fall within a specific range, the probability P of any one number satisfying the criteria is

$$P = \frac{M}{N}, \qquad 0 < P < 1$$

When making a trade, or forecasting prices, we can only talk in terms of probabilities or ranges. We expect prices to rise 30 to 40 points, or we have a 65% chance of a $400 profit from a trade. Nothing is certain, but a high probability of success is very attractive.

Laws of Probability

Two basic principles in probability are easily explained by using examples with playing cards. In a deck of 52 cards, there are 4 suits of 13 cards each. The probability of drawing a specific card on any one turn is $\frac{1}{52}$. Similarly, the chances of drawing a particular suit or card number are $\frac{1}{4}$ and $\frac{1}{13}$, respectively. *The probability of any one of these three possibilities occurring is the sum of their individual probabilities.* This is known as the *law of addition.* The probability of success in choosing a numbered card, suit, or specific card is

$$P = \frac{1}{13} + \frac{1}{4} + \frac{1}{52} = \frac{18}{52} = 35\%$$

Another basic principle, the *law of multiplications,* states that the *probability of two occurrences happening simultaneously or in succession is equal to the product of their separate probabilities.* The likelihood of drawing a three and a club from the same deck in two consecutive turns (replacing the card after each draw) or of drawing the same cards from two decks simultaneously is

$$P = \frac{1}{13} \times \frac{1}{4} = \frac{1}{52} = 2\%$$

Joint and Marginal Probability

Price movement is not as clearly defined as a deck of cards. There is often a relationship between successive events. For example, over two consecutive days, prices must have one of the following sequences or *joint events:* (up, up), (down, down), (up, down), (down, up), with the *joint probabilities* of .40, .10, .35, and .15, respectively. In this example, there is the greatest expectation that prices will rise. The *marginal probability* of a price rise on the first day is shown in Table 2-2. Thus there is a 75% chance of higher prices on the first day and a 55% chance of higher prices on the second day.

Contingent Probability

What is the probability of an outcome contingent on the result of a prior event? In the example of joint probability, this might be the chance of a price increase on the second day

TABLE 2-2   Marginal Probability

		Day 2 Up	Day 2 Down			
Day 1	Up	.40	.35	.75	Up	Marginal Probability on Day 1
	Down	.15	.10	.25	Down	
		.55	.45			
		Up	Down			

Marginal Probability
on Day 2

when prices declined on the first day. The notation for this situation (the probability of A conditioned on B) is

$$P(A|B) = \frac{P(A \text{ and } B)}{P(B)} = \frac{\text{joint probability of } A \text{ and } B}{\text{marginal probability of } B}$$

then

$$P(\text{up Day 2}|\text{down Day 1}) = \frac{\text{joint probability of (down, up)}}{\text{marginal probability of (down Day 1)}}$$

$$= \frac{.15}{.25} = .60$$

The probability of either a price increase on Day 1 or a price increase on Day 2 is

$$P(\text{either}) = P(\text{up Day 1}) + P(\text{up Day 2}) - P(\text{up Day 1 and up Day 2})$$

$$= .75 + .55 - .40$$

$$= .90$$

Markov Chains

If we believe that today's price movement is based in some part on what happened yesterday, we have a situation called *conditional probability*. This can be expressed as a *Markov process,* or *Markov chain.* The results, or outcomes, of a Markov chain express the probability of a state or condition occurring. For example, the possibility of a clear, cloudy, or rainy day tomorrow might be related to today's weather.

The different combinations of dependent possibilities are given by a *transition matrix.* In our weather prediction example, a clear day has a 70% chance of being followed by another clear day, a 25% chance of a cloudy day, and only a 5% chance of rain. In Table 2-3, each possibility today is shown on the left, and its probability of changing tomorrow is indicated across the top. Each row totals 100%, accounting for all weather combinations. The relationship between these events can be shown as a continuous network (see Figure 2-6).

The Markov process can reduce intricate relationships to a simpler form. First, consider a two-state process. Using the markets as an example, what is the probability of an up or down day following an up day, or following a down day? If there is a 70% chance of a higher day following a higher day and a 55% chance of a higher day following a lower day, what is the probability of any day within an uptrend being up?

TABLE 2-3   Transition Matrix

		Tomorrow		
		Clear	Cloudy	Rainy
	Clear	.70	.25	.05
Today	Cloudy	.20	.60	.20
	Rainy	.20	.40	.40

Start with either an up or down day, and then calculate the probability of the next day being up or down. This is done easily by simply counting the number of cases, given in Table 2-4a, then dividing to get the percentages, as shown in Table 2-4b.

Because the first day may be designated arbitrarily as up or down, it is an exception to the general rule and, therefore, is given the weight of 50%. The probability of the second day being up or down is the sum of the joint probabilities

$$P(\text{UP})_2 = (.50 \times .70) + (.50 \times .55)$$

$$= .625$$

The probability of the second day being up is 62.5%. Continuing in the same manner, use the probability of an up day as .625, the down as .375, and calculate the third day,

$$P(\text{UP})_3 = (.625 \times .70) + (.375 \times .55)$$

$$= .64375$$

and the fourth day,

$$P(\text{UP})_4 = (.64375 \times .70) + (.35625 \times .55)$$

$$= .64656$$

which can now be seen to be converging. To generalize the probability of an up day, look at what happens on the ith day:

$$P(\text{up})_{i+i} = [P(\text{up})_i \times .70] + [(1 - P(\text{up})_i) \times .55]$$

FIGURE 2-6   Probability network.

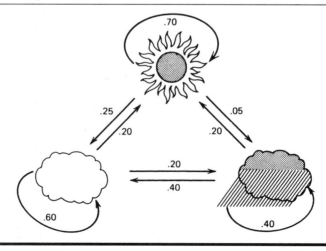

TABLE 2-4a   Counting the Occurrences of Up and Down Days

		Today		
		Up	Down	Total
Previous day	Up	75	60	135
	Down	60	65	125

TABLE 2-4b   Starting Transition Matrix

		Today		
		Up	Down	Total
Previous day	Up	.555	.444	1.00
	Down	.480	.520	1.00

Because the probability is converging, the relationship

$$P(\text{up})_{i+1} = P(\text{up})_i$$

can be substituted and used to solve the equation

$$P(\text{up})_i = [P(\text{up})_i \times .70] + [.55 - P(\text{up})_i \times .55]$$

giving the probability of any day being up within an uptrend as

$$P(\text{up})_i = .64705$$

We can find the chance of an up or down day if the 5-day trend is up simply by substituting the direction of the 5-day trend (or n-day trend) for the previous day's direction in the example just given.

Predicting the weather is a more involved case of multiple situations converging and may be very representative of the way prices react to past prices. By approaching the problem in the same manner as the two-state process, a ⅓ probability is assigned to each situation for the first day; the second day's probability is

$$P(\text{clear})_2 = (.333 \times .70) + (.333 \times .20) + (.333 \times .20)$$
$$= .3663$$

$$P(\text{cloudy})_2 = (.333 \times .25) + (.333 \times .60) + (.333 \times .40)$$
$$= .41625$$

$$P(\text{rainy})_2 = (.333 \times .05) + (.333 \times .20) + (.333 \times .40)$$
$$= .21645$$

Then using the second-day results, the third day is

$$P(\text{clear})_3 = (.3663 \times .70) + (.41625 \times .20) + (.21645 \times .20)$$
$$= .38295$$

$$P(\text{cloudy})_3 = (.3663 \times .25) + (.41625 \times .60) + (.21645 \times .40)$$
$$= .42791$$

$$P(\text{rainy})_3 = (.3663 \times .05) + (.41625 \times .20) + (.21645 \times .40)$$

$$= .18815$$

The general form for solving these three equations is

$$P(\text{clear})_{i+i} = [P(\text{clear})_i \times .70] + [P(\text{cloudy})_i \times .20] + [P(\text{rainy})_i \times .20]$$

$$P(\text{cloudy})_{i+i} = [P(\text{clear})_i \times .25] + [P(\text{cloudy})_i \times .60] + [P(\text{rainy})_i \times .40]$$

$$P(\text{rainy})_{i+i} = [P(\text{clear})_i \times .05] + [P(\text{cloudy})_i \times .20] + [P(\text{rainy})_i \times .40]$$

where each $i + 1$ element can be set equal to the corresponding ith values; there are then three equations in three unknowns, which can be solved directly or by matrix multiplication, as shown in Appendix 3 ("Solution to Weather Probabilities Expressed as a Markov Chain").[2] Otherwise, it will be necessary to use the additional relationship

$$P(\text{clear})_i + P(\text{cloudy})_i + P(\text{rainy})_i = 1.00$$

The results are

$$P(\text{clear}) = .400$$

$$P(\text{cloudy}) = .425$$

$$P(\text{rainy}) = .175$$

Bayes Theorem

Although historic generalization exists concerning the outcome of an event, a specific current market situation may alter the probabilities. *Bayes theorem* combines the *original probability* estimates with the *added-event probability* (the reliability of the new information) to get a *posterior* or *revised probability,*

$$\frac{P(\text{original and added-event})}{P(\text{added-event})}$$

Assume that the price changes $P(\text{up})$ and $P(\text{down})$ are both original probabilities and that an added-event probability, such as a crop report, inventory stocks, or money supply announcement, is expected to have an overriding effect on tomorrow's movement. Then

New probability $P(\text{up} \mid \text{added-event}) =$

$$\frac{P(\text{up and added-event})}{P(\text{up and added-event}) + P(\text{down and added-event})}$$

where *up* and *down* refer to the original historic probabilities, and $P(A \text{ and } B)$ is a joint probability.

Bayes theorem finds the conditional probability even if the joint and marginal probabilities are not known.

New probability $P(\text{up} \mid \text{added-event}) =$

$$\frac{P(\text{up}) \times P(\text{added-event} \mid \text{up})}{P(\text{up}) \times P(\text{added-event} \mid \text{up}) + P(\text{down}) \times P(\text{added-event} \mid \text{down})}$$

where $P(\text{added-event} \mid \text{up})$ is the reliability of the new event being a correct predictor of an upwards move, and $P(\text{added-event} \mid \text{down})$ is the probability of prices going down

---

[2] A full mathematical treatment of Markov chains can be found in John G. Kemeny's and J. Laurie Snell's *Finite Markov Chains* (Springer-Verlag, New York, 1976).

when the added news indicates up. For example, if a decline in soybean planting by more than 10% has a 90% chance of causing prices to move higher, then

P(added-event | up) = .90

and

P(added-event | down) = .10

would be used in Bayes theorem.

SUPPLY AND DEMAND

Price is the balancing point of supply and demand. To estimate the future price of any product or explain its historic patterns, it will be necessary to relate the factors of supply and demand and then adjust for inflation, technological improvement, and other indicators common to econometric analysis. The following sections briefly describe these factors.

Demand

The demand for a product declines as price increases. The rate of decline is always dependent on the need for the product and its available substitutes at different price levels. In Figure 2-7a, D represents normal demand for a product over some fixed period. As prices rise, demand declines fairly rapidly. D' represents increased demand, resulting in higher prices at all levels.

Figure 2-7b represents the demand relationship for potatoes for the years 1929–1939. In most cases, the demand relationship is not a straight line; production costs and minimum demand prevent the price estimate from going to zero. On the higher end of the scale, there is a lag in the response to increased prices and a consumer reluctance to reduce purchasing even at higher prices (called *inelastic demand*). Figure 2-7c shows a

FIGURE 2-7   (a) Shift in demand. (b) Potatoes: U.S. average farm price on December 15th versus total production: 1929–1939. (c) Demand curve, including extremes.

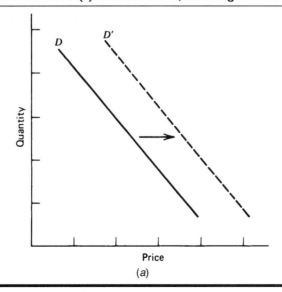

Source: Shepherd, Geoffrey S., and G.A. Futrell. *Agricultural Price Analysis.* (Ames, IA: Iowa State University, 1969, p. 53.)

FIGURE 2-7 *(Continued)*

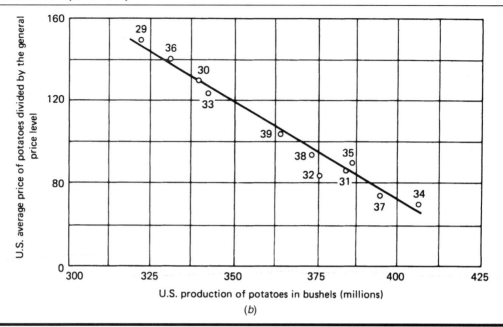

(b)

more representative demand curve, including extremes, where 100 represents the minimum acceptable income for a producer. The demand curve, therefore, shows the rate at which a change in quantity demanded brings about a change in price.

Elasticity of Demand

Elasticity is the key factor in expressing the relationship between price and demand. It is the relative change in demand as price increases,

FIGURE 2-7 *(Continued)*

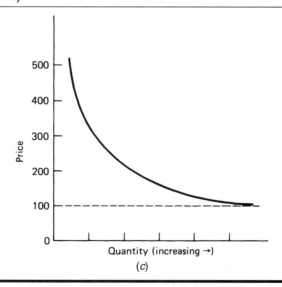

(c)

$$E_D = \frac{\text{relative change (\%) in demand}}{\text{relative change (\%) in price}}$$

A market that always consumes the same amount of a product, regardless of price, is called *inelastic:* as price rises, the demand remains the same and E_D is negatively very small. An *elastic* market is just the opposite: as demand increases, price remains the same and E_D is negatively very large. Figure 2-8 shows the demand curve for various demand elasticities.

If supply increases for a product that has existed in short supply for many years, consumer purchasing habits will require time to adjust. The demand elasticity will gradually shift from relatively inelastic (Figure 2-8*b*) to relatively elastic (Figure 2-8*a*).

Supply

The supply side of the economic equation is the normal counterpart of demand. Figure 2-9*a* shows that, as price increases, the supplier will respond by offering greater amounts of the product. Figure 2-9*b* demonstrates the supply at price extremes. At low levels, below production costs, there is a nominal supply by those producers who must maintain operations due to high fixed costs and difficulty restarting after a shutdown. At high-price levels, supply is erratic. There may be insufficient supply in the short term, followed by the appearance of new supplies or substitutes, as in the case of a location shortage. In most cases, however, it is demand that brings price down.

Elasticity of Supply

The elasticity of supply E_S is the relationship between the change in supply and the change in price,

$$E_S = \frac{\text{relative change (\%) in supply}}{\text{relative change (\%) in price}}$$

The elasticity of supply, the counterpart of *demand elasticity,* is a positive number, because price and quantity move in the same direction at the same time.

Equilibrium

The demand for a product and the supply of that product meet at a point of *equilibrium.* The current price of any commodity, or any market, represents the point of equilibrium for that product at that moment in time. Figure 2-10 shows a constant demand line D and a shifting supply, increasing to the right from S to S'.

FIGURE 2-8   Demand elasticity. (*a*) Relatively elastic. (*b*) Relatively inelastic. (*c*) Normal market.

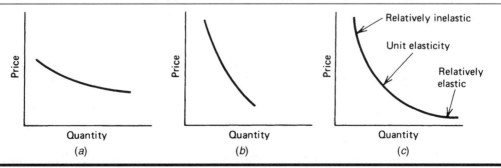

FIGURE 2-9   Supply-price relationship (a) Shift in supply. (b) Supply curve, including extremes.

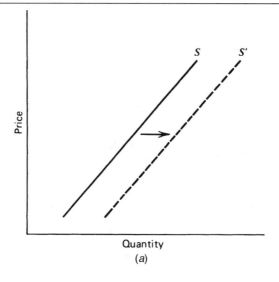

(a)

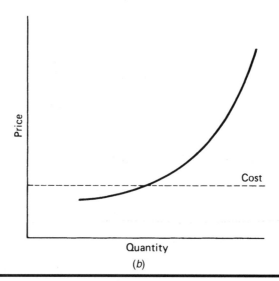

(b)

The demand line D and the original supply line S meet at the equilibrium price P; after the increase in supply, the supply line shifts to S'. The point of equilibrium P' represents a lower price, the consequence of larger supply with unchanged demand. Because supply and demand each have varying elasticities and are best represented by curves, the point of equilibrium can shift in any direction in a market with changing factors.

Equilibrium will be an important concept in developing trading strategies. Although the supply and demand balance may not be calculated, in practical terms equilibrium is a balance between buyers and sellers, a price level at which everyone is willing to trade, although always happy. Equilibrium is associated with lower volatility and often lower volume, because the urgency to buy or sell has been removed.

FIGURE 2-10   Equilibrium with shifting supply.

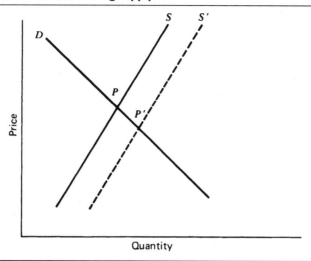

Cobweb Charts

The point at which the supply and demand lines cross is easily translated into a place on a price chart where the direction is sideways. The amount of price volatility during this sideways period depends upon the price level, market participation (called *noise*), and various undertones of instability caused by other factors. Very little is discussed about how price patterns reflect the shift in sentiment between the supply and demand lines, yet there is a clear representation of this action using *cobweb charts.*

Figure 2-11*a* shows a static (symmetric) supply-demand chart with dotted lines representing the cobweb.[3] A shift in the perceived importance of supply and demand factors can

[3] McKallip, Curtis, Jr. "Fundamentals behind technical analysis," *Technical Analysis of Stocks & Commodities* (November 1989).

FIGURE 2-11   Static supply-demand cobweb. (*a*) Dotted lines represent a shift of sentiment from supply to demand to supply, and so forth. (*b*) The price pattern likely to result from the cobweb in (*a*).

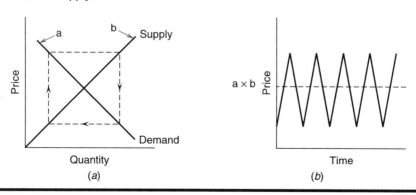

cause prices to reflect the pattern shown by the direction of the arrows on the cobweb, producing the sideways market shown in Figure 2-11b. If the cobweb was closer to the intersection of the supply and demand lines, the volatility of the sideways price pattern would be lower; if the cobweb was further away from the intersection, the pattern would be more volatile.

Most supply-demand relationships are not static and can be represented by lines that cross at oblique angles. In Figure 2-12a, the cobweb is shown to begin near the intersection and move outward, each shift forming a different length strand of the web, moving away from equilibrium. Figure 2-12b shows that the corresponding price pattern is one that shifts from equilibrium to increasing volatility. A reversal in the arrows on the cobweb would show decreasing volatility moving toward equilibrium.

Building a Model

A model can be created to *explain* or *forecast* price changes. Most models explain rather than forecast. Explanatory models analyze sets of data at concurrent times, that is, they look for relationships between multiple factors and their effect on price at the same moment in time. They can also look for *causal,* or lagged relationships, in which prices *respond* to other factors after one or more days. It is possible to use the explanatory model to determine the normal price at a particular moment. Although not considered forecasting, any variation in the actual market price from the normal or expected price could present trading opportunities.

Methods of selecting the best forecasting model can affect its credibility. An *analytic* approach selects the factors and specifies the relationships in advance. Tests are then performed on the data to verify the premise. Many models, though, are refined by *fitting* the data, using regression analysis or *shotgun* testing, which applies a broad selection of variables and weighting to find the best fit. These models do not necessarily forecast but are definitely using perfect hindsight. Even an analytic approach that is subsequently *fine-tuned* could be in danger of losing its forecasting qualities.

The factors that comprise a model can be both numerous and difficult to obtain. Figure 2-13 shows the interrelationship between factors in the cocoa industry. Although this chart is comprehensive in its intramarket relationships, it does not emphasize the global influences that have become a major part of price movement since the mid-1970s. The

---

FIGURE 2-12   Dynamic supply-demand cobweb. (a) Dotted lines represent a cobweb moving away from equilibrium. (b) The price pattern shows increasing volatility.

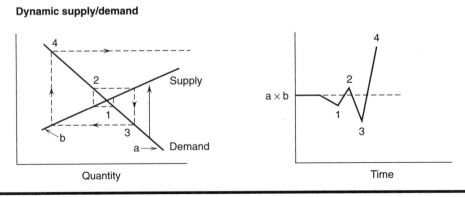

Source: Curtis McKallip, Jr., "Fundamentals behind technical analysis," *Technical Analysis of Stocks & Commodities,* 7, no. 11 (November 1989). © 1989 by Technical Analysis, Inc. Used with permission.

change in value of the U.S. dollar and the volatility of interest rates have had far greater influence on price than normal fundamental factors for many commodities.

Models that explain price movements must be constructed from the primary factors of supply and demand. A simple example for estimating the price of fall potatoes[4] is

$$P/\text{PPI} = a + bS + cD$$

[4] J.D. Schwager, "A Trader's Guide to Analyzing the Potato Futures Market," *1981 Commodity Yearbook* (Commodity Research Bureau, New York, 1981).

FIGURE 2-13   Cocoa factors.

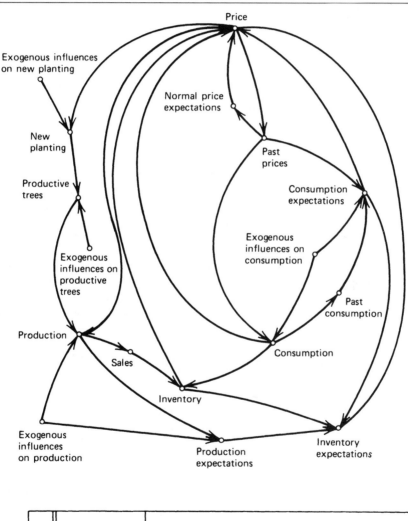

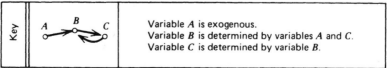

Key		
$A \xrightarrow{B} C$	Variable A is exogenous. Variable B is determined by variables A and C. Variable C is determined by variable B.	

Source: F. N. Weymar, *The Dynamics of the World Cocoa Market* (Cambridge, MA: MIT Press, 1968, p. 2).

where P is the average price of fall potatoes received by farmers; PPI is the Producer Price Index; S is the apparent domestic free supply (production less exports and diversions); D is the estimated deliverable supply; and a, b, and c are constants determined by regression analysis.

This model implies that consumption must be constant (i.e., inelastic demand); demand factors are only implicitly included in the estimated deliverable supply. Exports and diversion represent a small part of the total production. The use of the PPI gives the results in *relative* terms based on whether the index was used as an *inflator* or *deflator* of price.

A general model, presented by Weymar,[5] may be written as three behavior-based equations and one identity:

(a) *Consumption*

$$C_t = f_C(P_t, P_t^{\mathrm{L}}) + e_{C_t}$$

(b) *Production*

$$H_t = f_H(P_t, P_t^{\mathrm{L}}) + e_{H_t}$$

(c) *Inventory*

$$I_t = I_{t-1} + H_t - C_t$$

(d) *Supply of storage*

$$P_t' - P_t = f_P(I_t) + e_P$$

where C is the consumption, P is the price, P^{L} is the lagged price, H is the production (harvest), I is the inventory, P' is the expected price at some point in the future, and e is the corresponding error factor.

The first two equations show that both demand and supply depend on current and/or lagged prices, the traditional macroeconomic theory; production and consumption are thus dependent on past prices. The third equation, inventory level, is simply the total of previous inventories, plus new production, less current consumption. The last equation, *supply of storage*, demonstrates that people are willing to carry larger inventories if they expect prices to increase substantially. The inventory function itself, equation **(c)**, is composed of two separate relationships—manufacturers' inventories and speculators' inventories. Each reacts differently to expected price change.

[5] F.H. Weymar, *The Dynamics of the World Cocoa Market* (MIT Press, Cambridge, MA, 1968).

3

Regression Analysis

Regression analysis is a way of measuring the relationship between two or more sets of data. An economist might want to know how the supply of wheat affects wheat prices, or the relationship among gold, inflation, and the value of the U.S. dollar. A hedger or arbitrageur could use the relationship between two related products, such as palm oil and soybean oil, to select the cheaper product or to profit from the difference, or you can find the pattern that binds the Producer Price Index to interest rates. Regression analysis involves statistical measurements that determine the type of relationship that exists between the data studied. Many of the concepts are important in technical analysis and should be understood by all technicians, even if they are not used frequently. The techniques may also be directly used to trade, as will be shown later in this chapter.

Regression analysis is often applied separately to the basic components of a *time series,* that is, the *trend, seasonal* (or secular trend), and *cyclic* elements. These three factors are present in all price data. The part of the data that cannot be explained by these three elements is considered *random,* or unaccountable.

Trends are the basis of many trading systems. Long-term trends can be related to economic factors, such as inflation or shifts in the value of the U.S. dollar due to the balance of trade or changing interest rates. The reasons for the existence of short-term trends are not always clear. A sharp decline in oil supply would quickly send prices soaring, and a Soviet wheat embargo would force grain prices into a decline; however, trends that exist over periods of a few days cannot always be related to economic factors but may be strictly behavioral.

Major fluctuations about the long-term trend are attributed to *cycles.* Both business and industrial cycles respond slowly to changes in supply and demand. The decision to close a factory or shift to a new crop cannot be made immediately, nor can the decision be easily changed once it is made. Stimulating economic growth by lowering interest rates is not a cure that works overnight. Opening a new mine, finding crude oil deposits, or building an additional soybean processing plant makes the response to increased demand slower than the act of cutting back on production. Moreover, once the investment has been made, business is not inclined to stop production, even at returns below production costs.

The random element of price movement is a composite of everything unexplainable. In later sections ARIMA, or Box-Jenkins methods, will be used to find shorter trends and cycles that may exist in these leftover data. This chapter will concentrate on trend identification, using the methods of regression analysis. Seasonality and cycles will be discussed in Chapters 7 and 8. Because the basis of a strong trading strategy is its foundation in real phenomena, serious students of price movement and traders should understand the tools of regression analysis to avoid incorporating erroneous relationships into their strategies.

CHARACTERISTICS OF THE PRICE DATA

A time series is not just a series of numbers, but *ordered pairs* of price and time. There is a special relationship in the way price moves over various time intervals, the way price reacts to periodic reports, and the way prices fluctuate due to the time of year. Most trading strategies use one price per day, usually the closing price, although some methods will average the high, low, and closing prices. Economic analysis operates on weekly or monthly average

FIGURE 3-1   A basic regression analysis results in a straight line through the center of prices.

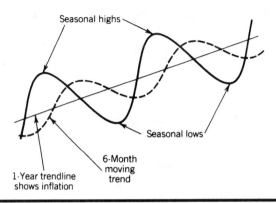

data, but might use a single price (e.g., "week on Friday") for convenience. Two reasons for the infrequent data are the availability of most major statistics on supply and demand, and the intrinsic long-term perspective of the analysis. The use of less frequent data will cause a smoothing effect. The highest and lowest prices will no longer appear, and the data will seem more stable. Even when using daily data, the intraday highs and lows have been elim-inated, and the closing prices show less erratic movement.

A regression analysis, which identifies the trend over a specific time period, will not be influenced by cyclic patterns or short-term trends that are the same length as the time interval used in the analysis. For example, if wide seasonal swings occurred during the year but prices ended at about the same level (shifted only by inflation), a 1-year regression line would be a straight line that split the fluctuations in half (see Figure 3-1).

The time interval used in regression analysis is selected to be long (or multiples of other cycles) if the impact of short-term patterns is to be reduced. To emphasize the move-ment caused by other phenomena, the time interval should be less than one-half of that period (e.g., a 3- or 6-month trend will exaggerate the seasonal factors). In this way, a trend technique may be used to identify a seasonal or cyclic element.

LINEAR REGRESSION

When most people talk about regression, they think about a straight line, which is the most popular application. A *linear regression* is the straight-line relationship of two sets of data.

TABLE 3-1   Annual Average Corn and Soybean Prices

	1956	1957	1958	1959	1960	1961	1962	1963	1964	1965
Corn	1.27	1.19	1.10	1.10	1.05	1.00	.98	1.09	1.12	1.18
Soybeans	2.43	2.26	2.15	2.07	2.03	2.45	2.36	2.44	2.52	2.74
	1966	1967	1968	1969	1970	1971	1972	1973	1974	1975
Corn	1.16	1.24	1.03	1.08	1.15	1.33	1.08	1.57	2.55	3.02
Soybeans	2.98	2.93	2.69	2.63	2.63	3.08	3.24	6.22	6.12	6.33
	1976	1977	1978	1979	1980	1981	1982			
Corn	2.54	2.15	2.02	2.25	2.52	3.11	2.50			
Soybeans	4.92	6.81	5.88	6.61	6.28	7.61	6.05			

Source: 1956–1965: Illinois Statistical Service; 1966–1982: Commodity Research Bureau *Commodity Yearbook.*

It is most often found using a technique called a *best fit*, which selects the straight line that comes closest to most of the data points. Using the prices of corn and soybeans as an example, their linear relationship is the straight-line (or *first-order*) equation (see Table 3-1).

$$Y = a + bX$$

where Y is the price of corn (dependent variable)
X is the price of soybeans (independent variable)
a is the Y-intercept (where the line crosses the Y-axis)
b is the slope (angle of the line)

METHOD OF LEAST SQUARES

The most popular technique in statistics for finding the best fit is the *method of least squares.* This approach produces the straight line from which the actual data points vary the least. To do this, calculate the *sum of the squares* of all the deviations from the line value and choose the line that has the smallest total deviation. The mathematical expression for this is

$$S = \sum (y_i - \hat{y}_i)^2, \qquad \text{while all uses of } \sum \text{ imply } \sum_{i=1}^{N}$$

S is the sum of the squares of the error of each of the data sets, and the value $y_i - \hat{y}_i$ is the difference between the actual value of y_i at x_i and the predicted line value $\hat{y}_i$. Graphically, the individual deviations, or errors, for four points may look like those in Figure 3-2. Each actual data point is (x_1, y_1), (x_2, y_2), (x_3, y_3) and (x_4, y_4), and the approximated position on the line is $(x_1 \hat{y}_1)$, $(x_2, \hat{y}_2)$, $(x_3, \hat{y}_3)$ and $(x_4, \hat{y}_4)$. The sum of the squares of the errors is

$$S = \sum (y_i - \hat{y}_i)^2$$
$$= (y_1 - \hat{y}_1)^2 + (y_2 - \hat{y}_2)^2 + (y_3 - \hat{y}_3)^2 + (y_4 - \hat{y}_4)^2$$

FIGURE 3-2   Error deviation for method of least squares.

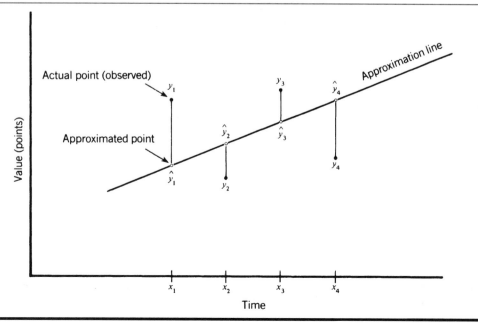

The line that causes S to be the smallest possible value will be the best choice for these data points. The square of $y_i - \hat{y}_i$ is always positive, thereby magnifying the importance of those data points that are farther from the approximated line on either side and reducing the significance of those points for which the approximation is good.

To use the least-squares method for solving the corn-soybean price relationship, look for the solution to the straight line, $y = a + bx$, expressed as

$$b = \frac{N \sum xy - \sum x \sum y}{N \sum x^2 - \left(\sum x\right)^2}$$

$$a = \frac{1}{N}\left(\sum y - b \sum x\right)$$

Here, N is the number of data points and $\sum$ represents the sum over N points. To solve these equations, construct a table of corn and soybean values and calculate all the unique sums in the preceding formulas individually[1] (Table 3-2).

Substitute these values into the formulas and solve for a and b.

$$b = \frac{27(202.35) - (106.46)(43.38)}{27(512.95) - (106.46)(106.46)}$$

$$= \frac{5463.45 - 4618.23}{13849.65 - 11333.73}$$

$$= .336$$

$$a = \frac{1}{27}(43.38 - .336 \times 106.46)$$

$$= \frac{7.61}{27}$$

$$= .282$$

The equation for the least-squares approximation is

$$y = .282 + .336x$$

Selecting values of x and solving for y gives the results shown in Table 3-3.

The results of the linear approximation are shown in Figure 3-3. The slope of .336 indicates that for every $1 increase in the price of soybeans, there is a corresponding increase of 33.6¢ in corn. This is not far from what would be expected for farm income. Because the corn yield per acre is 2.5 times greater than the soybean yield in most parts of the United States, the ratio 1/2.5 should yield a slope of about .4. Considering areas where soybeans are alternatives to cotton and other crops, and the tendency for midwest farmers to plant mostly corn, a relatively higher price for soybeans is not surprising.

Letting the Computer Do the Work

Having methodically worked through the calculations for linear regression, it should not be a surprise that the solution is readily available on any spreadsheet program or in strat-

---

[1] Appendix 2 offers a computer program to solve the straight-line equation using the method of least squares, as well as the nonlinear examples.

TABLE 3-2 Totals for Least-Squares Solution

		Corn	Soybeans			
	i	y_i	x_i	x_i^2	$x_i y_i$	y_i^2
1956	1	1.27	2.43	5.90	3.09	1.61
1957	2	1.19	2.26	5.11	2.69	1.42
1958	3	1.10	2.15	4.62	2.36	1.21
1959	4	1.10	2.07	4.28	2.28	1.21
1960	5	1.05	2.03	4.12	2.13	1.10
1961	6	1.00	2.45	6.00	2.45	1.00
1962	7	.98	2.36	5.57	2.31	.96
1963	8	1.09	2.44	5.95	2.66	1.19
1964	9	1.12	2.52	6.35	2.82	1.25
1965	10	1.18	2.74	7.51	3.23	1.39
1966	11	1.16	2.98	8.88	3.46	1.34
1967	12	1.24	2.93	8.58	3.63	1.54
1968	13	1.03	2.69	7.24	2.77	1.06
1969	14	1.08	2.63	6.92	2.84	1.17
1970	15	1.15	2.63	6.92	3.02	1.32
1971	16	1.33	3.08	9.49	4.10	1.77
1972	17	1.08	3.24	10.50	3.50	1.17
1973	18	1.57	6.22	38.69	9.76	2.46
1974	19	2.55	6.12	37.45	15.61	6.50
1975	20	3.02	6.33	40.07	19.12	9.12
1976	21	2.54	4.92	24.21	12.50	6.45
1977	22	2.15	6.81	46.38	14.64	4.62
1978	23	2.02	5.88	34.57	11.88	4.08
1979	24	2.25	6.61	43.69	14.87	5.06
1980	25	2.52	6.28	39.44	15.83	6.35
1981	26	3.11	7.61	57.91	23.67	9.67
1982	27	2.50	6.05	36.60	15.13	6.25
		Σy	Σx	Σx^2	Σxy	Σy^2
Σ sums		43.38	106.46	512.95	202.35	82.27

egy testing software. Nevertheless, it is difficult to use the results of these programs unless you can interpret the answer. Spreadsheet programs simply require that you indicate the two columns that represent the independent and dependent variables. If you simply want to have time as the independent variable, you can create a column of sequential numbers: 1, 2, 3, and so forth. The spreadsheet program will give you a table of statistics including the slope, y-intercept, and correlation coefficient (discussed in the next section), and a level of confidence. Look for a Regression Dialog Box in your spreadsheet program and follow the instructions. It is often found under Tools|Numeric Tools|Regression.

Programming Tools

More specific tools are available in strategy testing software, although all of it is restricted to linear regression. You should expect to find functions that will find the following:

TABLE 3-3 Least-Squares Relationship for Corn and Soybeans: 1956–1982

Soybeans	x	1.00	2.00	3.00	4.00	5.00	6.00	7.00
Corn	y	.61	.95	1.29	1.63	1.97	2.31	2.65

FIGURE 3-3   **Scatter diagram of corn, soybean pairs with linear regression solution.**

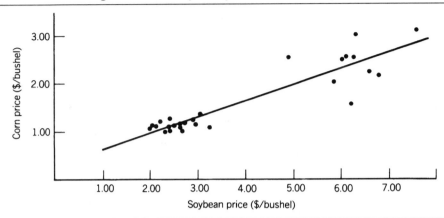

Linear regression slope—returns the slope of the straight line given the data series (e.g., the closing prices) and the period over which the line will be drawn (e.g., 20 days).

Linear regression angle—the same as the slope function but the answer is expressed in degrees.

Linear regression value—calculates the slope of the regression line then projects that line into the future, returning the value of the future point. This requires the user to specify the data series, the period over which the line will be calculated, and the number of periods into the future. Projecting the value can also be done by finding the slope, *s,* and performing the following calculation:

Projected price = starting price + *s* × (calculation period + projection period)

where the starting price is at the beginning of the calculation period.

LINEAR CORRELATION

Solving the least-squares equation for the best fit does not mean that the answer can be used. There is always a solution to the least squares method, but there might not be a valid linear relationship between the two sets of data. You may think that two data items affect one another, such as the amount of disposable income and the purchase of television sets, but that might not be the case. The *linear correlation,* which uses a value called the *coefficient of determination r^2,* or the *correlation coefficient,* expresses the relationship of the data on a scale from +1 (perfect positive correlation), to 0 (no relationship between the data), to −1 (perfect negative correlation), as shown in Figure 3-4.

The correlation coefficient is derived from the deviation, or variation, in the data. It is based on the relationship

Total deviation = explained deviation + unexplained deviation

where   *total deviation* is $\sum (y_i - \bar{y})$, the sum of the individual differences from the average;
explained deviation is $\sum (\hat{y}_i - \bar{y})$, the sum of the differences between the points on the fitted line and the average;
unexplained deviation is $\sum (y_i - \hat{y}_i)$, the sum of the remaining forecast error terms.

Changing this into a ratio gives

$$r^2 = 1 - \frac{\text{unexplained deviation}}{\text{total deviation}} = 1 - \frac{\sum (y_i - \hat{y}_i)^2}{\sum (y_i - \bar{y}_i)^2}$$

FIGURE 3-4   Degrees of correlation. (*a*) **Perfect positive linear correlation** ($r^2 = 1$). (*b*) **Somewhat positive linear correlation** ($r^2 = .5$). (*c*) **and** (*d*) **No correlation** ($r^2 = 0$). (*e*) **Perfect negative
linear correlation** ($r^2 = -1$).

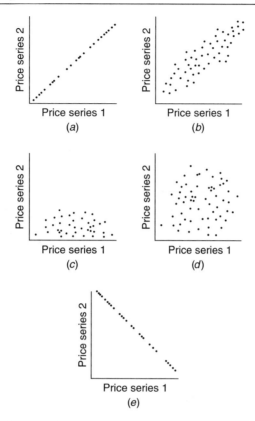

The value r^2 can also be determined using sums already calculated in Table 3-2, by applying the following formula:

$$r^2 = \frac{\left(N \sum xy - \sum x \sum \hat{y}\right)^2}{\left[N \sum x^2 - \left(\sum x\right)^2\right]\left[N \sum y^2 - \left(\sum y\right)^2\right]}$$

This is easy to calculate; it requires only one sum in addition to the solution of the least-
squares problem. The results r^2 are interpreted as follows:

$r^2 = +1$ — A perfect positive linear correlation. The data points are along a straight
line going upward to the right (Figure 3-4*a*).

$+1 > r^2 > 0$ — The scattered points become more uniformly distributed about a positive
approximation line as the value of r^2 becomes closer to +1 (Figure 3-4*b*).

$r^2 = 0$ — No linear correlation exists (Figures 3-4*c*, 3-4*d*).

$-1 < r^2 < 0$ — The scattered points become more uniformly distributed about a negative
approximation line as the value of r^2 becomes closer to −1.

$r^2 = -1$ — A perfect negative linear correlation, the line going downward to the right
(Figure 3-4*e*).

Applying the formula to the corn-soybean data and using the sums from Table 3-2 gives

$$r^2 = \frac{[27(202.35) - (106.46)(43.38)]^2}{[27(512.95) - (106.46)^2][27(82.27) - (43.38)^2]}$$

$$= \frac{(5463.45 - 4618.23)^2}{(13849.65 - 11333.73)(2221.29 - 1881.82)}$$

$$= \frac{714396.84}{(2515.92)(339.47)}$$

$$= 83.6$$

The results show a strong relationship between the prices of soybeans and corn. The value of r^2 may also be considered as having accounted for 83.6% of the price relationship between the two products.

Computer Programs to Find Correlations

Just as with a linear regression, both spreadsheets and trading strategy software have functions to return the correlation coefficient with no calculations on your part. Spreadsheets include the correlation as part of the statistics given when the regression tool is used. If only the correlation is needed, for example, to create a correlation matrix, then you can use the function @correl(col1,col2), which calculates only the correlation coefficient for the two series in columns 1 and 2.

The same facility exists in trading strategy software, in which you can use a function that specifies the independent series, dependent series, and the time period over which the regression will be calculated. For example, you might specify the correlation, R2, of two series, *data1* and *data2,* over the past 45 days as:

```
R2 = @correlation(close of data1, close of data2, 45)
```

Correlation Adjustments When Using a Time Series

Because most price analyses involve the use of two time series, precautions should be taken to avoid a dominant trend that can distort the results. A long-term upward or downward trend will overshadow the smaller movements around the trend and exaggerate the correlation. The following methods may be used to correct the problem:

1. The deviations from the trend $(\hat{y}_i - y_i)$ may be correlated.
2. The first differences $[(\hat{y}_i - \hat{y}_{i-1}), (y_i - y_{i-1})$ may be correlated.
3. The two series may be adjusted for trend.

The simplest method is number 2, which is also very effective. You should expect any commercial software to detrend the data before calculating the correlation coefficient; however, it is always a good habit to check it.

Forecasting Using Regression

A distinct advantage of regression analysis is that it allows the analyst to forecast price movement. In the case of the linear regression, the forecast will simply be an extension of the line. Later in this book, there will be other *nonlinear* solutions that are used to predict more complex patterns.

The regression forecast is the basis for the *probabilistic model.* Instead of the corn-soybean relationship, regress the price of soybeans against time using the linear least-squares method on the data in Table 3-2. The result is

$$y = .987 + .221x$$

where y is the price of soybeans for the year x. Because the solution substituted the value of 1 for 1956 and 27 for 1982, the average farm income per bushel of soybeans is forecast as 7.32 in 1985 ($x = 30$) and 8.38 in 1990 ($x = 35$).

Confidence Bands

Regression analysis includes its own measure of accuracy called *confidence bands.* It is based on a probability distribution of the errors in the fitted equation and the size of the data sample. Looking at Figure 3-3, the straight line cannot touch all the points, but its *goodness of fit* may be measured by using the *standard deviation of the errors* to determine the variance over the total number of data points N. If the actual data points are y_i and their corresponding value on the fitted line $\hat{y}_i$, then

$$\sigma = \sqrt{\frac{\Sigma e^2}{N}}$$

where

$$e_i = y_i - \hat{y}_i$$

Referring to the table of normal distribution (Appendix 1), the 95% level is equivalent to 1.96 standard deviations. Then, a confidence band of 95%, placed around the forecast line, is written

95% upper band $= y_i + 1.96\sigma$

95% lower band $= y_i - 1.96\sigma$

Figure 3-5*a* shows the soybean forecast with a 95% confidence band. The points that are outside the band are of particular interest and can be interpreted in either of two ways.

1. They are not representative of normal price behavior and are expected to correct the levels within the bands.
2. The model was not performed on representative or adequate data and should be reestimated.

Figure 3-5*b* also indicates that the forecast loses accuracy as it is further projected; the forecast is based on the size of the sample used to find the regression coefficients. The more data included in the original solution, the longer the forecast will maintain its accuracy.

NONLINEAR APPROXIMATIONS FOR TWO VARIABLES

Data points that cannot be related linearly may be approximated using a curve. The general polynomial form that approximates any curve is

$$y = a_0 + a_1 x + a_2 x^2 + \cdots + a_n x^n$$

The first two terms on the right side of the equal sign form the first-order equation for a straight line. By adding the next term $a_2 x^2$, the shape of the resulting line changes to a *parabolic* curve, one with a single, smooth change of direction. The third term $a_3 x^3$ adds an *inflection* to the pattern. For most price forecasting, the *second-order* equation, also called *curvilinear,* is sufficient (Figure 3-6). The corn and soybean prices from Table 3-1 will be used to give examples of this and other nonlinear approximations.

The curvilinear form

$$y = a + bx + cx^2$$

must be solved for the coefficients a, b, and c using the simultaneous equations

FIGURE 3-5   Confidence bands. (*a*) Soybeans with 95% confidence band. (*b*) Out-of-sample forecasts lose confidence.

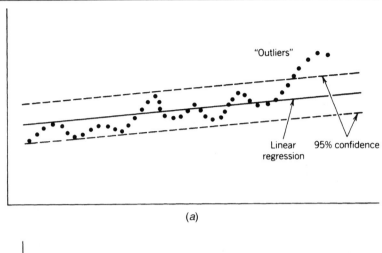

(*a*)

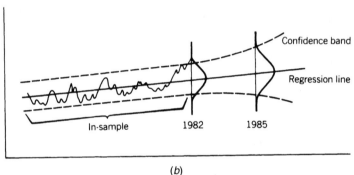

(*b*)

$$Na + b \sum x + c \sum x^2 = \sum y$$
$$a \sum x + b \sum x^2 + c \sum x^3 = \sum xy$$
$$a \sum x^2 + b \sum x^3 + c \sum x^4 = \sum x^2 y$$

The calculations from Table 3-2, including the additional sums for x^3, x^4, and $x^2 y$, can be substituted into the preceding equations. The system of simultaneous linear equations can be solved by the process of matrix elimination,[2] a technique that should not be performed without the help of a computer. An alternate solution can be obtained by continuing with the already familiar least-squares method.

SECOND-ORDER LEAST SQUARES

The concepts of least squares can be extended to the curvilinear (second-order) equation by minimizing the sum of the errors[3]

$$S = \sum_{i=1}^{N} (y_i - a - bx_i - cx_i^2)^2$$

---

[2] See Appendix 3 for examples of matrix solutions.

[3] F.R. Ruckdeschel, *BASIC Scientific Subroutines*. Vol. I. (Byte/McGraw-Hill, Peterborough, NH, 1981).

FIGURE 3-6   Curvilinear (parabolas).

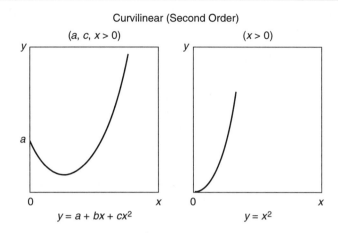

Curvilinear (Second Order)

$(a, c, x > 0)$

$(x > 0)$

$y = a + bx + cx^2$

$y = x^2$

First, it is necessary to separate the various intermediate sums before expressing the solution for a, b, and c.

$$S_{xx} = \frac{1}{N} \sum_{i=1}^{N} (x_i - \bar{x})^2$$

$$S_{xy} = \frac{1}{N} \sum_{i=1}^{N} (x_i - \bar{x})(y_i - \bar{y})$$

$$S_{yy} = \frac{1}{N} \sum_{i=1}^{N} (y_i - \bar{y})^2$$

$$S_{xx^2} = \frac{1}{N} \sum_{i=1}^{N} (x_i - \bar{x})(x_i^2 - \bar{x}^2)$$

$$S_{x^2x^2} = \frac{1}{N} \sum_{i=1}^{N} (x_i^2 - \bar{x}^2)^2$$

$$S_{yx^2} = \frac{1}{N} \sum_{i=1}^{N} (y_i - \bar{y})(x_i^2 - \bar{x}^2)$$

The constant values can then be found by substitution into the following equations

$$b = \frac{S_{xy}S_{x^2x^2} - S_{yx^2}S_{xx^2}}{S_{xx}S_{x^2x^2} - (S_{xx^2})^2}$$

$$c = \frac{S_{xx}S_{yx^2} - S_{xx^2}S_{xy}}{S_{xx}S_{x^2x^2} - (S_{xx^2})^2}$$

$$a = \bar{y} - b\bar{x} - c\bar{x}^2$$

The procedure is identical to the linear least-squares solution. Fortunately, there are simple computer programs that have already been written to solve these problems. Using the program found in Appendix 2, the result is

$$y = .310 + .323x + .002x^2$$

Table 3-4 shows the relationship using selected values of x. Notice that this relationship is essentially linear due to the small second-order coefficient. It is not necessary to solve both the linear and curvilinear models, because the second-order equation can be used in the linear form when this situation occurs.

Transforming Nonlinear to Linear

Two curves that are often used to forecast prices are *logarithmic* (*power*) and *exponential* relationships (see Figure 3-7). The exponential, curving up, is used to scale price data that become more volatile at higher levels. Each of these forms can be solved with unique equations; however, both can be easily transformed into linear relationships and solved using the method of least squares. This will allow you to fool the computer into solving a nonlinear problem using a linear regression tool.

	Logarithmic	Exponential
General form	$y = ax^b$	$y = ae^{bx}$
Transformed	$\ln y = \ln a + b \ln x$	$\ln y = \ln a + bx$
Linear form	$y = a + bx$	$y = a + bx$
	where $y = \ln y$	where $y = \ln y$
	$a = \ln a$	$a = \ln a$
	$x = \ln x$	

The significant difference in the transformations is that the value of x is not scaled for the exponential. Taking the original data and performing the appropriate natural log functions, ln results in the linear form that can be solved using least squares. Selected results from the computer program in Appendix 2 are shown in Table 3-5.

EVALUATION OF 2-VARIABLE TECHNIQUES

Of the three curve-fitting techniques, the curvilinear and exponential results are very similar, both curving upward and passing through the main cluster of data points at about the same incline. The log approximation curves downward after passing through the main group of data points at about the same place as the other approximations. To evaluate objectively whether any of the nonlinear methods are a better fit than the linear approximation, find the standard deviation of the errors, which gives a statistical measurement of how close the fitted line comes to the original data points. The results show that the curvilinear is best; the logarithmic, which curves downward, is noticeably the worst (see Figure 3-8).

In the case of the corn-soybean relationship, the model with the smallest variance makes the most sense. Prices will usually remain within the range tested, and the realities of the production-price relationship support the selection of the linear (or curvilinear) values.

The use of regression analysis for forecasting the price of soybeans alone has a different conclusion. Although 27 years were used, the last 10 showed a noticeable increase in soybean prices. This rising pattern is best fit by the curvilinear and exponential models. However, forecasts using these formulas show prices continuing to rise at an increasing rate. Had inflation maintained its double-digit rate, these forecasts would still lead to unrealistically high prices. The logarithmic model, which leveled off after the rise, turned out to

TABLE 3-4 Curvilinear Values for Corn and Soybeans

Soybeans	x	1.00	2.00	3.00	4.00	5.00	6.00	7.00
Corn	y	.63	.96	1.29	1.63	1.97	2.31	2.66

FIGURE 3-7 Logarithmic and exponential.

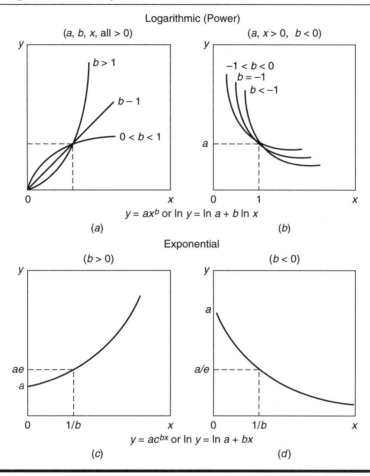

Logarithmic (Power)

$(a, b, x, \text{all} > 0)$ $(a, x > 0, \ b < 0)$

$y = ax^b$ or $\ln y = \ln a + b \ln x$

(a) (b)

Exponential

$(b > 0)$ $(b < 0)$

$y = ac^{bx}$ or $\ln y = \ln a + bx$

(c) (d)

Source: Cuthbert Daniel and Fred S. Wood, *Fitting Equations to Data: Computer Analysis of Multifactor Data*, 2nd ed. (New York: John Wiley & Sons, 1980, pp. 20, 21). Reprinted with permission.

be the best for the actual situation. This shows that the problem of forecasting is more complex than this naive solution. The logarithmic model, which showed the worst statistical results, provided the best forecast. Major factors that cause significant price shifts, such as interest rates, inflation, and the value of the U.S. dollar, must be monitored carefully. The model must be reestimated whenever these factors change. The section "Multivariate Approximations" will discuss this in more detail.

Direct Relationships

The price at which a market trades is limited by the cost of production and dependent upon the prices of other markets that provide a substitute product. Arbitrage is based on

TABLE 3-5 Log and Exponential Values for Corn and Soybeans

Soybeans	x	1.00	2.00	3.00	4.00	5.00	6.00	7.00
Corn (log)	y	.54	.94	1.30	1.64	1.96	2.26	2.56
(exp)	y	.84	1.02	1.24	1.50	1.83	2.22	2.70

FIGURE 3-8 **Least-squares approximation for soybeans using linear, curvilinear, logarithmic, and exponential models.**

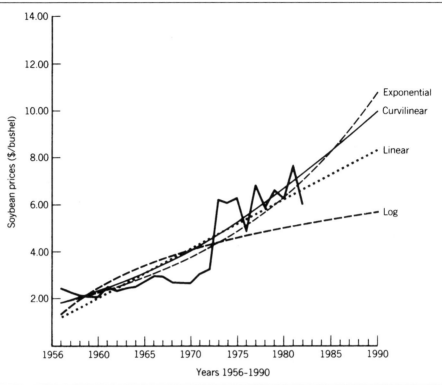

the ability to substitute one product for another after transaction costs, which can include carrying charges, shipping, inspection, and commissions. These relationships are carefully monitored and arbitrage opportunities are quickly acted upon by traders. This process keeps futures and cash prices together and prevents the price of gold in New York, London, and Hong Kong from drifting apart any further than the cost of buying gold in one location and delivering it to another. For interest rate markets, *strips* prevent the large pool of 3-month vehicles, notes, and bonds from offering widely different returns for the same maturity. The Interbank market provides the same stability for foreign exchange markets, while in agriculture the soybean crush and other processing margins do not stay out-of-line for long. The following nonfinancial markets have close relationships that can be found using regression analysis.

Products Related	Reason
All crops	Relative income for farmers
Grains	Protein substitution for feed
Livestock to feedgrains	Feed, cost of production
Livestock	Food substitution
Sugar and corn	Sweetener substitution
Hogs and pork bellies	Product dependency
Silver, gold, and platinum	Investor's inflation hedge
Interest rates and financials	The stock market and foreign exchange are strongly influenced by changes in interest rates.

MULTIVARIATE APPROXIMATIONS

Regression analysis is most often used in complex economic models to find the combination of two or more independent variables that best explain or forecast prices. A simple application of annual production and distribution of soybeans will determine whether these factors are significant in determination of soybean prices. Because the demand for soybeans and its products is complex, a high correlation should not be expected between the data. However, there is no way of knowing how much impact other factors have on the prices over a long term.

Using the method of least squares, which was employed for a simple linear regression, the new equation is

$$y = a + bx_1 + cx_2$$

where y is the resulting price
x_1 is the total production (supply)
x_2 is the total distribution (demand)
a, b, and c are constants to be calculated

As in the linear approximation, the solution to this problem will be found by minimizing the sum of the squares of the errors at each point

$$S = \sum_{i=1}^{n} (y_i - \hat{y}_i)^2$$

Substituting $\hat{y}$ from the previous equation,

$$S = \sum_{i=1}^{n} (y_i - (a + bx_1 + cx_2))^2$$

The solution to the multivariate problem of two independent variables x_1 and x_2 requires the following three least-squares equations:

$$an + b \sum x_1 + c \sum x_2 = \sum y$$
$$a \sum x_1 + b \sum x_1^2 + c \sum x_1 x_2 = \sum x_1 y$$
$$a \sum x_2 + b \sum x_1 x_2 + c \sum x_2^2 = \sum x_2 y$$

The procedure for solving the three simultaneous equations is the same as the curvilinear method of coefficient elimination. The sums are calculated in Table 3-6, then substituted into the last three equations:

$$12.00a + 13.546b + 12.582c = 44.4$$
$$13.55a + 15.980b + 14.75c = 53.28$$
$$12.58a + 14.75b + 13.86c = 49.264$$

The coefficient matrix solution is[4]

$$\begin{pmatrix} 12.00 & 13.55 & 12.58 & 44.40 \\ 13.55 & 15.98 & 14.74 & 53.28 \\ 12.58 & 14.74 & 13.86 & 49.26 \end{pmatrix}$$

$$\begin{pmatrix} 1 & 1.239 & 1.048 & 3.700 \\ 0 & .6798 & .5451 & 3.145 \\ 0 & .5451 & .6720 & 2.714 \end{pmatrix}$$

[4] Matrix elimination is the necessary solution to the multivariate problem. Appendix 3 contains the computer programs necessary to perform this operation.

TABLE 3-6   Totals for Multivariate Solution

			Supply	Demand					
			x_1	x_2	x_1^2	x_2^2	$x_1 x_2$	$x_1 y$	$x_2 y$
	y		(Billions)			(Billions)		(Millions)	
1964	1	2.67	.700	.677	.490	.458	.474	1.869	1.808
1965	2	2.88	.845	.738	.714	.545	.624	2.434	2.125
1966	3	2.98	.928	.839	.861	.704	.779	2.765	2.500
1967	4	2.93	.976	.874	.953	.764	.853	2.860	2.561
1968	5	2.69	1.107	.900	1.225	.810	.996	2.978	2.421
1969	6	2.63	1.133	.946	1.284	.895	1.072	2.980	2.488
1970	7	2.63	1.127	1.230	1.270	1.513	1.386	2.964	3.235
1971	8	3.08	1.176	1.258	1.383	1.583	1.479	3.622	3.875
1972	9	3.24	1.271	1.202	1.615	1.445	1.528	4.118	3.894
1973	10	6.22	1.547	1.283	2.393	1.646	1.985	9.622	7.980
1974	11	6.12	1.215	1.435	1.476	2.059	1.744	7.436	8.782
1975	12	6.33	1.521	1.200	2.313	1.440	1.825	9.628	7.596
Σ		44.40	13.546	12.582	15.977	13.862	14.745	53.276	49.265

$$\begin{pmatrix} 1 & 0 & .1429 & -1.5240 \\ 0 & 1 & .8018 & 4.6264 \\ 0 & 0 & .2349 & .1922 \end{pmatrix}$$

$$\begin{pmatrix} 1 & 0 & 0 & -1.641 \\ 0 & 1 & 0 & 3.9703 \\ 0 & 0 & 1 & .8183 \end{pmatrix}$$

The results show $a = -1.641$, $b = 3.9703$, and $c = .8183$, so that the multiple linear approximation of the price is

$$\hat{y} = -1.641 + 3.9703x_1 + .8183x_2$$

where x_1 is the production in billions of bushels and x_2 demand in billions of bushels. The coefficient of supply is the principal factor in the determination of price. Had either coefficient of x_1 or x_2 been small, it would have indicated a lack of significance. The selection of which data to try when determining price components is not obvious and may result in a useless answer. In the example, supply-and-demand figures were chosen to determine price, but perhaps supply and inflation or demand and inflation would have been better. To find out which sets of data are best, each combination would have to be tested and the results compared.

Computer programs are available that perform multivariate analysis and allow a large number of items to be input as potentially relevant factors. This program is available in special mathematical applications packages. You should be warned that the calculation time increases quickly as more data relationships are included. Recently, neural networks are used to find solutions to complex problems of supply and demand. Neural nets have the advantage of not being bound to a solution that fixes the relationships of each of the inputs to a constant value. That is, the multivariate answer to the soybean problem says that the effect of supply is always four times greater than the effect of demand; but the neural net solution may say that, in most years when supply is not threatened by weather, the demand is the primary factor. Neural nets are discussed in Chapter 20.

Selecting Data for an S&P Model

The stock market is driven by a healthy economy and by lower interest rates. A good economy means that there is high employment and consumers are actively buying homes, durable goods, and frivolous items. Low interest rates result in more corporate profitability, which is also influenced by controlled growth and low inflation, both delicate issues orchestrated by the Central Bank.

To create a robust S&P model, whether using multiple regression or, as we will discuss later, neural networks, it is necessary to select the most meaningful data. The following was suggested by Lincoln to be used for a 6-month S&P forecast:[5]

1. *S&P prices*—the closing prices of the Standard & Poor's 500 cash index
2. *Corporate bonds/Treasury bonds*—the BAA corporate bond yield divided by the 30-year Treasury bond yield, normalized by subtracting the historical mean
3. *Annual change in the dollar*—the 12-month change in the dollar, minus 1, which might be based on the Dollar Index traded on the New York Futures Exchange, or a comparable weighting of major currencies
4. *Annual change in Federal funds rate*—the 12-month change in the Fed funds rate, minus 1
5. *Federal funds rate/discount rate*—the Fed funds rate divided by the discount rate, normalized by subtracting the historical mean
6. *Money supply*—M1 money supply, not seasonally adjusted
7. *Annual Consumer Price Index*—the 12-month change in the CPI, minus 1
8. *Inflation/disinflation index*—the annualized 1-month change in the CPI divided by the 12-month change in the CPI, minus 1
9. *Leading economic indicators*—the 12-month change in the leading economic indicators, minus 1
10. *One-month versus 10-month oscillator for the S&P cash index*—the difference between the monthly average and the past 10 months, approximately 200 days
11. *Inflation-adjusted commercial loans*—the inflation-adjusted 12-month growth in commercial loans

Lincoln used 20 years of monthly values to forecast the S&P price 6 months ahead. Some of this data is available on a weekly basis and might be adapted to a shorter time frame; however, it is unreasonable to think that an accurate daily forecast is possible using weekly or monthly data. It is also likely that the use of more frequent S&P price data is inconsistent with the monthly statistics and will introduce more noise and make the results less reliable.

One element that is missing from the 11 items listed is a volatility adjustment. There has been a 600% increase in the S&P price over 20 years, and volatility is clearly much higher. A simple percentage relationship may not describe this change adequately, but may be used until a better one is substituted. Therefore, those items that become more or less volatile as prices move higher and lower must be corrected using a volatility-normalizing factor. For example, if we consider the initial volatility when the S&P was 100 at the beginning of the data as normal, then when the price is 800 we will divide the current volatility by 8 to normalize, or even take the square root if the increase in volatility is nonlinear. This type of adjustment would apply to nearly all the items except money supply and the inflation/disinflation index. Don't forget that, where applicable, yields must always be used, not prices.

[5] Thomas H. Lincoln, "Time Series Forecasting: ARMAX," *Technical Analysis of Stocks and Commodities* (September 1991).

Generalized Multivariate

In general, the relationship between n independent variables is expressed as

$$y = a_0 + a_1 x_1 + a_2 x_2 + \cdots + a_n x_n$$

The solution to this equation is an extension of the problems in two variables. The $n + 1$ equations in $n + 1$ variables are created by summing the $n + 1$ equations developed from the general equation by multiplying the second equation by x_1, the third by x_2, and so on:

$$
\begin{aligned}
a_0 n & + a_1 \sum x_1 + a_2 \sum x_2 + \cdots + a_n \sum x_n = \sum y \\
a_0 \sum x_1 & + a_1 \sum x_1^2 + a_2 \sum x_1 x_2 + \cdots + a_n \sum x_1 x_n = \sum x_1 y \\
a_0 \sum x_2 & + a_1 \sum x_1 x_2 + a_2 \sum x_2^2 + \cdots + a_n \sum x_2 x_n = \sum x_2 y \\
& \qquad\qquad\qquad\qquad \vdots \\
a_0 \sum x_n & + a_1 \sum x_1 x_n + a_2 \sum x_n + \cdots + a_n \sum x_n^2 = \sum x_n y
\end{aligned}
$$

The solution to this system of equations can be calculated on most computers using a standard program available for this purpose (see Appendix 2). Those with only a little experience in regression analysis should remember that the model is most accurate within the range of the data points; when projecting outside the bounds of the sample data, the predictive qualities of the regression formula decrease with time. It is most likely that a good solution will be found for interest rates and grain prices, which are trading at the same levels as previous years, but may not be reliable for index markets that have made erratic new highs over the years.

Many dependent variables (x_i) may be used to increase the possibility of finding a good correlation. The predictive quality of this solution will depend on the relevance of the independent variables. It is best to start with the obvious components of a time series, such as inflation, then add standard economic statistics, as the Consumer Price Index and industrial product, as well as supply-and-demand information specific to the market being evaluated. For both grain and energy markets, the accumulation of inventory, or stocks, is a strong influence on price; these factors also have an expected seasonal variation, which is represented in terms of an index of adjustment. Measuring the error of the estimates will help determine whether additional factors are necessary.

Least-Squares Sinusoidal

A special case of the multiple linear predictor occurs when periodic peaks can be observed in the sample time series data. These peaks and valleys suggest that the time series may have a cyclic pattern. One of the more well-known uses of cyclic analysis was performed by Hurst in *The Profit Magic of Stock Transaction Timing* (Prentice-Hall), in which there is an interesting example of Fourier analysis applied to the Dow Jones Industrial Averages.

The equation for the approximation of a periodic movement is

$$y_t = a_0 + a_1 t + a_2 \cos \frac{2\pi t}{P} + a_3 \sin \frac{2\pi t}{P} + a_4 t \cos \frac{2\pi t}{P} + a_5 t \sin \frac{2\pi t}{P}$$

which is a special case of the generalized multivariate approximation

$$y = a_0 + a_1 x_1 + a_2 x_2 + a_3 x_3 + a_4 x_4 + a_5 x_5$$

where P is the number of data points in each cycle and

> $x_1 = t$, the incremental time element
> $x_2 = \cos(2\pi t/P)$, a cyclic element
> $x_3 = \sin(2\pi t/P)$, a cyclic element
> $x_4 = t \cos(2\pi t/P)$, an amplitude-variation element
> $x_5 = t \sin(2\pi t/P)$, an amplitude-variation element

The term a_1t will allow for the linear tendencies of the sequence. The term 2π refers to an entire cycle and $2\pi t/P$ designates a section $(1/P)$ of a specific cycle t; this in turn adds weight to either the sin or cos functions at different points within a cycle.

The solution is calculated in the tabular manner of the other methods, using simultaneous linear equations derived in the same way as the generalized multivariate equation, substituting from the table of sums and solving the coefficient matrix for $a_0, \ldots, a_5$. A complete discussion of curve fitting using trigonometric functions appears in Chapter 7 ("Seasonality").

ARIMA

An *Autoregressive Integrated Moving Average* (ARIMA) model is created by a process of repeated regression analysis over a moving time window, resulting in a forecast value. An ARIMA process automatically applies the most important features of regression analysis in a preset order and continues to reanalyze results until an optimum set of parameters or coefficients is found. In Chapter 21, the selection and testing of individual parameters within a trading strategy are discussed. This involves approximating their initial value and identifying a testing range. An ARIMA model does all of this as part of its special process. Because it is used to recalculate the best fit each time a new piece of data appears, it may be thought of as the first *adaptive process.*

G.E.P. Box and G.M. Jenkins refined ARIMA at the University of Wisconsin,[6] and their procedures for solution have become the industry standard. This technique is often referred to as the *Box-Jenkins* forecast. The two important terms in ARIMA are "autoregression" and "moving average." *Autoregression* refers to the use of the same data to self-predict, for example, using only gold prices to arrive at a gold price forecast. *Moving average* refers to the normal concept of smoothing price fluctuations, using an average of the past n days. The moving average and popular variations are discussed thoroughly in Chapters 4 and 5. This process uses an exponential smoothing technique, which is among the most popular methods.

In the ARIMA process, the autocorrelation is used to determine to what extent past prices will forecast future prices. In a first-order autocorrelation, only the prices on the previous day are used to determine the forecast. This would be expressed as

$$P_t = a \times P_{t-1} + e$$

where P_t is the price being forecast (dependent variable)
    P_{t-1} is the price being used to forecast (independent variable)
    a is the coefficient (constant percentage)
    e is the forecast error

In a second-order autoregression, the previous two prices are used as follows:

$$P_t = a_1 \times P_{t-1} + a_2 \times P_{t-2} + e$$

where the current forecast P_t is based on the two previous prices P_{t-1} and P_{t-2}; there are two unique coefficients and a forecast error. The moving average is used to correct for the forecast error, e. There is also the choice of a first- or second-order moving average process,

First-order: $E_t = e_t - b \times e_{t-1}$

Second-order: $E_t = e_t - b_1 \times e_{t-1} - b_2 \times e_{t-2}$

where E_t is the approximated error term
    e_t is today's forecast error

[6] G.E.P. Box and G.M. Jenkins. *Time Series Analysis: Forecasting and Control,* 2nd ed. (Holden-Day, San Francisco, 1976).

e_{t-1} and e_{t-2} are the two previous forecast errors
b_1 and b_2 are the two regression coefficients

Because the two constant coefficients, b_1 and b_2, can be considered percentages, the moving average process is similar to exponential smoothing.

The success of the ARIMA model is determined by two factors: high correlation in the autoregression and low variance in the final forecast errors. The determination of whether to use a first- or second-order autoregression is based on a comparison of the *correlation coefficients* of the two regressions. If there is little improvement using the second-order process, it is not used due to its time-consuming calculations. The final forecast is constructed by adding the moving average term, which approximates the errors, back into the autoregressive process

$$P'_t = P_t + E_t + e'$$

where P'_t is the new forecast, and e' is the new forecast error. The moving average process is again repeated for the new errors e', added back into the forecast to get a new value P'' and another error e''. When the variance of the errors becomes sufficiently small, the ARIMA process is complete.

The contribution of Box and Jenkins was to stress the simplicity of the solution. They determined that the autoregression and moving average steps could be limited to first- or second-order processes. To do this, it was first necessary to detrend the data, thereby making it *stationary*. Detrending can be accomplished most easily by *differencing* the data, that is, creating a new series by subtracting each previous term P_{t-1} from the next P_t. Of course, the ARIMA program must remember all of these changes, or *transformations*, to restore the final forecast to the proper price notation by applying these operations in reverse. If a satisfactory solution is not found in the Box-Jenkins process, it is because the data are still not stationary and further differencing is necessary.

Because of the three features just discussed, the Box-Jenkins forecast is usually shown as *ARIMA(p,d,q)*, where p is the number of autoregressive terms, d is the number of differences, and q is the number of moving average terms. The expression *ARIMA(0,1,1)* is equivalent to simple exponential smoothing, a common technique discussed in the next chapter. In its normal form, the Box-Jenkins ARIMA process performs the following steps:

1. *Specification.* Preliminary steps for determining the order of the autoregression and moving average to be used.

   a. *The variance must be stabilized.* In many price series, increased volatility is directly related to increased price. In stocks, the common assumption is that this relationship is *log-normal.* A simple test for variance stability, using the log function, is checked before more complex transformations are used.

   b. *Prices are detrended.* This uses the technique of first differences; however, a second difference (or more) will be performed if it helps to remove further trending properties in the series (this is determined by later steps).

   c. *Specify the order of the autoregressive and moving average components.* This fixes the number of prior terms to be used in these approximations (not necessarily the same number). In the Box-Jenkins approach, these numbers are usually small, often one for both. Large numbers require a rapidly expanding amount of calculation, even for a computer.

      How many terms are necessary? This is a critical part of the ARIMA solution and may require manual intervention in the computer program. The object of this step is to find the fewest terms necessary to solve the problem. All ARIMA programs will print a *correlogram,* a display of the autocorrelation coefficients. The correlogram is used to find whether all the trends and well-defined periodic movements have been removed from the series by differencing. Figure 3-9 shows three patterns of correlograms printed by *EASI/ARIMA* on a PC. The top scale shows the importance of the coefficients. If they fall within the brackets, they have no importance; if they fall outside the brackets, they are *highly significant* (greater than two standard deviations, or 95%). The left scale gives the *lag* relationship, that is, the relationship of the current price to the price *n* days ago. An asterisk will appear on line 3 outside the bracket (see Figure 3-9*b*) if a strong pattern in the lag 3 relationship to current prices has not yet been removed. To remove this, additional differencing of the data must be performed. If successful, the resulting correlogram will appear as in Figure 3-9*a*, where only the lag 1 and 2 values are outside the bracket. If further differencing results in a pattern shown in Figure 3-9*c*, all correlation of any importance in the data have been lost. If the pattern in Figure 3-9*c* were to occur in the first step, it would mean that there is no relationship to be found by autoregression. If it occurs after some differencing has been performed, the data have been differenced too many times.[7]

2. *Estimation: determining the coefficients.* The previous step was used to reduce the number of autoregressive and moving average terms necessary to the estimation process. The ARIMA method of solution is one of minimizing the errors in the forecast. In minimization, it will perform a linear or nonlinear regression on price (de-

[7] Examples of the correlogram come from Eric Weiss, "Applying ARIMA Forecasts," *Technical Analysis of Stocks & Commodities* (May 1983). Refer to Weiss's two other articles on ARIMA in earlier volumes of the same magazine, especially "ARIMA Forecasting" (January 1983).

FIGURE 3-9 ARIMA correlograms. (*a*) Ideal correlogram results, showing significance in the first and seconds lags only. (*b*) Significance in the first and third lags, indicating that further trend elimination is necessary. (*c*) No significant correlations at any lag values.

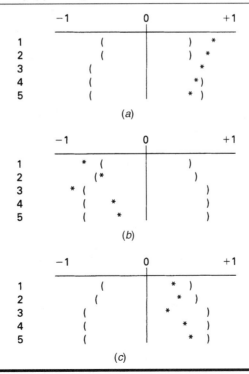

pending on the number of coefficients selected), determine the errors in the estimation, and then approximate those errors using a moving average. It will next look at the resulting new error series, attempt to estimate and correct the errors in that one, and repeat the process until it accounts for all price movement.

To determine when an ARIMA process is completed, three tests are performed at the end of each estimation pass:

a. *Compare the change in the coefficient value.* If the last estimation has caused little or no change in the value of the coefficient(s), the model has successfully converged to a solution.

b. *Compare the sum of the squares of the error.* If the error value is small or if it stays relatively unchanged, the model is completed.

c. *Perform a set number of estimations.* Unless a maximum number of estimations is set, an ARIMA process might continue indefinitely. This safety check is necessary in the event the model is not converging to a solution.

Once completed, the errors can be examined using an O-statistic to check for any trend. If one exists, an additional moving average term may be used to eliminate it.

Forecast Results

Once the coefficients have been determined, they are used to calculate the forecast value. These forecasts are most accurate for the next day and should be used with less confidence for subsequent days (see Figure 3-10).

What if the forecast does not work? First, the process should be checked to be certain that it was performed properly. Pay particular attention to the removal of trends using the correlogram. Next, check the data used in the process. If the data sample is changing (which can be observed on a price chart), select either a shorter or longer period that contains more homogeneous data, that is, data similar to the current market period.

Trading Strategies

In the article that originally piqued the interest of traders,[8] Anon uses a 5-day-ahead forecast. If the ARIMA process forecasts an uptrend and if prices fall below the forecast value,

[8] Louis J. Anon, "Catch Short-Term Profits with ARIMA," *Commodities Magazine* (December 1981).

FIGURE 3-10   ARIMA forecast becomes less accurate as it is used farther ahead.

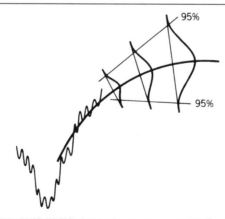

the market can be bought with added confidence (expecting lower risk and more profit). This technique of selecting better entry points may compensate for some of the inaccuracies latent in any forecasting method. The danger of this approach is that prices may continue to move counter to the forecast, so that caution and a stop-loss are also necessary.

Following the Trend

Use the 1-day-ahead forecast to determine the trend position. If the forecast is for higher prices, a long position should be held; if it is predicting lower prices, shorts are necessary.

Countertrend Indicator

Use the ARIMA confidence bands to determine overbought/oversold levels. Not only can a long position be entered when prices penetrate the lowest 95% confidence band, but they can be closed out when they return to the normal 50% level. A conservative trader will enter the market only in the direction of the ARIMA trend forecast. As shown in Figure 3-10, if the trend is up, only the penetrations of the lower band will be used to enter new long positions.

Use of Highs and Lows

Both the implied highs and lows as well as the independently forecasted highs and lows can be the basis for other interesting strategies.[9] The following two are used with intraday prices.

1. Using confidence bands based on the closing prices, buy an intraday penetration of the expected high or sell a penetration of the expected low, and liquidate the position on the close. Use a stop-loss. Consider taking positions only in the direction of the ARIMA trend.
2. Using the separate ARIMA models based on the daily high and low prices, buy a penetration of the 50% level of the high and sell a penetration of the 50% level of the lows. Liquidate positions on the close. Use a stop-loss.

Slope

The one-day-ahead forecast suggested in "Following the Trend," a few paragraphs earlier, is essentially a projection of the slope of the trendline. Because of the frequent erratic price movement, also called *noise,* the purpose of directional analysis, whether regression or moving averages, is to uncover the true direction of prices. Therefore, the slope of the trendline, or the direction of the regression forecast, is the logical answer.

The popular alternate for triggering a new directional signal is a price penetration of an envelope or band value. Using regression analysis that band can be replaced by a confidence level. While it is true that the number of random, or false, penetrations declines as the confidence band gets farther away from the trendline, so does the total number of penetrations. At any band distance there are still a large number of erroneous signals. The slope itself should be viewed as the best approximation of direction.

Kalman Filters

Kalman offers an alternative approach to ARIMA, allowing an underlying forecasting model (*message model*) to be combined with other timely information (*observation model*). The message model may be any trading strategy, moving average, or regression approach. The observation model may be the floor broker's opening calls, market liquidity, or, in the case of existing foreign markets, earlier trading activity—all of which have been determined to have some overriding importance in forecasting.

[9] John F. Kepka, "Trading With ARIMA Forecasts," *Technical Analysis of Stocks & Commodities* (August 1985).

Assume that the original forecast (message) model can be described as

$$M(P_t) = c_f P_{t-1} + me_t$$

and the observation model as

$$O(P_t) = c_0 P_t + oe_t$$

where *me* and *oe* are the message and observation model errors, respectively. The combined forecast would then use the observation model error to modify the result

$$P'_{t+1} = c_f P'_t + K_{t+1} oe_t$$

where K is the Kalman gain coefficient,[10] a factor that adjusts the error term.

LINEAR REGRESSION MODEL

A linear regression, or straight-line fit, could be the basis for a simple trading strategy similar to a moving average. For example, an *n*-day linear regression, applied to the closing prices, could be used with the following rules:

1. *Buy* when the closing price moves above the forecasted value of today's close.
2. *Sell* when the closing price moves below the forecasted value of today's close.[11]

There is an important difference between a model based on linear regression and one founded on a moving average. There is no lag in a regression strategy. If prices continue higher at the same rate, a moving average system will initially lag behind, then increase at the same rate. The lag creates a safety zone to absorb some changes in the direction of prices, without getting stopped out. (See Chapter 4 for a complete discussion of moving averages, and Chapter 5 for a comparison of a Linear Regression Slope trading system with five other popular trending methods.)

A regression model, on the other hand, identifies a change of direction sooner by measuring future movement against a straight-line projection in which the current price value has little influence. A steady price move, however, will place the fitted line right in the center of market movement, subject to frequent whipsaws. The area at which a uniform trend changes from one direction to another is a difficult case for a linear regression system (see Figure 3-11) and points out the need for using bands. Even with bands, the turning point of an orderly trend will appear to have much greater variance than during the direction period over the same calculation interval.

In Figure 3-11a, the three positions of the regression line all show numerous penetrations of the price, resulting in many losing trades. This is natural because the regression line is fitted best when it goes through the center of price movement. For prices to remain on one side of a regression line it must be constantly accelerating or decelerating, an unlikely situation. It is possible that this approach would work better using very few calculation periods; however, the use of only a few days is inconsistent with the nature of such a statistical measurement, which gains significance with more data. Figure 3-11b shows the more practical use of a *confidence band* spaced equally around the regression line. Using a high-confidence band (e.g., 95%), it is possible to turn the erratic performance in Figure 3-11a into two clearly identifiable trends. Interestingly, the use of a confi-

[10] For a more complete discussion, see Andrew D. Seidel and Philip D. Ginsberg's *Commodities Trading* (Prentice-Hall, Englewood Cliffs, NJ, 1983), or R.E. Kalman's "A New Approach to Linear Filtering and Prediction Problems," *Journal of Basic Engineering* (March 1960).

[11] These rules were used by Frank Hochheimer in *Computerized Trading Techniques 1982* (Merrill Lynch Commodities, New York, 1982).

FIGURE 3-11   Linear regression model. (*a*) Simple penetration of the regression lines. (*b*) Penetration of the channel formed by confidence bands.

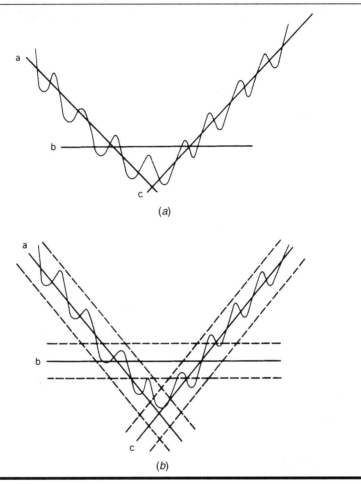

(*a*)

(*b*)

dence band with the regression analysis looks remarkably similar to a channel on a standard bar chart.

Hochheimer's 1982 study, performed without a channel or confidence band, shows the best selection of the regression interval at 60 to 70 days (the maximum tested was 70 days). Silver had a remarkable 1,615 trades—one each day. Only two markets showed average trade duration greater than 2 days. We can draw the conclusion that successful regression-based systems seek out longer time periods.

4

Trend Calculations

The purpose of all trend identification methods is to see past the underlying noise in the market, those erratic moves that seem to be meaningless, and find the current direction of prices. Because there may be more than one trend at any one time, caused by short-term events and long-term policy, it is possible to search for the strongest, or most dominant trend, or a minor trend that corresponds to your expected time frame. The technique that is used to uncover the right trend depends upon whether any of the trend characteristics are known. Does it have a seasonal or cyclic component, is it based on long-term monetary policy, or is it an overnight effect? The more you know about the reasons why prices trend, the better you will be able to find the most reliable calculation for separating the price direction from market noise.

Chapter 3, "Regression Analysis," produced forecasts by finding relationships between two or more price series. Once you know that there is a fundamental relationship between data, based on measuring the properties of dependence and correlation, a formula can be found that expresses one price movement in terms of the other prices and data. The predictive qualities of these methods are best when applied to data that has been seen before, that is, prices that are within the range of historic data. Forecasting reliability decreases sharply when values are based on extrapolation outside the previous occurrences. This phenomenon will also be true of other trending methods. Because of the way we test and define the final trend calculation, it is based on the movement of historical data; when prices move to new levels, the results of the model will often deteriorate.

FORECASTING AND FOLLOWING

There is a clear distinction between forecasting the trend and determining the current trend. Forecasting, predicting the future price, is much more desirable but very complex. As shown in the previous chapter, it may involve combining many pieces of data and result in a forecasted price with a confidence level. The further you try to forecast into the future, the lower the confidence.

The techniques most commonly used for evaluating the direction or tendency of prices both within prior ranges or at new levels are called *autoregressive* functions. Unlike forecasting models, they are only concerned with evaluating the current price direction. This analysis is normally used to conclude that prices are moving in an upward, downward, or sideways direction. From this simple building block, it will be possible to form rules of action and develop complex strategies of anticipation. From a practical viewpoint, these trending methods are more flexible than the traditional regression models, but to achieve success they introduce a lag. A great effort has been spent trying to reduce this lag.

In an autoregressive model, one or more of the previous day's prices determine the next sequential price. If P_t represents today's price, P_{t-1} yesterday's, and so on, then tomorrow's expected price will be

$$P_{t-1} = a_0 + a_1 P_t + a_2 P_{t-1} + \cdots + a_t P_1 + e$$

where each price is given a corresponding weighting a_i and combined to give the resultant price for tomorrow $P_{t+1} \pm e$ (where e represents an error factor). The simplest example is the use of yesterday's price alone to generate tomorrow's price:

$$P_{t+1} = a_0 + a_1 P_t + e$$

which you may also recognize as the formula for a straight line, $y = a + bx$.

The autoregressive model does not have to be linear; each prior day can have a nonlinear predictive quality. Thus each expected price P_{t+1} could be represented by a curvilinear expression, $P_{t+1} = a_0 + a_1 P_t + a_2 P_{t-1}^2 + e$, or by an exponential or logarithmic formula, $\ln P_{t+1} = a_0 + a_1 \ln P_t + a_2 \ln P_{t-1} + e$, which is commonly used in equity analysis. All of these expressions could then be combined to form an autoregressive forecasting model for P_{t+1}. In going from the simple to the complex, it is natural to want to know which of these choices will perform best. The answer can only be found by application to a specific problem, validation, and experience. Various methods, based on a sound premise, must be attempted and applied to actual data in real-time or extrapolated situations to determine the predictive quality of any model. Chapters 5 and 15 will discuss which choices have been most popular and Chapter 21 will show testing methods that are most likely to lead to robust results.

LEAST-SQUARES MODEL

The least-squares regression model is the same technique that was used in the previous chapter to find the relationship between two dependent markets, corn and soybeans, or to find how prices moved when driven by known related factors such as supply and demand. Here, the least-squares model will be used to find the relationship between time and price, rather than between two prices, where the price forecast that we are seeking is dependent upon time. The regression model will also be applied in an autoregressive way by recalculating the expected price daily and using the slope of the resulting straight line or curvilinear fit to determine the direction of the trend.

A simple error analysis can be used to evaluate the predictive qualities of this method. Assume that there is a lengthy price series for a market and that we would like to know how many prior days are optimum for predicting the next day's price. The answer is found by looking at the average error in the predictions. If the number of days in the calculation increases and if the predictive error decreases, the answer is improving; if the error stops decreasing, the accuracy limit has been reached. Error analysis can improve most trend calculations, and it is also covered in the section on exponential smoothing later in this chapter. As an example, start by using only one prior day to find the price forecast

$$P_{t+1} = a_0 + a_1 P_t$$

$$P_t = a_0 + a_1 P_{t-1}$$

$$P_{t-1} = a_0 + a_1 P_{t-2}$$

$$\vdots$$

$$P_2 = a_0 + a_1 P_1$$

and work up to a large number of days:

$$P_{t+1} = a_0 + a_1 P_t + a_2 P_{t-1} + \cdots + a_n P_{t-n+1}$$

$$P_t = a_0 + a_1 P_{t-1} + a_2 P_{t-2} + \cdots + a_n P_{t-n}$$

$$P_{t-1} = a_0 + a_1 P_{t-2} + a_2 P_{t-3} + \cdots + a_n P_{t-n-1}$$

In the last case, it takes n days of prior prices to generate each new prediction. In all cases, $n + 2$ equations can be written to solve the $n + 1$ coefficients $a_0, a_1, a_2, \ldots, a_n$, using the matrix elimination method found in Appendix 3. The result is a predicted price P_t' for each actual price P_t. We will use the notation $P'(n)_t$ to mean the predicted price for day t using an n-day linear regression; therefore, $P'(3)_{25} = 58.00$ means that the predicted value of P on day 25 was 58.00 using a 3-day linear regression analysis (a straight-line fit of the 3 prior days). The error occurring in each prediction is defined as

$$E(n)_t = P - P'(n)_t$$

the difference between the actual and predicted values for that day using the n-day linear regression. As an example of error analysis, a copper sequence was selected for a period of 20 trading days that included a slight upward and a slight downward move, with some intermediate changes of direction. Table 4-1 shows the actual predictions using linear regressions for 2 through 7 prior prices and a prediction of one day forward. Table 4-2 shows the relative error in these predictions and an analysis of the errors. The *mean*, shown at the bottom of Table 4-2, is a simple average of all the points and gives the net trend bias during the sample period; the small range from negative to positive shows very little bias. The *standard deviation* measures the accuracy of the forecast. When the standard deviation is small, the predicted values are closer to the actual values and the forecast error is smaller.

The standard deviation and variance are both measurements of the distribution of points around the fitted line. As discussed in Chapter 2, the standard deviation measures the occurrence of points near the predictions; the smaller the value, the closer the grouping and the better the estimation. The variance is another way of looking at the deviations; the smaller the variance, the better the forecast. The copper error analysis shows the smallest values for $E(4)_t$, the 4-day linear regression. This is an interesting result because we would expect the shortest forecasting interval to produce the smallest error simply because prices cannot move as far from the forecast in 2 days as they can in 7 days. Therefore, we should expect the absolute size of the error, as measured by the standard deviation or variance, to get larger as the forecasting period gets larger. The smaller error produced by the 4-day regression shows that there was a pattern during this short test that could be fit better by the 4-day model than by any of the others.

Determination of the best predictive model using error analysis can be applied to any forecasting technique. This works particularly well when comparing the errors of two different forecasting methods evaluated over the same number of periods, eliminating the bias caused by longer and shorter intervals. It is also practical to carry the error analysis one step further and include the results of the prediction error on day $t + 1$, $t + 2$, and so on. This gives a measure of out-of-sample forecast accuracy and lends confidence to the predictive qualities of the technique.

Having selected the most accurate forecast model, the size of the prior day predictive error can be used to resolve trading decisions. Consider the following situations:

1. The prediction and the actual price are very close (high confidence level). For example, the long-term copper error may have 1 standard deviation = .25.
2. Today's forecast error is within 1 standard deviation of expectations; therefore, we continue to follow the trend strategy.
3. Today's forecast error is between 1 and 3 standard deviations of expectations; therefore, we are cautious, yet understand that this is normal but less frequent.
4. Today's forecast error is greater than 3 standard deviations. This is unusual, indicates high risk, and may identify a price shock. Alternately, it could indicate a trend turning point.

TABLE 4-1   Analysis of Predictive Error for Copper

Date	Sequence (t)	Price P_t	Price Predictions for n-Day Linear Regression					
			$P'(2)_t$	$P'(3)_t$	$P'(4)_t$	$P'(5)_t$	$P'(6)_t$	$P'(7)_t$
10-21	1	60.30						
10-22	2	59.30						
10-25	3	58.70						
10-26	4	57.80						
10-27	5	59.80						
10-28	6	58.20						
10-29	7	58.40						
11-01	8	58.90	58.60	57.40	58.60	58.52	58.30	57.95
11-03	9	59.10	59.40	59.20	58.20	58.86	58.75	58.53
11-04	10	61.00	59.30	59.50	59.45	58.67	59.10	58.98
11-05	11	62.10	61.90	61.77	61.35	60.15	60.15	60.30
11-08	12	62.00	63.20	63.73	63.15	62.75	62.37	61.53
11-09	13	62.50	61.90	62.70	63.50	63.38	63.20	62.94
11-10	14	63.50	63.00	62.60	63.00	63.68	63.71	63.64
11-11	15	61.30	64.50	64.16	63.70	63.84	64.34	64.38
11-12	16	61.70	60.10	61.23	62.05	62.25	62.69	63.36
11-15	17	62.00	62.10	60.36	61.10	61.66	61.87	62.30
11-16	18	62.20	62.30	62.37	61.10	61.36	61.71	61.86
11-17	19	61.70	62.40	62.47	62.55	61.57	61.64	61.85
11-18	20	61.50	61.20	61.67	61.95	62.17	61.47	61.51
11-19	21	62.40	61.30	61.10	61.35	61.61	61.85	61.31
11-22	22	61.40	63.30	62.57	62.05	61.99	62.07	62.20
11-23	23	59.90	60.40	61.67	61.75	61.57	61.61	61.73
11-24	24	59.80	58.40	58.73	59.85	60.29	60.37	60.58
11-26	25	59.10	59.70	58.76	58.85	59.22	59.59	59.71
11-29	26	59.50	58.40	58.85	58.30	58.06	58.55	58.87
11-30	27	59.10	59.90	59.17	59.10	58.56	58.20	58.48

THE MOVING AVERAGE

The simplest and most well-known of all smoothing techniques is called the *moving average* (MA). Using this method, the number of elements to be averaged remains the same, but the time interval advances. Using a generalized time series as an example, P_0, P_1, P_2, ..., P_t are a sequence of prices. A moving average measured over n of these prices, or data points, at time t would be

$$\text{MA}_t = \frac{P_t + P_{t-1} + \cdots + P_{t-n+1}}{n} = \frac{\sum_{i=1}^{n} P_{t-i+1}}{n}, \qquad n \le t$$

In other words, the most recent moving average calculation is the average (arithmetic mean) of the prior n data points. For example, using three points ($n = 3$) to generate a moving average:

$$\text{MA}_3 = (P_1 + P_2 + P_3)/3$$
$$\text{MA}_4 = (P_2 + P_3 + P_4)/3$$
$$\vdots$$
$$\text{MA}_t = (P_{t-2} + P_{t-1} + P_t)/3$$

TABLE 4-2   Analysis of Predictive Error for Copper

Date	Sequence (t)	Price P_t	$E(2)_t$	$E(3)_t$	$E(4)_t$	$E(5)_t$	$E(6)_t$	$E(7)_t$
					Predictive Error for an n-Day Linear Regression			
10-21	1	60.30						
10-22	2	59.30						
10-25	3	58.70						
10-26	4	57.80						
10-27	5	59.80						
10-28	6	58.20						
10-29	7	58.40						
11-01	8	58.90	−.30	−1.50	−.30	−.38	−.60	−.95
11-03	9	59.10	.30	.10	−.90	−.24	−.35	−.57
11-04	10	61.00	−1.70	−1.50	−1.55	−2.33	−1.90	−2.02
11-05	11	62.10	−.20	−.33	−.75	−1.95	−1.95	−1.80
11-08	12	62.00	1.20	1.73	1.15	.75	.37	−.47
11-09	13	62.50	−.60	.20	1.00	.88	.70	.44
11-10	14	63.50	−.50	−.90	−.50	.18	.21	.14
11-11	15	61.30	3.20	2.86	2.40	2.54	3.04	3.08
11-12	16	61.70	−1.60	−.47	.35	.55	.99	1.66
11-15	17	62.00	.10	−1.64	−.90	−.34	−.13	.30
11-16	18	62.20	.10	.17	−1.10	−.84	−.49	−.34
11-17	19	61.70	.70	.77	.85	−.13	−.06	.15
11-18	20	61.50	−.30	.17	.45	.67	−.03	.01
11-19	21	62.40	−1.10	−1.30	−1.05	−.79	−.65	−1.09
11-22	22	61.40	1.90	1.17	.65	.59	.67	.80
11-23	23	59.90	.50	1.77	1.85	1.67	1.71	1.83
11-24	24	59.80	−1.40	−1.07	.05	.49	.57	.78
11-26	25	59.10	.60	−.34	−.25	.12	.49	.61
11-29	26	59.50	−1.10	−.70	−1.20	−1.44	−.95	−.63
11-30	27	59.10	.80	.07	.00	−.54	−.90	−.62
σ (Standard deviation)			1.209	1.217	1.069	1.151	1.149	1.220
M (Mean)			.030	−.037	.012	−.027	.037	.065
V (Variance)			1.389	1.406	1.086	1.260	1.255	1.415

If P_t represented a price at a specific time, the moving average would smooth the price movement. When more prices are used, the new price will be a smaller part of the average and have less effect on the final value. Five successive prices form a five-day moving average. When the next sequential price is added and the oldest is dropped off, the prior average is changed by ⅕ of the difference between the old and the new values. If

$$\text{MA}_5 = (P_1 + P_2 + P_3 + P_4 + P_5)/5$$

and

$$\text{MA}_6 = (P_2 + P_3 + P_4 + P_5 + P_6)/5$$

then $c = P_2 + P_3 + P_4 + P_5$ can be substituted for the common part of the moving average, solved for c, and substituted to get

$$\text{MA}_6 = \text{MA}_5 + (P_t - P_{t-n})/5$$

This also gives a faster way to calculate a moving average. It can be seen that the more terms in the moving average, the less effect the addition of a new term is likely to have:

$$\text{MA}_t = \text{MA}_{t-1} + (P_t - P_{t-n})/n$$

The selection of the proper number of terms is based on both the technical consideration of the predictive quality of the choice (measured by the error) and the need to determine price trends over specific time periods for commercial use. The more days or data points used in the moving average, the more smoothing will occur; variation lasting only a short while will have less effect. There is also a danger of losing cyclic or seasonal price patterns by selecting the wrong value of n. For example, a repeating cycle of four data points 5, 8, 3, 6, 9, 4, 7, . . . , which advances by the value 1 each complete cycle, will appear as a straight line if a moving average of 4 days is used. If there is a possibility of a cyclic or seasonal pattern within the data, care should be taken to select a moving average that is out of phase with the possible pattern (that is, not equal to the cycle period).

The length of the moving average must also relate to its use. A jeweler may purchase silver each week to produce bracelets. Frequent purchases of small amounts keep the company's cash outlay small. The purchaser can wait as long as possible while prices continue to trend downward during any one week but will buy immediately when prices turn upward. A 6-month trend cannot help his problem, because it gives a long-term answer to a short-term issue; however, a 5-day moving average may give the trend direction within the jeweler's time frame.

User-Friendly Software

Fortunately, we have reached a time when it is not necessary to perform these calculations the long way. Spreadsheet programs and specialized testing software provide simple tools for performing trend calculations as well as many other more complex functions discussed in this book. The notation for many of the different spreadsheets and software is very similar and self-explanatory:

Function	Spreadsheet	Omega
Sum	@sum(list, period)	@summation(value, period)
Moving average	@avg(list, period)	@average(value, period)
Standard deviation	@std(list, period)	@stddev(value, period)

What Do You Average?

The closing or daily settlement is the most common price applied to a moving average. It is generally accepted as the true price of the day and is used by many analysts for calculation of trends. But other alternatives exist. The average of the high and low prices of the day will smooth the results by preventing the maximum difference from occurring when the close is also the high or low. Similarly, the closing price may be added to the high and low, and an average of the three used as the basis for the moving average.

Another valid component of a moving average can be other averages. For example, if P_1 through P_n are prices, and MA_n is a 3-day moving average, then

$$MA_3 = (P_1 + P_2 + P_3)/3$$

$$MA_4 = (P_2 + P_3 + P_4)/3$$

$$MA_5 = (P_3 + P_4 + P_5)/3$$

and

$$MA_5' = (MA_3 + MA_4 + MA_5)/3$$

MA_5' is a *double-smoothed* moving average, which gives added weight to the center points. More on double smoothing can be found later in this chapter. Smoothing the highs and lows independently is another technique that creates a representation of the daily trading range, or volatility. This has been used to identify normal and extreme moves, and will also be discussed in Chapter 5 ("Trend Systems").

Types of Moving Averages

Besides varying the length of the moving average and the elements that are to be averaged, there are a great number of variations on the moving average.

An *accumulative average* may be used for a long-term trend. It does not satisfy our strict definition of a moving average, because it adds data but does not discard any; therefore, it is cumulative. It is traditionally started at the beginning of a futures contract and continued until the contract expires. It may be applied to stocks after each dividend notice. Due to the accumulation of prices and the constant increase in the length of the average, the effect of the additional price at day t on the moving average will be $(P_t - AVG)/t$, where AVG is the average of all prices from the beginning through t. The impact of 1 day becomes very small toward the end of a 1-year contract, which has approximately 250 trading days. A *reset accumulative average* is a modification of the standard accumulative average and attempts to correct for the loss of sensitivity as the number of trading days becomes large. This alternative allows you to reset or restart the moving average whenever a new trend begins, a significant event occurs, or at some specified time interval.

Truncated moving averages are the most common, and they are often called *simple moving averages.* The most basic has already been discussed in detail. An alternate method of calculating a daily moving average calculation is to keep the total of the past n days. Each new day then only requires the addition of the new value and subtraction of the oldest one. The new total is saved for the next day and is also divided by n to get the new moving average value. An interesting twist to this technique is the *average-modified method,* in which the price of the new day is added and the last moving average value is subtracted. Returning to the example of a 5-day moving average, day 6 was

$$MA_6 = MA_5 + (P_6 - P_1)/5$$

This becomes

$$MA_6 = MA_5 + (P_6 - MA_5)/5$$

The average-modified version is convenient, because only the prior moving average value and the new price are necessary for each calculation. The substitution of the moving average value tends to smooth the results even more than a simple moving average. Its use prevents the difference $(P_6 - P_1)$ from becoming too extreme; it effectively cuts the possible range in half and dampens the end-off impact.

The *weighted moving average* opens many possibilities. It allows the significance of individual or groups of data to be changed. It may restore proper value to parts of a data sample, or it may incorrectly bias the data. A weighted moving average is expressed in its general form as

$$W_t = \frac{w_1 P_t + w_2 P_{t-1} + \cdots + w_n P_{t-n+1}}{w_1 + w_2 + \cdots + w_n} = \frac{\sum_{i=1}^{n} w_i P_{t-i+1}}{\sum_{i=1}^{n} w_i}$$

This gives the weighted moving average at time t as the average of the previous n prices, each with its own weighting factor w_i. The most popular form of this technique is called *front-loaded,* because it gives more weight to the most recent data and reduces the significance of the older elements. Therefore, for the front-loaded weighted moving average (see Figure 4-1)

$$w_1 \geq w_2 \geq \cdots \geq w_n$$

The weighting factors w_i may also be determined by regression analysis, but then they may not necessarily be front-loaded. A common modification to front loading is called *step weighting* in which each successive w_i differs from the previous weighting factor w_{i-1} by a fixed increment

$$c = w_i - w_{i-1}$$

The simplest case takes integer values for an *n*-day step-weighted moving average:

$$w_1 = n$$
$$w_2 = n - 1$$
$$\vdots$$
$$w_n = 1$$

This gives the weighting factors the values of 5, 4, 3, 2, and 1 for a 5-day average. A computer program for calculating a linearly weighted moving average is

FIGURE 4-1   A comparison of moving averages.

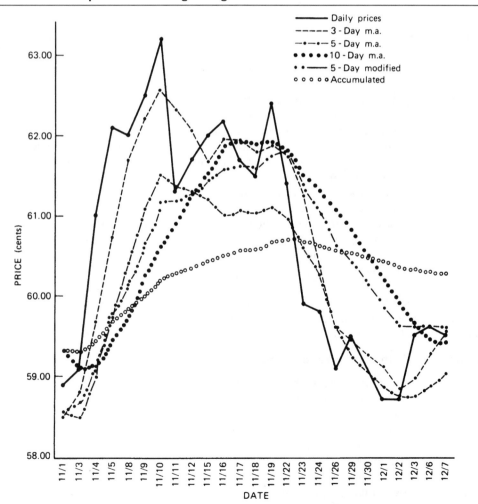

```
1      sum = 0;
2      for I = 1 to N begin
3          M = N - I + 1;
4          sum = sum + M*price;
5          end;
6      LWMA = sum/ ( N* (N+1) /2)
```

In line 6, the divisor $(N*(N+1))/2$ is the arithmetic formula for the sum of $1 + 2 + \cdots + N$. Another approach would be a percentage relationship between w_i elements,

$$w_{i-1} = a \times w_i$$

where $a = .90$; then, $w_5 = 5$, $w_4 = 4.5$, $w_3 = 4.05$, $w_2 = 3.645$, and $w_1 = 3.2805$.

Prices may also be weighted in groups. If every two consecutive data elements have the same weighting factor,

$$W_t = \frac{w_1 P_t + w_1 P_{t-1} + w_2 P_{t-2} + w_3 P_t - 3 + \cdots + w_{n/2} P_{t-n+1}}{2 \times (w_1 + w_2 + \cdots + w_{n/2})}$$

or, grouped with n even,

$$W_t = \frac{w_1(P_t + P_{t-1}) + w_2(P_{t-2} + P_{t-3}) + \cdots + w_{n/2}(P_{t-n+2} + P_{t-n+1})}{2 \times (w_1 + w_2 + \cdots + w_{n/2})}$$

Any number of consecutive data elements can be grouped for a step-weighted moving average. Because there can be any number of combinations, there is no simple, automatic method for calculating anything other than a linearly weighted average, which is the function @WAverage(price, length) in Omega's *Easy Language*. If the purpose of weighting is to duplicate a pattern that is intrinsic to price movement, then the following sections on geometric averages and exponential smoothing may provide better tools.

These moving averages can also be plotted in different ways, each way having a major impact on their interpretation. The conventional plot places the moving average value MA_t on the same vertical line as the last entry P_6 of the moving average. When prices have been trending higher over the period of calculation, this will cause the value MA_t to lag behind (or below) the actual prices; when prices are declining, the moving average will be above the prices (see Figure 4-2).

The plotted moving average can either *lead* or *lag* the last price recorded. If it is to lead by 3 days, the value MA_t is plotted on the vertical line $t + 3$; if it is to lag by 2 days, it is plotted at $t - 2$. In the case of leading moving averages, the analysis attempts to compensate for the time delay by judging price direction using a forecast based on current rate of change and direction. A penetration of the forecasted line by the price may be used to signal a change of direction. The lag technique may also serve the more sophisticated purpose of *phasing* the moving average. A 10-day moving average, when lagged by 5 days, will be plotted in the middle of the actual price data. This technique will be covered later.

Comparison of Moving Average Methods

The comparison seen in Table 4-3 confirms that simple moving averages taken over shorter periods identify shorter trends. The 3-day moving average trendline had 9 separate trends, while the 10-day had only 5. The 5-day average modified method was very similar to the 10-day simple moving average due to removing the average price each day. The cumulative average showed the fewest trends even though it began its accumulation process only 10 days prior; as time increases, this trend will become less responsive. For this short sample interval, the 10-day linearly weighted average was identical to the average modified method and very similar to the 10-day simple average; however, because it weights the recent data 10 times greater than the oldest, this similarity will not continue. A closer look will show that the trend values are very different.

FIGURE 4-2 Plotting lag and lead for a 10-day step-weighted moving average with weighting factors of 10, 9, 8, ...

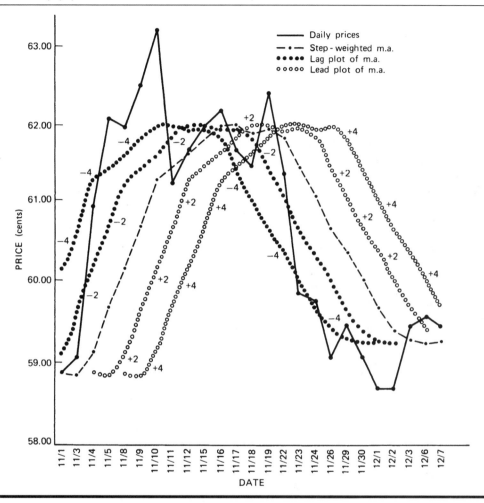

Triangular Weighting

While the simple moving average or linear regression treats each price equally, exponential smoothing and linear step weighting puts greater weight on the most recent data. There is an entire area of study in which the period of the dominant cycle is the basis for determining the best trend period. Triangular filtering[1] is a related concept that attempts to uncover the trend by reducing the noise on both the front and rear of the trend window, where it is expected to have the greatest interference. Therefore, if a 20-day weighted average is used, the 10th day will have the greatest weight, while days 1 and 20 will have the smallest.

To implement triangular weighting, begin with the standard formula for a weighted average,

$$W_t = \frac{\sum\limits_{i=1}^{n} w_i P_{t-i+1}}{\sum\limits_{i=1}^{n} w_i}$$

[1] J.J. Payne, "A better way to smooth data," *Technical Analysis of Stocks & Commodities* (October 1989).

TABLE 4-3 Comparison of Moving Averages Methods*

	Price	Simple Moving Averages			5-Day Average Modified	Cum Average	10-Day Linearly Weighted
		3-Day	5-Day	10-Day			
930316	64.59						
930317	64.23						
930318	65.26						
930319	65.24						
930322	65.07						
930323	65.14						
930324	64.98						
930325	64.76						
930326	65.11						
930329	65.46	65.11	65.09	64.98	78.10	65.46	65.08
930330	65.94	65.50	65.25	65.12	75.67	65.07	65.26
930331	66.10	65.83	65.47	65.31	73.76	65.16	65.43
930401	66.87	66.30	65.90	65.47	72.38	65.29	65.72
930402	66.56	66.51	66.19	65.60	71.22	65.38	65.92
930405	66.71	66.71	66.44	65.76	70.31	65.47	66.12
930406	66.19	66.49	66.49	65.87	69.49	65.51	66.20
930407	66.14	66.35	66.49	65.98	68.82	65.55	66.25
930408	66.64	66.32	66.45	66.17	68.38	65.61	66.37
930412	67.33	66.70	66.60	66.39	68.17	65.70	66.58
930413	68.18	67.38	66.90	66.67	68.17	65.83	66.90
930414	67.48	67.66	67.15	66.82	68.04	65.90	67.05
930415	67.19	67.62	67.36	66.93	67.87	65.96	67.12
930416	66.46	67.04	67.33	66.89	67.59	65.98	67.03
930419	67.20	66.95	67.30	66.95	67.51	66.03	67.09
930420	67.62	67.09	67.19	67.04	67.53	66.10	67.21
930421	67.66	67.49	67.23	67.19	67.56	66.16	67.32
930422	67.89	67.72	67.37	67.37	67.62	66.22	67.45
930423	69.19	68.25	67.91	67.62	67.94	66.33	67.78
930426	69.68	68.92	68.41	67.86	68.29	66.44	68.15
930427	69.31	69.39	68.75	67.97	68.49	66.54	68.42
930428	69.11	69.37	69.04	68.13	68.61	66.62	68.63
930429	69.27	69.23	69.31	68.34	68.75	66.71	68.83
930430	68.97	69.12	69.27	68.59	68.79	66.77	68.95
930503	69.11	69.12	69.15	68.78	68.85	66.84	69.04
930504	69.50	69.19	69.19	68.97	68.98	66.92	69.17
930505	69.70	69.44	69.31	69.17	69.13	67.00	69.31
930506	69.94	69.71	69.44	69.38	69.29	67.08	69.45
930507	69.11	69.58	69.47	69.37	69.25	67.13	69.40
930510	67.64	68.90	69.18	69.17	68.93	67.14	69.08
930511	67.75	68.17	68.83	69.01	68.69	67.16	68.83
930512	67.47	67.62	68.38	68.85	68.45	67.16	68.55
930513	67.50	67.57	67.89	68.67	68.26	67.17	68.30
930514	68.18	67.72	67.71	68.59	68.24	67.20	68.21
930517	67.35	67.68	67.65	68.41	68.07	67.20	67.99
930518	66.74	67.42	67.45	68.14	67.80	67.19	67.68
930519	67.00	67.03	67.35	67.87	67.64	67.19	67.48
930520	67.46	67.07	67.35	67.62	67.60	67.19	67.40
930521	67.36	67.27	67.18	67.45	67.56	67.19	67.35
930524	67.37	67.40	67.19	67.42	67.52	67.20	67.34
930525	67.78	67.50	67.39	67.42	67.57	67.21	67.41
930526	67.96	67.70	67.59	67.47	67.65	67.22	67.50
No. Trends		11	9	5	5	3	5

* The gray areas of the table show downtrends.

where n is the size, or width, of the window. The weighting factors w_i will increase linearly from 1 to the middle of the window, at $n/2$, then decrease to the end at n. This has a slightly different form when the period is odd or even,

$w_i = i,$ `for i = 1 to @intportion((n+2)/2)`

   $n - i + 1,$ `for i = @intportion((n+2)/2) + 1 to n`   (even values of n)

   $n - i,$ `for i = @intportion((n+2)/2) + 1 to n`   (odd values of n)

where, for odd values of n, the weight factor has the value i when i ranges from 1 to $n/2$ (rounded up using the function for the integer portion) and the value of $n - i$ from $n/2$ to n. Instead of a triangular filter, which is very precise about the middle value having the greatest importance, we may choose a Gaussian filter, which weights the data in a form similar to a bell curve. Here, the weighting factors are more complex,

$$w_i = 10^x \quad \text{and} \quad x = \frac{3}{2}\left(1 - \frac{2i}{n}\right)^2$$

Pivot-Point Weighting

Too often we limit ourselves by our training. When a weighted moving average is used, it is normal to assume that all the weighting factors should be positive; however, that is not a requirement. The *pivot-point moving average* uses linear weights (e.g., 5, 4, . . .) that begin with a positive value and continue to decline even when they become negative.[2] This method treats the oldest data in a manner opposite to their direction. In the following formula, a pivot point, where the weighting is zero, is reached about ⅔ of the way through the data interval. For a pivot-point moving average of 11 values, the 8th data point is weighted with 0:

$$\text{PPMA}_t(11) = (7P_t + 6P_t + 5P_t + 4P_t + 3P_t + 2P_t + 1P_t + 0P_t - 1P_t - 2P_t - 3P_t)/22$$

This technique is intended to limit the lag by front loading the prices and reducing the divisor of the weighting formula by the sum of the negative weighting factors. The general formula for an n-day pivot-point moving average is[3]

$$\text{PPMA}_t(n) = \frac{2}{n(n + 1)} \sum_{i=1}^{n} (3i - n - 1)P_i$$

To implement this in a computer program, the following steps would be used:

```
1    sum = 0;
2    for I = 1 to N begin
3        M = N - I + 1;
4        sum = sum + P[M]*(3*I - N - 1);
5        end;
6    PPMA = sum*(2/(N* (N+1)))
```

where lines 2 through 5 calculate the sum of the prices times the weighting factor, and line 6 divides that sum by the sum of the weighting factors (after multiplying the top and bottom of the fraction by the value 2).

The negative weighting factors reverse the impact of the price move for the oldest data points rather than just give them less importance. For a short interval this can cause the trendline to be out-of-phase with prices. The application of this method should be limited to longer-term cyclic markets, where the reflection point, at which the weighting factor becomes zero, aligns with the cyclic turn or can be fixed at the point of the last trend change.

[2] Patrick E. Lafferty, "End-Point Moving Average," *Technical Analysis of Stocks & Commodities* (October 1995).

[3] Don Kraska, "Letters To S&C," *Technical Analysis of Stocks & Commodities* (February 1996, p. 12).

GEOMETRIC MOVING AVERAGES

The *geometric mean* is a growth function that is very applicable to long-term price movement, introduced in Chapter 2 ("Basic Concepts"). It is especially useful calculating the components of an index. The geometric mean can also be applied to the most recent n points at time t to get a geometric average similar to a moving average

$$G_t = (P_t \times P_{t-1} \times \cdots \times P_{t-n+1})^{(1/n)} = \left(\prod_{i=1}^{n} P_{t-i+1}\right)^{(1/n)}$$

The daily calculation is more complicated but, as shown in Chapter 2, could be rewritten as

$$\ln G_t = \frac{\ln P_t + \ln P_{t-1} + \cdots + \ln P_{t-n+1}}{n}$$

$$= \frac{1}{n}\left(\sum_{i=1}^{n} \ln P_{t-i+1}\right)$$

This is similar in form to the summation of a standard moving average based on the arithmetic mean and can be written for either spreadsheet or program code as

```
GA = @average(@log(price),n)
```

Note that some software will use "log" although the calculation is actually the natural log, ln. Other programs will allow the choice of @log(value) or @ln(value). A weighted geometric moving average would have the form

$$\ln G_t = \frac{w_1 \ln P_t + w_2 \ln P_{t-1} + \cdots + w_n \ln P_{t-n+1}}{w_1 + w_2 + \cdots + w_n}$$

$$= \frac{\displaystyle\sum_{i=1}^{n} w_i \ln P_{t-i+1}}{\displaystyle\sum_{i=1}^{n} w_i}$$

The geometric moving average itself would give greater weight to smaller values without the need for a discrete weighting function. In applying the technique to actual commodity prices, this distinction may not be obvious. For widely ranging values such as 1,000 and 10, the simple average is 505 and the geometric average is 100, but for the three sequential cocoa prices, 56.20, 58.30, and 57.15, the arithmetic mean is 57.2166 and the geometric is 57.1871. A similar test of 5, 10, or 20 days of commodity prices will show a negligible difference between the results of the two averages. If the geometric moving average is to be helpful, it would be best applied to long-term historic data with wide variance, using yearly or quarterly average prices.

DROP-OFF EFFECT

Two types of trending methods can be distinguished by the *drop-off effect,* a common way of expressing the abrupt change in value when a fixed-period calculation drops off a significant value. A simple moving average, linear regression, and weighted averages all use a fixed period, or window, for determining the trend. When an unusually volatile piece of data becomes old and drops off, there can be a sudden jump in the trend value, called the drop-off effect. For an n-period moving average, this value is the difference between the first and the last items, divided by the number of periods,

$$\text{drop-off effect} = (P_t - P_{t-n})/n$$

   A weighted average, in which the oldest values have less importance, reduces this effect because the high-volatility data slowly become a smaller part of the result before being dropped off. Exponential smoothing, discussed next, is immune from this problem by its very nature.

EXPONENTIAL SMOOTHING

Exponential smoothing may appear to be more complex than other techniques, but it is only another form of a weighted moving average. It has the added advantage of being simpler to calculate than any other method discussed; only the last exponentially smoothed value E_{t-1} and the smoothing constant a are necessary to compute the new value. The technique of exponential smoothing was developed during World War II for tracking aircraft and projecting their position—the immediate past is used to predict the immediate future.

   The geometric progression

$$1, a, a^2, a^3, \ldots, a^{n-1}$$

applied to the terms of a weighted moving average

$$W_t = \frac{w_1 P_t + w_2 P_{t-1} + \cdots + w_n P_{t-n+1}}{w_1 + w_2 + \cdots + w_n}$$

gives $w_1 = 1$, $w_2 = a$, $w_3 = a^2$, $\ldots$, $w_n = a^{n-1}$. If $a = \frac{1}{2}$, also said to be 50% smoothed, the resulting sequence is

$$1, \frac{1}{2}, \frac{1}{4}, \frac{1}{8}, \ldots, (\tfrac{1}{2})^{n-1}$$

This shows the rapidly decreasing importance of each older price. Substituting the geometric progression into the equation for the weighted moving average gives

$$E_t = \frac{1 P_t + a P_{t-1} + a^2 P_{t-2} + \cdots + a^{n-1} P_{t-n+1}}{1 + a + a^2 + \cdots + a^{n-1}}$$

   By a lengthy arithmetic process using the formula for the sum of a geometric progression, the same equation can be stated as

$$E_t = (1 - a)P_t + aE_{t-1}$$

where P_t is the most recent price and $0 \leq a \leq 1$. It can be seen that 100% of the combined value of past prices is distributed such that $a \times 100\%$ goes to the previous exponential moving average and the balance to the most recent price. If $a = .70$, the current price P_t will receive a weighting of 30% of the total moving average. An equally popular form that reverses the weighting notations and has one less calculation, but gives identical results, is:

$$E_t = E_{t-1} + a\,(P_t - E_{t-1})$$

The smoothing process can be started by letting $E_1 = P_1$ and calculate the next value:

$$E_2 = E_1 + a\,(P_2 - E_1)$$

   The smoothing constant, a, will determine the number of calculations necessary to wind up the data. A longer-term smoothing, where a is closer to 0, will take more data for the smoothed line, E_t, to reach a stable value. The interpretation of this last equation can be seen in Figure 4-3 as

New exponential value = prior exponential value

+ some % of (today's price − prior exponential value)

FIGURE 4-3   Exponential smoothing.

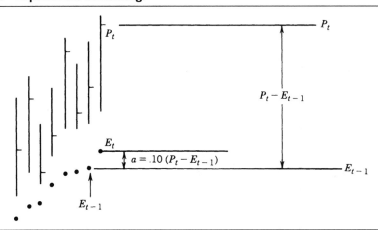

An important feature of the exponentially smoothed moving average is that all data previously used are always part of the new result, although with diminishing significance. In general:

$$E_t = a \left(P_t + (1 - a)P_{t-1} + (1 - a)^2 P_{t-2} + \cdots + (1 - a)^n P_{t-n} + \cdots \right)$$

For example, if the smoothing constant $a = .10$, add 10% of the new difference to the old average:

$$E_t = E_{t-1} + .10 \, (P_t - E_{t-1})$$

Each new calculation reduces all data from points 1 through $t - 1$ by 10%; the next calculation for $t + 1$ will cause the data from t through 1 to be reduced again by 10%. Therefore, at any time t the impact of data used at a previous time k is based on the number of days elapsed, $t - k$, and the smoothing constant a. Let the significance $P_k - E_{k-1} = k = D_k$. Then on day k we have

$$k = a \cdot D_k$$

$$k + 1 = a \cdot D_k - a \cdot a \cdot D_k$$

$$\vdots$$

$$k + n = a \cdot D_k - (a^2 \cdot D_k + a^3 \cdot D_k + \cdots + a^{n=1} \cdot D_k)$$

$$= a \cdot D_k - \sum_{i=2}^{n+1} a^i D_k \qquad \text{(written in summation form)}$$

$$= d_k \left(a - \sum_{i=2}^{n+1} a^i \right) \to 0 \qquad \text{as} \qquad n \to \infty$$

This shows that the significance of the data on day k goes to zero as n gets infinitely large. Consider the following example. An investor makes a deal to buy 10% of the outstanding shares of stock in a corporation in which there are $t - 1$ investors. The corporation decides to take in another investor and gives that investor 10% of the total outstanding shares. There are now $t + 1$ investors, and the original t share owners are all diluted by 10%; the investor t who bought 10% now owns 9%. Another investor buys in at 10% of the total; there are now $t + 2$ investors, and the investor t has 8.1% of the stock (10% less). As more investors are added, t's stock holding dwindles to 7.29%, 6.561%, and 5.9049%. Even though the number of shares that are held remain the same, each previous owner holds a less significant part of the whole. No matter how many investors are added at 10%, the original shareholders will always have some small percent of the whole. In exactly the same way, the original price used in an exponentially smoothed moving average always retains some relevance; with a standard moving average of n days, the $(n + 1)$th day is dropped off and ceases to have any impact.

Smoothing and Restoring the Lag

As a trend continues in its direction, the exponentially smoothed moving average will lag farther behind. By selecting a smoothing constant nearer to 1, the magnitude of this lag will be lessened but it will still increase, just as using a smaller number of days, or shorter period, will limit the lag of a simple moving average. If the lag is considered the predictive error e_t in the exponential smoothing calculation, then

$$e_t = P_t - E_t$$

where E_t is the exponential smoothing approximation of the price P_t. The same exponential smoothing technique can be applied to the pattern of increasing or decreasing errors to get

$$\text{ERR}_t = \text{ERR}_{t-1} + a(e_t - \text{ERR}_{t-1})$$

and then add the difference between the original smoothing value and this second-order smoothing back into the approximation:

$$EE_t = E_t + \text{ERR}_t$$

By measuring the new error, the difference between the first-order exponential E_t and the second-order EE_t, it can be seen whether there has been an improvement in the forecast. This process can be continued to *third-order* smoothing by applying the same method to the difference between the current price and the second-order trend EE_t. A comparison of this method, restoring the forecast error, is compared with other exponential smoothing techniques in Figure 4-4 and Table 4-4.

Double Smoothing

To make a trendline smoother, the period of a moving average or the exponential smoothing constant is normally increased. This succeeds in reducing the short-term market noise at the cost of increasing the lag. It has been suggested that each of these trending methods could be *double-smoothed,* that is, the trend values can themselves be smoothed. This will slow down the trendline, but gives weight to the previous values in a way that may be unexpected.

A double-smoothed simple 3-day moving average, MA, would take the original three moving average values and average them to get a double-smoothed moving average, DMA:

$$MA_3 = (P_1 + P_2 + P_3)/3$$

$$MA_4 = (P_2 + P_3 + P_4)/3$$

$$MA_5 = (P_3 + P_4 + P_5)/3$$

then

$$DMA_5 = (MA_3 + MA_4 + MA_5)/3$$

TABLE 4-4 Comparison of exponential smoothing techniques applied to Swiss franc from *TradeStation* **continuous daily data**

	Price	Exp	Dbl Exp	Exp Err	Exp Error	Smoothed Error	Price Change	Exp Change	Dbl Exp Change
930316	64.59	64.59	64.59	64.59	0.00	0			
930317	64.23	64.55	64.59	64.52	−0.32	−0.03	−0.36	−0.04	−0.04
930318	65.26	64.62	64.59	64.66	0.64	0.03	1.03	0.07	−0.03
930319	65.24	64.69	64.60	64.77	0.55	0.09	−0.02	0.06	−0.02
930322	65.07	64.72	64.61	64.84	0.35	0.11	−0.17	0.04	−0.01
930323	65.14	64.77	64.63	64.90	0.37	0.14	0.07	0.04	−0.01
930324	64.98	64.79	64.64	64.93	0.19	0.14	−0.16	0.02	−0.01
930325	64.76	64.78	64.66	64.91	−0.02	0.13	−0.22	−0.00	−0.01
930326	65.11	64.82	64.67	64.96	0.29	0.14	0.35	0.03	−0.00
930329	65.46	64.88	64.69	65.07	0.58	0.19	0.35	0.06	0.01
930330	65.94	64.99	64.72	65.25	0.95	0.26	0.48	0.11	0.02
930331	66.10	65.10	64.76	65.44	1.00	0.34	0.16	0.11	0.02
930401	66.87	65.28	64.81	65.74	1.59	0.46	0.77	0.18	0.04
930402	66.56	65.40	64.87	65.94	1.16	0.53	−0.31	0.13	0.05
930405	66.71	65.53	64.94	66.13	1.18	0.60	0.15	0.13	0.06
930406	66.19	65.60	65.00	66.20	0.59	0.60	−0.52	0.07	0.06
930407	66.14	65.65	65.07	66.24	0.49	0.58	−0.05	0.05	0.06
930408	66.64	65.75	65.14	66.37	0.89	0.62	0.50	0.10	0.06
930412	67.33	65.91	65.21	66.61	1.42	0.70	0.69	0.16	0.07
930413	68.18	66.14	65.31	66.97	2.04	0.83	0.85	0.23	0.09
930414	67.48	66.27	65.40	67.14	1.21	0.87	−0.70	0.13	0.09
930415	67.19	66.36	65.50	67.23	0.83	0.86	−0.29	0.09	0.09
930416	66.46	66.37	65.59	67.16	0.09	0.79	−0.73	0.01	0.08
930419	67.20	66.46	65.67	67.24	0.74	0.78	0.74	0.08	0.08
930420	67.62	66.57	65.76	67.38	1.05	0.81	0.42	0.12	0.09
930421	67.66	66.68	65.86	67.51	0.98	0.83	0.04	0.11	0.09
930422	67.89	66.80	65.95	67.65	1.09	0.85	0.23	0.12	0.09
930423	69.19	67.04	66.06	68.02	2.15	0.98	1.30	0.24	0.11
930426	69.68	67.30	66.18	68.43	2.38	1.12	0.49	0.26	0.12
930427	69.31	67.51	66.32	68.69	1.80	1.19	−0.37	0.20	0.13
930428	69.11	67.67	66.45	68.88	1.44	1.21	−0.20	0.16	0.13
930429	69.27	67.83	66.59	69.06	1.44	1.24	0.16	0.16	0.14
930430	68.97	67.94	66.72	69.16	1.03	1.22	−0.30	0.11	0.13
930503	69.11	68.06	66.86	69.26	1.05	1.20	0.14	0.12	0.13
930504	69.50	68.20	66.99	69.41	1.30	1.21	0.39	0.14	0.13
930505	69.70	68.35	67.13	69.58	1.35	1.22	0.20	0.15	0.13
930506	69.94	68.51	67.27	69.76	1.43	1.24	0.24	0.16	0.14
930507	69.11	68.57	67.40	69.74	0.54	1.17	−0.83	0.06	0.13
930510	67.64	68.48	67.50	69.45	−0.84	0.97	−1.47	−0.09	0.11
930511	67.75	68.40	67.59	69.21	−0.65	0.81	0.11	−0.07	0.09
930512	67.47	68.31	67.67	68.96	−0.84	0.65	−0.28	−0.09	0.07
930513	67.50	68.23	67.72	68.74	−0.73	0.51	0.03	−0.08	0.06
930514	68.18	68.23	67.77	68.68	−0.05	0.45	0.68	−0.01	0.05
930517	67.35	68.14	67.81	68.47	−0.79	0.33	−0.83	−0.09	0.04
930518	66.74	68.00	67.83	68.17	−1.26	0.17	−0.61	−0.14	0.02
930519	67.00	67.90	67.84	67.96	−0.90	0.06	0.26	−0.10	0.01
930520	67.46	67.85	67.84	67.87	−0.39	0.02	0.46	−0.04	0.00

TABLE 4-4 *(Continued)*

	Price	Exp	Dbl Exp	Exp Err	Exp Error	Smoothed Error	Price Change	Exp Change	Dbl Exp Change
930521	67.36	67.80	67.83	67.78	−0.44	−0.03	−0.10	−0.05	−0.00
930524	67.37	67.76	67.83	67.70	−0.39	−0.07	0.01	−0.04	−0.01
930525	67.78	67.76	67.82	67.71	0.02	−0.06	0.41	0.00	−0.01
930526	67.96	67.78	67.82	67.75	0.18	−0.03	0.18	0.02	−0.00
930527	68.97	67.90	67.82	67.98	1.07	0.08	1.01	0.12	0.01
930528	69.79	68.09	67.85	68.33	1.70	0.24	0.82	0.19	0.03
930601	69.53	68.23	67.89	68.58	1.30	0.34	−0.26	0.14	0.04
930602	69.52	68.36	67.94	68.79	1.16	0.43	−0.01	0.13	0.05
930603	69.17	68.44	67.99	68.90	0.73	0.46	−0.35	0.08	0.05
930604	67.41	68.34	68.02	68.66	−0.93	0.32	−1.76	−0.10	0.04
930607	67.96	68.30	68.05	68.55	−0.34	0.25	0.55	−0.04	0.03
930608	67.62	68.23	68.07	68.40	−0.61	0.16	−0.34	−0.07	0.02
930609	67.18	68.13	68.08	68.18	−0.95	0.05	−0.44	−0.11	0.01
930610	67.65	68.08	68.08	68.09	−0.43	0.01	0.47	−0.05	0.00
930611	68.08	68.08	68.08	68.09	−0.00	0.00	0.43	−0.00	0.00
930614	68.06	68.08	68.08	68.08	−0.02	0.00	−0.02	−0.00	0.00
930615	67.16	67.99	68.07	67.91	−0.83	−0.08	−0.90	−0.09	−0.01
930616	66.59	67.85	68.05	67.65	−1.26	−0.20	−0.57	−0.14	−0.02
930617	66.77	67.74	68.01	67.46	−0.97	−0.28	0.18	−0.11	−0.03
930618	65.95	67.56	67.97	67.15	−1.61	−0.41	−0.82	−0.18	−0.05
930621	65.89	67.39	67.91	66.87	−1.50	−0.52	−0.06	−0.17	−0.06
930622	65.48	67.20	67.84	66.56	−1.72	−0.64	−0.41	−0.19	−0.07
930623	65.69	67.05	67.76	66.34	−1.36	−0.71	0.21	−0.15	−0.08
930624	65.30	66.88	67.67	66.08	−1.58	−0.80	−0.39	−0.18	−0.09
930625	65.37	66.73	67.58	65.87	−1.36	−0.85	0.07	−0.15	−0.09
930628	65.70	66.62	67.48	65.76	−0.92	−0.86	0.33	−0.10	−0.10
930629	66.12	66.57	67.39	65.75	−0.45	−0.82	0.42	−0.05	−0.09
930630	65.37	66.45	67.30	65.61	−1.08	−0.85	−0.75	−0.12	−0.09
930701	65.64	66.37	67.21	65.54	−0.73	−0.83	0.27	−0.08	−0.09
930702	65.54	66.29	67.11	65.46	−0.75	−0.83	−0.10	−0.08	−0.09
930706	65.47	66.21	67.02	65.39	−0.74	−0.82	−0.07	−0.08	−0.09
930707	65.45	66.13	66.93	65.33	−0.68	−0.80	−0.02	−0.08	−0.09
930708	65.50	66.07	66.85	65.29	−0.57	−0.78	0.05	−0.06	−0.09
930709	64.70	65.93	66.76	65.11	−1.23	−0.82	−0.80	−0.14	−0.09
930712	64.82	65.82	66.66	64.98	−1.00	−0.84	0.12	−0.11	−0.09
930713	65.27	65.76	66.57	64.96	−0.49	−0.81	0.45	−0.05	−0.09
930714	65.62	65.75	66.49	65.01	−0.13	−0.74	0.35	−0.01	−0.08
930715	65.36	65.71	66.41	65.01	−0.35	−0.70	−0.26	−0.04	−0.08
930716	65.85	65.73	66.34	65.11	0.12	−0.62	0.49	0.01	−0.07
930719	66.09	65.76	66.29	65.24	0.33	−0.52	0.24	0.04	−0.06
930720	66.28	65.81	66.24	65.39	0.47	−0.42	0.19	0.05	−0.05
930721	66.07	65.84	66.20	65.48	0.23	−0.36	−0.21	0.03	−0.04
930722	66.03	65.86	66.16	65.55	0.17	−0.31	−0.04	0.02	−0.03
930723	65.22	65.79	66.13	65.46	−0.57	−0.33	−0.81	−0.06	−0.04
930726	65.19	65.73	66.09	65.38	−0.54	−0.35	−0.03	−0.06	−0.04
930727	65.19	65.68	66.05	65.31	−0.49	−0.37	0.00	−0.05	−0.04
930728	65.59	65.67	66.01	65.33	−0.08	−0.34	0.40	−0.01	−0.04
930729	64.80	65.58	65.97	65.20	−0.78	−0.38	−0.79	−0.09	−0.04

FIGURE 4-4   Comparison of exponential smoothing techniques. A simple .10 smoothing (Exp) is compared with a double-smoothed series (Dbl Exp), which applies the smoothing constant .10 first to prices, then to the smoothed series, and also to a smoothed series with the error restored (Exp Err).

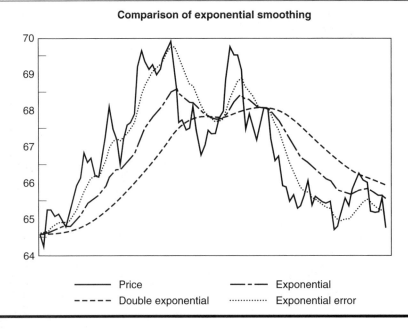

Comparison of exponential smoothing

Legend:
——— Price
— · — Exponential
- - - - Double exponential
············ Exponential error

If we substitute the original prices, $P_1, \ldots, P_5$, into the equation for DMA_5 we find out that

$$DMA_5 = (P_1 + 2P_2 + 3P_3 + 2P_4 + P_5) / 9$$

This shows that double smoothing results in weighting the middle values more than the end values, rather than the original equal weighting of the simple moving average. For exponential smoothing the result is different. Because the most recent value receives the weight of the smoothing constant, a, the double smoothing

$$DE_t = DE_{t-1} + a(E_t - DE_{t-1})$$

causes the nearby value t to be smoothed twice by a, or $a \times a$, and older values as well. Therefore, the net effect of using a smoothing of $a = .10$ for double smoothing will result much more closely to using the square root of a, approximately .031. Figure 4-4 and Table 4-4 give an example of this method.

Blau's Double Smoothing

To avoid this compounded lag, William Blau has substituted the price changes, $P_t - P_{t-n}$, for the price itself.[4] The smoothing is then performed on an accelerated price series, and the smoothed result restores the speed of the series back to normal. When $n = 1$, the price changes are called the *first difference*, or *speed*. In effect, the smoothed series does not have a lag. Blau has found this to be a successful proxy for long-term trends, in which the first smoothing may be as long as 300 periods and the second a much shorter 5 periods (also see Table 4-4).

[4] William Blau, *Momentum, Direction, and Divergence* (John Wiley & Sons, New York, 1995).

Comparing Exponential Smoothing Methods

Figure 4-4 and Table 4-4 illustrate the differences between a simple exponential smoothing (Exp) with smoothing constant $a = .10$, smoothing with the lag (or forecast error) restored (Exp Err) using the same $a = .10$, and double smoothing (Dbl Exp) with the same smoothing constant. In the following example, a trend was defined as the direction of the unfiltered trendline. When the change in the trendline value was positive, the trend was up; when it was negative, the trend was down.

The single exponential, Exp, appears as the medium-term trend in the sample period of about 4½ months. It had 9 distinct trend periods and a net profit, without any transaction costs, of 2.59 points. Double smoothing was predictably slower, showing a much smoother curve and only 4 trend changes. It netted only .07 points, but this particular data sample had a change of direction midway, which does not allow for long-term profits. Restoring the error, Exp Err, only increased the number of trends to 12 and gave a profit of .83 points, despite its appearance as a very fast trend.

Blau's double smoothing of the price changes was especially interesting. It performed differently from the other smoothing methods, yet posted 10 trends, making it similar in speed to the simple exponential, rather than the double-smoothed. Profits of 1.67 points were also high for this short sample, and the trend patterns that it identified were significantly different.

These alternatives all offer good possibilities for identifying the trend and should not be judged by the small sample used in the example.

RELATING EXPONENTIAL SMOOTHING AND STANDARD MOVING AVERAGES

It is much easier to visualize the amount of smoothing in a 10-day moving average than exponential smoothing in which $a = .10$ (which can be called *10% smoothing*). Although we try to relate the speed of both techniques, the simple moving average is equally weighted, and the exponential is front-weighted; therefore, they will produce a very different pattern. Because of the inclusion of old data, a 50% smoothing appears slower than a 2-day moving average, a 10% smoothing is slower than a 10-day moving average, and a 5% smoothing is slower than a 20-day moving average. The important factor is that for any specified smoothing constant, the exponential moving average includes all prior data. If a 5-day moving average was compared with an exponential with only 5 total days included, the relationship would be closer to a straight moving average than if the exponential had 10 or 20 days of elapsed calculations.

Instead of using prices, a series of numbers from 1 through 15 and back to 1 will be used to compare a 5-day moving average with an exponential moving. The exponential is calculated two ways: once using only the last five prices (a modified approach for our example); the other using all prices from the beginning (the standard method).

Figures 4-5 and 4-6 and Table 4-5 show the relationship between the standard exponential and the modified exponential using 5 points. During the period of constant price increase and decrease of at least 5 consecutive days, both the 5-day moving average and exponential with five points stabilize; those 5 days represent their entire set of calculation values. At the peak, the standard moving average reacts more quickly than the other methods in staying closer to the current price; the 5-point exponential gives 20% of its weight to the most recent price, and less to prior prices, causing it to react more slowly than the standard moving average.

The standard exponential smoothing is different, lagging farther behind each day but increasingly *approaching* the value of one, as the data increase by one, for long time periods. The weighting of the near values is offset by the retained significance of the oldest data, which is never fully lost, causing the exponentially smoothed moving average to lag

FIGURE 4-5   Daily price with moving averages.

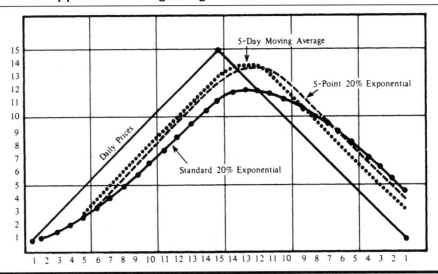

the farthest behind the current prices. Although there are 14 days of constant decline, the standard exponential has not yet stabilized, still reflecting the turning of prices from up to down at 15.

To form the specific relationship between exponential smoothing and standard moving averages, create a table showing the significance of each oldest day in the exponential calculation. In Table 4-6, the .50 smoothing constant gives 50% of the total value to the current price, 25% to the prior day, 12.5% to the next oldest, until the 7th oldest day adds only .8% to the total value of the exponential moving average. Table 4-7 accumulates these weights to show how much of the calculation has been completed by the elapsed days printed across the top. Table 4-7 is plotted in Figure 4-7. The most recent days (on the left) receive the bulk of the significance; the oldest prices are of little impact. The .10 smoothing calculation is 90.1% complete by day 22; the total remaining days added together only account for 9.9% of the value.

FIGURE 4-6   Comparative changes in straight and exponential moving averages.

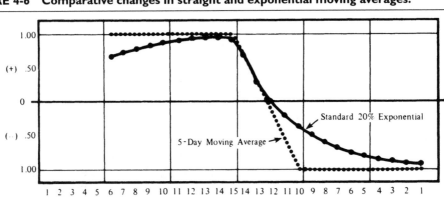

TABLE 4-5 Comparison of Lag between Standard and Exponentially Smoothed Moving Averages

Price	Standard 5-Day	5-Point 20% Exp	Standard 20% Exp	Change 5-Day	Change 5–20% Exp	Change 20% Exp
1	—	1.00	1.00	—	—	—
2	—	1.20	1.20	—	—	—
3	—	1.56	1.56	—	Not enough	—
4	—	2.05	2.05	—	data	—
5	3	2.64	2.64	—	—	—
6	4	3.64	3.31	1.00	1.00	.67
7	5	4.64	4.05	1.00	1.00	.74
8	6	5.64	4.84	1.00	1.00	.79
9	7	6.64	5.67	1.00	1.00	.83
10	8	7.64	6.54	1.00	1.00	.87
11	9	8.64	7.43	1.00	1.00	.89
12	10	9.64	8.34	1.00	1.00	.91
13	11	10.64	9.27	1.00	1.00	.93
14	12	11.64	10.22	1.00	1.00	.95
15	13	12.64	11.17	1.00	1.00	.95
14	13.6	13.24	11.74	.60	.60	.57
13	13.8	13.52	11.99	.20	.28	.25
12	13.6	13.54	11.99	−.20	.02	.00
11	13	13.36	11.79	−.60	−.18	−.20
10	12	12.36	11.43	−1.00	−1.00	−.36
9	11	11.36	10.95	−1.00	−1.00	−.48
8	10	10.36	10.36	−1.00	−1.00	−.59
7	9	9.36	9.69	−1.00	−1.00	−.67
6	8	8.36	8.95	−1.00	−1.00	−.74
5	7	7.36	8.16	−1.00	−1.00	−.79
4	6	6.36	7.33	−1.00	−1.00	−.83
3	5	5.36	6.46	−1.00	−1.00	−.87
2	4	4.36	5.57	−1.00	−1.00	−.89
1	3	3.36	4.65	−1.00	−1.00	−.92

Figure 4-7 relates the fully calculated exponential smoothing (within 1%) to the standard moving average. Find the smoothing constant on the left and the number of days in a standard moving average along the bottom. Observe that, if you perform an optimization with equally spaced exponential smoothing constants, there is an unexpected distribution relative to past days.

Equating Standard Moving Averages to Exponential Smoothing

Smoothing constant (%)	.10	.20	.30	.40	.50	.60	.70	.80	.90
Standard (*n*-day average)	20	10	6	4	3	2.25	1.75	1.40	1.15

If the equally distributed smoothing constants shown above are used for testing, half of the tests will analyze moving averages of 3 days or less. If the testing program is to relate to the standard moving average, reverse the process, finding the smoothing constant for a known

TABLE 4-6 Evaluation of Exponential Smoothing—Significance of Prior Data

Weighting (%)	Past Number of Days																						
	1	2	3	4	5	6	7	8	9	10	11	12	13	14	15	16	17	18	19	20	21	22	23
1.00	100.0	—																					
.90	90.0	9.0	.9																				
.80	80.0	16.0	3.2	.6																			
.70	70.0	21.0	6.3	1.9	.6																		
.60	60.0	24.0	9.6	3.8	1.5	.6																	
.50	50.0	25.0	12.5	6.3	3.1	1.6	.8																
.40	40.0	24.0	14.4	8.6	5.2	3.1	1.9	1.1	.7														
.30	30.0	21.0	14.7	10.3	7.2	5.0	3.5	2.5	1.7	1.2	.8												
.20	20.0	16.0	12.8	10.2	8.2	6.5	5.2	4.2	3.3	2.7	2.1	1.7	1.4	1.1	.9								
.10	10.0	9.0	8.1	7.3	6.6	5.9	5.3	4.8	4.3	3.9	3.5	3.1	2.8	2.5	2.3	2.1	1.8	1.7	1.5	1.3	1.2	1.1	1.0

TABLE 4-7 Evaluation of Exponential Smoothing—Significance of Prior Data

Weighting (%)	Total Inclusion through Nth Day																						
	1	2	3	4	5	6	7	8	9	10	11	12	13	14	15	16	17	18	19	20	21	22	23
1.00	100.0	—	—	—	—	—	—	—	—	—	—	—	—	—	—	—	—	—	—	—	—	—	—
.90	90.0	99.0	99.9	—	—	—	—	—	—	—	—	—	—	—	—	—	—	—	—	—	—	—	—
.80	80.0	96.0	99.2	—	—	—	—	—	—	—	—	—	—	—	—	—	—	—	—	—	—	—	—
.70	70.0	91.0	97.3	99.2	99.8	—	—	—	—	—	—	—	—	—	—	—	—	—	—	—	—	—	—
.60	60.0	84.0	93.6	97.4	99.0	99.6	—	—	—	—	—	—	—	—	—	—	—	—	—	—	—	—	—
.50	50.0	75.0	87.5	93.8	96.9	98.5	99.3	—	—	—	—	—	—	—	—	—	—	—	—	—	—	—	—
.40	40.0	64.0	78.4	87.0	92.2	95.3	97.2	98.3	99.0	—	—	—	—	—	—	—	—	—	—	—	—	—	—
.30	30.0	51.0	65.7	76.0	83.2	88.2	91.8	94.2	96.0	—	—	—	—	—	—	—	—	—	—	—	—	—	—
.20	20.0	36.0	48.8	59.0	67.2	73.8	79.0	83.2	86.6	89.3	91.4	93.1	94.5	95.6	96.5	—	—	—	—	—	—	—	—
.10	10.0	19.0	27.1	34.4	41.0	46.8	52.2	57.0	61.3	65.1	68.6	71.8	74.6	77.1	79.4	81.5	83.3	85.0	86.5	87.8	89.1	90.1	91.1

FIGURE 4-7   **Evaluation of exponential smoothing.**

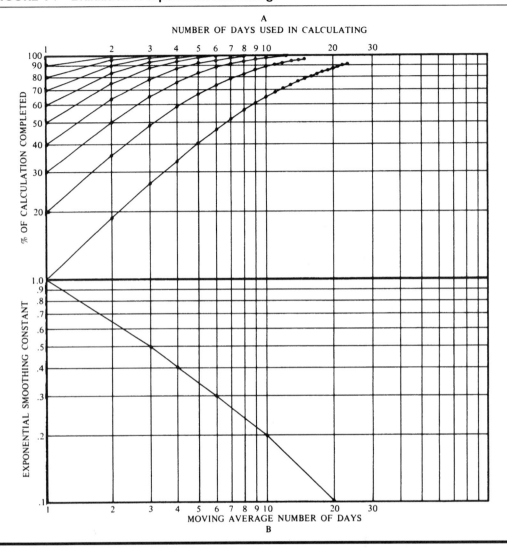

number of days. This process will be important when finding robust system parameters and will be discussed in Chapter 21 ("Testing and Optimization").

Equating Exponential Smoothing to Standard Moving Averages

Standard (n-day average)	2	4	6	8	10	12	14	16	18	20
Smoothing constant (%)	.65	.40	.30	.235	.20	.165	.14	.125	.11	.10

The distribution of smoothing constants is very close to logarithmic and is plotted on a log scale in Figure 4-6. To test exponential smoothing within a range of days, use a logarithmic distribution of smoothing constants across that range, with closer values taken at the smaller numbers, if necessary. This may seem an unnecessary precaution, but it is not.

TABLE 4-8 Comparison of Exponential Smoothing Values

Moving Average Days (n)	1st-Order p = 1	2nd-Order p = 2	3rd-Order p = 3
3	.500	.293	.206
5	.333	.184	.126
7	.250	.134	.091
9	.200	.106	.072
11	.167	.087	.059
13	.143	.074	.050
15	.125	.065	.044
17	.111	.057	.039
19	.100	.051	.035
21	.091	.047	.031

Best Approximation of Smoothing Constants

The standard conversion from the number of days to a smoothing constant *s* was given by Hutson[5] as

$$s = \frac{2}{n+1}$$

where *n* is the equivalent number of days in the standard (linearly weighted) moving average. In addition, 2nd- or 3rd-order exponential smoothing, based on the weighting of the past 2 or 3 days' prices, may be desirable. This is the exponential equivalent to step weighting. Its general form is

$$s_p = 1 - \left(1 - \frac{2}{n+1}\right)^{(1/p)}$$

A comparison of the standard moving average days with 1st-, 2nd-, and 3rd-order exponential smoothing is shown in Table 4-8.

Estimating Residual Impact

The primary difference between the standard moving average and exponential smoothing is that prices impact the exponentially smoothed value indefinitely. For practical purposes, the effect of the oldest data may be limited. A general method of approximating the smoothing constant *s* for a given level of residual impact is given by

$$s = 1 - RI^{1/n}$$

[5] Jack K. Hutson, "Filter Price Data: Moving Averages vs. Exponential Moving Averages," *Technical Analysis of Stocks & Commodities* (May/June 1984).

TABLE 4-9 Comparison of Exponential Smoothing Residual Impact

n	2/(n + 1)	RI (%)	10% RI	5% RI
5	.333	13.17	.369	.451
10	.182	13.44	.206	.259
15	.125	13.49	.142	.181
20	.095	13.51	.109	.139

where RI is the level of residual impact (e.g., .05, .10, .20). A lower percent level implies more residual impact, and n is the equivalent number of moving average days.[6]

The approximation for the smoothing constant, given in the previous section as $2/(n + 1)$, can be shown to have a consistent residual impact of between 13 and 14%. The use of the preceding formula, as shown in Table 4-9, would allow the specific adjustment of residual impact.

[6] Donald R. Lambert, "Exponentially Smoothed Moving Averages," *Technical Analysis of Stocks & Commodities* (September/October 1984).

5

Trend Systems

The previous chapter developed the tools for calculating trends—a standard moving average, weighted averages, exponential smoothing, and regression-based values. To profit from identifying the trend requires the use of trading rules and the selection of specific parameters that define the trend speed and position risk, among other factors. Often, the selection of rules is seen to be dependent on additional parameters. This chapter will first discuss those rules that are necessary to all trading strategies, then give examples of actual systems. The selection of trend speed is handled only briefly here, but it is continued with a detailed analysis of these and other systems throughout the book, and especially in Chapter 21 ("Testing"). Toward the end of this chapter, a section on viewing sequences of trends may prove interesting to the analyst trying to be more innovative.

BASIC BUY AND SELL SIGNALS

Regardless of the selection of moving averages, the smoothed trend calculation will lag behind the actual current market price. In rising markets, this lag will cause the moving average to be below the price; in falling markets, it will be above. When prices change direction, the trendline and the actual market prices cross because the trend is slow to reflect the new market direction. These crossings provide the opportunity for the basic trading signals

Buy when rising prices cross the trendline.

Sell when declining prices cross the trendline.

It is also necessary to decide what prices are to be used. The answer depends on the construction of the average and the testing of the system. If the average is composed only of closing prices, it is reasonable to start testing with the modified signals

Buy when rising prices close above the trendline.

Sell when declining prices close below the trendline.

If an average of high and low prices were used, or the high, low, and close, a buy or sell would be signaled when the new average (*high* + *low*)/2 or (*high* + *low* + *close*)/3 was above or below the corresponding moving average value. In all cases, consistency is important. The system that is tested and the one that is traded should be the same. In the following discussion, the term *close* will be used. To find out if a trading signal occurred on any day, wait until the close of trading, calculate the new moving average or trend value, and then see whether a crossing occurred according to the basic buy and sell rules.

You may have realized that using the closing price to generate a signal usually requires that calculations occur after the market has closed, and orders must be placed in the after-hours market or on the next day's open. If the system is actually generating signals as of the closing price, then you are not following the system. To correct this problem, the value of the closing price that would cause a new signal should be calculated in advance. This would allow execution on or near the close of the current day. The rules of the system can also be changed to buy or sell on today's close if that price is above or below yesterday's moving average value. A small amount of testing will determine which approach works best. Another choice would be to test today's close against yesterday's projected moving average; therefore, if the moving average values for the past 2 days were

$$M_{t-1} = 432$$

$$M_{t-2} = 429$$

the difference $M_{t-1} - M_{t-2} = 3$ would be added to M_{t-1} to get the estimated turning criterion of M'_t for today. That means that the *rate of change* must differ for a signal to occur. More sophisticated approaches to projecting the moving average will be covered later.

Variations in Timing

Lead and *lag* are features common to the trend calculations discussed in Chapter 4. The opposite in purpose, a lead of n days advances the plotted value of, for example, the moving average M_t from the same time as the current price P_t to the position n periods ahead. In actual trading, this gives an advance criterion for a trading signal; prices must remain above this level to maintain the current position. A lag time of n days plots the current moving average value at the same time as P_{t-n}, n days sooner. This indicates that a signal has already occurred, but no action may be taken for n days. The lead plot tries to anticipate a trend change, while a lag is a commitment to holding a position. Both lead and lag techniques may use the same basic buy and sell signals as standard trends.

Entry and exit timing may be improved by a *delay* in taking action on a signal, usually from 1 to 3 days. This technique allows a number of days for the newly developed trend to reverse and show a *false signal* at the cost of missing the beginning of the trend. Systems that have a large number of short-lived losing trades and a high profit/loss ratio can benefit from a delay of 1, 2, or 3 days.

Reversing a position on each trade signal results in a constant commitment to being in the market. This philosophy will show greater profits when the trade is successful, but more frequent losses because of the constant commitment to trend changes during whipsaw periods. An entry delay may also improve a reversal system.

BANDS AND CHANNELS

Thus far, modifications have been based on a simple moving average or trendline. The plot can be adjusted forward or backward, the position can be reversed, or the entry or exit delayed in an attempt to begin the new trade at the time when the trend has decidedly taken a new direction. Even if prices have begun what will become a major downtrend, an entry into a short position too soon may be subjected to sharp reversals caused by conflicting fundamental and technical elements at these turning points. The simplest way to avoid these price variations is by using a band.

A *band* is an area surrounding a trendline above and below that acts as a zone of commitment for the trader and allows time, as measured by price movement and risk, for prices to settle into their new direction. Also called *channels,* bands can be created in many ways, one of the most popular being a percentage of the current price or the current trendline value. A band that is formed from the trendline will be

(upper band) $B_U = M_t + cM_t$

(lower band) $B_L = M_t - cM_t$

where c is a percentage, $0 \le c \le 1$, and M_t is today's moving average value. Since the moving average is much smoother than the price patterns, the band will be fairly uniform as well. If the current price is used instead of the moving average then

$$B_U = M_t + cP_t$$

$$B_L = M_t - cP_t$$

The band will vary in width at a much faster rate using price. During an uptrend, the band based on prices can get very wide. Another popular type of band is based on *absolute point value,* for example, silver 5¢, corn 5¢, or cattle 25 points; each represents a dollar risk to the trader. The use of this type of band is usually found coordinated with a money management program that limits losses on trades to a specific number or to a maximum percentage of the portfolio being managed.

The *independent smoothing* of the high and low prices for any period forms a *volatility band.* Although it may be practical to use the same technique or the same relative smoothing (e.g., 10-day or 10% smoothing constant) for the high, low, and closing prices, it is not a requirement. If the same smoothing criterion is used, the band will be uniform with respect to the moving average of the closing price; if not, all three trendlines may weave around one another. A *volatility function* can also be used to create a band. Rather than the simple percentage calculation shown first, the band may be increased at rates equal to a price-volatility relationship. All of the methods of forming bands are subject to *scaling.* Scaling is accomplished using a value as a multiplier or *scaling factor;* it will increase or reduce the sensitivity of any technique used for calculating the band. If S is a scaling factor, then the following bands can be constructed:

$B = M_t \pm S \times c \times M_t$ (percentage smoothing)

$B = M_t \pm S \times c \times P_t$ (percentage smoothing using price)

$B = M_t \pm S \times R$ (fixed risk using absolute point value)

$\left.\begin{array}{l} B_U = S \times f(H_t) \\ B_L = S \times f(L_t) \end{array}\right\}$ (independent smoothing of highs or lows)

$B = M_t \pm S \times (H_t - L_t)$ (volatility of high-low)

$B = M_t \pm S \times V(P_t)$ (volatility function at price level)

$B = M_t \pm S \times V(M_t)$ (volatility at moving average level)

When $S = 1$, the scaling effect is nullified; for $S > 1$, the width of the band is magnified; and for $S < 1$, the band is reduced.

Different bands are not mutually exclusive. A variable band may be used to time the entries and exits subject to a maximum risk established by another band. It may also be convenient to have separate exit and entry bands, the first more sensitive, such that a reversal of position is not always necessary. An exit band may be based on the intraday high or low prices while entries are determined by closing prices.

Bollinger Bands

Perhaps the simplest and most robust measurement of price volatility is the standard deviation of the prices themselves over recent price history. Originally introduced by John Bollinger and popularly called *Bollinger bands,* the value of 2 standard deviations of price movement over the past 20 periods are plotted above and below a 20-day moving average. As with other techniques, the popularity of the computer has allowed users to change both the calculation period and the number of standard deviations that form the band. Because the standard deviation represents a confidence level, the choice of 2 standard deviations equates to a 95% confidence band, while 3 standard deviations give a confidence band of 99%.

Another way of viewing Bollinger bands is as a percentage, seen as %*b*:

%*b* = (Close − Lower band) / (Upper band − Lower band)

In *TradeStation,* a function that returns the upper and lower generalized Bollinger bands, given the calculation period and standard deviation factor, is

```
{Function Bollinger_Band
 Returns the width of the Bollinger band as measured from the moving average value}
 inputs:period(numericsimple), nsd(numeric);
 Bollinger_Band = nds * @stddev(close,period);
```

From the main program, the bands are created with the following instructions:

```
bandwidth = Bollinger_Band(period,nsd);
highband = @average(close,period) + band width;
lowband = @average(close,period) - band width;
```

An excellent example of Bollinger bands uses a combination of weekly and daily data applied to the S&P 500, as seen in Figure 5-1. The price pattern follows the weekly Bollinger band higher, where the daily and weekly come together during the week of July 14.

Rules for Using Bands

Regardless of the type of band that is constructed, rules for using bands to generate trading signals are limited. The first decision to be made is whether a current position will be liquidated or reversed, causing the entry into a new position in the opposite direction. Assuming a reversal from long to short and from short to long, the following rules apply:

Buy (close out shorts and go long) when the price penetrates (closes above) the upper band.

Sell (close out longs and go short) when the price penetrates (closes below) the lower band.

This technique is always in the market with a maximum risk (without execution costs) equal to the width of the band at the time of entry (see Figure 5-2). If a neutral position is preferred after exiting from each trade, there are the alternative rules:

Buy (go long) when prices penetrate the upper band. Close out longs when prices reverse and go below the moving average value (the center of the band).

Sell (go short) when prices break below the lower band. Cover your shorts when prices penetrate upward through the moving average value.

The band is then used to enter into new long or short trades, and the actual trendline within the band is used only for liquidation. If prices are not strong enough to penetrate the opposite band on the close of the same day, the trade is closed out but not reversed. The next day, penetration of either the upper or lower band will signal a new long or short trade, respectively.

This technique allows a trade to be reentered in the same direction in the event of a *false breakout.* If a pullback occurs after a closeout while no position is being held (as shown in Figure 5-3), an entry at a later date might be at a better price. A disadvantage occurs when the price changes direction and moves so fast that both the closeout and the new signal occur on the same day. Reversing the position immediately would be better in a fast market.

The high and low of the day may also be used as penetration criteria. Again, using the outer bands for entry and the moving average for exit, apply the following rules:

FIGURE 5-1 Combining daily and weekly Bollinger bands.

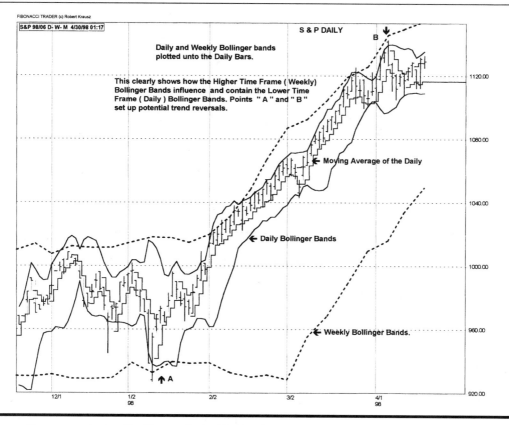

FIBONACCI TRADER (c) Robert Krausz

S&P 98/06 D- W- M 4/30/98 01:17

S & P DAILY

Daily and Weekly Bollinger bands
plotted unto the Daily Bars.

This clearly shows how the Higher Time Frame (Weekly)
Bollinger Bands influence and contain the Lower Time
Frame (Daily) Bollinger Bands. Points " A " and " B "
set up potential trend reversals.

← Moving Average of the Daily

← Daily Bollinger Bands

← Weekly Bollinger Bands.

Source: Chart created using *The Fibonacci Trader.* Used with permission from Fibonacci Trader Corporation, 757 SE 17th Street, Suite 272, Ft. Lauderdale, FL 33316. www.fibonaccitrader.com.

FIGURE 5-2 Simple trading rules for moving averages.

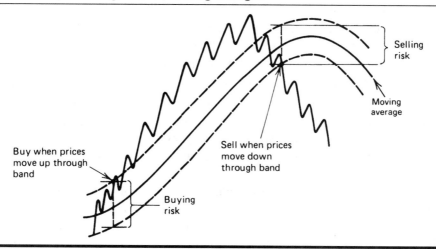

Selling
risk

Moving
average

Buy when prices
move up through
band

Sell when prices
move down
through band

Buying
risk

FIGURE 5-3   Basic rules for using bands.

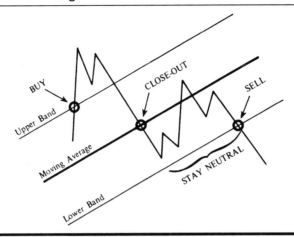

Buy when the high of the day penetrates the upper band, and close out longs when the low of the day penetrates the moving average.

Sell when the low of the day penetrates the lower band, and cover shorts when the high penetrates the moving average.

With both the first and second set of rules, risk is limited to half of the full band width. In the second case, the chances of exiting one trade and remaining neutral are greater than the first.

Timing the Order

The type of execution order placed when following a system will have a long-term effect on its results. The use of a band with a single moving average identifies change of trends when a breakout occurs. Buying during an upside break or selling during a downside break often results in poor entry prices, and has been known to place the trader in a new trend at the point where prices are ready for a *technical adjustment.* The most frequent complaint of trend followers is that their new positions usually show losses and that it takes a long time before the technical adjustment ends and the new trend returns to its entry price level. This reasoning has caused many variations from the original rules:

> *Buy* (or *sell*) on the close after an entry signal has been indicated.
>
> *Buy* (or *sell*) on the next market open following a signal.
>
> *Buy* (or *sell*) with a delay of 1, 2, or 3 days after the signal.
>
> *Buy* (or *sell*) after a price retracement of 50% (or some other value) following a signal.
>
> *Buy* (or *sell*) when prices move to within a specified risk relative to a stop-loss point.

These modifications are for the purpose of entering a new position with an immediate profit or preventing excessive risk. Some can be categorized as *timing* and others as *risk management.* If intraday prices are used to signal new entries and exits, a rule may be added that states:

> Only one order can be executed in one day—either the liquidation of a current position or an entry into a new position.

The goal of improving exit and entry points is well worth spending time and effort. With limited capital, the conservation of the investment is important when the greater number of trades are expected to lose money. Better entry points will reduce the risk on a larger part of the trades and allow longer strings of poor performance.

Waiting for the right time to enter a trade may have more disadvantages than is apparent. In tests on trend-following systems conducted over many years, it can be shown that positions entered at the market opening on the day following the system signal improved fill prices about 75% of the time but resulted in smaller overall profits for the year. Why? Fast breakouts never adjusted back to allow the trader to enter at a better price. The three out of four better fills were more than offset by the one breakout that kept going.

APPLICATIONS OF SINGLE TRENDS

The selection of the trend speed (calculation period) is as important as any of the system's rules. The speed determines the activity of trading and the nature of the trend to be isolated. To help this decision, some of the preceding sections have shown comparisons of the different speeds as well as approaches, based on minimizing the magnitude of the forecast errors. Without a computer, extensive examination of alternatives is impossible. Chapter 21 concentrates on the use of the computer for selection of trend speed and risk parameters for single- and multiple-trend systems, as well as breakout systems. It also includes an analysis of results.

Prior to being able to *optimize,* the trend period was based on multiples of calendar periods, expressed as trading days. In doing this, there is an opportunity to be in phase with behavioral patterns of traders and brokerage houses, who may work within weekly or monthly spans. The most popular intervals for selection have been 3 days, the expected duration of a short price move; 5 days, a trading week; 20 to 23 days, a trading month, and so on. Included in the next sections are well-known systems using single trends, followed by examples of multiple-trend systems.

MPTDI (A Step-Weighted Moving Average)

In 1972, Robert Joel Taylor published a system called the "Major Price Trend Directional Indicator" (MPTDI), which was reprinted in summary form in the September 1973 issue of *Commodities Magazine.* The system was promoted and implemented through Enterex Commodities in Dallas and was tested in 1972 on historical data by Dunn and Hargitt Financial Services in West Lafayette, Indiana. It was one of the few well-defined published systems, and it served as the basis for much experimentation for current technicians and aspiring analysts.

MPTDI is based on a step-weighted moving average of varying lengths, with a band of changing widths relative to volatility. It is unique in its complete dependence on incremental values for all aspects of the system: the moving average, entry, and stop-loss points. For example, Table 5-1 shows what conditions might be assigned to gold.

If gold were trading in an average range of 250 to 350 points each day, the weighting factor for the moving average would be TYPE C, indicating medium volatility (TYPE A is lowest). Using TYPE C with a 15-day moving average, the most recent 5 days are given the weight 3, the next 5 days 2, and the last 5 days are weighted by 1. The buy and sell signals use the corresponding entry-signal penetration of 250 points above the moving average as a buy signal and 250 below as a sell entry. The highs or lows of intraday trading are used to activate the entry based on values calculated after the close of trading on the prior day. A stop-loss point is fixed at the time of entry equal to the value on the same line as the proper volatility. The penetration of the stop-loss will cause the liquidation of the current trade. A new signal in the reverse direction will serve as both a stop-loss and reentry point.

TABLE 5-1   MPTDI Variables*

Average Trading Range	Number of Days in Calculation	Weighting Factors Progression	Entry-Signal Penetration	Approximate Stop-Loss Point
50–150	25 days	TYPE A	100 pts	150 pts
150–250	20 days	TYPE B	200 pts	300 pts
250–350	15 days	TYPE C	250 pts	350 pts
350–450	10 days	TYPE D	350 pts	450 pts
450+	5 days	TYPE E	450 pts	550 pts

*100 points = $1 per ounce.

There is a lot to say in favor of the principles of MPTDI. It is individualized with respect to markets and self-adjusting with changing volatility. The stop-loss serves to limit the initial risk of the trade and allow the coordination of a money management approach. The fixed risk differs from moving averages using standard bands, because a moving average and its band can back away from system-entry points on a gradual reversal of the price trend. But there are some rough edges to the system. The incremental ranges for volatility, entry points, and stops seem a crude measure. Even if they are accurate in the center of the range, they must get doubtful at the extremes at the point of change from one range to another. Analysts will find that they may need to study price movement at discrete levels, such as those shown in MPTDI, to be able to generalize a price or volatility pattern.

The Volatility System

Another method that includes volatility and is computationally simple is the Volatility System.[1] Signals are generated when a price change is accompanied by an unusually large move relative to average volatility. If the average volatility measured over N days is

$$V_t(N) = \frac{1}{N} \sum_{i=1}^{N} D_{t-i+1}$$

where D is the maximum of

(a) $|H_t - C_{i-1}|$

(b) $|H_i - L_i|$

(c) $|L_1 - C_{i-1}|$

and H_i is the high on day i
  C_i is the close on day i
  L_t is the low on day i

Trading rules are given as

  Sell if the close drops by more than $K \times V(N)$ from the previous close.

  Buy if the close rises by more than $K \times V(N)$ from the previous close.

The value of K is generally about 3.0.

---

[1] Richard Bookstaber, *The Complete Investment Book* (Scott, Foresman, Glenview, IL, 1984, p. 231).

Note that the average volatility should not include the current day t. A comparison of today's volatility using an average containing that value might cause inconsistent signals.

The 10-Day Moving Average Rule

The most basic application of a moving average system was proposed by Keltner in his 1960 publication, *How to Make Money in Commodities* (The Keltner Statistical Service, Kansas City, 1960). Of three mechanical systems presented by Keltner, his choice of a moving average was based on performance and experience. The system itself is quite simple: a 10-day moving average based on the average of the daily high, low, and closing prices, with a band on each side formed from the 10-day moving average of the high-low range. A buy signal occurs on penetration of the upper band and a sell signal when the lower band is broken; positions are always reversed.

The 10-Day Moving Average Rule is basic, but it does account for the fundamental volatility principle and serves as an example of the actual use of moving averages. Keltner expresses his preference for this particular technique because of its identification of minor rather than medium- or long-term trends, and there are some performance figures that substantiate his conclusion. As an experienced trader, he prefers the speed of the 10-day moving average, which follows the market prices with more reasonable risk than slower methods. A side benefit to the selection is that the usual division required by a moving average calculation can be substituted by a simple shift of the decimal place; in an era before the pocket calculator, who knows how much impact that convenience had on Keltner's choice?

Triple Exponential Smoothing

A triple exponential smoothing technique was described by Hutson as another approach to trend following.[2] Substituting the log of the price for the price itself, he applied an exponential smoothing three times using the same smoothing constant. A buy signal was generated when the triple-smoothed series rose for 2 consecutive days; a sell signal followed a 2-day decline.

The smoothing constant selected would normally be faster (less than a 20-day equivalent, when $2/(n + 1)$ is used to convert the n days to a smoothing constant) for a triple smoothing than for a single smoothed line. It is interesting to see what actually happens when a series is smoothed three times. For example, a triple smoothing of a straight 3-day moving average gives the following:

$$P = (P_1, P_2, \cdots, P_n)$$

The single moving average at day n is

$$M_n = \frac{(P_{n-2} + P_{n-1} + P_n)}{3}$$

Smoothing the new series M gives

$$M_n' = \frac{(M_{n-2} + M_{n-1} + M_n)}{3}$$

$$= \frac{(P_{n-4} + 2P_{n-3} + 3P_{n-2} + 2P_{n-1} + P_n)}{9}$$

and the third smoothing gives

[2] Jack K. Hutson, "Good TRIX," *Technical Analysis of Stocks & Commodities* (July 1983).

$$M_n'' = \frac{(M_{n-2}' + M_{n-1}' + M_n')}{3}$$

$$= \frac{(P_{n-6} + 3P_{n-5} + 6P_{n-4} + 7P_{n-3} + 6P_{n-2} + 3P_{n-1} + P_n)}{27}$$

The effect of the weighting puts increased importance on the middle values, reducing the significance of both ends. With exponential smoothing as well, the increased emphasis will be placed on the $n - 2$ value, the price which is repeated most often.

The Parabolic Time/Price System

One of the primary complaints about trend-following systems is that the built-in lag destroys the trade. In the Parabolic Time/Price System,[3] Wilder has reduced the lag by increasing the speed of the trend (shortening the days) whenever prices achieve new profitable levels. The philosophy of the Parabolic System is that time is an enemy. Once a position is entered, it must continue to be profitable or it will be liquidated.

The Parabolic Time/Price System is always in the market; whenever a position is closed out, it is also reversed. The point at which this occurs is called the Stop and Reverse (SAR). When plotted, it is similar to a trendline, although it has a decreasing lag (the distance between the current price and the trendline, or SAR point), as shown in Figure 5-4.

To calculate the SAR value, first assume a long or short position. If the market has recently moved lower and is now above the lows of that move, assume a *long*. Call the lowest point of the previous trade the SAR initial point (SIP), because it will be the starting point for the SAR calculation ($SAR_1 = SIP$).

Calculate each following SAR as

$$SAR(tomorrow) = SAR(prior) + AF \times [High(today) - SAR(prior)]$$

This is an exponential smoothing using the prior high price. It is unique because the smoothing constant *AF,* called the acceleration factor, changes. *AF* is set to .02 at the beginning of the trade. Each day that a new extreme occurs (a new high when long, or a new low

[3] J. Welles Wilder, Jr., *New Concepts in Technical Trading Systems* (Trend Research, Greensboro, NC, 1978).

FIGURE 5-4   Parabolic Time/Price System.

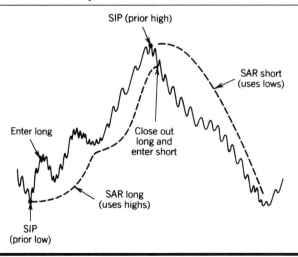

when short), *AF* is increased by .02. In moving average days, *AF* begins at 99 days and increases in speed to a maximum of a 9-day moving average, but not in a linear fashion.

In the SAR calculation, High(today) is used when a long position is held, and Low(today) is used when a short is held. An additional rule also prevents premature reversal by not allowing the SAR to enter the price range of the most recent 2 days:

> If *long,* the SAR may never be greater than the low of today or the prior day. If it is greater than this low, set the SAR to that low value. A reversal will occur on a new intra-day low that penetrates the SAR.

> If *short,* the SAR is calculated in the same way based on the highs.

Wilder's Parabolic Time/Price System was a new and interesting idea—varying the exponential smoothing constant. This could also be accomplished by varying the moving average days, but not as effectively. The constant increment of .02 and the limitations of the range, .02 to .20, are likely to be shortcomings. Traders might want to relate the changing speed to more basic price phenomena such as volatility or momentum. For those readers interested in the further development of this method, the Parabolic Time/Price System is combined with Directional Movement (described in Chapter 23) to form the Directional Parabolic System discussed in Chapter 6.

The Master Trading Formula

Another method of variable speed is Mart's *The Master Trading Formula.*[4] It uses an exponential smoothing formula in which the smoothing constant and band are calculated daily, based on market volatility. Mart averages the extended daily range (using the maximum of yesterday's close and today's high and low) and the net price movement over the same interval to define a *correlated volatility factor.* This value is then used to look up a smoothing constant in a modified log-scale table, in which an 8% smoothing (24-day equivalent) is used for the lowest volatility and a 33% smoothing (2-day equivalent) for the greatest volatility, with the median value at 14% (13-day equivalent).

A band is also placed around the trendline, based on an inverse relationship to the correlated volatility factor. The band is widest when there is low volatility and the smoothing constant produces a slow trend; it is narrowest in fast, highly volatile markets.

Rules for trading Mart's Master Formula are centered around the basic band trading rules. The system is always in the market, taking long positions when the upper band is broken and short positions when the lower band is crossed.

Raschke's First Cross

Although we usually trade a trend from the beginning to end based on some smoothing method, Linda Bradford Raschke has shown that a selected piece of the trend move can be a very reliable trade. Her First Cross system enters a trend trade on the first pullback after an initial trend signal based on a faster momentum indicator. She did not offer any exit rules, but there are some that can be suggested. To create this program we need

```
slowMA    Slow-moving average, part of oscillator calculation
fastMA    Fast-moving average, part of oscillator calculation
osc       Moving average oscillator, fastMA - slowMA
trend     Moving average of osc
```

The oscillator is the difference between the fast- and slow-moving averages

```
osc = fastMA - slowMA
```

[4] Donald S. Mart, *The Master Trading Formula* (Winsor Books, Brightwaters, NY, 1981).

To generate a buy or sell entry signal, use the following steps (comments on the right):

> **B1.** `osc[1]> trend and osc <= trend`   osc **crosses** trend **moving down**
> **B2.** `low > low[1]`   low of bar rises
> **B3.** `buy`
>
> **S1.** `osc[1] < trend and osc >= trend`   osc **crosses** trend **moving up**
> **S2.** `high < high[1]`   high of the bar declines
> **S3.** `sell`

A likely exit rule for the First Cross system should maintain the short-term nature of the selection. You might simply consider the entry on the first pullback as better entry timing for a longer-term trend. Or, you might want to trade only the short period isolated by the first pullback until this initial impulse is exhausted. If you chose the second method, you might try the following exit condition:

Exit for a long position

> **X1.** `close[1] > close[2]`   close of bar turns up (confirms trend)
> **X2.** `close < close[1]`   after going up, the close turns down
> **X3.** `exit long`

Raschke's idea is an excellent example of selectivity. First, you recognize that the beginning of a trend is different from other times. As traders recognize a change of direction there is an increasingly strong move. Because most systems lag the market, they are often too late or miss the first part of the turn, which could create large profits. As an alternative, this technique waits for the first move to be exhausted, then enters in anticipation of another fast surge as the new trend reasserts itself. Once these early moves are over, the general trend move may not be as easy to work with, and you may find yourself trying to enter as the trend comes to an end.

COMPARISON OF MAJOR TREND SYSTEMS

A section on trends cannot be complete without looking at the comparative performance of the six most popular approaches:

1. Simple moving average
2. Exponential smoothing
3. Linear regression slope
4. *N*-day breakout
5. Swing breakout
6. Point-and-figure

Trading Rules

To see the characteristics of each system, the trading rules will be as simple as possible. All six systems are always in the market. That is, once they enter a long or short position, they always reverse on a new signal, going from long to short, or short to long. There are no stop-losses or other risk control rules; therefore, each system has its own, natural risk profile. A $100 round-turn charge was applied to each trade to cover commissions and slippage. Table 5-2 summarizes the type of system, calculation method, and trading rules.

Varying the Speed of the Trend

Each system must be tested with a wide range of fast and slow trends. For systems 1 through 4, the period, or number of days, *n*, determines the trend speed. For the swing

TABLE 5-2 Summary of Six Major Trending Systems

System Type	Formulas	Rules
1. Simple moving average MA is the average of previous *n*-day closing prices.	`MA = @Sum(close,n) / n` `MA = @Average(close,n)` `MAchange = MA - MA[1]`	`BUY if MAchange > 0` `SELL if MAchange < 0` (the moving average turns up or down)
2. Exponential smoothing EXP is a weighting of the recent closing price by a percentage, *s* (called the *smoothing constant*).	`EXP= EXP[1]+s*(close-EXP[1])` `EXPchange = EXP - EXP[1]`	`BUY if EXPchange > 0` `SELL if EXPchange < 0` (the trend turns up or down)
3. Linear regression slope LRS is the slope (angle) of a straight line found using a least-squares regression.	$$\text{LRS} = \frac{n*\text{Sum}(x*c) \ -\text{Sum}(x)*\text{Sum}(c)}{n*\text{Sum}(x*x) \ -\text{Sum}(x)*\text{Sum}(x)}$$ where c is the `close`, and x are the integers, 1, 2, 3, . . . , *n*, representing the time intervals.	`BUY if LRS > 0` `SELL if LRS < 0` *Buy* when the LRS is up (slope is positive), and *sell* when the LRS is down (slope is negative).
4. *N*-day breakout Signals occur when the current price reaches a new high or low (a "breakout") for both intraday and end of day, based on the previous *n*-days.	`nhigh = @high-` `  est(high[1],n-1)` `nlow =` `@lowest(low[1],n-1)`	`BUY if high > nhigh` `     and close > close[1]` `SELL if low < nlow` `     and close < close[1]` *Buy* when the current high price is greater than the highest price of the past *n* days, and the `close` is higher than the previous `close[1]`.
5. Swing breakout Signals occur when the current high or low price exceeds the previous swing high or low price. A swing is a price move that begins with a reversal of a minimum percentage value.	`swhigh` is the highest price that occurs before a price decline of `p*swhigh`, where p is a percent `swlow` is the lowest price that occurs before a rally of `p*swlow`, where p is a percent.	`BUY if high > swhigh` `SELL if low < swlow` *Buy* when the current high exceeds the previous swing high. *Sell* when the current low falls below the previous swing low.
6. Point-and-figure Signals occur when the current high or low price exceeds the previous high or low, which is formed by filling boxes of a preset point size.	Same rules as Swing Breakout, except that new highs and lows are recorded only if they exceed a preset box size. A reversal is recorded if a minimum of 3 boxes can be filled, not including the current box	`BUY if high > PFhigh + 1 box` `SELL if low < PFlow - 1 box` *Buy* when the current high exceeds the previous PF swing high by at least one box. *Sell* when the current low falls below the previous PF swing low by at least 1 box.

TABLE 5-3 Eurodollar Results for Six Systems (1985–1994)

Systems	Rules
1. Moving average (MA)	1. TradeStation closed-out trades only
2. Exponential smoothing (EXP)	2. First 200 days used for initialization
3. Linear regression slope (LRS)	3. Commissions and slippage at $100 per trade
4. Swing breakout (SWG)	4. Test data from 1/1/84 to 3/31/94 unless indicated
5. Point-and-figure (P&F)	5. TYPE = 0, standard; 1, 3-month rate; 2, bonds
6. N-day breakout (NDAY)	

1. MOVING AVERAGE	2. EXPONENTIAL SMOOTHING	3. LINEAR REGRESSION SLOPE
1. No memory of past period.	1. Some memory of past prices.	1. Projects direction as mean (economics).
2. Whips limit minimum number of trades (need filter).	2. Whips limit minimum number of trades (need filter).	2. Price penetration does not cause whips.
3. Mostly small losses.	3. Mostly small losses.	3. Losses can be larger than MA or EXP.

1. MOVING AVERAGE

	Days	#Prf	#Trds	Rel	Radj%	%Tr
ED	4	131	433	30.3	-79	-0.18
	8	88	274	32.1	51	0.19
	16	51	182	28.0	134	0.74
	32	37	111	33.3	566	5.10
	50	31	95	32.6	208	2.19
	75	17	65	26.2	267	4.11
	100	15	43	34.9	281	6.53
	150	8	21	38.1	468	22.29
	200	9	44	20.5	5	0.11
Avg	70.6	43.0	141	30.6	211.2	4.56
SD				4.9	199.4	
A-sd				25.7	11.7	

2. EXPONENTIAL SMOOTHING

Days	#Prf	#Trds	Rel	Radj%	%Tr
4	136	515	26.4	-88	-0.17
8	90	316	28.5	-17	-0.05
16	51	214	23.8	44	0.21
32	32	117	27.4	365	3.12
50	25	87	28.7	91	1.05
75	19	73	26.0	135	1.85
100	22	51	43.1	257	5.04
150	12	27	44.4	472	17.48
200	9	42	21.4	5	0.12
70.56	44.0	160.2	30	140.4	3.18
			7.7	176.7	
			22.3	-36.3	

3. LINEAR REGRESSION SLOPE

Days	#Prf	#Trds	Rel	Radj%	%Tr
4	171	557	30.7	-90	-0.16
8	91	259	35.1	-4	-0.02
16	41	127	32.3	27	0.21
32	21	55	38.2	238	4.33
50	16	39	41.0	216	5.54
75	13	29	44.8	156	5.38
100	5	15	33.3	141	9.40
150	8	11	72.7	279	25.36
200	1	6	16.7	105	17.50
70.56	40.8	122	38.3	118.7	7.50
			14.3	114.7	
			24.0	3.9	

(handwritten notes: "BEST RETURN", "MA turns up or down", "Goes L & Short!")

TABLE 5-3 *(Continued)*

1. Signals on natural level without memory.
2. Whips mostly on expanding market swings.
3. Risk increases with range.

1. Uses natural levels to give signals.
2. Fewer whips unless expanding market.
3. Risk increases with swing size.

1. Signals on natural level plus filter.
2. Fewer whips unless expanding market.
3. Risk increases with swing size.

4. N-DAY BREAKOUT

	Days	#Prf	#Trds	Rel	Radj%	%/Tr
ED	4	108	283	38.2	84	0.30
	8	58	143	40.6	240	1.68
	16	29	77	37.7	188	2.44
	32	17	37	45.9	459	12.41
	50	12	27	44.4	347	12.85
	75	8	15	53.3	423	28.20
	100	6	13	46.2	215	16.54
	150	4	7	57.1	431	61.57
	200	1	6	16.7	106	17.67
Avg	70.6	27.0	67.6	42.2	277.0	17.07
SD				10.9	134.4	
A-sd				31.3	142.6	

5. SWING BREAKOUT (type=1)

%	#Prf	#Trds	Rel	Radj%	%/Tr
0.25	134	381	35.2	-67	-0.18
0.50	132	371	35.6	-47	-0.13
0.75	105	279	37.6	36	0.13
1.00	80	217	36.9	157	0.72
1.50	57	137	41.6	69	0.50
2.00	34	83	41.0	94	1.13
2.50	18	51	35.3	404	7.92
3.00	14	33	42.4	375	11.36
4.00	10	17	58.8	458	26.94
5.00	7	15	46.7	123	8.20
2.1	59.1	158.4	41.1	160.2	5.7
			6.9	178.4	
			34.2	-18.2	

6. POINT-AND-FIGURE

Box	#Prf	#Trds	Rel	Radj%	%/Tr
0.004	126	406	31.0	-78	-0.19
0.008	124	368	33.7	-60	-0.16
0.016	96	275	34.9	-15	-0.05
0.025	70	180	38.9	84	0.47
0.033	59	147	40.1	133	0.90
0.050	34	83	41.0	115	1.39
0.067	23	62	37.1	73	1.18
0.083	17	40	42.5	337	8.43
0.100	11	28	39.3	307	10.96
0.133	7	16	43.8	264	16.50
0.167	2	10	20.0	-4	-0.40
0.062	51.7	146.8	36.6	105.1	3.55
			6.4	121.7	
			30.2	-16.6	

EXPLANATION OF COLUMNS:
Column 1: days, number of days in the calculation period; %, percentage of price for minimum swing criteria; box, box size in points; reversal criteria is 3 × box. Column 2: #Prf, number of profitable trades. Column 3: #Trds, total number of trades. Column 4: Rel, reliability, the percentage of profitable trades. Column 5: Radj%, risk-adjusted 10-year returns, Radj% = PL/MaxDrawdown. Column 6: %/Tr, profit per trade in %.

breakout, a percentage swing makes it more or less sensitive to price movements. Point-and-figure uses a constant box size, which is then multiplied by 3 to get the reversal size.

Tests shown in Table 5-3 for the Eurodollar confirm a broad range of trading from very short-term to very long-term. The number of trades varies from over 500 in 10 years (about 2,500 days) to 6 trades in 10 years. Some showed a fairly high minimum number of trades for the longest periods.

Different Trend Philosophies

The moving average, exponential, and linear regression are time-series processes; that is, each day is a small part of the total calculation. This can make it very difficult for a single large price jump to cause a change of signal. For very fast trends, each price will have more importance than for slower trends.

The N-day breakout, swing breakout, and point-and-figure systems all depend on a price breakout. A signal occurs when the market makes a new high or low. Therefore, a single big move often causes a new signal. Breakout systems can be considered *event driven,* while a moving average system requires a trend to *evolve.*

Different Risk Profiles

Each of the six systems fall into particular categories of risk profiles.

Moving Averages and Exponential Smoothing

Both the moving average and exponential smoothing return a weighted average. The simple moving average uses equal weighting, and the exponential gives more importance to the most recent value, according to the smoothing constant, *s.*

Both systems are considered *conservation-of-capital* methods because they keep losses small. When current price levels are trading near the *n*-day average, it takes very little to change the trend from up to down and back to up. Although this is annoying to traders, it is part of the conservation-of-capital benefit. Table 5-3 shows that the minimum number of trades were 42 to 44 for these systems, far greater than the other four strategies. The whipsaws seem to increase as the trends become very slow, which is the reason for using a filter, or band, in most trend systems. In Table 5-3 the number of trades doubled when the trend slowed from 150 to 200 days.

Breakout Systems

The swing breakout, point-and-figure, and N-day breakout systems can all be grouped as high-risk strategies. Once a buy signal has occurred because of new high prices, the trade is reversed only when new low prices occur. The initial risk is

breakout risk = highest high − lowest low

for the N-day period. The rate at which risk declines is different for each of the systems. The swing breakout and point and figure systems reduce risk each time a new swing low occurs only if that low is higher than the previous swing low (see Figure 5-5). The N-day breakout reduces risk if the oldest days, which are dropped off, were also the lowest prices. Otherwise, its risk is the same as the other breakout systems.

Linear Regression Risk

The linear regression method, which creates a straight-line forecast, is very different from other trending systems. It does not change direction when prices move up or down through the trendline (as in the smoothing systems). It is possible that a very large, but fast price drop, which recovers quickly, will not cause a long position signal to reverse.

FIGURE 5-5 Swing breakout risk pattern. As prices move lower, the swing highs become the point at which signals reverse. This pattern is the same for point-and-figure.

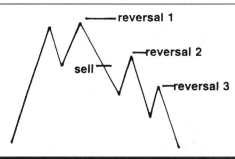

Least squares puts the greatest importance on those prices closest to the straight-line estimate. It is very sluggish to change direction when a larger number of days is used. Because of this pattern, it can have a mixture of large and small losses.

Frequency of Trades

You might notice that the number of trades varies considerably across systems. This reflects their risk. The longer you hold a trade, the greater the risk exposure. The two smoothing systems (moving average and exponential smoothing) cut losses short; therefore, they show the largest number of trades for a slow trend.

Breakout systems can trade very little if they enter on a new high after a volatile market period. A long position can be held for months waiting for the swing low to move up. An expanding range, one that makes a new high, followed by a new low and another new high, can be devastating.

Expectations

We form expectations so that we can recognize when test results are wrong. It is the same as an engineer estimating the length of a bridge before a computer program produces the final numbers. An accidental shift of a decimal point may give you plans for a 10-foot bridge over a 100-foot river.

Similar Systems Give Similar Results

We expect the first two and last two systems to be very similar. In each case the rules are nearly the same. We expect the *N*-day breakout to have the highest risk because volatility increases over time. The *n*-day high and low should create a much larger range than the most recent swing high and low. Of course, we expect slower systems to be more profitable than faster ones, because longer periods often reflect fundamental price movements.

Robust Testing

To get the most value from these tests (an approach covered in detail in Chapter 21), there needs to be as much consistency as possible between tests. The following standards are set:

1. *Test periods.* All markets and all tests covered the same 10-year period, ending March 31, 1994 (except the OEX, which began in 1986 and totaled 9 years).
2. *Range of trend speeds.* Those systems that used days were tested from 4 to 200. Systems 5 and 6, swing breakout and point-and-figure, used values that produced a similar number of trades.

3. *Adjusted rate of return.* Returns were specified as the 10-year return divided by the maximum intraday drawdown.

4. *Test averages.* Below each test group are the averages of all tests, the standard deviation of the total returns, and the average minus one standard deviation. The best result is the system with the highest average return and the smallest standard deviation.

Which System Is Best?

Table 5-4 gives only the average returns by system and market. It then averages those results down and to the right, giving the average of averages. Results show that Eurodollars were profitable for all systems and that the *N*-day breakout had the best returns for all markets. In trying to understand the results, it is useful to remove those tests that resulted in very few trades or too many trades to be practical. Table 5-5 presents the same results for all results with the number of trades from 24 through 260 over the 10-year period (from 2.5 per year to 1 every 2 weeks). The table shows that the simple moving average was much better and the *N*-day breakout much worse. Total results were better, showing that the fast trends were big losers. This is particularly true of the smoothing methods.

A Different View of Results

The average results give a reasonable picture of performance, but it is clear that each type of system has a different distribution of trades. For example, doubling the swing percent-

TABLE 5-4 Average Returns

	MA	EXP	LRS	SWG	P&F	NDAY	Avg
ED	211	140	119	160	105	277	169
US	108	72	17	−24	−6	123	48
DM	133	95	141	16	81	106	95
SP	−57	−44	−66	−24	−27	−49	−44
OEX	−35	−23	−29	−12	−17	−7	−21
CL	135	112	47	−18	−30	152	66
SY	16	−14	108	39	47	78	45
Avg	73	48	48	20	22	97	51

The average of all tests gives a better picture of the robustness of the systems and the trendiness of the markets. Each value is a 10-year risk-adjusted return.

TABLE 5-5 Average Returns for Tests with 24–260 Trades

	MA	EXP	LRS	SWG	P&F	NDAY	Avg
ED	276	196	127	220	175	309	217
US	153	111	26	13	27	28	59
DM	192	139	285	−1	123	57	132
SP	−44	−31	−60	−18	−48	−80	−47
OEX	−11	−2	−11	18	1	−46	−8
CL	196	165	153	13	−16	215	121
SY	47	22	14	53	93	−69	27
Avg	116	86	76	43	51	59	72

By limiting the test periods to a more popular range, we see that the simple moving average is best, although the markets perform relatively the same way.

age does not reduce trades as quickly as doubling the days in the *N*-day breakout. This causes the average results of the two systems to be biased differently toward faster or slower trends. This is corrected by comparing the systems when they have the same number of trades.

Aligning Test Results Graphically

Figure 5-6 shows the Eurodollar results when we attempt to align each of the six systems by their test periods. The patterns are similar, but somewhat out of phase. This is especially true for the breakout systems. By displaying performance of all systems by total trades, shown in Figure 5-7, we see a steady decline from left to right. As the number of trades increases, profits disappear.

We can conclude that trending systems, in general, are a robust trading vehicle for Eurodollars, but only if we apply a longer time horizon. The patterns clearly show that increasing trades result in overall losses. This should be a very comforting conclusion for systems traders.

Programming the Six Systems

Omega Easy Language Code

A general systems approach to programming *TradeStation's Easy Language* has been taken in this example. The strategies are written as User Functions rather than systems. This adds flexibility and allows us to use the same programs at another time. A *User Function* is a small program or subprogram that can be referenced (called) from other programs. This shared program saves you from repeating the rules and calculations for each new program.

FIGURE 5-6 Eurodollar results by test period. The rising pattern of profits from left to right is not clear because of the difficulty in aligning the test period, in days, with the swing size, in percent.

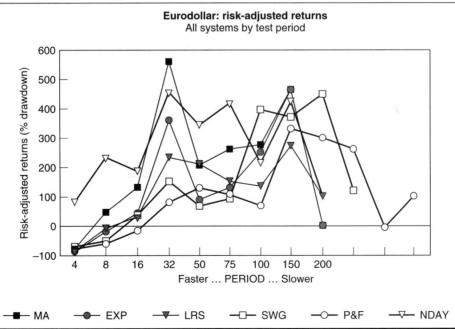

FIGURE 5-7   Eurodollar results by total trades. Plotting all systems by total trades (the bottom scale) shows a clear drop in performance as trading becomes more frequent.

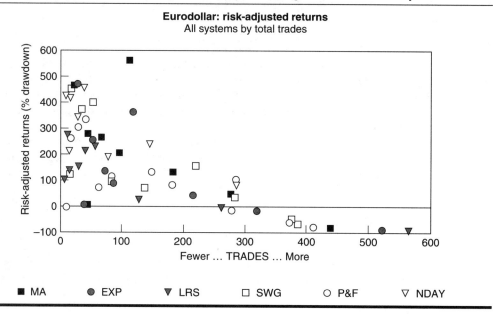

The following User Functions perform the unique calculations for each of the six strategies, and return the value

signal = 0, no position

= 1, buy or hold long position

= −1, sell or hold short position

Note that the final statement of the User Function sets the User Function name equal to the value of the signal. Each program also references a variable *type,* which indicates that the market being processed is, or is not, an interest rate.

type = 0, default

= 1, 3-month interest rate (e.g., Eurodollars, Matif Pibor, Short sterling)

= 2, long-term interest rate (e.g., U.S. T-bonds, T-notes, U.K. Gilt, German bund)

System

A system has buy and sell orders, equity calculations, and other statistics. Parameter values can be set from the appropriate menu. Our systems will reference a User Function to find the signal for each strategy. Because each of the systems would be identical, except for the one line that calls the user function, only one system is shown.

Indicator

An indicator is a program that displays the value of key points or calculations on a chart. An indicator can position the high and low points of a swing (Kswing) or show a separate graph on a split page (KLRS).

```
{KMA : Moving Average User Function
 Copyright 1994-1998, P J Kaufman. All rights reserved.}
```

```
{period = length of moving average trend
 filter = whole % trend change to give signal
 lag  = 0 to enter on close, n to enter n-days later
}
input:  period(numericsimple), filter(numeric), lag(numericsimple);
vars:   ma(0), change(0), signal(0);

signal = signal[1];
{moving average for testing anticipation}
ma = @Average(close,period);
change = (ma - ma[1])*100/close[1];
{long signal}
if lag >= 0 and change[lag]>filter then signal=1;
{short signal}
if lag >= 0 and change[lag]<-filter then signal= -1;
KMA = signal;
```

```
{KEXP exponential User Function
 Copyright 1994-1998, P J Kaufman. All rights reserved.}

{period = length of exponential trend
 filter = whole percent trend change to give signal
 lag = 0 to enter on close, n to enter n-days later
}
input:  period(numericsimple), filter(numeric), lag(numericsimple);
vars:   exp(0), change(0), signal(0);

signal = signal[1];
{Exponential smoothing for testing anticipation}
Exp = @SmoothedAverage(close,period);
change = (Exp - Exp[1])*100/close[1];
{long signal}
if lag >= 0 and change[lag]>filter then signal=1;
{short signal}
if lag >= 0 and change[lag]<-filter then signal= -1;
KEXP = signal;
```

```
{KLRS : Linear Regression Slope User Function
 Copyright 1994-1998, P J Kaufman. All rights reserved.
 Method of least squares to calculate slope}
Inputs: period(numericsimple);
vars:   sumx(0), sumx2(0), sumy(0), sumxy(0), n(0), k(0), top(0), bot(0),
slope(0), yint(0);

{Time = x, the independent variable, e.g., 1, 2, 3, . . .
 Close = y, the dependent variable}

{standard sum of integer series}
  sumx = period*(period+1) / 2;
  sumx2 = period*(period+1)*(2*period+1) / 6;
  sumy = @summation(close,period);
  sumxy = 0;
  n = period;
  for k = 0 to period-1 begin
      sumxy = sumxy + n*close[k];
      n = n - 1;
      end;
 top = period*sumxy - sumx*sumy;
 bot = period*sumx2 - sumx*sumx;
 if bot<>0 then slope = top / bot;
{yint = (sumy - slope*sumx) / period;}
 KLRS = slope;
```

```
{KLRSignal : Linear Regression Slope signal User Function
 Copyright 1994-1998, P J Kaufman. All rights reserved.}

{period = length of exponential trend
 filter = whole % trend change to give signal
 }
input:  period(numericsimple), filter(numeric), lag(numeric);
vars:   slope(0), signal(0);

{Call linear regression slope User Function}
slope = KLRS(close,period);
signal = signal[1];
{long signal : slope is up by more than filter}
if lag >= 0 and slope[lag]>filter then signal = 1;
{short signal : slope is down by more than filter}
if lag >= 0 and slope[lag]<-filter then signal = -1;
KLRSignal = signal;
```

```
{KNDB : N-Day Breakout User Function
 Copyright 1994-1998, P J Kaufman. All rights reserved.}

{INPUT for N-day Breakout System signal rules:
 BUY when high is above N-day high and close > prior close
 SELL when low is below N-day low and close < prior close}

input: period(numeric);
vars: nhigh(0), nlow(0), signal(0);

nhigh = highest(high[1],period - 1);
nlow = lowest(low[1],period - 1);
{Buy and sell signals}
signal = signal[1];
if high > nhigh and close > close[1] then signal = 1;
if low < nlow and close < close[1] then signal = -1;
KNDB = signal;
```

```
{KSWG : User Function to determine swing direction and new swing highs or lows
 Copyright 1994-1998, P J Kaufman. All rights reserved.}
{INPUT for KSWG
 swing in whole percent
 direction & breakout:
    +1 up, +2 up breakout
    0 none
    -1 dn, -2 dnbreakout
 type : 0= normal, 1= 3 month rate, 2= bond
 signal rules:
     buy when upswing is above prior upswing
     sell when downswing is below prior downswing}
input: swing(numeric), type(numericsimple);
vars: minswing(0), last(0) , curhigh(0) , curlow(0), swhigh(0), swlow(0),
swingdir(0), signal(0);

minswing = swing*close/100;
if type=1 then minswing = swing*(100 - close) / 100;
if type=2 then minswing = swing*(8./close)
{SWINGS: Initialize most recent high and low}
if (currentbar = 1)then begin
    curhigh = close;      {current high}
    curlow = close;       {current low}
    end;
{Search for a new high}
if last<>1 then begin
```

```
        if high > curhigh then curhigh = high;        {new current high}
        if low < curhigh - minswing then begin
            last = 1;              {last high fixed}
            swhigh = curhigh;      {new verified high}
            curlow = low;          {initialize new lows}
            end;
    end
{Search for a new low}
 else begin
    if last <> -1 then begin
        if low < curlow then curlow = low;
        if high > curlow + minswing then begin
            last = -1;
            swlow = curlow;
            curhigh = high; {initialize current high}
            end;
        end;
    end;
{Buy and sell signals}
 signal = signal[1];
 swingdir = 0;
 if last = 1 then begin
     swingdir = -1;
     if curlow < swlow then signal = -1;
     end;
 if last = -1 then begin
     swingdir = 1;
     if curhigh > swhigh then signal = 1;
     end;
 KSWG = signal;
```

```
{KPF : Point & Figure User Function
 Copyright 1994-1998, P J Kaufman. All rights reserved.}
{INPUT for KMA_PF_System, swing in whole percent
 direction & breakout:
   +1 up, +2 up breakout
    0 none
   -1 dn, -2 dnbreakout
 type : 0= normal, 1= 3 month rate, 2= bond
 signal rules:
    buy when upswing is above prior upswing
    sell when downswing is below prior
        downswing}

input: box(numeric), revboxes(numeric);
vars: minswing(0), last(0), curhigh(0), curlow(0), swhigh(0), swlow(0),
swingdir(0), signal(0);

{For percentage calculations:
 minswing = swing*close/100;
 if type=1 then minswing = swing*(100-close) / 100;
 if type=2 then minswing = swing*(8./close)}
 minswing = box*revboxes;
{SWINGS: Initialize most recent high and low}
if currentbar = 1 then begin
    curhigh = close;        {current high}
    curlow = close;         {current low}
    end;
{Search for a new high}
if last<> 1 then begin
    if high > curhigh+boxsize then curhigh = high; {new current high}
```

```
        if low < curhigh - minswing then begin
            last = 1;                {last high fixed}
            swhigh = curhigh;        {new verified high}
            curlow = low;            {initialize new lows}
            end;
        end
{Search for a new low}
 else begin
   if last <> -1 then begin
        if low < curlow-boxsize then curlow=low;
        if high > curlow+minswing then begin
        last = -1;
        swlow = curlow;
        curhigh = high; {initialize current high}
        end;
      end;
    end;
{Buy and sell signals}
 signal = signal[1];
 swingdir = 0;
 if last = 1 then begin
     swingdir = -1;
     if curlow < swlow then signal = -1;
     end;
 if last = -1 then begin
     swingdir = 1;
     if curhigh > swhigh then signal = 1;
     end;
 KPF = signal;
```

SYSTEM

The following system can be used for any of the six methods by changing the braces (comment notation)

```
{System Signals.
 Copyright 1994-1998, P J Kaufman. All rights reserved.}

{type = 0, default,
        1, 3-month rate
        2, long-term rates
 period = length of calculation
 swing = swing filter in whole percent (i.e., 1.5 = 1½ percent)
 filter  = whole % trend change to give signal
}
 input:  type(0), period(0), swing(0), box(0), revboxes(0), filter(0), lag(0);
 vars:   signal(0);

{Call User Function}
   signal = KMA(period,filter,lag);
   {signal = KLRSignal(period);}
   {signal = KNDB(period);}
   {signal = KSWG(type);}
   {signal = KPF(box, revboxes);}
   if signal = 1 then buy at close;
   if signal = -1 then sell at close;
```

INDICATOR

The KMA Swing Indicator plots the high and low swing points above and below the corresponding prices. Select the *scale-by-price* feature.

```
{KMA SWING: Finds most recent swing
 highs and lows.
 Copyright 1994-1998, P J Kaufman. All rights reserved.

 Inputs for KMA SWING:
    swing = price swing in %
    type  = 0, normal; 1, 3-month rate; 2, bond rate
    index = 0, treat as price;
          1, create index series
}
input: swing(1.5), type(0), index(1);
vars:  pcswing(0), last(0), curhigh(0), curlow(0),
       swhigh(0), swlow(0), highbar(0), lowbar(0),
       chighbar(0), clowbar(0), lowp(0), highp(0),
       aclose(0), ahigh(0), alow(0), xclose(0),
       xhigh(0), xlow(0), factor(1);

pcswing = swing/100.;
aclose = close;
ahigh = high;
alow = low;
factor = 1;
if type <> 0 then factor = -1;
{Adjust prices if interest rates}
if type = 1 then begin
   aclose = 100. - close;
   ahigh = 100. - low;
   alow = 100. - high;
   end;
if type = 2 then begin;
   aclose = 800./close;
   ahigh = 800./close;
   alow = 800./close;
   end;
{Initialize most recent high and low}
if currentbar = 1 then begin
   if index = 0 then begin
        xclose = aclose;
        xhigh = ahigh;
        xlow = alow;
        end
      else begin
        xclose = 100.;
          xhigh = ahigh*100 / aclose;
          xlow = alow*100 / aclose;
          end;
      curhigh = xclose;           {current high}
      curlow = xclose;            {current low}
      end
      else begin
        if index = 0 then begin
          xclose = aclose;
          xhigh = ahigh;
          xlow = alow;
          end
        else begin
          xclose = xclose[1] + (aclose - aclose[1])*100 / aclose[1];
          xhigh = xclose[1] + (ahigh - aclose[1])*100 / aclose[1];
          xlow = xclose[1] + (alow - aclose[1])*100 / aclose[1];
          end;
```

```
        end;
        {Search for a new high - favor reversals}
        if last<>1 then begin
        {Reverse from high if minimum % swing}
      if xlow < curhigh - curhigh*pcswing then begin
        last = 1;              {last high fixed}
        swhigh = curhigh;   {new verified high}
        highbar = chighbar;
        curlow = xlow;        {initialize new lows}
        lowp = low;
        clowbar = currentbar;
        plot1[currentbar - highbar](high[currentbar - highbar]
           + factor*highp*pcswing/4,"swinghigh");
        end
      else begin
      if xhigh > curhigh then begin
        curhigh = xhigh;      {new current high}
        chighbar = currentbar;
        end;
      end;
   end;
{Search for a new low - favor reversal}
if last <> -1 then begin
{Reversal from low if minimum % swing}
 if xhigh > curlow + curlow*pcswing then begin
    last = -1;
    swlow = curlow;
    lowbar = clowbar;
    curhigh = xhigh;       {initialize current high}
    highp = high;
    chighbar = currentbar;
    plot2[currentbar - lowbar](low[currentbar - lowbar]-
       factor*lowp*pcswing/4,"swinglow");
    end
 else begin
    if xlow < curlow then begin
       curlow = xlow;
       clowbar = currentbar;
       end;
    end;
 end;
```

Spreadsheet Code

In the following QUATTRO code, the "$" precedes a row or column that is fixed (i.e., it does not get copied down).

Moving average, exponential, and *N*-day breakout share the same page, as do the swing breakout and point-and-figure system.

The price data is not repeated to save space.

GENERAL DESCRIPTION

A6	Date (YYMMDD)
B6	High price
C6	Low price
D6	Closing price
C3	Test period, swing %, or box size
C5	Point-and-figure number of reversal boxes

All data starts in row 7

```
MOVING AVERAGE
C3     period (e.g., 5 day)
E3     filter (e.g.,.10 for OEX data)
```

```
Repeated process (copy down)
E11    MA    @Avg(D7..D11)
F11    Dir   @IF(E11 - E10>$E$3,1,@IF(E11 - E10<-$E$3,-1,F10))
G11    Entry @IF(F11=_1#AND#F10<>-1,"Sell",@IF(F11=1#AND#F10<>1,"Buy",""))

EXPONENTIAL SMOOTHING
C3     period (e.g., 5 day)
E3     filter (e.g.,.10 for OEX data)
G3     smoothing constant    1 / (C3+1)
Initialize
E6     EXP    +D6
Repeated process (copy down)
E7     EXP    +E6+$G$3*(D7 - E6)
F7     Dir    @IF(E7 - E6>$E$3,1,@IF(E7 - E6<-$E$3,-1,F6))
G7     Entry  @IF(F7=-1#AND#F6<>-1,"Sell",@IF(F7=1#AND#F6<>-1,"Buy",""))

N-DAY BREAKOUT
Repeated process (copy down). There are no constants and no initialization
E11    Nhigh @Max(B6..B10)
F11    Nlow  @Min(C6..C10)
G11    Dir   @IF(B11>E11#AND#D11>D10,1,@IF(C11<F11#AND#D11<D10,-1,G10))
H11    Entry @IF(G11=-1#AND#G10<>-1,"Sell",@IF(G11=1#AND#G10<>1,"Buy",""))

SWING BREAKOUT
C3        Minimum swing percentage
E6 CurH   +B6
F6 CurL   +C6
G6 H/L    @IF(D6>(E6+F6)/2,-1,1)

E7 CurH  @IF($G6=-1#AND#B7>E6,B7,@IF($G6=1,B7,E6))
F7 CurL  @IF($G6=1#AND#C7<F6,C7,@IF($G6=-1,C7,F6))
G7 H/L   @IF($G6=-1, @IF(C7<E7 - $C$3*D7,1,$G6),@IF(B7>F7+$C$3*D7,-1,$G6))
H7 SwH   @IF($G7=1#AND#G6=-1,E7,H6)
I7 SwL   @IF($G7=1#AND#G6=1,F7,I6)
J7 Entry @IF($G7=-1#AND#B7>H7#AND#D7>D6,"Buy",
         @IF($G7=1#AND#C7<i7#AND#D7<D6,"Sell",""))
```

NOTE: The point-and-figure spreadsheet code varies slightly from the TradeStation code. It is a more accurate representation of the exact point-and-figure charting method (favoring reversals when possible).

```
POINT AND FIGURE
C3        Point and figure box size
C5        Number of reversal boxes
E6 CurH   @INT(B6/$C$3)
F6 CurL   @INT((C6+$C$3)/$C$3)
G6 Dir    @IF(D6>(E6+F6)/2,1,-1)

E7 CurH  @IF($G6=1,@IF(@INT(b7/$C$3)>E6,@INT(B7/$C$3),E6),@INT(B7/$C$3))
F7 CurL  @IF($G6=-1,@IF(@INT((C7+$C$3)/$C$3)<F6,@INT((C7+$C$3)/$C$3)),
         F6,@INT((C7+$C$3)/$C$3))
G7 Dir   @IF(G6=-1#AND#@INT(B7/$C$3)>F7+$D$3-1),1,@IF(G6=1#AND#
         @INT((C7+$C$3)/$C$3)<E7 - ($D$3-1),-1,G6))
H7 LastH @IF(G7=-1#AND#G6=1,E7,H6)
I7 LastL @IF(G7=1#AND#G6=-1,F7,I6)
J7 Entry @IF(G7=-1#AND#@INT((C7 - $C$3)/$C$3)<I7,"Sell",
         @IF(G7=1#AND#@INT(B7/$C$3)>H7,"Buy",""))

LINEAR REGRESSION SLOPE
C3     period (e.g.,5)
E3     filter (e.g.,0)
Initialize
```

```
E6       TimeX  1
G6       X^2    E6*E6 (copy down)
J6       XY     E6*D6 (copy down)
Normal processing (copy down all cells)
E7       TimeX  +E6+1
F10      SumX   @Sum(E6..E10)
G10      X^2    +E10*E10
H10      SumX^2 @Sum(G6..G10)
I10      SumY   @Sum(D6..D10)
J10      XY     +E10*D10
K10      SumXY  @Sum(J6..J10)
L10      Slope  ($C$3*K10 - F10*I10) / ($C$3*H10 - F10*F10)
M10      Dir    @IF(L10>$E$3#AND#L9<$E$3,1,@IF(L10<-$E$3#AND#L9> - $E$3, - 1,M10))
N10      Entry  @IF(M10=-1#AND#M9<>-1,"Sell",@IF(M10=1#AND#M9<>1,"Buy",""))
```

To verify that the correct code was entered into the spreadsheet, Figure 5-8 shows a sample of the opening lines of the spreadsheet using sample data. The columns E, F, G, and H have been repeated for each of the moving average, exponential smoothing, and N-day breakout systems. In Figure 5-9, this approach has been taken for the swing breakout and point-and-figure systems using the same data.

TECHNIQUES USING TWO TRENDLINES

This section is restricted to applications of trendlines; however, do not assume that trendlines constitute the only timing methods. Any secondary system that analyzes a shorter time period than the primary system can be considered as a timing device. Typically, a 3-day moving average could act as a timing technique for a 10-day average; however, the delays of 1, 2, 3, or more days, discussed earlier, are also for timing. A 5-day delay would not be a sensible choice to be used with a 3-day moving average, because the two periods would be incompatible. Plotting of lag and lead moving average values is another possible timing method. In this section, the use of more than one moving average will be examined (any type of trend approach would apply) to create a system.

In using two averages, the slower one, requiring a longer calculation period, will determine the long-term trend. The faster average will be used for timing. The long-term moving average generates a signal compatible with the long-term trend, regardless of recent patterns. A trader would be more comfortable knowing that there is a recent short-term surge of prices in the direction of the new position at the moment of entry. To implement this idea, select two moving averages, one noticeably faster than the other, and apply either of the two following rules:

1. *Buy* when the faster moving average crosses the slower moving average going up. *Sell* when the faster moving average crosses the slower moving average going down.
2. *Buy* when the current price crosses above both moving averages, and close out long positions when prices cross below either moving average. *Sell* when the current price crosses below both moving averages, and close out short positions when prices cross above either moving average (Figure 5-10).

The first set of rules results in constant trading, going from long to short and back again as the long-term trend is violated by the faster trend. The second set of rules allows for a neutral position when the current position is closed out and the long-term trend is not penetrated. One problem with this second approach is that the faster moving average may cause whipsaws by being too close to the current price. This can be solved in the same way as the single moving average by placing a band around one or both of the trendlines. There are other variations of these rules that can be listed, but they are not materially different from these two.

FIGURE 5-8 Sample spreadsheet results for the moving average, exponential, and N-day breakout systems.

| | Data | | | | Moving Avg | | | Exponential | | | N-day Breakout | | | |
| | A | B | C | D | E | F | G | E | F | G | E | F | G | H |
Row	Date	High	Low	Close	MA	Dir	Entry	EXP	Dir	Entry	Nhigh	Nlow	Dir	Entry
6	921231	400.88	396.64	396.64				396.64						
7	930104	398.72	395.71	396.28				396.58						
8	930105	396.50	394.72	395.65				396.43						
9	930106	396.61	394.37	395.78				396.32						
10	930107	396.68	390.26	391.30	395.13			395.48						
11	930108	391.31	387.30	389.93	393.79	-1	Sell	394.56	-1	Sell	400.88	390.26	-1	Sell
12	930111	391.75	389.61	391.16	392.76	-1		393.99	-1		398.72	387.30	-1	
13	930112	391.72	388.25	391.65	391.96	-1		393.60	-1		396.68	387.30	-1	
14	930113	394.11	390.72	393.50	391.51	-1		393.58	-1		396.68	387.30	-1	
15	930114	396.33	393.36	396.25	392.50	1	Buy	394.03	1	Buy	396.68	387.30	-1	
16	930115	400.33	395.75	397.17	393.95	1		394.55	1		396.33	388.25	1	Buy
17	930118	397.47	396.19	397.18	395.15	1		394.99	1		400.33	388.25	1	
18	930119	398.44	394.88	395.92	396.00	1		395.14	1		400.33	388.25	1	
19	930120	397.23	394.01	394.06	396.12	1		394.96	-1	Sell	400.33	390.72	1	
20	930121	395.97	392.67	395.51	395.97	-1	Sell	395.05	-1		400.33	393.36	1	
21	930122	398.11	395.33	396.75	395.88	-1		395.34	1	Buy	400.33	392.67	1	
22	930125	400.99	396.75	400.61	396.57	1	Buy	396.22	1		398.44	392.67	1	
23	930126	403.93	400.49	401.14	397.61	1		397.04	1		400.99	392.67	1	
24	930127	401.23	397.70	399.41	398.68	1		397.43	1		403.93	392.67	1	
25	930128	400.69	398.51	400.40	399.66	1		397.93	1		403.93	392.67	1	
26	930129	401.91	399.14	401.57	400.63	1		398.53	1		403.93	395.33	1	
27	930201	404.84	401.57	404.84	401.47	1		399.59	1		403.93	396.75	1	
28	930202	404.84	402.70	404.19	402.08	1		400.35	1		404.84	397.70	1	
29	930203	408.42	404.19	408.02	403.80	1		401.63	1		404.84	397.70	1	
30	930204	410.02	408.02	409.39	405.60	1		402.92	1		408.42	398.51	1	
31	930205	409.69	407.33	409.39	407.17	1		404.00	1		410.02	399.14	1	

FIGURE 5-9 Sample spreadsheet results for the swing breakout and point-and-figure systems.

| Row | Data | | | | Swing Breakout | | | | | | Point-and-Figure | | | | | |
	A Date	B High	C Low	D Close	E CurH	F CurL	G H/L	H SwHi	I SwLo	J Entry	E CurH	F CurL	G Dir	H LastH	I LastL	J Entry
6	921231	400.88	396.64	396.64	400.88	396.64	1	0.00	0.00		200	199	−1	200	0	
7	930104	398.72	395.71	396.28	398.72	395.71	1	0.00	0.00		199	198	−1	200	0	
8	930105	396.50	394.72	395.65	396.50	394.72	1	0.00	0.00		198	198	−1	200	0	
9	930106	396.61	394.37	395.78	396.61	394.37	1	0.00	0.00		198	198	−1	200	0	
10	930107	396.68	390.26	391.30	396.68	390.26	−1	0.00	390.26		198	196	−1	200	0	
11	930108	391.31	387.30	389.93	396.68	387.30	−1	0.00	390.26	Sell	198	194	−1	200	0	
12	930111	391.75	389.61	391.16	391.75	387.30	−1	396.68	390.26		195	194	−1	200	0	
13	930112	391.72	388.25	391.65	391.75	388.25	−1	396.68	387.30		195	194	−1	200	0	
14	930113	394.11	390.72	393.50	394.11	390.72	−1	396.68	387.30		197	194	−1	200	194	
15	930114	396.33	393.36	396.25	396.33	393.36	−1	396.68	387.30		198	197	−1	200	194	
16	930115	400.33	395.75	397.17	400.33	395.75	1	400.33	387.30		200	198	1	200	194	
17	930118	397.47	396.19	397.18	397.47	395.75	1	400.33	387.30		200	199	1	200	194	
18	930119	398.44	394.88	395.92	398.44	394.88	1	400.33	387.30		200	198	1	200	194	
19	930120	397.23	394.01	394.06	397.23	394.01	1	400.33	387.30		200	198	1	200	194	
20	930121	395.97	392.67	395.51	395.97	392.67	1	400.33	387.30		200	197	1	200	194	
21	930122	398.11	395.33	396.75	398.11	392.67	1	400.33	392.67		199	197	−1	200	194	
22	930125	400.99	396.75	400.61	400.99	396.75	1	400.99	392.67		200	197	1	200	197	
23	930126	403.93	400.49	401.14	403.93	396.75	1	400.99	396.75	Buy	201	201	1	200	197	Buy
24	930127	401.23	397.70	399.41	403.93	397.70	1	403.93	396.75		201	199	1	200	197	
25	930128	400.69	398.51	400.40	400.69	397.70	1	403.93	396.75		201	200	1	200	197	
26	930129	401.91	399.14	401.57	401.91	397.70	1	403.93	397.70		201	200	1	200	197	
27	930201	404.84	401.57	404.84	404.84	401.57	1	403.93	397.70	Buy	202	201	1	200	197	Buy
28	930202	404.84	402.70	404.19	404.84	402.70	1	403.93	397.70		202	202	1	200	197	Buy
29	930203	408.42	404.19	408.02	408.42	404.19	1	408.42	397.70		204	203	1	200	197	Buy
30	930204	410.02	408.02	409.39	410.02	404.19	1	408.42	404.19	Buy	205	205	1	200	197	Buy
31	930205	409.69	407.33	409.39	410.02	407.33	1	408.42	404.19		205	204	1	200	197	Buy
32	930208	411.51	408.58	409.62	411.51	408.58	1	408.42	404.19	Buy	205	205	1	200	197	Buy
33	930209	409.62	406.80	407.78	411.51	406.80	1	411.51	404.19		205	204	1	200	197	Buy
34	930210	408.46	405.77	408.10	408.46	405.77	1	411.51	404.19		205	203	1	200	197	Buy
35	930211	410.90	408.10	409.08	410.90	405.77	1	411.51	405.77		205	205	1	200	197	Buy
36	930212	409.23	406.26	406.26	410.90	406.26	1	410.90	405.77		205	204	1	200	197	Buy
37	930216	406.26	396.38	397.08	406.26	396.38	−1	410.90	396.38		205	199	−1	205	197	Sell
38	930217	397.30	394.34	396.82	406.26	394.34	−1	406.26	396.38	Sell	198	198	−1	205	197	
39	930218	401.01	391.60	396.10	401.01	391.60	−1	406.26	391.60		200	196	1	205	196	

FIGURE 5-10   Trading system using two moving averages.

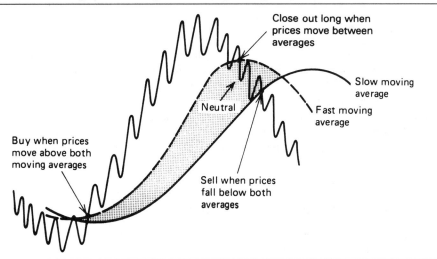

Close out long when prices move between averages

Slow moving average

Fast moving average

Neutral

Buy when prices move above both moving averages

Sell when prices fall below both averages

Donchian's 5- and 20-Day Moving Average System

The combined use of two moving averages has been popular among professional advisors. Of these, the most well-known is Donchian's 5- and 20-Day Moving Average,[5] a method claiming one of the longest recorded operational results, beginning January 1, 1961. There is no explanation for the selection of these two values, but in 1961 when moving averages were considered state-of-the-art, they were a reasonable choice. The selections can be justified because of their close relationship to the number of trading days in a week and a month; even now, similar calendar periods might add some desirable features to a system.

Donchian's idea is to use a volatility-penetration criterion relative to the 20-day moving average, but with some added complication. The current penetration must not only cross the 20-day moving average but also exceed any previous 1-day penetration of a closing price by at least one volatility measure.

The 5-day moving average serves as a liquidation criterion (along with others) and is also modified by prior penetration and volatility. These features tend to make Donchian's volatility measurement self-adjusting. Even if selected poorly, the new penetration must exceed prior breakouts; without thorough testing, it may be difficult to determine which rule has more significance. To maintain a human element, Donchian requires execution of certain orders to be delayed a day if the signals occurred on specific weekdays or before a holiday. The combination of different factors is generally the result of refinement over years of actual operation, but neither complexity nor sophistication guarantees success; only the results will tell.

More Than Two Moving Averages

If two moving averages improve trading, it should follow that three or more are even better—but it doesn't. With the use of two moving averages, there is a main trend identifier and a timing device; the addition of one or more averages or indicators must fulfill a distinct purpose. When multiple moving averages must agree on the same signal, there is less

[5] Richard D. Donchian, "Donchian's 5- and 20-Day Moving Averages," *Commodities Magazine* (December 1974).

chance of getting a trading signal and less time holding the trade. The results of moving average systems using two and three moving averages are covered in Chapter 21.

COMPREHENSIVE STUDIES

Because computerized testing programs have made it easy for anyone to test any number of trends in combination, there have been very few comprehensive studies published within the past 10 years. Nevertheless, there is a great deal to learn from putting the results of various systems and markets side by side. Earlier in this chapter there is an informative comparison of six major trending systems; others studies have been included in Chapter 21 ("Testing"). Among them are systems similar to the single and double moving average methods just discussed, as well as the selection of a third trend for entry timing. An important objective of the testing process is the longevity of the parameters selected; this discussion can also be found in Chapter 21.

SELECTING THE RIGHT MOVING AVERAGE[6]

Up to now, the selection of the *right* moving average, the one that will work in the future, has only been discussed in general terms. The best moving average speed for a hedger may not be the same as for a speculator. For example, a hedger may be marketing cattle each month and may need to choose a time at which to preprice his or her product. A 3-day moving average might generate five sell signals in 1 month, each the result of a 2-day price move—an ineffective tool for the hedger. The hedger needs an average of one sell signal per month to be a useful timing tool; the speculator has no such concerns.

For the speculator, the right moving average speed is the one that produces the best performance profile. This profile could be simply maximum profits, or it could be a more complex combination of profits, equity variation, and use of margin. In Chapter 21, the computer is used to find the combination of speed, stop-loss, and other rules that best satisfies a preset criterion; a computer, however, is not always necessary.

Computer testing of a trend system or other trading strategies sometimes leads to solutions that are highly fitted. The computer may find that a 3-day moving average was more profitable with lower risk than a 20-day trend, which was only slightly worse in performance. Our logic tells us that the results of the 3-day system will be more difficult to attain in real trading, because execution costs in fast markets with many trades may be higher than expected. A slower selection is more conservative and more likely to return the expected results. However, the trader must be the judge of whether the selection is reasonable.

A grain trader knows that the seasonal price pattern forms a complete cycle each year. At best we can expect one long upward move followed by a shorter, faster decline. Not all trend speeds can capture the profits in this pattern. For example, if the uptrend lasts for six months, a 6-month moving average won't see any of it; therefore, you will need a moving average not much longer than ¼ of the length of the trend and perhaps shorter. If mass testing of moving averages using an optimizer results in a *best* moving average period of 6 months, that choice must be understood as a failure of the system to find any shorter period that worked.

Selecting the Trend Speed

Observation of a price chart will show the trends of the market. The trends that two traders see will often be different. Some traders immediately focus on long-term price trends;

---

[6] Perry J. Kaufman, "Moving Averages," in *Trading Tactics: A Livestock Futures Anthology,* Todd Lofton (ed.) (Chicago Mercantile Exchange, Chicago, 1986).

others see much shorter movements. To find your own best moving average speed without the use of a computer, look at a price chart and mark the beginning and end of each price move that you would like to capture. These trends may occur every few days, or only three or four times each year. In this exercise, the major trends were selected from the chart for August 1985 pork bellies (Figure 5-11).

Use the fact that a moving average of n-day speed will be neutral over a period of n days in which the price returns to the same level. (Remember that a 1-year moving average is used to remove the annual seasonal effects.) If the daily price changes are nearly equal, one leg of this move (the trends identified in Figure 5-5) will occur in $n/2$ days. To be cautious, select moving average intervals slightly longer than two times the worst retracement within the trend to prevent being *stopped-out* of the trend.

When calculating profits generated by a moving average, part of the trend movement is lost at the beginning and end of the trade. This part is equivalent to the price change over ½ of the moving average period, because it requires that much time for the moving average to *break even,* or become neutral with respect to the price move.

Keeping these two points in mind, the best trend speed can be selected from presenting the largest moves and largest reversals, as shown in Table 5-6.

The longest period needed to offset the largest reversal is 3.1 weeks (each week is 5 days), and it takes a 16-day moving average to neutralize the largest move. A 16-day moving average usually requires 8 days to break even. Allowing 2 weeks (10 days) of price movement to reach the break-even point, the following profitability remains:

Trade	Move/Week	Profitable Weeks	Total Profit
1	1.30	8	10.4
2	1.25	6	7.5
3	1.40	3	4.2
4	1.70	5	8.5
Total			30.6

Naturally, there will be periods of uncertain direction and small losing trades with this or any price series; however, capturing these four price trends will go a long way toward profitability.

MOVING AVERAGE SEQUENCES: SIGNAL PROGRESSION

Consider the case in which you have selected a 20-day moving average to trade. You enter the day with a long bond position and you get a sell signal. However, you don't know because you are not looking, but the 19-day and 21-day moving averages did not get sell signals. This means that the day that was dropped off the calculation 20 days ago caused a slight shift not seen by the other neighboring trends. Is this important? Yes.

A moving average is simply a consensus of direction. It is an approximation of values intended to put you on the right side of the market more often than not. It is most fallible at the time prices are changing direction or going sideways. Any information that clears up the problem is helpful. For any moving average system, we would like to see a steady progression of trend change from the short term to the long term. This is seen in the following illustration:

Example E1. Moving Average Period in Days

```
        1 2 3 4 5 6 7 8 9 10 11 12 13 14 15 16 17 18 19 20 21 22 23 24 25
Trend   u u u u u u u u u  u  u  u  u  u  u  u  u  u  u  u  d  d  d  d  d
```

FIGURE 5-11 Selected trends and reversals.

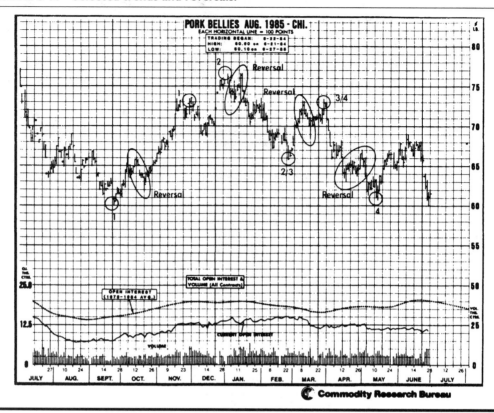

Unfortunately, not everything is as uniform as this example. The shorter-term trends can be very erratic, and they often appear in small groups of uptrends and downtrends (see Example E2). This is easily explainable because adding and subtracting 1 day, when only 2, 3, or 4 days are used in the moving average calculation, can quickly change the direction of the trend. As you get to longer intervals, such as 20, 30, and 50 days, this is not the case, and in reality, it doesn't happen often. Yet, when it does, it is clearly an odd case not to be trusted.

TABLE 5-6 Selecting Trends and Reversals

Trade		Range (cents)	Total Move (cents)	Duration (weeks)	Move per Week	Needed to Offset (weeks)*
1. Sustained move	up	60–73	13	10	1.3	3.1
Largest reversal	down	66–62	4	1	4.0	
2. Sustained move	down	76–66	10	8	1.25	2.4
Largest reversal	up	73–76	3	1	3.0	
3. Sustained move	up	66–73	7	5	1.4	2.9
Largest reversal	down	73–69	4	1	4.0	
4. Sustained move	down	73–61	12	7	1.7	1.2
Largest reversal	up	63–67	4	2	2.0	

*The number of weeks of profitable movement needed to recover the loss due to the largest reversal.

Example E2. Moving Average Period in Days

```
        1 2 3 4 5 6 7 8 9 10 11 12 13 14 15 16 17 18 19 20 21 22 23 24 25
Trend   u u d d u d u u u  u  u  u  u  u  u  u  u  u  u  d  d  d  d  d  d
```

There are also cases in which the longer trend begins to reassert itself and the results appear the same as in Example E1; however, the trend change occurs from the longer term down (from right to left instead of left to right). The case we must watch for satisfies neither of these, but occurs in erratic pattern, such as in Example E3. Here we see a dominant long-term uptrend with the very short end turning down. Because of another downturn a few days ago, which then disappeared, this most recent downturn also caused a *shadow* turn in the 20-day range. Is it a leading indicator or a false signal? All indications are that smooth changes in a trend are a more reliable indicator. Another case is given in the second line of Example E3. Here, the smooth trend change from up to down is occurring from left to right; however, as it gets to 13 days, it also jumps ahead to 19 and 20 days, leaving the 14th through 18th days still in an uptrend. Again, we favor the orderly approach and would wait for all trends to change below the one we are using.

Example E3. Unreliable Turns in Trend

<Moving Average Period in Days>

```
        1 2 3 4 5 6 7 8 9 10 11 12 13 14 15 16 17 18 19 20 21 22 23 24 25
Trend   d d d d u u u u u  u  u  u  u  u  u  u  u  u  d  d  u  u  u  u  d
Trend   d d d d d d d d d  d  d  d  d  u  u  u  u  u  d  d  u  u  u  u  u
```

An example of this process is shown in Figure 5-12. Moving average calculation periods of 5 to 50 days are shown in increments of 5 days for a total of 44 consecutive days. This illustration points out how the long-term uptrend (X) is breached by shorter-term, less consistent trends. Perhaps the best trend is the one with the majority of Xs or Os on the same line.

LIVING WITH A TREND-FOLLOWING PHILOSOPHY

The advantages and disadvantages of trend systems are similar to most other types of trading strategies. The first question that a trader should ask is, "What can I expect from a trend approach?" The calculation period of trend will change the profitability, size of individual profits and losses, and reliability. This is covered thoroughly in Chapter 22. Fast trends enter trades on the first strong move following a price reversal; slower averages take more time to identify a trend change. No matter what its speed or how well-timed, a trend signal can never occur at the *right* point; consequently, watching prices vary with respect to the trendline will be frustrating. The moving average system will rarely enter or close out a position at just the right place; it can only extract profits from the middle of a trend and hold losses to a minimum. The risks and magnitude of reward are intrinsic to the speed of the moving average although the risk/reward ratio may be similar for many moving averages. The success of such a system can only be judged by its actual performance; thus, the weekly or monthly accumulated results should be studied rather than simply observing the relationship of the trendline to prices.

The slower the trend, the further it will lag behind a sustained price move. Professional traders lean toward the faster trends and portfolio managers toward the slower. When trading only one market, individual trade risks can be kept small using faster trends. The portfolio trader can offset the long-term adverse move in one market with an equally long favorable trend in another. The advantage of diversification and long-term trends is that each market will move in the direction of the trend a majority of days, even though that

FIGURE 5-12 Sequences of moving averages.

Day	5	10	15	20	25	30	35	40	45	50
					Moving Average Period					
1	X	X	X	X	X	X	X	X	X	X
2	O	O	X	X	X	X	X	X	X	X
3	O	X	X	X	X	X	X	X	X	X
4	X	X	X	X	X	X	X	X	X	X
5	X	X	X	X	X	X	X	X	X	X
6	X	X	X	X	X	X	X	X	X	X
7	X	X	X	X	X	X	X	X	X	X
8	O	X	X	X	X	X	X	X	X	X
9	X	O	O	O	X	X	X	X	X	X
10	O	O	O	O	O	X	X	X	X	X
11	O	O	O	O	X	X	X	X	X	X
12	O	O	O	O	O	O	O	X	X	X
13	O	O	O	O	X	X	X	X	X	X
14	X	O	O	O	O	O	X	X	X	X
15	O	O	O	O	O	O	O	O	O	X
16	O	O	O	O	O	O	O	O	O	O
17	O	O	O	O	O	O	O	O	O	O
18	O	O	O	O	O	O	O	O	O	O
19	X	O	O	O	O	O	O	O	O	O
20	X	O	O	O	O	O	O	O	O	O
21	X	X	X	O	O	O	O	X	X	X
22	X	X	X	X	O	X	X	X	X	X
23	X	X	X	O	O	O	O	X	X	X
24	X	X	X	X	O	O	O	X	X	X
25	X	X	X	X	O	O	O	X	X	X
26	O	X	X	O	O	O	O	O	O	X
27	O	O	O	O	O	O	O	O	O	O
28	O	O	O	O	O	O	O	O	O	O
29	O	X	X	X	O	O	O	O	O	X
30	X	X	X	X	X	O	O	O	X	X
31	X	X	X	X	X	O	O	O	O	X
32	X	X	X	X	X	X	X	X	X	X
33	X	X	X	X	X	X	X	X	X	X
34	X	X	X	X	X	X	X	X	X	X
35	X	X	X	X	X	X	X	X	X	X
36	X	X	X	X	X	X	X	X	X	X
37	X	X	X	X	X	X	X	X	X	X
38	O	X	X	X	X	X	X	X	X	X
39	O	O	X	X	X	X	X	X	X	X
40	O	O	X	X	X	X	X	X	X	X
41	O	X	X	X	X	X	X	X	X	X
42	X	X	X	X	X	X	X	X	X	X
43	X	X	X	X	X	X	X	X	X	X
44	X	X	X	X	X	X	X	X	X	X

may mean only 6 out of 10. A portfolio of 10 markets, each with a 60% probability of a move in the trend direction, should result in 6 of them moving in a profitable direction. It is more likely that all of them will be profitable on the same day than it is that all will be losers.

Slower trends are more likely to endure than faster ones. These slower trends often profit from fundamental market changes, such as seasonality, production cycles, and inflation. They stick to a trend while it develops. The faster trends are attempting to catch shifts in market psychology, short-term cycles caused by trading patterns and current events, and wide swings in high-priced, uncertain markets. The patterns that make fast trading profitable also change quickly. A 3-day moving average may be highly profitable for one month, then produce consistently losing trades.

"Take Your Profits and Let Your Losses Run"

Many traders are guilty of profit-taking using trend systems. Cutting losses short is an intrinsic quality of a trend-based system as is its lag. It is inevitable that a trader will want to close out a trade that has a $1,000 profit and a stop-loss at a level that captures only $300. However, this places an arbitrary limit on potential profits while letting losses remain at their natural size. A trend-following system compensates for many small losses when prices sustain a large trending move. Don't cut it short.

Using Other Reasons to Exit a Trend Trade

A very long-term trend will often find the direction of the underlying economic fundamentals. For example, a 1-year Treasury bond trend would have been long for about five years during the late-1980s. Once you understand that the position you are holding is based on a sustained economic situation, you can exit the position when that situation changes. Looking at the T-bond example, prices continued to rise (interest rates fall) to offset slow economic growth and high unemployment. Once the Central Bank (the "Fed") raises rates, it is a good indication that the uptrend is nearly over. Because the very slow trend lags far behind the actual market price, it may be another year before prices cross the trendline and signal a change of position. This is also likely to occur after a large part of your profits have been given back to the market. Exiting the trade when the fundamentals change would be a safe way of capturing more profits and being exposed to less market risk—provided the fundamentals are the ones that were driving the market and your profits.

6

Momentum and Oscillators

The study of momentum and oscillators is an analysis of price changes rather than price levels. Among technicians, momentum establishes the speed of price movement and the rate of ascent or descent. Analysts use *momentum* interchangeably with *slope,* a straight-line angle of inclination of price movement as measured from a horizontal line representing time. Momentum is also thought of as force or impact; it is often considered, as in Newton's Law, that once started prices tend to remain in motion in a somewhat straight line.

Rate-of-change indicators, such as momentum and oscillators, are used as leading indicators of price change. They can identify when the current trend is no longer maintaining its same level of strength. This gives the trader an opportunity to begin liquidating the open-trend trades before prices actually reverse. As the time period for the momentum calculation shortens, this technique of leading a trend changes to become more aggressive and is interpreted as a *countertrend* method. Use of a rate-of-change indicator anticipates change even sooner.

Before beginning a discussion of various momentum calculations, a brief comment on terminology will be helpful to understand how various techniques are grouped together. We begin with a single price, which has no movement. When we talk about bonds at 110 or gold at $400 per ounce, we are relating a price level and not implying that prices are going up or down. Next, we describe the speed at which prices are rising or falling. It is not enough to say that the S&P rose 3 points; rather, you must specify the time interval over which this happened "The S&P rose 3 points in one hour." When you say that you drove your car at 60, you really imply that you were going 60 miles per hour, or 60 kilometers per hour. This description of speed, or distance covered over time, is the same information that is given by a single momentum value.

The last measure is one of *change in speed,* which is either acceleration or deceleration. The price of the Deutschemark may have risen by .0150 dollars per mark in the past week, indicating an average speed of .0150/5, or a rise of .0030 dollars/mark per day; however, it started rising slowly and increasing its speed over the week. Perhaps the mark rose .0010 on Monday, .0020 on Tuesday, .0030 on Wednesday, .0040 on Thursday, and .0050 on Friday, increasing in speed (or accelerating) by .0010 each day. The term *rate of change* (ROC) will also be used to describe acceleration; when the rate of change is zero, we are talking about speed and momentum.

You will see in this chapter that speed is a more sensitive measurement than price level, and acceleration is more sensitive than speed. The various techniques described here are presented in order of speed and then rate of change. Following that is *divergence,* the most popular use of momentum indicators.

MOMENTUM

Momentum is the difference between two prices taken over a fixed interval. It is another word for *speed,* the distance covered over time. For example, today's 5-day momentum value M would be the difference between today's price P_t and the price 5 days ago:

(5-day) $M = P_t - P_{t-5}$

Using notation familiar to many programmers:

```
momentum = price - price[5]
```

or

```
momentum = price - price[N]
```

where the notation [N] refers to the (closing) price N days ago.

The momentum value M_t increases as the change in price increases over the 5-day period. Figure 6-1 shows that momentum is also related to slope; that is, a faster price increase will cause both angle a to become larger and the hypotenuse of the triangle, marked "momentum," to increase. If the 5-day momentum is 100, the slope of the momentum line can be expressed as 100/5 = 20. If prices had increased by 150 points over the same time interval, the slope would be 150/5 = 30 and the momentum would be 150.

The 5-day momentum M_t can range in value from the maximum upward move to the maximum downward move that the price can make in 5 days; the momentum is zero if prices are unchanged after 5 days. Figure 6-2 shows the possible moves in the momentum calculation. Consider a commodity with a 20-point daily limit. Starting at point A, the 5-day price change *increased at a faster rate* for 8 days (up 2, up 4, etc.) until at point B, prices were moving at their fastest 5-day rate. At point B the 5-day price change was three-fifths of the maximum 100-point change, or 60 points. From point B to point C prices still increased, but at a slower rate, until the 5-day difference at point C was zero. Prices then declined at an increasing rate until at point D the maximum 5-day decline of 40 points was reached; at point E the 5-day difference was again zero. Note that at point B prices did not start down but only increased at a slower rate; only at C did prices first begin their 5-day decline.

Momentum as a Percentage

Momentum, as most other calculations, can be expressed as a percentage rather than a raw value of its components. This is usually done by dividing the current value by the previous price or index level, so that a 5-day momentum may be

$$\%M = \frac{P_t - P_{t-5}}{P_{t-1}} \quad \text{or} \quad \frac{P_t - P_{t-5}}{P_{t-5}}$$

FIGURE 6-1   Geometric representation of momentum.

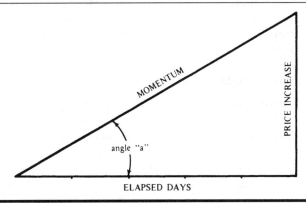

FIGURE 6-2   Momentum range.

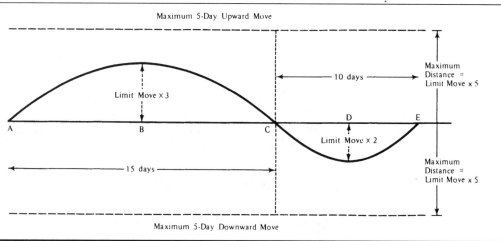

The difference in the two approaches is limited by the percentage change in the underlying price over the 4-day period between $t-1$ and $t-5$. It is not likely that the change will even be noticeable on a chart of %M, and it is best to standardize the approach to taking percentages using $t-1$.

Price and Trend Difference

It is common for the term *momentum* to refer to the difference between today's price and a corresponding moving average value. The properties of this new value remain the same. As the momentum becomes larger, prices are moving away from the moving average at a faster rate. When it gets smaller, the prices are converging with the moving average. Unlike the first definition of momentum, a value that is positive but converging toward the moving average may actually represent declining prices rather than prices that are advancing at a slower rate. The major similarity is that the peak of the price move is near the extreme points of the momentum chart.

Figure 6-3a (upper panel) shows 10-period and 40-period moving averages plotted on a 15-minute German bund chart. Figure 6-3b (center panel) shows the difference between the price and the 40-period moving average; the momentum value is fairly uniform, varying by about .50 above and below zero. Because the moving average tends to catch up to prices over time, the maximum variation of the momentum measured this way is not as extreme as when momentum is calculated as the difference between two prices. This momentum calculation has also been called *relative strength*, because it is measured relative to a moving average.

Moving Average Convergence/Divergence (MACD)

Momentum may also be seen as the difference between two moving averages, a technique developed by Gerald Appel and named the *Moving Average Convergence/Divergence* (MACD).[1] In its original form, the two trendlines were produced using exponential smoothing, and their difference resulted in the MACD value. This was further smoothed to give a signal line. The most common presentation of MACD uses the difference between a 12-day and 26-day exponential smoothing. The signal line, used to produce trading rec-

[1] From John D. Becker, "Value of oscillators in determining price action," *Futures* (May 1994).

FIGURE 6-3 Momentum as relative strength, the difference between prices and a moving average, or between two moving averages (MACD). (*a*, top panel) 10-day and 40-day moving averages plotted with 15-minute German bund prices. (*b*, center panel) Momentum as the difference between prices and the 40-day moving average. (*c*, bottom panel) MACD as the difference between the 10-day and 40-day moving average values.

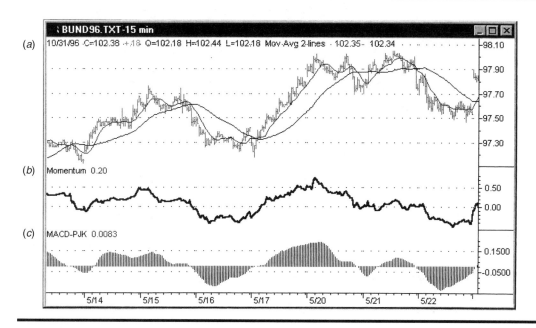

Source: Chart created with *TradeStation*® by Omega Research, Inc.

ommendations, is a 9-day smoothing of today's MACD subtracted from today's MACD. In programming code, the function @SmoothedAverage refers to an exponential smoothing:

```
MACD = @SmoothedAverage(close,12) - @SmoothedAverage(close,26)
signal_line = MACD - @SmoothedAverage(MACD,9)
```

The basic rules for trading the MACD would enter trend positions by referring only to the signal line calculation. *Buy* when the signal line moves above zero, and *sell* when the signal line falls below zero. Many traders, however, prefer to use the combination of MACD and signal line for signals, buying when the signal line crosses above the MACD line and selling when it crosses below. The signal line could be used to produce countertrend signals, as is common when using the stochastic (discussed in the section "Oscillators" in this chapter), by selling when the MACD crosses the signal line heading down while still above zero.

Because both moving averages are lagged, the peaks identified by the difference between the two will also be lagged. This is contrary to the usual purpose of the momentum indicator, which is to identify the precise time when an extreme has been reached. Looking at Figure 6-3*c* (bottom panel), the difference between the 10-day and 40-day moving averages is shown as a histogram, a form most commonly used for the MACD. It can be seen that the peak formed by the widest difference between the two moving averages is generally a few bars to the right of the peak seen on the price chart and the simple momentum line in Figure 6-3*b*.

An advantage of using MACD, as shown in Figure 6-3, is that the pattern is very smooth compared with both prices and the single momentum line, and the trend of the MACD pattern is often a leading indicator of price change. The peak prices that occur on both May

15th and May 20th are followed by a sideways price pattern over the remaining part of the day; however, the MACD declines smoothly, indicating price weakness. It would be difficult to use the momentum calculation in Figure 6-3*b*, because it still contains much of the erratic price movements.

Timing an Entry

Momentum is a convenient way of identifying a good entry point caused by a price reversal during a trend. By choosing a much shorter time period for the momentum calculation, for example 6 days, to work in conjunction with a longer trend of 30 to 50 days, the momentum indicator will show frequent opportunities within the trend. The short time period for the momentum calculation assures you that there will be an entry opportunity within about 3 days of the entry signal; therefore, it becomes a practical timing tool.

Momentum as a Trend Indicator

The momentum value is a smoothing of price changes and can be very similar to a standard moving average. Most applications use momentum as a substitute for a price trend. By looking at the net increase in prices over the number of days designated by an *n*-day momentum indicator, intermediate fluctuations are ignored, and the pattern in price trend can be seen. The longer the span between the observed points, the smoother the results. This is equivalent to faster and slower moving averages.

To use momentum as a trend indicator, the momentum span is selected and plotted as in Figure 6-4. A buy signal occurs whenever the value of the momentum turns from negative to positive, and a sell signal is when the opposite occurs. If a band is used to establish a neutral position or a commitment zone, as discussed in Chapter 5, it should be drawn around the horizontal line representing the midpoint momentum value, usually zero.

Buy and sell signals that occur sooner and are likely to be stopped out more often, use a signal line created by smoothing the momentum values, in this case using a simple 3-day moving average. Once the momentum value moves above a threshold level of, for example, 70, a sell occurs when the momentum crosses below the signal line. The position may be stopped out when the momentum crosses above the signal line, or when momentum moves above its entry level.

To find the best choice of a momentum span, a sampling of different values could be tested for optimum performance, or a chart could be examined for some natural price cycle. Identify the significant tops and bottoms of any bar chart, and average the number of days between these cycles, or find the number of days that would closely approximate

FIGURE 6-4   Price momentum signals with and without a signal line.

the occurrences of these peaks and valleys. These natural cycles will often be the best choice of a momentum calculation interval (Figure 6-5a).

Momentum and oscillators, however, are used just as often to identify abnormal price movements and for timing of entries and exits in conjunction with a longer-term trend.

Identifying Extremes

An equally popular and more interesting interpretation of the momentum chart is based on an analysis of tops and bottoms. All momentum values are bounded in both directions by the maximum move possible during the time interval represented by the span of the momentum. The conditions at the points of high positive and negative momentum are called *overbought* and *oversold*, respectively. A market is overbought when it can no longer sustain the strength of the current trend and a downward price reaction is imminent; an oversold market is ready for an upward move. Faster momentum calculations will reach these maximum values more often and stay there for extended periods of high upward or downward momentum. The use of a slow momentum period, however, will produce values that rarely test its limits. If the momentum system uses the horizontal zero line to enter and exit trades, it is of no consequence how often the bounds are touched; once a position is entered, the high-momentum condition serves as a positive reinforcement for the trade. However, the maximum positive and negative momentum values can be measured and used to anticipate the end of a trend. For this purpose, momentum values that are too fast will obscure the trading signals—the momentum *index* must be allowed to reach its full value.

A system that takes advantage of the momentum extremes may be created by drawing two horizontal lines on the momentum graph (Figure 6-5b), above and below the zero line

FIGURE 6-5   Relationship of momentum to prices. (a) Tops and bottoms determine momentum value. (b) Corresponding momentum.

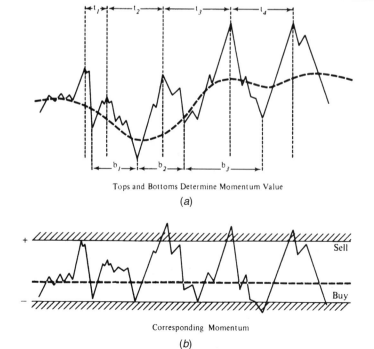

Tops and Bottoms Determine Momentum Value

(a)

Corresponding Momentum

(b)

in such a way that the tops and bottoms of the major moves are isolated. These lines may be selected visually so that once the line is penetrated, prices reverse shortly afterward. Another selection might simply be based on a percentage of the maximum possible momentum value. A third statistical approach would be to use a multiple of the standard deviation, or some other probability distribution function, so that the band is formed by the zero line plus or minus two standard deviations. That is, about 95% of all values within the area are bounded by the two horizontal lines.

When positioning these bands, there is always a trade-off between finding more trading opportunities and entering the market too soon. This can be a complicated choice and is discussed in Chapter 22 ("System Trade-Offs"). Once these lines have been drawn, the basic trading rules will be one of the following:

1. *Aggressive.* Enter a new long position when the momentum value penetrates the lower bound; enter a new short position when the value penetrates the upper bound.
2. *Minor confirmation.* Enter a new short position on the first day the momentum value turns down after penetrating the upper bound (the opposite for longs).
3. *Major confirmation.* Enter a new short position when the momentum value penetrates the upper bound coming down (the opposite for longs).
4. *Timing.* Enter a new short position after the momentum value has remained above the upper bound for *t* days (the opposite for longs).

To close out a profitable position there are the following alternatives:

1. Close out long positions or cover short positions when the momentum value satisfies the entry condition for a reverse position.
2. Cover a short position when the momentum penetrates the zero line minus one standard deviation, or some target point (e.g., halfway between the zero line and the lower bound).
3. Cover a short position if the momentum recrosses the zero line, moving up after penetrating that line moving down.

A protective stop-loss order may be used to prevent giving up all profits (as in the last point) or to protect the trader from a sustained move that causes the momentum value to remain on the outside of the overbought/oversold lines.

1. Place a protective stop above or below the most extreme high or low momentum value.
2. Follow a profitable move with a nonretreating stop based on fixed points or a percentage.
3. Establish zones that act as levels of attainment (using horizontal lines of equal spacing), and do not permit reverse penetrations once entered.

These precautions are due to both normal price variability and volatility. As prices reach higher levels, increased volatility will cause momentum tops and bottoms to widen; at lower levels, they may not be active enough to penetrate the bounds. A penetration level established when coffee prices were 50¢ per pound and the maximum daily range was 2¢ would not work with coffee at $2.50 per pound and limits of 4¢. A reasonable modification to the momentum plot would be the use of a band or stop-loss, which is a percentage of price, or a percentage of the permissible limit move (a volatility function). The tops and bottoms would remain more in-line although the risk would increase appreciably. This, however, is the intention of the oscillator.

When selecting trading rules for a countertrend technique, risk must be the primary concern. Using entry option 1, a short signal will occur upon penetration of the upper level; this may happen when the market is very strong. If an immediate reversal does not occur, large open losses may accrue. One solution might be to place a fixed stop-loss at the time of each entry. To determine the proper stop-loss amount, a computer test was performed using an immediate entry based on penetration of an extreme boundary, with a close stop-loss for risk protection. The first results were thought to have outstanding profits and consistency until it was discovered that the computer had done exactly the opposite of what was intended: It *bought* when the momentum crossed the upper bound and placed a close stop-loss *below* the entry. It did prove, for a good sampling of commodities, that high-momentum periods continued for enough time to capture small but consistent profits. It also showed that entry rule 1, anticipating an early reversal, would be a losing strategy. One should never forget that declining momentum does not mean that prices are falling.

OSCILLATORS

Because the representation of the momentum index is that of a line fluctuating above and below a zero value, this technique has often been termed an *oscillator*. Even though it does oscillate, the use of that word is confusing. In this presentation, the term oscillator will be restricted to a specific form of momentum, or rate-of-change indicator, which is normalized and expressed in terms of values that are limited to the ranges between +1 and −1, +1 and 0, or 100 and 0, as in percent.

To transform a standard momentum calculation into the normalized form (maximum value of +1, minimum value of −1), divide the momentum calculation by the maximum attainable value of the momentum index. A 5-day index for silver with a 20-limit move could be divided by $1.00 to find the normalized value. If silver were to move its limit up for 5 days, the oscillator would have the value of +1 rather than the momentum value of 100. If the limits were to expand, the divisor would change as well, giving the technique a means of adjusting for varying volatility. Using the normalized momentum, or oscillator, the top and bottom zones become volatility-adjusted at any level.

Erratic movements in the simple momentum and oscillator make it a very difficult tool to apply without additional work. Some of these problems can be eliminated by making the buying and selling zones more extreme or by smoothing the indicator values. In the following sections, a few of the applications of this technique are shown.

Relative Strength Index

One of the most popular indicators for denoting overbought and oversold conditions is the *Relative Strength Index* (RSI) developed by Wilder.[2] It provides added value to the momentum indicator by scaling all values between 0 and 100. It is more stable than momentum because it uses all the values in the period rather than just the first and last. It is a simple measurement that expresses the relative strength of the current price movement as increasing from 0 to 100. It is calculated as

$$RSI = 100 - \left(\frac{100}{1 + RS} \right) = 100 \times \left(\frac{RS}{1 + RS} \right)$$

where $RS = \dfrac{AU}{AD}$

AU = the total of those days closing higher during the past 14 days
AD = the total of those days closing lower during the past 14 days

Once the first calculation has been made, both the *AU* and *AD* values can be calculated daily using an *average-off* method:

[2] J. Welles Wilder, Jr., *New Concepts in Technical Trading Systems* (Trend Research, Greensboro, NC, 1978).

$$AU_{today} = AU_{prior} - \frac{AU_{prior}}{14} + \text{today's up close or } 0$$

$$AD_{today} = AD_{prior} - \frac{AD_{prior}}{14} + \text{today's down close or } 0$$

This method essentially drops an average value and adds the new value, if any. The daily calculation of the RSI becomes simple.

Wilder has favored the use of the 14-day measurement because it represents one-half of a natural cycle. He has set the significant levels for the RSI at 30 and 70. The lower level is indicative of an imminent upturn and the upper level of a pending downturn. A plot of the RSI can be interpreted in the same manner as a bar chart, with the *head-and-shoulders* formation as the primary confirmation of a change in direction (Figure 6-6).

In fact, Wilder relies heavily on top and bottom formations for RSI signals. More often than head and shoulders, the *failure swing* or divergence denotes an unsuccessful test of a recent high or low RSI value.

Modifying the RSI

An obvious objection to the RSI might be the selection of a 14-day *half-cycle.* Maximum divergence is achieved by the use of a moving average that is exactly one-half the length of the dominant cycle, but 14 days may not be that half-cycle. In addition, common-use chart interpretation might mean that the RSI value remains outside the 70–30 zones for extended periods rather than signaling an immediate turn.

In practical terms, a 14-day criterion means that a sustained move in one direction that exceeds 14 days will retain a very high RSI value and may result in losses if a short position was entered. If the trading of the RSI seems to have high risk, increase the overbought and oversold levels by moving them from 70–30 to 80–20. This will cause a signal to be given at a more extreme level.

The generalized program code for an *n*-day RSI is given as

```
sumup = 0;
sumdn = 0;
for i = 1 to n begin
    if close - close[i] > 0 then
        sumup = sumup + close - close[1]
        else sumdn = sumdn + close[1] - close;
    end;
RSI = 100 - (100 / (1 + (sumup/sumdn)));
```

FIGURE 6-6   RSI top formation.

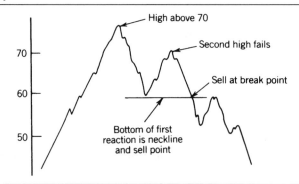

A study by Aan[3] on the distribution of the RSI showed that the average value of an RSI top and bottom was consistently grouped near 72 and 32, respectively. Therefore, 50% of all RSI values lie between 72 and 32, which is evenly distributed and similar in proportion to a standard deviation. This would suggest that the 70–30 levels proposed by Wilder are too close together to act as selective overbought/oversold values, but should be moved farther apart.

The frequency at which the market will reach these extreme levels can be adjusted by changing the 14-day criteria. If the interval is shortened, the RSI will reach extremes more often and trades will have higher risk. If the time period is increased, there will be safer but fewer trades based on RSI extremes (discussed in more detail in Chapter 22). It is always safer to err on the side of less risk. If there are too many trades being generated by the RSI, a combination of a longer interval and higher confidence bands will be an improvement.[4]

Further Smoothing with N-Day Ups and Downs

Instead of increasing the number of days in the RSI calculation period, a smoother indicator can be found by increasing the period over which each of the *up* and *down* values are determined. The original RSI method uses 14 individual days, where an up day is a day in which the price change was positive. Instead, we can replace each 1-day change with a 2-day change, or an *n*-day change. If we use 2-day changes, then a total of 28 days will be needed, so that each 2-day period does not overlap another; there will be 14 sets of 2 days. Using 14 sets of 2 will give a smoother indicator than using 28 single day changes.

Net Momentum Oscillator

Another variation on the RSI is the use of the difference between the sum of the up days and the sum of the down days, called a *net momentum oscillator*.[5] If you consider the unsmoothed RSI = $100 \times (S_u/(S_u + S_d))$, then the net momentum oscillator would be CMO = $100 \times (S_u - S_d)/(S_u + S_d)$. This method replaces some of the indicator movement lost to smoothing in the normal RSI and shows more extremes. This may also be done by shortening the number of periods in the RSI calculation.

Stochastics

The *stochastic,* created by George Lane, is an oscillator that measures the relative position of the closing price within a past high-low range. It is based on the commonly accepted observation that closing prices tend to resist penetrating the day's high prices as an upward move gains strength; similarly, closing prices often remain above the lows during a decline. When the market is about to turn from up to down, for instance, it is often the case that the highs are higher, but the closing price settles within the previous range. This makes the stochastic oscillator different from most oscillators, which are normalized representations of the *relative strength*, the difference between the closing price and a selected trend speed.

The three indicators that result from the stochastic measurement are called *%K, %D,* and *%D-slow*. The first two calculations form the normal concept of the stochastic oscillator and are calculated for today *t* as

$$\text{Initial } \%K_t = 100 \times \frac{C_t - L_t\,(5)}{R_t\,(5)}$$

[3] Peter W. Aan, "How RSI Behaves," *Futures* (January 1985).

[4] For a more sophisticated approach to RSI optimization, see John F. Ehlers, "Optimizing RSI with Cycles," *Technical Analysis of Stocks & Commodities* (February 1986).

[5] Tushar S. Chande and Stanley Kroll, *The New Technical Trader* (John Wiley & Sons, New York, 1994).

$$\%D = \text{``}\%K_t\text{-slow''} = \frac{\%K_t + \%K_{t-1} + \%K_{t-2}}{3} = \frac{\left(\sum_{i=t-2}^{t} \%K_i\right)}{3}$$

$$\%D_t\text{-slow} = \frac{\left(\sum_{i=t-2}^{t} \%D_i\right)}{3}$$

where C_t is today's closing price

$L_t(5)$ is the low price of the last 5 days

$R_t(5)$ is the range of the last 5 days (highest high minus lowest low) as of today.[6]

Notice that %D is a 3-day moving average of %K, and %D-slow is a 3-day moving average of %D. The 5-day high, low, and range selections tend to make the smoothed stochastics, %D and %D-slow, front-loaded calculations. Figure 6-7 shows the price of July 1984 cotton plotted with the corresponding %D-slow and %D (%K-slow) stochastic. Notice that the extremes do not correspond to what would be expected using a 5-day simple momentum. Points A and B appear much weaker in the stochastic than on the line chart, while points C and D are more pronounced. The low at point E is confusing, perhaps due to the gap in data; otherwise, the stochastic would seem a unique and useful tool. The smoothed value %D-slow does not lag as much as the 3-day average would imply, supporting the premise that there is significant weighting given to the more recent prices. The first calculation, %K, is not used due to its instability.[7]

Interpreting the Stochastic

The initial trading signal occurs when the %D-slow crosses the extreme bands, suggested in the range of 75 to 85 on the upside, and 15 to 25 on the downside. The order, however, is not placed until the %K-slow line crosses the %D-slow line (considered the *signal line*). Even though the extreme zone helps assure an adverse reaction of minimum size, the crossing of the two lines acts in a way similar to a dual moving average system. By waiting for the crossover, the trader cannot be trapped into shorting an extremely bullish move or buying a bearish one.

The emphasis in interpretation of the stochastic is its divergence from the apparent direction of prices. Referring again to Figure 6-7, points A and B are declining while new high prices at A are tested at B. This divergence is an important confirmation of the sell indication.

Patterns noted by Lane[8] are more extensive than other writings. They include:

Left and Right Crossovers

Typically, the faster %K-slow will change direction sooner than the %D-slow, crossing the %D-slow line while it is still moving in the prior trend direction. The opposite case, when the %D-slow turns first, indicates a slow, stable change of direction and is a more favorable pattern (Figure 6-8*a*).

---

[6] Harry Schirding, "Stochastic Oscillator," *Technical Analysis of Stocks & Commodities* (May/June 1984). For a pocket computer version of these calculations, see C.F. Johnson, "Stochastic Oscillator Program for the HP-41C(V)," *Technical Analysis of Stocks & Commodities* (September/October 1984).

[7] It is common practice to use the notation %K and %D to mean *%K-slow* and *%D-slow*, respectively. All writings on the stochastic use the smoothed values, rather than the initial %K calculation, regardless of the omission of "slow." Any use of %K in this text will also refer to %K-slow, unless specifically stated.

[8] George C. Lane, "Lane's Stochastics," *Technical Analysis of Stocks & Commodities* (May/June 1984).

FIGURE 6-7   The stochastic. A 5-minute bar chart of July 1984 cotton futures (New York Cotton Exchange) as recorded by a Commodity Quote-Graphics TQ-20/20 satellite system. Cotton's 5-period stochastic is plotted below the bar chart.

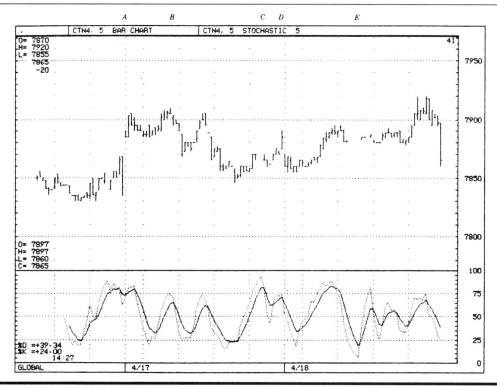

Hinge

A reduction in the speed of either the %K-slow or %D-slow lines, shown as a flattening out, indicates a reversal on the next day (Figure 6-8*b*).

Warning

An extreme turn in the faster %K-slow (2 to 12%) indicates at most 2 days remaining in the old trend.

Extremes

Reaching the extreme %K-slow values of 0 and 100 requires 7 consecutive days of closes at the highs (lows). The test of this extreme, following a pullback, is an excellent entry point.

Setup

Although the line chart shows higher highs and lows, if the %D-slow line has lower lows, a *bear market setup* has occurred. Look for a selling opportunity on the next rally (Figure 6-8*c*).

Failure

An excellent confirmation of a change in direction occurs when %K-slow crosses %D-slow (after penetrating the extreme level) then pulls back to the %D-slow line, but fails to cross it again (Figure 6-8*d*).

FIGURE 6-8 Lane's patterns. (*a*) Left and right crossings. (*b*) Hinge. (*c*) Bear market setup. (*d*) %*K*-slow failure.

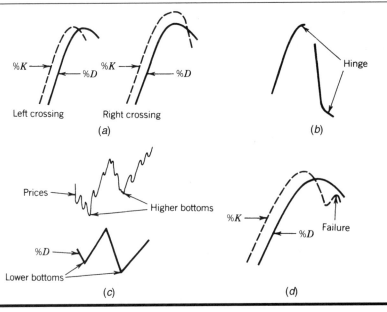

Relative Speed and Patterns of the Stochastic and RSI

Increasing the calculation period is a way of smoothing the values of indicator, whether it is viewing weekly instead of daily prices, using a 200-day average instead of a 10-day, or selecting a 20-day stochastic over a 5-day. The two most popular oscillators, the RSI and stochastic, can be very similar if the time periods are chosen correctly. In Figure 6-9, a Treasury bond chart for June 1996 delivery is used to show how the RSI and stochastic patterns change by varying the number of days in the calculation.

The 5-day raw stochastic is shown in panel *b* of Figure 6-9. Its characteristic is that whenever prices close on a 5-day high or low, the stochastic value is 100 or 0 and the indicator cannot provide any value. Smoothing the raw value offsets this problem at the cost of introducing a lag; this example will avoid that additional problem and use only the raw stochastic. Figure 6-9 (panel *c*) contains a 5-day RSI that tends to show similarities to the 5-day stochastic as bond prices become more actively traded toward the right part of the chart. Nevertheless, the RSI does not tend to approach peak values. Smoothing the stochastic by using 20 days, as shown in Figure 6-9 (panel *d*), gives a very similar picture as the 5-period RSI in panel *c* of Figure 6-9. The pattern has all the same ups and downs, although the stochastic continues to show more extreme values. The last two panels of Figure 6-9 (panels *e* and *f*) compare the standard 14-period RSI with a much longer 40-day stochastic with similar results as in Figure 6-9 (panels *c* and *d*). The patterns are very similar, but the stochastic moves to extremes more often.

Creating a Stochastic from the RSI

Any series or indicator value can be converted to a raw stochastic, %*K*, without adding lag by replacing the closing price with the indicator value. This creates a measure of where that indicator lies in its high-low range over the period selected and may simplify the comparison needed to generate buy and sell signals. A stochastic created from an RSI would be[9]

---

[9] Tushar Chande and Stanley Kroll, *The New Technical Trader* (John Wiley & Sons, New York, 1994).

FIGURE 6-9 Comparison of RSI and stochastic. (Panel *a*) Treasury bond prices for the June 1996 delivery. (Panel *b*) The 5-day raw stochastic often reaches maximum and minimum values. (Panels *c* and *d*) Comparing the 5-day RSI with the 20-day stochastic. (Panels *e* and *f*) Comparing the 14-day RSI with the 40-day stochastic.

(*a*)

(*b*)

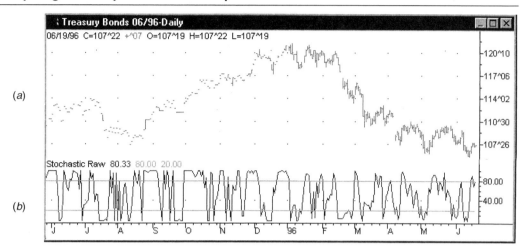

(*c*)

(*d*)

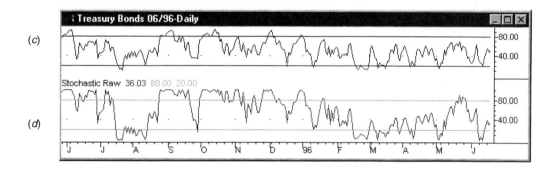

(*e*)

(*f*)

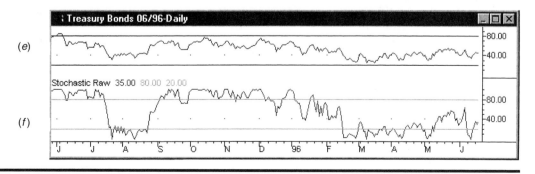

Source: Charts created with *TradeStation*® by Omega Research, Inc.

$$n\text{-day StochRSI} = \frac{\text{RSI}_{\text{today}} - \text{RSI}_{n\text{-day low}}}{\text{RSI}_{n\text{-day high}} - \text{RSI}_{n\text{-day low}}}$$

Larry Williams' Oscillators

Larry Williams has been known for his development of trading methods based on oscillators since his publication of the *A/D Oscillator* in 1972. Although they have changed over the 14 years spanning these systems, some similarities are apparent in Williams' three techniques that follow.

A/D Oscillator

In 1972, Jim Waters and Larry Williams published a description of their *A/D Oscillator* in *Commodities* magazine. For their system, A/D means *accumulation/distribution* rather than the usual notation of advance/decline, a well-known interpretive index for stocks. They used a unique form of relative strength, defining *buying power* (BP) and *selling power* (SP) as

BP = high − open   SP = close − low

where the values used were today's open, high, low, and closing prices. The two values, BP and SP, show the additional buying strength (relative to the open) and selling strength (compared with the close) in an effort to measure the implied direction of the day's trading. The combined measurement, called the *daily raw figure* (DRF) is calculated as

$$\text{DRF} = \frac{\text{BP} + \text{SP}}{2 \times (\text{high} - \text{low})}$$

The maximum value of 1 is reached when a market opens trading at the low and closes at the high: BP − SP = high − low. When the opposite occurs and the market opens at the high and closes on the lows, the DRF will be 0. Each price series will develop its own patterns, which can be smoothed or traded in many ways similar to a momentum index. The Waters/Williams A/D Oscillator solves problems of volatility and physical limits. The daily raw figure completely adjusts to higher or lower trading ranges because the divisor itself is a multiple of the day's range; and because each day is treated independently, the cumulative values of the momentum index are not part of the results. This day-to-day evaluation causes the DRF to vary radically and requires some smoothing technique or cycle interpretation to make it useable. As an example, look at the January 1977 soybean contract for the two months before delivery, November and December 1976. Table 6-1 shows the calculations for the DRF and for the smoothed DRF using an exponential moving average with a smoothing constant of 30% (selected arbitrarily). The daily raw figure is plotted as the solid line on a scale of .00 to 1.00 in Figure 6-10 and is extremely erratic in its movements. The dotted line is the smoothed DRF. Once plotted, two horizontal lines can be drawn to isolate the peaks and bottoms of the DRF; the top part becomes a zone representing an overbought condition and the bottom zone represents oversold. Bear in mind that these lines were drawn after the DRF was plotted and cannot be construed as predictive; however, in the article by Waters and Williams, their example of soybean oil had lines drawn in a similar place. Corresponding broken lines were drawn to indicate the overbought and oversold state for the smoothed DRF.

The rules for using the A/D Oscillator were not defined in the *Commodities* magazine presentation, but some simple rules could be:

Sell when the DRF (or smoothed DRF) penetrates into the overbought zone. Close out all accumulated long positions, if any, and go short on the open of the next trading day.

Buy when the opposite condition occurs.

TABLE 6-1 A/D Oscillator—January 1977 Soybeans

1976 Date	Open	High	Low	Close	DRF	DRF* Signal	Price	30% Smoothed DRF	30% Smoothed Signal*	Price
11-01	682	686	674¾	678½	.34			.34		
11-03	679	683	655	658½	.13			.28		
11-04	658	676	658	671½	.87	Sell		.45		
11-05	674	678	665	673½	.48		674	.46		
11-08	673	685	671	674¼	.54			.48		
11-09	673	673	660	666	.23			.41		
11-10	667	676½	665	675	.85	Sell		.54		
11-11	660	662½	645	651	.24		660	.45		
11-12	652	658	650½	653	.57			.49		
11-15	652	652	627	632½	.11	Buy		.37	Buy	
11-16	639½	655	636½	654¼	.90	Sell	639½	.53		639½
11-17	653	671	649	668½	.85		653	.63		
11-18	667	674½	658	666½	.48			.58		
11-19	670	691	669½	678¾	.70			.62		
11-22	680	691	675½	690½	.84	Sell		.68	Sell	
11-23	689	696½	674½	675¾	.20	Buy	689	.54		689
11-24	681	686	678½	680	.43		681	.51		
11-26	678	681½	670½	671¾	.21	Buy		.42		
11-29	670	675	661½	672	.57		670	.46		
11-30	668	677½	666	674½	.78			.56		
12-01	676	681½	673	677	.56			.56		
12-02	678	681½	675	679½	.61			.57		
12-03	679	687	679	685¾	.92	Sell		.68	Sell	
12-06	690	698½	689	696½	.84		690	.73		690
12-07	700	700	690	690½	.02	Buy		.51		
12-08	691	708	691	706	.94	Sell	691	.64		
12-09	705	712	702	703	.40		705	.57		
12-10	704	704	696	696½	.03	Buy		.41		
12-13	693	695	690½	691½	.33		693	.38	Buy	
12-14	696	701½	694	701	.83	Sell		.52		696
12-15	701	702	684	687	.11	Buy	701	.39	Buy	
12-16	688½	692	685	690½	.64		688½	.47		688½
12-17	690	690	676	677½	.05	Buy		.34	Buy	
12-20	680	684½	679½	683¼	.82	Sell	680	.49		680
12-21	682	688	679	687½	.80		682	.58		
12-22	688	693	686½	689¼	.60			.59		
12-23	689	693	684½	692½	.71			.62		
12-27	695	705	694	700¾	.76			.66		
12-28	701	706½	697½	705¾	.76			.69	Sell	
12-29	708	710	699	699½	.11	Buy		.52		708
12-30	703½	708	698	706½	.65		703½	.56		

Basic DRF Performance[†]		30% Smoothed DRF Performance[†]	
16 signals		7 signals	
4 compounded signals		3 compounded signals	
12 profits		5 profits	
Average profit	13.08¢	Average profit	22.10¢
4 losses		2 losses	
Average loss	14.25¢	Average loss	6.50¢
Net profit/loss	99.96¢	Net profit/loss	97.50¢

* Signals taken the following day on open.
[†] No commissions have been deducted.

FIGURE 6-10   A/D Oscillator.

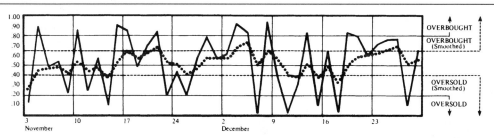

If the DRF (or smoothed DRF) enters an overbought or oversold zone more than once without the opposite zone being entered, one additional position is added at each reentry. Following these rules, the A/D Oscillator showed excellent success for both the raw and smoothed values. Accepting the after-the-fact designation of zones, the results still show that the method is viable and that a smoothing technique can be applied to the DRF to vary the speed of trading.

Waters and Williams used a simple 10-day momentum for their example of the A/D Oscillator. The choice of interval can be determined by examining the tops and bottoms of a chart for the natural cycle of the prices.

In reviewing the A/D Oscillator, there are modifications to be considered. Conceptually, the value of the oscillator should be +1 when prices are rising rapidly. The most extreme example is a locked-limit no-trading day, representative of the strongest (or weakest) market. But for that case, the open, high, low, and closing prices are all the same and the DRF cannot be determined (since the divisor is zero). A more basic problem concerns gap openings. A much higher opening with a stronger close would also upset the resulting DRF. For example, the following trading occurs:

	Open	High	Low	Close	DRF	ΔDRF	Σ ΔDRF
Monday	43.00	44.00	40.00	41.00	.25		
Tuesday	42.00	42.00	39.00	40.00	.17	−.17	−.17
Wednesday	38.50	38.50	38.00	38.00	.00	+.17	.00
Thursday	42.00	42.00	39.00	40.00	.17	−.33	−.33
Friday	40.00	43.00	40.00	42.00	.83	+.50	+.17

Note that on Wednesday, the DRF indicates that the momentum has reversed, but in fact the price is falling rapidly and gives no indication of recovering; it may actually be gaining momentum. On Thursday the price soars up and closes in the midrange, but the DRF shows a new downward momentum. The problem seems to be related to lack of association with the prior closing price. The daily movement can take on different appearances if the entire range was above or below the closing price. To form this link, replace the current high or low with the prior closing price if that price was outside the current trading range. The following example shows the results smoothed out and leaves the trend intact.

	Open	High	Low	Close	DRF	ΔDRF	Σ ΔDRF
Monday	43.00	44.00	40.00	41.00	.25		
Tuesday	42.00	42.00	39.00	40.00	.17	−.17	−.17
Wednesday	38.50	(40.00)	38.00	38.00	.37	+.04	−.13
Thursday	42.00	42.00	(38.00)	40.00	.25	−.12	−.25
Friday	40.00	43.00	40.00	42.00	.83	+.58	+.33

Another construction of an oscillator can be made using the highs and lows relative to the prior close:

$$O_t = \frac{H_t - C_{t-1}}{H_t - L_t}$$

The two days are linked together and the ratio of the high price relative to the prior close is measured against the total range for the day. For the normal case, $H_t \geq C_{t-1} \geq L_t$; but if $C_{t-1} > H_t$ or $L_t > C_{t-1}$, C_{t-1} replaces either H_t or L_t to extend the range. The value of O_t will be either 1 or 0 for these extreme cases. As with the A/D Oscillator, the values derived from this method may also be smoothed.

Oscillators are not the only tools for measuring momentum or for determining over-bought or oversold conditions. Because it is very different from either a charting technique or a moving average, it is valuable either on its own or as a confirmation of another method.

A word of caution: Trading against the trend can be exciting and profitable, but at con-siderably greater risk than a trend-following system. The problem with selling an over-bought condition is that there is no way to hold losses to a minimum. Once a short position is entered, the momentum or the oscillator value could sustain its strength and move against the position.

%R Method

After the publication of Williams' *How I Made One Million Dollars . . . Last Year . . . Trad-ing Commodities* (Conceptual Management, 1973), the *%R* oscillator became well known. It is a simple way of calculating where today's closing price fits into the recent trading range. Using the last 10 days, define

$$\%R = \frac{\text{buying power}}{\text{range}} = \frac{\text{high}_{10} - \text{close}_{\text{today}}}{\text{high}_{10} - \text{low}_{10}}$$

Williams' 10-day *%R* is actually a *10-day stochastic,* using the high price rather than the low price in the numerator; therefore, it is the complement (100 minus the 10-day sto-chastic) of the original stochastic calculation. With a chart that has 0 at the top and 100 at the bottom, a value below 95% will give a buy signal, and one over 10% will give a sell sig-nal. Williams viewed this as a timing device to add positions within a major technical or fundamental trend. Trades were not to be entered if they contradicted the major market direction. Readers should refer to the earlier section in this chapter, "Stochastics," for more information.

The Ultimate Oscillator

In the *Ultimate Oscillator,* Williams seems to combine his original idea of the A/D Oscilla-tor with a great deal of Wilder's RSI.[10] He adds the unique feature of three concurrent time periods to offset the negative qualities of the short time period of the *%R,* without slowing the system too much. The Ultimate Oscillator works as follows:

1. Calculate today's *buying pressure* B_t by subtracting the *true low* from the closing price. The true low is today's low or yesterday's close, whichever is lower.
2. Calculate today's *true range* R_t by taking either the greater of today's high and low, today's high and yesterday's close, or yesterday's close and today's low.
3. Total the buying pressure B_t separately over the three intervals of 7, 14, and 28 days, designated as SB_7, SB_{14}, and SB_{28}.
4. Total the true range R_t over the same three periods, SR_7, SR_{14}, and SR_{28}.

---

[10] Larry Williams, "The Ultimate Oscillator," *Technical Analysis of Stocks & Commodities* (August 1985).

5. Divide the sum of the buying pressures by the corresponding true range, that is, SB_7/SR_7 and scale by multiplying the 7-day value by 4 and the 14-day value by 2. All three calculations are now in the same scale.

Notice that the nearest seven values for the buying pressure and the true range are each used seven times; that is, they are multiplied by both the scaling factors of 4 and 2, and used once more in the 28-day calculation. Williams has created a step-weighted momentum, assigning values of 7, 3, and 1 to the first 7 days, second 7 days, and last 14 days, respectively. The last 14 days account for only 10% of the total.

The rules for using this oscillator (see Figure 6-11) are:

1. A sell signal occurs when the oscillator moves above the 50% line (an upward divergence), and the oscillator peaks and then fails to break the peak on the next rally. Then, a sell order can be placed when the oscillator fails (on the right shoulder).
2. If holding a short position, close out the short when a long signal occurs, or when the 30% level is reached, or if the oscillator rises above 65% (the stop-loss point) after being below 50%.
3. A buy signal occurs using the opposite techniques as the short signal (rule 1).
4. If a long position is held, close out longs when a short signal occurs, or when the 70% level is reached, or if the oscillator falls below 30% (after being above 50%).

Williams' Ultimate Oscillator has combined many important features, including weighting time periods, setting objectives, stop-loss points, and chart interpretation. There are two obvious weaknesses in this approach.

1. The chart rules add a great deal of subjectiveness to the method. Waiting for a failure of a second peak is another way of looking for a broadening top—a slower rise followed by a rounding pattern. Waiting for a pattern may add reliability if interpreted properly, but it defeats the effect of the oscillator being a *leading indicator.*
2. The stop-loss rules apply only after the oscillator has crossed 50%. If it moves the wrong way immediately, there is no risk control.

DOUBLE-SMOOTHED MOMENTUM

The most recent contributions to the study of momentum have been made by William Blau.[11] In addition to creating new momentum indicators, he has added substantial value to the old ones. Also refer to his work on double smoothing of momentum in Chapter 4 ("Trend Calculations").

[11] William Blau, *Momentum, Direction and Divergence* (John Wiley & Sons, New York, 1995).

FIGURE 6-11   Williams' Ultimate Oscillator.

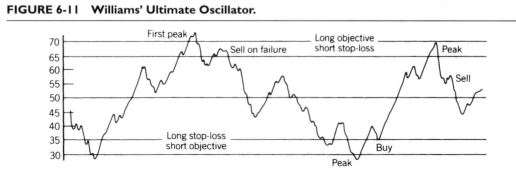

True Strength Index

Much of Blau's work combines double smoothing of momentum values (1-period price differences), which has surprisingly little calculation lag. By using the momentum, he has based the calculations on values more sensitive than price, then slowed them down by smoothing. He refers to this as using momentum as a proxy for price. One of Blau's most popular indicators is the True Strength Index (TSI), which combines these features:

$$\text{TSI}(close,r,s) = \frac{100 \times @\text{SmoothedAverage}(@\text{SmoothedAverage}(close - close[1],r)s)}{@\text{SmoothedAverage}(@\text{SmoothedAverage}(@\text{abs}(close - close[1]),r),s)}$$

where r is the period of the first momentum smoothing
s is the period of the second momentum smoothing
close-close[1] is the 1-day momentum

Written in *TradeStation* format, where the two smoothing periods are *smooth1* and *smooth2,* this formula is:

```
num = @smoothedaverage(@smoothedaverage(close-close[1],smooth1),smooth2);
denom = @smoothedaverage(@smoothedaverage(@absvalue(close-close[1]),
                smooth1),smooth2);
TSI = 100*num / denom;
```

The numerator is the scaled value of the double-smoothed momentum, and the denominator is the double smoothing of the absolute value of momentum. The 1-day momentum is first smoothed over the period r, and then over the period s. The relationship between the standard momentum (the difference in prices over r days) and the TSI can be seen in Figure 6-12. The momentum indicator, formed by using an MACD indicator with moving average values of 1 and 20, has the typical erratic pattern of prices, and a slight lead ahead of the peaks, formed by the pending crossing of the prices and moving average. The TSI is much smoother with peaks and valleys aligning with those of the prices. Buy and sell signals are created by smoothing the TSI signal line and buying when the TSI crosses above the signal line.

Double-Smoothed Stochastics

Because of Blau's great interest in double smoothing, he defines the general form of a double-smoothed stochastic as:

$DS(q,r,s) =$

$$\frac{100 \times @\text{SmoothedAverage}(@\text{SmoothedAverage}(close - @\text{Lowest}(low,q),r),s)}{@\text{SmoothedAverage}(@\text{SmoothedAverage}(@\text{Highest}(high,q) - @\text{Lowest}(low,q),r),s)}$$

where *close – @Lowest(low,q)* is the numerator of Lane's raw stochastic, the lowest low over the past q periods
@Highest(high,q) – @Lowest(low,q) is the denominator of Lane's stochastic, the greatest high-low range over the past q periods
@SmoothedAverage(. . . ,r),s) is an exponential smoothing first over r periods, then over s periods, of the numerator

Forecast Oscillator

In Chapter 4 ("Trend Calculations"), the difference between the price and the trendline value was smoothed and added to the trend value to get what was originally considered a double-smoothed trendline. Instead, the difference between the current price and the cor-

FIGURE 6-12   Comparing the TSI with a standard momentum over the same period.

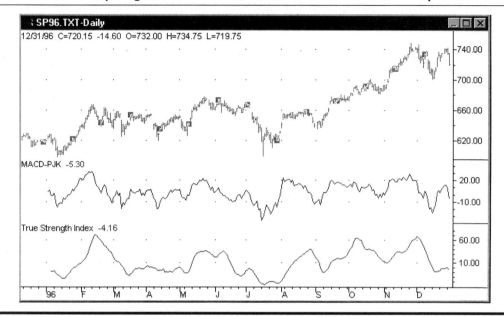

Source: Chart created with *TradeStation*® by Omega Research, Inc.

responding forecast (trendline) price can be calculated as a percentage and treated as a momentum indicator %F.[12] This oscillator is not bounded; however, by giving the value as a percentage, there will be more consistency over very long test periods.

$$\%F = 100 \times \frac{\text{close}_{\text{today}} - \text{close}_{\text{previous}}}{\text{close}_{\text{today}}}$$

For practical purposes, a 3-period smoothing of %F gives more consistency. When %F = 0, then the trendline and prices are moving parallel to one another; when %F > 0, the market is accelerating away from the trendline; and when %F < 0, prices are slowing down and the two series are converging. Traders interested in this technique should also read the section on acceleration.

An Oscillator to Distinguish between Trending and Sideways Markets

The lack of predictability of trending markets is the greatest problem for the analyst. The work found under the topics "Directional Movement" and "Ranking" in Chapter 23 ("Risk Control") this book discusses that issue. Based on the idea that the trend component is stronger when price is farther from fair value, and the noise (sideways movement) is greater when price is near value, an oscillator can be created to show the strength of the trend component based on this concept,

$$\text{Strength Oscillator} = \frac{@\text{avg}(\text{close}_{\text{today}} - \text{close}_{\text{previous}}, n)}{@\text{avg}(\text{high}_{\text{today}} - \text{low}_{\text{today}}, n)}$$

As the trend increases, the average change in closing prices becomes larger relative to the high-low range for the day. In an unusual period, when the market gaps open, it would be possible for the closes to become larger than the daily range. In a sideways market both the

[12] Tushar Chande and Stanley Kroll, *The New Technical Trader* (John Wiley & Sons, New York, 1994).

change in the closes and daily range will get smaller, but the net price change over the period n should be close to zero. This oscillator can be smoothed by taking the change in price over 2 or 3 days, rather than the most recent day, as well as the high-low range over the same number of days.

ADDING VOLUME TO MOMENTUM

A momentum indicator can also incorporate volume by multiplying the price change over n periods by the total volume over that same period. The use of a cumulative period will help to stabilize the volume, which is often erratic. Although the sum of the volume over the period can be used, the average will appear more familiar and can be plotted against a volume chart. In standard and programming notation, that gives the momentum times the volume MV as:

$$MV = (\text{price}_t - \text{price}_{t-n}) \times \frac{\sum_{i=t-n}^{t} \text{volume}_i}{n}$$

```
MV = (close - close[n])*@Average(volume,n)
```

Alternately, the price change of n periods could have been divided by n to give a per-unit value. This section will include those techniques that combine price change and volume; for methods that do not use price, see Chapter 10 ("Volume, Open Interest, and Breadth").

Scaling by a Percentage or Volatility

The same conversions can be applied to momentum with and without volume. Using a percentage, rather than price, will add some robustness over long test periods. Because volatility often increases when prices rise faster than the percentage would show, momentum can be scaled according to a shorter measure of true range. If the true range is averaged over 20 to 65 days, approximately one month to one quarter, then the 1-day change in price will become a relative momentum value. By using a much longer period for averaging the true range, you can create a stable profile of the volatility changes in the underlying market.

(Percentage momentum with volume)

```
%MV = (close - close[n]) / close[n] * @Average(volume,n)
```

(Momentum with volume scaled by true range)

```
TRMV = (close - close[n]) / @Average(@TrueRange,p)) * @Average(volume,n)
```

where `@TrueRange` is always calculated for the most recent period, and
`@Average(@TrueRange,p))` is the average of the 1-day true range for the past p days.

Volume-Weighted RSI   *MONEY FLOW*

In the same way that the RSI adds the positive days and divides by the sum of the negative days, it is possible to weight each day by its volume to add another factor, called *money flow*,[13] to the calculation. A positive or upward day is when the average of today's high, low, and close (high + low + close/3) is greater than the previous average. Each average is then multiplied by the volume, giving the daily money flow, and a ratio of the past 14 days is used to create a *money ratio* and finally a *money flow index,* both steps similar to Wilder's RSI.

[13] Gene Quong and Avrum Soudack, "Volume-Weighted RSI: Money Flow," *Technical Analysis of Stocks & Commodities* (March 1989).

$$\text{Money Flow} = \text{volume} \times \frac{\text{high} + \text{low} + \text{close}}{3}$$

$$\text{Money Ratio} = \frac{\text{14-day positive money flow}}{\text{14-day negative money flow}}$$

$$\text{Money Flow Index} = 100 - \frac{100}{1 + \text{Money Ratio}}$$

Herrick Payoff Index

Using the change in the underlying value of the futures contract, rather than only the change in price, the Herrick Payoff Index (HPI)[14] combines volume and open interest to generate an indicator that, as the basic momentum calculation, is not bounded but scaled down to a manageable value and smoothed using a .10 smoothing factor, s (about 19 days). The daily value is:

$$\text{HP} = cf \times V_t \times (M_t - M_{t-1}) \times \left[1 + \left(\frac{M_t - M_{t-1}}{|M_t - M_{t-1}|} \right) \left(\frac{2 \times |OI_t - OI_{t-1}|}{\min(OI_t, OI_{t-1})} \right) \right]$$

and the index is an exponential smoothing of the individual daily calculations:

$$\text{HPI}_{\text{today}} = \text{HPI}_{\text{previous}} + s \times (\text{HPI}_{\text{today}} - \text{HPI}_{\text{previous}})$$

where t is today

$t - 1$ is the previous day

cf is the conversion factor (value of a basis point move)

V_t is today's volume

$(M_t - M_{t-1})$ is the difference in the mean prices $\frac{\text{high} + \text{low}}{2}$

$|\ |$ (vertical bars) are for absolute value

$|OI_t - OI_{t-1}|$ is the absolute value of the change in open interest

$\min(OI_t, OI_{t-1})$ is the smaller of today and the previous open interest

s is a smoothing constant (default 10)

The expression that divides the change in mean prices by the absolute value of the same change is used to create a +1 or −1 value. This complex formula can also be written in programming code as

```
HP = @BigPointValue * volume * ((high-low)/2 - (high[1]-low[1])/2) *
     (1 - (((high-low)/2 - (high[1]-low[1])/2) / @Abs((high-low)/2 -
     (high[1]-low[1])/2))* 2 * (@Abs(opint - opint[1]) /@Lowest(opint,2)))

HPI = @SmoothedAverage(HP,19)
```

Most analysts who use the Herrick Payoff Index divide the HPI by 100,000 to reduce the value to a more useable level. The final series, when seen along with prices, may appear volatile and require an interpretation using trendlines. This is due to the fluctuations in volume and open interest, which are smoothed over 20 days, rather than longer. The HPI may be helpful, despite the volatility, because it is a combination of factors not included in most other indices. It will have patterns that appear to lead price change to compensate for market noise.

---

[14] From the original *CompuTrac* manual, which is now the Bridge Telerate division.

Comments on the Use of Volume

Volume is an important piece of information, but it can be difficult to interpret. It fluctuates in a much larger range than price, and may be one-third higher or lower from day to day. Although it indicates market interest and potential volatility, there are many days for which a high or low volume does not have a consistent reaction.

In general, adding volume to an indicator will result in a more volatile, erratic series. Therefore, the first steps in using volume would be

1. Create a long-term, smoothed volume series.
2. Compare current volume for extremes to identify only those exceptional days that should be followed by high volatility.
3. Low volume should not be determined by a single day, but by either a few unusually low days together or by a volume decay over a modest time period.

VELOCITY AND ACCELERATION

A method conceptually similar to momentum is derived from the concepts in physics of velocity and acceleration, both elements in the science of motion. *Velocity,* as defined in mechanics, is the rate of change of position with respect to time (also called *speed*). There are two types of velocity, *average* and *instantaneous.* The average velocity is simply calculated as the mean velocity over a fixed distance and for a fixed time interval. In working with commodity prices, the time interval used will be days and the distance is measured in points; so that if silver moved 40 points in 6 days, its average velocity is

$$\bar{v} = \frac{40}{6} = 6\,\frac{2}{3} \text{ points per day}$$

In general, the average velocity is expressed

$$\bar{v} = \frac{D}{T}$$

where D is the total elapsed distance over the time interval T. For a geometric interpretation of momentum, D (the change in price) can be related to T (the length of the momentum span) to get exactly the same results for average velocity as for slope (see Figure 6-13).

The instantaneous velocity v, which is the velocity calculated at a specific point in time, will be different. To determine the instantaneous velocity, a mathematical technique called *differentiation* is used. It effectively looks at smaller and smaller time intervals and consequently smaller distances on the price curve until the slope calculation is reduced to a single point. The results of the process of differentiation is called the *derivative* and is expressed

$$v_t = \lim_{\Delta t \to 0} \frac{\Delta D}{\Delta t} = \frac{dD}{dt}$$

This shows that the velocity taken at any point is the result of the time interval (t) becoming progressively smaller without reaching zero. The rules for differentiation can be found in any advanced mathematics book. Only the results will be presented. The velocity v_t represents the speed or momentum of the price at the point in time t. If v gets larger for t, t_1, $t_2, \ldots$, then the velocity is increasing; if v gets smaller, the velocity is decreasing. Because the velocity also denotes direction, it can be both positive and negative in value and appear similar to a momentum indicator. Systems applied to momentum may equally be applied to velocity. Of course, some of the basic equations have constant velocity and cannot be used for a velocity trading plan, because the values never change. The straight line, simple

FIGURE 6-13   (a) Average velocity. (b) Instantaneous velocity.

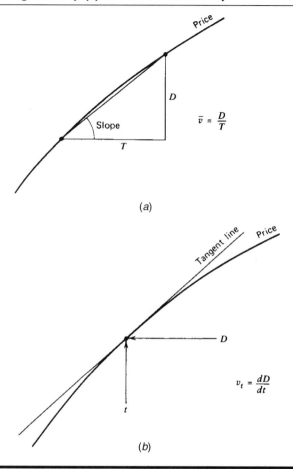

(a)

(b)

and weighted moving averages, and exponential smoothing all have constant velocities. Only those equations with *second-order smoothing* will work.

When the process of differentiation is reapplied to the equation for velocity, it results in the rate of change of the speed with respect to time, or *acceleration*. This type of acceleration tells whether the velocity is increasing or decreasing at any point in time. The acceleration, also called the *second derivative*, adds another dimension to momentum and may improve the timing of trades.

Let's assume that the velocity and acceleration have been calculated (Table 6-2). The following are the possible combinations that can occur:

Vel	Acc	Price Movement
+	+	Price is moving up at an increasing rate
+	0	Price is moving up at a constant rate
+	−	Price is moving up at a decreasing rate
0	0	Price is static
−	+	Price is moving down at a decreasing rate
−	0	Price is moving down at a constant rate
−	−	Price is moving down at an increasing rate

TABLE 6-2 Equations for Velocity and Acceleration

	Basic Equation	Velocity at x_t*	Acceleration at x_t*
Straight line	$y_t = a + bx_t$	$v_t = b$	$a_t = 0$
Curvilinear	$y_t = a + bx_t + cx_t^2$	$v_t = b + 2cx_t$	$a_t = 2c$
Logarithmic (base a)	$y_t = \log_a x_t$	$v_t = (\log_a e)/x_t$ or $v_t = 1/(x_t \ln a)$	$a_t = -1/(x_t^2 \ln a)$
Logarithmic (natural log)	$y_t = \ln x_t$	$v_t = 1/x_t$	$a_t = -1/x_t^2$
Exponential	$y_t = e^{ax_t}$	$v_t = ae^{ax_t}$	$a_t = a^2 e^{ax_t}$
Moving average	$y_t = \dfrac{x_t + x_{t-1} + \cdots + x_{t-n+1}}{n}$	$v_t = 1$	$a_t = 0$
Weighted moving average	$y_t = \dfrac{a_1 x_t + a_2 x_{t-1} + \cdots + a_n x_{t-n+1}}{n}$	$v_t = \dfrac{a_1 + a_2 + \cdots + a_n}{n}$	$a_t = 0$
Exponential smoothing	$y_t = y_{t-1} + c(x_t - y_{t-1})$	$v_t = c$	$a_t = 0$

* Because velocity and acceleration are time derivatives, all equations implicitly include the factor $\dfrac{d(x_t)}{d_t}$ as part of the right member.

Using the acceleration feature, a change of velocity (or momentum) can be detected, or the strength of a current price move can be confirmed.

Quick Calculation of Velocity and Acceleration

A less precise but very convenient way of determining velocity and acceleration is the calculation of first and second differences. The purpose of these values is to find more sensitive indicators of price change, and most traders will find this quick calculation satisfactory. The results can be used in exactly the same way as the formal mathematical results. Consider the following examples:

1. A price series 10, 20, 30, 40, . . . is moving higher by a constant value each day. The first differences are 10, 10, 10, . . . , showing a consistent velocity of 10. The second differences, formed by subtracting sequential values in the first-difference series, are 0, 0, 0, . . . , showing that there is no change in speed; therefore, the acceleration is 0.

2. Another price series is shown with its first and second differences as

t	1	2	3	4	5	6	7	8	9	10	11	12
S	10	15	20	30	45	50	45	35	25	20	25	40
V		+5	+5	+10	+15	+5	-5	-10	-10	-5	+5	+15
A			0	+5	+5	-10	-10	-5	0	+5	+10	+10

where S is the price series
    V is the velocity (first differences)
    A is the acceleration (second differences)

The original series S has two turns in trend clearly shown by the velocity and acceleration. The velocity V continues to be positive through the sixth value as the underlying price moves from 10 to 50. Whenever prices change direction, the velocity changes sign. The basic upward trend can be associated with a positive velocity and a downward trend with a negative one.

The acceleration, or second difference, shows the change in speed. At the sixth item, the acceleration becomes negative, even though the velocity was positive, because prices moved higher at a slower rate. They had been gaining by 5, 10, and 15 points each day, but on day 6, the gain was only 5 points. This reversal in acceleration was a leading indicator of a trend change. A similar situation occurred on day 8, when the acceleration slowed and reversed on day 10, one day ahead of the actual price reversal.

The relationship between velocity and acceleration using first and second differences can be interpreted using the same logic as previously discussed. Velocity and acceleration are increasingly more sensitive directional indicators; the slightest variation in price movement will cause the acceleration to reverse. It is an indicator of great value when it is used selectively.

OTHER RATE-OF-CHANGE INDICATORS

Projected Crossovers

If moving averages can successfully be used to identify the trend direction, it follows that a projection of the moving average will be valuable in anticipating when the trends will change. If a moving average trading strategy used a single trend, the price at which the standard N-day moving average line would cross the price CP1 is

$$\text{CP1} = \frac{\text{sum of last } N - 1 \text{ prices}}{N - 1} = \frac{\left(\sum_{t-N+2}^{t} P_i \right)}{(N - 1)}$$

To calculate the price at which two moving averages would cross requires the following:

$$\text{CP2} = \frac{N \times (\text{sum of last } N - 1 \text{ prices}) - M \times (\text{sum of last } M - 1 \text{ prices})}{(M - N)}$$

where N and M are the lengths of the two moving averages.[15]

The projected crossover price is most useful when it is likely that a trend change will occur within a few days, that is, when the two moving averages begin converging and become close in value. Acting on the expected price would give the trader a great advantage in order execution. A plot of this, however, may not be much different than a simple *relative strength* measurement. The difference between the price and the moving average line constitutes the relative strength.

The change in the projected crossover is considered a more valuable tool by Lambert. He creates a *Market Direction Indicator* (MDI) with the following formula:

$$\text{MDI} = \frac{100 \times (\text{crossover price}_{previous} - \text{crossover price}_{today})}{\text{average of past 2 day's prices}}$$

The point at which the MDI crosses the zero line moving higher is a buy signal, and the point at which it crosses moving lower is a sell signal.

Combining a Trend and Oscillator

Directional Parabolic System

The *Directional Parabolic System*[16] is a combination of two of Wilder's well-known techniques, Directional Movement and the Parabolic Time/Price System. Directional Movement is covered fully in Chapter 23. It gained popularity as a method of selecting the commodi-

---

[15] Donald R. Lambert, "The Market Directional Indicator," *Technical Analysis of Stocks & Commodities* (November/December 1983). This article also contains a BASIC computer program to calculate the MDI.

[16] J. Welles Wilder, Jr., *Chart Trading Workshop 1980* (Trend Research, Greensboro, NC, 1980).

ties that were most likely candidates for trend-following systems. The Parabolic Time/Price System is covered in Chapter 17 ("Adaptive Techniques"). Although a full reading of both techniques are necessary, the essence of the combined systems can be understood with the following definitions:

+DI14   The 14-day upward Directional Index

−DI14   The 14-day downward Directional Index

ADX   The average Directional Movement Index

DPS   The Directional Parabolic stop

Although shown as −DI14, the downward Directional Index is a positive number based on the sum of those days that closed lower. The ADX is a ratio of those days that closed higher with those that closed lower over the past 14 days. The ADX is an oscillator based on the scaled ratio of +DI/−DI. The two systems combine according to the following rules:

1. If the ADX is up (the +DM14 is greater than the −DM14), take only long Parabolic System trades; if the ADX is down, take only short trades.
2. If the two systems conflict, no trade is entered. A trade may be entered at the time they agree.
3. If a position is held, the Parabolic stop is used. (The stop is now called the DPS instead of the SAR, because it no longer requires a reversal of position.)
4. If no position is held, the Directional Movement *equilibrium point* is used (the high or low of the day on which the +DM14 crosses the −DM14).

Directional Parabolic Revision

In 1980, the entry rules were revised to include an added use of the ADX when it is greater than the +DI14 or the −DI14. Because the ADX serves as an oscillator and indicates turning points in the trend, when the ADX exceeds the magnitude of the current +DI14 or −DI14 and reverses, the current position should be closed out. If the ADX remains above both the +DI14 and −DI14, the market is extremely strong and liquidation should stop. The ADX is intended to be a leading indicator for liquidation only. Reversal of the current position only occurs when the Parabolic stop has been penetrated, and the new trade agrees with the direction of the Parabolic System.

The addition of an oscillator to a trend-following system allows trades to be closed out at more favorable positions than the usual trend exits. If the new direction carries through and the position is reversed, the added feature has worked perfectly; however, if prices turn back in the original direction, a reentry may not be possible. The revised rules are unclear concerning reentry into a position if prices fail to penetrate the DPS and signal a reversal. A reentry might occur if the ADX falls below both the +DI14 and −DI14, indicating that prices are no longer extreme, then turns back in the trend direction. Once reestablished, the DPS can be used and additional exits using the revised rules would apply.

Cambridge Hook

A combined indicator that has received some promotion is the *Cambridge Hook,* used by one commodity trading advisor.[17] It is intended to identify an early reversal of the current trend by combining the following indicators (applied to an existing uptrend):

1. An outside reversal day (a higher high followed by a lower close)
2. Wilder's RSI must exceed 60% (moderately overbought)
3. Volume and open interest must be increasing

[17] Elias Crim, "Are You Watching the 'Right' Signals?" *Futures* (June 1985).

The result is a high likelihood of a downward trend reversal (the opposite applies to upward trend reversals). Protective stops are placed above the high of the hook on the day that signaled a downward reversal.

MOMENTUM DIVERGENCE

Divergence is a concept familiar to most traders. It is frequently seen in the Dow Jones Industrials versus the Dow Jones Utilities, when the Utilities indicate a downturn in the economy in advance of any sign in the DJIA price pattern. The prices of the S&P 500 are also watched closely in conjunction with the 30-year U.S. Treasury bonds. When bond prices fall, the S&P can't be far behind. The underlying relationship of two markets that make divergence important can also be represented technically by the slope of trendlines and the alignment of relative peak prices.

An unsmoothed momentum chart has as many irregular ups and downs as a normal price chart and is often subjected to the same analysis. Trendlines are drawn across the tops and bottoms of chart sections and can be interpreted in a manner similar to their price counterparts (as shown in Figure 6-14), with two significant differences:

1. The trend of a momentum chart shows the *speed* of the trend, but allows us to see the *rate of change* of price. For example, an unchanged momentum value of +.10 is actually a steady increase of +.10 in the relative price level; that is, a price sequence of 102.20, 102.30, 102.40, . . . would show a momentum of +.10 and would appear as a horizontal line on a chart. In this example, the change (momentum) is .10, but the rate of change (acceleration or deceleration) is 0. When the momentum increases, the rate of change is positive; a downtrend in the momentum means that the rate of change is negative. A steady uptrend in the momentum means that price

FIGURE 6-14 Divergence of price and momentum. The trendline drawn across the price moves (panel *a*) and the corresponding momentum (panel *b*) and MACD (panel *c*) indicators shows that the directions diverge.

Source: Chart created with *TradeStation*® by Omega Research, Inc.

movement is accelerating at a steady rate (for example, a gain of .10 the first day, .20 the second day, .30 the third, and so on), moving faster and faster, a situation that is not likely to continue; therefore, these periods are relatively short-lived.

2. The divergence between the price trend and momentum trend creates a very strong indicator of impending change in the direction of the price trend. A bearish divergence occurs when prices continue higher, while momentum moves lower. This is typically seen by drawing a trendline above the rising tops of the prices, as shown in panel *a* of Figure 6-14, and above the falling tops of the momentum indicator, seen in panels *b* and *c* of Figure 6-14. The reason for this pattern is that prices are actually rising at a slower rate, causing the new price peaks to be farther apart.

Figure 6-14 gives three examples of divergence using two different momentum indicators, the difference between prices and a single moving average (Figure 6-14, panel *b*), and an MACD, the difference between two moving averages (Figure 6-14, panel *c*). The classic example is in the center of the chart, where prices make new highs near the close of 10/22, while both of the momentum indicators show lower peaks. In classic divergence the trendlines drawn on the price chart must be in absolute contrast to the direction of those drawn on the momentum chart. That is, one must be going up and the other down. The failure of momentum to make a corresponding high peak indicates a downturn in prices.

On the left side of Figure 6-14 is a bullish divergence, in which prices make new lows while the momentum indicators rise. In this case, the MACD is much stronger than the standard momentum. On the far right, a bullish divergence appears in the center panel but not in the MACD indicator. Standard momentum indicates a modest rise in value while the MACD declines quickly. Not all changes in price direction are identified by the divergence of price and momentum, but it remains a valuable tool.

We can distinguish between a stronger and weaker divergence by measuring the difference in the relative angles of the two trendlines, but mostly by the momentum trendline. In a bearish divergence situation, the price trend is normally increasing at a slow rate, and becoming slower. When the momentum drops quickly there is a strong divergence and the price rise is quickly ending.

Slope Divergence

To change an interpretive analysis to one that can be computerized, there are two techniques, one using slopes and the other based on the analysis of peaks. A comparison between the rate at which prices and a momentum indicator are rising or falling will give enough information to automatically identify a divergence. Using a linear regression feature in either a spreadsheet (@Slope) or a strategy testing program (@LinearRegSlope), the slope of any time interval can be found for both momentum and price over the same period. Because momentum is a detrended series, the period compared should not be too long; otherwise, the slope of the trendline will be zero, a horizontal line. Instead of the trendlines that appear above and below prices and momentum in Figure 6-14, the regression lines will pass through the center of the price movement.

Divergence can be any combination of conflicting directions between the slope of price and the slope of momentum, including prices rising faster than momentum, momentum rising faster than prices, or the opposite. However, classic analysis has focused on momentum as a leading indicator of a change in the price trend, which limits the combinations to:

1. Prices rising and momentum falling (a *bearish* divergence)
2. Prices falling and momentum rising (a *bullish* divergence)

The *strength* of a bearish divergence, which can be used to select which situations are best for trading, can be determined by the momentum slope provided prices are rising, or the net of the rising slope of prices and the falling slope of momentum. In the second case, the difference between the slopes must be converted to a common denominator, because the angle of price movement can cover a far wider range than the angle of momentum movement.

Divergence Using Peak Comparisons

The identification of divergence for a short-term trader is very different from the slope technique that applies to the major moves seen in the Dow Jones Industrials and Utilities. In this application, the peaks (or valleys) of any momentum indicator are compared against the corresponding peaks (or valleys) of the price series (upon which the momentum was calculated). If the momentum peaks are declining and the price peaks are rising there is a divergence. In Figure 6-14 the ups and downs between the peaks are ignored, and only the points at which the prices form swing highs and lows are compared with corresponding momentum values.

It is easier to find divergence by looking at a chart on a quote screen than to program it into a computer. Translating what you see into a systematic analysis of divergence signals is very difficult. There are a number of steps necessary for signaling a bearish divergence:

1. **Identify each momentum peak and record its value, MP_i.** The standard approach to finding a momentum peak is to locate each momentum value that is higher than the previous n values and higher than the next n values. In addition, the first momentum peak of a sequence must be above a threshold level, for example 80, to assure that an overbought situation has occurred. It seems reasonable that all momentum peak values should be greater than some level, for example 50, to avoid having already reached the correction objective before a position can be entered (see Step 4).

2. **Identify the price peaks corresponding to each momentum peak, PP_i.** This is done in the same way as Step 1 or the corresponding value of the price can be used, assuming that it produced a peak.

3. **Compare the last momentum peak, MP_i, with the previous momentum peak, MP_{i-1}, and their corresponding prices, PP_i and PP_{i-1}.** A bearish divergence exists if $PP_i > PP_{i-1}$ and $MP_i < MP_{i-1}$. A stronger divergence exists if $MP_{i-1} - MP_i$ is larger.

4. **Enter a short position when the divergence is identified, provided prices have not already reached the correction level or anticipated profit.** This fourth step points out a problem in this method of finding a divergence. The need to wait a number of days after a momentum high will cause many of the signals to be too late. Although the price may have been higher at the time of the second peak, the lag needed to recognize the next declining momentum peak gives the price a chance to correct before a signal can be generated.

5. **Exit the short position when the current momentum moves above the last momentum peak.** This new momentum high indicates that the divergence, used as the entry criteria, has disappeared and there is no basis for this trade. The exact price at which this occurs cannot be calculated in advance.

6. **Exit the short position when the market has corrected or an objective has been reached.** Once the momentum has declined to the midpoint level of 50 for the RSI and stochastic, it should be considered neutral and cannot be expected to continue on to negative values. A price objective can be set using volatility or support levels.

Single, Double, and Triple Divergences

In fewer cases, double and triple divergences will occur. A double divergence is one in which three momentum peaks are declining and price is rising in each case. Most often, the second momentum peak is only slightly lower than the first, and the last peak drops off indicating that price is soon to follow. Multiple divergences are expected to be more reliable than single, and represent a prolonged period in which prices are rising at a slower and slower rate.

Alternating Divergence Peaks

A common pattern is that there is a lower momentum peak between two declining peaks. For example, the first momentum peak is at 90, the next at 60, and the last at 75. When studying the chart manually, most analysts will ignore the lower peak in the middle and consider the 90-75 divergence. This combination can be automated by looking at the most recent momentum peak, i, and the one back 2, $i - 2$, along with their corresponding prices.

Converting a Divergence into a Trend Trade

Divergence trades represent a clear chart pattern of slowing price direction. At the same time they are countertrend trades and have a higher degree of risk. Before the October 1987 stock plunge, there were numerous divergence signals in the S&P, both long-term and short-term, and many traders posted losses trying to sell what might have been the top of the market. Most gave up before the decline. If, in fact, the greatest opportunities come when the divergence is strong, that is, the decline in the momentum peaks is large, then the best results will come from entering a short position, then holding that short when a long trend turns to a short one. By entering the trend trade early (and exiting the old long position), a divergence can become a large profit rather than a small one.

MOMENTUM SMOOTHING

When Blau's work on double smoothing was discussed in the section "True Strength Index," it was still being compared with other momentum indicators. The most important part of his work, however, is in using price change as a substitute, or proxy, for prices themselves, then smoothing them to define the trend. A long-term moving average, applied to prices, produces a lag of one-half the period of the moving average; that is, a 200-day moving average has a lag of 100 days.

The same moving average technique applied to price change, or momentum, gives very different results because price changes, also called *first differences,* remove the underlying trend and make price movement more sensitive. Applying a long-term moving average to momentum is an excellent substitute for price, yet it oscillates around the average value of zero in a manner similar to other momentum indicators.

Double Smoothing of Momentum

Double smoothing of momentum is an extension of normal momentum smoothing, and results in a value that has less noise than the original momentum series, and retains its low-lag characteristics, provided that one of the smoothing periods is very large. Double smoothing of momentum can be a smooth substitute for price, without a significant lag (see Figure 6-12). The shape of Blau's True Strength Index (TSI), first smoothed over a 300-day period, then smoothed again over a 5-day period, closely approximates the result of a 5-day exponential smoothing (EMA). When applied using the same smoothing periods, this can be very useful for identifying divergence between two markets. In Figure 6-15 the trend of the TSI line is still up at the end of February 1994, making a new high in both

FIGURE 6-15 Double-smoothed momentum applied to the Dow Jones Average and Dow Jones Utilities, showing divergence.

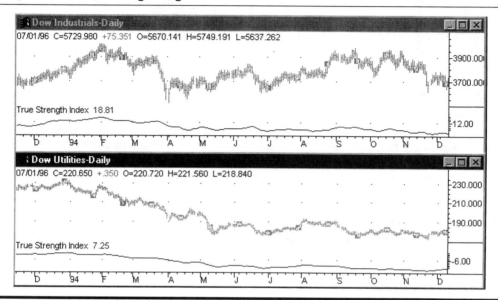

Source: Chart created with *TradeStation*® by Omega Research, Inc.

the prices and indicator, while the utilities are steadily heading lower. In December 1994 there is a turn up in the TSI for the utilities that will lead the DJIA throughout 1995.

$$TSI(close,300,5) =$$

$$\frac{100 \times @SmoothedAverage(@SmoothedAverage(close - close[1]),300),5)}{@SmoothedAverage(@SmoothedAverage(@abs(close - close[1]),300),5)}$$

When the 5-day momentum is replaced by a 1-day momentum, or the daily price changes, the second smoothing can be any length, and the result is a very effective substitute for a moving average of price with the significant added advantages of a detrended series, lower noise, and less lag. When plotted, the series fluctuates around the value zero unless there has been a strong trend during the full period, as in the stock index.

SOME FINAL COMMENTS ON MOMENTUM

Momentum and oscillators are not the only tools for determining overbought and oversold conditions. Because they can be very different from either a charting technique or moving averages, they have taken their place as timing indicators within other more structured systems. When the time interval for calculation is small, these indicators can be highly unstable, jumping from frequent overbought signals to just as frequent oversold ones. Both faster and slower speeds have the problem of risk control. The method implies that a position be entered contrary to the direction of price movement. Although chart interpretations attempt to remedy this, unusually large losses may result.

It is not likely that an indicator can be found that will identify only the trades that will be profitable. It is far more likely that an indicator will add more patterns to the already difficult combinations that are seen in price; therefore, it is not clear whether an indicator will simplify trading or make it more complex. If you need to interpret the indicator because each situation creates new decisions, then you've got the wrong one.

Indicators can be designed to reach extremes when a specific situation occurs. During other times it tells us nothing. One practical use of any oscillator is to show when a market is relatively overbought or oversold. If you are using a trending approach, and each trade is held about 20 days, an oscillator can be tuned to provide entry timing. For example, if you are willing to wait up to 2 days to enter a long position based on the daily close, then construct a 10-period oscillator of 5-, 10-, or 15-minute data. Test the oscillator to see if it generates at least one, but preferably two, oversold signals during each 2-day period. If so, use it to time your entry and you are likely to be buying dips rather than rallies.

7

Seasonality

Chapter 3 introduced prices as a time series and identified its four components as the trend, the seasonal pattern, the cycle, and the chance movement; it included various ways of finding the trend using statistical analysis and forecasting techniques. Chapter 4 then showed various ways to calculate trends. Of all techniques, the trend is overwhelmingly the most popular foundation for trading systems. In this and Chapter 8 we will turn our attention to two other principal components, the seasonal and cyclic movements.

Seasonality is a cycle that occurs yearly. It is most often associated with the planting and harvesting of crops, which can directly affect the feeding and marketing of livestock. Normally, prices are higher when a product is not as readily available, or when there is a greater demand relative to the supply, as often occurs with food during the winter months. For grain, the season is dominated by planting, harvesting, and weather-related events that occur in between. Most crops have been produced in the Northern Hemisphere, but South American soybeans and orange juice have become significant factors since the early 1980s, as have Australian and New Zealand beef and lamb, resulting in a structural change in seasonal patterns. Globalization has not only affected financial markets, but nearly everything we purchase.

Consumer habits can cause a seasonal pattern in metals and stocks as weather does for agricultural products. Passenger airline traffic is much heavier in the summer than in the winter, and profits of that industry, especially companies not diversified, reflect seasonality. Eastman Kodak once had a classic pattern caused by much more active picture taking during the summer months, when most workers take vacations. This seasonal activity also increased demand on silver, a major ingredient of film coating, which developed a co-dependent pattern before a substitute was found.

A CONSISTENT FACTOR

Even when the impact of seasonality on agricultural products is not clear from the price patterns, it is still there. Consider the following factors that do not change:

1. More corn, wheat, and soybeans are sold during harvest than at any other time of year because there is not enough available storage to hold all of the new crop. Rental storage, when available, requires a minimum three-month charge. Lack of storage and the need for immediate income result in greater sales and cause prices to decline.
2. Because feedgrains are harvested only once each year, forward contracts include a storage cost as part of the total carrying charge. Therefore, each forward delivery price should be higher within the same crop year.

Sometimes the price pattern of forward months does not seem to reflect the added costs of carry. Occasionally these markets will even invert and the nearest delivery will trade at a price higher than the deferred months, a situation familiar to crude oil and copper. The cost of carry, however, still exists in an inverted or *backwardation* market. Extreme short-term demand pushes the nearest delivery much higher, while the events causing price disruption are expected to be temporary. The normal carry is still there, it is just overwhelmed by temporary demand.

It is important to be able to identify seasonal patterns. The methods for finding them are simple, and made more so by the use of a spreadsheet and a computer. These will be discussed in this chapter along with some practical applications.

THE SEASONAL PATTERN

Seasonal patterns are easier to find than the longer-term cycles or economic trends, because they must repeat each calendar year. Although any 12-month period can be used to find the seasonal pattern, academic studies usually begin with the new crop year for grains, just following harvest, when prices tend to be lowest. This approach will make the carrying charges, which increase steadily throughout the new crop year, more apparent. For uniformity, the examples in this chapter will always begin with a calendar year, which assumes no knowledge of where the season starts, and can be equally applied to stocks. It will always include carrying charges as an integral part of the market price.

United States agricultural production is considered to be the standard for *seasonal,* even though a wheat crop is harvested continuously throughout the year in different parts of the world. Prices are expected to be lower during the U.S. harvest and highest during the middle of the growing season. The influence of world stocks and anticipated harvest from other major producers in South America or Russia will cause an overall dampening or inflating of prices, rather than change the seasonal pattern. While the costs of transporting grain to the United States is not practical, except for special products, each purchaser in the world market will select a supplier at the best price. This fungibility has a direct impact on the U.S. market, which must alter its local price based on export demand.

Industrial commodities have seasonal price variation based on demand. Silver, although increasingly used in electronics as a conductor, is also consumed for jewelry and photography, and has served as a general hedge against inflation. It still shows a seasonal pattern of greater demand during the summer months. Almost half of all copper is used in electrical and heat conductivity, with much of it in the form of an alloy with nickel and silver. Its seasonality is heavily related to the housing industry, where it is required for both electrical and water systems. New sources of ore are introduced infrequently, and the possibility of discovery or expansion is rarely seen in price movement as short-term anticipation. The primary supply problems in copper are related to labor as well as social and political changes in producing countries.

There are many businesses with finished products that have seasonal demand and their publicly traded stock prices will reflect that tendency. Because the shares in a company are far removed from buying and selling the raw materials that they use, even major oil companies, such as Exxon, may not show a seasonal pattern similar to crude oil or its refined products. As with Eastman Kodak, these firms have thoroughly diversified, and the impact of a $1.00 increase in a barrel of oil or a $.50 increase in an ounce of silver will have only a small effect on the profitability of the firm, and may be the cause of stock prices advancing or declining. Yet some industries, such as airlines, still show seasonal patterns, and the same procedures given here can be used to find them.

POPULAR METHODS FOR CALCULATING SEASONALITY

Seasonal patterns are most often calculated using monthly data, although some studies have tried to pinpoint their periodic turns to specific days. As with most other analysis, closer observation or shorter time periods also bring more noise and erratic results. With this in mind, the seasonal studies in this chapter will use monthly data and keep an eye toward the big picture.

There is one important caveat about the prices used in some of these examples: they were created using a computer program that averaged the prices of a TradeStation continuous contract. This contract is gap-adjusted to remove the price jumps in futures when delivery months change; therefore, in the earlier years prices may be higher or lower than they actually were at the time. In the case of soybeans you will see that the prices in the mid-1970s are about $2 per bushel higher. In some cases, such as interest rates, prices that are 25 years in the past can actually become negative because of gap adjusting. A precise seasonal analysis will need to use continuous cash prices, rather than a constructed series, to have valid percentages. Results of these examples, however, show seasonality similar to studies that use cash data. The following terminology and concepts will also be of help.

Basic Calculation Components

Average Prices

Finding the seasonal pattern does not need to be complicated; however, some basic rules must be followed to get sound results. For most analysts, it is easiest to begin with a spreadsheet, where the months are recorded in each column and the rows represent years (see Table 7-1). The average monthly price, placed in each cell, can give a good indication of seasonal patterns by simply averaging each column and plotting the results as shown in the first of four summary lines at the bottom. The major criticism of this technique is that it ignores the changing price levels over time. For example, a 25-year study of soybeans will use prices that vary from $6 to $15 per bushel; price changes at the $15 level could overwhelm other years.

Indexing the Data

A simple way to adjust for price differences over time is by indexing data, where each new entry is based on a percentage change from the previous value. This method will also work with seasonal studies, but must use unadjusted cash data. Because the monthly average prices for these examples were created from *TradeStation* continuous data, they cannot be used for this purpose.

Percentage Change

Over the many years needed for a seasonal study, prices may increase by a factor of two or three, and the magnitude of volatility at these different levels will vary significantly, distorting the results. To correct for the problems associated with a long-term increase or decline in price, a monthly percentage change can be substituted for the average price. The use of percentages adjusts for most of the volatility changes and, at the same time, removes any long-term trend bias. It is a simple and very credible method for finding seasonality, but its results can be more erratic than the sophisticated calculations found in the next section.

Detrending

Removing the trend using a moving average, then comparing the percentage differences between the price and the corresponding trend value, is a classic approach to evaluating seasonality.

Median Price

The median is the *middle price* of a series of values that have been sorted in numerical order. Instead of using an average monthly price, or the average of, for example, all June average prices, using the median value should improve results. The median ignores the extreme prices that occur during some unusual years and gives a typical price. For example, if the average September price of heating oil was 50 cents per gallon for four years, but reached $1.00 per gallon during one year, then the average would be 60 cents and the median would be 50 cents. Later in this chapter you might note that a large difference between the median and the average prices indicates that there were a few volatile years mixed with mostly normal patterns.

TABLE 7-1 A Simple Spreadsheet of Soybean Continuous Prices Used to Calculate Seasonality, January 1969–March 1994

Year	Jan	Feb	Mar	Apr	May	Jun	Jul	Aug	Sep	Oct	Nov	Dec
1969		864.25	861.49	862.19	863.01	858.69	858.80	860.54	861.87	867.16	868.03	864.93
1970	867.63	869.54	869.60	872.78	874.63	884.77	897.16	886.76	886.35	899.88	903.66	893.26
1971	898.53	897.55	893.45	880.20	886.94	904.42	921.19	914.26	906.00	910.26	902.01	901.48
1972	895.65	902.05	919.41	929.94	926.67	921.09	923.55	933.46	938.41	939.28	964.17	1,014.17
1973	1,041.85	1,160.47	1,207.83	1,237.30	1,479.24	1,742.11	1,614.95	1,625.46	1,447.32	1,386.66	1,366.76	1,400.54
1974	1,421.55	1,440.51	1,421.02	1,349.11	1,333.74	1,338.68	1,494.40	1,564.05	1,550.65	1,641.64	1,557.45	1,502.73
1975	1,397.31	1,316.00	1,296.59	1,309.60	1,259.08	1,257.19	1,309.94	1,362.02	1,322.94	1,274.00	1,223.55	1,200.99
1976	1,202.23	1,206.63	1,198.87	1,199.08	1,242.14	1,346.01	1,390.06	1,343.23	1,374.02	1,334.56	1,354.56	1,378.63
1977	1,405.80	1,429.39	1,530.15	1,674.19	1,654.75	1,528.26	1,338.09	1,282.88	1,276.89	1,281.76	1,341.63	1,339.57
1978	1,318.89	1,308.17	1,405.67	1,432.15	1,457.25	1,430.45	1,402.49	1,401.79	1,429.71	1,462.75	1,450.14	1,454.29
1979	1,455.56	1,507.17	1,512.11	1,487.64	1,468.67	1,512.75	1,490.85	1,444.92	1,443.93	1,402.70	1,385.35	1,372.22
1980	1,349.35	1,345.31	1,296.90	1,258.64	1,265.33	1,273.88	1,381.11	1,389.58	1,443.61	1,462.46	1,503.93	1,376.24
1981	1,331.45	1,295.86	1,274.55	1,303.43	1,265.01	1,215.83	1,217.81	1,166.05	1,128.24	1,120.83	1,099.49	1,073.70
1982	1,071.16	1,061.58	1,043.26	1,069.54	1,066.54	1,031.98	1,014.69	970.88	942.15	925.95	952.31	946.44
1983	962.06	966.88	966.84	997.69	975.11	946.78	1,001.16	1,180.75	1,219.30	1,161.25	1,126.77	1,087.83
1984	1,050.26	1,013.08	1,063.32	1,061.60	1,115.75	1,044.36	925.35	905.08	881.33	884.79	882.83	851.28
1985	839.61	828.53	827.95	832.40	801.97	802.49	783.00	749.13	749.08	741.63	734.20	744.80
1986	751.60	732.11	734.80	727.88	736.89	731.60	729.80	712.85	721.77	723.93	738.30	730.17
1987	730.95	721.58	724.00	746.27	786.56	790.14	760.89	745.75	765.98	779.60	801.36	827.67
1988	844.45	839.96	845.47	884.14	941.81	1,141.24	1,089.10	1,054.39	1,047.42	983.19	947.68	955.57
1989	944.82	908.12	921.08	878.15	871.92	865.17	853.74	803.79	799.35	784.18	793.12	784.49
1990	765.99	759.18	775.75	782.14	794.74	766.06	764.33	760.61	762.74	749.39	707.18	703.31
1991	676.36	676.92	677.86	678.95	657.93	647.31	618.11	645.13	657.74	623.35	612.85	607.04
1992	617.61	623.71	634.11	616.58	638.74	646.25	600.35	581.62	585.24	575.91	592.95	601.81
1993	604.95	595.58	606.53	614.75	623.34	624.38	723.39	690.78	656.85	633.55	678.65	697.77
1994	705.29	685.07	683.95									
Average (Avg)	1,006.04	998.28	1,007.41	1,027.45	1,039.51	1,050.08	1,044.17	1,039.03	1,031.96	1,022.03	1,019.54	1,012.44
Adj Avg (Nrm)	-1.83	-2.59	-1.70	0.26	1.43	2.46	1.89	1.39	0.70	-0.27	-0.52	-1.21
Median (Mdn)	944.82	905.085	920.245	929.94	941.81	946.78	925.35	933.46	938.41	925.95	947.68	946.44
Adj Median (NMdn)	1.18	-3.08	-1.45	-0.42	0.85	1.39	-0.91	-0.04	0.49	-0.84	1.48	1.35

Effects of a Few Volatile Years

All seasonal calculations can be distorted by a few very volatile years that show large percentage price changes, especially during a time when there is not normally a strong seasonal bias. For example, if heating oil prices were stable for four years, or tended slightly lower, then jump 100% in one unusual period, the result of an OPEC announcement coupled with low inventories, the average will show a seasonal increase of 20%. In fact, that is what happens in many markets in which one or two unrelated events cause a price change that can be interpreted as seasonal. In a computerized environment, the use of the median (discussed above) or more data can prevent mistakes; however, common sense will also show that a single odd year will erroneously distort the average.

Yearly Averages

The most basic way of measuring or describing seasonality is by the monthly variation from the yearly average or crop average (for agricultural products), usually calculated as a ratio or percentage. The results of this technique using the 1975 corn prices can be seen in Table 7-2. During this one year, the highest prices occur in January and August and the lowest at the end of the year after harvest, confirming what we might expect of the corn season, with the exception of the January high. The average price for 1975 was 2.92, and the extent of variation throughout the year ranges, coincidentally, 13.7% above and below the average. By applying this method to the 20 years of data for corn shown in Table 7-3, the percentage variation can be shown in the corresponding Table 7-4. For those who prefer using negative percentages to show when values are below the average, simply subtract 100 from each number.

The long-term seasonality, called the *seasonal adjustment factor*, is the monthly average of the percentages shown in Table 7-4 and appears at the bottom of Table 7-4 and in Figure 7-1. These values must be divided by 100 before they can be correctly used as percentages. In both cases, the analysis has been separated into the two periods, 1956–1970 and 1971–1975, to indicate the changing volatility and slight change in pattern. The shaded area in Figure 7-1 represents the range in the percentage variation for the 1956–1970 period, and the broken lines show the corresponding 1971–1975 results. Figure 7-1 shows that the traditional seasonality can also have sharp fluctuations, reduced to intervals of short duration. The more recent period reflects the traditional seasonal highs and lows, but shows that there is a considerable wide range of other possibilities. All methods of determining seasonality will be influenced by those years in which unusual, overwhelming factors caused prices to move counter to normal seasonal patterns. A later section will discuss the advantages of distinguishing seasonal and nonseasonal years.

TABLE 7-2   Percentage of Monthly Corn Prices to the Average

	Avg	Jan	Feb	Mar	Apr	May	Jun
Price*	2.70	3.07	2.86	2.67	2.68	2.66	2.68
Percent	100.0	113.7	105.9	98.9	99.2	98.5	99.2

	Jul	Aug	Sep	Oct	Nov	Dec
Price	2.72	2.95	2.76	2.62	2.33	2.37
Percent	100.7	109.2	102.2	97.0	86.3	87.8

*Midmonth U.S. farm price, 1975.

TABLE 7-3   Corn Cash Prices

Year	Avg	Jan	Feb	Mar	Apr	May	Jun	Jul	Aug	Sep	Oct	Nov	Dec
1956*	1.30	1.14	1.16	1.19	1.32	1.41	1.44	1.45	1.46	1.45	1.12	1.22	1.23
1957	1.25	1.22	1.16	1.18	1.18	1.20	1.20	1.21	1.22	1.13	1.04	.98	1.01
1958	1.10	.97	.98	1.04	1.18	1.20	1.23	1.23	1.24	1.15	1.02	.94	1.04
1959	1.09	1.05	1.06	1.08	1.17	1.18	1.19	1.17	1.17	1.09	.96	1.00	.99
1960	1.03	1.03	1.04	1.04	1.09	1.11	1.11	1.11	1.09	1.07	.97	.82	.92
1961	1.01	.99	1.03	1.04	.98	1.04	1.04	1.06	1.04	1.02	1.00	.91	.94
1962	.98	.94	.95	.96	.98	1.03	1.03	1.02	1.01	1.00	.94	.91	1.00
1963	1.11	1.03	1.05	1.06	1.09	1.12	1.19	1.21	1.21	1.23	1.04	1.02	1.20
1964	1.13	1.12	1.09	1.13	1.15	1.18	1.17	1.14	1.14	1.17	1.05	1.04	1.14
1965	1.18	1.16	1.17	1.19	1.22	1.25	1.26	1.24	1.20	1.18	1.10	1.04	1.13
1966†	1.25	1.19	1.20	1.17	1.19	1.21	1.20	1.27	1.34	1.35	1.29	1.26	1.29
1967	1.17	1.28	1.26	1.28	1.26	1.25	1.26	1.21	1.11	1.12	1.04	.97	1.03
1968	1.04	1.04	1.06	1.06	1.06	1.09	1.07	1.04	.99	1.01	.96	1.04	1.05
1969	1.12	1.08	1.09	1.09	1.12	1.19	1.18	1.08	1.18	1.15	1.12	1.07	1.09
1970	1.24	1.12	1.14	1.13	1.15	1.18	1.21	1.24	1.27	1.38	1.34	1.29	1.39
1971	1.27	1.42	1.43	1.43	1.41	1.38	1.43	1.36	1.19	1.11	1.00	.97	1.08
1972	1.17	1.09	1.09	1.10	1.13	1.15	1.13	1.14	1.15	1.22	1.19	1.20	1.42
1973	1.86	1.39	1.35	1.37	1.42	1.16	1.99	2.03	2.68	2.15	2.17	2.18	2.39
1974	2.92	2.59	2.76	2.68	2.41	2.45	2.57	2.91	3.37	3.30	3.45	3.32	3.27
1975	2.70	3.07	2.86	2.67	2.68	2.66	2.68	2.72	2.95	2.76	2.62	2.33	2.37
Average		1.30	1.30	1.29	1.31	1.32	1.38	1.39	1.45	1.40	1.32	1.28	1.34
1976		2.44	2.48	2.50									

*1956–1965 midmonth Illinois farm prices (U of I).
†1966–1975 midmonth U.S. farm prices (CRB Yearbook).

A general formula for the monthly average is:[1]

$$\text{APP}_i = 100 \left\{ \frac{1}{N} \left[12 \sum_{n=1}^{N} \left(P_{in} / \sum_{j=1}^{12} P_{jn} \right) \right] \right\}, \qquad i = 1, 12$$

where APP_i is the average percentage price in month i
  i is the calendar month from 1 to 12
  N is the number of years in the analysis
  P_{jn} is the average price for month j of year n

This formula may be applied to weekly or quarterly average prices by changing the 12 to 52 or 4, respectively.

The use of an annual average price can bias a clear seasonal pattern because of its inability to account for a long-term trend in the price of the commodity. If the rate of inflation in the United States is 6%, there will be a tendency for each month to be ½% higher, resulting in a trend toward higher prices at the end of the year. Longer trends, such as the steady rise in grain prices from 1972–1975, followed by a longer decline in the 1980s, will obscure or even distort the seasonality unless the trend is removed.

[1] David Handmaker, "Low-Frequency Filters for Seasonal Analysis," in *Handbook of Futures Markets*, Perry J. Kaufman (ed.) (John Wiley & Sons, New York, 1984).

TABLE 7-4   Corn Price as Percentage Average (Annual)

Year	Avg	Jan	Feb	Mar	Apr	May	Jun	Jul	Aug	Sep	Oct	Nov	Dec
1956	1.30	87.6	89.2	91.5	101.5	108.5	110.8	111.5	112.3	111.5	86.1	93.8	94.6
1957	1.25	97.6	92.8	94.4	94.4	96.0	96.0	96.8	97.6	86.9	86.9	75.4	80.8
1958	1.10	88.2	89.1	94.5	107.3	109.1	111.8	111.8	112.7	88.5	92.7	85.4	94.5
1959	1.09	96.3	97.2	99.1	107.3	108.2	109.2	107.3	107.3	100.0	88.1	91.7	90.1
1960	1.03	100.0	101.0	101.0	105.8	107.8	107.8	107.8	105.8	103.9	94.2	79.6	89.3
1961	1.01	98.0	102.0	103.0	97.0	103.0	103.0	104.9	103.0	101.0	99.0	90.1	93.1
1962	.98	95.9	96.9	97.9	100.0	105.1	105.1	104.1	103.1	102.0	95.9	92.8	102.0
1963	1.11	92.8	94.6	95.5	98.2	101.0	107.2	109.0	109.0	110.8	93.7	91.9	99.1
1964	1.13	99.1	96.5	100.0	101.8	104.4	103.5	100.9	100.9	103.5	92.9	92.0	100.9
1965	1.18	98.3	99.1	100.8	103.4	105.9	106.8	105.1	101.7	100.0	93.2	88.1	95.8
1966	1.25	95.2	96.0	93.6	95.2	96.8	96.0	101.6	107.2	108.0	103.2	100.8	103.2
1967	1.17	109.4	107.7	109.4	107.7	106.8	107.7	103.4	94.9	95.7	88.9	82.9	88.0
1968	1.04	100.0	101.9	101.9	101.9	104.8	102.9	100.0	95.2	97.1	92.3	100.0	101.0
1969	1.12	96.4	97.3	97.3	100.0	106.2	105.3	96.4	105.3	102.7	100.0	95.5	97.3
1970	1.24	90.3	91.9	91.1	92.7	95.2	97.6	100.0	102.4	111.3	108.1	104.0	112.1
1956–1970	Avg	96.3	96.9	98.1	100.9	103.9	104.7	104.0	103.9	101.5	94.3	90.9	96.1
1971	1.27	111.8	112.6	112.6	111.0	108.7	112.6	107.1	93.7	87.4	78.7	76.4	85.0
1972	1.17	93.2	93.2	94.0	96.6	98.3	96.6	97.4	98.3	104.3	101.7	102.6	121.4
1973	1.86	74.7	72.6	73.6	76.3	62.4	107.0	109.1	144.1	115.6	116.7	117.2	128.5
1974	2.92	88.7	94.5	91.8	82.5	83.9	88.0	99.6	115.4	113.0	118.1	113.7	112.0
1975	2.70	113.7	105.9	98.9	99.2	98.5	99.2	100.7	109.2	102.2	97.0	86.3	87.8
1971–1975	Avg	96.4	95.8	94.2	93.1	90.1	100.7	102.8	112.1	104.5	102.4	99.2	106.9

Removing the Trend

Jake Bernstein, most well known for his seasonal studies,[2] uses the method of first differences to remove the trend from prices before calculating the seasonal adjustment factor. He offers the following steps for determining the cash price seasonality:

1. Arrange the data used in a table with each row as one year. Columns can be daily, weekly, or monthly, although most analyses will use monthly. Average prices are preferred for each period (see Table 7-1).
2. Compute a second table of month-to-month differences by subtracting month 1 from month 2, month 2 from month 3, and so on. This new table contains detrended values.
3. Calculate the sum of the price differences in each column (month) in the new table. Find the average for that column by dividing the number of years of data (columns may have different numbers of entries). This is the average price change for that month.
4. From the table, count the times during each month (column) that prices were up, down, or unchanged. This will give the frequency (expressed as a percent) of movement in each direction.

Bernstein adds the average monthly changes together, expresses the frequency of upward price changes, and presents the results of corn in Figure 7-2.

[2] Jacob Bernstein, *Seasonal Concepts in Futures Trading* (John Wiley & Sons, New York, 1986).

FIGURE 7-1 Changes in volatility and variations in seasonal patterns for corn.

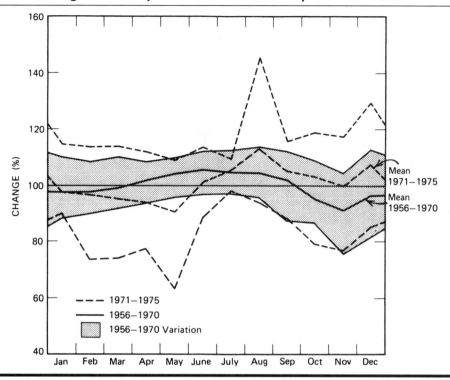

FIGURE 7-2 Seasonal price tendency in monthly cash average corn prices (1936–1983).

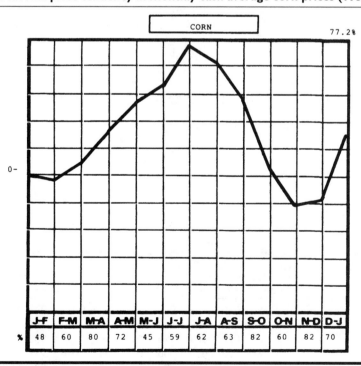

Source: Jacob Bernstein, *Seasonal Concepts in Futures Trading* (New York: John Wiley & Sons, 1986, p. 31). Reprinted with permission of John Wiley & Sons, Inc.

The Method of Link Relatives

Another interesting and important way of identifying the seasonal price variations and separating them from other price components involves the use of *link relatives*. In Table 7-5 each month during 1960 and 1961 is expressed as a percentage by taking the ratio of that average monthly price to the average price of the preceding month (found in Table 7-3) in a manner similar to an index.

After the initial calculation of 1960 and 1961 link relatives, it is necessary to find the average (or the median, which is preferred if an adequate sample is used) of the monthly ratios expressed in rows (1) and (2). The average in row (3) represents monthly variation as a percentage of change; each calculation is a function of the preceding month. Thus far, this is the same as Bernstein's average monthly price changes, expressed as a percent of the prior price.

To establish a fixed base in the manner of an index, *chain relatives* are constructed using January as 100; each monthly chain relative is calculated by multiplying its average link relative by the average link relative of the preceding month. The March chain relative is then $1.005 \times 1.025 = 1.030$, and February remains the same because it uses January as a base.

A constant trend throughout the test period can be found by multiplying the December chain relative (4) by the January average link relative. If prices show no tendency for either upward or downward movement, the result would be 1.00; however, inflation should cause an upward bias and, therefore, the results are expected to be higher. From line (4), the December entry multiplied by the January entry on line (3) gives $.946 \times 1.047 = .990$, leaving a negative factor of .1% unaccounted. This means that the 1960–1961 years showed a .1% downward bias; therefore, the expected rate of inflation was offset by some other economic factor, such as the accumulation of grain stocks by the U.S. government.

The chain relatives must be corrected by adding the negative bias back into the values, using the same technique as in computing compound interest. For example, from 1967–1977, the Consumer Price Index increased from 100 to 175, a total of 75% in 10 years. To calculate the annual compounded growth rate for that period, apply the formula:

$$\text{Compound rate of growth} = \sqrt[N]{\frac{\text{ending value}}{\text{starting value}}} - 1$$

where N is the number of years or the number of periods over which the growth is compounded.

$$R = \sqrt[10]{\frac{175}{100}} - 1$$

$$= 1.05755 - 1$$

$$= .05755$$

TABLE 7-5 Corn Prices Expressed as Link Relatives

	Jan	Feb	Mar	Apr	May	Jun	Jul	Aug	Sep	Oct	Nov	Dec
(1) 1960	1.040	1.010	1.000	1.048	1.018	1.000	1.000	.982	.982	.907	.845	1.122
(2) 1961	1.053	1.040	1.010	.942	1.061	1.000	1.019	.981	.981	.980	.910	1.031
(3) Average	1.047	1.025	1.005	.995	1.040	1.000	1.010	.982	.982	.944	.878	1.077
(4) Chain relatives	1.000	1.025	1.030	1.000	1.035	1.040	1.010	.992	.964	.927	.829	.946
(5) Corrected chain relatives	1.000	1.024	1.028	.997	1.032	1.036	1.005	.986	.958	.920	.822	.937
(6) Indices of seasonal variations	1.022	1.046	1.050	1.019	1.054	1058	1.027	1.007	.979	.940	.840	.957

This indicates a compounded rate of inflation equal to 5.75% per year. In the case of corn, if the trend had been positive, that is, greater than 1.00 instead of .990, the growth rate would be subtracted from each month to offset the upward bias. In this case, the results are added back into the chain relative to compensate for the negative influence. A .1% decline, compounded over 12 consecutive entries gives:

$$R = \sqrt[12]{\frac{.99}{1.00}} - 1$$

$$= .99916 - 1$$

$$= -.00084$$

This is a compounded deflation of about 8/100 of 1%. The corrected chain relative was found by multiplying the February entry by $(1 + R) = .99916$, March by $(1 + R)^2 = .99832$, and December by $(1 + R)^{11} = .99076$.

The chain relatives have been calculated on a base of January, which was important to correct the compounded bias throughout the test period. The final step is to switch the corrected chain relatives to a base of the average value. The average (.97875) of line (5) is used to create line (6), taking the ratio of the corrected chain relative entries to their average. The final result is the *Index of Seasonal Variation.* The accuracy of this result can be proved by averaging the entries of line (6), which will be 1.00. A complete study of seasonality using this method can be found in Courtney Smith, *Seasonal Charts For Futures Traders* (Wiley, 1987).

The Moving Average Method

The moving average is a much simpler, yet very good technique for determining seasonal patterns. Looking again at the cash corn prices in Table 7-3, take the average quarterly prices for the years 1960–1965 rounded to the nearest cent. More practical results may be obtained by repeating this procedure for monthly prices.

Because every four entries completes a season, a 4-quarter moving average is calculated and recorded in such a way that each value lags 2½ quarters, corresponding to the center of the 4 points used in the calculation. Column 2 of Table 7-6 shows the 4-quarter moving average positioned properly; Figure 7-3 is a plot of both the quarterly corn prices and the lagged moving average. By using the exact number of entries in the season, the moving average line is not affected by any seasonal pattern.

Because there was an even number of points in the moving average, each calculation falls between two original data points. Column 3 of Table 7-6 is constructed by averaging every two adjacent entries in column 2 and placing the results in a position corresponding to the original data points. This avoids smoothing the initial prices. The difference of column 1 minus column 3 is the seasonal adjustment factor (column 4) in cents per bushel; the *seasonal index* (column 5) is the ratio of column 1 divided by column 3. The periodic fluctuation of prices becomes obvious once these values have been recorded. A generalized seasonal adjustment factor and seasonal index are calculated by taking the average of the quarterly entries for the five complete years (Table 7-7).

X-11

The seasonal adjustment method X-11 (Census Method II-X-11) is most widely used for creating a seasonally adjusted series of such information as car and housing sales, as well as other consumer products. It is very extensive, involving both an initial estima-

TABLE 7-6 Seasonal Adjustment by the Moving Average Method

		Average Quarterly Price	4-Point Moving Average	Corresponding 4-Point Values	Seasonal Adjustment Factor	Seasonal Index
1960	Jan–Mar	104				
	Apr–Jun	110				
	Jul–Sep	109	103¼	103	+6	1.06
	Oct–Dec	90	102¾	101¾	−11¾	.88
1961	Jan–Mar	102	100¾	100⅛	+1⅞	1.02
	Apr–Jun	102	99½	100⅛	+1⅞	1.02
	Jul–Sep	104	100¾	99⅞	+4⅛	1.04
	Oct–Dec	95	99	98⅞	−3⅞	.96
1962	Jan–Mar	95	98¾	98⅜	−3⅜	.96
	Apr–Jun	101	98	98	+3	1.03
	Jul–Sep	101	98	99¼	+1¾	1.02
	Oct–Dec	95	100½	102	−7	.93
1963	Jan–Mar	105	103½	106⅛	−1⅛	.99
	Apr–Jun	113	108¾	110¾	+2¼	1.12
	Jul–Sep	122	112¼	113¼	+8¾	1.08
	Oct–Dec	109	113¾	114¼	−5¼	.95
1964	Jan–Mar	111	114¾	113⅞	−2⅞	.97
	Apr–Jun	117	113	113⅞	+4⅛	1.04
	Jul–Sep	115	112¾	112⅞	+1½	1.01
	Oct–Dec	108	114¼	113½	−7⅛	.94
1965	Jan–Mar	117	116	116¾	−¼	1.00
	Apr–Jun	124	117½	117⅝	+6⅜	1.05
	Jul–Sep	121				
	Oct–Dec	109				

TABLE 7-7 Average Seasonal Variation Using the Moving Average Method

Average of All Years	Seasonal Adjustment Factor	Seasonal Index
Jan–Mar	−1.15	.988
Apr–Jun	+3.53	1.052
Jul–Sep	+4.43	1.042
Oct–Dec	−7.00	.932

tion and reestimation. Because it is widely used by economists, an outline of its procedure follows.[3]

1. Calculate a centered 12-month moving average (MA). Subtract this MA from the original series to get an initial detrended seasonal series.

---

[3] A more detailed account of X-11 and Henderson's weighted moving average (step 9) can be found in Bovas Abraham and Johannes Ledolter, *Statistical Methods for Forecasting* (John Wiley & Sons, New York, pp. 178–191). Their book also includes a computer program for *seasonal exponential smoothing*.

FIGURE 7-3   Detrending corn using a moving average with a yearly period.

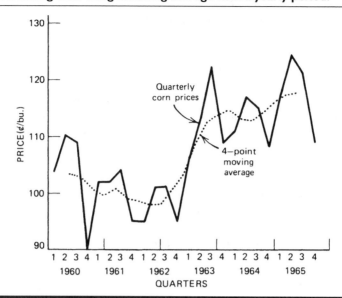

2. Apply a weighted 5-period MA to *each month separately* to get an estimate of the seasonal factors.
3. Compute a centered 12-month MA of the seasonal factors (step 2) for the entire series. Fill in the six missing values at either end by repeating the first and last available MA values. Adjust the seasonal factors from step 2 by subtracting the centered 12-term MA. The *adjusted seasonal factors* will total approximately zero over any 12-month period.
4. Subtract the seasonal factor estimates (step 3) from the initial detrended seasonal series (step 1). This is the *irregular component series* used for outlier adjustment.
5. Adjust the outliers in step 4 by the following procedure:

   a. Compute a 5-year moving standard deviation s of the irregular component series (step 4).

   b. Assign weights to the series components c_i as follows:

      0 if $c_i > 2.5s$

      linearly scaled from 0 to 1 if $2.5s \geq c_i \geq 1.5s$

      1 if $c_i < 1.5s$

   Use this weighting function to adjust the detrended series in step 1.
6. Apply a weighted 7-period MA to the adjusted series (step 5) to get the *preliminary seasonal factor.*
7. Repeat step 3 to standardize the seasonal factors.
8. Subtract the series resulting in step 7 from the original series to find the *preliminary seasonally adjusted series.*
9. To get the trend estimate, apply a 9-, 13-, or 23-period *Henderson's weighted moving average*[4] to the seasonally adjusted series (step 8). Subtract this series from the original data to find a second estimate of the detrended series.

[4] A specialized symmetric assignment of weighting values. A specific example can be found in Bovas Abraham and Johannes Ledolter, *Statistical Methods for Forecasting* (John Wiley & Sons, New York, p. 178).

10. Apply a weighted 7-period MA to each month separately to get a second estimate of the seasonal component.
11. Repeat step 3 to standardize the *seasonal factors.*
12. Subtract the final seasonal factors from the original series to get the final *seasonally adjusted series.*

Winter's Method

Another technique for forecasting prices with a seasonal component is *Winter's method,* a self-generating, heuristic approach.[5] It assumes that the only relevant characteristics of price movement are the trend and seasonal components, which are represented by the formula

$$X_t = (a + bt)S_t + e_t$$

where X_t is the estimated value at time t
          $(a + bt)$ is a straight line that represents the trend
          S_t is the seasonal weighting factor
          e_t is the error in the estimate at each point

If each season is represented by N data points, S_t repeats every N entries, and

$$\sum_{t=1}^{N} S_t = t$$

The unique feature of Winter's model is that each new observation is used to correct the previous components a, b, and S_t. Without that feature, it would have no applicability to commodity price forecasting. Starting with 2 or 3 years of price data, the yearly (seasonal) price average can be used to calculate both values a and b of the linear trend. Each subsequent year can be used to correct the equation $a + bt$ using any regression analysis. Winter's method actually uses a technique similar to exponential smoothing to estimate the next a and b components individually. The seasonal adjustment factors are assigned by calculating the average variance from the linear component, expressed as a ratio, at each point desired. As more observations are made, each component can be refined, and it will take on the form of the general long-term seasonal pattern.

A Comparison of Seasonality Using Different Methods

Heating oil and soybeans represent two fundamentally sound seasonal markets. Even before we analyze the patterns, we can expect heating oil to post higher prices during the winter months and soybeans to be high during the summer. Heating oil is accumulated beginning in midsummer in anticipation of the winter season, while soybeans are subject to speculative volatility during planting and growing seasons.

For the purposes of comparison, we will use four basic methods of calculating seasonality: average price, median price, percentage change from the previous month, and the moving average deseasonalizing. For our purposes, more complicated methods are unnecessary.

Figure 7-4*a* shows that the peak price for heating oil is most likely to come in October, well below the coldest months of the year. According to these techniques, it is the anticipation of winter that drives prices up, while February and March, typically colder, show lower average prices as most consumers use up the oil they had committed to buy during the previous September and October. Three of the methods for calculation gave similar results, while *%Change* seems to lead by one month.

---

[5] Winter's method, as well as other advanced models, can be found in Douglas C. Montgomery and Lynwood A. Johnson's *Forecasting and Time Series* (McGraw-Hill, New York, 1976), and Bovas Abraham and Johannes Ledolter's *Statistical Methods for Forecasting* (John Wiley & Sons, New York, 1983).

FIGURE 7-4 (*a*) **Heating oil seasonal patterns. Results are very uniform with %Change leading the other methods by one month. Peak prices come in October, during the time of greatest accumulation, with lower prices in February and March when consumers are normally depleting inventory.** (*b*) **Soybean seasonal patterns. The four basic calculations show soybean prices peaking in June and reaching lows in February. The use of the median gives results in July that are much lower than the average, and higher during the period November through January, indicating that there were unusually extreme moves during those months that distort the average.**

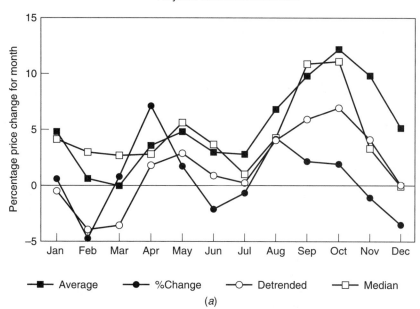

(*a*)

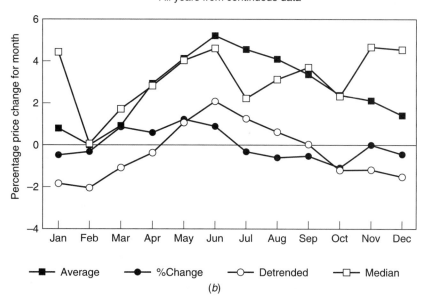

(*b*)

When applied to soybeans, all four basic seasonal calculations produce patterns that show the expected winter and summer cycles, with most lines rising and falling smoothly throughout the year (see Figure 7-4*b*). Again, it should be noted that the seasonal pattern of the percentage price changes leads the normal and detrended methods because it acts in the same way as momentum; a decline in the percentage change does not mean that current prices are lower than the previous month, but that prices did not increase by as much as the previous month.

Seasonal Volatility

Consistent seasonal patterns can be confirmed by a corresponding increase in volatility as the season reaches its peak as seen in Figure 7-5. In this soybean chart, the peak volatility in June, represented by one standard deviation of price equal to about 12%, shows that there is a 68% chance that soybeans will vary by 24% in June. For the purpose of confirming the validity of the seasonal results, the steady increase and decrease in volatility surrounding the peak month of June indicates a building of the seasonal concerns that cause wide fluctuations. If a single price shock had occurred, unrelated to seasonality, there would be a sharp increase in volatility during one month, perhaps declining afterward, but with no steady growth of volatility leading up to this event.

WEATHER SENSITIVITY

The effects of changes in weather, especially extremes in weather, are an inseparable part of seasonal effects. Without weather, the price of an agricultural commodity would lack the surprises that cause them to jump around during the growing period. Once planted, you would have a very good idea of the expected supply; one-half of the supply-demand equation would be constant each year.

Each agricultural product has its own particular sensitivity to weather. Grain planting can be delayed due to rain, causing some farmers to switch from corn to soybeans; hot weather during pollination will significantly reduce yields; a freeze in September can stop the ripening

FIGURE 7-5   Soybean monthly price variation.

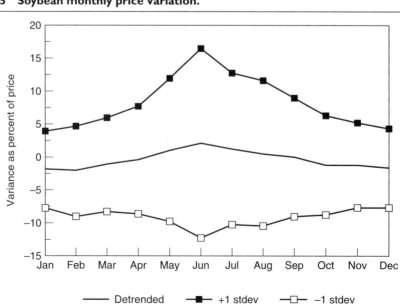

process and damage production. Freezes are of greater concern than droughts and affect more products. In general, patterns for crop sensitivity to weather depend upon their location in the Northern or Southern Hemisphere. Active trade between world markets shows that crops grown primarily in the Northern Hemisphere are affected by weather developments in the Southern Hemisphere. In Table 7-8 major weather events are shown separated into Southern and Northern Hemisphere. Figure 7-6 combines the soybean and corn weather sensitivity charts[6] to show the effects of both Southern and Northern Hemisphere weather.

Measuring Weather Sensitivity

While a weather sensitivity chart, such as shown in Figure 7-6, may appear to have a strong similarity to a standard seasonal chart, they are actually very different. Weather sensitivity is a measurement of potential price volatility. It could simply be the highest price that the market reached during a period in which the weather event occurred. Those more adept at statistics would want to record the increase in price from the average during those months in which weather was a factor, then show the price representing the 95% confidence level.

A thorough approach to measuring weather sensitivity is to record the temperature each day and find out whether it is unusually far above or below the average. Information available from the U.S. weather or meteorological service will give you both regional weather and measurements of effective heat. It is the cumulative effect of heat that is damaging to a crop, rather than a high temperature for one day. In addition, the amount of crop damage is not simply a linear relationship with rising temperatures; rather, it is more likely to start slowly and increase quickly once critical levels of time and heat are reached.

[6] Jon Davis, *Weather Sensitivity in the Markets* (Smith Barney, October 1994).

TABLE 7-8   Weather-Related Events in the Southern and Northern Hemispheres

	Southern Hemisphere	Northern Hemisphere
January		OJ peak for Florida freeze
		Heating oil cold or hot
February	Corn pollination in S. Africa and Argentina	Heating oil cold or hot
	Soybean pod development	
March		
April		Cotton planting
May		Soybean planting
June		Cotton boll development
July	Coffee freeze Brazil	Sugar: heat in Russia
	OJ freeze Brazil	Corn pollination
	Cocoa pod development in W. Africa and pod rot in Brazil	
August		Soybean pod development
September		Atlantic hurricanes affect sugar, orange juice, heating oil
		Corn freeze
October		Soybean freeze
		Cotton harvest
November	Coffee in Brazil rainy season	Soybean harvest
		Corn harvest
December		Heating oil cold or hot

FIGURE 7-6   Weather sensitivity for soybeans and corn.

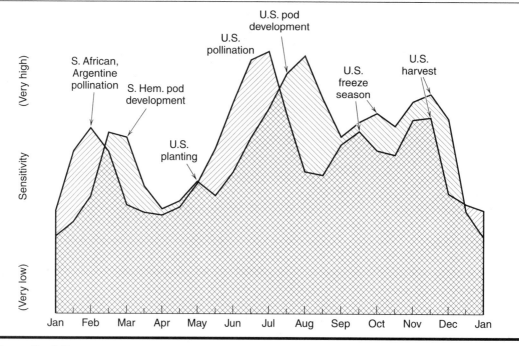

Source: Smith Barney.

SEASONAL FILTERS

Seasonal filters identify periods during the year in which you would favor either a long or short position in a market based upon a clear seasonal component. These periods are normally chosen from the results of a calculation that uses detrended data; however, where there is a large difference between the median value and the average value, we should expect the median value to be more representative of expected price movement. The large difference between the median and average also tells us to expect extreme prices and high volatility during those months. This can be seen in Table 7-9, showing monthly soybean prices as a percentage of the annual average price. The double-digit values in 1973, 1977, and 1988 are enough to cause the averages at the beginning of the year to be lower than the median, and June, July, and August to be higher than the median. This bias is mainly the result of only 3 of 24 years.

Using the examples of heating oil and soybeans, which have been discussed in the previous section, we can select the months with the largest and most reliable seasonal price moves as the best choice for seasonal filters. We can also separate the year into upward and downward cycles to allow for a wider range of trades. The following periods could be considered for heating oil and soybeans:

	Best Choice (Partial Year)	Full-Year Seasonal Patterns
Heating oil	Long from August 1 to November 1 Short from November 1 to March 1	Long from April 1 to October 1 Short from November 1 to March 1
Soybeans	Long from March 1 to July 1 Short from July 1 to November 1	Long from March 1 to July 1 Short from July 1 to March 1

TABLE 7-9 Monthly Soybean Prices as a Percentage Difference from the Average Annual Price, February 1969–December 1993

Year	Jan	Feb	Mar	Apr	May	Jun	Jul	Aug	Sep	Oct	Nov	Dec
69		0.17	−0.15	−0.07	0.02	−0.48	−0.47	−0.26	−0.11	0.50	0.60	0.25
70	−1.83	−1.62	−1.61	−1.25	−1.04	0.11	1.51	0.33	0.28	1.82	2.24	1.07
71	−0.31	−0.42	−0.88	−2.35	−1.60	0.34	2.20	1.43	0.52	0.99	0.07	0.01
72	−4.10	−3.42	−1.56	−0.43	−0.78	−1.38	−1.12	−0.06	0.47	0.57	3.23	8.58
73	−25.18	−16.67	−13.26	−11.15	6.23	25.10	15.97	16.73	3.93	−0.42	−1.85	0.57
74	−3.16	−1.87	−3.20	−8.10	−9.14	−8.81	1.80	6.55	5.63	11.83	6.10	2.37
75	7.98	1.69	0.19	1.20	−2.71	−2.85	1.22	5.25	2.23	−1.55	−5.45	−7.20
76	−7.34	−7.00	−7.60	−7.58	−4.26	3.74	7.14	3.53	5.90	2.86	4.36	6.26
77	−1.25	0.41	7.48	17.60	16.24	7.35	−6.01	−9.89	−10.31	−9.96	−5.76	−5.90
78	−6.65	−7.41	−0.51	1.37	3.15	1.25	−0.73	−0.78	1.20	3.53	2.64	2.94
79	−0.10	3.44	3.78	2.10	0.80	3.83	2.32	−0.83	−0.90	−3.73	−4.92	−5.82
80	−0.94	−1.24	−4.79	−7.60	−7.11	−6.48	1.39	2.01	5.98	7.36	10.40	1.03
81	10.25	7.30	5.54	7.93	4.75	0.67	0.84	−3.45	−6.58	−7.19	−8.96	−11.09
82	6.26	5.31	3.49	6.10	5.80	2.37	0.66	−3.69	−6.54	−8.14	−5.53	−6.11
83	−8.32	−7.86	−7.86	−4.92	−7.08	−9.78	−4.59	12.52	16.19	10.66	7.38	3.67
84	7.91	4.09	9.25	9.08	14.64	7.31	−4.92	−7.00	−9.44	−9.09	−9.29	−12.53
85	6.79	5.38	5.31	5.87	2.00	2.07	−0.41	−4.72	−4.73	−5.67	−6.62	−5.27
86	2.82	0.16	0.52	−0.42	0.81	0.09	−0.16	−2.48	−1.26	−0.96	1.00	−0.11
87	−4.46	−5.68	−5.37	−2.46	2.81	3.28	−0.55	−2.52	0.12	1.90	4.74	8.18
88	−12.45	−12.92	−12.34	−8.34	−2.36	18.32	12.91	9.32	8.59	1.93	−1.75	−0.93
89	11.07	6.75	8.28	3.23	2.50	1.71	0.36	−5.51	−6.03	−7.82	−6.76	−7.78
90	1.10	0.21	2.39	3.24	4.90	1.11	0.89	0.39	0.68	−1.09	−6.66	−7.17
91	4.33	4.42	4.56	4.73	1.49	−0.15	−4.66	−0.49	1.46	−3.85	−5.47	−6.36
92	1.32	2.32	4.03	1.15	4.78	6.02	−1.51	−4.59	−3.99	−5.52	−2.73	−1.27
93	−6.34	−7.79	−6.09	−4.82	−3.49	−3.33	12.00	6.95	1.70	−1.91	5.07	8.03
Avg	−0.94	−1.29	−0.42	0.16	1.25	2.06	1.44	0.75	0.20	−0.92	−0.96	−1.38
Mdn	−0.63	0.16	−0.15	−0.07	0.81	1.11	0.66	−0.26	0.47	−0.96	−1.75	−0.11

One practical note is needed here. Although there may appear to be a statistical benefit to selling heating oil in the later part of winter, there is also extreme risk. Prices jumped 40% from March to April 1982, and 20% during the same period in 1983. We must also consider that the Gulf War, which pushed prices higher from August 1990, conformed by chance to the seasonal pattern; in reality, it could have happened any time during the year. These special situations do not always cause prices to rise. In 1986, Saudi Arabia decided to dump oil in a politically motivated effort to drive prices down, successfully pushing crude oil under $10 per barrel.

Years with Similar Characteristics

Seasonal studies often yield results that are not as clear as desirable, and these results may be rejected because of the obvious lack of consistency. Often, this is caused by a few years that conflict with the normal seasonal patterns due to special events. David Handmaker shows that separating the data into analogous years can give strikingly better results.[7]

[7] David Handmaker, "Low-Frequency Filters in Seasonal Analysis," *Journal of Futures Markets*, Vol. 1, No. 3 (John Wiley & Sons, New York, 1981).

For example, crop production is primarily determined by weather. Poor weather will cause sharp rallies during the growing season, whereas good weather results in a dull, sideways market. Bad weather develops slowly. A drought is not caused by the first hot day but prolonged days of sunshine and no rain. Similarly, delayed planting due to wet fields or a late winter will set the stage for an underdeveloped crop. A trader can see the characteristics of a *weather market* in time to act on it.

In Figure 7-7a, the seasonal corn pattern has been separated into those years with good weather and those with bad weather. In a later study by ContiCommodity,[8] soybean seasonality was separated into *bull* and *bear* years (Figure 7-7b). Bull years include all bad weather years but also years with such incidents as the 1973 Soviet grain sale. Because other events are not confined to the growing months, they may distort rather than clarify the patterns. Bear would represent mostly good weather patterns; however, markets that decline steadily during the year following a bull market would also be included.

During the bad weather years, the corn chart shows a prolonged rise during the primary growing months, May through August. The study of bull years for soybeans shows a longer sustained rise from the beginning of the new crop in October into the following June. In the case of good weather and bear markets, corn shows a rise from May to June, some sideways hesitation from June to July (possibly the last anticipation of bad weather), then a return to previous price levels. For bear years soybeans have steady declines through April and then a short rally through the summer.

The corn analysis shows a critical point around July 1, when the market decides that the weather is not a factor. The soybean analysis is completely different showing nearly the opposite patterns for bull and bear markets. Because the resulting pattern of combining both bull and bear markets looks very similar to the bull pattern, the magnitude of the bull moves must overwhelm the overall picture. In fact, the magnitude of the bull moves are often three to four times greater than the price change in bear markets.

Updating Bull, Bear, and Nonseasonal Market Patterns

Both the Handmaker and ContiCommodity studies ended in the early 1980s and while grain fundamentals have essentially remained the same, the use of more data and recent years can only help understand seasonality better. Using the soybean average prices expressed as a percentage of average annual price in Table 7-9, we separated the years from 1969 to 1993 into bull and bear categories, where bull years (and bear years) had significantly higher (or lower) prices at the end of the year than at the beginning. Table 7-10, parts (a) and (b), which also give the prices as a percent of the average annual price, show that there were about the same number of years in each category. The averages at the bottom of those tables indicate that both bull and bear years had a price swing of about 10% over the year.

Bull and bear years are nearly opposite in pattern, as seen in Figure 7-8, and cross at about the same price in June. This makes the seasonal pattern using all years peak in June. As interesting as it is to know that there are an equal number of years going the opposite directions within a seasonal pattern, the bull and bear tables were created after the fact and can not be traded unless you know in advance that a bull or bear year will occur. Instead, it is possible to look at *nonseasonal* years, those in which the price of soybeans was higher during the harvest months of September and October than during the previous summer months.

One important quality of crops is that each year we begin again; a shortage one year does not mean a shortage the next year. This is seen in the chart of nonseasonal years in Figure 7-8. After a nonseasonal year, prices rally early, nervous about planting and shortages,

---

[8] ContiCommodity, *Seasonality in Agricultural Futures Markets* (ContiCommodity Services, Chicago, 1983).

FIGURE 7-7 (*a*) Corn price seasonality separated into all years, years with good weather, and years with bad weather. (*b*) Soybeans (10 years) shown with separate bull years (5 years) and bear years (5 years).

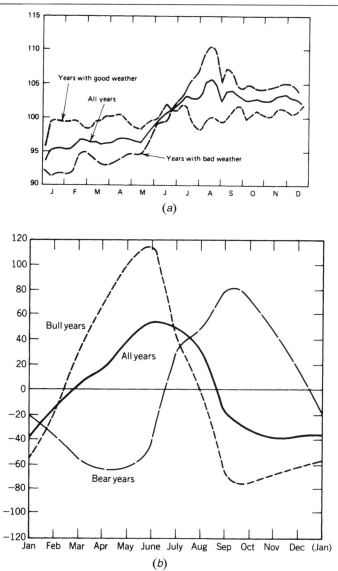

but the reality of a good crop and normal demand drive prices steadily lower during the second half of the year. The pattern is typically seasonal and very well defined by large swings.

Seasonality for Trading

Whatever method is used to find the seasonal pattern, it is equally important to apply it properly when trading. Select a market that has a dominant seasonal pattern. The crops always qualify, with the exception of potatoes, which are fully stored and do not react to the harvest depression. Livestock tends to be more complex than other commodities

TABLE 7-10   Bull, Bear, and Nonseasonal Market Patterns

(a) Bull years begin at relatively low levels, peak during the summer but remain high at the end of the year. (b) Bear years decline steadily after April and do not reflect the concerns that often drive prices higher during the summer. (c) Nonseasonal years follow years in which the harvest months of September–October posted higher prices than the summer months. These years revert back to what we expect of normal seasonal patterns.

(a) Soybean Bullish Years (Prices Higher at the End of the Year)

Year	Jan	Feb	Mar	Apr	May	Jun	Jul	Aug	Sep	Oct	Nov	Dec
70	−1.83	−1.62	−1.61	−1.25	−1.04	0.11	1.51	0.33	0.28	1.82	2.24	1.07
72	−4.10	−3.42	−1.56	−0.43	−0.78	−1.38	−1.12	−0.06	0.47	0.57	3.23	8.58
73	−25.18	−16.67	−13.26	−11.15	6.23	25.10	15.97	16.73	3.93	−0.42	−1.85	0.57
74	−3.16	−1.87	−3.20	−8.10	−9.14	−8.81	1.80	6.55	5.63	11.83	6.10	2.37
76	−7.34	−7.00	−7.60	−7.58	−4.26	3.74	7.14	3.53	5.90	2.86	4.36	6.26
78	−6.65	−7.41	−0.51	1.37	3.15	1.25	−0.73	−0.78	1.20	3.53	2.64	2.94
80	−0.94	−1.24	−4.79	−7.60	−7.11	−6.48	1.39	2.01	5.98	7.36	10.40	1.03
83	−8.32	−7.86	−7.86	−4.92	−7.08	−9.78	−4.59	12.52	16.19	10.66	7.38	3.67
87	−4.46	−5.68	−5.37	−2.46	2.81	3.28	−0.55	−2.52	0.12	1.90	4.74	8.18
88	−12.45	−12.92	−12.34	−8.34	−2.36	18.32	12.91	9.32	8.59	1.93	−1.75	−0.93
93	−6.34	−7.79	−6.09	−4.82	−3.49	−3.33	12.00	6.95	1.70	−1.91	5.07	8.03
Average	−7.34	−6.68	−5.84	−5.03	−2.10	2.00	4.16	4.96	4.55	3.65	3.87	3.80

(b) Soybean Bearish Years (Prices Lower at the End of the Year)

Year	Jan	Feb	Mar	Apr	May	Jun	Jul	Aug	Sep	Oct	Nov	Dec
75	7.98	1.69	0.19	1.20	−2.71	−2.85	1.22	5.25	2.23	−1.55	−5.45	−7.20
77	−1.25	0.41	7.48	17.60	16.24	7.35	−6.01	−9.89	−10.31	−9.96	−5.76	−5.90
79	−0.10	3.44	3.78	2.10	0.80	3.83	2.32	−0.83	−0.90	−3.73	−4.92	−5.82
81	10.25	7.30	5.54	7.93	4.75	0.67	0.84	−3.45	−6.58	−7.19	−8.96	−11.09
82	6.26	5.31	3.49	6.10	5.80	2.37	0.66	−3.69	−6.54	−8.14	−5.53	−6.11
84	7.91	4.09	9.25	9.08	14.64	7.31	−4.92	−7.00	−9.44	−9.09	−9.29	−12.53
85	6.79	5.38	5.31	5.87	2.00	2.07	−0.41	−4.72	−4.73	−5.67	−6.62	−5.27
86	2.82	0.16	0.52	−0.42	0.81	0.09	−0.16	−2.48	−1.26	−0.96	1.00	−0.11
89	11.07	6.75	8.28	3.23	2.50	1.71	0.36	−5.51	−6.03	−7.82	−6.76	−7.78
90	1.10	0.21	2.39	3.24	4.90	1.11	0.89	0.39	0.68	−1.09	−6.66	−7.17
91	4.33	4.42	4.56	4.73	1.49	−0.15	−4.66	−0.49	1.46	−3.85	−5.47	−6.36
92	1.32	2.32	4.03	1.15	4.78	6.02	−1.51	−4.59	−3.99	−5.52	−2.73	−1.27
Average	4.87	3.46	4.57	5.15	4.67	2.46	−0.95	−3.08	−3.78	−5.38	−5.59	−6.38

(c) Soybean Nonseasonal (Prices Higher during the Previous September-October than Summer)

Year	Jan	Feb	Mar	Apr	May	Jun	Jul	Aug	Sep	Oct	Nov	Dec
71	−0.31	−0.42	−0.88	−2.35	−1.60	0.34	2.20	1.43	0.52	0.99	0.07	0.01
73	−25.18	−16.67	−13.26	−11.15	6.23	25.10	15.97	16.73	3.93	−0.42	−1.85	0.57
75	7.98	1.69	0.19	1.20	−2.71	−2.85	1.22	5.25	2.23	−1.55	−5.45	−7.20
77	−1.25	0.41	7.48	17.60	16.24	7.35	−6.01	−9.89	−10.31	−9.96	−5.76	−5.90
79	−0.10	3.44	3.78	2.10	0.80	3.83	2.32	−0.83	−0.90	−3.73	−4.92	−5.82
81	10.25	7.30	5.54	7.93	4.75	0.67	0.84	−3.45	−6.58	−7.19	−8.96	−11.09
84	7.91	4.09	9.25	9.08	14.64	7.31	−4.92	−7.00	−9.44	−9.09	−9.29	−12.53
Average	−0.10	−0.02	1.73	3.49	5.48	5.96	1.66	0.32	−2.94	−4.42	−5.17	−5.99

FIGURE 7-8   Soybean seasonality, a comparison of filtered years.

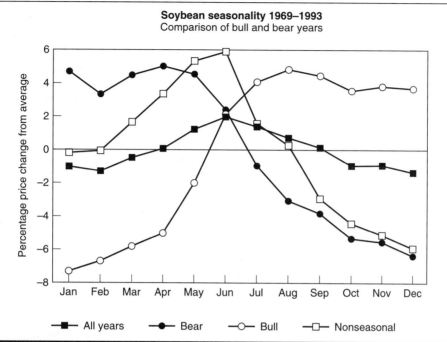

Soybean seasonality 1969–1993
Comparison of bull and bear years

because of the joint dependency on both feedgrain prices as well as their own production and consumption factors. Both crops and livestock have primarily supply-oriented seasonal trends, depressed at harvest and highest during the growing months—or depressed in the fall when the livestock supply becomes greatest due to liquidation before winter. Metals patterns are caused by demand, because they have no dependence on weather and production is usually constant. The summer months still see the highest prices due to increased consumption—copper in housing and silver in photography.

Select a delivery month most likely to reflect the pattern to be traded. If a sharp rise in soybeans is expected in July, trade the August contract. Prices of the November delivery, which will also be active, will not move as much because it is both deferred and a new crop. In more extreme cases, February pork bellies do not reflect events occurring in the previous July or August contracts.

Exceptions occur in seasonal patterns as they do in any model. There are events that may overwhelm normal seasonality such as runaway interest rates or inflation, rapid change in the U.S. dollar, or Soviet grain embargoes. Even though the seasonal variation still exists, the size of the price change resulting from these other factors is much greater and tends to obscure the seasonality. It is usually easy to recognize a nonseasonal pattern—prices simply go steadily up when they normally go down, or down when they are expected to go up. From 1972–1974, corn prices increased steadily with only small adjustments in September and October. Once this variation occurs, it may be wise to wait until another season has reestablished the normal pattern.

The systems and methods that follow are based entirely on seasonal patterns and may be used alone or to filter other methods.

Seasonal Studies and Key Dates

Most agricultural commodities exhibit traditional, reliable price moves at one or more periods throughout the year. The grains grown in the Northern Hemisphere have a high likelihood of a rally during the late spring and early summer, when the chance of drought will have the greatest effect on yield. When prices show the normal harvest lows, followed by a modest rise and sideways pattern throughout the winter, the potential is good for a rally during the early growing season. Because prices start at relatively low levels, the risk of holding a long position is small. Once prices have moved higher, there is rarely a season in which a short sale of corn, soybeans, cotton, or sugar will not net a good profit within the two months before harvest begins.

Seasonal studies are intended to provide information on when the largest move will occur. The following studies—(1) Grushcow and Smith (1980), (2) ContiCommodity (1983), and (3) Bernstein (1986)—will be used to compare the seasonality in some of the more active commodities. A summary of the results is shown in Table 7-11. Each study offers a different perspective on seasonality. Grushcow and Smith analyze both cash and individual futures markets over a fairly long period and present complete statistics; ContiCommodity used mostly the past 10 years, but included a unique volatility analysis; Bernstein, the most recently published study (*Seasonal Concepts in Futures Trading*), gave the most complete background on calculations, including separate studies of bullish and bearish years and an exceptionally long time period for cash market analysis.

The number of years in the seasonal analysis counts heavily in determining the normal patterns. As Table 7-11 shows, the ContiCommodity results, based on a maximum of 10 years, is often quite different from the other two studies. For trading safety, it would be best to select those patterns that have proved reliable over many years; however, because inconsistency in the past 10 years cannot be ignored, a trader must be able to identify nonseasonal, bullish, or bearish patterns.

The periods that seem consistent throughout all studies are:

Corn and soybeans. September and October show major harvest pressure.

Cattle. An end-of-the-year liquidation and midwinter rally.

Coffee and juice. No common moves in the three studies.

Some commodities are clearly more seasonally consistent than others. Both the coffee and orange juice markets were expected to show patterns that reflect a rise as the possibilities of a freeze increase. It must be that the normal seasonality of these products is distorted by the inconsistent and highly volatile periods that follow a freeze. These markets would be candidates for an *analogous years* study in which you compare only those years with common factors.

The three studies shown here, as well as most others, include recommended trades based on key dates, which reflect the patterns in Table 7-10a. By selecting those trades common to all of them, you have found those that are most reliable. In a summary by Bernstein, which catalogues commodities by those months with the highest reliability, the agricultural products are clearly the most seasonal. The only nonagricultural market that shows any consistent seasonality is copper. Although there may be interesting arguments for the forces of demand on silver, currencies, and financial markets, their inconsistency is apparent and they are not candidates for seasonal trading.

Seasonal Calendar

Because Bernstein's work covers the cash markets over an extremely long period, it must be considered the most reliable source of basic seasonal patterns. Table 7-12 is part of the

TABLE 7-11   Results of Seasonal Studies

	J-F	F-M	M-A	A-M	M-J	J-J	J-A	A-S	S-O	O-N	N-D	D-J
						Corn						
24 years*	.5	−1.1	1.6	3.6	3.4	.5	1.5	−5.3	−8.5	−1.3	.5	2.1
10 years†	2.2	−1.3	−2.3	−1.2	2.3	7.7	4.5	1.4	−7.5	−1.3	−6.4	1.8
46 years‡	−.6	2.0	3.0	2.9	2.3	3.8	−1.5	−3.2	−6.7	−3.7	5.4	1.5
%*	58	58	67	92	50	46	50	54	88	63	83	71
%‡	52	60	80	72	45	59	62	63	82	60	82	70
						Soybeans						
24 years*	7.4	7.5	8.4	9.5	6.4	−.7	−1.3	−25.8	−7.5	4.2	5.8	.3
10 years†	−2.3	21.1	23.7	12.6	20.0	14.7	−11.7	−14.9	−46.7	−9.8	−8.9	2.1
42 years‡§	3	11	8	8	3	−1	−5	−20	−8	10	3	2
%*	67	50	67	50	42	38	58	83	63	75	67	79
%‡	62	53	57	51	42	37	64	74	64	76	72	70
						Cattle						
25 years*	−.4	.1	.6	.1	−.1	.4	.4	−.3	−.4	−.5	−.1	.4
10 years†	1.4	.2	.8	1.8	.4	−1.2	−.4	−.7	−1.3	−.5	−.3	−.2
50 years‡§	1	12	13	4	−1	7	3	4	−9	−9	−2	2
%*	64	60	48	44	56	60	56	44	76	64	52	72
%‡	52	70	59	52	52	59	55	42	60	71	51	62
						Orange Juice						
10 years*	−1.6	−.1	−.3	−.9	−.9	−.3	.1	−.2	1.2	−2.3	−.3	1.7
10 years†	−1.9	2.4	−1.1	−.7	.0	1.6	1.8	2.3	.2	.0	.0	−4.7
34 years‡	27	14	4	−3	−8	−1	1	3	−2	−2	−13	−4
%*	78	45	67	56	45	45	56	67	45	45	56	56
%‡	61	64	50	58	50	65	66	81	61	40	67	62
						Coffee						
22 years*	−.2	.9	−.5	−.4	.1	.1	−.7	−.3	.1	.3	−.5	.1
8 years†	−6.5	1.8	7.6	5.0	−.3	3.3	−11.5	−2.0	4.3	−8.6	4.7	2.2
53 years‡§	0	−10	2	−4	1	4	18	2	19	−10	−4	−2
%*	41	64	50	50	59	46	46	55	41	64	50	77
%‡	56	58	43	53	50	48	56	56	51	59	54	49

*Grushcow and Smith (change in price).
†ContiCommodity (% change in seasonal factor).
‡Bernstein (% change in seasonal factor).
§Approximate values.
% refers to the reliability of monthly seasonality.

weekly seasonal calendar, which appears in *Seasonal Concepts in Futures Trading*. The numbers that appear show those weeks with consistent historic moves. Weeks of 64% and higher represent upward moves; weeks of 36% and lower display downward trends. This calendar can be extremely useful when combined with some simple trading logic which asks, "Is the market acting in a seasonal manner?" before the position is entered.

TABLE 7-12 Seasonal Calendar

	Mar Corn	May Corn	Jul Corn	Sep Corn	Dec Corn	Mar Wheat	May Wheat	Jul Wheat	Sep Wheat	Dec Wheat	Mar Oats	May Oats	Jul Oats	Sep Oats	Dec Oats	Jan Soybeans	Mar Soybeans	May Soybeans
1 Jan				76			29				66	66					29	
2												66		66				
3	66							22	23	37							66	
4						27				33	37						37	
5 Feb					31		35	37	31									66
6		27			64					75	66							
7	35										31	37	33					
8	35	29				22	27				27						70	
9 Mar	66						35		31	25		23	37	37			35	
10								27	37	31								
11				72		35	35		23	29								
12																		37
13 Apr			66	66			72		79		76	64	81					78
14		77										66	64					70
15							37		33									35
16							33							25	37			26
17			27					22			22							
18 May							37		29	18	83							76
19	35										82	76						
20	70				66		33											
21						37	33										66	
22 Jun				37					31	29				37		64	35	
23	33		33	35		76			35	28			37	37				
24	76		76		33				64	82							70	
25	33		27	36					37	29						76		64
26 Jul	66		70	66	63									64				
27			66						64					29	26			
28		35						64						35		13		23
29	22	22			21									31		25	17	29
30		27		23	36		27											
31 Aug				35	33													
32												70		66				
33												66		66				
34							83		64			64		66	66	37		
35 Sep				35			72		70	64		66		37				
36									64									66
37			31								70					29		29
38	29				31										35		33	
39																		
40 Oct											64				64	76		64
41						66		72		64						25		35
42				63								66						
43						27	33				70							
44 Nov			27		66	37	33		26			72				31	33	
45										35					79	64		
46																29	33	35
47			64						64									
48 Dec							29		35						66	64		
49	18		35								33					66		
50												35				29	66	25
51												64			35	35	27	37
52							66											

TABLE 7-12 *(Continued)*

Jul Soybeans	Aug Soybeans	Sep Soybeans	Nov Soybeans	Jan Soybean Meal	Mar Soybean Meal	May Soybean Meal	Jul Soybean Meal	Sep Soybean Meal	Dec Soybean Meal	Mar Soybean Oil	May Soybean Oil	Jul Soybean Oil	Sep Soybean Oil	Dec Soybean Oil	Feb Live Cattle	Apr Live Cattle	Jun Live Cattle	Aug Live Cattle	Oct Live Cattle
37							33			35									
64	64									66						64			
								29			77	66						64	
	37				33				66	66					66			66	
	64	70	28				37	37	70	64	62				64		76		
			37												66				75
64	64												66		76			64	
								35		33								37	
	35				66	35	23	23	35							77	76	66	
			66		64		70			70	66							66	66
							37	35							66	70			
37											33							37	
	64					70	70				72					72	76	71	
64		63					70		66						64	66	76		
		25							37								64	75	66
23						29	17			33			66						
		36					29	29		70			64					66	
75											27						64		33
70	64	66				64				70			70						66
							64	75	27			33					70	75	66
23	33	37	66		66	31	31				27	33	22		64			64	
64									76			33	66	66					
37			64	81	66		66	66	70	33			66	66					33
	70		72								72							66	
75		66				64			66	70		72		72	66	77		73	
		63			66	29	64								33				
33	25	15	33	20	35		29	25		29									
		28					35	35					64						
							35	35										66	
			37					37											
							70	75		33									
	37				37			29	35	27	64		29	10					37
64	35					64				64					64	66	35		70
29		66				29		76	66	27				37					
										37				66		37			
64		36	72												35	33			
35		73	66			36		76	64					72					
		35								23						27		31	
								64							33		35		
64		77	66		70										70	72	13	64	
	76	75	64												64	70	75		
			66							16					66	70	76		
	37							35		37	29	66		27				66	
		66					66		72	66	33								
									70					33					
33	29		35	31						66	29				66		66		
37	35	31								11	27	22			64			66	

TABLE 7-12 *(Continued)*

	Dec Live Cattle	Mar Feeder Cattle	Apr Feeder Cattle	Sep Feeder Cattle	Oct Feeder Cattle	Nov Feeder Cattle	Feb Live Hogs	Apr Live Hogs	Jun Live Hogs	Jul Live Hogs	Aug Live Hogs	Oct Live Hogs	Dec Live Hogs	Feb Pork Bellies	Mar Pork Bellies	May Pork Bellies	Jul Pork Bellies	Aug Pork Bellies	Mar Cocoa	May Cocoa	Jul Cocoa	Dec Cocoa
1 Jan									66					64		37						
2							70	77			76			70	66						33	
3			66						66	80	76				66	64	64		35			
4									73	64						66	62					
5 Feb		70							64	66				64	81							
6	66						64								37				64			
7																	35		35	33		
8		20		36				35	66									66		66		
9 Mar	80	80	70	63				66									70		75		66	
10				63	70																	
11				35					33										64	35	27	27
12	37			63								73					66				68	
13 Apr									66		70	64						79				
14	72		90	80	63	90		77	78	87		71				33	31				38	
15			80	81	72	66						33				66	78				66	
16				81													23	23			22	38
17											64	64										
18 May				30	33	30					66	73										
19				27							80					27			37	29	27	
20				70						29	31						35			64	66	
21				63	81	80											17	35				33
22 Jun						77					35	26	27	35			35	23				
23	33			36		30				31					37				37			33
24	70			36						70				70			70				66	
25			72	63							64	66					70			76	77	
26 Jul	66			72	66						35				66		75					72
27				36	80								64						64	77	66	72
28				36	27												66				77	64
29											35					37						
30				27																		
31 Aug				36								66					64		64	66		
32				72	63						76	66	72						64	36		
33				36								70		76	66			64	64	33		
34				63		30							37	38					64	83		
35 Sep	70			63		80							73	66		70	66	81	70			77
36				63	72	70								66						33		66
37						70											37					
38						30																
39	27																			33		
40 Oct	33					70						31		29		33	29	23		29	33	
41													27		31					29	33	
42	35				36															37	70	
43	22													66	33		75				72	64
44 Nov							82	83	71			72		64	66	72		66	70	29		
45	70											77			70		80		25	33	33	
46		70					84					77										27
47																						
48 Dec							64								35		35		64	66		72
49	33		66										66									
50													76	76		37	66	64				
51									64					73			77	76				
52																						

TABLE 7-12 *(Continued)*

Jan Orange Juice	May Orange Juice	Sep Orange Juice	Nov Orange Juice	Mar Sugar	May Sugar	Jul Sugar	Oct Sugar	Mar Coffee	May Coffee	Jul Coffee	Sep Coffee	Dec Coffee	Mar Cotton	May Cotton	Jul Cotton	Oct Cotton	Dec Cotton	Jan Lumber	Mar Lumber	May Lumber	Jul Lumber	Sep Lumber	Nov Lumber
31	35	29								63				75	87	86			66				
	35					77	70	63		66						75		66		28			
37								27	18	27						64			30	69			
	35			35						66	75				35	33					69	64	
						35		63		63	72	81							71	69	69	66	
						70			66	91	75	63							15		64	63	
	35									72		33	70	35	37	18	37						76
	35	29	33	62	72	35		36	25		66		64	64	70	68			21	7	28	72	28
								70	66		72								30	35	16		
25	31		64	29	37	36	36	36	33		33				37	35	31					33	
26	29	12	16		27	37	36	80	75		83	72			35				35	69			30
				22							66	33			70	75			15			25	35
31	64		70							75	36	36										36	7
31	37	37					36			66	66	66	72	66								33	
75						33	37				63	63										70	
75	64	76	76					63	66	75		27			29	26							
																	30						
	77					33	36	72		72	80			75		68			27	30	7	25	23
						35		72		66	63			76	70			35	33	35			
68	35							36		75	72	72			70	66			23			25	
68										66		36	35		37	31	35	69			28	83	14
33		64					64						29			29					78	33	83
35		33	33					36	36		33				70	37		66					35
35											33	36	27	70		75	69					75	64
66	35	27				29		36			33												
						35							36	64									
73		66									36				68		37	30					35
	64										29		70			35	72	15		35			28
	64							36	63		66			76					?			66	71
								36						64									
	70							63			66	80											28
37								72			66	63	37			37							71
73		66						66	27			36	64	64		37						66	
73	82	66				76		36	75			36						66					
	70	66								72	66	36		35	35				30				69
								36			63	33	63	35	35	37			25	7		25	28
75						27	37	36		63	66	63	23	37	29	12			35	23			28
												63					23						
81	82		64	11		35		36	33			81							33				28
			64													81	66	75					
	76			72	66	70	68	36			63	27	70		68	68			76				
75	64		66	72	64	75		66		75	83				37							69	28
80		72						90	66	75	83	63	64	64				66	66	71	76	71	
									63	63													71
			70		72	70		63		63	66		35	35	35	37		35	84	69	69		64
					66	64						63			64	66				64			
						64		72	75	75	66	63			35	37							
						64	70	72		66		63							33			30	
					66	33				72	83	83	75	63	64	35				69	76	85	83
26	18			33		35						63									76		66

COMMON SENSE AND SEASONALITY

Nonseasonal Markets

Most comprehensive works on seasonality include not only agricultural markets but currencies, interest rates, and indices. Common sense tells us that the primary feedgrains follow a clear seasonal pattern based upon a single crop year. This calendar cycle also applies to coffee, cocoa, and oranges, although competition from South America has limited the extreme moves that resulted from a freeze in Florida's orange groves. Grain seasonality has been slowly changing as well, as Brazil improves their production of soybeans. Cattle and hog prices, dependent upon the cost of feed, and still marketed more actively in the fall because of weather, show a strong seasonal trend even though they have a growth and feeding cycle that is not confined to a calendar year. Livestock patterns have adjusted to long-term competition from Australia and New Zealand.

These agricultural markets are reasonable candidates for seasonal analysis, but may require careful study to identify shifting patterns in competition and storage. What about Treasury bonds or the Japanese yen? Should we look for seasonal patterns in the financial markets? While we can argue that certain stocks are highly dependent upon seasonal business, can we say that the demand on money is higher in the summer than in the winter, or that enough tourists convert their currencies to yen when they visit Japan during the summer that this effect drives the value of the yen consistently higher? Are automobile exports from Japan stronger or weaker during a certain season, so that there is a predictable pattern? These scenarios are highly unlikely and have no assurance, such as the coming of winter, that cars must be sold the way grain must be harvested. In financial markets the players can choose their time to act; they can hedge their commitments or wait for a better opportunity. This choice makes any pattern that might exist uncertain. The study of seasonality should be limited to those markets that depend on weather and seasons, either directly or indirectly.

Being Too Specific about Targets

Nature is not precise and selecting an optimal day of the year to set a long position is not likely to work. Small shifts in fundamentals, such as the building of additional storage, will allow farmers to change their selling habits slightly. The right day to buy or sell in 1975 is not likely to be the right day this year. Even weekly data may be a little too specific. Seasonal patterns are best seen using monthly data. The most we might expect is to know that the seasonal high in corn usually occurs in July but sometimes in June or August; the harvest lows are likely in September but could be in October or November. We must first be aware of the big picture, then study how the specific pattern develops each year.

Recognizing Nonseasonal Years and External Factors

The studies of bull and bear market years shown in this book should make it clear that seasonality is not at all consistent. It is only a few years that cause prices to show extreme highs during the summer, while there are years in which the patterns are influenced by external factors and do not show normal seasonality. Seasonality, although a clear concept and a fact of nature, is not a trivial analysis when applied to trading. Each year must be observed and categorized, then a reasonable trading plan must be defined for that situation.

8

Cycle Analysis

The cycle is another basic element of price movement, along with the trend and seasonality, but it is more difficult to evaluate; therefore, it is often overlooked. Cycles
come in many forms—seasonality, production start-up and shutdown, inventory or
stocks, behavioral, and astronomical. Seasonality is a special case of a calendar or annual
cycle. Seasonality was covered in the previous chapter and its special features are not considered here. Some of the cycles are clearly *periodic,* having regular intervals between
peaks and valleys; others are more uniform in their *amplitude* or height but irregular in
period. The most definitive and regular cycle remains the seasonal, which is determined by
periodic physical phenomena.

This chapter will discuss the major commodity cycles that result from business decisions, government programs, long-term market characteristics, and phenomena. Short-term
cycles are usually attributed to behavior and will be covered in a later chapter on pattern
recognition. There are a few important ways to find the cycle, the most common being
trigonometric curve fitting and *Fourier (spectral) analysis.* Both will require a computer
and will be explained in the following sections. Examples of solutions will be included in
the explanation of the methods and applications will follow. Computer programs that solve
the trigonometric problems can be found in Appendix 4 along with additional examples.

CYCLE BASICS

Even when the seasonal pattern is eliminated, most cycles are still based on the periodic
effects in our solar system. After the 1-year orbit of our planet around the sun, there is the
28-day lunar cycle; converted to business days, this gives the very familiar 20-day reference,
which remains overwhelmingly popular among all analysts. Other planetary effects, which
should by no means be discarded offhand, can be found in Chapter 14 under the topic
"Financial Astrology." Throughout this chapter, there should be the undercurrent that planetary motion may account for the consistency of any cycle that repeats with a fixed period.

Cycles can be complex and difficult to see because there are often larger and smaller
patterns, and cycles within cycles, all acting at the same time. Nevertheless, they exist and
they are real. The cycles that appear to be most important are either long-term or the sum
of a number of subcycles that come together at peaks or bottoms. This gives us a way to
identify one point on a cycle; we must remember that, when the individual components
are found, there may be a number of smaller patterns that cause this effect. A reference to
harmonics, just as in music, means that a smaller cycle is a fraction of the larger (for example, its cycle length is ½, ⅓, ¼, . . . of the larger). When two cycles are synchronized, their
peaks or valleys occur at the same time. Any price series can be decomposed into individual cycles, although there may be many cycles needed.

Observing the Cycle

Before selecting a market for cycle analysis, it is necessary to observe that a dominant cycle
exists; it is also useful to know why it exists to avoid uncovering spurious patterns. This is

most easily done for markets in which you can clearly identify the fundamental and/or industrial reasons for cycles. The basis for a cycle could be a pattern of holding inventory, the fixed time needed for breeding and feeding of livestock, seasonality, or other economic factors. Figure 8-1 shows a clear 9- to 11-month cycle in live cattle futures prices[1] over a past 6-year period. The peaks and valleys vary by up to 1 month, making the pattern reliable for use as part of a long-term trading strategy.

The Swiss franc cycle demonstrated in Figure 8-2 is quite different.[2] It ranges from 24 to 35 weeks with a 40% variance compared with 20% for cattle. Most important, the cycle in the Swiss franc cannot be related to any specific fundamental reason. Given enough variance, a repeating pattern can be found in any data. To rationally trade a cyclic pattern, there must be a reason for its existence and the confidence that it should continue.

A simple way to begin the search for major cycles is to look at a long-term chart, displayed as weekly rather than daily prices. The dominant half-cycle can be found by locating the obvious price peaks and valleys, then averaging the distance between them. A convenient tool for estimating the cycle length is the Ehrlich Cycle Finder.[3] It is an expanding device with evenly spaced points, allowing you to align the peaks and valleys to observe the consistency in the cycle. For finding a single pattern, it is just as good as some of the mathematical methods that follow. It is best to have at least eight cycle repetitions before concluding that you have a valid cycle.

Cycles can be obscured by other price patterns. A strong trend, such as the one in Swiss francs (Figure 8-2) or the seasonal movement of crops, may overwhelm a less pronounced cycle. Proper cycle identification requires that these factors first be removed by detrending and by deseasonalizing. The resulting data will then be analyzed and the trend and seasonal factors added back once the cycle has been found. To find a subcycle, the primary cycle should be removed and a second cycle analysis performed on the data. The methods that follow (trigonometric regression and spectral analysis) locate the dominant cycles at one time using integrated processes.

The Kondratieff Wave

Much of the popularity of cycles is due to the publicity of Nicolai Kondratieff's 54-year cycle, known as the *K-wave*. During its documented span from about 1780 to the present, it appears to be very regular, moving from highs to lows and back again. In Figure 8-3 the Kondratieff wave is shown with the Wholesale Price Index as a measure of economic health.[4] With only three full cycles completed, it is difficult to tell if the overall trend is moving upward or whether the entire pattern is just a coincidence.

The forecast of the K-wave, shown in Figure 8-3, indicates a sharp decline in wholesale prices due at about the year 1990, the millenium's equivalent to the depression of the 1930s. In fact, the early 1990s have posted remarkable gains in the stock market, and at the end of the 1990s there is talk of *disinflation* from the U.S. Federal Reserve; this may serve as some support for a continued cycle. Although interesting, a cycle of this length is impractical other than to point out that the peaks and valleys could vary by as much as 10% from the predicted values without diminishing the validity of the theory. For the Kondratieff wave, a shift of 10%, as seen in the 1930s, would cause a trading signal to buy 5 years too soon or too late. Determining cycles for any market has the same problem—the actual

[1] Jacob Bernstein, "Cyclic and Seasonal Price Tendencies in Meat and Livestock Markets," in *Trading Tactics: A Livestock Futures Anthology*, Todd Lofton (ed.) (Chicago Mercantile Exchange, Chicago, 1986).

[2] Jacob Bernstein, *The Handbook of Commodity Cycles* (John Wiley & Sons, New York, 1982).

[3] Ehrlich Cycle Finder Company, 2220 Noyes Street, Evanston, IL 60201.

[4] Jeff Walker, "What K-wave?," *Technical Analysis of Stocks & Commodities* (July 1990).

FIGURE 8-1 Nine- to 11-month cycle in live cattle futures prices.

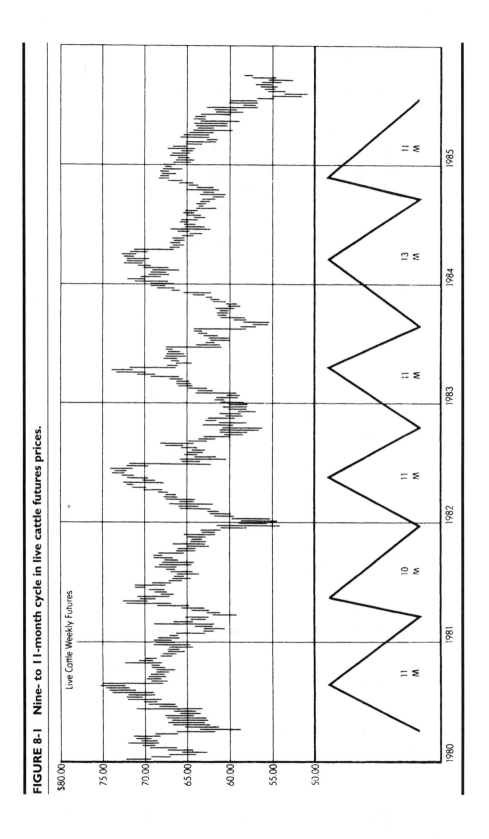

FIGURE 8-2   Cycles in Swiss franc futures.

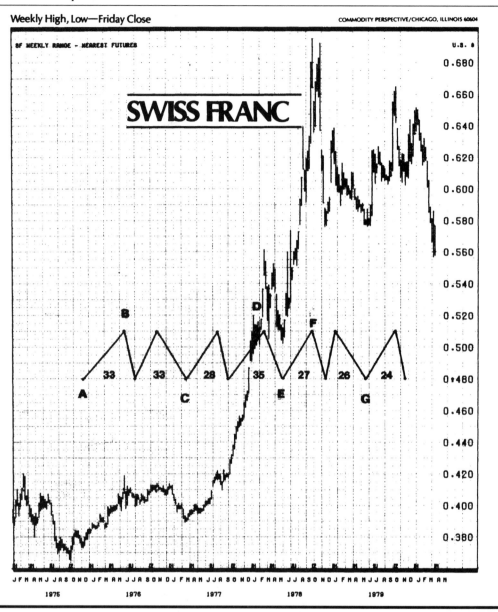

Weekly High, Low—Friday Close

Source: J. Bernstein, *The Handbook of Commodity Cycles* (New York: John Wiley & Sons, 1982).

price pattern will never correspond exactly to the predicted peaks and valleys, which, because they are a mathematical *cycle,* must come at regular intervals.

Terminology

Before getting very technical about the measurement and calculation of cycles, there are a few terms that describe most of the concepts discussed throughout this chapter. Note that the use of *wave* and *cycle* is interchangeable.

FIGURE 8-3   The Kondratieff Wave.

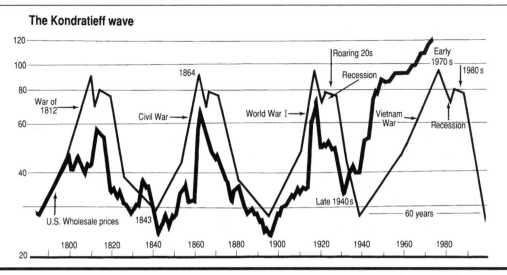

Source: Jeff Walker, "What K-wave?" *Technical Analysis of Stocks & Commodities,* 8, no. 7 (July 1989). © 1989 Technical Analysis, Inc. Used with permission.

Amplitude—the height of the wave (cycle)

Period—the time needed to finish one wave (one cycle)

Frequency—(for the more mathematical) the number of cycles that repeat every 360°

Phase—a measurement of the separation of tops or bottoms of two waves with the same period

Left and right translation—the tendency for a cycle peak to fall to the left or right of the center of the cycle

UNCOVERING THE CYCLE

Before resorting to the highly mathematical methods for finding cycles, there are some simple approaches that may serve many traders. For example, if you believe that there is a dominant 20-day cycle, then you simply create a new price series by subtracting the current data from a 20-day moving average. This removes the trend that may obscure the cycle. Most oscillators, such as a stochastic or RSI, also serve to identify a price cycle.

Enhancing the Cycle by Removing the Trend

The cycle can become more obvious by removing the price trend. The use of two trend-lines seems to work very well in most cases.[5] First, smooth the data using two exponential moving averages, in which the longer average is half the period of the dominant cycle (using your best guess), and the shorter one is half the period of the other. Then create an

---

[5] In his article, "Finding Cycles in Time Series Data" (*Technical Analysis of Stocks & Commodities* (August 1990)), A. Bruce Johnson credits John Ehlers for his work in the use of two exponential trends. See John Ehlers, "Moving Averages, Part 1" and "Moving Averages, Part 2," *Technical Analysis of Stocks & Commodities* (1988).

MACD index by subtracting the value of one exponential trend from the other; the resulting *synthetic* series avoids the lag inherent in most methods.

A technique that enhances the cycle is the use of triangular weighting instead of exponential smoothing. This method creates a set of weighting factors that are smallest at the ends and peak in the middle of the weighted average. For example, if you wanted a 10-period triangular average, the peak weighting factor would always be 2.0 and is assigned to the price just before the middle (there is no middle value for an even number of periods; therefore, the first value is eliminated), then weighting factors would begin and increase by $2.0/(P/2)$, where $P = 10$. This creates the series of weighting factors, beginning at $t - P + 2$ (to get a center value you need to have an odd number of entries), .4, .8, 1.2, 1.6, 2.0, 1.6, 1.2, .8, .4. Once the weighting factors, w, are known, the sum of the weighting factors is P (the same as the period), and the triangular average is

$$\text{TMA}_t = (W_1 \times P_{t-P+2} + W_2 \times P_{t-P+3} + \cdots + W_{P-1} \times P_t)/P$$

When applying a triangular average, each of the two averages used (one of which is half the period of the other) get triangular weights and the difference is taken. The smooth curve of the triangular MACD in Figure 8-4 shows what appears to be a regular cyclic pattern in the price of IBM.

Trigonometric Price Analysis

Most cycles can be found using the trigonometric functions sine and cosine. These functions are also called *periodic waves,* because they repeat every 360° or 2 radians (where π = 3.141592). Because radians can be converted to degrees using the relationship

$$1 \text{ degree} = \frac{2\pi}{360}$$

all work that follows will be in degrees. Some other necessary terms are:

Amplitude (a)—the height of the wave from the center (x = axis)

Frequency (ω)—the number of wavelengths that repeat every 360°, calculated as $\omega = 1/T$

Period (T)—the number of time units necessary to complete one wavelength (cycle)

A simple sine wave fluctuates back and forth from +1 to −1 (0, +1, 0, −1, 0) for each cycle (one wavelength) as the degrees increase from 0° to 360° (see Figure 8-5). To relate the wavelength to a specific distance in boxes (on graph paper), simply divide 360° by the number of boxes in a full wavelength, resulting in the box size (in degrees). For example, a 100-box cycle would give a value of 3.6° to each box. The wavelength can be changed to other than 360° by using the frequency as a multiplier of the angle of the sine wave

$$\sin \omega\phi$$

If $\omega > 1$, the frequency increases and the wavelength shortens to less than 360°; if $\omega <$ 1, the frequency decreases and the wavelength increases. Because ω is the frequency, it gives the number of wavelengths in each 360° cycle. To change the *phase* of the wave (the starting point), the value b is added to the angle

$$\sin (\omega\phi + b)$$

If b is 180°, the sine wave will start in the second half of the cycle; b serves to shift the wave to the left. The *amplitude* can be changed by multiplying the resulting value by a con-

FIGURE 8-4 A triangular MACD shows an apparent cycle in IBM.

Johnson indicator on IBM 2/1/88-3/30/90, IBM 2/1/88-3/30/90

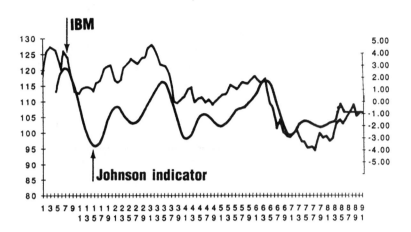

Triangular MACD vs. MADL

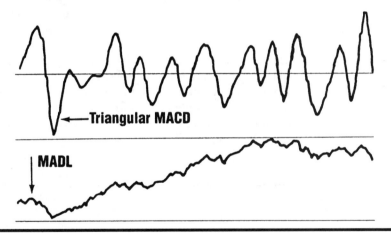

Source: A. Bruce Johnson, "Finding cycles in time series data," *Technical Analysis of Stocks & Commodities,* 8, no. 8 (August 1990). © 1990 Technical Analysis, Inc. Used with permission.

stant *a*. Because the sine ranges from +1 to −1, the new range will be +*a* to −*a* (Figure 8-6). This is written $a\sin(\omega\phi + b)$.

There are few examples of price movement that can be represented by a single wave; thus, two sine waves must be added together to form a *compound wave:*

$$y = a_1 \sin(\omega_1\phi + b_1) + a_2 \sin(\omega_2\phi + b_2)$$

Each set of characteristic variables, a_1, ω_1, b_1, and a_2, ω_2, b_2, can be different, but both waves are measured at the same point ϕ at the same time. Consider an example that lets the phase constants b_1 and b_2 be zero:

FIGURE 8-5   Sinusoidal wave.

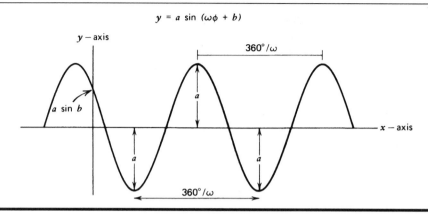

$$y = a \sin (\omega\phi + b)$$

$y_1 = 3 \sin 4\phi$

$y_2 = 5 \sin 6\phi$

$y = y_1 + y_2$

Figure 8-6 shows the individual regular waves y_1 and y_2, and the compound wave y over the interval 0° to 180°. Note that both y_1 and y_2 began the normal upward cycle at 0°; but by 180°, they are perfectly out-of-phase. During the next 180°, the two waves come back into phase.

When combining periodic waves, it is useful to know the maximum and minimum amplitude of the resulting wave. Because the peaks of the two elementary waves do not necessarily fall at the same point, the maximum amplitude of either wave may not be reached. A mathematical technique, called *differentiation*, is used to find the maximum and minimum amplitudes. The first derivative, with respect to angle ϕ, is written $dy/d\phi$ or y', where y is the formula to be differentiated. The rules are:

FIGURE 8-6   Compound sine wave.

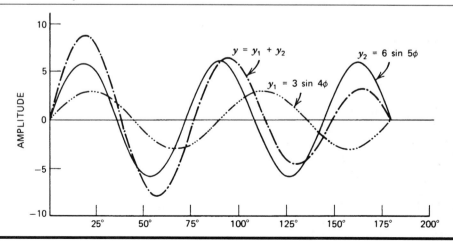

$$\frac{d}{d\phi} (\sin \phi) = \cos \phi; \qquad \frac{d}{d\phi} (\cos \phi) = -\sin \phi$$

$$\frac{d}{d\phi} (\sin \omega\phi) = \omega \cos \omega\phi$$

$$\frac{d}{d\phi} (\sin (\omega\phi + b)) = \omega \cos (\omega\phi + b)$$

$$\frac{d}{d\phi} (a_1 \sin (\omega_1\phi + b_1) + a_2 \sin (\omega_2\phi + b_2))$$

$$= a_1\omega_1 \cos (\omega_1\phi + b_1) + a_2\omega_2 \cos (\omega_2\phi + b_2)$$

Applying this method to the previous example,

$$y = 3 \sin 4\phi + 6 \sin 5\phi$$

$$\frac{dy}{d\phi} = y' = 12 \cos 4\phi + 30 \cos 5\phi$$

The points of maximum and/or minimum value occur when $y' = 0$. For $y_1' = 12 \cos 4\phi$, the maxima and minima occur when $4\phi = 90°$ and $270°$ ($\phi = 22\frac{1}{2}°$ and $67\frac{1}{2}°$) (Figure 8-6). For $y_2' = 30 \cos 5\phi$, the maximum and minimum values occur at $5\phi = 90°$ and $270°$ ($\phi = 18°$ and $54°$). It must be pointed out that the first derivative identifies the location of the extreme highs and lows, but does not tell which one is the maximum and which is the minimum. The second derivative, y'', calculated by taking the derivative of y', is used for this purpose as follows:

If $y'(x) = 0$ and $y''(x) > 0$, then $y(x)$ is a minimum.

If $y'(x) = 0$ and $y''(x) < 0$, then $y(x)$ is a maximum.

Then, $y_1 = 22\frac{1}{2}°$ and $y_2 = 18°$ are maxima and $y_1 = 67\frac{1}{2}°$ and $y_2 = 54°$ are minima.

Anyone interested in pursuing the analysis of extrema will find more complete discussions in a text on calculus. Rather than concentrating on these theoretical aspects of curves,[6] consider a practical example of finding a cycle in the price of scrap copper, shown in Table 8-1 and charted in Figure 8-7. The price peaks seem evenly spaced, occurring at mid-1966, January 1970, and January 1974, about 4 years apart. The solutions to these problems are tedious; therefore, calculations will be performed using the computer programs in Appendix 4.

The results obtained by using actual copper prices will not be as clear as using fictitious data. It is important to be able to understand the significance of practical results and apply them effectively.

Because trigonometric curves fluctuate above and below a horizontal line of value zero, the first step is to detrend the data using the least-squares method. This results in the equation for a straight line representing the upward bias of the data. The value of the detrending line is then subtracted from the original data to produce copper prices that vary equally above and below the line from positive to negative values.

The straight line $y = a + bx$, which best represents the trend, can be found by solving the least-squares equations:

---

[6] A more specific presentation of trigonometric curve fitting can be found in Claude Cleeton, *The Art of Independent Investing* (Prentice-Hall, 1976, Chapter 8). The material covered in this section is carried further in that work.

TABLE 8-1   Dealer's Buying Price, No. 2 Heavy Copper Scrap at New York*

	Average Quarterly Price (¢/lb)			
Year	1st	2nd	3rd	4th
1963	22.12	22.46	22.17	22.00
1964	23.18	24.56	25.57	30.59
1965	28.23	33.77	35.90	40.05
1966	46.22	51.48	40.76	40.16
1967	36.51	29.30	30.36	36.42
1968	39.75	30.07	29.08	32.13
1969	38.94	42.95	43.38	46.23
1970	47.70	46.98	35.78	27.35
1971	25.40	29.45	27.15	28.48
1972	32.74	33.53	30.01	29.25
1973	36.82	45.07	55.13	65.51
1974	66.56	70.06	47.30	35.62
1975	32.06	31.46	35.75	36.46
1976	38.22	43.24	45.46	38.96
1977	37.08	38.72	34.01	33.00
1978	35.07	40.23	41.63	44.95
1979	51.12	63.71	59.56	63.38

*Based on prices from the American Metal Market.

$$b = \frac{N \sum xy - \sum x \sum y}{N \sum x^2 - \left(\sum x\right)^2}$$

$$a = \frac{1}{N}\left(\sum y - b \sum x\right)$$

To do this, let x be the date and y be the price on that date. For convenience, instead of letting $x = 1967, 1967\frac{1}{4}, 1967\frac{1}{2}, \ldots$, let $x = 1, 2, 3, \ldots$. The solution, using a computer program in Appendix 2 (also an integral part of the programs in Appendix 4) or the hand-calculation method, is

$$y = 28.89 + .267x$$

Figure 8-7 displays the original copper prices and the regression line. The original prices can now be detrended using the equation above, subtracting the line values from the corresponding prices. Complete step-by-step results for this example can be found in Appendix 4. The detrended data is now used in the general trigonometric single-frequency wave:

$$y_t = a \cos \omega t + b \sin \omega t$$

The variable t replaces ϕ to express the angle in integer units rather than in degrees. This will be more convenient to visualize and to chart.

To find the frequency ω, it will be necessary to first solve the equation:

$$\cos \omega - \frac{1}{2}\alpha = 0$$

using the system of equations,

FIGURE 8-7   Copper prices 1963–1979.

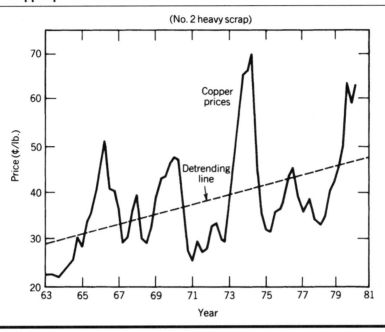

$$\alpha y_2 = y_1 + y_3$$

$$\alpha y_3 = y_2 + y_4$$

$$\vdots$$

$$\alpha y_{n-1} = y_{n-2} + y_n$$

This is expressed as a summation (similar to least-squares) in which the values for c and d must be found:

$$\alpha \sum c^2 = \sum cd$$

where $c = y_n$ and $d = y_{n-1} + y_{n+1}$. Summing the detrended values c^2 and cd gives $\sum c^2 = 6338.4$ and $\sum cd = 9282.2$, resulting in $\alpha = 1.464$. The value for α is substituted into the intermediate equation and solved for the frequency ω:

$$\cos \omega - \frac{1}{2}(1.464) = 0$$

$$\cos \omega = .732$$

$$\omega = 42.9$$

The period T is $360/42.9 = 8.4$ calendar quarters. The last step in solving the equation for a single frequency is to write the normal equations:

$$a \sum \cos^2 \omega t + b \sum \cos \omega t \sin \omega t = \sum y_t \cos \omega t$$

$$a \sum \sin \omega t \cos \omega t + b \sum \sin^2 \omega t = \sum y_t \sin \omega t$$

and solve for a and b, where $t = 1, \ldots, 40$, and $\omega = 42.9$. As in the other solutions, a computer program is best for finding the sums (using detrended data) necessary to solve the equations. The sums are

$$a \sum \cos^2 \omega t \qquad \sum \sin \omega t \cos \omega t \qquad \sum y_t \cos \omega t$$

$$\sum \sin^2 \omega t \qquad \sum y_t \sin \omega t$$

Then, a and b can be found by substituting in the following equations:

$$b = \frac{\sum y_t \sin \omega t \sum \cos^2 \omega t - \sum y_t \cos \omega t}{\sum \sin^2 \omega t \sum \cos^2 \omega t - \sum \cos \omega t \sin \omega t}$$

$$a = \frac{\sum y_t \cos \omega t - b \sum \cos \omega t \sin \omega t}{\sum \cos^2 \omega t}$$

The results $a = -.603$ and $b = 1.831$ give the single-frequency curve as:

$$y_t = -.603 \cos 42.9t + 1.831 \sin 42.1t$$

Taking $t = 1$ to be 1967 and $t = 68$ to be 1979¾ and adding back the trend, the resulting periodic curve is shown in Figure 8-8.

The single-frequency curve shown in Figure 8-8 matches seven out of the eight peaks in copper; however, it is not much more than could have been done using the Ehrlich

FIGURE 8-8 Copper prices 1963–1979: single-frequency copper cycle manually scaled to approximate amplitude.

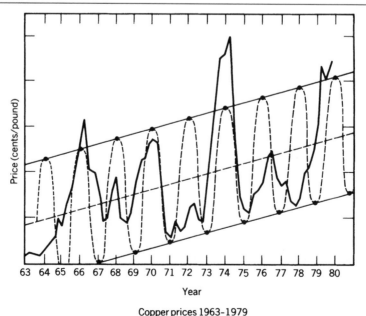

Copper prices 1963-1979

Cycle Finder mentioned in a previous section. A single-frequency curve can be created simply by identifying the most dominant peaks, averaging the distance (period), and applying the single-frequency formula.

Two-Frequency Trigonometric Regression

The combination of more than one set of sine and cosine waves of varying amplitudes and frequencies will create a better fit than a single-frequency solution. This is analogous to the use of a second-order (curvilinear) solution instead of the first-order linear. The equation for the two-frequency cycle is

$$y_t = a_1 \cos \omega_1 t + b_1 \sin \omega_1 t + a_2 \cos \omega_2 t + b_2 \sin \omega_2 t$$

To find the results of this complex wave, apply the same techniques used in the single-frequency approach to the detrended copper data. The algebra for solving this problem is an expanded form of the previous solution, and the use of a computer is a requirement. The programs necessary to solve this one appear in Appendix 4. The frequencies ω_1 and ω_2 are found by solving the quadratic equation:

$$2x^2 - \alpha_1 x - (1 + \alpha_2/2) = 0$$

where $x = \cos \omega$, using the standard formula:

$$x = \frac{\alpha_1 \pm \sqrt{\alpha_1^2 + 8(1 + \alpha_2/2)}}{4}$$

The same least-squares method as before can be used, derived from the general form:

$$\alpha_1(y_n + y_{n+2}) + \alpha_2 y_{n+1} = y_{n-1} + y_{n+3}$$

The least-squares equations for finding α_1 and α_2 are:

$$\alpha_1 \sum c^2 + \alpha_2 \sum cd = \sum cp$$

$$\alpha_1 \sum cd + \alpha_2 \sum d^2 = \sum dp$$

where $c = y_n + y_{n+2}$, $d = y_{n+1}$, and $p = y_{n-1} + y_{n+3}$. These equations can be solved for α_1 and α_2 using:

$$\alpha_2 = \frac{\sum dp \sum c^2 - \sum cp \sum cd}{\sum d^2 \sum c^2 - \left(\sum cd\right)^2}$$

$$\alpha_1 = \frac{\sum cp - \alpha_2 \sum cd}{\sum c^2}$$

Then, ω_1 and ω_2 are calculated from the two solutions x_1 and x_2 of the quadratic equation. The next step is to solve the normal equations to find the amplitudes a_1, b_1, a_2, and b_2:

$$a_1 \sum \cos^2 \omega_1 t + b_1 \sum \cos \omega_1 t \sin \omega_1 t + a_2 \sum \cos \omega_1 t \cos \omega_2 t$$

$$+ b_2 \sum \cos \omega_1 t \sin \omega_2 t = \sum y_t \cos \omega_1 t$$

$$a_1 \sum \sin \omega_1 t \cos \omega_1 t + b_1 \sum \sin^2 \omega_1 t + a_2 \sum \sin \omega_1 t \cos \omega_2 t$$

$$+ b_2 \sum \sin \omega_1 t \sin \omega_2 t = \sum y_t \sin \omega_1 t$$

$$a_1 \sum \cos \omega_2 t \cos \omega_1 t + b_1 \sum \cos \omega_2 t \sin \omega_1 t + a_2 \sum \cos^2 \omega_2 t$$

$$+ b_2 \sum \cos \omega_2 t \sin \omega_2 t = \sum y_t \cos \omega_2 t$$

$$a_1 \sum \sin \omega_2 t \cos \omega_1 t + b_1 \sum \sin \omega_2 t \sin \omega_1 t + a_2 \sum \sin \omega_2 t \cos \omega_2 t$$

$$+ b_2 \sum \sin^2 \omega_2 t = \sum y_t \sin \omega_2 t$$

Once the sums are obtained, the final step is to create a 4×5 matrix to solve the four normal equations for the coefficients a_1, b_1, a_2, and b_2. When plotting the answer it will be best to plot the original two-frequency equation in its component forms as well as in combination:

$$y_t' = a_1 \cos \omega_1 t + b_1 \sin \omega_1 t$$

$$y_t'' = a_2 \cos \omega_2 t + b_2 \sin \omega_2 t$$

$$y_t = y_t' + y_t''$$

where $a_1 = 3.635$, $b_1 = -.317$, $a_2 = -.930$, and $b_2 = .762$. The solution to the two-frequency problem gives the following values:

$$\alpha_1 = .535 \qquad x_1 = .830$$

and

$$\alpha_2 = .133 \qquad x_2 = -.764$$

and finally the frequencies:

$$\omega_1 = 33.9 \quad \text{and} \quad \omega_2 = 139.8$$

correspond to 10.6 and 2.6 calendar quarters (Figure 8-9).

Fourier Analysis: Complex Trigonometric Regression

Developed by the French mathematician John Baptiste Joseph Fourier, *Fourier analysis* is a method of complex trigonometric regression, which expresses any data set as a series of sine and cosine waves of the same type as discussed in the previous section.

Assuming that there is a cycle and that there are N data points in each repetition of this cycle, the Fourier method of analysis shows that the N points lie on the regression curve:

$$y_i = 1 + \sum_{k=1}^{(N/2)} \left(u_k \cos \frac{2\pi ki}{(N/2)} + v_k \sin \frac{2\pi ki}{(N/2)} \right)$$

where the regression coefficients u_k and v_k are given by:

$$u_k = \frac{1}{(N/2)} \sum_{i=1}^{N} y_i \cos \frac{2\pi ki}{(N/2)} \qquad k = 1, 2, \ldots, \frac{N}{2}$$

$$v_k = \frac{1}{(N/2)} \sum_{i=1}^{N} y_i \sin \frac{2\pi ki}{(N/2)} \qquad k = 1, 2, \ldots, \frac{N}{2}$$

$$v_{N/2} = 0$$

FIGURE 8-9   Two-frequency trigonometric approximation.

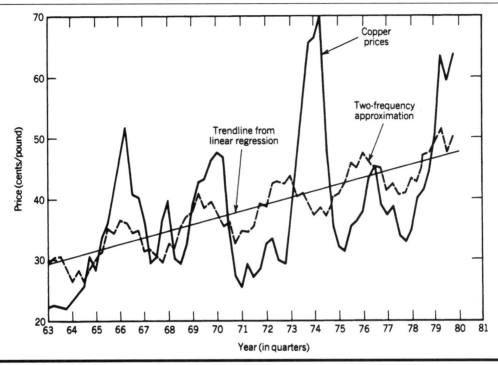

It is important to see that the mean of all the points on one cycle is equal to 1. The N values of y_i will have the property

$$\sum_{i=1}^{N} y_i = N$$

Applying the Fourier series to the seasonal component will help clarify this method. Seasonal data form the most obvious cycle. Using average monthly prices, detrended to avoid letting the trend overwhelm the cycle, let $N = 12$. It is also known that seasonally adjusted prices will vary about the mean; hence, the weighting factors will have the same property as the above equation. With this information, the trigonometric curve, which approximates the seasonals, can be generated and compared with the results of other methods.[7]

Spectral Analysis

Derived from the word *spectrum,* spectral analysis is a statistical procedure that isolates and measures the cycles within a data series. The specific technique used is the Fourier series as previously discussed, although other series have also been used.

When studying the cycles that comprise a data series, it is important to refer to their *phase* with respect to each other. Phase is the relationship of the starting points of different cycles. For example, if one cycle has the same period as another but its peaks and val-

---

[7] A continuation of this development can be found in Warren Gilchrist, *Statistical Forecasting* (John Wiley & Sons, London, 1976, pp. 139–148); a more theoretical approach is to be found in C. Chatfield, *The Analysis of a Time Series: Theory and Practice* (Chapman and Hall, London, 1975, Chapter 7).

leys are exactly opposite, it is 180° *out-of-phase.* If the two cycles are identical in phase, they are *coincident.* Cycles with the same period may lead or lag the other by being out-of-phase to various degrees.

A tool used in spectral analysis to visualize the relative significance of a series' cyclic components is the *periodogram.* Weighting the cyclic components in the periodogram will give the more popular *spectral density* diagram, which will be used to illustrate the results of the spectral analysis. *Density* refers to the frequency of occurrence. Figures 8-10*a* and 8-10*b* show the spectral density of a series composed of three simple waves (*D* is the Fourier series made up of waves *A, B,* and *C*).[8] The cycle length, shown at the bottom of the spectral density chart, corresponds exactly to the cycle length of the component waves *A, B,* and *C.* The spectral density, measured along the left side of Figure 8-10*b*, varies with the amplitude squared of the cycle and the magnitude of the noise, or random price movements, which obscures the cycle. In Figure 8-10*b*, the result is based on a series composed of only three pure waves. Had there been noise of the same magnitude as the underlying cycle amplitude, those cycles identified by the spectral analysis would have been completely obscured. Readers who have studied ARIMA will recognize the similarity between the spectral density and the correlogram.

As in trigonometric regression analysis, the other basic price components can distort the results. A noticeable trend in the data must be removed or it will be interpreted as the dominant cycle. The familiar methods of first differencing or linear regression can be used to accomplish this. The seasonal component is itself a cycle and does not need to be removed from the series. Because spectral analysis will identify both the seasonal and cyclic components, the success of the results will depend on the strength of these waves compared with the noise that remains. In applying this technique to real data, it would not be surprising to see the results demonstrated in Figure 8-11. Three subcycles of length 10, 20, and 40 days are shown as part of a 250-day (seasonal) cycle. Notice that, as the cycle lengthens, the width of the spectral density representation widens. This does not mean that the wider peaks are more important.

The trader is most interested in those cycles with greater spectral density, corresponding to a larger price move. The minimum amount of data necessary to find these cycles must include the full cycle that might be identified. For example, to see any seasonal pattern, a minimum of 12 months is needed. More data is better when using spectral analysis to confirm the consistency of the cycle. A single year is not adequate to support any seasonal findings.

Weighting Factors

The most important part of spectral analysis is finding the proper estimators, or weighting factors, for the single-frequency series of cosine waves. When looking for long-term cycles, it is worth being reminded that the trend and seasonal components must be removed, because the method of spectral analysis will consider these the dominant characteristics, and other cycles may be obscured.

As in the other trigonometric formulas, the basic time series notation is used, where y_t, $t = 1, 2, \ldots, N$ are the data points and $\hat{y}_t$ will be the resulting estimated points on the spectral analysis. Then

$$\hat{y}_t(\omega) = \frac{1}{\pi}\left(c_0 + 2\sum_{k=1}^{N-1} c_k \cos \omega k\right)$$

where

$$c_k = \sum_{i=1}^{N-k} \frac{(y_t - \overline{y})(y_{t+k} - \overline{y})}{N}$$

[8] William T. Taylor, "Fourier Spectral Analysis," *Technical Analysis of Stocks & Commodities* (July/August 1984).

FIGURE 8-10 Spectral density. (*a*) A compound wave *D*, formed from three primary waves, *A*, *B*, and *C*. (*b*) Spectral density of compound wave *D*.

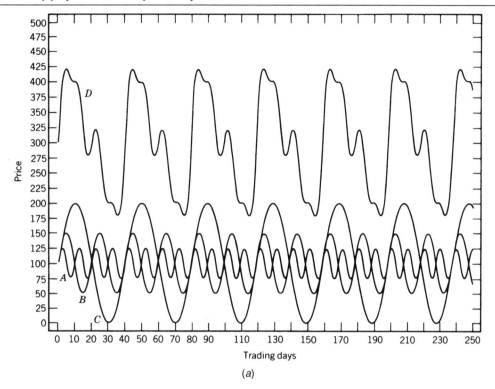

(*a*)

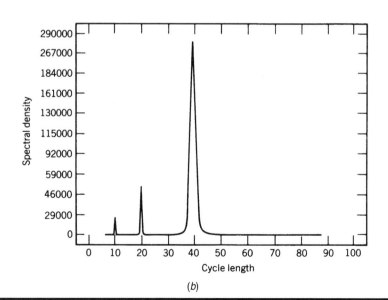

(*b*)

FIGURE 8-11   10-, 20-, and 40-day cycles, within a 250-day seasonal.

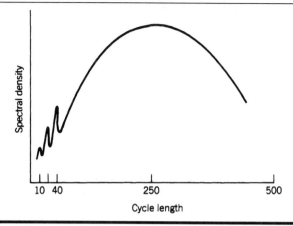

Methods of performing spectral analysis vary due to the choice of weighting functions that compensate for the fact that the accuracy of c_k decreases as k increases. The two most popular techniques for adjusting for this problem introduce an estimator λ_k called a *lag window* and a truncation point $M < N$ so that the values of c_k for $M < k < N$ are no longer used and the values of c_k for $k \leq M$ are weighted by λ_k.

The spectral analysis approximation is then written:

$$\hat{y}_t(\omega) = \frac{1}{\pi} \left(\lambda_0 c_0 + 2 \sum_{k=1}^{M} \lambda_k c_k \cos \omega k \right)$$

where λ_k can be either of the following:

(a) *Tukey window*

$$\lambda_k = \frac{1}{2} \left(1 + \cos \frac{\pi k}{M} \right) \qquad k = 0, 1, \ldots, M$$

(b) *Parzen window*

$$\lambda_k = \begin{cases} 1 - 6 \left(\dfrac{k}{M} \right)^2 + 6 \left(\dfrac{k}{M} \right)^3 & 0 \leq k \leq \dfrac{M}{2} \\[3mm] 2 \left(1 - \dfrac{k}{M} \right)^3 & \dfrac{M}{2} \leq k \leq M \end{cases}$$

Using a Fast Fourier Transform Program

There are computer programs that apply a *Fast Fourier Transform* to perform a spectral analysis and create a Fourier power spectrum such as the one in Figure 8-10b. Anthony Warren's approach[9] can be found in Appendix 5 written in BASIC program code. The pro-

---

[9] Anthony Warren, "A Mini Guide to Fourier Spectrum Analysis," *Technical Analysis of Stocks & Commodities* (January 1983). A very useful series of articles on spectral analysis has been published in *Technical Analysis* beginning in January 1983, authored by both Anthony W. Warren and Jack K. Hutson. Much of the information in this section was drawn from that material.

gram detrends the data and reduces endpoint discontinuity, which can produce large unwanted cycles. This is accomplished by multiplying the data by a bell-shaped *window* and extending the endpoints to give a more definitive structure to the detrended data, without affecting the results (as discussed in the previous section).

A second filter is applied using selected moving averages. The moving average will reduce or eliminate the importance of those cycles, which are equal to or shorter than two times the length of the moving average, letting the more dominant cycles appear. For example, the use of a 10-day moving average will eliminate cycles of length less than 20 days (frequencies greater than 12.5 per year). Figure 8-12 shows the output of the computer program.

Subsequent works by Warren and Hutson[10] present a computer program to calculate moving average weighted filters using linear, triangular, and Hanning weights.

Interpreting the Results of the Fourier Power Spectrum

Both Figures 8-10*b* and 8-12 show a power spectrum resulting from a Fourier transform. Figure 8-10*b* is an ideal representation, in which the cycles stand out with no ambiguity; Figure 8-12 is more realistic, showing both the dominant cycles and a certain amount of variance around those values. In the power spectrum, the cycle power shown along the *y*-axis is the cycle amplitude squared. In Figure 8-10*a*, cycle *D* peaks at a price of about 425, which yields a spectral density, or *spectral power,* of 180,625 when squared, corresponding roughly to the 40-day cycle in Figure 8-10*b*.

Using the information from the beginning of this chapter, the frequency is the inverse of the cycle length; therefore, if the cycle length is 40 days, the frequency $F = 360/40 = 9$.

---

[10] Anthony Warren and Jack K. Hutson, "Finite Impulse Response Filter," *Technical Analysis of Stocks & Commodities* (May 1983).

FIGURE 8-12   Output of spectral analysis program.

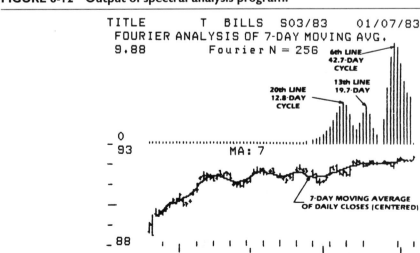

Source: Jack K. Hutson, "Using Fourier," *Technical Analysis of Stocks & Commodities,* 1, no. 2 (January & February 1983). © 1983 Technical Analysis, Inc. Used with permission.

The sine wave changes phase at the rate of 9 degrees per day, completing one full cycle every 40 days.

A fast method for observing the possible results is to use weekly rather than daily data. This will be a close approximation for low-frequency waves but will be less representative for the high frequencies. Averaging the data points can yield results very similar to the daily analysis.

MAXIMUM ENTROPY

Maximum Entropy Spectral Analysis (MESA) is a technique that filters noise (*entropy*) from a time series and exposes the useful cycles;[11] it provides a very practical alternative to Fourier analysis that makes it possible to find cycles using a very small amount of data. The use of Fourier transforms requires at least 256 data points and a minimum of 16 consistent cycles of 16 bars. That would eliminate the possibility of uncovering cycles for the short-term trader.

John Ehlers describes the existence of short-term cycles as a natural phenomenon.[12] It is part of the process that causes rivers to meander back and forth as water seeks to flow in a straight line, or a drunkard who walks through an alley bumping against the walls but moving steadily forward. From these patterns, useful cycles can be found about 20% of the time.

Using the Phase Angle

In an ideal situation, in which the market cycle can be shown as a pure sine wave, the phase angle constantly increases throughout the cycle, beginning at 0 and ending at 360°. The phase angle then drops to 0 when the new cycle begins and increases again at a constant rate until it ends at 360°. This repeated pattern forms a *sawtooth* chart, as shown in Figure 8-13. Although the cycle goes from peak to value, the phase angle moves constantly in one direction.

In the practical analysis of short-term cycles, Ehlers compresses tick data into bars of equal numbers of ticks, then examines the phase for uniformity. Once found, the uniform phase, which appears as a sawtooth chart, will become erratic as the short-term cycle begins to break down, marking the end of a current market event.

Ehlers's Lateral Shift in Thinking

At first glance, the use of only a small amount of data needed by MESA seems to contradict the basic rules of statistics, which demand that results be based on as much data as possible to be reliable. But Ehlers, who has been the dominant influence in cycles since about 1990, is too knowledgeable to have made a mistake so simple. His book *MESA and Trading Market Cycles*[13] focuses on the use of short-term cycles based on short sample time periods. Instead, he has used this very attribute to apply cycles inside out.

Ehlers's objective is to find very short-term cycles. By definition, these cycles must be the result of human behavior, rather than based on market economics, because fundamentals are not usually relevant to periods of only a few days, and they are not likely to have a regular pattern when they make a rare appearance. If very short-term cycles exist,

---

[11] Anthony Warren, "An Introduction to Maximum Entropy Method (MEM)," *Technical Analysis of Stocks & Commodities* (February 1984). See the bibliography for other articles on this topic.

[12] John F. Ehlers, "How to Use Maximum Entropy," *Technical Analysis of Stocks & Commodities* (November 1987).

[13] John F. Ehlers, *MESA and Trading Market Cycles* (John Wiley & Sons, New York, 1992).

FIGURE 8-13   The phase angle forms a sawtooth pattern.

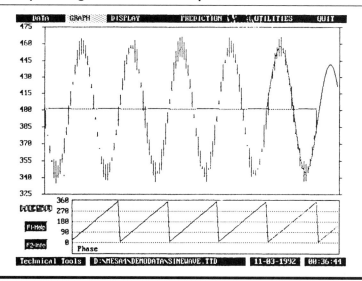

Source: John Ehlers, "Cycle Analysis and Intraday Trading," *Technical Analysis of Stocks & Commodities,* 11, no. 4 (February 1993). © 1993 Technical Analysis, Inc. Used with permission.

they will not continue for long periods, and you must recognize them quickly if they are to be useful; therefore, short-term cycles are found by analyzing only a small amount of recent data.

Then how does it help to find a short-term cycle based on a small amount of data, if it is not statistically dependable? In a lateral shift, Ehlers uses the existence of a short-term cycle to tell if prices are in a sideways pattern or trending. If a short-term cycle exists, then the market trend should be weak. Ehlers has no interest in trading the cycle, which is surprising for a cycle expert, but prefers the dependability of the trend. He has, instead, attempted to solve one of the most difficult problems facing the analyst, trying to distinguish between a trending and sideways market. If a short-term cycle exists, then we cannot rely on the trend. Ehlers develops this method throughout his book.

CYCLE CHANNEL INDEX

A trend-following system that operates for a market with a well-defined cyclic pattern should have specific qualities that do not necessarily exist in a generalized smoothing model. To confirm the cyclic turning points, which do not often occur precisely where they are expected, a standard moving average should be used, rather than an exponentially smoothed one. Although exponential smoothing always includes some residual effect of older data, the determination of a cyclic turning point must be limited to data that is nearer to one-fourth of the period, combined with a measure of the relative noise in the series, which may obscure the turn.

These features have been combined by Lambert[14] into a *Commodity Cycle Index* (CCI), which is calculated as follows:

---

[14] Donald R. Lambert, "Commodity Channel Index Tools for Trading Cyclic Trends," *Commodities* (1980), reprinted in *Technical Analysis of Stocks & Commodities.*

$$CCI_t = \frac{x_t - \bar{x}_t}{.015MD}$$

where $x_t = (H_t + L_t + C_t)/3$ is the average of the daily high, low, and close

$\bar{x}_t = \sum\limits_{i=t-N+1}^{t} x_i$ is the moving average over the past N days

$MD = \sum\limits_{i=t-N+1}^{t} |x_i - x|$ is the mean deviation over the past N days

N is the number of days selected (less than ¼ cycle)

Because all terms are divided by N, that value has been omitted. In the CCI calculations, the use of .015MD as a divisor scales the result so that 70% to 80% of the values fall within a +100 to −100 channel. The rules for using the CCI state that a value greater than +100 indicates a cyclic turn upward; a value lower than −100 defines a turn downward. Improvements in timing rest in the selection of N as short as possible but with a mean deviation calculation that is a consistent representation of the noise. The CCI concept of identifying cyclic turns is good because of the substantial latitude in the variance of peaks and valleys, even with regular cycles.

PHASING

One of the most interesting applications of the cyclic element of a time series is presented by J.M. Hurst in *The Profit Magic of Stock Transaction Timing* (Prentice-Hall); it is the *phasing* or synchronization of a moving average to represent cycles. This section will highlight some of the concepts and present a simplified example of the method. It is already known that to isolate the cycle from the other elements, the trending and seasonal factors should be subtracted, reducing the resulting series to its cyclic and chance parts. In many cases, the seasonal and cyclic components are similar, but the trend is unique. Hurst treats the cyclic component as the dominant component of price movement and uses a moving average in a unique way to identify the combined trend-cycle.

The system can be visualized as measuring the oscillation about a straight-line approximation of the trend (centered line), anticipating equal moves above and below. Prices have many long- and short-term trends, depending on the interval of analysis. Because this technique was originally applied to stocks, most of the examples used by Hurst are long-term trends expressed in weeks. For commodities the same technique could be used by applying the nearest futures contract on a continuous basis.

As a simple example of the concept, choose a moving average of medium length for the trending component. The *full-span* moving average may be selected by averaging the distance between the tops on a price chart. The *half-span* moving average is then equal to half the days used in the full-span average.

The problem with using moving averages is that they aways lag. A 40-day moving average is always 20 days behind the price movement. The current average is plotted under the most recent price, although it actually represents the price pattern if the plot were lagged by one-half the value of the average. This method applies a process called *phasing*, which aligns the tops and bottoms of the moving average with the corresponding tops and bottoms of the price movement. To phase the full- and half-span moving averages, lag each plot by half the days in the average; this causes the curve to overlay the prices (Figure 8-14). Then project the phased full- and half-span moving averages until they cross. A line or curve connecting two or more of the most recent intersections will be the major trendline. The more points used, the more complicated the regression formula for calculating the trend; Chapter 3 discusses a variety of linear and nonlinear techniques for finding the *best fit* for these intersections. Once the trendline is calculated, it is projected as the center of the next price cycle.

With the trend identified and projected, the next step is to reflect the cycle about the trend. When the phased half-span average turns down at point *A* (Figure 8-15), measure the greatest distance *D* of the actual prices above the projected trendline. The system then anticipates the actual price crossing the trendline at point *X* and declining an equal distance *D* below the projected trendline. Once the projected crossing becomes an actual crossing, the distance *D* can be measured exactly and the price objective firmed. Rules for using this technique can be listed as follows:

1. Calculate the full-span moving average for the selected number of days; lag the plot by half the days. If the full-span moving average uses *F* days, the value of the average is calculated at $t - F/2$, where t is the current day. Call this phased point PH_t.
2. The half-span moving average is calculated for *H* days and plotted at $t - H/2 + PH_t$.
3. Record the points where the two phased averages PH_i and PF_i cross and call these points $X_n, X_{n-1}, \ldots$.
4. Find the trend by performing a linear regression on the crossing points X_n, $X_{n-1}, \ldots$. If a straight line, then $Y_T = a + bX_T$.

FIGURE 8-14   Phasing.

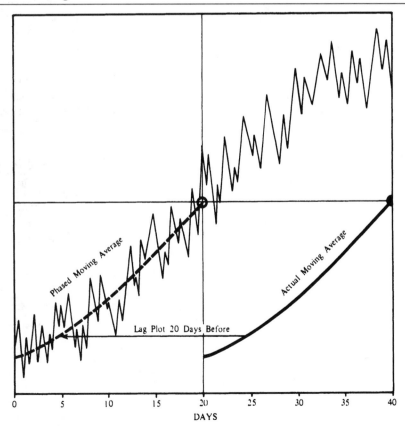

FIGURE 8-15   Finding the target price.

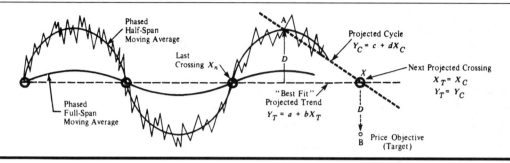

5. Record the highest (or lowest) values of the price since the last crossing, X_n.

6. Calculate the projection of the half-span by creating a straight line from the highest (or lowest) half-span value since the last crossing (A) to the last calculated half-span value. This equation will be $Y_C = c + dX_C$.

7. Find the point at which the projected trendline crosses the projected cyclic line by setting the equations equal to one another and solving for X and Y. At the point of crossing $(X_T, Y_T) = (X_C, Y_C)$, giving two equations in two unknowns, which is easily solvable (X is time in days; Y is price).

8. If the half-span is moving down, the maximum price reached by the commodity since the last crossing is subtracted from the Y coordinate of the projected crossing. This distance D is subtracted again from the Y coordinate to determine the price objective. If the half-span is moving up, the price objective uses the minimum price and reflects the distance above the projected crossing. It should be noted that this calculation of distance is simplified because the trend is established by a straight line; for nonlinear fits, the measurement of D will be more complicated.

9. Recalculate the moving averages, the half-span projection (6), the projected crossing (7), and price objective (8) each day until the actual crossing occurs. At that time D is fixed.

10. Follow the trading rules:

    a. Enter a new long position when the half-span moving average turns up; cover any existing short positions regardless of the price objective.

    b. Enter a new short position when the half-span moving average turns down; close out any long positions.

    c. Close out both long and short positions if the price objective is reached. An allowable error factor is considered as 10% of the height of the full cycle (lowest to highest point).

This approach to cycles should be studied carefully as an example of a complex problem solved using elementary mathematics. There are many techniques for determining trends and a number of seasonally oriented systems, but a cyclic approach is rare. Whereas Hurst's explanation is more complete and more sophisticated, the interpretation presented in this section should be considered only a reasonable approximation.

9

Charting

Nowhere can a picture be more valuable than in price forecasting. Elaborate theories and complex formulas may ultimately be successful, but the loss of perspective is rarely corrected without a simple chart. We should remember the investor who, anxious after a long technical presentation by a research analyst, could only blurt out, "But is it going up or down?" Even the most sophisticated market strategies must capture the obvious trends or countertrends. Before any trading method is used, the past buy and sell signals should be plotted on a chart. Those signals should appear at logical points; otherwise, the basis of the strategy or the testing method should be questioned.

Through the mid-1980s technical analysis was considered chart interpretation. In the equities industry that perception is still strong. Most traders begin as chartists, and many return to it or use it along with their other methods. William L. Jiler, a great trader and founder of Commodity Research Bureau, wrote:

> One of the most significant and intriguing concepts derived from intensive chart studies by this writer is that of characterization, or habit. Generally speaking, charts of the same commodity tend to have similar pattern sequences which may be different from those of another commodity. In other words, charts of one particular commodity may appear to have an identity or a character peculiar to that commodity. For example, cotton charts display many round tops and bottoms, and even a series of these constructions, which are seldom observed in soybeans and wheat. The examination of soybean charts over the years reveals that triangles are especially favored. Head and shoulders formations abound throughout the wheat charts. All commodities seem to favor certain behavior patterns.[1]

In addition to Jiler's observation, the cattle market is recognized as also having the unusual occurrence of "V" bottoms. Both the silver and pork belly markets have tendencies to look very similar, with long periods of sideways movement and short-lived, violent *price shocks,* where prices leap rather than trend to a new level. The financial markets have equally unique personalities. The S&P traditionally makes new highs, then immediately falls back; it has fast, short-lived drops and slower, steady gains. Currencies show intermediate trends bounded by noticeable major stopping levels, while long-term interest rates have long-term direction.

Charting remains a most popular and practical form for evaluating commodity price movement, and numerous works have been written on methods of interpretation. This chapter will summarize some of the accepted approaches to charting, and then consider advanced concepts of both standard charting methods and systems designed to take advantage of behavioral patterns found in charts. Some conclusions will be drawn as to what is most likely to work and why.

---

[1] William L. Jiler, *How Charts Are Used in Commodity Price Forecasting* (Commodity Research Publications, New York, 1977).

FINDING CONSISTENT PATTERNS

A price chart is often considered a representation of human behavior. The goal of any chart analyst is to find consistent, reliable, and logical patterns that predict price movement. In the classic approaches to charting, there are consolidation forms, trend channels, top-and-bottom formations, and a multitude of other patterns that can only be created by the repeated action of large groups of people in similar circumstances or with similar objectives. As of this date, quantitative studies relating the psychology of behavior to the reliability of chart formations have not been reliable. Traditional trading techniques found in the most popular stocks and commodities literature may themselves be the cause of the repeated patterns. Novice speculators approach the problem with great enthusiasm and often some rigidity in an effort to stick to the rules. They will sell double and triple tops, buy breakouts, and generally do everything to propagate the standard formations. In that sense, it is wise to know the most popular and well-read techniques and act accordingly.

Speculators have many habits which, taken as a whole, can be used to interpret charts and help trading. The typical screen trader (not on the exchange floor) will place an order at an even number, from 5¢ to $1.00 per bushel in the grains, 10 to 50 points in other products. This pattern far outweighs the number of orders entering the market to buy at odd numbers, for example the S&P at 863.50 rather than 863.35 or bonds at 105 16/32 instead of 105 19/32. The public is also known to enter into the bull markets always at the wrong time. When the major media, such as television news, syndicated newspapers, and radio, carry stories of outrageous prices in cattle, sugar, or coffee, the public enters in what W.D. Gann calls the *grand rush,* causing the final runaway move before the collapse; this behavior is easily identifiable on a chart. Gann also talks of *lost motion,* the effect of momentum that carries prices slightly past its goal. A common notion of the professional trader who is close to the market is that a large move may carry 10% over its objective. A downward swing in the U.S. dollar/Japanese yen from 1.2000 to a support level of 1.1000 could overshoot the bottom by .0100 without being considered significant.

The behavioral aspects of prices appear rational. In the great bull markets, the repeated price patterns and variations from chance movement are indications of the effects of mass psychology. The greatest single source of information on this topic is Mackay's *Extraordinary Popular Delusions and the Madness of Crowds,* originally published in 1841.[2] In the preface to the edition of 1852 the author says:

> We find that whole communities suddenly fix their minds on one object, and go mad in its pursuit; that millions of people become simultaneously impressed with one delusion. . . .

In 1975, sugar was being rationed in supermarkets at the highest price ever known. The public was so concerned that there would not be enough at any price that they would buy (and horde) as much as possible. This extreme case of public demand coincided with the peak prices, and shortly afterward the public found itself with an abundant supply of high-priced sugar in a rapidly declining market. The world stock markets are often the target of acts of mass psychology. Many have taken their turn reaching incredible heights, only to drop suddenly at a time when buyers are most confident, to start the long climb up again. It should not be difficult to understand why contrary thinking has developed.

Charting is a broad topic taken to great detail; the chart paper itself and its scaling are sources of controversy. A standard bar chart (or line chart) representing highs and lows can be plotted for daily, weekly, or monthly intervals to smooth out the price movement over time. The use of large increments representing price levels will reduce the volatile appear-

---

[2] Reprinted in 1995 by John Wiley & Sons, Inc.

ance of price fluctuations. Bar charts have been drawn on logarithmic and exponential scales,[3] where the significance of greater volatility at higher price levels is put into proportion with the quieter movement in the low ranges by using percentage changes. Each variation gives the chartist a unique representation of price action. The shape of the box and its ratio of height/width will alter subsequent interpretations based on angles. Standard techniques applied to bar graphs, point-and-figure charts, and other representations use support and resistance trendlines, frequently measured at 45-degree angles (and at various other angles in more complex theories). Selection of the charting paper may have a major effect on the results. This chapter will use daily price charts and square boxes unless otherwise noted.

It may be a concern to today's chartist that the principles and rules that govern chart interpretations were based on the early stock market, using averages instead of individual contracts. This will be discussed in the next section. For now, refer to Edwards and Magee, who said that the similarity of an organized exchange trading, "anything whose market value is determined solely by the free interplay of supply and demand," will form the same graphic representation. They continued to say that the aims and psychology of speculators in either a stock or commodity environment would be essentially the same; the effect of postwar government regulations have caused a "more orderly" market in which these same charting techniques can be used.[4]

INTERPRETING THE BAR CHART

The *bar chart,* also called the *line chart,* became known through the theories of Charles H. Dow, who expressed them in the editorials of the *Wall Street Journal.* Dow first formulated his ideas in 1897 when he created the stock averages for the purpose of evaluating the movements of stock groups. After Dow's death in 1902, William P. Hamilton succeeded him and continued the development of his work into the theory that is known today. Those who have used charts extensively and understand their weak and strong points might be interested in just how far our acceptance has come. In the 1920s, a New York newspaper was reported to have written:

> One leading banker deplores the growing use of charts by professional stock traders and customers' men, who, he says, are causing unwarranted market declines by purely mechanical interpretation of a meaningless set of lines. It is impossible, he contends, to figure values by plotting prices actually based on supply and demand; but, he adds, if too many persons play with the same set of charts, they tend to create the very unbalanced supply and demand which upsets market trends. In his opinion, all charts should be confiscated, piled at the intersection of Broad and Wall and burned with much shouting and rejoicing.[5]

This same newspaper may have repeated this idea applied to program trading after the stock market plunge in October 1987. Nevertheless, charting has become part of the financial industry, whether the analyst is interested in the fundamentals of supply and demand or pure price movement. The earliest authoritative works on chart analysis are long out of print, but the essential material has been recounted in newer publications. If, however, a copy should cross your path, read the original *Dow Theory* by Robert Rhea;[6] most of all, read Richard W. Schabacker's outstanding work *Stock Market Theory and Practice,* which is probably the basis for most subsequent texts on the use of the stock market for invest-

[3] R.W. Schabacker, *Stock Market Theory and Practice* (Forbes, New York, 1930, pp. 595–600).

[4] Robert D. Edwards and John Magee, *Technical Analysis of Stock Trends* (John Magee, Springfield, MA, 1948, Chapter 16).

[5] Richard D. Wyckoff, *Stock Market Technique, Number One* (Wyckoff, New York, 1933, p. 105).

[6] Robert Rhea, *Dow Theory* (Vail-Ballou, Binghamton, NY, 1932).

ment or speculation. The most available book that is both comprehensive and well written is *Technical Analysis of Stock Trends* by Robert D. Edwards and John Magee. It is confined entirely to chart analysis with related management implications and a small section on commodities. For the reader who prefers concise information with few examples, the monograph by W.L. Jiler, *Forecasting Commodity Prices with Vertical Line Charts,* and a complementary piece, *Volume and Open Interest, A Key to Commodity Price Forecasting,* can still be found.[7] A valuable recent addition is Jack Schwager's, *Schwager on Futures: Technical Analysis* (Wiley, 1996), the first of a three-volume set.

The Dow Theory

In its basic form, the Dow theory is still the foundation of chart interpretation and applies equally to stocks, financial markets, commodities, and the wide variety of vehicles used to trade them. Its major premise is that averages remove a large amount of extraneous price motion; therefore, Dow's original work applied exclusively to averages and not to individual stocks. In fact, Dow's Industrial, Utility, and Transportation averages have survived the test of time. The difficulty with interpreting stock movement is in the thinness of a specific issue especially in the early part of the twentieth century; its fixed number of shares and light volume made the movement of one stock an unreliable indicator of an economic turn. Taken in total, it would be improbable to move the average by the manipulation of a single issue; hence, the averages become the subject of analysis. Commodities, especially the financial and index markets, differ from stocks in their enormous volume, as demonstrated by the Eurodollars, which can trade exceptionally high volume with only the slightest price movement. In futures, trading can be limited to one primary contract with little distortion because of constant massive arbitrage between futures and cash, and between one bank and another, especially in the interest rate and currency markets. The possibility of one trader influencing the U.S. bond market (other than the Chairman of the Federal Reserve) for more than a few seconds is remote to the point of no concern. When working in financial markets a single product is often given the same significance as a sector in the stock market when constructing a portfolio or index, yet in the footsteps of Dow, a group of international interest rates, with similar maturities, or a U.S. dollar index, can still be a valuable substitute for a single market.

The Dow theory defines price motion, as represented by the average, in three distinct primary, secondary, and minor trends. These elements have often been compared with the tide, the wave, and the ripple. The primary trend denotes the main move that exceeds 20% of the original price; the secondary trend is an adjustment or correction, and the minor movements are day-to-day fluctuations. The theory emphasizes the main move. As Angas said: "Be simple. Take the grand view." It is easier to identify the dominant trend than to worry about every change in direction.

Accumulation and *distribution* are the beginning phases of a bull or bear market. Accumulation is the period in which the insiders begin to acquire a long position in anticipation of a bull move. In charting, this is traditionally seen as a wide formation at a low price with increasing open interest and erratic peaks in volume representing large purchases. The distribution phase serves the same function for anticipated bear moves.

A unique part of the original Dow theory that prevents it from being applied to commodities markets is the *principle of confirmation,* requiring that a signal be produced by more than one average. There has been some criticism with regard to the significance of an industrial group being confirmed by a rail, but the concept seems sound. If the purpose of

---

[7] Two other works worth studying are Gerald Appel, *Winning Market Systems: 83 Ways to Beat the Market* (Signalert, Great Neck, NY, 1974), and Gerald Appel and Martin E. Zweig, *New Directions in Technical Analysis* (Signalert, Great Neck, NY, 1976).

the Dow theory is to identify major trends in the economy, it is unlikely that the average of one stock group would be going up and the other group moving down in a well-defined inflationary or deflationary period. In the same way, one would not expect the price of corn to increase and the price of wheat to decrease in absolute terms. A period of inflation should uniformly affect stocks and commodities; any items varying from the total pattern should be explained on an individual basis.

The relationship of the number of shares or contracts traded to the development of a price move is characterized by saying that "volume expands with the trend." Whether a bull or bear market, activity increases as the trend becomes clear. In futures, the open interest has been treated in the same manner, with increased open interest, especially during the accumulation and distribution phases, a sign of a new move forming.

The Dow theory has other points that have been incorporated into chart interpretation. The exclusive use of closing prices is important for two reasons: (1) they are most closely followed by the typical speculator, and (2) they discount the effects of any positions taken by floor traders who are day-trading. Support and resistance lines were introduced as a substitute for the secondary move, which may have been difficult to define. Lastly, the theory expressed a trading philosophy by stating that a trend should be assumed to be intact until a reversal occurred.

CHART FORMATIONS

Chart analysis applies straight lines and geometric formations extensively. They can be classified into broader groups of trendlines and channels, accumulation and distribution, and other patterns. In addition, chart formations can apply to major or minor price changes and to different time frames.

Trendlines

The trendline remains the most popular and readily recognized tool of chart analysis. It can be any of the following:

A *support line* is drawn to connect the bottom points of a price move. A *horizontal support line* is extremely common and represents a firm price level that has withheld market penetration. It may be the most significant of all chart lines.

A *resistance line* is drawn across the price peaks of a sustained move, or a horizontal resistance line representing the fixed level that resists upward movement. Resistance lines are not normally as clear as support lines because they are associated with higher volatility, which causes erratic price movement.

A *channel* is the area between parallel support and resistance lines that serves to contain a sustained price move. When the support and resistance lines are relatively horizontal, or sideways, the channel is called a *trading range*.

A *bullish support line* would then be a rising line drawn across the lowest points of a price move, and a *bearish resistance line* is a declining line drawn across the highest peaks of a price move.

Formations for Accumulation and Distribution

Most of the effort in charting goes into the identification of tops and bottoms. Because many of these formations unfold over fairly long periods, they have been called accumulation at the bottom, where typical stock investors slowly buy into their position, and distribution at the top, where the invested positions are sold off. The most popular of these formations are:

Head-and-shoulders bottom and top

Common rounded upward or downward turn

Triangular bottom and top of an ascending, descending, or symmetric shape, such as a triangle, flag, or pennant

Ascending bottom and top

"V"-bottom (a "V"-top is usually referred to as a *spike*)

Double bottom and top

Complex bottom and top, including a triple bottom or top, or a combination of other formations

Broadening bottom and top

Most of these patterns are self-explanatory and are covered in detail in many books devoted entirely to the topic. In addition to the classic by Edwards and Magee and the monograph by Jiler, the reader can find considerable value in John Murphy's "Bar Charting" in Kaufman, *Handbook of Futures Markets,*[8] and more recently *Schwager on Futures: Technical Analysis.*[9] Instead of giving examples of these formations, we will look at them in the context of trading rules.

Individual Patterns

In addition to the broader patterns noted above, there are specific situations of short duration that have been noted by the chartist, including:

Gaps

Spikes

Reversal days

Thrust days

Cups and caps

These will be covered in the following sections.

Major and Minor Formations

Throughout the study of charting, it is important to remember that the same patterns will appear in short- as well as long-term charts. An upward trendline can be drawn across the bottom of a price move that only began last week; it can represent a sustained 3-year trend in the financial markets, or a 6-month move in coffee. In general, the longer the time interval, the more significant the formation. Contract highs and lows, well-defined trading ranges, trendlines using weekly charts, and head-and-shoulder formations are carefully watched by traders. Obscure patterns and new formations are not of interest to most chartists, and without the support of the traders, conclusions drawn from those formations have no substance. The basic charting course also includes interpretation of volume and open interest and a variety of rules for using the formations.

BASIC TRADING RULES

The simplest formations to recognize are the most commonly used and most important: horizontal support and resistance lines, bullish and bearish support and resistance lines, and channels. Proper use of these basic lines is essential for identifying the overall direc-

[8] Arthur Sklarew, *Techniques of a Professional Commodity Chart Analyst* (Commodity Research Bureau, New York, 1980), and John Murphy, "Bar Charting" in *Handbook of Futures Markets,* Perry J. Kaufman (ed.) (John Wiley & Sons, New York, 1984).

[9] Jack D. Schwager, *Schwager on Futures: Technical Analysis* (John Wiley & Sons, New York, 1996).

tion of the market and how it gets there. An understanding of these patterns will be helpful to computer-oriented analysts, many of whose techniques have been modeled after chart formation. More complex formations are likely to enhance good performance but cannot compensate for poor trend identification.

Once the support and resistance lines have been drawn, a price penetration of those lines creates the basic trend signal (Figure 9-1*a*). The bullish support line defines the upward trend, and the bearish resistance line denotes the downward one. For long-term charts and major trends this is often sufficient, but frequent small penetrations of both long- and short-term trendlines can be avoided by placing a band around both lines (Figure 9-1*b*). A short signal occurs when both the trendline and the band have been penetrated. Because of the basic charting rule—"Once broken, a resistance level becomes a support level and a support level becomes a resistance level"—the original trendline (or a trendline plus and minus a band) can be used as a stop-loss. If prices penetrate the stop-loss point, then return to the original formation; there has been a false breakout and the original trendlines are still valid.

A Classic Dilemma

The use of bands around a trendline is more popular than the use of the trendline alone because price movement is not *clean*. Larger bands produce more reliable trend signals;

FIGURE 9-1 Basic trading rules. (*a*) Line signals. (*b*) Bands.

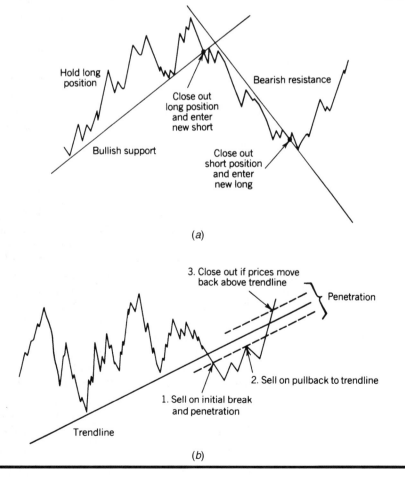

(*a*)

(*b*)

however, they need more time to generate a signal resulting in smaller profits and larger risk. This produces a classic dilemma for the trader, one that cannot be resolved except by personal choice.

Experienced traders often wait for the first pullback after the breakout before entering their position. This technique results in a higher percentage of profitable trades. The position is set when the new direction is confirmed following a test of the old support or resistance levels (and the theoretic stop-loss). If the test fails, which frequently occurs, the trade is not entered and a loss is prevented (Figure 9-1*b*). Unfortunately, most of the biggest profits result from breakouts that never pull back. Catching only one of these breakouts can compensate for all the small losses due to false signals. Many professional traders may be steady winners, but they do not often profit from the biggest moves.

Identifying Direction from Consolidation Patterns

It is said that markets move sideways about 80% of the time, which means that directional breakouts do not occur often, or that most breakouts are false and fail to identify a new market direction. Classic accumulation and distribution formations, which occur at long-term lows and highs, attempt to find evolving changes in market sentiment. Because these formations occur only at extremes, and may extend for a long time, they represent the most obvious consolidation of price movement. Even a rounded, or saucer, bottom may have a number of false starts; it may seem to turn up in a uniform pattern, then fall back and begin another slow move up. In the long run the pattern looks as if it is a somewhat irregular but extended rounded bottom; however, using this pattern to enter a trade in a timely fashion can be disappointing and has resulted in the safe but conservative technique of *averaging in.*

Most other consolidation formations are best viewed in the same way as a simply horizontal sideways pattern, bounded above by a resistance line and below by a support line. If this pattern occurs at reasonably low prices, we can eventually expect a breakout upward when the fundamentals change. Occasionally prices seem to become less volatile within the sideways pattern, and chartists take this opportunity to redefine the support and resistance levels so that they are narrower. Breakouts based on these more sensitive lines tend to be less reliable because they represent a temporary quiet period inside the normal level of market noise.

Market Noise

All markets have a normal level of noise. The stock index markets have the greatest amount of irregular movement due to its extensive participation, the high level of anticipation built into the prices, and because it is an index. This is contrasted to short-term interest rates, which have large participation but little anticipation and a strong tie to the underlying cash market. In comparison, long-term rates allow for greater movement away from the cash market. The normal level of noise can be seen as the consistent daily or weekly trading range on a chart of the DJIA or S&P. When volatility declines below the normal level of noise, the market is experiencing short-term inactivity. An increase in volatility back to normal levels of noise should not be confused with a breakout.

This same situation can be applied to a triangular formation, which has traditionally been interpreted as a pause within a trend. This pattern often follows a fast rise and represents a short period of declining volatility. If volatility declines in a consistent fashion, it appears as a triangle; however, if the point of the triangle is smaller than the normal level of market noise, then a breakout from this point is likely to restore price movement to a range typical of noise, resulting in a flag or pennant formation. Both of these latter patterns have uniform height that can include a normal level of noise.

TOPS AND BOTTOMS

Most of the formations important to bar charting can be traded using a penetration of one of the support or resistance lines as a signal. The most interesting and potentially profitable trades occur on breakouts from major top or bottom formations. The simplest of all bottom formations, as well as one that offers great opportunities, is the extended rectangle at contract lows. Fortunes have been made by applying patience, some available capital, and the following plan:

1. Find a market with a long consolidating base and low volatility (with futures it should also have increasing open interest). When evaluating interest rates, use the yield rather than the price, and avoid currencies that have no base price; that is, they have no level considered low, but instead have a point of equilibrium.
2. Buy whenever there is a test of its major support level, placing a stop-loss to liquidate all positions on a new, low price.
3. After the initial breakout, buy again when prices pull back to the original resistance line (now a support level). Close out all positions if prices penetrate back into the consolidation area, and start again at step 2.
4. Buy whenever there is a major price adjustment in the bull move. These adjustments, or pullbacks, will become shorter and less frequent as the move develops. They will usually be proportional to current volatility or the size of the price as measured from the original breakout.
5. Liquidate all positions at a prior major resistance point, a top formation, or the breaking of a major bullish support line.

Building positions in this way can be done with a relatively small amount of capital and risk. The closer the price comes to major support, the shorter the distance from the stop-loss; however, fewer positions can be placed. In his book, *The Professional Commodity Trader* (Harper & Row), Stanley Kroll discussed "The Copper Caper—How We're Going to Make a Million," using a similar technique for building positions. It can be done, but it requires patience, planning, and capital. The opportunities continue to be there.

This example of patiently building a large position does not usually apply to bear markets. Although there is a great deal of money to be made on the short side of the market, prices move faster and may not permit the accumulation of a large position. There is also exceptionally high risk and the increased risk of false signals caused by greater volatility. Within consolidation areas at low levels, there is an underlying demand for a product, the cost of production, government price support (for agricultural products), and low volatility. There is also a well-defined trendline that may have been tested many times. A careful trader will not enter a large short-sale position at an anticipated top, but will join the buyers who contribute to the growing volume and open interest at a well-defined major support level.

Head and Shoulders

The classic top and bottom formation is the *head and shoulders,* accepted as a major reversal indicator. This pattern, well-known to chartists, appears as a left shoulder, a head, and a right shoulder (Figure 9-2).

The head-and-shoulders top is developed in the following manner:

1. A strong upward breakout reaching new highs on increased volume. The move appears to be the continuation of a long-term bull move.
2. A consolidation area formed with diminishing volume. This can look much like a descending flag predicting an upward breakout, or a descending triangle indicating a downward breakout.

FIGURE 9-2   Head-and-shoulders formation.

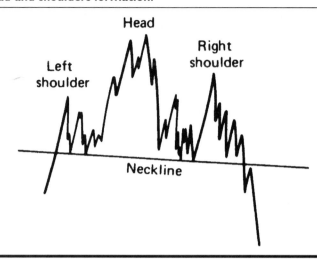

3. Another upward breakout on continued reduced volume forms the head. This is the key point of the formation. The new high is not confirmed by increased volume, and prices fall off quickly.

4. Another descending flag or triangle is formed on further reduced volume followed by a minor breakout without increased volume. This last move forms the right shoulder and is the third attempt at new highs for the move.

5. The lowest points of the two flags, pennants, or triangles become the *neckline* of the formation. A sale is indicated when this neckline is broken.

Trading Rules for Head and Shoulders

There are three approaches to trading a head-and-shoulders top formation involving increasing degrees of anticipation:

1a. Sell when the final dip of the right shoulder penetrates the neckline. This represents the completion of the head-and-shoulders formation. Place a stop-loss just above the entry if the trade is to be held only for a fast profit, or place the stop-loss above the right shoulder or above the head to liquidate on new strength, allowing a longer holding period.

  b. Sell on the first rally after the neckline is broken. (Although more conservative, the lost opportunities usually outweigh the improved entry prices.) Use the same stops as in Step 1a.

2a. Sell when the right shoulder is being formed. A likely place would be when prices have retraced their way half of the distance to the head. A stop-loss can be placed above the top of the head.

  b. Wait until the top of the right shoulder is formed and sell with a stop either above the high of the right shoulder or above the high of the head.

Both steps 2a and 2b allow positions to be taken well in advance of the neckline penetration with logical stop-loss points. Using the high of the head for a protective stop is conservative.

3. Sell when the right part of the head is forming, with a stop-loss at about the high of the move. Although this represents a small risk, it has less chance of success. It is for traders who prefer to find tops and are willing to suffer frequent small losses

to do it. Even if the current prices become the head of the formation, there may be numerous small corrections that will look like absolute tops to an anxious seller.

Other Top and Bottom Formations

The experienced trader is most successful when prices are testing a major support or resistance level, usually a contract or seasonal high or low. The more often those levels are tested the clearer they become and the less likely prices will break through to a new level without a change in the fundamental supply and demand factors.

Repeated tests of tops are visually clearer, but not as exact as bottoms because of the added volatility of higher prices. The double top is a more speculative trade than successive multiple tops; it is more frequent than the other formations and is the first opportunity for picking the top of a bull move. It is also easy to position a stop-loss above the previous highs. As with other chart patterns, declining volume would be a welcome confirmation after the formation of the first top and accompanying each additional test of the top (Figure 9-3).

Triple tops are frequently used as opportunities for selling. Because they are easily seen, there is anticipation that causes the third top to look similar to a right shoulder, lower than the previous highs. Traders waiting for a near-test of the highs to enter a trade with less risk could find themselves without any position at all. Among professionals, the fourth top is considered the final test; whichever direction prices turn at that time will determine the new major trend.

Double and triple bottoms also occur but are generally of lesser magnitude than tops. Because low prices can be sustained at value or cost-of-production levels, it is not necessary for the new upward trend to begin in the near future. In most markets, the profitability associated with these bottom formations is much lower and is proportional to the lower risk. With the exception of the financial markets, for which bottoms are really tops (peak interest rates), double and triple bottom formations are most often found in the currency and cattle markets.

When using top formations, we must consider why a three- or four-peak combination is so rare. There are two possibilities. When it is evident that the previous peaks occurred under extreme conditions, such as a temporary supply shortage, or demand caused by a news-related item, the following tests of the high are met with active selling. This causes any attempt at an upward move to be sharply halted. The greater the conviction that the rally is over, the greater the selling.

Multiple tops also fail to appear because prices simply move higher. The market does not see the previous tops as significant, and new buying renews the upward trend. If you see a single, interim top on a chart, formed by a pullback within a trend, there must have been a potential double top when prices resumed their direction. It may be that two or

FIGURE 9-3 Double and triple tops.

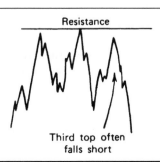

three peaks at very similar prices are very unusual and a poor way to trade. A perfect test of the top means that there is uncertainty at that moment and significant selling developed after the fact.

Now You See It, Now You Don't!

The "V"-top (actually an inverted *V*), or *spike,* is the most difficult top formation to anticipate and trade. Its frequency in the 1974 and 1980 markets tended to deceive a generation of new speculators. V-tops are caused by critical shortage and demand and magnified by public awareness. In 1974, it was a combination of domestic crop shortage, severe pressure on the U.S. dollar abroad, and foreign purchases of U.S. grain that combined to draw public attention. The news was so well publicized that novice commodity traders withdrew their funds from their declining stock portfolios and bought any commodity available as a hedge against inflation.

It could not continue for long. When the top came in soybeans, silver, and most other commodities, there was no trading for days in locked-limit markets; paper profits dwindled faster than they were made, and the latecomers found their investments unrecoverable. The public often seems to enter at the wrong time. The case of cattle is an example.

Live cattle prices are based on a combination of consumer demand, substitute foods, current health news, and the price of various feed grains. During 1973 as the price of feed increased, cattle prices rose steadily from under 40¢ per pound to almost 54¢ in August. Prior to that, live beef prices had never been over 37¢ (in 1952). The price of soybean meal, used as a high-protein feed, continued to move prices higher. How high could it go? Between August and October, live-cattle prices formed a V-top and declined back to under 40¢, giving up the 8-month gain in 2 months. How could the supply-and-demand factors change so quickly? They can't. Fast rises are always followed by fast, usually extensive declines.

The psychology of the runaway market is fascinating. In some way, every V-top shares a similarity with the examples in Mackay's *Extraordinary Popular Delusions and the Madness of Crowds.* With beef, the consumers do not tend to consider pork, fowl, or fish as an adequate substitute and will bear increased costs longer than expected. As prices neared the top, the following changes occurred:

- The cost became an increasing factor in the standard household budget.
- Rising prices received more publicity.
- Movements for public beef boycotts began.
- Grain prices declined due to the new harvest.

This becomes a matter explained by the *Elastic Theory.* It can be applied to the 1973 soybean and 1980 silver markets as well. The Elastic Theory is based on the principle that when prices get high enough, a number of phenomena occur:

1. Previously higher-priced substitutes become practical (synthetics for cotton, reclaimed silver).
2. Competition becomes more feasible (corn sweetener as a sugar substitute, alternate energy).
3. Inactive operations start up (Southwest gold mines, marginal production of oil).
4. Consumers avoid the products (beef, bacon, silver).

Consequently, the demand suddenly disappears (the same conclusion arrived at by economists).

Announcements of additional production, more acreage, new products, boycotts, and a cancellation of orders all coming at once cause highly inflated prices to reverse sharply.

These factors form a V-top that is impossible to anticipate with reasonable risk. There is a natural reluctance to take profits while they are still growing. Further impetus is given to the reversal because of the scramble to liquidate after the first reversal day. This is followed by those latecomers or pyramiders who entered their most recent positions near the top and cannot afford a continued adverse move. The rush to close out long positions, put on new shorts, and liquidate deficit accounts only prolongs the sharpness of the V-top, causing a liquidity void at many points during the decline.

Quantifying Spikes

A spike is often the focal point of a trade. Most often it represents a severe reaction to an event, but it may be an island reversal representing a new direction. A spike is important because it always indicates high volatility and exceptional risk and cannot be ignored. A spike has only one dominant feature, a price high or low much higher or lower than recent prices. This must result in volatility that is equally extreme. The easiest way to identify an upside spike is to compare the day's trading range with previous ranges and to the next day. This can be done by using the average true range and satisfying both the following conditions:

High today – @highest(high,n) > K × average true range(n)

High today – high tomorrow > K × average true range(n)

Today's spike high must be higher than the highs of the previous n-days by a multiple, K, of the average true range; it must also be higher than tomorrow's high if it is to stand out as a spike.

GAPS

A *gap* is a formation caused by a jump in price from one point to the next and can be calculated as

```
Gap = @AbsValue(open - close[1])
```

Gaps are phenomena that make sense only when trading is restricted to local business hours. A currency trader with 24-hour capability has, theoretically, a very small chance of confronting a gap. Most gaps are *overnight* moves, where continuous events cause changes in price levels; when the exchange or banks open for business the price immediately jumps to the new level. A market with very large relative gaps is the Japanese yen trading in Chicago. During the Japanese business day, when most relevant news occurs, the International Monetary Market (IMM) is closed; when the IMM is open, most businesses in Japan are closed. The Chicago market is therefore always trying to catch up to the price of the dollar/yen as seen by the Japanese.

There is also a technical situation associated with price gaps. Traders place more orders to buy at a point near or just above a resistance level; similarly, they place sell orders just below support lines. This causes fast moves and a void of orders when resistance and support are penetrated. Gaps also occur after a price shock or any unexpected new release or economic report.

A gap appears as an open area on a chart created by prices trading entirely above or below the prior trading range. Gaps will usually occur at the opening of the day, a news release, or where prices break out of a clearly identified formation, such as a long-term trendline, a consolidation area, or during a prolonged major price move. Regardless of the reason, it is the consequence of a lack of speculators willing to take the opposing position causing a thinly traded or illiquid market. In the most interesting situations, the *breakaway gap* is the name given to the result of many stop-loss orders placed at new highs or lows, at major trendlines as protection against unfavorable breakouts with respect to existing positions, or as an entry to a new position. The breakaway gap usually signifies a change from the previous, well-established pattern.

The *common gap* is the least glamorous. It occurs within a well-defined trading range or pattern, and is not indicative of a change of direction nor does it have other special attributes; hence it is called "common." Both *runaway gaps* and *midway gaps* refer to those price jumps occurring within a strong trend. They are associated with periods of illiquidity within a move; this could be the result of additional news to encourage the bulls or bears, or it could be a critical chart formation or anticipated reversal point that fails. Runaway gaps indicate stronger moves.

The *exhaustion gap* or *island reversal* is the culmination of a major move; unfortunately, it is a formation only identifiable after the fact. If the price move has been exceptionally extended, it is likely that the first gap reversal will be the beginning of the trend change; however, there is a great risk associated with it.

Gaps are a hindrance rather than an asset to trading. A breakaway gap usually causes stop-loss orders to be executed far away from the stated price. If a long position is entered in anticipation of a breakout, that breakout never occurs and a high price is guaranteed. If the breakaway gap occurs on light volume, a position might be entered on a pullback. In the final analysis, if the breakout represents a major change, a trade should be entered immediately at the market price. The poor executions will be offset by a single time when prices move quickly and no pullback occurs. A breakaway gap on high volume should be more indicative of such a major change.

Many traders believe that prices will retrace and "fill the gap" that occurred sometime earlier. There are analysts who never give up, but waiting to fill a gap that is more than two years old may be carrying this technique too far. There is no doubt that the gap represents an important point at which prices move out of their previous pattern and begin a new phase. The breakaway gap will often be a position just above the previous normal price level. Once the short-term demand situation has passed, prices should return to near normal (perhaps slightly above the old prices), but also slightly below the gap.

KEY REVERSAL DAYS

A formation that has been endowed with great forecasting power is the *key reversal day,* sometimes called an outside reversal day. It is a weaker form of an island reversal. A bearish key reversal is formed in one day by first making a new high in an upward trend, reversing to make a low that is lower than the previous low, and then closing below the previous close. It is considered more reliable when the prior trend is well established. This could be identified using *EasyLanguage* as

```
KeyReversalDown = 0;
@if close[1] > @average(close[1],n) and high >= @highest(high[1],n) and
        low < low[1] and close < close[1] then KeyReversalDown = 1;
```

where the first term tests for an uptrend over *n*-days, the second tests that this day is the highest price of the same *n*-days, the third verifies a lower low, and the last tests a lower close.

Studies have shown mixed results using the key reversal as a sole trading indicator. The most complete analysis,[10] similar to others, concluded that the performance was "strikingly unimpressive." Even though tests have not proved its importance, traders still pay close attention to key reversals. Based on this, it must be concluded that other factors unconsciously enter into the normal perception of a key reversal. A trader's senses should not be

---

[10] Eric Evans, "Why You Can't Rely on 'Key Reversal Days'," *Futures* (March 1985).

underestimated; the extent and speed of the prior trend, a change in liquidity, a quieter tone, or some external news may be essential in confirming the important reversals.

Pivot Point Reversals and Swings

A *pivot point* is a trading day, or a price bar, that is higher or lower than the bars that come before and after. It is the common form of an island reversal and a popular way of identifying turning points. The most frequent pivot point high is a bar that has a higher high than one day before and one day after. More significant *swing highs* can be found by comparing the high of any day with two or more days before and after. This is the method used in *TradeStation's* "Swing High Bar" function. The pattern of the days on either side of the high bar are not important as long as the middle bar has the highest high.

Pivot points are used as the basis for finding swing highs and lows, and they identify the extremes of both price and oscillator for *TradeStation's* divergence functions. For example, if the last two price pivot points correspond to the same days as the last two stochastic or RSI pivot points, and prices are rising while the momentum is falling, there is a bearish divergence. When more days are used to identify pivot points, these divergence signals are expected to be more significant; unfortunately, they take longer to identify.

Cups and Caps

Another name given to the pivot point reversals are *cups* and *caps,* each determined by only three price bars. These two formations are associated with trading rules that are identical to pivot point channels applied to the shortest time frame. Contrary to their names, a cup formation identifies a sell signal when the trend is up, while a cap is a setup for a buy signal in a downtrend. Once an uptrend is clear, a cup formation is found using either the daily closes or daily lows. For any 3 consecutive days, the middle day must have the lowest close or the lowest low. In a cap pattern the middle day must have the highest high or the highest close of the 3-day cluster. In both cases, the positioning of the highs and lows of the other 2 days are not important as long as the middle day is lower for the cup and higher for the cap.

The cup will generate a sell signal if:

1. The cup formation is the highest point of the uptrend.
2. The sell signal occurs within 3 days of the cup formation.
3. The current price closes below the lowest low (middle bar) of the cup formation.

The signal is false if prices reverse and close above the high of the cup formation, resuming the previous trend. This pattern is only expected to forecast a downward price move of two days; however, every change of direction must start somewhere, and this formation could offer an edge. A cap formation is traded with the opposite rules.

According to tests by Colby and Meyers,[11] entries that occur based on a breakout of the highs or lows of the pivot points, called *pivot point channels,* are much more reliable than simply entering in the direction of the reversal based on the close of the last bar of the pivot point, cup, or cap formation. For traders not interested in this very short-term strategy, a pivot point may help entry timing for any longer-term method.

EPISODIC PATTERNS

There is little argument that prices change quickly in response to unexpected news. The transition from one major level to another is termed an *episodic pattern;* when these tran-

---

[11] Tests of pivot point reversals and pivot point channels can be found in Robert W. Colby and Thomas A. Meyers, *The Encyclopedia of Technical Market Indicators* (Dow Jones-Irwin, 1988).

sitions are violent, they are called *shocks*. The coffee and oil markets have received the greatest number of shocks; however, all markets are continually adjusting to new price levels, and all experience occasional shocks.

The pattern that results from episodic movement is exactly what one might expect. Following the sharp price movement there is a period when volatility declines from its highs, narrowing until a normal volatility level is found and remains at that level (Figure 9-4).

Patterns that result from rising prices are not the same as falling prices. Although higher price moves usually overshoot the price level at which they normally settle, sharp declines do not reach their final levels during the first shock.

Price shocks have become the focus of much analytic work. Because a price shock is an unpredictable event, it cannot be forecast. This has a critical effect on the way in which systems are developed, especially with regard to the testing procedures. This topic is covered in other parts of this book under the topics "Price Shocks," "Robustness," and "Optimization."

PRICE OBJECTIVES FOR BAR CHARTING

There is some satisfaction in having a price objective for a trade that has just been entered. If this objective can be determined to a reliable degree, those trades would be selected that have the best profit potential as compared with the risk. It is also comforting to know that profits will be banked at a specific point. The most successful objectives will be based on straightforward concepts and not complex calculations.

The simplest and most logical price objective is a major support or resistance level established by previous trading. When entering a long position, look at the most well-defined resistance levels above the entry point. These have been discussed in a previous section of this chapter, "Tops and Bottoms." When those prior levels are tested, there is generally a technical adjustment or a reversal. In the case of a strong upward market, volatility often causes a short penetration before the setback occurs. Placing the price objective a reasonable distance below the identifiable major resistance level will always be safe; the intermediate resistance levels can be used for adding positions on technical reversals. The downside objective can be identified in a similar manner: Find the major support level and place a stop just above it.

FIGURE 9-4   Episodic patterns. (*a*) Upward price shocks. (*b*) Downward price shocks.

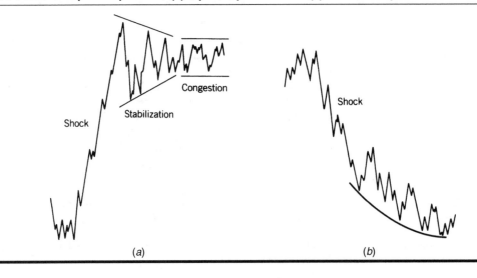

(*a*)   (*b*)

When using both support and resistance price objectives, watch carefully for a violation of the current trend; don't be rigid about the position. Take advantage of each reaction to add to the position, but get out if the major trendline is broken before the objective is reached. On the other hand, if the goal is reached and prices react as predicted but then reverse and break through the previous highs or lows, the trade may be reentered on the breakout and a new price objective calculated.

There are other, more analytic ways to determine the objective of a trade. Bear in mind that these methods are considered guidelines and are not precise. If you have set a single price target for a long position, and it falls slightly above a resistance level, then the resistance level (the closer point) should be substituted for an original price objective.

The head-and-shoulders top has a downside objective that is associated with its volatility. This objective is measured from the point where the right shoulder penetrates the neckline and is equal to the distance from the top of the head to the neckline (Figure 9-5). For a major top, this goal seems modest, but it will be a good measure of the initial reaction and will generally be safe, even if a new high price is reached later.

For a *consolidation area,* both top and bottom, a counting method based on the width of the rectangle or consolidation pattern is used to find the price target. For a basing formation, the objective is the vertical distance above the support line equal to the width of the consolidation area (Figure 9-6). For downside objectives, measure vertically downward from the resistance line forming the upper bound of the congestion area, a goal similar to the head-and-shoulders top. This technique implies that the longer the consolidation area, the bigger the subsequent breakout. The same method can be seen later in point-and-figure charting.

Trendlines can also be used to measure the expected price move. The most common techniques are based on channel volatility and, therefore, set very modest, realistic targets.

1. The channel width, which bounds a trend, will be equal to the price objective measured from the point of the channel breakout (Figure 9-7).

FIGURE 9-5   Head-and-shoulders top price objective.

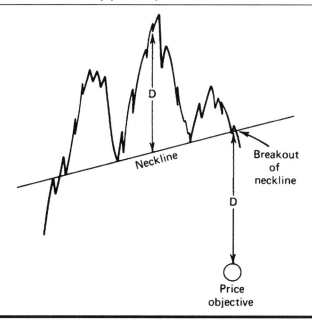

FIGURE 9-6   Consolidation price objective.

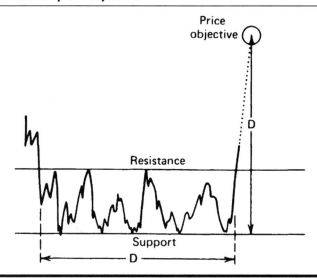

2. Once a breakout of an upward channel has occurred, construct a new descending channel. This is done by connecting the high of the uptrend with the high of the first reversal following the break, then drawing a parallel support line across the low of the first breakout. The new channel will be shallow but will serve as a guideline for the price change. A second channel, drawn after the next reversal, should indicate the final direction of the new move.

In Figure 9-8, the original channel around the uptrend was broken at the point marked by the black dot, followed by prices moving down to point *a* and reacting back up to point *b*. When a new high is not made at point *b*, a resistance line (1R) can be drawn from the prior high *b* to the top of the latest move *b*. A line parallel to 1R can be constructed at point *a*, forming the initial downward channel. Price objective 1 is on the support line of the new channel (1S) and is used once the top at point *b* is determined. Price objective 1 cannot be

FIGURE 9-7   The channel width as a price objective.

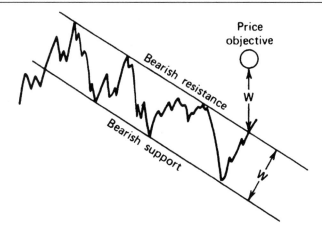

expected to be too precise due to the early development of the channel. If prices continue to point *c* and then rally to *d,* a more reasonable channel can now be defined using trendlines 2R and 2S. The support line will again become the point where the new price objective is placed. The upper and lower trendlines can be further refined as the new high and low reactions occur. The primary trendline is always drawn first, then the new price objective becomes a point on the parallel trendline.

Triangles and *flags* have objectives based on volatility in a manner consistent with other patterns. The triangle objective is equivalent in size to the initial reaction, which formed the largest end of the triangle (Figure 9-9*a*). The flag is assumed to occur midway in a price move; therefore, the objective of a new breakout must be equal to the size of the move preceding the flag (Figure 9-9*b*). Recalling the comments on the problems associated with the decreasing volatility of the triangular formation, the use of the first reaction as a measure of volatility is a safe way to avoid those problems.

The Rule of Seven

Another measurement of price objectives, the *Rule of Seven,* is credited to Arthur Sklarew.[12] It is based on the volatility of the prior consolidation formation and computes three successive price objectives in proportion to one another. The Rule of Seven is not symmetric for both uptrends and downtrends. Sklarew believes that, after the initial leg of a move, the downtrend reactions are closer together than the reactions in a bull market. Because the downside of a major bear market is limited, it is usually characterized by consolidation. Major bull markets tend to expand as they develop.

To calculate the objectives using the Rule of Seven, first measure the length *L* of the initial leg of a price move (from the previous high or low, the most extreme point before the first pullback). The objectives are:

1. In an *uptrend:*

$$OBJ\ 1 = \text{prior low} + (L \times 7/4)$$

$$OBJ\ 2 = \text{prior low} + (L \times 7/3)$$

$$OBJ\ 3 = \text{prior low} + (L \times 7/2)$$

---

[12] Sklarew. (See reference 8.)

FIGURE 9-8   Forming new channels to determine objectives.

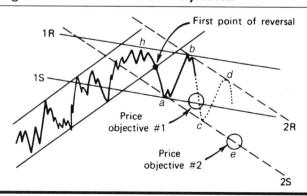

FIGURE 9-9 Triangle and flag objectives. (*a*) Triangle objective is based on the width of the initial side, *s*. (*b*) Flag objective is equal to the move prior to the flag formation.

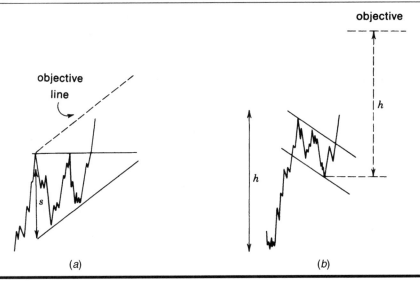

(*a*)   (*b*)

2. In a *downtrend*:

OBJ 1 = prior high − (*L* × 7/5)

OBJ 2 = prior high − (*L* × 7/4)

OBJ 3 = prior high − (*L* × 7/3)

The three objectives apply most clearly to major moves. During minor price swings it is likely that the first two objectives will be bypassed. In Sklarew's experience, regardless of whether any one objective is missed, the others still remain intact.

CANDLESTICK CHARTS

For a technique that is reported to have been used as early as the mid-1600s, Japanese candle charts were slow finding their way into the western method of analysis. In actuality, candle charts only differ from simple bar charts by *shading* the piece of the bar between the opening and closing prices—white if the close is higher than the open and black if the close is lower than the open. The shaded area is called the *body,* and the extended lines are the *shadows.* With this simple change, we get an entirely new way of looking at and interpreting charts. The patterns become much clearer than the western style of line chart. Over the centuries many of the candle formations have been given names representing their significance (see Figure 9-10):

Doji—in which the opening and closing prices are the same.

Hammer—a bullish reversal signal, showing the bottom of a swing, where the body is at the top of the candle, indicating an upward change of direction, and the shadow is below the body. The body may be black or white.

Hanging man—another bearish reversal pattern where the body of the candle represents the high of a swing, and the shadow lies below in the direction of the reversal. The body may be black or white.

FIGURE 9-10 Popular candle formations.

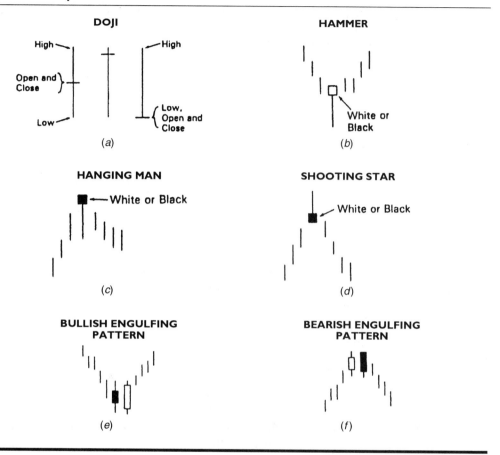

Source: Jack D. Schwager, *Schwager on Futures: Technical Analysis* (John Wiley & Sons, 1996, pp. 281–288).

Shooting star—a bearish signal, also occurs at the top of a swing and has its body at the bottom of the candle with the shadow above. The body may be black or white.

Engulfing pattern—occurring at a swing high or low, has the current body engulfing the entire prior candle.

Although these patterns are similar to western bar chart formation, none of them are exactly the same. The hammer, hanging man, and shooting star are reversal patterns but can only be compared with the simple pivot point, where the middle day is higher or lower than the bars on either side. None of these candle formations would be a key reversal or island reversal. The engulfing pattern is stronger than the typical outside day, because the spanning of the prior day's range must be done only by the current day's open-close range.

The analysis of candle charts is a skill involving the understanding of many complex and interrelated patterns. For a brief review of this method, readers are referred to *Schwager on Futures: Technical Analysis;* for full coverage, *Japanese Candlestick Charting Techniques* (New York Institute of Finance, 1991), and *Beyond Candlesticks—New Japanese Trading Techniques,* both by Steve Nison, are recommended.

Quantifying Candle Formations

The preciseness of the candle formations allows some patterns to be tested. One technique uses the shadows as confirmation of direction. We can interpret an increase in the size of the upper shadows as strengthening resistance (prices are closing lower each day); and an increase in the size of the lower shadows represents more support. One way to look at this is by defining

Upper shadow (white) = high − close   Lower shadow (white) = open − low

Upper shadow (black) = high − open   Lower shadow (black) = close − low

The sequences of upper and lower shadows can be smoothed separately using a moving average to find out whether they are rising or falling.[13]

Another method for determining whether black or white candles dominate recent price movement is to use only the body of the candle, $B = close - open$ and apply a momentum calculation

$$\text{Body momentum} = \frac{B_{\text{up}}}{B_{\text{up}} + B_{\text{down}}} \times 100$$

where B_{up} is the sum of the days where $B > 0$ (body is white)
  B_{down} is the sum of the days where $B < 0$ (body is black),
  the number of days is recommended as 14.

When the body momentum is greater than 70 the whites dominate; when the value is below 20 the blacks dominate.

USING THE BAR CHART

Charting is not precise and the construction of the trendlines, other geometric formations, and their interpretation can be performed with some latitude. When using the simplest trendline analysis, it often happens that there will be a small penetration of the channel or trendline followed by a movement back into the channel. Some think that this inaccuracy, with respect to the rules, makes charting useless; however, many experienced analysts interpret this action as confirmation of the trend. The trendline is not redrawn so that the penetration becomes the new low of the trend, but it is left in its original position.

We must always step back and look for the underlying purpose in each method of analysis, whether technical or fundamental. In the case of the trendline we are trying to identify the direction of prices over some time period. Chartists can use a simple straight line to visualize the direction; they draw the uptrend by connecting the lowest prices in a rising market even though each point used may represent varying levels of volatility and unique conditions. The chances of these points aligning perfectly, or forecasting the perfect price support level, is small. A trendline is simply a guide; it may be too conservative at one time and too aggressive another; you'll never know. Applied rigorously, charting rules should produce many incorrect signals but be right in the most important cases. The challenge of the chartist is to interpret the pattern of prices in context with the bigger picture.

Multiple Signals

Some of the impreciseness of charting can be offset with confirming signals. A simultaneous short- and long-term trend break is a much stronger signal than either one considered separately. The break of a head-and-shoulders neckline that corresponds to a channel sup-

---

[13] Both *shadow trends* and *body momentum* are adapted from Tushar Chande and Stanley Kroll, *The New Technical Trader* (John Wiley & Sons, 1994).

port line is likely to receive much attention. Whenever there are multiple signals converging at, or near, a single point, whether based on moving averages, Gann, cycles, or phases of the moon, that point gains significance. In chart analysis, the occurrence of multiple signals at one point can compensate for the quality of the interpretation.

Pattern Failures

The failure to adhere to a pattern is equally as important as the continuation of that pattern. Although a trader might anticipate a reversal as prices near a major support line, a break of that trendline is significant in continuing the downward move. A failure to stop at the support line should result in setting short positions and abandoning plans for higher prices.

A head-and-shoulders formation that breaks the neckline, declines for a day or two, then reverses and moves above the neckline is another pattern failure. *Postpattern* activity must confirm the pattern. Failure to do so means that the market refused to follow through and, therefore, should be traded in the opposite direction. This is not a case of identifying the wrong pattern; instead, price action actively opposed the completion of the pattern. Wyckoff calls this "Effort and Results," referring to the effort expended by the market to produce a pattern that explains the price direction. If this pattern is not followed by results that confirm the effort, the opposite position should be set.

Consider a trading day in which prices open above the previous close, move higher, then close lower. The expectation is for prices to open lower the next day. If an inside day or a higher open follows, there is a strong sign of higher prices to come. As Thompson concludes, "A strongly suggestive pattern that is aborted is just as valuable as a completed pattern."[14]

Change of Character

Thompson also discusses the completion of a pattern or price trend by identifying a *change of character* in the movement. As a trend develops, the reactions, or pullbacks, tend to become smaller. Traders looking to enter the trend wait for reactions to place their orders; as the move becomes more obvious, these reactions will get smaller and the increments of trend movement will become larger. When the reaction suddenly is larger, the move is ending; the change in the character of the move signals a prudent exit, even if prices continue erratically in the direction of the trend.

A similar example occurs in the way prices react to economic reports or government action. The first time the Federal Reserve acts to raise rates after a prolonged decline the market is not prepared and bond prices react sharply lower. Before the next meeting of the Fed the market may be more apprehensive, but is likely to be neutral with regard to expectation of policy. However, once there is a pattern of increasing rates following signs of inflation, the market begins to anticipate the action of the Fed. The sharp move occurs when the government fails to take action.

Testing Your Skill

Recognizing a pattern is both an art and a science. Not everyone has an eye for patterns; others will see formations where no one else would. The first decision may be the most important: How much of the chart do you use? It is perfectly normal for different time intervals to show different trends. In some cases, arbitrarily cutting the chart at some previous date might cause a clear trend to disappear. The price scale (the vertical axis) of the chart is another variable not considered by some chartists. When applying methods requir-

[14] Jesse H. Thompson, "What Textbooks Never Tell You," *Technical Analysis of Stocks & Commodities* (November/December 1983).

ing specific angles, the chart paper is expected to have square boxes. Regardless of the shape of the box, the formations will appear very different from one piece of chart paper, or computerized page, to another.

The timeliness of the pattern identification is the most serious problem. Can the formation be interpreted in time to act on a breakout, or is the pattern only seen afterward? At different stages of development, the lines may appear to form different patterns. Before using your charting skills to trade, practice simulating the day-to-day development of prices as follows:

1. Hold a piece of the paper over the right side of the chart, covering the most recent months, or better still, have someone else give you the partial chart.
2. Look at the chart and analyze the formations.
3. Determine what action will be based on your interpretation. Be specific.
4. Move the paper 1 day to the right, or have someone else give you the next day's price.
5. Record any orders that would have been filled based on the prior day's analysis. Don't cheat.
6. Determine whether the new day's price would have altered your formations and plans.
7. Return to step 3 until finished.

This simple exercise might save a lot of money but may be discouraging. With practice you will become better at finding and using formations and will learn to select the ones that work best. Very few traders base their trading decisions entirely on bar charts. Many refer to charts for confirmation of separate technical or fundamental analysis; others will only use the most obvious major trendlines, looking for points at which multiple indicators converge. The general acceptance of bar charting analysis and the need for visualization makes it a lasting tool.

10

Volume, Open Interest, and Breadth

Volume pattern has always been tied closely to chart analysis in both the stock and futures markets. It is a valuable piece of information that is not often used, and one of the few items, other than price, that is traditionally considered valid data for the technician. Nevertheless, there has been little research published that relates this factor to futures markets; its popular use has adopted the same conclusions as in stock market analysis.

The stock and futures markets have two other measures of participation that are related, yet not the same. In equities, the large number of shares being traded allow for measurements of *breadth*. In the same way that the stock index has become a popular measure of overall market trend, the breadth of the market is the total number of stocks that have risen or fallen during a specific period. When you have the ability to view the bigger picture of market movement, breadth seems to be the natural adjunct to the index.

In futures, *open interest* is the measurement of those participants with outstanding trades; it is the netting out of all open positions in any one market or contract, and it gives an understanding of the depth of volume that is possible. A market that trades only 10,000 contracts per day, but has an open interest of 250,000, is telling the trader that there are many participants who will enter the market when the price is right. These are most likely to be commercial traders, using the futures markets for hedging.

CONTRACT VOLUME VERSUS TOTAL VOLUME

In futures markets, in which individual contracts specify standard delivery months, the volume of each contract is available, along with the total volume of the market; that is, the total volume of all individual contracts. Spread transactions are not included in volume. This information is officially posted one day late, but estimates are available for many markets during the day. Total volume of crude oil is estimated every hour and released to on-line news services.

Individual contract volume is important to determine the delivery month that is most active. Traders find that the best execution fills are most likely where there is greatest liquidity. Analysts, however, have a difficult time assessing volume trends because there is a natural increase in volume as a contract moves from second month out to the nearby and traders shift their positions to the closest delivery month; there is a corresponding decline in volume as the delivery date becomes close. Looking only at the volume of one delivery month is equivalent to ignoring seasonality in an agricultural market.

Each futures market has its unique pattern of volume for individual contracts. Some, such as the interest rates, shift abruptly on the last day of the month prior to delivery, because the exchange raises margins dramatically for all traders holding positions in the delivery month. Currencies are very different and tend to trade actively in the nearest month up to one or two days before that contract goes *off the board*. While volume increases slightly in the next deferred contract, anyone trading sizable positions will need to stay with the nearby contract to the end.

Other than for determining which contract to trade, and perhaps the size order that the market can absorb, an analysis of volume as discussed in this chapter must use total volume, the aggregate of all contracts, to have a data series that does not suffer the patterns of increasing and decreasing participation based on the coming and going of individual delivery months. When traders roll from the nearby to the next deferred contract, the transactions are performed as a spread, and those trades are not included in the volume figures. Because positions are closed out in one contract and opened in another, there is no change in the open interest.

The stock market equivalent to using total volume would be to add the volume for all stocks in a similar group. This would help smooth over those periods when the volume of one stock is very low. If the group is not highly correlated in price movement, the end result might be a volume series that has very little to do with the stock you are trading.

Tick Volume

The popularity of quote machines and fast trading requires a measurement of volume that can be used immediately to make decisions. Because total volume is not available on a timely basis to day traders, *tick volume* has become a substitute. Tick volume is the number of changes in price, regardless of volume, that occur during any time interval. Tick volume relates directly to actual volume because, as markets become more active, prices change back and forth more often. If only two trades occur in a 5-minute period, then the market is not liquid, regardless of the size of the orders that changed hands. From an analytic view, tick volume gives a reasonable approximation of true volume and can be used as a substitute. From a practical view, it is the only choice. Tick volume patterns are discussed later in this chapter.

VARIATIONS FROM THE NORMAL PATTERNS

One final note of warning when using volume indicators to confirm price direction: markets have patterns in volume that cause the same effect as seasonality. To decide that a buy signal is more important because it came near the end of the trading day, when volume was much higher than midday, is not correct because volume is always higher at the beginning and end of the day. You may conclude, in general, that those two periods produce more reliable trading signals; however, a volume confirmation must be compared against the normal volume for that time period.

Open interest and market breadth also have seasonal patterns. In agricultural markets, farmers hedge in larger numbers during the growing season than in the winter, raising the open interest. In stocks, there is a lot of activity associated with the end-of-year positioning for tax purposes, and traditional rallying during holiday seasons. While this predictable market activity may be enough to confirm your positions, it does not indicate that something special is occurring. Identifying these variations will be discussed in detail later in this chapter.

Volume Drops and Spikes

Volume spikes are carefully watched because they are seen as a significant positive action by the traders. For a stock that has been relatively inactive, a volume spike is a warning that something is changing. In futures, a day of very high activity means that the market is sensitive to news. In both cases, a sharp increase in volume can be a predictor of change, or at least of higher volatility. This will be discussed in the section "Volume as a Predictor of Volatility," later in this chapter.

At this time it is worth remembering that a volume spike is a clear indicator of a positive action, while a volume drop can be ambiguous. Volume can decline because there is little interest in a stock or futures market; buying and selling pressure have been eliminated. When a currency, gold, or any traded product reaches a price that is considered fair (also called equilibrium), volume normally declines. Volume may also drop on the day before a holiday, or just by chance. While there are seasonal and other predictable patterns associated with volume drops, they are far less certain than large increases.

STANDARD INTERPRETATION

The interpretation of volume has been a part of market lore since charting began. The best consolidation of that information was published in the monograph by W.L. Jiler, *Volume and Open Interest: A Key to Commodity Price Forecasting,* a companion piece to his most popular *Forecasting Commodity Prices with Vertical Line Charts* (see references in Chapter 9 ("Charting")).

In both the futures and stock markets, volume has much the same interpretation, when volume increases it is said to confirm the direction of prices. Price changes that occur on very light volume are less dependable for indicating future direction than those changes associated with relatively heavy volume. An additional uncertainty exists for stocks that are not actively traded, and for low prices shares where the total dollar volume can be small. In these cases it might be best to look at the accumulated volume of similar companies, or its sector.

Open interest is a concept unique to futures markets, but helps to explain the depth of the market as well as trader expectation. New interest in a market brings new buyers or sellers, which increases the open interest, the net of all outstanding contracts being traded. When the open interest increases while prices rise quickly, it is commonly interpreted as more traders entering long positions. This may seem strange because for every new buyer of a futures contract there must be a new seller; however, the seller is likely to be someone looking to hold a position for a few hours or days, looking to profit from the normal ups and downs of price movement. The position trader, who is willing to sit for much more time holding a long position, is the one who is attributed with the open interest. In reality, no one knows. However, if prices keep rising, the shorts are more likely to be forced out while the longs have staying power.

The traditional interpretation of changes in volume and open interest (for futures markets) can be summarized as follows:

Volume	Open Interest	Interpretation
Rising	Rising	Confirmation of trend
Rising	Falling	Position liquidation (at extremes)
Falling	Rising	Slow accumulation
Falling	Falling	Congestion phase

Some of the generally accepted notions for the use of volume and open interest are:

1. Open interest increases during a trending period.
2. Volume may decline but open interest builds during an accumulation phase. Volume occasionally spikes.
3. Rising prices and declining volume/open interest indicate a pending change of direction.

In the stock market, when confirming the direction of the overall market, the breadth of trading (percentage of rising to total stocks) should be used if it closely approximates the stocks in the index. It would be inconsistent, for example, to use the total breadth of all stocks traded on the New York Stock Exchange, to confirm a move in a portfolio that contained only the 30 stocks of the Dow Industrials. In that case, you would need to construct an indicator of breadth that used only those 30 stocks.

Exceptions

No method is without exceptions, including volume patterns in the stock market. There are days or periods when volume is expected to change, and must be considered in the analysis. For example, volume is lighter:

On the first day of the week

On the day before a holiday

During the summer

It is equally difficult to forget that volume is heavier on *triple witching day,* when S&P 500 futures, options on futures, and options on the cash index all expire at the same time.

In the futures markets, there are similar patterns. Lighter volume will exist during holiday periods and summer months, but may be heavier on Fridays and Mondays during a trending market or a weather market for agricultural products. Liquidation often occurs before the weekend, and positions are reentered on the first day of the week.

Richard Arms's Equivolume

Most of the techniques for using volume discussed in this chapter will multiply or accumulate volume, creating an index that rises faster as volume increases. *Equivolume,* a charting method introduced by Richard Arms, takes the unique approach of substituting volume for time along the bottom scale of a chart. When volume increases, the price bar is elongated to the right, rather than the standard approach of extending the height of the bar.

There are no systematic methods for using this technique included here, and applications parallel standard chart interpretations; however, analysts can represent this type of chart by creating a new price series in which the daily closing price is repeated based on the relative volume. For example, if the normal volume day causes a closing price to be repeated 10 times, then a day with twice the volume will repeat that price 20 times, and a day with half the volume will show 5 prices. This approach may cause a short-term moving average trend to look strange; however, a linear regression or long-term trend should reflect the importance of varying time.

VOLUME INDICATORS

Both the stock and futures markets are familiar to indicators that use only volume, or those that add volume, intending to make other calculations more robust. The following section gives the most popular of these indicators, most of which originate in the stock market and many of which use the number of advancing and declining stocks. Readers should note the way in which the data is used from one technique to another and consider the significance of these changes. They will be discussed at the end of this section.

Volume Momentum and Percentage Change

The most basic of volume indicators are momentum and rate of change. These techniques treat volume as price. For momentum, this means finding the change in volume over a specific time interval; percentage change measures the size of the volume change relative to the starting value.

$$\text{Volume Momentum} = \text{volume today} - \text{volume}_{n\text{-days ago}}$$

$$\text{Volume \%} = \frac{\text{volume today} - \text{volume}_{n\text{-days ago}}}{\text{volume}_{n\text{-days ago}}}$$

On-Balance Volume

Made famous by Joseph Granville, *On-Balance Volume* (OBV)[1] is now a byword in stock analyst circles. On days when prices close higher, it is assumed that all volume is representative of the buyers; on lower days, the volume is controlled by the sellers. Although each day yields a new value, these values are added together to form a new series. The result is a volume-weighted series. In the following formula, the expression in parentheses simply uses the closing prices to produce a value of +1, 0, or −1, which then determines whether today's volume will be added or subtracted from the volume series:

$$\text{OBV}_{\text{today}} = \text{OBV}_{\text{previous}} + \left(\frac{\text{close} - \text{close}_{\text{previous}}}{@\text{abs}(\text{close} - \text{close}_{\text{previous}})} \right) \times \text{volume}$$

Determining the OBV manually is a simple accumulation process. In Table 10-1, there was greater volume on days in which prices rose and lower volume on declining days. This is expected in a market with a clear uptrend. The advantage of recording the OBV is in observing when the trend of the prices diverges from the OBV values. The general interpretation of OBV is given in Table 10-2.

Because a volume series has many erratic qualities, caused by large variations in volume from day to day, it is most often used by applying a trend from 1 to 100 weeks, then identifying a simple volume direction when the OBV value crosses the trend. An upward trend in volume is interpreted as a confirmation of the current price direction, while a downturn in volume can be liquidation or uncertainty.

Simple Variation

An indicator that closely resembles On-Balance Volume is a running total of the days when volume increases minus the days when volume delines. That is, add 1 to the cumulative value on a day when today's volume is greater than the previous day, otherwise subtract 1. This volume count indicator (VCI) can be written as:

[1] Robert W. Colby and Thomas A. Meyers, *The Encyclopedia of Technical Market Indicators* (Dow Jones-Irwin, 1988) is a comprehensive study of most market indicators, including On-Balance Volume and some other techniques included in this section.

TABLE 10-1   Calculating On-Balance Volume

Closing Price	Daily Volume (in 1,000s)	On-Balance Volume
310	25	25
315	30	55
318	27	82
316	15	67
314	12	55
320	28	83

TABLE 10-2   Interpreting On-Balance Volume

Price Direction	OBV Direction	Interpretation
Up	Up	Clear uptrend
	Sideways	Moderate uptrend
	Down	Weak uptrend near reversal
Sideways	Up	Accumulation period (bottom)
	Sideways	No determination
	Down	Distribution period (top)
Down	Up	Weak downtrend near reversal
	Sideways	Moderate downtrend
	Down	Clear downtrend

$$\text{VCI}_{\text{today}} = \text{VCI}_{\text{previous}} + \frac{\text{volume}_{\text{today}} - \text{volume}_{\text{previous}}}{@\text{abs}(\text{volume}_{\text{today}} - \text{volume}_{\text{previous}})}$$

Volume Accumulator

A modification to Granville's OBV system is Mark Chaiken's *Volume Accumulator* (VA). Instead of assigning all the volume to either the buyers or the sellers, the Volume Accumulator uses a proportional amount of volume corresponding to the relationship of the closing price to the intraday mean price. If prices close at the high or low of the day, all volume is given to the buyers or sellers as in the OBV calculation.[2] If the close is at the midrange, no volume is added.

$$\text{VA}_{\text{today}} = \text{VA}_{\text{previous}} + \left(\frac{\text{close} - \text{low}}{\text{high} - \text{low}} - .50 \right) \times 2 \times \text{volume}$$

Other Accumulation Index Techniques

The *Price and Volume Trend* (PVT) applies volume to the percentage price change from close to close, which can be positive or negative. The *Positive Volume Index* (PVI) and *Negative Volume Index* (NVI) take the approach that a single indicator, which adds and subtracts volume based on market direction, is not as informative as two separate series that can be viewed at the same time.

$$\text{PVT}_{\text{today}} = \text{PVT}_{\text{previous}} + \left(\frac{\text{close} - \text{close}_{\text{previous}}}{\text{close}_{\text{previous}}} \right) \times \text{volume}$$

if close < close$_{\text{previous}}$ then PVI$_{\text{today}}$ = PVI$_{\text{previous}}$ + volume

if close > close$_{\text{previous}}$ then NVI$_{\text{today}}$ = NVI$_{\text{previous}}$ + volume

Separating Advancing from Declining Volume

The most basic of all techniques for determining market breadth is the *Advance-Decline Index,* which creates a new series by adding the net of the number of advancing and declining stocks each day. Unchanged issues are ignored.

---

[2] Both OBV and the Volume Accumulator are characterized as momentum systems. See Chapter 6 for more information on similar techniques.

Advance-Decline Oscillator = Advances − Declines

Advance-Decline Index$_{today}$ = Advance-Decline Index$_{previous}$ + advance − decline

In some of the techniques that follow, only the oscillator, or single-period calculation, may be shown. An index can be created by accumulating these values.

Sibbett's Demand Index

One method that smooths out volume because it uses the total activity of the past 10 days is James Sibbett's *Demand Index.* The technique bears a resemblance to the approach used in Wilder's RSI. It can be used as an oscillator with individual daily values or accumulated into an index. The individual days are calculated as:

$$\text{Demand Index} = \frac{@\text{sum(upside volume, 10)}}{@\text{sum(downside volume, 10)}}$$

where @sum is a function that sums the past 10 days of upside and downside volume, found in the *Wall Street Journal* under the heading "Trading Activity." Arthur Merrill, another well-known stock analyst, has suggested applying 5 days to this same technique.

Aspray's Demand Oscillator

Using direction to separate volume into two series of *Buying Pressure* and *Selling Pressure,* Aspray then nets them into his own *Demand Oscillator.*[3] Note that during a rising market the selling pressure has been *divided* by a percentage of the volume, which has been scaled to be greater than 1. The following calculations show the separate steps needed to create Aspray's Demand Oscillator:

For rising prices:

Buying Pressure = volume

$$\text{Selling Pressure} = \frac{\text{volume}}{\left(K \times \dfrac{\text{close}_{today} - \text{close}_{previous}}{\text{close}_{previous}} \right)}$$

For declining prices:

$$\text{Buying Pressure} = \frac{\text{volume}}{\left(K \times \dfrac{\text{close}_{today} - \text{close}_{previous}}{\text{close}_{previous}} \right)}$$

and where

$$K = \frac{3 \times \text{close}}{@\text{avg}(@\text{highest(high, 2)} - @\text{lowest(low, 2), 10})}$$

and

Demand Oscillator = BP − SP

K is a volatility scaling factor, which is 3 times the closing price divided by the 10-day moving average of the 2-day high-low range, and has a value likely to be well over 100. For example, if the S&P is trading at 600 and the average volatility is 10 full basis points (which is very high for a 10-day average), then $K = 1,800/10 = 180$.

---

[3] Thomas Aspray, "Fine-tuning the Demand Index," *Technical Analysis of Stocks & Commodities* (June 1986), and "Demand Oscillator Momentum," *Technical Analysis of Stocks & Commodities* (September 1989).

Bolton-Tremblay

Introducing the net advancing stocks compared with the number of stocks that were unchanged, the Bolton-Tremblay approach also includes a form of geometric weighting of the results:

$$\text{Bolton-Tremblay}_{\text{today}} = \frac{\text{advancing} - \text{declining}}{\text{unchanged}}$$

if $\text{Bolton-Tremblay}_{\text{today}} > 0$ then Accum BT_{today} = Accum $\text{BT}_{\text{previous}} + \sqrt{\text{Bolton-Tremblay}_{\text{today}}}$

if $\text{Bolton-Tremblay}_{\text{today}} < 0$ then Accum BT_{today} = Accum $\text{BT}_{\text{previous}} - \sqrt{\text{Bolton-Tremblay}_{\text{today}}}$

Schultz

Schultz chose to look at the advancing stocks only as a percentage of the total stocks:

$$\text{Schultz A/T}_{\text{today}} = \text{Schultz A/T}_{\text{previous}} + \frac{\text{advancing}}{\text{advancing} + \text{declining} + \text{unchanged}}$$

McClellan Oscillator

Similar to the Advance-Decline Index, the *McClellan Oscillator* does not accumulate the net change in breadth, but looks at the individual changes as an oscillator:

$$\text{McClellan Oscillator} = \text{advances} - \text{declines}$$

Upside/Downside Ratio

A simple *upside/downside ratio* (UDR) has also been used; however, the ratio value has no symmetry. When the declining volume is very low, for example, only 20% of the total volume, the UDR will have a value of 4.0. In contrast, if the advancing volume is low, the ratio is limited to the range between 0 and 1.

$$\text{UDR} = \frac{\text{Advancing volume}}{\text{Declining volume}}$$

Tick Volume Indicator

In a manner similar to Wilder's RSI, Blau double smooths the tick volume as a way of confirming price direction. The Tick Volume Indicator (seen in Figure 10-1) is:

$$\text{TVI}(r, s) = \frac{100 \times \text{DEMA}(\text{upticks}, r, s) - \text{DEMA}(\text{downticks}, r, s)}{\text{DEMA}(\text{upticks}, r, s) + \text{DEMA}(\text{downticks}, r, s)}$$

which ranges from -100 to $+100$ and where DEMA is the double (EMA) smoothing of the downticks or upticks over the past *s* bars, with the initial smoothing over *r* bars.

Programming Volume Indicators

Volume indicators are easy programming on both a spreadsheet and Omega's *Easy Language.* The following examples include only some of the indicators discussed in this chapter; the others are very similar and can be added using the same form.

Spreadsheet Code

Using Corel's *Quattro,* the following spreadsheet shows the Eurodollars beginning in April 1993. The calculations for On-Balance Volume, Volume Accumulator, and Price-Volume

FIGURE 10-1   Blau's Tick Volume Indicator.

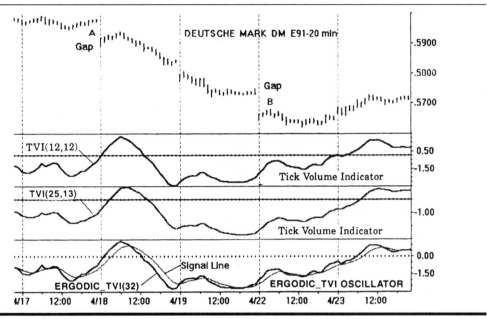

Source: William Blau, *Momentum, Direction, and Divergence* (John Wiley & Sons, 1995, p. 45). © 1995 William Blau. Reprinted by permission of John Wiley & Sons, Inc.

Trend are shown in the rightmost three columns. The spreadsheet code for these calculations are shown after the sample output.

Col	Name	Start Row	
A	Date	5	
B	High	5	
C	Low	5	
D	Close	5	
E	Volume	5	
F	OBV	7	@IF(D7-D6>0,F6+F7,@IF(D7-D6<0,F6-E7,F6))
G	VACC	7	+G6+(((D7-C7)/(B7-C7))-0.5)*2*E7
H	PVT	7	+H6+E7*(D7-D6)/D6
I	MAP	45	@AVG(D26.D45)
J	PX	48	(I48-I46)*100/I45
K	MA	45	@AVG(D6.D45)
L	MADIFF	48	+K48-K45
M	MAV	45	@AVG(F26.F45) [for OBV]
N	VX	48	(M48-M45)*100/M45
O	DVG	48	@IF(J48*N48<0,J48-N48,0)
P	OBV VX	Signal from row 49	

```
                @IF(L49>0#AND#L48<=0#AND#N49>=$D$3,"buy",
                    @IF(L49>0#AND#L48<=0,"exitS",
                    @IF(L49<=0#AND#L48>0#AND#N49>=$D$3,"sell",
                    @IF(L49<=0#AND#L48>0,"exitL",
                    @IF(L49<$D$3,"exitALL"," "))))
```

Q   OBV VX DVG Signal from row 49

```
                        @IF(L49>0#AND#L48<=0#AND#N49>=$D$3
                            #AND#@ABS(O49)<=$E$3,"buy",
                            @IF(L49>0#AND#L48<=0,"exitS",
                            @IF(L49<=0#AND#L48>0,#AND#N49>=$D$3
                            #AND#@ABS(O49)<=$E$3,"sell",
                            @IF(L49<=0#AND#L48>0,"exitL",
                            @IF(L49<$D$3#AND#@ABS(O49)>$E$3,
                            "exitALL"," ")))))
```

R	Mom Osc	25	(@AVG(E22.E25) - @AVG(E25.E6))*100/@AVG(E22-E25)
S	Avg Mom	45	@AVG(R26.R45)
T	StDev Mom	45	@STD(R26.R45)
U	Mom Signal	45	@IF(L45>0#AND#L44<=0#AND#R45>=S45-$F$3*T45,"buy",

```
                            @IF(L45>0#AND#L44<=0,"exitS",
                            @IF(L45<=0#AND#L44>0#AND#R45>=S45-$F$3*T45,"sell",
                            @IF(L45<=0#AND#L44>0,"exitL"," ")))))
```

V	ROC	25	(E25-E6)*100/E6
W	Avg ROC	45	@AVG(V26-V45)
X	StDev ROC	45	@STD(V26.V45)
Y	ROC Signal	45	@IF(L45>0#AND#L44<=0#AND#V45>=W45-$F$3*T45,"buy",

```
                            @IF(L45>0#AND#L44<=0,"exitS",
                            @IF(L45<=0#AND#L44>0#AND#V45>=
                            W45-$F$3*T45,"sell",@IF(L45<=0#AND#L44>0,"exitL","")))))
```

Omega's Easy Language Code

The following program code gives an example of a system that uses one of eight volume measurements to filter the entry or exit of a trade. When the input `ttype` is negative the input values are treated as an entry filter; when `ttype` is positive the values are used for an exit filter.

```
{PJK Volume: Create a volume filter
 Copyright 1995-1998, PJKaufman. All rights reserved.}

inputs: period(20), ttype(1), maxdn(0), maxdvg(0), npsd(.5), ddays(3);
vars:   px(0), vx(0), Kvol(0), map(0), mav(0),sdiff(0), madays(0),ma(0), dvg(0),
        nd(0), madiff(0), avgv(0), sdv(0), tentry(0), avg2(0), type(0), sc(0),
        avghl(0), signhl(0);
{Exit type      =1, On-Balance Volume
                =2, Chiaken Volume Accumulator
                =3, Negative Volume Index
                =4, Positive Volume Index
                =5, Price and Volume Trend
                =6, Volume oscillator (npsd used for exit level)
                =7, Volume rate of change
                =8, Low volume exit
For entry filter use negative type

{test exit}
type = ttype;
if type < 0 then begin
   tentry = 1;
   type = @absvalue(ttype);
   end;

{price index}
map = @average(close,period);

if ddays < 1 then nd = 1 else nd = ddays;
if map[nd] = 0 then px = 0 else px = (map - map[nd])*100/map[nd];

{On-Balance Volume}
if type = 1 then begin
```

```
       if close > close[1] then KMAvol = KMAvol + volume
              else if close < close[1] then Kvol = Kvol - volume;
    end;

{Chaikin Volume Accumulator }
if type = 2 then Kvol = Kvol +(((close - low) / (high - low)) - .5)*2*volume

{Negative Volume Index}
if type = 3 then begin
    if volume < volume[1] then Kvol = Kvol[1] + (close - close[1])*Kvol/close[1]
       else if Kvol = 0 then Kvol = volume
       else Kvol = Kvol[1];
    end;

{Positive Volume Index}
if type = 4 then begin
    if volume > volume[1] then Kvol = Kvol[1] + (close - close[1])*Kvol[1]/close[1]
       else if Kvol = 0 then Kvol = volume
       else Kvol = Kvol[1];
       end;

{Price and Volume Trend}
if type = 5 then Kvol = Kvol +volume*(close - close[1]) / close[1]

{Volume oscillator}
if type = 6 then
    Kvol = (@average(volume,ddays) -
    @average(volume,period))*100/@average(volume,ddays);

{Volume rate-of-change}
if type = 7 then begin
    if Kvol = 0 then Kvol = volume;
    if volume[period] = 0 then Kvol = Kvol[1] else
    Kvol = (volume - volume[period])*100/volume[period];
    end;

{Moving average of price}
madays = 2*period;
ma = @average(close,madays);
madiff = ma - ma[nd];

if type < 6 or type = 9 then begin
    mav = @average(Kvol,period);
    if mav[nd] = 0 then vx = 0 else vx = (mav - mav[nd])*100/mav[nd];
    sdiff = px - vx;
{record divergence only}
  if vx*px < 0 then dvg = sdiff else dvg = 0;
    if madiff > 0 and madiff[1] <= 0 then begin
       exitshort at market;
       if tentry = 0 and (vx >= maxdn and @absvalue(dvg) <= maxdvg) then
       buy at market;
       end;
    if madiff < 0 and madiff[1] >= 0 then begin
       exitlong at market;
       if tentry = 0 and (vx >= maxdn and @absvalue(dvg) <= maxdvg) then
       sell at market;
       end;
    if vx < maxdn and @absvalue(dvg) > maxdvg then begin
       exitlong at market;
       exitshort at market;
       end;
    end;
```

```
if type = 6 or type = 7 then begin
   avgv = @average(Kvol,period);
   sdv = @stddev(Kvol,period);
   if tentry = 0 then begin
      if (madiff > 0 and madiff[1] <= 0) or Kvol <= avgv-npsd*sdv then
      exitshort at market;
      if (madiff < 0 and madiff[1] >= 0) or Kvol <= avgv-npsd*sdv then
      exitlong at market;
      if madiff > 0 and madiff[1] <= 0 then buy at market;
      if madiff < 0 and madiff[1] >= 0 then sell at market;
      end
   else begin
      if madiff > 0 and madiff[1] <= 0 then exitshort at market;
      if madiff < 0 and madiff[1] >= 0 then exitlong at market;
      if madiff > 0 and madiff[1] <= 0 and Kvol <= avgv-npsd*sdv then
      buy at market;
      if madiff < 0 and madiff[1] >= 0 and Kvol <= avgv-npsd*sdv then
      sell at market;
      end;
   end;

{Low volume exit, comparing slow and fast average}
if type = 8 then begin
   avgv = @average(volume,period);
   avg2 = @average(volume,ddays);

if tentry = 0 then begin
      if (madiff > 0 and madiff[1] <= 0) or avg2 <= avgv*npsd
      then exitshort at market;
      if (madiff < 0 and madiff[1] >= 0) or avg2 <= avgv*npsd
      then exitlong at market;
        if madiff > 0 and madiff[1] <= 0 then buy at market;
        if madiff < 0 and madiff[1] >= 0 then sell at market;
      end
   else begin
      if madiff > 0 and madiff[1] <= 0 then exitshort at market;
      if madiff < 0 and madiff[1] >= 0 then exitlong at market;
      if madiff > 0 and madiff[1] <= 0 and avg2 <= avgv*npsd then buy at market;
      if madiff < 0 and madiff[1] >= 0 and avg2 <= avgv*npsd then sell at market;
      end;
   end;
```

Is One Volume/Breadth Indicator Better Than Another?

The final test of a successful indicator is whether it adds value to your trading decisions. This can be determined by programming the indicator into the total strategy and testing the rules over a reasonable historic time period. Before doing that, we should decide what the increase or decrease in volume or breadth is telling us. If performance testing does not confirm our expectations, than we must rethink the approach because the chance of an error has increased. What appears to be a profitable discovery may only be an unlikely coincidence.

Looking at the selection of indicators, we see that small net changes in price can result in all volume being designated to one market direction. This is the case with Granville's *On-Balance Volume* and Bolton-Tremblay. Is it reasonable to add all volume to the accumulated index if the S&P gained only a fraction of one point? On a single day this may seem to be arbitrary, but just as so many of the simple systems, over a long period of time the net effect of this approach is sound. In addition, we should not forget that these indicators fail to account for a range of noise that is similar to the erratic movement of prices; that is, there is a normal variation in volume that does not mean anything special. On the other side, these indicators fail to isolate outliers, the significant events or price shocks that are associated with high volatility.

The changes made by Mark Chaiken, which take a percentage of volume based on the relative close of prices within the daily range, have a very sensible basis and avoid the all-or-nothing technique used in *On-Balance Volume.* Sibbett's *Demand Index,* by using the sum of 10 days' volume, avoids this problem completely and smooths out results, a situation often needed when using the highly variable values of volume and breadth.

On the more confusing side, it has been suggested that the *Demand Index,* which simply accumulates the net of advances minus declines, be used with the absolute value of the daily calculation, *Advances – Declines.* That would give the same value when advances outnumbered declines by the same amount as declines outnumbering advances, which appears to lose information and fails to distinguish between market direction. Unless you clearly understand why taking the absolute value of any advance-decline formula makes sense, they should be avoided, even if historical testing shows a better result than other methods.

By seeing these indicators close together, they appear to be a collection of minor manipulations of data. The resulting series still requires interpretation using trendlines, divergence, or new highs and lows. Instead of having to interpret only the difficult movements of prices, we have added an equally difficult series of volume. While it is not clear that volume is always useful in analyzing price movement, it can impart valuable information in certain situations.

INTERPRETING VOLUME SYSTEMATICALLY

Most systematic approaches to volume apply a long-term smoothing method to the data, then identify trend changes to confirm price direction. This can be implemented with any of the accumulation indices, but not with single-day momentum or oscillator values. For the oscillators, most analysts have taken the approach that high volume confirms a new price direction; therefore, they look for a reversal signal at the same time as peak or near-peak volume. If they do not occur at the same time, a volume peak should precede a trend change. A decline in volume has also been used to confirm direction, but it is more likely to indicate that prices have reached equilibrium, and that a further advance or decline requires additional confirmation.

Moving Average Approaches

A straightforward way of using volume is to calculate a 10-day moving average of the volume to be used as a confirmation of a 20-day trend position.[4] By simply requiring the current volume to be greater than the average volume over that past 10 days, you introduce the idea of greater participation associated with the new trend. An additional important benefit is that this volume condition acts as a filter, eliminating a substantial number of trades. If the net returns are the same, the volume-filtered approach is far better because you are out of the market more, and are not reversing your position every time there is a new signal.

A similar method was proposed by Waxenberg.[5] A 10-day moving average of the volume is calculated as the normal level, and a change in trend must be confirmed by a 20%

---

[4] Alex Saitta, "A Price and Volume-Based System," *Technical Analysis of Stocks & Commodities* (March 1996).

[5] Howard K. Waxenberg, "Technical Analysis of Volume," *Technical Analysis of Stocks & Commodities* (March 1986).

increase in volume above this norm. (The 20% band acts as an additional smoothing filter, but may be replaced by a longer trend and smaller band.) Extremes in a trending move can be found at points that exceed approximately a 40% volume increase. Applied to the stock market, Waxenberg used the extreme volumes to indicate the end of a sell-off. To add more flexibility for longer test periods, and to adjust for volatility, Bollinger bands (based on about 2 standard deviations, or 95% probability) can be substituted for the fixed percentage bands.

Alternately, using 13 days of volume, subtract the total down volume from the total up volume. A plot of the results will serve as a momentum indicator from which overbought and oversold levels can be identified. If these values are unstable due to lack of liquidity, they may be smoothed using a short-term moving average.

Advance-Decline System

Advance and decline values, as with most volume figures, can be more useful if they are smoothed. By combining peak values of the net of smoothed advancing and declining shares with a directional move in price, Conners and Hayward have created a basic system structure that they named CHADTP[6] (Conners-Hayward Advance-Decline Trading Patterns™). This system tries to identify reversal patterns by applying the following steps:

1. Add the past 5 days of advancing issues (New York Stock Exchange)
2. Add the past 5 days of declining issues (New York Stock Exchange)
3. Subtract the 5-day sum of declining issues (1) from the advancing issues (2)
4. Divide by 5 to get the average daily value

```
CHADTP = (@sum(advNYSE,5) - @sum(declNYSE,5)) /5
```

To trade using this oscillator, Conners and Hayward have determined that ±400 are the extreme levels where the values have been overbought and oversold. Based on this, we can apply the following rules to the S&P futures:

1. Sell when CHADTP > +400 and the SP trades .10 below the low of the previous day; buy when CHADTP < −400 and the SP trades .10 above the high of the previous day.
2. Note that the oscillator does not have to exceed its recent extremes on the day of the buy or sell signal.
3. Timing is best if the signal corresponds to a newspaper commentary indicating "depressed volume" (which is seen as an excess of cash waiting to enter).

This system targets returns over a 5- to 7-day period. A drop in the oscillator, which results in values in the midrange, is an opportunity to exit, or a standard oscillator of price can be constructed to generate overbought and oversold signals within this time frame. An opposite entry signal would reverse the position.

AN INTEGRATED PROBABILITY MODEL

If there is a noticeable relationship between price, volume, and open interest (or market breadth), then a probability model can be constructed to test its importance.[7] To do this it is necessary to construct a one-day-ahead forecast using a simple linear regression model, then back-test weighting factors for each element. Because of the powerful software products, this has become a very manageable process. Using Omega's *Easy Language,* each one-day-ahead forecast is determined using *n* past days:

---

[6] Laurence A. Conners and Blake E. Hayward, *Investment Secrets of a Hedge Fund Manager* (Probus, 1995).

[7] Based on the May 1995 "CSI Technical Journal" (Commodity Systems, Inc., Boca Raton, FL).

1. **Price forecast:** `Pf = Price + LinearRegSlope(close,n)`
2. **Volume forecast:** `Vf = Volume + LinearRegSlope(volume,n)`
3. **Open interest forecast:** `Of = Opint + LinearRegSlope(opint,n)`
4. **On-Balance Volume forecast:** `OBVf = OBV + LinearRegSlope(OBV,n)`

The function *LinearRegSlope* gives the one-period increase or decrease in the value based on a straight-line fit of the past n days, and can be added to the current value to get the one-day-ahead forecast. The period n can be selected by subtracting the actual next-day value from the forecast and creating an error series that can be measured using a standard deviation. The number of days, n, that generates the smallest standard deviation is the best forecast period. It is likely that the optimal forecast period will differ for each of the four items above, and this becomes a matter of concern. Is there a reason why the forecast period be the same for all of the predictions? If we are independently trying to forecast volume, then fixing the periods at the same length does not seem necessary. If we are trying to discover whether a change in volume is related to a change in price, as we are here, then the same regression interval seems important. (These and other testing procedures are thoroughly discussed in Chapter 21 ("Testing").

Having found the four one-day-ahead forecasts, an index can be created that gives one weight w_1 to the price forecast and the balance, $1 - w_1$, to a combination of the other three factors. This assumes that price is the most important predictor of price.

$$\text{Forecast Index} = w_1 \times \text{Pf} + (1 - w_1) \times (w_2\text{Vf} + w_3\text{Of} + w_4\text{OBVf})$$

This formula can be backtested for values of w_1, w_2, w_3, and w_4 between 0 and 1. The final index can be used instead of price for determining the trend. It will still require a moving average, or some trendline, to signal new uptrends and downtrends; however, the results, if successful, should be more reliable than only using price.

One advantage of testing the weighting factors is that, if one of the four elements is not helpful in predicting a trend, the weighting factor should be zero. Another approach, that does not cluster the nonprice data together, would be to treat each item separately:

$$\text{Forecast Index} = w_1\text{Pf} + w_2\text{Vf} + w_3\text{Of} + w_4\text{OBVf}$$

$$\text{and where} \quad \sum_{i=1}^{4} w_i = 1$$

The sum of the weighting factors should always be 1, equal to 100%.

INTRADAY VOLUME PATTERNS

Identifying increases and decreases in volume during the trading day must consider over-riding patterns caused by the way traders enter orders. The pattern of intraday volume can be seen using tick volume as a practical substitute for actual volume, which is usually not available until the next day. To create a meanful chart of 30-minute volume patterns, each interval was compared with the first 30 minutes of the day and recorded as a percentage of that initial tick volume. Figure 10-2 shows the results of three futures markets, Eurodollars, S&P 500, and Deutschemarks taken over a 1-year period using the nearest delivery.

The patterns of the three markets shown in Figure 10-2 are similar in that the greatest volume is at the beginning and end of the trading day, yet very different in their internal patterns. Eurodollars, which have the highest volume of all futures markets, show much larger volume on the opening and closing 30-minute periods.

It should not be surprising to see the extreme clustering at both ends of the trading day. Orders enter the market early in reaction to news and events that occurred since the close of the previous day's trading. There are also orders resulting from trading decisions based on the previous day's data but calculated after the close. The end of day is active

FIGURE 10-2 Patterns of 30-minute tick volume, 1993. (*a*) Eurodollars. (*b*) S&P 500.
(*c*) Deutschemarks.

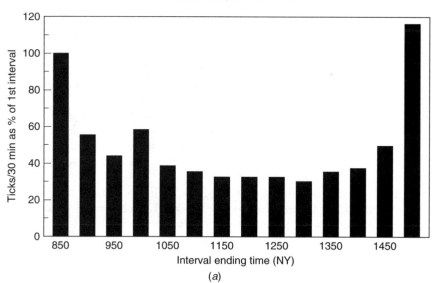

(*a*)

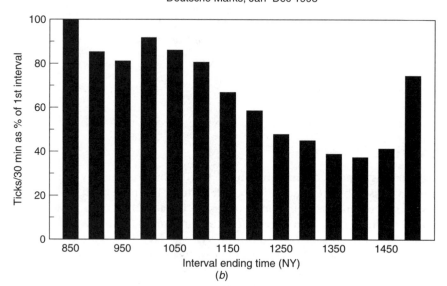

(*b*)

FIGURE 10-2 *(Continued)*

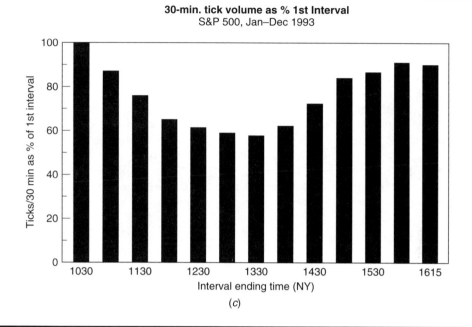

30-min. tick volume as % 1st Interval
S&P 500, Jan–Dec 1993

(c)

because of juggling for position based on today's price movements. For most traders, the closing price is the most dependable value of the day.

There is a typical rounded bottom formation on most charts, with lowest volume in the late morning when traders take their breaks. Deutsche marks (Figure 10-2*c*) differ from the others by showing more sustained high volume through late morning. This is because the European markets are open during that period. London interbank markets are likely to be open at 5 P.M. (12 noon in New York), to overlap U.S. trading as much as possible. Volume on the IMM Deutschemark contract tapers off after European business hours end.

When trading based on an increase in volume, these patterns must serve as the norm. To decide whether there is a volume confirmation for a trade to be entered at 11 A.M., you must compare today's 30-minute volume for the 11 A.M. interval with the previous average volume for this *same period only*. This is equivalent to deseasonalizing or detrending the data. Even with this precaution, an increase in volume for a thinly traded market, such as cocoa, may appear significant because the 30-minute volume jumped from 100 contracts to 300 contracts during midday. This can easily be misleading. You will need to consider the sample error in low-volume markets or demand much larger volume changes to be more certain.

FILTERING LOW VOLUME

It seems clear that minutes, hours, or even days that have little market activity are likely to be associated with uncertain price direction. If the British pound moves the equivalent of $.50 in the early afternoon of the U.S. market, we know that volume is normally light and the London and European markets are closed. If the intention of a volume indicator is to identify positive moves in volume that can be used as a confirmation of price direction, then eliminating those days with low volume, or with marginal price moves, may make the volume indicator dependable.

Removing Low-Volume Periods

The inclusion of low-volume periods into a volume index may make the index movements unreliable. There is a similar situation in statistics, where a number of statistical values are slightly skewed to one side. Each value on its own is not noticeably important, but collectively they cause a bias. Some analysts believe that the collective weight creates a significant situation, while others favor ignoring any statistic that is too close to the norm to be distinguished. When you ignore the individual values, there is no collective value. In the same way, by ignoring days with low volume, you do not have to risk the chance of posting a series of days, all of which may be uncertain, that result in a confirmation of a new price direction. Days may be filtered if the volume falls one standard deviation below the average (removing 16% of the total days), or two standard deviations (removing only 2.5% of the days), or any other combination. The use of absolute volume numbers, such as a day on the New York Stock Exchange with volume under 200 million, will not allow consistent filtering over any prolonged test. Then, on any day, the Volume-Filtered On-Balance Volume would be found by the following program or spreadsheet steps:

```
volume_threshold = @AVG(volume, n) + f*@STD(volume - volume[1], n)
if volume < volume_threshold then VFOBV = VFOBV[1]
    else VFOBV = VFOBV[1] + ((close - close[1])/(@ABS(close - close[1]))) * volume
```

where n is the number of periods in the average and standard deviation
     f is the number of standard deviations used to filter minimum volume

Removing Volume Associated with Small Price Moves

Indicators such as On-Balance Volume post all volume as either a positive or negative contribution to the index, based on the direction of prices on that day. It is fair to question the validity of posting all volume to the upside when the S&P 500 closed up a minimum move of one-twentieth of one point (+.05). It could just as easily have closed down that amount. In a manner similar to filtering low-volume periods, in the section above, periods in which prices moved very little may be eliminated by using a standard deviation of the price changes as a filter. Days which are within ±.5 or ±1.0 standard deviations of the average would be ignored. The Price-Filtered On-Balance Volume would then be found as follows:

```
price_threshold = @AVG(price - price[1], n) + f*@STD(price - price[1],n)
if @ABS(price - price[1]) < price_threshold then PFOBV = PFOBV[1]
    else PFOBV = PFOBV[1] + ((close - close[1])/(@ABS(close - close[1]))) * volume
```

where n is the number of periods in the average and standard deviation
     f is the number of standard deviations used to filter minimum volume

Note that, in the case of a minimum price threshold, the rules look at price change, which can be positive or negative. For a volume threshold there is only a one-sided test.

MARKET FACILITATION INDEX

In weighing the likelihood that prices are indicating a direction, rather than a false start, the tick volume compared with the price range for the same period, called the *Market Facilitation Index*,[8] can measure the willingness of the market to move the price. This concept is interesting because it is not clear that high volume results in a large price move, although it appears to set up the conditions for high volatility. If the Market Facilitation Index increases, then the market is willing to move the price; therefore, trading profits are more likely.

[8] Bill Williams, *Trading Chaos* (John Wiley & Sons, 1995).

$$\text{Market Facilitation Index} = \frac{\text{range}}{\text{volume}} = \frac{\text{high} - \text{low}}{\text{volume}}$$

The results of combining the change in tick volume and the Market Facilitation Index are interpreted as:

Tick Volume	Market Facilitation Index	Interpretation
Up	Up	Confirmation of direction
Down	Down	False direction, do not take trade
Down	Up	Poor entry timing, approach with caution
Up	Down	Potential new trend, end of old trend

SOURCES OF INFORMATION

In addition to the various references in this chapter, the following is a list of sources containing useful information on volume:

Steven B. Achelis, *Technical Analysis from A to Z* (Probus, 1995)

Colby and Meyers, *The Encyclopedia of Technical Market Indicators* (Dow Jones-Irwin, 1988)

CompuTrac Manual (Telerate, 1990)

Edwards and Magee, *Technical Analysis of Stock Trends* (Edwards and Magee, 1948)

Dr. Alexander Elder, *Trading for a Living* (John Wiley & Sons, 1994)

Omega TradeStation, *Easy Language Manual* (Omega Research, 1995)

Martin J. Pring, *Technical Analysis Explained* (McGraw-Hill, 1991)

Kenneth H. Shaleen, *Volume and Open Interest* (Probus, 1991)

11

Point-and-Figure Charting

oint-and-figure charting is credited to Charles Dow, who is said to have used it just
prior to the turn of the twentieth century. This method differs from ordinary charting
in three important ways:

1. It has simple, well-defined trading rules.
2. It eliminates price reversals that are below a minimum (box) value.
3. It has no time factor. As long as prices fail to change direction by the *reversal value,* the trend is intact.

When point-and-figure charting first appeared, it did not contain the familiar boxes of
Xs and Os. The earliest book containing the subject is reported to be *The Game in Wall
Street and How to Play it Successfully,* published by Hoyle (not Edmond Hoyle, the
English writer) in 1898. The first definitive work on the subject was by Victor de Villiers,
who in 1933 published *The Point and Figure Method of Anticipating Stock Price Movement.* De Villiers worked with Owen Taylor to publish and promote a weekly point-and-
figure service, maintaining their own charts; he was impressed by the simple scientific
methodology. As with many of the original technical systems, the application was intended
for the stock market, and the rules required the use of every price change appearing on the
ticker. The rationale for a purely technical system has been told many times by now, but an
original source is often refreshing. De Villiers said:

"The Method takes for granted:

1. That the price of a stock at any given time is its correct valuation up to the
   instant of purchase and sales (a) by the consensus of opinion of *all* buyers
   and sellers in the world and (b) by the verdict of *all* the forces governing
   the laws of supply and demand.
2. That the last price of a stock reflects or crystalizes *everything* known about
   or bearing on it from its first sale on the Exchange (or prior), up to that
   time.
3. That those who know more about it than the observer *cannot* conceal their
   future intentions regarding it. Their plans will be revealed in time by the
   stock's subsequent action."[1]

The unique aspect of the point-and-figure method is that it ignores the passage of time.
Unlike bar charts, you do not make a single vertical mark and then move to the right a uniform distance. Each column of a point-and-figure chart can represent any length of time.
The measurement of a significant change in price direction alone determines the pattern
of the chart.

The original *figure charts* were plotted with only dots or with the exact price in each
box or with a combination of Xs and occasional digits (usually 0s and 5s every 5 boxes) to

---

[1] Victor De Villiers, *The Point and Figure Method of Anticipating Stock Price Movements* (Trader Press, New York, 1966 (Reprint of 1933 edition), p. 8).

help keep the chart aligned. A geometric representation was also created by connecting the points in each column with a vertical line and closing the gap between columns with a crossbar on top for a reversal down and a bar at the bottom if the next column goes up. This would later be called a *swing chart*. Charts using 1, 3, and 5 points were popular, in which each point represented a minimum price move. In the 5-point method, no entry was recorded unless the price change spanned 5 points.

Point-and-figure charts, which are still commonly used on the floor of the Chicago Mercantile Exchange and the Chicago Board of Trade, are recorded to show the greatest detail. Each box represents the minimum allowable price move, and reversals of direction use the traditional 3-box criteria. Floor traders use the charts to show only the short-term sustained price moves and leave a lot to the interpretation of patterns.

PLOTTING PRICES USING THE POINT-AND-FIGURE METHOD

To plot prices on a point-and-figure chart, start with a piece of graph paper and mark the left scale using a conveniently small price increment. For example, each box may be set at $1 for gold and platinum, one-eighth of a point (4 ticks) for 30-year bonds, 1¢ for soybeans and silver, and so forth (see Figure 11-1). The choice of a box size will make the chart more or less sensitive to changes in price direction, as will be seen in later examples. The smaller the price increment, the more changes in direction will be seen. This also corresponds to longer and shorter trends or major and minor trends. Therefore, a point-and-figure chartist looking for a long-term price movement will use a larger box size. Box sizes are often related to the current volatility of the markets.

Once the graph paper has been scaled and the prices entered along the left side, the chartist can begin. The first box to be entered is that of the current closing price of the market. If the price of silver is 852.50 and a 1¢ box is being used, a mark is placed in the box beside the value 852. An X or an O is used to indicate that the current price trend is up or down, respectively. Either an X or O may be used to begin—after that, it will be determined by the method.

The rules for plotting point-and-figure charts are easily shown as a flowchart (Figure 11-2). Preference is given to price movements that continue in the direction of the current trend. Therefore, if the trend is up (represented by a column of Xs), the new high price is tested first; if the trend is down, the low price is of greatest importance. The opposite price is checked only if the new price fails to increase the length of the column showing the current trend.

FIGURE 11-1   Point-and-figure chart.

Silver

854.0	X										
853.0	X	O	X								
852.0	X	O	X	O							
851.0		O	X	O	X						
850.0		O		O	X	O					
849.0				O	X	O					
848.0				O	X	O					
847.0				O							
846.0											

FIGURE 11-2   Point-and-figure daily rules.

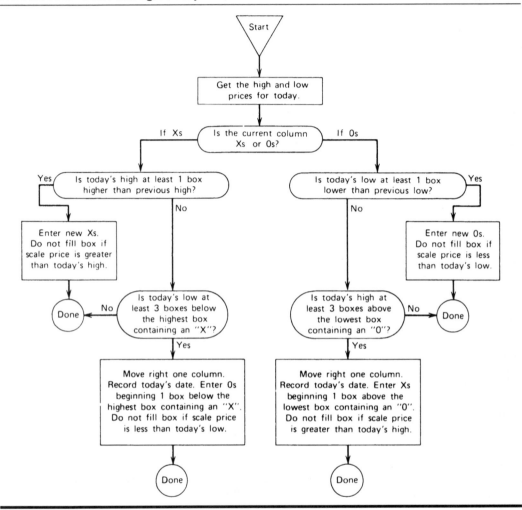

The traditional point-and-figure method calls for the use of a *3-box reversal;* that is, the price must reverse direction by an amount equal to 3 boxes from the most extreme box of the last column before a new column can begin (it actually must fill the 4th box since the extreme box is left blank). The importance of keeping the 3-box reversal has long been questioned by experienced point-and-figure traders. It should be noted that the net reversal amount (the box size times the number of boxes in the reversal) is the critical value. For example, a $4 box for gold with a 3-box reversal means that gold must reverse by $12 to indicate a trend change. The opposite combination, a $3 box and a 4-box reversal, would actually signal a reversal of trend at the same time. The proper selection is based on the subsequent sensitivity of the box size following the reversal. Therefore, a smaller box size may interpret the smallest price movements as a continuation of the trend and ultimately capture more of the price move; it is considered the preferable alternative. The choice of box size and reversal boxes will be considered later in more detail.

CHART FORMATIONS

It would be impossible for the average speculator to follow the original method of recording every change in price. When applied to stocks, those charts became so lengthy that interpretations similar to those used for the traditional bar chart were necessary to select the best patterns. In 1969, Robert E. Davis published *Profit and Profitability*, a point-and-figure study that detailed eight unique buy and sell signals. The study covered two stocks for the years 1914–1964, and 1,100 stocks for 1954–1964. The intention was to find specific bull and bear patterns that were more reliable than others. The best buy signal was an ascending triple top, and the best sell signal was the breakout of a triple bottom (Figures 11-3 and 11-4).

Plotted daily, futures prices do not offer the variety of formations available in the stock market. The small number of markets and the high correlation of movement between many of the delivery months make the limitations of signal selection impractical. Instead, the most basic approach is used, in which a buy signal occurs when an X in the current column is 1 box above the highest X in the last column of Xs, and the simple sell signal is an O plotted below the lowest O of the last descending column. The variability in the system lies in the size of the box; the smaller the size, the more sensitive the chart will be to price moves. In 1933, Wyckoff noted that it was advisable to use a chart with a different box size when the price of the stock varied substantially.[2]

Trendlines

The bullish and bearish trendlines important to bar charting also exist for point-and-figure charts. The top or bottom box that remains blank when a reversal occurs often forms the beginning of a descending or ascending pattern at a 45° angle (diagonally through the boxes, providing the graph paper has square boxes). These 45° lines represent the major anticipated trends of the market. Once a top or bottom has been identified, a 45° line can be drawn down from the upper corner of the top boxes of Xs toward the right, or up from the bottom of the lowest box of Os toward the right (Figure 11-5). These trendlines are used to *confirm* the direction of price movement and often *filter* the basic point-and-figure trading signals so that only long positions are taken when the 45° trendline is up and only shorts are entered when the trendline is down.

Point-and-Figure Studies

In 1970, Charles C. Thiel, Jr., with Robert E. Davis, completed the first purely futures market point-and-figure study[3] that calculated profitability of a reasonably large sample of markets

---

[2] Richard D. Wyckoff, *Stock Market Technique, Number One* (Wyckoff, New York, 1933, p. 89).
[3] Charles Thiel and R.E. Davis, *Point and Figure Commodity Trading: A Computer Evaluation* (Dunn & Hargitt, West Lafayette, IN, 1970).

FIGURE 11-3   Best formations from Davis's study.

```
        Ascending Triple Top          Breakout of a Triple Bottom
                X ← BUY                      X   X
              X   X                        O X O X O
            X   X O X                      O X O X O
            X O X O X                      O     O     O
            X O X O                                  O ← SELL
              O
```

FIGURE 11-4 (a) Compound point-and-figure buy signals. (b) Compound point-and-figure sell signals.

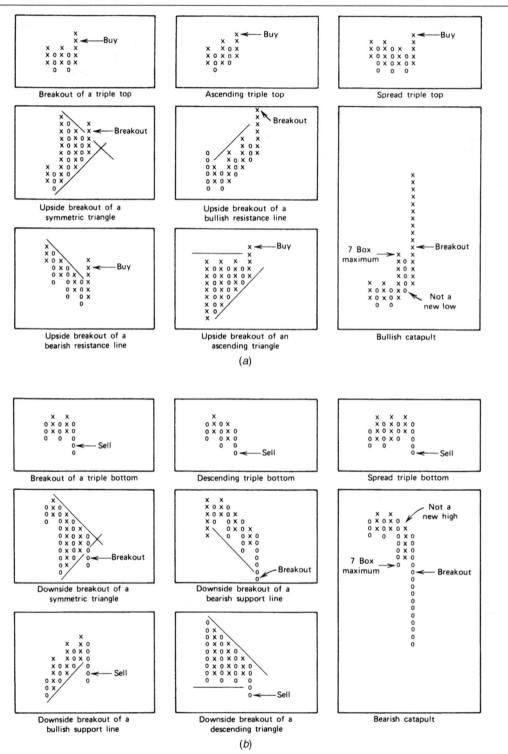

FIGURE 11-5   Point-and-figure trendlines.

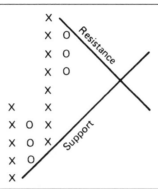

by varying both the value of a box and the reversal criteria (the number of boxes necessary to start a new column). With the standard 3-box reversal and only simple buy and sell formations, the tests showed 799 signals, of which 53% were profitable; the average net profit on all trades was $311 realized in approximately 50 days. The period studied was 1960 through 1969. In the mid-1970s, Zieg and Kaufman[4] performed a computerized study using the same rules but limiting the test period to 6 months ending May 1974, an extremely active market period. For the 22 commodities tested, 375 signals showed 40% of the trades were profitable; the net profit over all the trades was $306 and the average duration was 12.4 days. It is interesting to note that the most significant difference in the results of the two studies is in the average length of a trade, from 50 to 12.4 days, indicating a change apparently induced by more volatile markets. Although the two tests varied in many of the details, the results are a strong argument for the consistency of the point-and-figure method as a trading tool.

In its current role, point-and-figure differs from other forms of charting because it provides a rigid set of rules for entering long and short positions. Many of the formations are still subjected to interpretation and are frequently used in the original sense by floor traders; but as a tool for the speculator without access to intraday prices and the experience to understand the subtleties of chart analysis, point-and-figure fills an important gap. It will tell the trader exactly what penetration of a resistance or support level is necessary to generate a buy or sell signal and exactly where the stop-loss order should be placed to limit risk. It is this well-defined nature of point-and-figure charting that allows computer testing and evaluation.

The basic study of the point-and-figure method involves rules of charting, buy and sell signals, trendlines, geometric formations, and price objectives. Since these points have been covered effectively in at least two books currently available,[5] they will not be repeated here. More advanced point-and-figure topics will be discussed, including its relationship to bar charting, alternate plotting rules, risk-limited trading, and varying box size.

POINT-AND-FIGURE BOX SIZE

The box size used in a point-and-figure chart determines the sensitivity, or frequency of signals, and allows the identification of trends and trading ranges of various duration. For many years Chartcraft was the only major service that produced a full set of point-and-figure charts (see Table 11-1).

---

[4] Kermit C. Zieg, Jr., and Perry J. Kaufman, *Point and Figure Commodity Trading Techniques* (Investors Intelligence, Larchmont, NY, 1975). This book contains complete tabularized results of both point-and-figure tests.

[5] A.W. Cohen, *How to Use the Three-Point Reversal Method of Point and Figure Stock Market Trading* (Chartcraft, Larchmont, NY, 1972), and Zieg and Kaufman, *Point and Figure Commodity Trading Techniques* (1975).

TABLE 11-1a   Point-and-Figure Box Sizes*

Commodity	Year	Prior to 1975[†] Box Size	1975[‡] Box Size	1977[‡] Box Size	1977[§] Box Size	1986[‡] Box Size
			Grains			
Corn	1971	½¢	2¢	2¢	2¢	1¢
Oats	1965	½¢	1¢	1¢		1¢
Soybeans	1971	1¢	10¢	10¢	5¢	5¢
Soybean meal	1964	50 pts	500 pts	500 pts		100 pts
Soybean oil	1965	10 pts	20 pts	20 pts		10 pts
Wheat	1964	1¢	2¢	2¢	2¢	1¢
			Livestock and Meats			
Cattle	1967	20 pts	20 pts	20 pts		20 pts
Hogs	1968	20 pts	20 pts	20 pts		20 pts
Pork bellies	1965	20 pts	20 pts	20 pts		20 pts
			Other Agricultural Products			
Cocoa[¶]	1964	20 pts	100 pts	100 pts	50 pts	10 pts
Coffee		(20) pts	100 pts	100 pts	50 pts	100 pts
Cotton		(20) pts	100 pts	100 pts		50 pts
Lumber		(100) pts	100 pts	100 pts		100 pts
Orange juice	1968	20 pts	20 pts	100 pts		100 pts
Sugar	1965	5 pts	20 pts	20 pts	20 pts	10 pts
			Metals			
Aluminum						50 pts
Copper	1964	20 pts	100 pts	100 pts	50 pts	50 pts
Gold			50 pts	100 pts		400 pts
Palladium						100 pts
Platinum	1968	200 pts	100 pts	200 pts	200 pts	400 pts
Silver	1971	100 pts	200 pts	200 pts	400 pts	1000 pts

* All box sizes use a 3-box reversal and are in *points* (decimal fractions treated as whole numbers) unless otherwise indicated.
[†] Cohen (1972); parentheses indicate approximate values.
[‡] Courtesy of Chartcraft Commodity Service, Chartcraft, Inc., Larchmont, NY.
[§] Chart Analysis Limited, Bishopgate, London. Values are for long-term continuation charts.
[¶] Cocoa contract changed from cents/pound to dollars/ton.

Over the past 10 years, all markets have had one or more major price moves reaching levels often greater than twice their normal price. Sugar and silver each topped at 10 times their starting value. These moves necessitate changes in box size to control the impact of the increased, and later decreased, volatility.

Alternating with extremely high prices are periods in which many commodities fall to levels near their production costs. Table 11-1 shows part of the history of changing box sizes based on a 3-box reversal, for agricultural markets during the late 1960s compared with the mid-1980s. By noting the historic price moves, the change in volatility can be related to the change in box size. Whereas most agricultural markets show a pattern of small to large to small box sizes, coffee and orange juice have remained volatile. Silver and gold maintain large box sizes through the mid-1980s, as a result of their long steady

TABLE 11-1b   Point-and-Figure Box Sizes

Commodity	1986 Box Size	Commodity	1986 Box Size
Oils		*Currencies*	
Crude	10 pts	British pound	50 pts
Gasoline	50 pts	Canadian dollar	10 pts
Heating oil	50 pts	Japanese yen	10 pts
		Swiss franc	10 pts
		Deutschemark	10 pts
Financials		*Index*	
Eurodollars	10 pts	S&P 500	50 pts
GNMAs	$^{16}/_{32}$ pts	Major market	50 pts
Treasury bonds	$^{16}/_{32}$ pts	NYSE	50 pts
Treasure bills	10 pts	Value line	50 pts
Certificates of deposit	10 pts		

declines; however, current levels would require a reduction. Rules for varying box sizes and risks associated with these changes will be discussed in the next sections.

The Nature of Markets

Financial markets have underlying differences from agricultural ones. Interest rates have the greatest similarity, with the exception that a low volatility level for rates is associated with high prices. To create a point-and-figure chart for Eurodollars with the same orientation as soybeans, it is necessary to plot the yield, rather than the price, of the market. This is easy for any 3-month rate, because the current price can be subtracted from 100; for longer maturity bonds this is more difficult, but could be estimated by subtracting the current price from 164, or by dividing 800 by the futures price.

Currencies present another unique problem, because there is no low or high price for foreign exchange, only what the market decides. When an economy strengthens, the value of the currency increases; when the economy falters, its currency devalues. Sometimes, as happened in the U.S. from 1985 to 1995, the government may choose to allow the currency to decline as a way to reduce its debt. Does this mean that the U.S. dollar is low and that its volatility will decline? No. With agricultural products, when prices fall to production levels there is less trading and lower volatility, the result of lack of interest. The dollar, however, can continue to decline and its volatility can increase as long as traders believe that the current situation is changing. Therefore, the volatility of a currency is low when market participants see its price as correct, at equilibrium. If prices move away from equilibrium, and the government disapproves of what is happening, economic policy will attempt to move it back; therefore, currency prices can be volatile when they move in either direction away from equilibrium. This makes it difficult to scale prices by a percentage, as we will do in later sections.

THE PROBLEM OF RISK

I go long or short as close as I can to the danger point, and if the danger becomes real I close out and take a small loss.

Jesse Livermore to Richard Wyckoff[6]

---

[6] Wyckoff, *Stock Market Technique, Number One* (Wyckoff, New York, 1933, p. 2).

If the point-and-figure method is accepted as successful, why is it necessary to modify the basic signal and use trendlines and geometric formations to interpret new signals? The answer involves the risk of an individual trade. The difference in treatment of the same price move can be seen by looking at both a bar chart and a corresponding point-and-figure chart for the same period (Figure 11-6). The most basic bar chart trading method uses horizontal support and resistance trendlines to define a rectangular trading range; when the resistance line is penetrated, a long position is taken. A stop-loss is placed below the resistance line to close out the position in the event of a false breakout. An alternate place for the stop-loss could have been below the support line allowing the new bull move some latitude to develop. The interpreted bar chart makes the selection of the entry point and the placement of stops seem obvious; however, when trading, the placement of the support and resistance lines is not as clear. The time to enter a trade after a breakout is never certain, and the position for the stop depends on the volatility of prices and the risk that can be assumed.

In contrast to the ambiguity of the bar chart, the point-and-figure method defines the support and resistance levels exactly, establishes a place to buy in advance, and designates the position for the stop-loss below the rectangular congestion area. The rigidity of the method allows only one place for the stop-loss and fixes the risk as the difference between the support and resistance lines, a total of 5 boxes in this example. In the bar chart, the risk might have been held to the equivalent of 2 boxes using the first strategy; however, a very small risk often results in being stopped out of the trend prematurely.

TRADING TECHNIQUES

There are alternate methods for selecting point-and-figure entry and exit points that have become popular. Buying or selling on a pullback after an initial point-and-figure signal is one of the more common modifications to the system, because it can limit risk to any level and still maintain a logical stop-loss point. Of course, the smaller the risk, the fewer the opportunities and the more likely you will be stopped out. There are two approaches that are recommended for entering on limited risk:

1. *Wait for a reversal back to within an acceptable risk, then buy or sell immediately with the normal point-and-figure stop.* Figure 11-7 shows various levels of risk using corn (a 5,000-bushel contract, with $50 for each 1¢ move). The initial buy signal is at 258, with the simple sell signal for liquidation at 249, giving a risk of 9¢, or

FIGURE 11-6   Placement of stops.

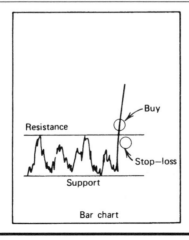

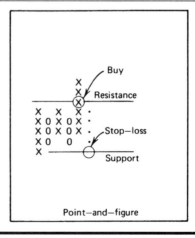

FIGURE 11-7 Entering on a pullback.

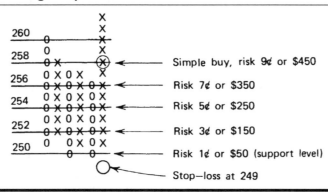

$450 per contract. Wait for a reversal following the breakout, and buy when the low for the day penetrates the box corresponding to the predetermined risk. Buying into a declining market assumes that the support level will hold, preventing the stop-loss point from being reached. Because of this, the base of the formation should be as broad as possible. The test of a triple bottom or a spread triple bottom after a buy signal is a more reasonable place to go long than a simple buy after a small reversal in the middle of a move.

It is not advisable to reduce risk by entering on the simple buy signal and placing a stop-loss at the point of the first reversal (3 boxes below the highs). The advantage of waiting for the pullback is that it uses the logical support level as a stop. A stop-loss placed nearby following a breakout has no logical basis and will quickly result in a losing trade.

2. *Enter the market on the second reversal back in the direction of the original signal.* As shown in Figure 11-8, the first reversal following a signal may not be within the desirable risk, but by placing a trailing entry order using the point-and-figure reversal value, while prices are moving counter to the direction of the signal, an entry will occur on a confirmation of the original direction with a stop-loss at the minimum 4-box distance.

FIGURE 11-8 Entering on a confirmation of a new trend after a pullback.

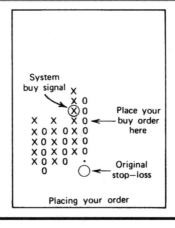

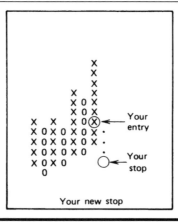

This technique is frequently used by traders who firmly believe that a reversal follows immediately after a breakout and prevents both high risk and false signals. If the pullback that follows the breakout continues in an adverse direction, penetrates the other support or resistance level, and triggers the original system stop-loss, no entry occurs, thus saving a substantial whipsaw loss.

The reversal principle in step 2 can also be effective for building positions. In bar charting, a pullback to a bullish support line or a bearish resistance line was a point for adding to a position with a risk limited to penetration of the major trendline. The equivalent procedure using point-and-figure is to add on each reversal back in the direction of the trend using the newly formed stop-loss point to exit the entire position as shown in Figure 11-9.

3. *Allowing for irregular patterns.* Price patterns are not always as orderly as we want them to be, and the price activity at time of a trend change can be very indecisive. One basic trading principle demands that the market confirms a new high before buying; the first new high might simply be an erratic sideways pattern, or an expanding formation after a period of low volatility. If we require prices to make a new high by more than 1 box on the next upward thrust, and increase the minimum by another box on the third upward thrust, we can actually demand that the momentum increase before a position is set.[7]

This technique, which tends to minimize false breakouts, may be modified to increase the confirmation threshold from 2 to 3 or 4 boxes as market volatility increases. If the box size is changed according to volatility, as discussed later in this chapter, confirmation can remain at 2 boxes.

Take It and Run!

There comes a time in most substantial moves when there is ample profit and apprehension about how much of the paper profit will be returned before the system close-out signal is reached. Some traders prefer to take the profits. These are decisions that go beyond the area of technical analysis. If the profit currently held in open positions is enough to sustain a life of leisure, a home in the mountains or South Seas, a country club, and a small investment in a hotel or restaurant to occupy your time, then take it and run! A trading sys-

[7] Adam Hewison, "The Will Rogers Theory of Point & Figure Trading," *Technical Analysis of Stocks & Commodities* (August 1991).

FIGURE 11-9   Three ways to compound positions.

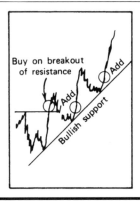
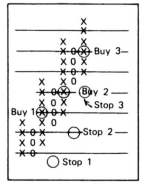
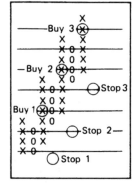

tem should not depend on a single, very large profit, to work over time. It should have a successful, consistent profile. We can, therefore, reason that any extremely large profit is a windfall and should be taken.

If you cannot sleep nights because you need money to meet personal commitments, you have just the right amount in unrealized profits, and 1 or 2 adverse days would ruin the opportunity, take the profits and begin again with a small investment. Technically, that is an issue of investor *risk preference*. If you want a logical place to cash in on current open profits but you have some time and latitude, as long as you do not lose more than 10 to 25% of the existing profits, use the point-and-figure reversal value. The *reversal value,* the box size times the number of boxes in a reversal (usually three), is meant to indicate a significant contrary move and can be used as an objective indication of a change of direction. One approach to taking profits is shown in Figure 11-10.

In Figure 11-10a, a trailing 3-box reversal value is used for the stop-loss once there is a sustained move of at least 10 boxes. To reenter the move in the same direction, the same technique is used (Figure 11-10b), adding another 4 boxes of profits while keeping the new risk small. In Figure 11-10c, this method lost 4 boxes of the potential profits when the reversal was short-lived.

In general, taking small profits in this way does not improve profits, because it most often misses the biggest moves. It may, however, reduce the risk of loss at a rate even faster than the reduction in profits, yielding a better reward-to-risk ratio. A new rule should be carefully tested to know its effect on different market conditions. If successful, it should always be used. Selective use is more likely to limit potential profits without reducing losses. This topic is covered thoroughly in Chapter 21 ("Testing").

Alternate Treatment of Reversals

Traditional point-and-figure charting favors the continuing trend. On highly volatile days, or *outside days,* it is possible for both a trend continuation and a reversal to occur. Point-and-figure rules require that the trend continuation be recorded and the reversal ignored. Figure 11-11 shows a comparison of the two choices. In the example, prices are in an uptrend when a new 1-box high and a 3-box reversal both occur on day 6. In Figure 11-11b, the traditional approach is taken, resulting in a continuous upward trend with a stop-loss at 790. Taking the reversal first as an alternate rule, Figure 11-11c shows the same trend with a stop-loss at 805.

FIGURE 11-10   Cashing in on profits.

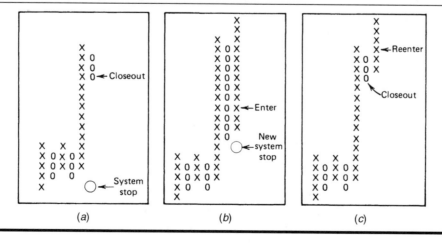

FIGURE 11-11 Alternate methods of plotting point-and-figure reversals. (*a*) Sample prices for plotting. (*b*) Traditional method. (*c*) Alternate rule taken on day 6.

Day	High	Low
1	802	790
2	811	795
3	813	792
4	818	796
5	825	810
6	832	808
7	840	825

(*a*)

```
840          X                          X
835          X                          X
830          X                          X
825          X                    X      X
820          X                    X  O   X
815          X                    X  O   X
810   X      X           X        X  O
805   X  O   X           X  O     X
800   X  O   X           X  O     X
795   X  O               X  O
790   X                  X
```

(*b*)   (*c*)

Plotting the reversal first will usually work to the benefit of the trader; both the stop-loss and change of trend will occur sooner. Subsequent computer testing proved this to be true. The alternate rule will not help when the reversal value is small and the optional reversals, or outside days, occur frequently.

PRICE OBJECTIVES

Point-and-figure charting has two unique methods for calculating price objectives: *horizontal and vertical counts.* These techniques do not eliminate the use of the standard bar charting objectives, such as support and resistance levels, which apply here as well.

The Horizontal Count

The time that prices spend in a consolidation area is considered important in determining its potential move. One technique for calculating price objectives is to measure the width of the consolidation (the number of columns) and project the same measurement up or down as the target of the move. The point-and-figure horizontal count method is a more exact approach to the same idea.

The upside price objective is calculated as

$$H_U = P_L + (W \times R)$$

where H_U is the upside horizontal count price objective
   P_L is the price of the lowest box of the base
   W is the width of the bottom formation (number of columns)
   R is the reversal value (number of boxes times the value of one box)

To complete this formula, the *base* (width of the bottom or top formation) needs to be identified. Count the number of columns, *W,* not including the breakout column and multiply that width by the value of a minimum reversal, *R;* then add that result to the bottom point of the base to get the upper price objective. The base can always be identified after the breakout has occurred. For example, Figure 11-12 shows the March 74 contract of London Cocoa

FIGURE 11-12 Horizontal count price objectives.

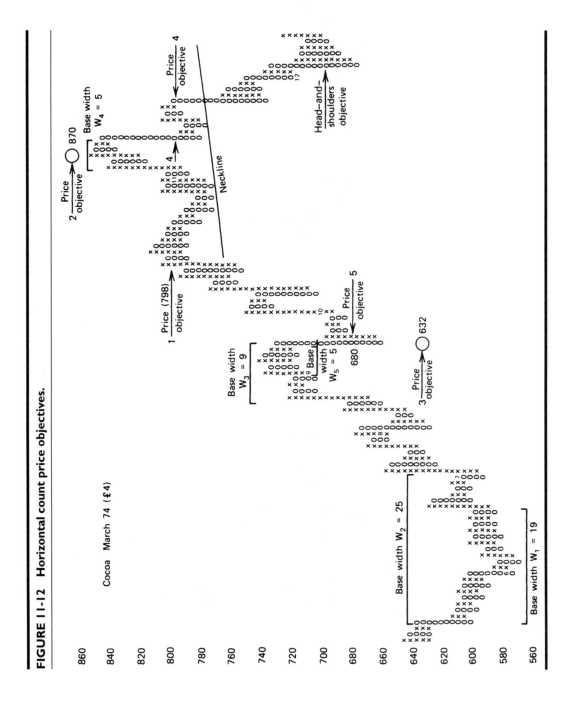

(£4 box) forming a very long but clear base. The reversal value is £12, and the width of the base is 19 columns (not counting the last column, which included the breakout). Added to the lowest point of the base (£570) this gives an objective of £798, reached on the left shoulder of the topping formation. Another alternative is the wider base, marked as $W_2 = 25$. Using this selection results in a price objective of £870, by adding $25 \times £12 = £300$ to £570, the lowest point of the base.

The downside objective is calculated in the same manner as the upside objective:

$$H_D = P_H - (W \times R)$$

where H_D is the downside horizontal count price objective

P_H is the price of the highest box of the top formation

W is the width of the top formation (number of columns)

R is the reversal value

Some examples are given for downside objectives in the same cocoa diagram (Figure 11-12). A small correction top could be isolated at the £720 level and two possible top widths, W_3 and W_5, could be chosen. W_3, the broader top, has a width of 9 and a downside objective of £632. W_5 has a smaller width of 5 and a downside objective of £680. Although the lesser objective, calculated from W_5, is easy to reach, the farther one is reasonable because it coincides with a strong intermediate support level at about £640.

The very top formation was small and only produced a nearby price objective similar to the first downside example; there would be no indication that prices were ready for a major reversal. The top also forms a clear head-and-shoulders pattern, which could be used in the same manner as in bar charting to find an objective. The height of the top of the head to the point on the neckline directly below is 20 boxes; the downside price objective is 20 boxes below the point where the neckline was penetrated by the breakout of the right shoulder, at £776, giving £696 as an objective.

The horizontal count can also be applied to a breakout from a triangular formation, similar to the one on the very far right in Figure 11-12 (marked "Head-and-shoulders objective"). The width of the formation, W, is the widest point in the center of the triangle, and the upward objective is also measured from the center, rather than from the bottom of the triangle.

The Vertical Count

The vertical count is a simpler and more definitive calculation than the horizontal count. As with the horizontal count, there is adequate time to identify the formations and establish a price objective before it is reached. The vertical count is a measure of volatility, the amount of rebound from a top or bottom, and can be used to determine the size of a retracement after a major price move. To calculate the upside vertical count price objective, locate the first reversal column after a bottom. To do this, a bottom must be established with one or more tests or a major resistance line must be broken. The vertical count price objective is then calculated:

V_{up} = lowest box + (number of boxes in first reversal

$\times$ minimum number of boxes in a chart reversal)

The downside vertical count price objective is just the opposite:

V_{down} = highest box − (number of boxes in the first reversal

$\times$ minimum number of boxes in a chart reversal)

Examples illustrating the vertical count are easy to find. Consider the following cases:

1. A cattle chart (Figure 11-13*a*) has an obvious bottom at 36.66 and a 13-box reversal immediately following. Using the vertical count, a retracement of three times the primary reversal (13 boxes) is added to the low of the bottom. The price objective is then 41.73, 39 boxes above the low.
2. Following that upward move in cattle, there is a top of 43.42 followed by a downward column of 9 boxes. The price objective becomes 27 boxes below the high, or

FIGURE 11-13 (*a*) Cattle point-and-figure chart.

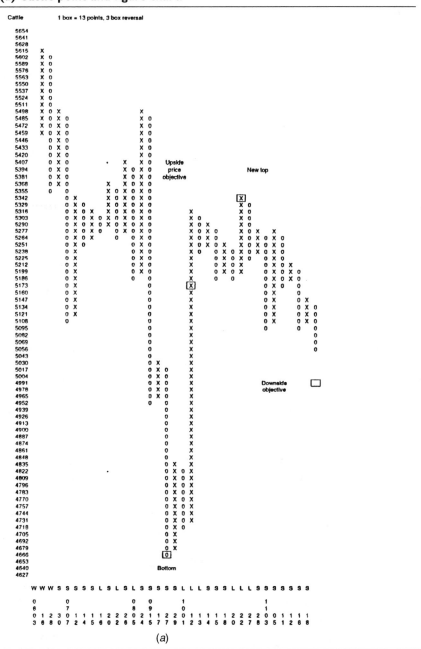

(*a*)

FIGURE 11-13 *(Continued) (b)* **Corn point-and-figure chart.**

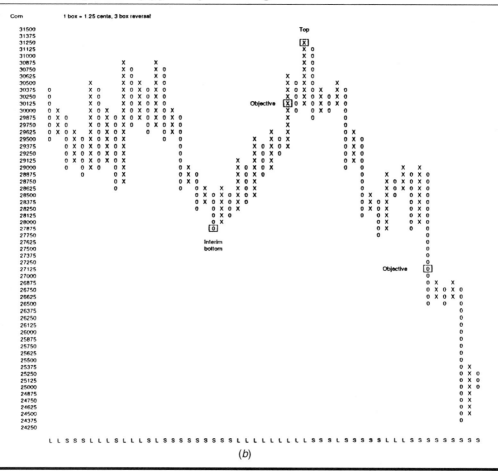

(b)

39.91, a likely goal on the chart because it is also the center of the only technical adjustment during the downtrend.

3. Corn (Figure 11-13b) topped at 312½ and had an 11-box reversal in the next column; the price objective is 33 boxes lower at 271¼. Although that goal fell short of the lows by quite a distance, it netted about a 27¢ profit from the system sell signal. Earlier in the contract, there was an intermediate bottom at 278¾ with a 6-box reversal. The price objective of 301¼ was in the center of the prior major resistance level and resulted in another good trade.

As a simple measurement tool from contract highs or lows, this technique seems to have some reliability once the bottom or top becomes clear. It is, however, far from perfect.

A STUDY IN POINT-AND-FIGURE OPTIMIZATION

Throughout the point-and-figure discussion, there has been constant reference to reversal value or 3-box reversal, although there has been no explicit suggestion of any alternative. In looking back at Table 11-1, it can be seen that the box sizes used prior to 1971 were generally smaller than the 1975 box sizes. In addition, larger boxes are used for long-term continuation charts and smaller ones for individual contracts of maximum term

1 to 1½ years. These differences are due to changing price levels and volatility as Wyckoff had suggested.

Prior to 1971, prices had been steadily increasing, but at a much slower rate than 1974–1976. In a single year, the price fluctuation of any one market was easy to anticipate. Since 1969, prices have moved to unprecedented levels and back, with high volatility. The stock market, represented by a wide range of indices, has continued to gain and expand in dollar volatility throughout the early 1990s.

In 1969, sugar prices were plotted on a 5-point scale while prices ranged from 2.86¢ to 3.95¢ per pound; the possible span of point-and-figure boxes that could be filled was 22. In 1973, sugar prices went to almost 60¢ per pound, approximately 20 times their 1969 price. The daily limits were expanded from ½¢ to 2¢—more than the price had moved in 1 year. The use of a 5¢ point-and-figure box would result in a new reversal column on any day the market failed to continue its prior direction, and it no longer served the function of smoothing the price movement. It took 1,200 boxes (10 feet of graph paper) to record the moves all the way up to 60¢.

One reason why the sugar scale changed from 5¢ to 20¢ boxes or soybeans from 1¢ to 10¢ was the practical need to fit the point-and-figure chart on a single page. Oddly enough, rescaling to fit a piece of paper of constant size has considerable merit. Look at soybeans in 1970. The range of the January 71 futures contract was 251⅛ to 315 and required a page of graph paper with only 64 boxes and an assigned value of 1¢ per box. Table 11-2a shows what happens if the same number of boxes is used each year and if the scale is changed to accommodate the full price range. The reversal value is forced to increase so that the size of the point-and-figure chart and formations will look the same regardless of the price level. This is called *keeping the sensitivity constant.* The point-and-figure method, with its increased reversal value due to larger box size, will generate about the same number of reversals and buy and sell signals at any price level. Had prices increased without the box size increasing, the system would have had more frequent reversals, as in the sugar example, and it would be considered *more sensitive* to price changes. Table 11-2b shows the comparable scaling for the S&P 500 from 1988 (after the "crash") through 1996. During this period, the stock index had an equal number of years with slightly higher volatility, as well as years with as much as 50% lower volatility. During the quieter years there would have been very few trading signals.

The relationship of reversal value to the average price for soybeans from 1971 through 1977, and the S&P from 1988 through 1996 gives a price-volatility relationship, shown in the last column of Table 11-2a. It is important to know to what degree prices will fluctuate as they advance and decline. This can become a valuable risk management tool.

Before continuing, certain questions must be asked of this method:

Why were soybeans started with a 1¢ box . . . why not ½¢ or 5¢?

Does this price-volatility relationship represent the best approach to rescaling?

How can it be used?

It can only be assumed that the original selection of a 1¢ box for soybeans was a combination of both a smoothing attempt (chosen as a multiple of the minimum move) and convenience. The convenience part is easy to see; all the box sizes in Table 11-1 were even numbers. The first point-and-figure charts were drawn using the smallest allowable move and later refined to larger increments to identify long-term trends, and major support and resistance levels. However, it is necessary to find a more logical selection of starting parameters.

To answer the second question, the impact of rescaling on trading must be considered. As prices rise, boxes become larger and the minimum risk becomes proportionately greater.

TABLE 11-2   Keeping the Size of the Chart the Same

(a) Soybeans (January Futures Contract)

Year	High	Low	Average	Box Size	Reversal	Total Number of Boxes	Reversal Value	Reversal as Percentage of Average %
1971	315	251	283	1.00	3	64	3.00	1.06
1972	346	282	314	1.00	3	64	3.00	0.96
1973	444	300	372	2.25	3	64	6.75	1.81
1974	915	349	632	8.84	3	64	26.53	4.20
1975	961	509	735	7.06	3	64	21.19	2.88
1976	705	439	572	4.16	3	64	12.47	2.18
1977	782	490	636	4.56	3	64	13.69	2.15

(b) S&P 500 Futures (Continuous Daily Prices)

Year	High	Low	Average	Box Size	Reversal	Total Number of Boxes	Reversal Value	Reversal as Percentage of Average %
1986	250	205	228	0.70	3	64	2.11	0.93
1987	330	175	253	2.42	3	64	7.27	2.88
1988	280	240	260	0.63	3	64	1.88	0.72
1989	350	280	315	1.09	3	64	3.28	1.04
1990	365	285	325	1.25	3	64	3.75	1.15
1991	410	310	360	1.56	3	64	4.69	1.30
1992	440	390	415	0.78	3	64	2.34	0.56
1993	470	425	448	0.70	3	64	2.11	0.47
1994	480	435	458	0.70	3	64	2.11	0.46
1995	610	460	535	2.34	3	64	7.03	1.31
1996	745	600	673	2.27	3	64	6.80	1.01

The risk of trading one contract increases at the same rate as the volatility expressed as a percentage of average price. If the box sizes are not increased when prices rise, risk can be kept small, but frequent losses will occur and trading will be based on extremely short-term trends.

There are few alternatives to rescaling, the two most reasonable being:

Method 1—Rechart at new price levels using larger box values to keep the size of the chart constant and the sensitivity fixed as shown in Table 11-2.

Method 2—Increase the box value at a rate based on a fixed percentage of the current price so that a chart with a box value of 3 points at a price of 300 (1% value) would have a 6-point box at a price of 600.

Both approaches effectively increase the box value and risk while reducing the sensitivity of the chart as prices increase.

Solving the Scaling Problem

To avoid being arbitrary in selecting a price-volatility scaling relationship, we perform a regression analysis on the average price and box size to get a formula for the relationship. A linear approximation was performed using the soybean values in Table 11-2a, based on a 3-box reversal, with the following results:

$$100 \times \text{volatility} = -28.8 + .485 \times \text{average price}$$

$$\text{box size} = -3.347 + .0147 \times \text{price}$$

The exact figures for the box size corresponding to specific price levels are shown in Table 11-3. Understanding that box sizes must be in practical increments, a variable box point-

and-figure chart can be constructed that changes box size as the price increases according to the table. These box sizes are shown with their corresponding price levels in Table 11-4.

Scaling by Constant Rate

The second choice of scaling requires answering the question: "Why were soybeans started with a 1¢ box?" The long-term charts show that prior to 1970, prices were relatively stable and fluctuated in normal ranges. Finding the proper box size for the initial interval forms the basis for continuing into more volatile years. In the 1970 study by Thiel and Davis entitled *Point and Figure Commodity Trading: A Computer Evaluation* (Dunn & Hargitt), they approach the problem of variable box size and reversal value strictly scientifically. They proceeded to test a good sampling of commodity futures markets, varying both the box size and reversal value, and recorded the resulting profits or losses and the reliability of the combination (percentage of profitable trades). For example, the January 66 soybean contract test results are presented in Table 11-5.

TABLE 11-3 Point-and-Figure Price-Volatility Relationship (Method 1)

Average price	250	300	350	400	450	500	550	600
Percentage volatility	92	117	140	165	189	214	240	262
Box size	.328	1.06	1.80	2.54	3.20	4.01	4.75	5.49
Average price	650	700	750	800	850	900	950	1000
Percentage volatility	286	311	335	359	383	408	432	456
Box size	6.22	6.96	7.70	8.43	9.17	9.91	10.65	11.38

TABLE 11-4 Point-and-Figure Variable Box Size for Specific Price Levels (Method 1)

Box	Price	Box	Price	Box	Price	Box	Price	Box	Price
¼	245	2¼	380	4¼	516	6¼	652	8¼	787
½	262	2½	397	4½	533	6½	669	8½	804
¾	279	2¾	414	4¾	550	6¾	686	8¾	821
1	295	3	431	5	567	7	703	9	838
1¼	312	3¼	448	5¼	584	7¼	720	9¼	855
1½	329	3½	465	5½	601	7½	736	9½	872
1¾	346	3¾	482	5¾	618	7¾	753	9¾	889
2	363	4	499	6	634	8	770	10	906

TABLE 11-5 Thiel and Davis's Results, January 66 Soybeans

Box Size	Reversal Boxes	Results		
		Profitability	Profit	Per Trade
0.500	4	2 of 12	−14.874	−1.239
0.500	5	2 of 12	−14.874	−1.239
0.500	6	2 of 10	−15.124	−1.512
⋮	⋮	⋮	⋮	⋮
1.000	4	1 of 2	3.00	1.500
⋮	⋮	⋮	⋮	⋮
4.000	1	1 of 1	7.25	7.25
⋮	⋮	⋮	⋮	⋮

The study included the years 1960–1969, with data supplied by Dunn and Hargitt.[8] This coincides exactly with the time interval needed to determine the basic box size and reversal. In their study, Thiel and Davis draw conclusions and present alternatives for their selections, but the interests of this analysis are slightly different. Table 11-6 shows the final choice. The most important part of Table 11-6 is the reversal value, expressed as a percentage of the 10-year fluctuation. This figure represents the best choice of value for rescaling as a fixed percentage of the market's average price. The proper reversal criteria for each price level can now be selected using the rate of increase shown in the first and second formulas and the base price from Table 11-6.

For convenience, all box sizes will be chosen to correspond to the standard 3-box reversal. In general, a reversal value of 6¢ for soybeans would be profitable if plotted on a scale of 2×3, 3×2, 6×1, or 1×6, where the first number is the box size and the second is the number of boxes for a reversal. By having the percentage reversal value, the box and reversal criteria can be varied in a logical manner as the prices rise or fall. Using the January soybean contract, boxes can be assigned in such a way that the reversal value is close to 2.38% of the annual range (taken from Table 11-6). The results are the parameters shown in Table 11-7.

[8] Dunn & Hargitt Financial Services, Inc., West Lafayette, IN.

TABLE 11-6   Optimum Box and Reversal Criteria for 10 Years—1960–1969 (Davis and Thiel)

	Approximate Price Range 1960–1969	Average	Box Size	Reversal	Reversal Value	10-Year Fluctuation (%)
Wheat	113–225	169.0	1½¢	3 boxes	4½¢ = $225	2.66
Corn	88–154	121.0	1½¢	4 boxes	6¢ = $300	4.95
Soybeans	196–309	252.0	2¢	3 boxes	6¢ = $300	2.38
Soybean meal	48–102	75.0	75 pts	2 boxes	150 = $150	2.00
Soybean oil	7.3–12.3	9.8	25 pts	1 box	25 = $150	2.55
Cattle	19–34	26.5	20 pts	2 boxes	40 = $160	1.50
Pork bellies	18–55	36.5	25 pts	6 boxes	150 = $540	4.10
Potatoes	1.9–8.4	5.15	5 pts	3 boxes	15 = $75	2.91
Copper	29–52	40.5	50 pts	4 boxes	200 = $500	4.93
Sugar	2–12	7.0	10 pts	5 boxes	54 = $560	7.14
Cocoa	12–51	31.5	25 pts	7 boxes	175 = $525	5.55
Silver	85–245	165.0	100 pts	2 boxes	200 = $200	1.21

TABLE 11-7   Holding the Chart to a 2.38% Reversal Value*

Soybean Contract	Highest Price	Lowest Price	Annual Range	Reversal Value	Box Size
Jan 71	315	251⅝	63⅜	1½	½
Jan 72	346	284⅞	61⅛	1½	½
Jan 73	444	300	144	3½	1⅛
Jan 74	915	354¼	560¾	13⅜	4½
Jan 75	961	509	452	10¾	3½
Jan 76	705	439½	265½	6⅜	2⅛
Jan 77	782½	490	292½	7	2⅜

* All values in cents.

Indexing and Logarithmic Scale

One way to transform prices into a percentage is by indexing. The steps needed to create an index can be found in Chapter 2 ("Basic Concepts"). The results of plotting a point-and-figure chart on an index will be very close to trying to create a chart with boxes that vary in price by an amount equal to a percentage, and much simpler. If boxes represent a percentage change, they can be marked 95, 96, 97, . . . , 103, 104, . . . and so forth, each box representing a 1% change in price. Because orders are placed as prices, not percentages, you will need to know the corresponding price whenever you buy and sell.

A logarithmic scale represents a constant 2.33% change in price, equal to a proportional 0.01 logarithmic box size.[9] It is interesting that the results of the Davis and Thiel study determined that the optimal box size would be the equivalent of a 2.38% price change over a 10-year period, remarkably close to the logarithmic equivalent.

Price Objectives Using Percentages

If the entire price series has been converted to an index, and plotted on a point-and-figure chart with percentage boxes, then the calculations for horizontal and vertical price objectives are applied to the index values in the normal manner. If prices are used instead of index values or percentages, then the price objectives must also be put into a compounded growth form. For example, a price objective of 5 boxes, each box equal to 2.33%, would be compounded (in spreadsheet notation) as:

Objective = 100 * ((1 + .0233)^5 − 1) = 12.20%

instead of simply $5 \times .0233 = .1165$, or 11.65%.

Stock Dividends and Splits

For those applying point-and-figure charts to stocks, an adjustment must be made whenever a stock dividend is issued or the stock splits, because the chart represents the price of one share. Splits and dividends result in stock multiplying factors:[10]

Activity	Stock Multiplication Factor
10% stock dividend	1.1
30% stock dividend	1.3
2-for-1 stock split	2.0
3-for-2 stock split	1.5

These multiplication factors can be used to correct the box size of a percentage, or logarithmic point-and-figure chart by *dividing* all the boxes by the multiplication factor; therefore, the new box sizes represent the value of one share.

---

[9] See Luis Ballesca Loyo, "Price projections on point and figure charts," *Technical Analysis of Stocks & Commodities* (July 1989).

[10] William G.S. Brown, "Logarithmic Point & Figure Charting," *Technical Analysis of Stocks & Commodities* (July 1995).

Variable-Scale Comparative Results

A simple way of determining the best selection of scaling is to plot the results. The choice of equal percentage increases presented no problem. A standard point-and-figure chart was drawn with incremental price ranges assigned the necessary box size as follows:

Price range (¢/bu)	Box size (¢/bu)
240–286	2¢
286–351	2½¢
351–417	3¢
417–480	3½¢
480–544	4¢
544–598	4½¢
598–648	5¢
648–725	5½¢
725–917	6¢

Once the master chart is constructed, it will never have to be changed. If prices rise above the top of the scale, additional boxes can be numbered with larger increments. Using the standard 3-box method of charting, each January soybean futures contract was plotted in Figure 11-14 and the results are shown in Table 11-8. The profits were consistently good except for 1976. It should be noted that the number of trades increased as the average price increased throughout the test period. This can be expected since the box size does not increase as quickly at higher prices as does the price-volatility relationship. Because of this steady lag, the sensitivity of the system will increase noticeably at peak levels.

The size of the chart based on the price-volatility approximation taken from Tables 11-3 and 11-4 is much smaller than the one used for equal percentage increases. Because the box sizes increase so rapidly, the formations appear more uniform at all price levels, and the number of trades occurring during each contract was reasonably constant. The results of this method show that its application to a long-term chart would be practical. Any one contract contained only a small number of reversals and was able to generate from one to three trades (Table 11-9).

TABLE 11-8   Results Using Equal Percentage Increases (Method 2)

	Trades		Net P/L*
	Total	Profitable	(¢/bu)
January 1966	2	1	+22
January 1971	4	3	+21
January 1972	3	2	+8½
January 1973	2	1	+93⅝
January 1974	20	9	+23⅝
January 1975	12	7	+554⅝
January 1976	16	7	−175¼
			Total +548⅛

* 1¢ commissions deducted.

FIGURE 11-14   Point-and-figure chart for January soybeans using price-volatility scaling.

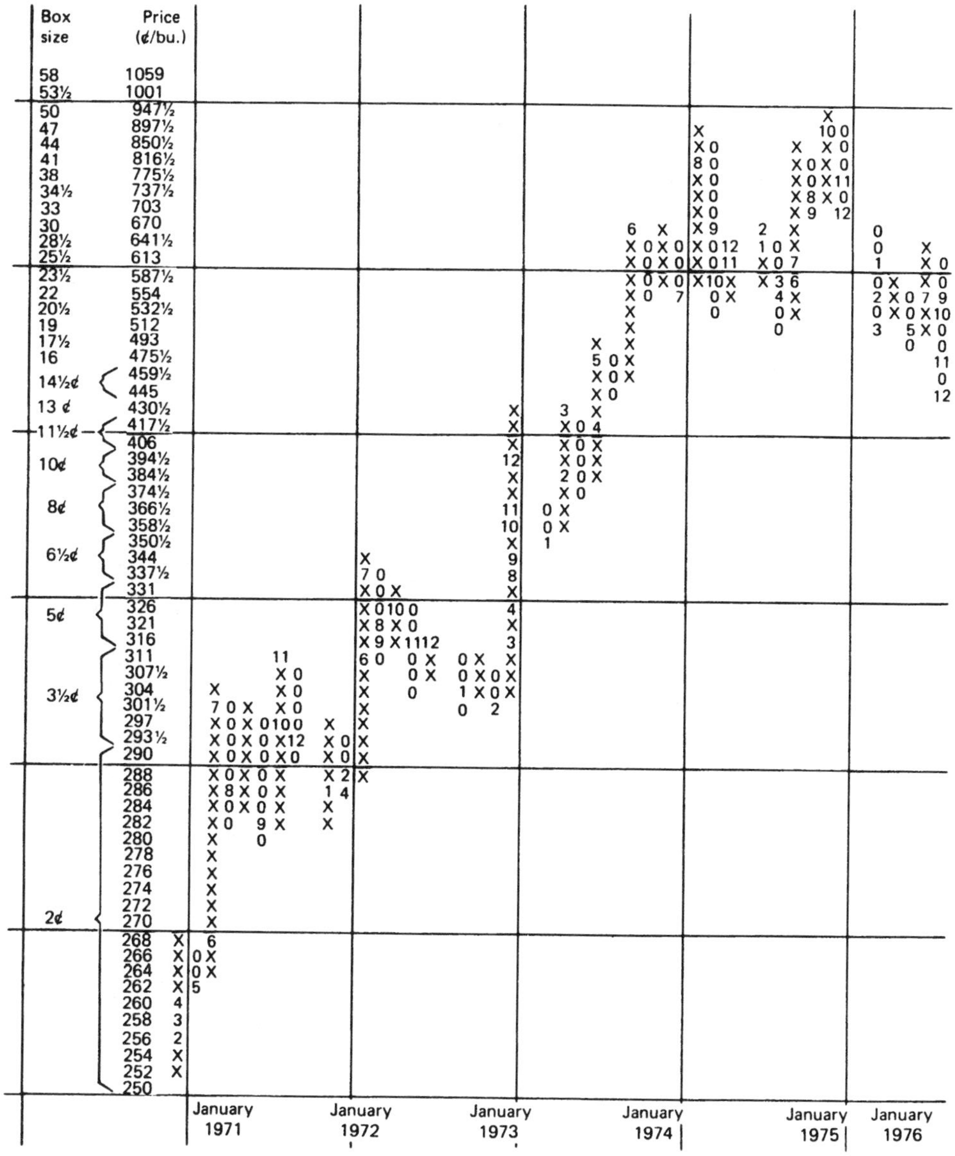

Box size	Price (¢/bu.)					
58	1059					
53½	1001					
50	947½					X
47	897½				X	10 0
44	850½				X 0	X X 0
41	816½				8 0	X 0 X 0
38	775½				X 0	X 0 X 11
34½	737½				X 0	X 8 X 0
33	703				X 0	X 9 12
30	670			6 X	X 9	2 X
28½	641½			X 0 X 0	X 0 12	1 0 X
25½	613			X 0 X 0	X 0 11	X 0 7
23½	587½			X 0 X 0	X 10 X	X 3 6
22	554			X 0 7	0 X	4 X
20½	532½			X	0	0 X
19	512			X		0
17½	493		X X		
16	475½		5 0 X		
14½¢	459½		X 0 X		
13 ¢	445		X 0		
	430½		3 X		
11½¢	417½	X	X 0 4		
	406	X	X 0 X		
10¢	394½	12	X 0 X		
	384½	X	2 0 X		
	374½	X	X 0		
8¢	366½	11	0 X		
	358½	10	0 X		
	350½	X	1		
6½¢	344	X	9		
	337½	7 0 X	8		
	331	X 0 X	X		
5¢	326	X 0 10 0	4		
	321	X 8 X 0	X		
	316	X 9 X 11 12	3		
	311	6 0 0 X	0 X X		
	307½	X 0 X	0 X 0 X		
3½¢	304	X X 0	0 X 0 X		
	301½	7 0 X X 0	1 X 0 X		
	297	X 0 X 0 10 0	0 2		
	293½	X 0 X 0 X 12	X 0 X		
	290	X 0 X 0 X 0	X 0 X		
	288	X 0 X 0 X	X 2 X		
	286	X 8 X 0 X	1 4		
	284	X 0 X 0 X	X		
	282	X 0 9 X	X		
	280	X 0			
	278	X			
	276	X			
	274	X			
	272	X			
2¢	270	X			
	268	X 6			
	266	X 0 X			
	264	X 0 X			
	262	X 5			
	260	4			
	258	3			
	256	2			
	254	X			
	252	X			
	250				
		January 1971	January 1972	January 1973	January 1974	January 1975 January 1976

TABLE 11-9   Results Using Price-Volatility Scaling

Individual Contracts	Trades		Net P/L* (¢/bu)
	Total	Profitable	
January 1971	3	1	−28
January 1972	2	1	+¼
January 1973	1	1	+109
January 1974	2	1	+32
January 1975	1	0	−24
January 1976	3	1	−234
			Total −144¾
Continuous trading 1971–1976	10	5	−70

* 1¢ commission deducted.

The plotted results appear to be much better than the tabulated results. This can be attributed to the increased risk at higher price levels. Although the number of boxes in a losing reversal remained small, the value of the loss increased by a factor of 25 from the bottom to the top of the chart. The few profits and losses that occur at higher price levels will be so significant in the final results that the earlier trading performance is unimportant.

Both variable box approaches offer unique possibilities for identifying trends but increase the problems of risk management. Some of these effects can be offset by reducing the invested margin as prices rise. Other techniques are discussed in Chapter 23.

12

Charting Systems

The rapid growth of computerization has had a great impact on technical trading. The first to be affected were the moving average, or mathematical trending methods, as well as easy-to-program indicators, followed by systematic optimization. More recently, econometric analysis, cycles, and pattern recognition have been the subject of new computerized research. Many quote services that offer graphics can convert a bar chart to a point-and-figure chart at the push of a button. Yet the techniques normally used in classic charting, such as trendlines, channels, and special patterns, have not yet been bombarded with automated analyses.

The systems included in this chapter are those that might be used by a traditional chartist. They do not all require the presence of a chart to be followed, but they are clearly interpretations of natural price patterns. The time that it takes for a price to move from one level to the next is not significant in many of these charting systems; it is only the level itself that is important. The only restriction is that the systems presented could all be verified and tested using a computer.

SWING TRADING

The foundation for the largest number of chart-based systems is the *swing chart*. Similar to point-and-figure, a swing is an upward or downward movement of a minimum size, regardless of the time it takes to achieve that move. Unlike point-and-figure, there are no boxes, and the notation does not use Xs and Os. The only difference between one swing chart and another is the *swing filter*. Once prices have reversed from a high or low point by the minimum amount specified by the swing filter, a new vertical line is drawn in a column to the right of the current one. An example of a swing chart is given in Figure 12-1.

Rules for using the swing chart generally follow those of point-and-figure. New buy and sell signals occur at points where the new swing penetrates the level of the prior swing in the same direction. Secondary signals are given if the new signal is in the same direction as the existing trend. Stop-loss orders can be placed at trend reversal levels or at a point of fixed dollar loss.

A swing method is very different from a moving average technique because it does not require prices to move to a new level to maintain the existing trend. In a swing philosophy, prices can move sideways or stand still within a trend. Analysts will find its attributes similar to a breakout method.

The following systems are all unique, but at the same time they are clearly simple variations of the swing method of charting.

A Classic Chartist's Swing Method

Originally, all swing charts were the product of analyzing a price chart. They were observed patterns that preceded the more modern percentage retracements that now need a pocket calculator. A classic technique for finding the swing highs and lows uses the following steps[1] and is shown in Figure 12.2.

---

[1] Based on William F. Eng, "A Mechanical Trading System," *Technical Analysis of Stocks & Commodities* (July 1986). Further information can be found in Eng, *The Technical Analysis of Stocks, Options & Futures* (Probus, 1988).

**FIGURE 12-1   Standard bar chart with corresponding swing chart. (a) Bar chart.
(b) Swing chart.**

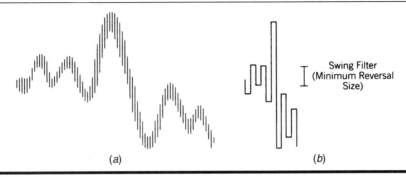

1. Begin at a bar (or new day) where the highs and lows are both higher than the highs and lows of the previous bar (an upswing), or both lower than the highs and lows of the previous bar (a downswing).
2. If an upswing, connect the highs of the two periods.
3. If the next period continues to have higher highs and lows, connect the highs.
4. Continue until a bar occurs that has a lower low without making a higher high. This indicates a possible swing change based on the pattern of the next bar.
5. If the next bar has a lower high and lower low, the highest high of the swing is connected to the new lowest low and a swing change has occurred.

FIGURE 12-2   Constructing a classic swing chart.

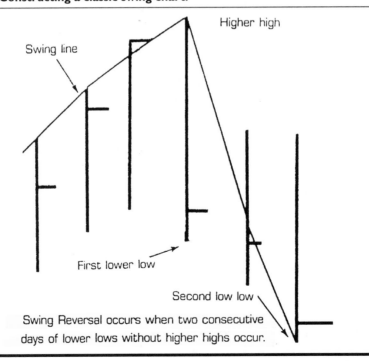

Source: William Eng, "A Mechanical Trading System," *Technical Analysis of Stocks & Commodities,* 4, no. 7 (July 1986). © 1986 Technical Analysis, Inc. Used with permission.

6. If the swing reversal fails, the upswing continues when a new higher high and higher low occurs.

This particular method is called a "2-day" (2-period) technique, because it requires two periods to identify a swing change. The greatest benefit of this swing method is that it finds fast changes in market direction; however, it is recommended for its ability to identify stop-loss points and control risk rather than for its entry timing.

The Livermore System

Known as the greatest trader on Wall Street, Jesse Livermore was associated with every major move in both stocks and commodities during the 30-year period from 1910 to 1940. Livermore began his career as a board boy, marking prices on the high slate boards that surrounded the New York Stock Exchange floor. During this time, he began to notice the distinct patterns, or habits, in the price movement that appeared in the columns of numbers.[2]

As Livermore developed his trading skills and eventually took his position as a professional trader, he maintained the habit of writing prices in columns headed Secondary Rally, Natural Rally, Up Trend, Down Trend, Natural Reaction, and Secondary Reaction. This may have been the basis for what is now considered a swing chart.

Livermore's approach to swing trading required two filters, a larger *swing filter* and a *penetration filter* one-half the size of the swing filter. Penetrations were significant at price levels he called "pivot points." A pivot point is defined in retrospect as the top and bottom of each new swing and are marked with letters in Figure 12-3.[3]

As mentioned earlier, the swing chart differs primarily from the point-and-figure chart by having no box size. By measuring the change in trend as a reversal of the minimum swing filter size from the last high or low swing, the pivot points are always posted at the exact price at which they occurred. In point-and-figure charting, using a 10-point box, a price rally that fails 5 points above the previous box will not be posted; a point-and-figure reversal is measured from the last posted box; therefore, the size of the price reversal needed to indicate a directional change may vary up to the size of one box.

Livermore's trading technique is a unique interpretation of the swing chart. Positions are taken only in the direction of the major trend. This trend is defined by confirming higher highs and higher lows (uptrend), or lower lows and lower highs (downtrend), where the penetration filter is not broken in the reverse direction. That is, an uptrend is still intact as long as prices do not decline below the previous pivot point by as much as the penetration filter size (seen in Figure 12-2). Once the trend is identified, positions are added each time a new penetration occurs, confirming the trend direction. A stop-loss is placed at the point of penetration beyond the prior pivot point. Unfortunately, the penetration filter is not the same as a pivot point, and Livermore never revealed how it was calculated. It seems, however, to be a minor percentage (for example, 20%) of the current swing size.

Failed Reversal

In the Livermore system, the first penetration of the stop-loss calls for liquidation of the current position. A second penetration is necessary to confirm the new trend. If the second penetration fails (at point *K* in Figure 12-4), it is considered a *secondary reaction* within the old trend. The downtrend may be reentered at a distance of the swing filter below *K*, guaranteeing that point *K* is defined, and again on the next swing, following pivot point *M*,

---

[2] Edwin Lefevre, *Reminiscences of a Stock Operator* (Books of Wall Street, Burlington, VT, 1980). First published by George H. Doran in 1923.

[3] Jesse Thompson, "The Livermore System," *Technical Analysis of Stocks & Commodities* (May 1983).

FIGURE 12-3   Trend change.

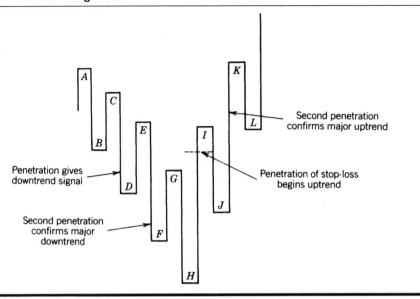

when prices reach the penetration level below pivot point *L*. It is easier to reenter an old trend than to establish a position in a new one.

Percentage Swings

The minimum swing value, which is the only determinate of the swing high and low points, can be more robust if it is a percentage of price rather than a fixed number of points or fixed dollar value. Many markets have doubled in value over the past 10 years—in stocks the price of a technology issue could have increased 20 times and then split. A fixed value for finding the swing highs and lows will be far apart at low price levels and too frequent at higher prices, unless that minimum is calculated as a percentage, *p*.

FIGURE 12-4   Failed reversal.

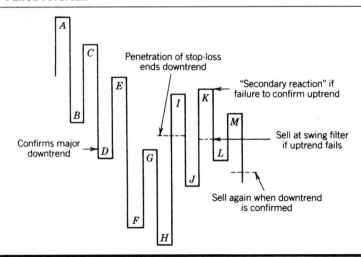

Minimum swing value $MSV_t = p \times price_t$

The most basic systematic approach to trading a swing method is simply to buy when prices move up from the recent lows by the minimum swing value (MSV), and sell when prices fall by the MSV from the recent high. The risk of each trade is always equal to the current value of MSV.

Finding the Swing High and Low Points

The following *Easy Language* program, *KSWING,* plots the swing high and low based on a percentage minimum swing value. For percentage swings, the interest rate *yield* should be used rather than *price.*

```
{KSWING: Finds most recent swing highs and lows.
 Plots values on a TradeStation chart. Copyright 1994-95, P.J. Kaufman. All rights
reserved.

Inputs for KSWING:
  swing = price swing in %}

  input: swing(2.5);
  vars: pcswing(0), last(0), curhigh(0), curlow(0), swhigh(0), swlow(0),
        highbar(0), lowbar(0), chighbar(0), clowbar(0), lowp(0), highp(0),
        xclose(0), xhigh(0), xlow(0), divide(4);

 pcswing = swing / 100.;
{"divide" positions the high or low market on the plot }
 divide = 4;
 factor = 1;

{INITIALIZE MOST RECENT HIGH AND LOW}
 if currentbar = 1 then begin
     curhigh = close;        {current high}
     curlow = close;         {current low}
     end;

{SEARCH FOR A NEW HIGH -- favor reversals}
 if last<>1 then begin
{REVERSE FROM HIGH IF MINIMUM % SWING}
 if low < curhigh - curhigh*pcswing then begin
     last = 1;               {last high fixed}
     swhigh  = curhigh;      {new verified high}
     highbar  = chighbar;
     curlow = low;           {initialize new lows}
     lowp = low;             {swing low for plot}
     clowbar = currentbar;
     plot1[currentbar-highbar](high[currentbar-highbar] + highp*pcswing/divide,
     "swinghigh");
     end
   else begin
    if high > curhigh then begin
     curhigh = high;         {new current high}
     chighbar = currentbar;
     end;
   end;
 end;

{SEARCH FOR A NEW LOW - favor reversal}
 if last <> -1 then begin
{REVERSAL FROM LOW IF MINIMUM % SWING}
 if high > curlow + curlow*pcswing then begin
     last = -1;
```

```
  swlow  = curlow;
  lowbar = clowbar;
  curhigh = high;        {initialize current high}
  highp = high;          {swing high for plot}
  chighbar = currentbar;
  plot2[currentbar-lowbar](low[currentbar-lowbar] - lowp*pcswing/divide,
  "swinglow");
  end
else begin
  if low < curlow then begin
     curlow = low;
     clowbar = currentbar;
     end;
  end;
end;
```

Wilder's Swing Index

An automated way of determining swings is presented with trading rules in Wilder's *Swing Index System.*[4] Wilder has determined that the five most important positive patterns in an uptrend are:

1. Today's close is higher than the prior close.
2. Today's close is higher than today's open.
3. Today's high is greater than the prior close.
4. Today's low is greater than the prior close.
5. The prior close was above the prior open.

In a downtrend, these patterns are reversed.

The Swing Index (SI) combines these five factors, then scales the resulting value to fall between -100 and $+100$ as follows:

$$SI = 50 \left(\frac{(C_t - C_{t-1}) + .5(C_t - O_t) + .25(C_{t-1} - O_{t-1})}{R} \right) \frac{K}{M}$$

where K is the largest of $H_t - C_{t-1}$ and $L_t - C_{t-1}$

  M is the value of a limit move

  R is calculated from the following two steps:

1. Determine which is the largest of

   a. $H_t - C_{t-1}$

   b. $L_t - C_{t-1}$

   c. $H_t - L_t$

2. Calculate R according to the corresponding formula:

   a. $R = (H_t - C_{t-1}) - .5(L_t - C_{t-1}) + .25(C_{t-1} - O_{t-1})$

   b. $R = (L_t - C_{t-1}) .5(H_t - C_{t-1}) + .25(C_{t-1} - O_{t-1})$

   c. $R = (H_t - L_t) + .25(C_{t-1} - O_{t-1})$

Although the usefulness of the SI cannot be determined without proper testing, the formulas combine factors that have a great deal of interest. The SI calculation uses three

[4] J. Welles Wilder, Jr., *New Concepts in Technical Trading Systems* (Trend Research, Greensboro, NC, 1978).

price relationships, the net price direction (close-to-close), the strength of today's trading (open-to-close), and the memory of yesterday's strength (prior open-to-close). It then employs the additional factor of volatility as a percentage of the maximum possible move (K/M). The rest of the formula simply scales the results to within the required −100 to +100 range. In the first step of the calculation of R, the concept of the *true range* reappears.

The daily values are added together to form an *Accumulated Swing Index* (ASI), which substitutes for the price chart, allowing ready identification of the significant highs and lows, as well as clear application of Wilder's trading rules.

Terms used in the trading rules are as follows:

HSP   *High swing point*—Any day on which the ASI is higher than both the previous and the following day.

LSP   *Low swing point*—Any day on which the ASI is lower than both the previous and the following day.

SAR   *Stop-and-reverse points* (three types)—*Index SAR* points are generated by the ASI calculation, *SAR* points apply to a specific price, and *Trailing Index SAR*, which lags 60 ASI points behind the best ASI value during a trade.

The Swing Index System rules are:

1. Initial entry:

   a. Enter a new long position when the ASI crosses above the previous HSP.
   b. Enter a new short position when the ASI crosses below the previous LSP.

2. Setting the SAR point:

   a. On entering a new long trade, the SAR is the most recent LSP; the SAR is reset to the first LSP following each new HSP. A trailing SAR is determined as the lowest daily low occurring between the highest HSP and the close of the day on which the ASI dropped 60 points or more.

   b. On entering a new short trade, the SAR is the most recent HSP; the SAR is reset to the first HSP following each new LSP. The trailing SAR is determined as the highest daily high occurring between the lowest LSP and the close of the day on which the ASI rose by 60 points or more.

Keltner's Minor Trend Rule

One of the classic trading systems is the Minor Trend Rule published by Keltner in his book *How to Make Money in Commodities* (The Keltner Statistical Service). It is still followed closely by a great part of the agricultural community and should be understood for its simplicity and potential impact on markets. Sophisticated analysts must always remember that a large part of trading activity is the result of straightforward decisions that do not use high technology.

Keltner defines an upward trend by the failure to make new lows (comparing today's low with the prior day) and a downtrend by the absence of new highs. This notion is consistent with chart interpretation of trendlines by measuring upward moves along the bottom and downward moves along the tops. The Minor Trend Rule is a plan for using the daily trend as a trading guide. The rule states that the minor trend turns up when the daily trend sells above its most recent high; the minor trend stays up until the daily trend sells below its most recent low, when it is considered to have turned down. To trade using the Minor Trend Rule, buy when the minor trend turns up and sell when the minor trend turns down; always reverse the position.

The Minor Trend Rule is a simple, short-term trading tool, buying on new highs and selling on new lows. It is a breakout method in the style of swing trading and can be used as a leading indicator of the major trend. It requires frequent trading in most markets, with risk varying according to the volatility of the market. Keltner's Minor Trend Rule is the basis for a number of current technical systems that vary the time period over which prior highs and lows are established and consequently increase the interval between trades and the risk of each trade. An advantage of the Keltner approach is that it imposes no arbitrary restrictions on the analysis of prices (e.g., breakouts of 100 points).

Donchian's Four-Week Rule

In the mid-1970s, Playboy's *Investment Guide* reviewed Donchian's Four-Week Rule as "childishly simple . . . was recently discovered to rank premiere among a dozen widely followed mechanical techniques." And the rules are simple:

1. Go long (and cover shorts) when the current price exceeds the highs of the previous 4 full calendar weeks.
2. Go short (and liquidate longs) when the current price falls below the lows of the previous 4 full calendar weeks.
3. Roll forward if necessary into the next contract on the last day of the month preceding expiration.

In 1970, *The Traders Note Book* (Dunn and Hargitt Financial Services), rated the Four-Week Rule as the best of the popular systems of the day. Based on 16 years of history, the best performers were December wheat, June cattle, May copper, August bellies, January soybean oil, and May potatoes.

The system satisfies the basic concepts of trading with the trend, limiting losses and following well-defined rules. It bears a great resemblance to the principle of Keltner's Minor Trend Rule, modified to avoid trading too often. Over the years this technique, classified as a slow breakout system, has shown the greatest longevity. The system is so simple that the only comments about it must also be simple: can a Four-Week Rule work for all markets? If price volatility increases dramatically, the high and low for a 4-week period could become astronomical, while at the same time lower prices could cause narrow ranges in another market. That characteristic is both a key to its success and a problem for risk control. The solution may be a price level–modified rule (called *adaptive*) that reduces the number of weeks (or days) in the high-low measured period as prices and volatility increase. A change of this sort would keep risk on a more even level but still relate to the basic volatility principle of the original system. This approach is discussed in Chapter 17 ("Adaptive Techniques").

Modified for the Final Three Months

One system based on the Four-Week Rule uses only the last 3 months of each futures contract. Beginning 3 months before the delivery month, plot the highs and lows according to the Four-Week Rule. For example, trading December silver, start on September 1 and plot for 4 weeks. The first time the market price crosses the high or low of that 4-week period, take the appropriate long or short position and place a stop-loss of 2½% of the entry price. If not stopped out, liquidate the position on the last day of the month prior to delivery. If stopped out, reenter a new position using the high and low established during the original 4 weeks.

The theory behind the modification is that breakouts are more valid and larger in the period just prior to delivery. An advantage of the system is that it trades very little and has a low commission burden. The disadvantage is that the stop-loss counteracts the nature of the breakout system and imposes an artificial risk level on a method that uses highs and lows established by the market itself. This feature is likely to harm the robustness of the concept.

The *N*-Day Rule

Computers have allowed us to take many simple ideas and examine them in great detail, sometimes to excess. One of the earliest applications of computer power was to change the Four-Week Rule into the *N-Day Rule,* the predecessor of the *n*-minute and *n*-tick rules. The rationale seems logical. If the Four-Week Rule works but the equity drawdown is too large, shortening the time period should improve results.

The *N*-Day Rule states that a buy signal occurs when the current price exceeds the highest price of the past *N* days; a sell signal occurs when the current price falls below the lowest price of the past *N* days. The determination of *N* is critical to the success of this system. The most obvious approach to finding *N* is by testing a broad range of values (as will be shown in the next section). It has also been suggested that *N* could be variable based on the relationship of *normal* volatility to *current* volatility.[5]

$$N_t = N_I \times \frac{V_t}{V_c}$$

where N_t is the number of days used for today's calculation
  N_I is the initial number of days used for normal markets
  V_n is the normal volatility measured over historical data
  V_c is the current volatility measured over a fixed period shorter than the normal volatility, V_n

As the current volatility increases, the number of days used in today's calculation decreases. This may also be classified as an *adaptive* technique.

Testing the N-Day Rule

Weekly breakouts, a limited case of the *N*-Day Rule, were tested by Hochheimer and summarized in his report as the *Weekly Price Channel.* Weekly breakouts produce a slow trading system that depend on major moves for profits. About 75% of those futures markets tested in this 1982 study[6] showed higher risk (some very high), than the crossover systems tested earlier (also see Chapter 21).

The original purpose for the *Weekly Rule* was to look at prices only on Friday. The close on Friday is considered in the same sense as the daily close—more important because it is the *evening up* at the end of the day. Traders are attributed with the feeling that holding a position over a weekend is the only thing worse than holding it overnight. This evening up will prevent false signals that may never occur midday or midweek.

Typical trading rules for a Weekly Price Channel system would be

1. *Buy* (and close out shorts) if the closing price on Friday exceeds the highest closing price of the past *N* weeks.
2. *Sell* (and close out longs) if the close on Friday is below the lowest closing price of the past *N* weeks.

Because this model is always in the market, it is possible for the risk to become very high. The commitment to a new long position is the difference between the highest and lowest closing prices of the past *N* weeks. In addition, even if penetrated, the position is not liquidated until the close of Friday. This could be a very risky proposition; however, that risk is offset by the smoothing effect of only acting once each week. It may be that higher risk is better than being subjected to more frequent false signals.

[5] Andrew D. Seidel and Philip M. Ginsberg, *Commodities Trading* (Prentice-Hall, Englewood Cliffs, NJ, 1983).

[6] Frank L. Hochheimer and Richard J. Vaughn, *Computerized Trading Techniques 1982* (Merrill Lynch Commodities, New York, 1982).

Alternate rules were tested by Hochheimer in his study. Buy and sell signals were taken at the time that the intraday new high or new low occurred. No comparison was available to determine whether the risk was greater or less than the conventional approach. Hochheimer also tested the Weekly Rule with the week ending on days other than Friday. It was not apparent that any one day was better.

Traders will find this basic breakout method is important as a benchmark study. Chapter 5 ("Trend Systems") included the N-Day Breakout as one of the basic trending methods in "Comparison of Major Trend Systems," and shows 10 years of results for the Eurodollar. Included with the study is program code to help enter this program into a computer to allow further testing.

Avoiding Problems Programming the Weekly Breakout

The Weekly Rule is often thought of having signals only on Friday; however, when programming this method, it is important to remember that a number of weeks end on Thursdays due to holidays. Identifying the last day of the week in advance is a problem for a computer program. Although we can find the day of the week by simply using the function @DayOfWeek for *Easy Language,* or @WKDAY in *Quattro,* we have missed the day if the information returned jumps from Thursday to Monday.

The simpler and preferred method, using most intelligent market charting systems, is to request weekly data, or a weekly chart, rather than daily. The built-in conversion program will correctly change days to weeks. By looking at the high, low, and close of the weekly bar you can decide whether a signal has occurred, and executing on the close will be the last price of the week, regardless of the day on which it occurs.

WILLIAM DUNNIGAN AND THE THRUST METHOD

Dunnigan's work in the early 1950s is based on chart formations and is purely technical. Although an admirer of others' abilities to perform fundamental analysis, his practical approach is contained in the statements:

> "If the economists are interested in the price of beans, they should, first of all, learn all they can about the *price of beans.*" Then, by supporting their observations with the fundamental elements of supply and demand, they will be "certain that the bean *prices will reflect these things.*"[7]

Dunnigan did extensive research before his major publications in 1954. A follower of the Dow theory, he originally created a *breakaway system* of trading stocks and commodities, but was forced to drop this approach because of long strings of losses even though the net results of his system were profitable. He was also disappointed when his *2⅜ Swing Method* failed after its publication in *A Study in Wheat Trading.* But good often comes from failure and Dunnigan had realized by now that different measurements should be applied to each market at different price levels. His next system, the *Percentage Wheat Method,* combined a 2½% penetration and a 3-day swing, introducing the time element into his work and perhaps the first notion of *thrust,* a substantial move within a predefined time interval. With the 2½%, 3-day swing, a buy signal was generated if the price of wheat came within 2% of the lows, then reversed and moved up at least an additional 2½% over a period of at least 3 days.

For Dunnigan, the swing method of charting[8] represented a breakthrough; it allowed each market to develop its natural pattern of moves, more or less volatile than any other

---

[7] William Dunnigan, *Selected Studies in Speculation* (Dunnigan, San Francisco, 1954, p. 7).

[8] W.D. Gann, *How to Make Profits in Commodities* (Lambert-Gann, Pomeroy, WA, 1976). This book devotes a large section to swing charts and includes many examples of markets prior to Dunnigan's work.

market. He had a difficult time trying to find one criteria for his charts that satisfied all markets, or even all grains, but established a $2 swing for stocks where Rhea's *Dow Theory* used only $1 moves. His studies of percentage swings were of no help.

The Thrust Method

Dunnigan's final development of the *Thrust Method* combined both the use of percentage measurements with the interpretation of chart patterns, later modified with some mathematical price objectives. He defines a *downswing* as a decline in which the current day's high and low are both lower than the corresponding high and low of the highest day of the prior *upswing*. If currently in an upswing, a higher high or higher low will continue the same move. The reverse effect of having both a higher high and low would result in a change from a downswing to an upswing. The top and bottom of a swing are the highest high of an upswing and the lowest low of a downswing, respectively. It should be noted that a broadening or consolidation day, in which the highs and lows are both greater or both contained within any previous day of the same swing, has no effect on the direction.

In addition to the swings, Dunnigan defines the five key buy patterns:

1. *Test of the bottom*—where prices come within a predetermined percentage of a prior low
2. *Closing-price reversal*—a new low for the swing followed by a higher close than the prior day
3. *Narrow range*—where the current day's range is less than half of the largest range for the swing
4. *Inside range*—where both the high and low fall within the prior range
5. *Penetration of the top*—by any amount, conforming to the standard Dow theory buy signal

All of these conditions can be reversed for the sell patterns. An entry buy signal was generated by combining the patterns indicating a preliminary buy, with a thrust the next day confirming the move. The thrust was defined as a variable price gain based on the price level of the market (for 1954 wheat, this was from ½ to 1½¢). Dunnigan's system attempted to enter the market long near a bottom and short near a top, an improvement on the Dow theory. Because of the risks, the market was asked to give evidence of a change of direction by satisfying two of the first four patterns followed by a thrust on the next day. Any variance would not satisfy the conditions and an entry near the top or bottom would be passed.

The same buy and sell signals applied to changes in direction that did not occur at prior tops and bottoms but somewhere within the previous trading range. In the event all the conditions were not satisfied and prices penetrated either the top or bottom, moving into a new price area, the fifth pattern satisfied the preliminary signal and a thrust could occur on any day. This was not restricted to the day following the penetration. So that if nothing else happened, Dunnigan followed the rules of the Dow Theory to insure that a major move would not be missed.

It has been said by followers of Dunnigan's method that his *repeat* signals are the strongest part of his system; even Dunnigan states that they are more reliable although they limit the size of the profit by not taking full advantage of the trend from its start. Repeat signals use relaxed rules not requiring a new thrust because the trend has already been identified. Two key situations for repeat buy signals are:

1. A test of the bottom followed by an inside range (interpreted as market indecision)
2. A closing price reversal followed by an inside range

A *double thrust* occurs when the first thrust is followed immediately by a second thrust; or, after the first thrust, a congestion area develops, followed by a second thrust in the same direction as the first. Although Dunnigan used a fixed number of points to define his thrust, today's traders may find the standard deviation of the daily price changes or another volatility measure as a more practical basis for identifying significant price moves.

One-Way Formula

Dunnigan worked on what he hoped would be a generalized version of his successful Thrust Method and called it the *One-Way Formula*. Based on his conclusions that the Thrust Method was too sensitive, causing more false signals than he was prepared to accept, he modified the confirmation aspect of the signal and made the thrust into the preliminary signal. He also emphasized longer price trends which smooth performance and reduce signals.

With the upswing and downswing rules remaining the same, Dunnigan modified the thrust to require its entire range to be outside the range of the prior day. For a preliminary buy, the low of the day must be above the high of the prior day. This is a stronger condition than his original thrust, yet only constitutes a preliminary buy. The confirmation occurs only if an additional upthrust occurs after the formation of, or test of, a previous bottom. There must be a double bottom or ascending bottom followed by a thrust to get a buy signal near the lows. If the confirmation does not occur after the first bottom of an adjustment, it may still be valid on subsequent tests of the bottom.

For the One-Way Formula, repeat signals are identical to original confirming signals. Each one occurs on a pullback and test of a previous bottom, or ascending bottom, followed by an upthrust. Both the initial and repeat signals allow the trader to enter after a reaction to the main trend. The Dow approach to penetration is still allowable in the event all else fails. The refinement of the original thrust method satisfied Dunnigan's problem of getting in too soon.

The Square-Root Theory

The two previous methods show a conspicuous concentration of entry techniques and an absence of ways to exit. Although it is valid to reverse positions when an opposite entry condition appears, Dunnigan spends a great effort in portfolio management[9] and risk-reward conditions that were linked to exits. By his own definition, his technique would be considered *trap forecasting,* taking a quick or calculated profit rather than letting the trend run its course (the latter was called *continuous forecasting*).

A fascinating calculation of risk evaluation and profit objectives is the *Square-Root Theory*. He strongly supported this method, thinking of it as the golden[10] key, and claiming support of numerous esoteric sources such as *The Journal of the American Statistical Association, The Analysts Journal,* and *Econometrica.* The theory claims that prices move in a square root relationship. For example, a market trading at 81 (or 9^2) would move to 64 (8^2) or 100 (10^2); either would be one unit up or down based on the square root. The rule also states that a price may move to a level that is a multiple of its square root. A similar concept can be found greatly expanded in the works of Gann (Chapter 14).

NOFRI'S CONGESTION-PHASE SYSTEM

Markets spend the greater part of their time in nontrending motions, moving up and down within a range determined by near-stable equilibrium of supply and demand. Most trend

---

[9] Each of his writings on systems contained examples of multiple-fund management of varied risk.

[10] Refers to the Greek description of Fibonacci ratios.

followers complain about the poor performance that results from markets that fail to move continuously in one direction. However, their systems are designed to conserve capital by taking repeated small losses during these periods to capture the big move. Eugene Nofri's system, presented by Jeanette Nofri Steinberg, is used during the long period of congestion, returning steady but small profits. Nofri's system does not concern itself with the sustained directional move; therefore, the user of the Congestion-Phase System can wait to be certain of a well-defined congestion area before beginning a trading sequence.

The basis of the system is a 3rd-day reversal. If prices are within a congestion range and have closed in the same direction for 2 consecutive days, take the opposite position on the close of day 2, anticipating a reversal. If this is correct, take the profits on the close of trading the next (3rd) day. Nofri claims a 75% probability of success using this technique, and the Theory of Runs supports that figure. If there is a 50% chance of a move either up or down on day 1, there is a 25% chance of the same move on the next day, and 12½% chance on day 3. Considering both commissions and variation in the distribution, an assumption of 75% is reasonable.

Because the basis of the Congestion-Phase System is an unlikely run within a sideways price period, the substitution of a 4-day run instead of the current 3-day run should increase the profitability and reliability of the individual trades while reducing the number of opportunities.

The Congestion-Phase System is only applied to markets within a trading range specifically defined by Nofri. Users are cautioned not to be too anxious to trade in a newly formed range until adequate time has elapsed or a test of the support and resistance has failed. The top of the congestion area is defined as a high, which is immediately followed by 2 consecutive days of lower closing prices; the bottom of the congestion area is a low price followed by 2 higher days. A new high or low price cancels the congestion area. Any 2 consecutive days with prices closing almost unchanged (for example, ±2 ticks) are considered as 1 day for the purposes of the system. These ranges occur frequently and can be found by charting prices using the last 10 days. In cases in which the top or bottom has been formed following a major breakout or price run, a waiting period of 10 additional days is suggested to ensure the continuance of the congestion area and limit the risk during more volatile periods. Remember, systems that trade only within ranges offer many opportunities that should be exercised with patience.

A congestion area is not formed until both a top and bottom can be identified. Penetration of a previous top and formation of a new top redefines the range without altering the bottom point; the opposite case can occur for new bottoms. If a false breakout occurs lasting 2 or 3 days, safety suggests a waiting period of 7 days. Logical stops are also possible, the most obvious places being the top and bottom of the current congestion area, but closer stops could be formulated based on price volatility.

The Congestion-Phase System can stand alone as a short-term trading method or can be used to complement any longer technique. When trying to improve entry or exit fills, the system qualifies as a timing device but only within the congestion areas defined by the rules. It is not intended to be used in all situations. The converse of the system says that an entry signal given outside of a congestion area should be taken immediately because longer periods of prolonged movement in one direction are most likely. But in a trading range, the Congestion-Phase System may turn a moving average technique from a loser to a winner.

OUTSIDE DAYS WITH AN OUTSIDE CLOSE

There are numerous chart patterns that can be profitable if they are properly identified and traded consistently. Unfortunately, any one pattern may not appear very often and traders may become impatient waiting for the opportunities. For others who may feel that overall trading success is a combination of small victories, the *outside day with an outside close* is one such successful pattern.

An outside day has the high and low outside the range of the previous day; that is, the high is higher and the low is lower. An outside close is one in which the closing price is higher or lower than the prior day's high or low, respectively. This is considered an attempt to move in one direction followed by a strong push in the other direction. If the close was in the direction opposite to a recent price move, this is called a key reversal day;[11] however, because the previous price direction is not distinguished, it is not necessarily a reversal but may be a renewal of the trend direction.

A brief study by Arnold[12] showed that this pattern proved profitable for a small sample of currencies, metals, and financials using the following rules:

1. *Buy* on the close of an outside day if the close is above the prior high; *sell* if the close is below the prior low.
2. If buying, place a stop-loss just below the low of the outside day; if selling, place the stop just above the high.
3. Close out the position on the close 3 days after entry.

After studying exits on days 1 through 5 following the trade entry, Arnold concluded that this formation predicts reasonably consistent price movements for the next 3 days.

ACTION AND REACTION

The human element in the market is not responsible for the ultimate rise and fall of prices, but for the way in which prices find their proper level. Each move is a series of overreactions and adjustments. Many stock and commodity analysts have studied this phenomenon and base entire systems and trading rules on their observations. Elliott's *Wave Principle* is the clearest and most well-known of the theories founded entirely on this notion. Tubbs' *Stock Market Correspondence Course* is the first to define the magnitude of these reactions in the *Law of Proportion;* and, in 1975 the Trident System was based on both the patterns and the size of the action and reaction.

Retracement of a major bull campaign is the most familiar of the market reactions and the one to which almost every theory applies. It is virtually unanimous that a 100% retracement, back to the beginning of the move, encounters the most important support level. The 100% figure itself has been discussed in terms of unity, referring to its behavioral significance. The next most accepted retracement level is 50%, strongly supported by Gann and commonly discussed by experienced speculators. The other significant levels vary according to different theories:

Schabacker accepts an adjustment of $\frac{1}{3}$ or $\frac{1}{2}$, considering anything larger to be a trend reversal.

Angas anticipates 25% reactions for intermediate trends.

Dunnigan and *Tubbs* look at the larger $\frac{1}{2}$, $\frac{2}{3}$, or $\frac{3}{4}$ adjustment.

Gann takes inverse powers of 2 as behaviorally significant: $\frac{1}{2}$, $\frac{1}{4}$, $\frac{1}{8}$, ...

Elliott bases his projections on the Fibonacci ratio and its complement (.618 and .382).

Predicting advances into new ground is also based on prior moves. Gann believed in multiples of the lowest historic price as well as even numbers; prices would find natural resistance at $2, $3, . . . , at intermediate levels of $2.50, $3.50, . . . , or at two to three times the base price level. Elliott looked at moves of 1.618% based on a Fibonacci ratio.

[11] See the discussion of key reversals in Chapter 8.

[12] Curtis Arnold, "Your Computer Can Take You Beyond Charting," *Futures* (May 1984).

Fibonacci Ratios

Along with the most common 1, ½, ⅓, and ¼ retracement values, Fibonacci ratios are considered of equal importance. Fibonacci ratios are found by dividing one number in the *Fibonacci summation series*

1, 1, 2, 3, 5, 8, 13, 21, 34, 55, 89, 14 . . .

by the preceding or following value. The series is formed beginning with the values 1, 1, and adding the last two numbers in the series together to get the next value. The numbers in the series, especially those up to the value 21, are often found in nature's symmetry; however, the most important aspect of the Fibonacci sequence is the ratio of one value to the next. Called the *Golden Ratio,* this value F_N/F_{N+1} approaches 1.618 as N gets large. Oddly, the inverse $F_{N+1}/F_N = 0.618$, which is a feature that has drawn attention.

The Golden Ratio has a long history. The great pyramid of Giza, the Mexican pyramids, many Greek structures, and works of art have been constructed in the proportions of the Golden Ratio. These and some further examples are given in Chapter 14 where they are also shown in context with trading systems. At this time it is important to recognize that many analysts who consider human behavior as the primary reason for the size of a price move and their retracements, use the Fibonacci ratio .618 or its reciprocal $1 - .618 = .382$, as very likely targets. Elliott is the most well-known advocate, and applications of his Wave Theory are filled with these ratios.

Retracement rules have not been proved scientifically, but they are accepted by most traders. In general terms, the retracement theories, or *revelation methods,* can be categorized as either *proportional retracements* or *time-distance goals.* Proportional retracement states that prices will return to a level that is clearly related, by proportion or ratio, to the length of the prior price move. The larger the move, the clearer the retracement. The percentages and ratios expected to be successful are those that are most obvious: 100%, 50%, 33%, and so on, in addition to the Fibonacci ratio 1.618 and its inverse 0.618. The time-distance rule is popularized in the works of Gann (also found in Chapter 14). Gann's retracement objectives can best be thought of as forming an arc of a circle, with the center at the price peak. The goal is satisfied when prices touch any point on the circle.

Tubbs' Law of Proportion

The technical part of Tubbs course in stock market trading is intense chart interpretation. The *Law of Proportion* presented in Lesson 9 is a well-defined action-and-reaction law. In cases where the nearby highs or lows of a swing were not broken, Tubbs claims four out of five successful predictions with his principle. The law states:

> Aggregates and individual stocks tend to run on half, two-thirds, three-fourths of previous moves. First in relation to the next preceding move which was made. Then in relation to the move preceding that.

Applied to silver, an initial move from $4 to $6 would react ½ to $5, ⅔ to $4.67, or ¾ to $4.50. Tubbs does allow for traditional price support as a major obstacle to the measured price retracement, and so unity (a 100% retracement) may be added to the three proportions. Figure 12-5 shows subsequent reactions to the silver move just described; the second reversal could be any of three magnitudes (or back to major support at $4.00), ending at $4.50, a ¾ reversal. Reversals 3, 4, and 5 are shown with their possible objectives. The last reversal, 5, becomes so small that the major support levels (horizontal broken lines) are considered as having primary significance, along with proportions of moves 1 and 2. Major support at $4.00 coincides with ½ of move 1 and ⅔ of move 2. This would normally be sufficient to nominate that point as the most likely to succeed. Tubbs indicates that

FIGURE 12-5   Tubbs' Law of Proportion.

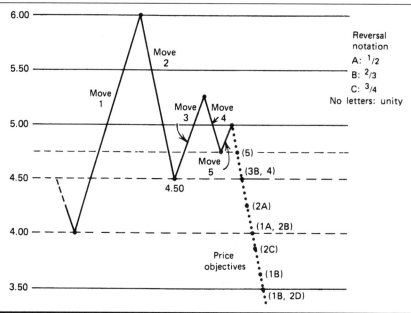

these points rarely occur with exactness, but proportions serve as a valuable guideline. The principle is one of reaction in relationship to an obvious preceding action.

Trident

The Trident Commodity-Trading System received its fair share of publicity when it was introduced at the beginning of 1975. An article in the 1977 *Dow Jones Commodities Handbook* had an excellent review of the background of the system and some of the conflicts surrounding its presentation and subsequent successes and failures. The system itself is not unique in concept but in its implementation. It is based upon the principle of price action and reaction with formations similar to the waves of R.N. Elliott. For each price move, there is a point of undervalue and overvalue with subsequent reaction, or adjustments, in price as it moves irregularly in the direction determined by the ultimate balance of supply and demand.

The object of the system is to trade in the direction of the main trend but take advantage of the reaction (or waves) to get favorable entry and exit points. The concept of trading with the trend and entering on reactions is discussed in the context of commodity technical analysis as early as 1942 by W.D. Gann and in the preceding section on action and reaction. The goal is to predict where the reactions will occur and what profit objective to set for each trade.[13] Trident's approach is easy to understand: Each wave in the direction of the main trend will be equal in length to the previous wave in the same direction. The target is calculated by adding this distance to the highest or lowest point of the completed reaction. As with Elliott's principle, the determination of the tops and bottoms of the waves is dependent on the time element used; the complex form of primary and intermediate waves would hold true with Trident (Figure 12-6).

Because there are inaccuracies in the measurement of behavioral phenomena, Trident emphasizes the practical side of its theory by offering latitude in its choice of entry and exit

---

[13] Gann's work also discusses this topic specifically.

FIGURE 12-6   Trident entry-exit.

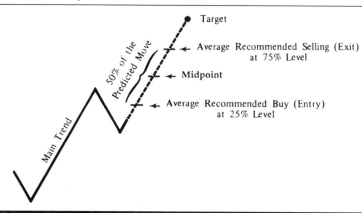

points. By entering after 25% of the anticipated move has occurred and exiting 25% before the target, there is ample time to determine that the downward reaction has ended before your long position is taken and enough caution to exit well before the next reaction. A critical point in each main trend is midway between the start of the move and the target. If the midpoint is not reached, there is a change in direction of the main trend causing a reevaluation of the main trend and the reactions. A change of direction is considered conclusive if a reversal equal in size to 25% of the last reaction occurs during what was expected to be an extension of the main trend. That 25% value becomes the trailing stop-loss on any trade in the event the objective is not reached.

This discussion is not intended to be a complete representation of the Trident System, but a brief description of its essential ideas. The actual system has substantial refinements and subtleties in target selection for major and minor trends and corrective moves; it includes points to reverse positions based on the trailing stop.

In a later bulletin to Trident users, it was suggested that a modification to the system be implemented with respect to money management. Using a technique similar to the Martingale System, each loss is followed by an increase in the number of positions traded. The trader only has to continue to extend his positions and stay with the system until he wins. A comprehensive version of this classic gambling approach can be found in the section "Theory of Runs," in Chapter 17. The Trident concepts are all reasonable and generally accepted by experienced traders. They include advance and retracement, trade the trend, don't pick tops and bottoms, take the center out of each move, and use a trailing stop.

Rethinking Retracements

Interesting observations were made by Tom DeMark[14] about identifying the price move that serves as the basis for measuring retracements. If the market is currently at a low, rather than judging the distance of this drop from the most recent swing high, he chooses to look for the highest point that has occurred since the last time the market traded at this low level. He then finds the most likely retracement points using the Fibonacci ratios .618, and 1.618, plus Fibonacci alternatives .382, .50, 1.382, 2.236, and 2.618 applied to the difference between the high and low, added to the current low price.

---

[14] Tom DeMark, "Retracing your steps," *Futures* (November 1995). Also see Chapter 2 of DeMark, *The New Science of Technical Analysis* (John Wiley & Sons, 1994).

CHANNEL BREAKOUT

The classic *channel* is formed by drawing a straight line along the bottom of an upward trend (or the tops of a downtrend), then constructing a parallel line that touches the extreme high price of that same time interval, forming an envelop, or channel, around a price move. It is easy to do this with a chart and a ruler, but not as simple to transfer this concept to a computer program. Because the concept of a channel breakout is basic to charting, an automated version may prove useful for identifying key market turning points. The steps to creating a program are as follows:

1. *Create a swing chart to identify key high and low points.* A construction of a swing chart was discussed in the first section of this chapter, "Finding the Swing High and Low Points." This method used a minimum swing value, MSV, to identify a swing high or low. For example, once a price had declined from its recent high by the MSV, that previous high becomes the last swing high. The swing highs and lows are therefore only found after-the-fact. When a larger MSV is used, the points identified as swing highs and lows become farther apart and are considered more important, or major swings. By creating two swing charts using a small and a large minimum swing value, we can show both major and minor market price swings (see Figure 12-7).

2. *Find a straight-line trend.* Beginning with the last swing high or swing low, use the least-squares linear regression to find the straight line through the center of prices that have occurred since that high or low:

    Straight-line value $Y = a \times \text{date} + b$

3. *Draw channel bands.* Beginning at the previous swing high or low, calculate the value Y of the linear regression line at all points up to the most recent date, and find the two prices that are the farthest above and below the regression line. These prices will define the upper and lower channel bands:

    Highest relative price $H \max = Ht - (aPt + b)$

    Lowest relative price $L \max = (aPt + b) - Lt$

FIGURE 12-7   Major and minor swings.

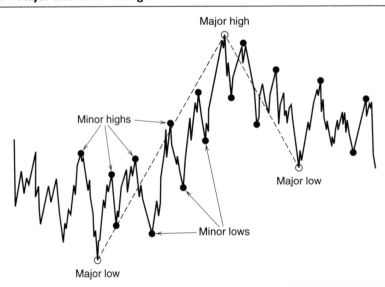

where a and b are the linear regression slope and y-intercept. The channel band is found by adding or subtracting H max and L max from the linear regression straight-line formula:

Upper channel band $= aPT + b + H$ max

Lower channel band $= aPt + b - L$ max

4. *Project the bands one period ahead.* To know whether the next price has broken the channel, indicating a change of trend, we project the channel one period ahead using the slope value, a,

Projected upper channel band $t + 1 = aPt + b + H$ max $+ a$

Projected lower channel band $t + 1 = aPt + b - L$ max $+ a$

If the trend is up (the slope $a > 0$) and the next price is *below* the projected *lower* band, then the trend has turned from up to down. If the trend is down ($a < 0$) and the next price is greater than the projected upper band, then the trend has turned up. When the slope, a, is very near 0, we have a sideways channel and the same rules still apply.

Because a major channel is considered a strong chart formation, prices that approach the channel, but have not penetrated the band, would be candidates for trades. For example, if the trend is down and prices come within 15% of the upper band, we would want additional short positions (see Figure 12-8). We do not necessarily want to lift those existing shorts at the bottom of the channel, especially if the downtrend is severe; however, this

FIGURE 12-8 Entering near the top of a declining channel. Points *A, B,* and *C* define the new channel. Trades can be entered at point *E1,* exited at *X1,* then entered at *E2* and *E3* and exited at *X2.*

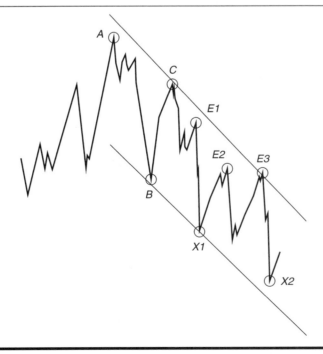

technique offers a clear and safe way to scale into a trade with more than one entry point. If the trend is sideways (the slope is near zero), then exiting shorts and reversing your position could work well.

A minor channel can also be used to signal buys and sells within a major channel. By finding swing points using a small minimum swing value, we can wait for a break of the minor channel to signal a trend direction within the major channel. This gives an added confirmation that prices are moving in your direction before entering.

MOVING CHANNELS

As computers have become common, channels are frequently constructed as moving bands around prices. Some of these, such as those using a standard deviation, can claim statistical significance (these are discussed in Chapter 5). A simple mathematical way of representing a channel might use the average of the high, low, and close to designate the center and a band based on the highs and lows. The midpoint of the price move M and height or range R of the move can be calculated

$$M_t = \frac{1}{3N} \sum_{1}^{N} (H_t + L_t + C_t)$$

$$R_t = \frac{1}{N} \sum_{1}^{N} (H_t - L_t)$$

Then, the upper and lower channel bands forecasted for the next day are

$$U'_{t+1} = M_t + (M_t - M_{t-1}) + wR_t$$

$$L'_{t+1} = M_t + (M_t - M_{t-1}) - wR_t$$

The bands are created by extrapolating the average midpoint and adding or subtracting the average daily range R multiplied by a scaling factor w. A long position is taken when the new price $P_{t+1} > U'_{t+1}$; a short is taken when $P_{t+1} < L'_{t+1}$. If a channel profit objective is needed, it can be calculated at a point equal in distance to the channel width from the channel breakout as follows

Long objective $UO_{t+1} = U'_{t+1} + 2wR_t$

Short objective $LO_{t+1} = L'_{t+1} - 2wR_t$

Because the value wR_t represents one-half the band width, $2wR_t$, the objective is an equal band width above or below the breakout point on any day. The objective may remain fixed at the price level determined on the day of the breakout, or preferably, will change each day to remain one band width from the new channel value (Figure 12-9). This method relates closely to volatility measures and more examples can be found in Chapter 20.

An alternate way of defining a channel would be to forecast 1 day ahead using the slope of a regression analysis (*linear* for a straight channel, *log* for a curved one) and use the standard deviation of the price changes to define the band. The other rules would remain the same.[15]

COMBINING TECHNIQUES

Richard D. Wyckoff, popular in the early 1930s, relied solely on charts to determine the motives behind price behavior. He combined the three most popular methods, bar chart-

[15] For a further discussion of channels, see Donald Lambert, "Commodity Channel Index: Tool for Trading Cyclic Trends," *Technical Analysis of Stocks & Commodities* (October 1980), and John F. Ehlers, "Trading Channels," *Technical Analysis of Stocks & Commodities* (April 1986).

ing, point charts (the predecessor of point-and-figure charts), and waves to identify the direction, extent, and timing of price behavior, respectively.[16]

To Wyckoff, the bar chart combined price and volume to show the direction of the price movement. In general terms, it shows the trading ranges in which supply and demand are balanced. The volume complemented this by giving the intensity of trading, which relates to the *quality* of the long or short position. Wyckoff used *group charts,* or indices, in the manner of Charles Dow, to select the stocks with the most potential, rather than looking only at individual stock price movement. This assures that the move is based on the broader nature of the business, rather than on company politics.

Point-and-figure charts are used to condense price action. If prices move from lower to higher levels due to events, the time it takes to reach the new level is unimportant. Point-and-figure charts record events, not time. As long as prices rise without a significant reversal, the chart uses only one column; when prices change direction, a new column is posted (see the point-and-figure section of Chapter 9 as well as the swing trading section of this chapter). Price objectives can be determined from formations in a point-and-figure chart usually related to the length of the sideways periods or *horizontal formations.* These objectives are very different and normally closer than objectives found using similar bar chart formations.

The *wave chart,* similar to Elliott's theories, represents the behavior of investors and the natural rhythm of the market. Wyckoff uses these waves to determine the points of buying and selling within the limitations defined by both the bar chart and point-and-figure charts. He considered it essential to use the wave charts as a leading indicator of price movement.

Wyckoff used many technical tools but not rigidly. He did not believe in unconfirmed fundamentals but insisted that the market action was all you needed—the market's primary forces of supply and demand could be found in charts. He did not use triangles, flags, and other formations, which he considered to be a type of Rorschach test, but limited his analysis to the most basic patterns—the horizontal or congestion areas. He used time-

---

[16] Jack K. Hutson, "Elements of Charting," *Technical Analysis of Stocks & Commodities* (March 1986).

FIGURE 12-9　Channel calculation.

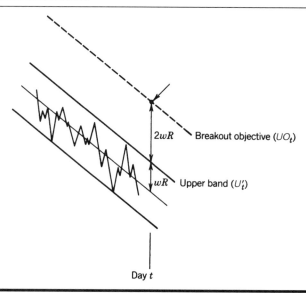

2wR　Breakout objective (UO_t)

wR　Upper band (U_t')

Day t

based and event-based charts to find the direction and forecast, then relied on human behavior (in the form of Elliott waves) for timing. His trading was successful and his principles have survived.

COMPLEX PATTERNS

Most charting systems involve a few simple rules, trying to model a price pattern that seems to have repeatedly resulted in a profitable move. The most popular systems are simply a breakout of a previous high or low, either a horizontal pattern or a trend channel. Over the years these approaches have proved to be steady performers. Another group of traders might argue that it is better to be more selective about each trade and increase the expectation of a larger profit, than to take many trades to win with the long-term probabilities.

DeMark's Sequential™

Tom DeMark has created a strategy, called a *sequential,* that finds a very overextended price move, one that is likely to change direction, and takes a countertrend position.[17] His selling objective is to identify the place where the last buyer has bought. His rules use counting and retracements rather than mathematical formulas or trendlines. To get a buy signal, the following steps are applied to daily data:

1. *Setup.* To begin, there must be a decline of at least nine or more consecutive closes that are lower than the corresponding closes 4 days earlier (close − close[4] < 0). In the case where today's close is equal or greater than the close 4 days before, the setup must begin again.
2. *Intersection.* To assure that prices are declining in an orderly fashion, rather than plunging, the high of any day on or after the 8th day of the setup must be greater than the low of any day 3 or more days earlier. Note that there can be a delay before the intersection occurs provided that the pattern is not negated by the following rules.
3. *Countdown.* Once the setup and intersection have been satisfied, we count the number of days in which the close was lower than the close 2 days ago (close < close[2]). The days that satisfy this countdown requirement do not need to be continuous. When the countdown reaches 13 we get a buy signal *unless* one of the following conditions occurs:
   a. There is a close that exceeds the highest intraday high that occurred during the setup stage.
   b. A sell setup occurs (nine consecutive closes above the corresponding closes 4 days earlier).
   c. Another buy setup occurs before the buy countdown is complete. In this case, the rules begin again at Step 2, the intersection. This condition is called *recycling.*

For the sequential pattern, the sell signal is the reverse of the buy. Traders should expect that the development of the entire formation will take no less than 21 days, but typically 24 to 39 days.

Entering the Sequential

Once the buy signal occurs, there are three choices for entering the market. The first is to enter on the close of the day on which the countdown is completed; however, this risks a new setup situation that will extend the conditions for an entry. The second requires a directional confirmation, the close greater than the close 4 days ago, but it avoids the possibility of recycling. The third is to enter a long when the close is greater than the high 2 days earlier, a compromise between the first two techniques.

[17] Thomas R. DeMark, *The New Science of Technical Analysis* (John Wiley & Sons, 1994).

FIGURE 12-10 A sequential buy signal in the Deutschemark.

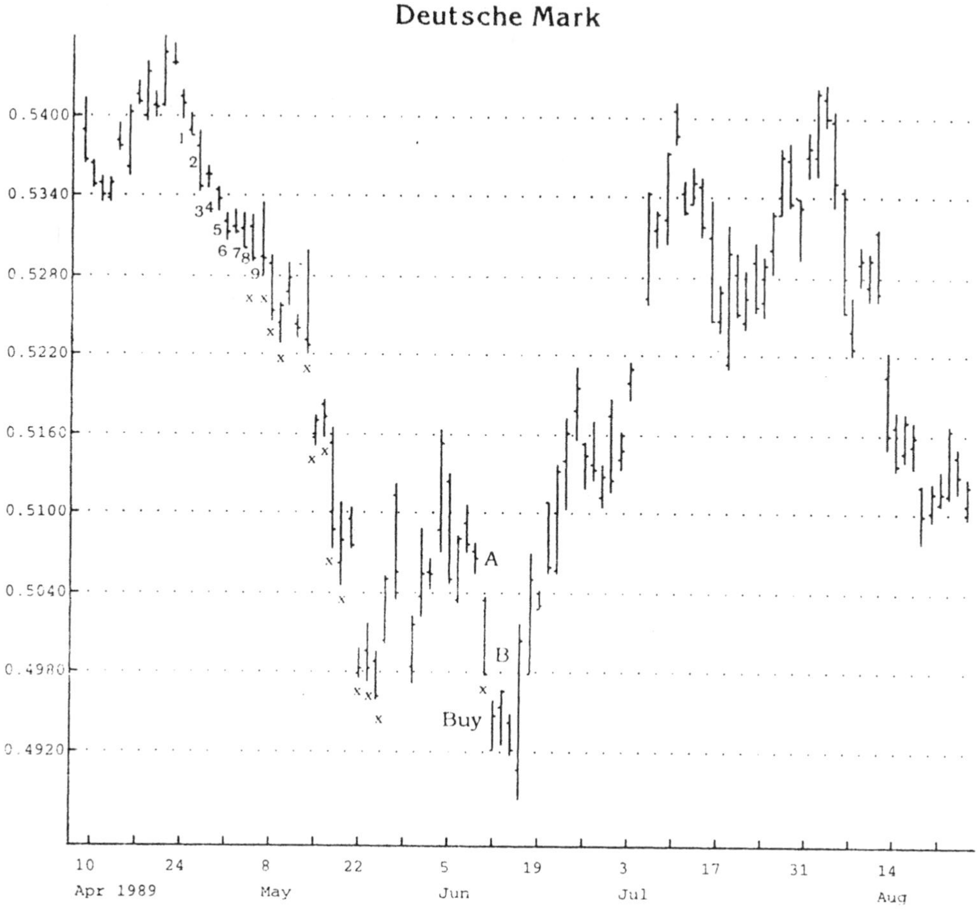

Deutsche Mark

Source: Logical Information Machines, Inc. (LIM), Chicago, IL.

Exiting the Sequential

A number of exit conditions, consistent with the type of patterns, provide the trader with clear rules to liquidate the current trade. First, the current buy setup is complete, and the lowest price recorded does not exceed the furthest price recorded by the recent inactive setup (normally the previous sell setup). If, on the other hand, any price recorded in the current buy setup exceeds the furthest price of the previous sell setup, then the position is held until a reverse signal occurs.

Two stop-losses are also recommended. For a buy signal, the true range for the lowest-range day of the combined setup and countdown period is subtracted from the low of that lowest day to create a stop-loss. Alternately, the difference between the close and the low of the lowest day is subtracted from the low of the lowest day to form a closer stop-loss.

Considering Complex Patterns

There seems to be an extreme contrast between the simple robustness of a breakout system and the very complex set of circumstances that produce a signal for DeMark's sequential. The philosophic consistency of the breakout system is demonstrated by applying increasingly larger breakout criteria to the same market and observing that the reliability and profits per trade both increase, indicating that it becomes more selective, and those trades that occur have a better performance profile. In the case of a single pattern, such as an island reversal or DeMark's sequential, there is no way to measure this robustness. For the sequential, the time taken to identify a signal must also limit the number of signals that are possible. Each trader must decide whether this pattern selection produces a better set of trades, or if it is too demanding to survive the test of time.

13

Spreads and Arbitrage

A position taken in opposing directions in related markets, contracts, options, or shares is called a *spread,* or *straddle.* When the dynamics of the spread can be definitively calculated, such as the price of two bonds of the same maturity and the same grade, or the price of gold in two different locations, the transaction can be considered an *arbitrage.* For futures markets, the most common use of the term *spread* relates to two delivery months of the same market. For example, a trader may take a long position in March Treasury bonds and a short position in the June contract (for the same year). The expectation is that prices will rise and that near-term delivery will rise faster than the deferred, netting a larger profit on the long position and a smaller loss on the short.

A spread is most often a way to reduce both the risk and, consequently, the potential profit that exists in an outright long or short position. A spread is commonly placed in two delivery months of the same market, a combination of futures and physicals in the same market, or in two options of different strike prices or maturities. The reduction in risk depends on the relationship between successive delivery months, which varies considerably with the market traded. These can be summarized as follows:

Financial markets nearest to delivery react more quickly and with greater magnitude to changing interest rates, economic data, and supply and demand situations. The deferred contracts will respond more slowly because the lasting effect on the market is not as clear.

Precious metals, such as gold, platinum, and silver, were once considered *pure carry* markets. Successive delivery months would always trade at a higher price due to the interest rate component of holding inventory. If the price of the metal rises or interest rates rise, the cost of carry increases and the spread between months widens. If metal prices or interest rates decline, the spread narrows. If metal prices and interest rates move in opposite ways, the effect on the spread is dampened to varying degrees. There has been an evolution in the industrial use of precious metals, primarily in electronics, which has increased the *consumption* and changed the patterns to reflect a more industrial look.

Industrial metals, such as copper, will show normal carrying charges under most circumstances, but they are affected by demand to the extent that prices have been known to *invert* for significant periods of time. Because of their fundamental changes, silver prices inverted for the first time in 1997.

Foreign exchange rates are dependent on the prevailing economic outlook for the specific country, combined with their balance of trade. A stable economy will show nearly unchanged forward rates; a weakening economy will cause the deferred contracts to be discounted. Prices tend to become more volatile as they move away from equilibrium, whether higher or lower. Because exchange rates are quoted in terms of other currencies, everything must be viewed as relative to another economy.

Agricultural products (crops) contain a well-defined carrying charge within each crop year. Expected variations in both supply and demand have made delivery month patterns differ from one another; however, prices rarely achieve *full carry.* (Note that potatoes are an exception to the normal patterns shown by agricultural products.)

Livestock markets are noted for products that cannot be stored and redelivered; therefore, the prices for any one contract month are based on anticipated supply and demand at the time of delivery. Feedlots and farmers have been known to deliver early when prices were high or when production costs were rising; however, this will cause an unreplaceable shortage in the nearest deferred months (Figure 13-1).[1] Patterns in

[1] Perry J. Kaufman, "Technical Analysis," in *The Handbook of Financial Futures,* Nancy H. Rothstein (ed.), (McGraw-Hill, New York, 1984).

FIGURE 13-1   Interdelivery price relationship and terminology. (*a*) Precious metals. (*b*) Industrial metals. (*c*) Foreign exchange. (*d*) Agricultural products. (*e*) Interest rates.

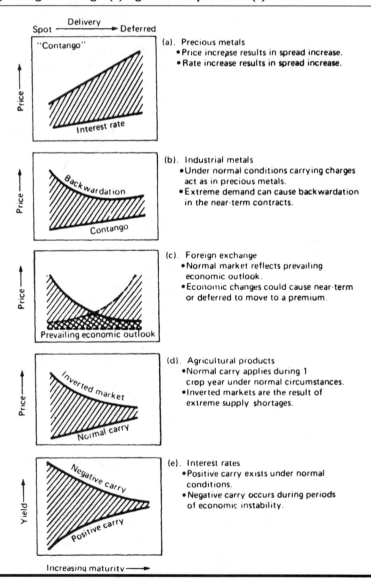

delivery months are a combination of livestock on feed, expectations of marketing, and the price of grain.

Spreads are actively traded between related products. As within a sector of the stock market, such as airlines or technology, there are groups of financial and agricultural markets that are interdependent. Globalization has made interest rates in the industrialized countries respond to changes in monetary policy by the United States, Germany, and Japan. Changing interest rates then cause changes in foreign exchange rates, which also impact the local equities markets. The meetings of the *Group of 7* (G7) further increase the chance of a unified policy by setting common expectations among the largest economies. While there is a clear dependence of one market on the other, the effects are highly variable.

Spreads are often unique to a specific market situation and cannot be generalized for all products. The trader must first understand the basis of the spread relationship before any technical analysis can be applied. It is most important that a trader understand the conditions under which a spread, or even an arbitrage, will fail. This chapter will present many approaches to spreading that very specific; examples are equally limited in scope and application.

SPREAD AND ARBITRAGE RELATIONSHIPS

The relationship between two markets, or between various deliveries and trading vehicles within the same market, will determine the type of trading strategy that may be applied. The types of spreads and arbitrage situations that are most often watched are:

1. *Substitute products,* such as wheat and corn or cattle and hogs. Product substitution ranges from those markets that are nearly identical (e.g., 3-month T-bills and 3-month Eurodollars), to cotton and soybeans, which share the same land and growing season.
2. *Location spreads,* including gold in New York, Chicago, and London; cocoa and heating oil (gasoil) in New York and London.
3. *Carrying charge spreads* and *cash-and-carry,* where one delivery month is out-of-line with others.
4. *Product relationships,* such as crude oil versus heating oil and gasoline, and soybeans versus soybean meal and oil.
5. *Usage spreads,* including the hog-corn ratio, feeder cattle-corn-fat cattle, cocoa-sugar, broilers-corn, and lumber-plywood.
6. *Pure price differences,* such as exchange and interbank currency rates, interest rates of the same maturity and the same grade, where there is no actual cost of delivery or carrying charges.

ARBITRAGE

When the two legs of a spread are highly correlated and, therefore, the opportunity for profit from price divergence is of short duration (less than 1 or 2 days), the trade is called an *arbitrage.* True arbitrage has, theoretically, no trading risk; however, it is offset by small profits and limited opportunity. For example, a *spacial* arbitrageur using the interbank market might call one bank in Tokyo and another in Frankfurt to find their rates on the Mexican peso. If they differ, the trader would buy the peso from one bank and sell the peso at another provided:

1. The price difference was greater than the bid-asked spread, representing the cost of converting the currencies.
2. The arbitrageur has proper credit established with both banks.

3. The transaction can be performed *simultaneously* (by telephone). This requires one trader with a telephone in each ear or two traders working side-by-side.

Large-scale arbitrage has become the domain of major financial institutions who employ many traders, each provided with high-tech computer displays, sophisticated analytic software, and lots of telephones. These traders specialize in specific interest rate markets, foreign exchange, individual stock selection, or less often, precious metals. They constantly scan quotes from across the world to find price differences, then act quickly using cash, forward and futures markets. They trade large quantities to profit from small variations. For the interest rate markets, there are computer programs that compare the various types of coupons and maturities to identify an opportunity quickly. Such operations have become an integral part of the banking industry; they keep rates in-line with other banks and generate steady profits.

Pricing of Futures Contracts

The relationship of one futures market delivery month to the spot price of that market is different according to the type of product, which has already been described in general terms. The mathematics of some of these relationships can become very complex, and the reader is referred to texts that deal specifically with these subjects.[2] The following sections describe the most important features of these relationships.

Storable Commodities

Storable commodities can be purchased in the cash market, stored, and sold at a later time. They can also be delivered on a futures contract, held in storage, and redelivered against another contract. This puts an upper limit on the amount of the carrying charges that can be added to futures prices. The difference in cost between holding the physical commodity and buying it on the futures market are:

1. The financing cost involved in the purchase of the physical commodity:

$$added\ interest\ cost = spot\ price\ ([1 + interest\ rate]^{life\ of\ futures\ contract} - 1)$$

Where *life of futures contract* is expressed in years.
2. The cost of storage, if any.
3. A convenience cost for not buying the physical product, and the ability to be able to sell it at any time.

These three costs are added to the futures spot price to get the fair value of the futures price at the time of delivery. The strategies that keep the spot and futures prices aligned, where F is the futures price, S is the spot price, r is the annualized interest rate, t is the life of the futures contract (in years) from today to the time of delivery, and k is the net annual storage cost (expressed as a percentage of the spot price) are:

Method 1: Buy the futures contract for F; take delivery at expiration. Margin cost can be collateralized. Net cost is F.

Method 2: Borrow the cost of the spot commodity S and buy the physical product; pay the interest, $S([1 + r]^t - 1)$, and the storage net-of-convenience cost, $S \times k \times t$, until the corresponding futures market delivery.

[2] See Aswath Damodaran, *Investment Valuation* (John Wiley & Sons, New York, 1996, pp. 448–458), which provided the basis for these formulas; also see Marsha Stigum, *Money Market Calculations* (Dow Jones-Irwin, 1981).

The two methods must have the same net cost; otherwise, everyone would choose the cheaper alternative. Therefore the two strategies are equal, and they form the basic arbitrage relationship between futures and spot prices:

$$F = S + S([1 + r]^t - 1) + Skt$$
$$= S([1 + r]^t + kt)$$

This relationship represents the ideal case. If you add more realistic features, including separate borrowing and lending rates, r_b and r_a, where $r_b > r_a$, and assume that the short seller cannot recover the saved storage costs and must pay transaction costs, t_s, as well, you get a normal range in which futures prices can fluctuate:

$$(S - t_s)(1 + r_a)^t < F < S([1 + r_b]^t + kt)$$

When futures prices move outside this range, there is a possibility of arbitrage.

Interest Rate Parity

One well-known, second-order arbitrage combines foreign exchange forward rates with interest rate parity. Consider the following: A U.S. corporation would like to invest $1 million for the next 6 months. The current U.S. T-bill return for the next 6 months is lower than the rate in West Germany, and the inflation rate is about the same. The corporation is faced with the decision of whether to convert U.S. dollars to Deutschemarks and invest in West German time deposits or accept the lower U.S. rates. The decision is made easier if the corporation purchases goods from West Germany, since it must eventually convert U.S. dollars to Deutschemarks to satisfy payments; the conversion cost will then exist with either choice.

What if the value of the Deutschemark loses 1% against the U.S. dollar during the 6-month investment period? A corporation whose payment is stated in Deutschemarks suffers a 1% loss in the total interest received. If the 6-month return was 4%, interest received is now valued at $400 less than the $40,000 total, a small amount for the corporation making payment in Deutschemarks. A speculator would face a different problem because the entire return of $1,040,000 would be reduced by 1% to $1,029,600, netting a return of only 2.96%, less the additional cost of conversion. For the speculator, shifts in exchange rates often overwhelm the relative improvement in interest rate return.

The *interest rate parity theorem* will normally explain the differences between the foreign exchange rates and the relative interest rates of countries. It states that

> the forward rate of a currency is equal to its present value plus the interest earned in that country for the period of the forward rate.[3]

Using the futures or interbank market for the forward rate ($DM_{1\,yr}$ is 1 year forward) and the spot rate for the current value (DM_{spot}), the annual interest rate in West Germany (I_{Ger}) is applied to obtain the relationship

$$DM_{1\,yr} = DM_{spot}\,(1 + I_{Ger})$$

Because the forward value of the U.S. dollar can be expressed similarly as

$$U.S._{1\,yr} = U.S._{spot}\,(1 + I_{U.S.})$$

Compute *the implied interest rate/forward rate parity* by dividing the second equation by the first:

[3] James E. Higgens and Allan M. Loosigian, "Foreign Exchange Futures," in *Handbook of Futures Markets,* Perry J. Kaufman (ed.) (John Wiley & Sons, New York, 1984).

$$U.S./DM_{1\,yr} = U.S./DM_{spot}\,\frac{1 + I_{U.S.}}{1 + I_{Ger}}$$

For example, if U.S. interest rates are 8%, West German rates are 6%, and the $U.S./DM_{spot}$ is 0.5000, the 1-year forward rate would be

$$U.S./DM_{1\,yr} = 0.5000\frac{1.08}{1.06}$$

$$U.S./DM_{1\,yr} = 0.5094$$

Crossrate Matrix Evaluation

Given the large number of currency exchange rates that can be quoted in terms of any other currency, there are many combinations of rates that might provide an opportunity for arbitrage. The process for uncovering those inconsistencies that offer opportunity is easier if you put all of the rates into a table format often seen in the newspapers. Using simplified values, this takes the form:

		USD	DEM	CHF	JPY
	USD	1.00			
T =	DEM	2.00	1.00		
	CHF	1.25	.625	1.00	
	JPY	.001	.00625	.0125	1.00

Every crossrate in table T is related to every other crossrate according to:

$$a_{ij} \times a_{jk} = a_{ik}, \qquad \text{for all } i, j, k,$$

where the first subscript is the row, the second is the column, and each value of a represents an element in the table, with a_{ij} representing currency i in terms of currency j. Because the top right triangle in the table is exactly the inverse of the lower left part, it is usually omitted. Whenever a value in the empty part of the table is referenced, substitute the inverse from the mirror image of that location:

$$a_{ij} = 1/a_{ji}$$

For the example in table T, $a_{31} \times a_{12} = a_{32}$. Because there is no a_{14}, we substitute $1/a_{43}$ and get $a_{31}/a_{21} = a_{32}$. Replacing this with values in the table gives $1.25/2.00 = .625$, showing that the exchange rates between the U.S. dollar (USD), Deutschemark (DEM), and Swiss franc (CHF) are equitable. If the two sides of the equation were not the same, there would be a potential arbitrage opportunity. As in all arbitrage, the transaction costs must be subtracted from the opportunity to determine the realistic minimum variance for a profitable trade.

Class B Arbitrage

To facilitate the process of keeping prices aligned, there is *Class B arbitrage*, which takes advantage of the difference between the futures and the interbank forward markets. *Class B* actually refers to the category of membership on the International Monetary Market of the Chicago Mercantile Exchange, which provides exclusively for this type of arbitrage.

Institutional Arbitrage

Arbitrage is most often associated with institutional trading. Because profits on individual positions are small, it is necessary to trade large numbers; hence, the capital requirements can be equally large. The most well-known of all arbitrages is called *program trading,* the process by which a stock index futures market and the cash index (the weighted average of the actual stock prices) are kept in the proper relationship to one another.

Program Trading

There is nothing secret about program trading. The premise is that cash and futures prices will come together (to within a small price difference) by the time the futures contract expires. At that time the buyers and sellers must settle in cash at the current cash market value. The price of the two markets at delivery will be:

$$F = S(1 + r - y)^t$$

where F is the futures price at delivery, r is the riskless interest rate, and y is the annualized dividend yield. In addition to a deviation from this relationship, you must know:

1. The transaction costs of executing both the stock and futures side of the trade. This includes both commissions and an estimated slippage for each of the stock issues that must be bought.
2. The trade can only be entered with a short sale in the futures and the purchase of stocks because of the *uptick rule.* The uptick rule requires that share prices only be sold on an uptick, which makes it impossible to guarantee that short positions can be entered in each stock, or that the trade can be completed in a preset time.

In addition to the large costs involved in setting a position in all of the 500 stocks that comprise the S&P Index, there is competition from other institutions. This limits the profit potential of the trade to the smallest acceptable amount over the break-even level. Adding the more realistic assumptions of distinct borrowing and lending rates made in the basic futures arbitrage discussed earlier, plus separate transaction costs for buying stock t_c and selling short t_s, the *normal* futures price at delivery can vary within the band:

$$(S - t_s)(1 + r_a - y)^t < F < (S + t_c)(1 + r_b - y)^t$$

Finding a Representative Subset of an Index

An arbitrage would be much easier and less costly if there was a smaller group of stocks or futures markets that performed the same as the entire index. If the index is weighted by capitalization, volatility, or some other characteristic, then sorting the components of the index in order of largest capitalization, or highest volatility, would allow you to find a reasonable subset. In the case of capitalization, it is likely that a smaller group of stocks would represent 90% of the index value; therefore, that subset would perform in a way very similar to the index. Unfortunately, the S&P 500 is comprised of companies that all have relatively high capitalization.

Another approach to finding a subset of markets that closely tracks the index value is by using stepwise regression, inputting all of the markets that compose the index, and examining the weighting factors assigned to each in the answer. Those markets with the highest weighting factors are the most significant in the movement of the overall index. By creating a smaller basket from those markets with the highest weighting factors, you can achieve a close approximation of the index with few components—at least temporarily. The influence of the components may change, causing the weighting factors to change; therefore, the regression would need to be rerun frequently, and the basket adjusted to stay aligned with the index. Unless you are sure that the subset of the index that represents 90% of the movement will continue to reflect the index movement until expiration, you have replaced an arbitrage with a simple speculative position.

Intermarket Spreads

The propagation of financial and stock index futures markets have expanded the number of markets that are interdependent upon one another. Prior to the influx of financial markets, product substitution (hogs and cattle, feedgrains) and location spreads were the most common activity; silver in New York, London, and Chicago, and gold in New York and Chicago received much attention. Now there are a large number of interest rate markets of all maturities in many countries, and stock index markets attempting to measure high cap, low cap, and sectors, as well as the old favorites, the S&P 500 and the DJIA. Every country seems to have introduced its equity index into the marketplace, all with the idea of competing for their share of hedgers, speculators, and investors.

Spreading two stock indices expresses a particular market opinion. If you consider three popular indices, the Dow, S&P 500, and the NYSE Index, we see that each represents an increasing picture of business economy. The Dow, limited to blue chips, includes very stable companies not affected by minor events. On the other end of the spectrum, the NYSE Index is the average of all shares and expresses the broadest view of the economic health. If you believe that the economy is headed for a downturn, but do not want to be net short the entire market, then a spread which is long the Dow and short the NYSE Index would be a lower-risk approach to implementing that position.

Figure 13-2 shows the spread between the Value Line Index, the first stock index market in Kansas City, and the S&P 500 in Chicago, once the most active stock spread. As is often the case, traders are attracted to the most active market, and there is significantly less liquidity in one leg of the spread.

There are many dependent relationships between futures markets. Because the basis for these are fundamentally sound, spreads are an excellent way to profit from short-term divergence. The most comprehensive study of these relationships can be found in John Murphy's *Intermarket Technical Analysis,*[4] in which he studies the leads and lags between markets and examines the interaction in their relationships. Of these, Figure 13-3 shows how two markets can trend in the same direction, but have short periods of extreme divergence. Interest rates, represented by U.S. bonds, are a dominant component in the carrying charges of most markets; therefore, when yields rise, physical commodity prices rise, as seen in the CRB Index. Other events, however, can overwhelm this relationship and cause violent distortions.

Traders must be cautious when attempting intermarket spreads. Because they are on different exchanges, the simultaneous execution of both legs cannot be guaranteed by either exchange. In addition, each leg must be entered *at the market* with orders placed at *almost* the same time. Further care must be taken to understand the differences in the contracts; for example, the three wheat contracts in Kansas City, Minneapolis, and Chicago trade wheat of different types for different purposes, and each of the stock index markets represents a different view of public participation. Intermarket wheat spreads can often go the wrong way. Even the Dow will shift relative to the S&P 500 when market participants concentrate on blue chips.

Additional care is needed when exchanges offer lower margins for intermarket spreads. A lower margin can result in extreme leverage, which may not always be justified for intermarket spreads. When prices diverge, the leverage can work against you.

Product Spreads

Product spreads are very actively traded. The *soybean crush,* the most popular among futures traders, has been used for many years. Product spreads usually involve three mar-

---

[4] John J. Murphy, *Intermarket Technical Analysis* (John Wiley & Sons, New York, 1991).

FIGURE 13-2 Intermarket spread between Value Line and S&P 500.

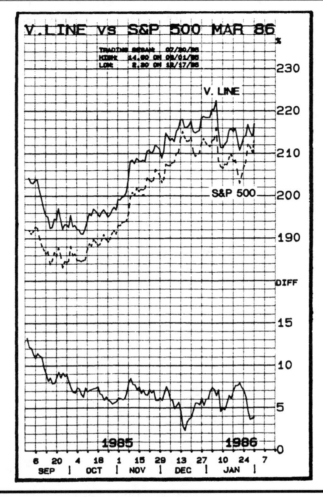

Source: Commodity Research Bureau Weekly Chart Service.

kets, which may be of different delivery months, depending on the processing time. The most common product spreads are:

Raw product(s)	Resulting primary product(s)
Soybeans	Meal and oil
Crude oil	Gasoline and #2 heating oil
Feeder cattle and grain	Fat cattle
Feeder pigs and corn	Live hogs
Live hogs	Pork bellies

Exchanges often allow reduced margins when these spreads are entered in the proper proportion at the same time.

FIGURE 13-3 A comparison of U.S. Treasury bond yields and the CRB Index, 1987–1993.
**A very similar trend is disrupted by an occasional large divergence. In most cases, a noticeable
rise or fall in the CRB Index is followed by a change in interest rates in a manner intended to
offset the effects of inflation.**

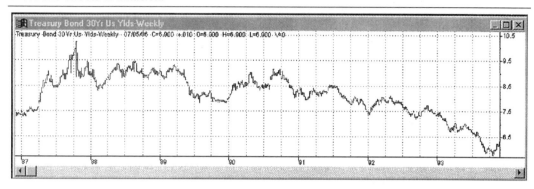

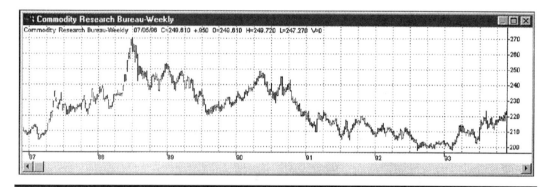

Source: Charts created with *TradeStation®* by Omega Research, Inc.

Product spreads do not always correct for distortions within the time needed to be profitable for the trader. When the combined return on soybean meal and oil is below the cost of crushing the soybeans, processors may execute a *reverse soybean crush* spread, in which they sell the soybeans and buy the products. Even though this appears to be a clever way of keeping prices in-line, it is not done until the crushing margin is very negative. Processors cannot readily reduce their level of operation and lay off employees; a reverse crush means that they are buying products as well as producing them—a position of significantly increased risk.

The Crack Spread

Crude oil is refined primarily into gasoline and heating oil. As with the soybean crush, where the processor buys soybeans and produces meal and oil, the refiner expects a profit from the business of buying crude oil and selling gasoline and heating oil. A speculator can theoretically participate in this process by buying crude oil and selling the products in the right proportion and in the correct delivery months. For example, if crude oil was trading at $20 per barrel, heating oil at 52.40¢ per gallon, and gasoline at 59.50¢ per gallon, then based on futures contracts of 1,000 barrels of crude and 42,000 gallons of heating oil and gasoline, we could calculate each contract value:

Gasoline component:	$59.50 \times 42,000 = \$24,990$
Heating oil component:	$52.40 \times 42,000 = \$22,008$
Total components:	$\$46,998$
Crude oil component:	$20.00 \times 1,000 = \$20,000$

Two other important facts are necessary to put this trade together:

1. It takes from 4 to 6 weeks to refine crude oil into its products; therefore, the prices used in the crack spread should always take the product prices quoted 1 month after the crude price.
2. While the refining ratios can vary during the year, based on the higher demand for gasoline in the summer, and the higher demand for heating oil in the winter, the standard ratios are found in Table 13-1.

Although there are many other by-products of the refining process, the major components of fuel oil and gasoline are produced in a ratio of slightly more than two parts gasoline to one part fuel oil on average each year. This ratio then accounts for the 3-2-1 crack spread, in which three contracts of crude oil are bought, and two contracts of gasoline and one contract of heating oil are sold. In the example above, we can complete the net transaction as follows:

	Market	Price Quantity	Unit Value	Total Units Cost
Sell 2	Gasoline contracts	$59.50 \times 42,000 =$	$\$24,990 \times 2 = \$49,980$	
Sell 1	Heating oil contract	$52.40 \times 42,000 =$	$\$22,008 \times 1 = \$22,008$	
Buy 3	Crude oil contracts	$20.00 \times 1,000 =$	$\$20,000 \times 3 = \$60,000$	
	Net transaction (without costs)			$\$11,998$

Transaction costs will include the expectation of buying crude oil higher and selling products lower than desired when the trade is entered, the commission, and the cost of holding the contracts until delivery.

TABLE 13-1 Fuel Oil and Gas Production and Ratios, 1984–1992

	Fuel Oil			Gases				Gas/ Fuel Oil Ratio
	Distillate	Resid-ual	Total	Gaso-line	Jet Fuel	Kero-sene	Total	
1984	981	326	1,307	2,371	414	42	2,827	2.16
1985	981	322	1,303	2,352	434	34	2,820	2.16
1986	1,021	324	1,345	2,476	472	33	2,981	2.22
1987	997	323	1,320	2,506	490	29	3,025	2.29
1988	1,046	339	1,355	2,555	501	29	3,085	2.28
1989	1,152	500	1,652	2,684	544	31	3,259	1.97
1990	1,067	347	1,414	2,650	556	16	3,222	2.28
1991	1,081	341	1,422	2,554	525	14	2,820	1.98
1992	1,088	326	1,414	2,591	512	15	3,118	2.20

Source: The CRB Commodity Yearbook, 1994 (John Wiley & Sons, 1994).

Reverse Crack

When the delivered price of the products totals to less than the cost of crude oil, the refiner has no reason to process the crude oil, and can go to the market to buy the products and sell crude. This is called a *reverse crack.* In reality, processors can perform a reverse crack to some degree, but shutting down operations to accommodate a temporary market condition is not a good policy. The process of shutting down and restarting a large refinery is not simple, and labor problems make matters more complicated. When executing a reverse crack, the same delivery months are used for both crude and products.

CHANGING SPREAD RELATIONSHIPS

Some spread relationships will always exist, while others may change due to:

1. Price level, such as during the silver bull market of 1980
2. Consumer tastes, such as a shift away from red meat
3. Health reasons, such as those often concerning nitrates in bacon
4. New competition, such as increased supply of edible oils from the Far East impacting the soybean product relationship, or the effect of high-fructose corn sweeteners on the sugar industry

Even though the market absorbs the anticipation of change in an orderly way, unexpected events relating to health or interruption of supply can produce a price shock that will affect many spreads.

Gold/Silver Ratio

A relationship that has always been followed with keen interest is the gold/silver ratio, traditionally considered normal at 33 : 1. It serves as a good example of the variability of many perceived spreads. When gold was $35 per ounce and silver about $1 per ounce, the relationship was never very stable. Between 1930 and 1945, silver prices dropped to about $.50 per ounce; from 1951 to 1962, they remained just under $1 per ounce, and afterward silver began its accelerating move to $38 per ounce in January 1980. Between 1944 (when the International Monetary Fund (IMF) was formed) and 1971, the price of gold was fixed at $35 per ounce, although in a few years before the cancellation of the agreement, the price varied above the designated value. From the late 1960s until the silver crisis of 1980, the gold/silver ratio ranged from about 20 : 1 to 45 : 1 in a slow cycle. During the crisis attributed to the Hunt brothers (September 1979–September 1980), the ratio fluctuated around 33 : 1 in a highly volatile pattern moving only slightly above and below its historic pattern. Following the silver crisis, the value of silver declined faster than gold, reaching a ratio of 56 : 1 in June 1982, with gold at $314 and silver at $5.57. A year later, the ratio touched 33 : 1 and rapidly widened to 66 : 1 in June 1986.

Is the gold/silver ratio a tradable spread? Was it ever a good spread trade? Probably not. The relationship is mainly dependent on public perception of both items as an enduring store of value. The same is true for the platinum/gold ratio (Figure 13-4) or the value of gems. Prices remain strong as long as the public confidence is unshaken. There is no fundamental reason for these prices to remain in the same ratio as there is for feedgrain prices to adjust relative to their protein content.

The public was hurt during the silver crisis. Many people made their purchases during the latter part of 1979, then lost heavily in 1980. At the same time that the U.S. dollar was gaining incredible strength and interest rates were still high, gold and silver prices were dropping rapidly.

Naturally, the value of gold did not decline as much as some other investments. Many countries still hold gold as a store of value. But times change and there has been a notice-

FIGURE 13-4 The platinum/gold spread, similar to gold/silver, shows periods where it might be successfully traded; however, markets such as 1980 always remain a possibility.

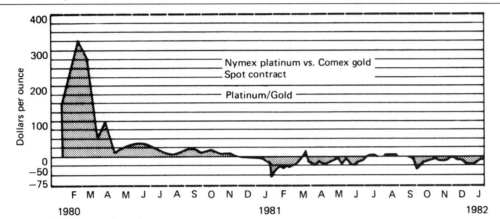

Source: New York Mercantile Exchange.

able shift to the U.S. dollar as an international standard. Investors feel safe with their money in U.S. banks and in U.S. dollars; they are willing to suffer short-term currency swings in exchange for security and diversification. For example, the price of oil, the largest traded commodity in the world, is quoted in U.S. dollars rather than gold.

There is no doubt the U.S. dollar will lose glamour if U.S. leadership or its economy weakens; if world peace becomes a reality, the security of the dollar will also be less important. If there is significant economic instability, there may be a return to gold and diamonds as an implied standard. However, these relationships are too uncertain to be tradable, except at great risk.

Intramarket and Intermarket Financial Spreads

Spread relationships in financial markets represent anticipation of economic policy. The spread values themselves are well defined by the interrelationship of all interest rate vehicles, but they will vary on the interpretation of the impact of government policy on money supply in reaction to the balance of trade, unemployment, and an expanding economy, and the time period in which the action will occur.

An *intramarket spread,* or *delivery month spread,* in a single financial instrument, such as T-bills, is a conservative speculation in changing policies as discussed in the previous section. A *bull spread,* long the nearby and short the deferred, shows a belief in temporarily declining interest rates. An *intermarket financial spread,* involving different maturities, is a speculation in the changing yield curve. A *long bonds/short bills* position favors a negative carry, while *long bills/short bonds* expects a return-to-normal carry (with respect to futures prices).

Intercrop Spreads

A special case involving carrying charges is the *intercrop spread,* which can be highly volatile, even though there is an old crop *carryover* that ties the two seasonal markets together. Soybeans, for example, are harvested mainly in September and October. The August delivery is clearly the old crop, and November is the first new crop month; the September contract often reflects the shift from old to new.

Normally, the old crop trades at a premium to the new crop. Carrying charges, accumulating since the previous winter, are part of the August price; export demand may cause shortages in the old crop, which moves prices further above the cost of carry. Figure 13-5*a* shows the anticipated price pattern resulting from carrying charges during a normal year. The minimum storage commitment for the 3 months immediately following harvest is shown as a larger increase in price. Normal carry adds equal amounts to the price until the following September, where old and new crop mix. Finally, any carryover must assume the price of the new crop, which is in greater supply.

The theory behind an intercrop spread is that prices must come together when the old crop merges with the new crop. But can it be a profitable trade? Examine the two possible events that affect this trade:

1. Problems involving development of the new crop making supply uncertain. This causes prices in the new crop to rise more quickly than the old crop (Figure 13-5*b*).
2. Export demand in the old crop results in old crop prices rising faster than new crop prices (Figure 13-5*c*).

In case 1, the spread between crops narrows and can only be traded as a spread that is *short the old crop, long the new crop.* This spread has limited potential since the November delivery cannot exceed the old crop by more than the normal carrying charge. At that

FIGURE 13-5 Intercrop spreads. (*a*) Normal carrying charge relationship. (*b*) New crop supply problems result in narrowing spreads. (*c*) Export affects the old crop more than the new, resulting in a widening spread.

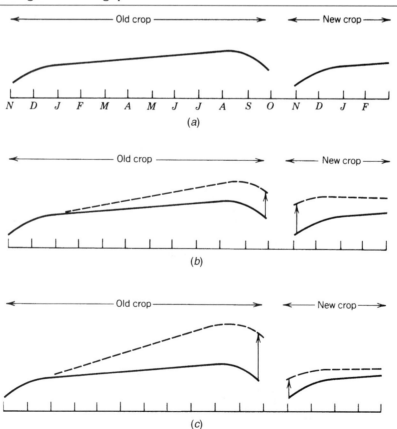

point, processors will buy, store, and redeliver the old crop against the new crop. When prices in the new crop are nearing the old crop value, it makes sense to liquidate or even to reverse the spread. Once reversed, there is little risk that the spread can move adversely. A revised crop estimate that showed better yield than originally expected would cause the new crop to decline sharply and the spread to widen.

In case 2, export demand in the old crop causes the intercrop spread to widen at first. A spread trader will typically wait until export commitments are complete, then sell the old crop and buy the new. When old crop prices rise to a large premium over the new crop, many processors will reduce purchasing based on:

1. Low or negative profit margins at the current price levels
2. Use of reserves or inventory to carry processing through until the lower new crop prices are available

It is remarkable how demand is inversely related to price, even when it is considered *inelastic*. When a delay in purchasing or processing will result in greater profits for the commercial, it is somehow achieved.

Butterfly Spreads

A *butterfly spread,* normally referred to as just a *butterfly,* is a low-risk technique for capturing short-term interdelivery distortions. It is most appropriate in highly volatile markets, where the concentration of trading in one or two delivery months causes those contract prices to move away from the normal delivery month relationship.

For example, in April a combination of poor planting, declines in the U.S. dollar, and new export agreements changes the soybean prices as shown in Figure 13-6. Increased demand results in sharply higher July futures prices with a tapering-off of the effect in the more deferred contracts. The normal carrying charge relationship is shown as a straight line in the old crop, beginning again in the new crop. A butterfly entered in the old crop would mean selling two contracts of July soybeans and buying one contract each of May and August. This is the same as executing two spreads: long May, short July and short July, long August.

Each spread in the butterfly has a good chance of being profitable; the combination of the two is exceptionally good. The July contract cannot remain out-of-line with the deliveries on both sides, because a trader could take delivery of the May contract and redeliver it in July at a profit exceeding the cost of carry. Under normal circumstances, commercial users of soybeans will defer their purchases to later months, depleting their reserves, to avoid paying a short-term premium and causing July prices to drop.

FIGURE 13-6   Delivery month distortions in the old crop making a *butterfly spread* possible.

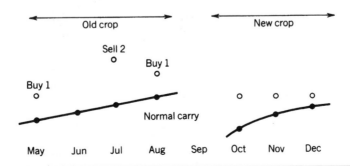

The butterfly spread guarantees that any adjustment in the three contracts back to a normal relationship will prove profitable. If the prices of both May and August rise to be in-line with July or if May rises to form an inverted relationship, the spread will be profitable (Figure 13-7).

The problem with such an ideal spread is the short life and difficult execution. Because profits are nearly riskless, opportunity is small. The beneficiaries of these trades are usually the floor traders who can act quickly. Once the position is entered, liquidation can be easily accomplished.

Pseudoarbitrage of S&P Day and Night Markets

Intended to take advantage of distortions caused by S&P Market-on-Close orders and GLOBEX session, Conners and Hayward have created a *GLOBEX/S&P Fair Value Program.*[5]

1. Determine the daily fair value difference between the S&P futures and cash markets, *FV = S&P futures − S&P cash.* Use the price as soon after the close of the NYSE as possible, for example, 4:03 EST, leaving 12 minutes to the close of futures trading.
2. Calculate your price entry target, *T,* as *T = S&P cash + FV + .50,* where the value .50 represents ½ an S&P point.
3. Place a sell order at price *T.* If the market is already trading above *T* just after the NYSE close, then entering the order as *Market-on-Close* of futures is likely to be best.
4. If filled, cover your short if your profit is .50 during the 16 hours of GLOBEX trading.
5. Close out the trade on the close of GLOBEX if your profit has not been reached. Do not carry the trade into the next session.

The justification for this situation is the investors' fear of an overnight drop in price. It depends on the lack of overnight news that would drive the market higher; however, analysts might note that S&P price shocks always cause prices to drop. It is strongly suggested that no position be taken on the evening that the President gives the State of the Union Message.

CARRYING CHARGES

The *carrying charge* structure of a market determines the underlying differences in the relative price of each contract. For metals and most storable commodities, these charges con-

---

[5] Laurence A. Conners and Blake E. Hayward, *Investment Secrets of a Hedge Fund Manager* (Probus, 1995).

FIGURE 13-7   Corrections to interdelivery patterns.

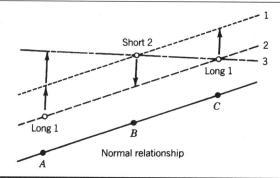

sist of interest, storage costs, and insurance. All else being equal, a market with *normal carry* can be expected to show steadily higher prices for deferred contracts based entirely on the cost of carry. Prices that move out-of-line may be corrected by taking delivery of the nearby and redelivering against the next contract.

It is always possible for changes in supply and demand to alter the relationship of futures contracts so that the carrying charge pattern no longer appears normal. Although this is not likely to occur in the metals, it often happens that an immediate demand for food can cause short-term increases in prices without substantial effect on more deferred months. This situation is called an *inverted market,* or *negative carry,* even though the carrying charges are implicit in the price regardless of the pattern.

In the financial markets, a similar situation occurs when the demand for money increases dramatically in the short term. If the market expects that the demand will be short-lived, the rates on short-term maturities are significantly affected, whereas the longer-term rates may show only a minor change.

In the metals markets, a normal carry is called *contango* (a term coined by the London Metals Exchange when referring to copper) and a negative carry is *backwardation.* Changes in supply and demand that lead to backwardation are most likely to occur in the industrial metals where the commodity is consumed at a greater rate. Gold, silver, and platinum, the precious metals markets, have traditionally had a uniform price relationship in the deferred delivery months. Any deferred delivery price can be calculated by adding the current rate of interest (plus storage and insurance) to the value in the cash market. If interest rates rise and the price of gold remains the same, the carrying charges and the spread will increase. If the price of gold rises but interest rates remain constant, the carrying charges and spread will also increase because the increased value of the contract results in higher interest costs. Similarly, lower carrying charges and a narrowing spread will occur if either or both the rate of interest or the price of gold declines.

The terms used in referring to carrying charges in the financial markets are the same as those just mentioned, but the concepts are different. *Carry* is a term describing the yield-curve relationship. The concept of positive or normal carry is a curve that increases in yield with the time of maturity. The longer an investor is willing to commit money, the greater the yield. Negative carry can also exist for short periods of time. When economic conditions become unstable, the interest on short-term investments may increase sharply, although longer-term rates will increase only slightly. Investors anticipate a correction in these short-term distortions, and do not often move money committed for longer periods for fear that rates will return to positive carry. The various relationships and terminology that exist in each market sector can be found in Figure 13-1.

Implied Interest Rates

A *pure carry* market is one in which the forward price is entirely comprised of the costs of holding the physical product until a predetermined delivery date. As previously mentioned, these costs are those of storage, insurance, and the loan rate. As an example, consider gold, which is a classic pure carry market.

Assume that spot gold is selling for $300 per ounce and the 6-month forward contract for $313.50, an increase of 4.5%. With interest rates at 7%, there is a possibility of increasing the return on investment by purchasing gold at the current spot price of $300 per ounce and selling a futures contract 6 months deferred for $313.50. The gross profit is the difference between the futures price and the value of a comparable cash investment. Compare this with an initial investment of $30,000, which corresponds to the size of a 100-ounce futures contract of gold. That is,

6-month return on $30,000 cash at 7% = $1,050

6-month futures price = 313.50

Less the spot price = −300.00

Gives the profit per oz. = 13.50

Times the contract size of 100 oz. = $1,350

The gross improvement over the cash investment is $300, or 1% over the 6-month investment period; however, there are costs involved in this cash-and-carry that do not exist in a straight time deposit. In addition to the storage and insurance of the physical gold, there are transaction costs involved in the trading of futures. Because these costs are relatively fixed, they are known in advance and the potential profit level of the cash-and-carry can be calculated.

The Limited-Risk Spread

If the nearby month of a storable commodity is at a discount to a deferred month by more than the cost of carry, a *limited-risk* spread may be entered by buying the nearby and selling the deferred. The trader then takes delivery of the nearby and redelivers it against the later contract. When trading commodities, which are significantly influenced by supply and demand, the outcome of this trade is never certain.

For example, the crude oil and copper markets are not affected by weather or planting conditions, and their supply is readily available. Demand has caused both markets to become inverted for long periods of time. Anticipation of lower prices, reduced demand, or a poor economy may result in a hand-to-mouth purchasing policy. This causes a concentrated short-term demand in the spot market and little activity in the deferred months, resulting in higher prices in the nearby months than further out. Carrying charges are still an integral part of the deferred price; if they were absent, the inversion would be more extreme. Even when they appear to have normal carry, these markets are not candidates for an implied interest rate or cash-and-carry spreads.

The limited-risk spread may be better termed a *limited-profit* spread. Whereas the carrying charges provide a theoretical limit to the premium that a deferred month may have over a nearby, there is no limit to the discount that a month may take on. An increase in the expected supply might change a normal carry market to an inverted one, resulting in large losses.

The Carrying Charge Spread

The *carrying charge spread* is a popular trade based on anticipation of interest rate change and is, therefore, a lower risk than a net long or short position in any market. Consider gold again as an example.

In 1978, the price of gold was low (under $200 per ounce) as were interest rates (about 6%). An investor who had the foresight to expect both gold and interest rates to rise but who wanted to limit the risk of a speculative position, could have entered a *bull spread* by buying a deferred contract and selling a nearby contract of gold. The number of months between the contracts would determine the potential for both profit and risk; the further apart, the larger the carrying charges and the greater the expected spread movement.

TECHNICAL ANALYSIS OF SPREADS

Once the spread components have been selected and there is full confidence in the underlying fundamental relationship (even if temporary), the extreme levels and trends may be found to determine which spread trades may be entered.

Most technical analysis of intramarket spreads (e.g., March–December T-bonds) is represented as variations or distortions from the *normal* price relationship. In this method of trading, the distortions are also called *overbought* and *oversold* conditions and the strategic approach taken is *countertrend*. By subtracting the deferred price from the nearby (e.g., December from March of the same year) over the life of the contract for many years, the investor can measure the historic patterns (see Figure 13-8). These spread relationships will vary in a manner that allows the trader to set objectives. When March is trading 1½ points over December, the spread can be sold; when March trades under December by 1¼ points, the spread can be bought.

Historical Comparisons

Those spreads with a sound fundamental basis will show clear patterns in their price history. Analysis of longer historic periods will result in a better understanding of the consistency and risk involved in trading the spread. A long-term study will reveal seasonal and cyclic moves as well as periods of lower and higher volatility.

Many spread opportunities result from understanding changing spread patterns. For example, Figure 13-9 shows a long-term spread that has three distinct ranges, marked along the bottom as *a, b,* and *c*. During period *a,* spread traders would have identified +1 and −1 as the extreme levels and entered positions at those points; the risk varied but remained within an acceptable range. The higher volatility during period *b* would have caused large losses for those traders still expecting the prior market patterns; unprecedented shifts in the spread relationship would prompt traders to liquidate spreads. As period *c* begins, traders change their objectives to wait for a spread opportunity at ±2. Although they could not profit from the original extreme moves because spreads were entered too early, they are prepared for the next time. But instead of repeating itself, the spread narrows until it settles in a range of ±½. If it is now traded in this range, an increase to the prior normal levels of period *a* will produce a large loss.

This dilemma is common to spreading; spread prices shift from one range to another. When the range decreases, few spreads are taken, and when it increases, a large loss occurs. The following outlines possible solutions to this problem:

1. *Underlying price-volatility relationship.* Higher prices allow the spread to widen, whereas lower prices force the spread price to narrow. The spread between heating oil and gasoline must be greater when those products are trading at $1.00 per gal-

FIGURE 13-8   Intramarket interest rate spread relationship.

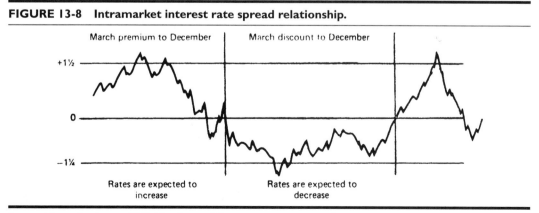

Source: Nancy Rothstein (Ed.), *Handbook of Financial Futures,* p. 359. © 1984 Nancy Rothstein. Reprinted by permission of The McGraw-Hill Companies.

FIGURE 13-9   Changing spread ranges.

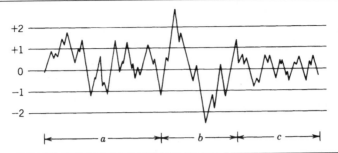

lon than when they are at one-half that price. Figure 13-8 could easily be related to changing price levels, where *a* is a long-term bull market, peaking in period *b*, and followed by a decline to lower levels in period *c*.

2. *Normal seasonal patterns.* Seasonality causes spreads to narrow and widen in predictable ways. During harvest, the *basis spread* (the difference between the spot and cash markets) widens, reflecting the available supply. After harvest, the basis will continue to narrow if demand fails to materialize.

3. *Specific events*

   a. A freeze in coffee or orange juice results in a prolonged shift in prices, which will then make the next year's crop even more sensitive to a potential freeze.

   b. Events that cause seasonal price changes, such as exceptional crop demand, will nullify the seasonal patterns for the remainder of the crop year and often into the next season.

   c. Combination of circumstances, such as low inventory, stocks, or carryover; prior year higher export demand; and dry, hot weather midway in the growing season will result in a *nervous* market, causing prices to rally in anticipation of problems becoming real. By observing past similar situations, the extent of the rally can be observed as large enough to use a medium to fast trend-following method, with profit taking either at the time the trend turns or 1 month before harvest begins, whichever comes first.

Relative Spread Opportunities

The long-term analysis of a spread relationship will show the extent of variability and include most patterns. When the spread range is wide due to shifts caused by inventory cycles, changing public opinion, and other factors, a *relative* measure will be of interest. Figure 13-10*a* shows a simple example of a more complicated spread pattern.

The safest spread trades are those taken at historic highs and lows (H_1, L_3, H_6), anticipating a return to normal levels; these trades do not occur often. Instead, there are many opportunities to sell a *relatively overbought* (H_2, H_3, H_4, . . .) level or buy a *relatively oversold* level (L_1, L_2, L_4, . . .). There is less risk if the relative level is closer to the historic extreme.

The relative spread levels can be found by taking the difference between the spread price and a moving average. The number and magnitude of the relative tops and bottoms will vary with the speed of the trend; the faster the moving average (3 to 5 days), the more relative highs and lows will appear and the smaller the magnitude of those moves. Figure 13-10*b* shows a detrended spread chart based on the patterns in Figure 13-10*a*. The highs and lows are clear; however, it is not possible to distinguish those that have less risk from those with greater risk. When actually trading, selling H_3 is more likely to result in a loss

FIGURE 13-10   *Relative* spread opportunities. (*a*) Spread prices showing relative swings. (*b*) Prices adjusted to identify relative spread opportunities.

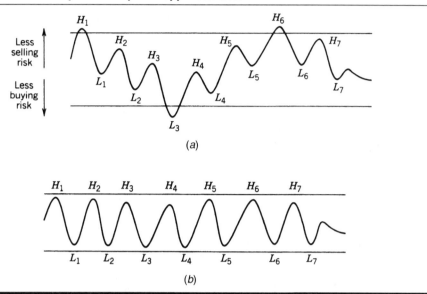

(*a*)

(*b*)

than a profit. It will be necessary to use both charts to select the proper trades: one to locate the relative highs and lows, the other to determine risk.

Trend Analysis of Spreads

Moving averages, point-and-figure, and other trend-following methods are usually inappropriate for intramarket spreads. The time needed to develop a buy or sell signal using a trending approach often takes most of the potential profit from the trade. The magnitude of the profits and losses resulting from these spread trades is usually small compared with an outright long- or short-market position.

Trend-following methods apply to spreads when the movement of the spread is large enough to justify sacrificing both the beginning and end of the move to determine the direction of the trend. Using T-bonds and T-notes as an example, the trader selects the delivery month to be analyzed (usually the same one) and subtracts the T-note price from the bond price. The resulting price is treated as a single new market; a moving average, point-and-figure method, or another trend-following technique can be applied to these new numbers. When a buy signal occurs, the spread is bought (bonds are increasing in price with respect to T-notes), and when a sell signal is generated, the spread is sold (bonds are decreasing in price with respect to T-notes). These techniques can work as well as any analysis of the individual markets and lower margin requirements boost the returns that may result from net moves of lower magnitude.

Spreads that typically allow trend analysis are those with very wide swings extending for long time intervals. Some examples of these spreads (Figure 13-11) are:

Short- versus long-term interest rates (trading the yield curve)

Index markets representing diverse market segments

Index markets in different countries

Hogs versus cattle

Gold versus silver

Currency crossrates

FIGURE 13-11 Trending spreads. (*a*) T-bills versus T-bonds, March 1986. (*b*) Cattle versus hogs, February 1986. (*c*) Gold versus silver, December 1986. (*d*) British pound versus Deutschemark, March 1986.

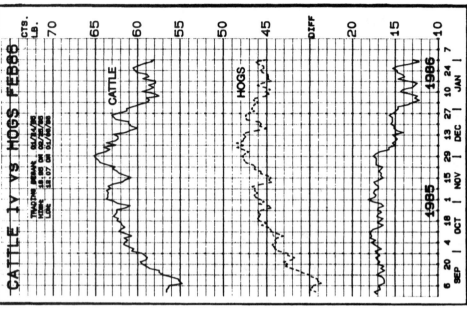

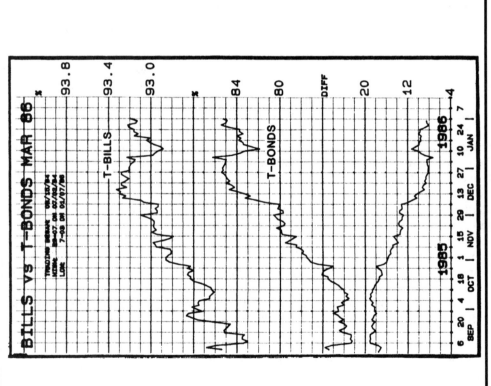

Source: Commodity Research Bureau Weekly Chart Service.

FIGURE 13-11 *(Continued)*

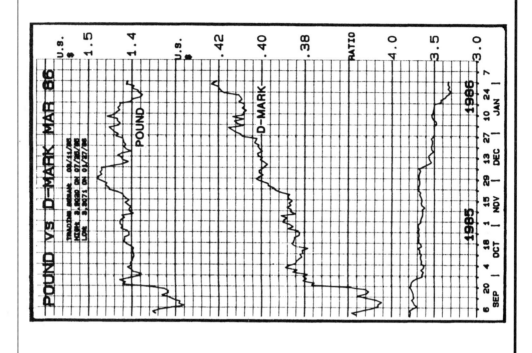

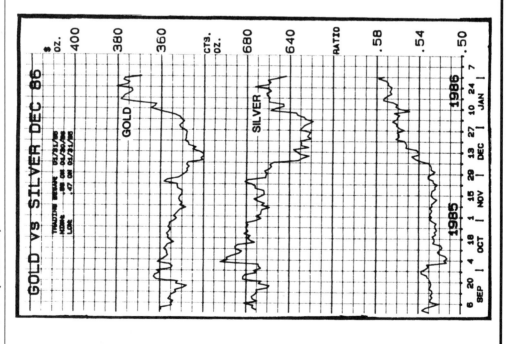

Bull and Bear Spreads

A spread can be a low-risk substitute for an outright long- or short-trend position. In grains and foods, a bull market will result in prices of the nearby delivery months rising faster than deferred months. A *bull spread* can be placed by entering a long position in the nearby and a short position in a deferred month. Both risk and reward are reduced; the greater the time between months, the more volatile the spread (Figure 13-12). As in an outright position, once the upward price peaks, the spread must be reversed because the nearby delivery will decline faster than the deferred. By selling the nearby and buying the deferred contract, a *bear spread* is established.

The analysis that identifies the time to enter a bull or bear spread can be a standard trend-following approach based on the nearby contract only. Many traders believe that the spread itself must also confirm the trend before a position is taken; therefore, a moderate-speed moving average may be applied to the spread series. This would provide a signal based on the relative change in spread direction. A simple 1-day change might be enough for the fast trader. An upward trend signal in the nearby delivery and a bear spread movement is a conflict that should be passed.

Legging In and Out of a Spread

When both contracts, or legs, of a spread are not entered or closed out at the same moment, trading risk is increased. An unprotected leg of a spread is simply an outright long or short position and must be managed carefully. Consider a bull spread in a fast-moving market. Although both legs can be entered simultaneously using a spread order, the long position (in the trend direction) might be entered first, followed by the short leg within a few minutes or a few days. If the market is trending steadily, profits in the long position can be protected when the short leg is entered. Legging-in is a rewarding philosophy when it works. When it doesn't work, there is a large loss on the outright

---

FIGURE 13-12   Interdelivery spread volatility. (*a*) Actual prices. (*b*) Relationship of interdelivery spreads.

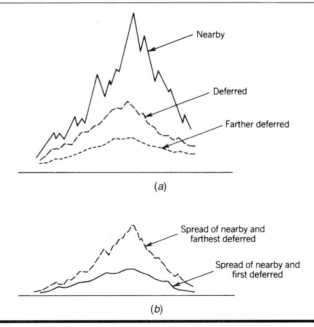

(*a*)

(*b*)

position, which will be difficult to offset with the lower profits from the spread. If the purpose of trading a spread is to reduce risk, legging-in or legging-out is not going to accomplish that goal.

Protecting an existing trend position in the nearby month by spreading with the next deferred delivery is not as good as simply liquidating the initial position. If the market has been going up and indicates a temporary downturn, some traders will *hedge* by selling the first deferred contract. The result is a bull spread instead of an outright long. If the anticipation of a price reversal was correct, the trade risk is reduced but there is still a loss. If the decision was wrong, profits are reduced. Converting a potentially losing outright position into a potentially losing hedge changes the size of the loss or profit. It is much simpler to close out the position rather than defer the decision.

When the trend turns from up to down, it is necessary to switch the spread from bull to bear. If large profits have been made in the bull move and both the trend and spread signal a downward turn, it could be tempting to lift the long leg and hold the outright short using accrued profits to offset the increased risk. A more conservative trader might enter a bear spread in the first and second deferred months rather than the spot and first deferred, thereby reducing risk even further and allowing smaller profits—conserving prior success.

Reverse Response to Trending Markets

Some spreads respond in just the opposite way to trends. For precious metals and potatoes, an upward trend results in the deferred contracts rising faster than the nearby. For example, consider the rising price of gold, which results in a larger total contract value and, consequently, a higher interest charge based on that value.

Traders familiar with the potato market will know that higher prices, which reflect greater demand and product disappearance, will result in critical tightness in the last winter trading month. The perishable potato crop must last to early June when the first spring potatoes reach the market. Early demand on the stored crop will magnify the volatility as end of spring approaches. For both metals and potatoes, a bull spread can be entered by selling the nearby and buying the deferred contracts.

Exceptions to the Rules

During a trending period, most markets exhibit a clear relationship between delivery months. Cattle, hogs, broilers, and eggs are nonstorable, however, and show little relationship in the response of deferred contracts to the same bullish or bearish news.

During periods of exceptional demand, livestock may be marketed early causing a strong similarity in the price patterns of cattle and hogs in the nearby contracts. Even in the most extreme cases, this pattern cannot be carried far into the future.

VOLATILITY AND SPREAD RATIOS

Higher price levels result in increased volatility in both individual markets and their related spreads. Fast price movements and large swings associated with high price levels will create spread opportunities that are more profitable than normal; markets with small movement are not candidates for spreads. The combination of two low-volatility markets produces spreads with such small potential that execution costs often exceed the expected profits.

The two sides of a spread rarely have the same volatility. When badly mismatched, a spread will act the same as if you had taken an outright position in the more volatile side of the spread. For example, Figure 13-13*a* shows what appears to be an excellent spread relationship; however, Figure 13-13*b* reveals that the pattern is the result of two sideways markets, one highly volatile (*A*) and the other with low volatility (*B*). Market *B* offers little protection if market *A* were to move sharply higher instead of sideways.

FIGURE 13-13   Poor spread selection. (*a*) Spread price. (*b*) Spread components.

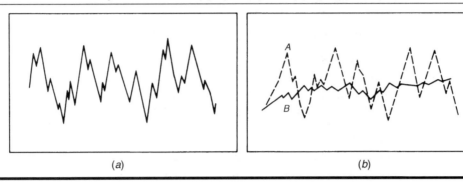

| (*a*) | (*b*) |

The same illustration would be appropriate if a gold-silver spread were created by subtracting the price of silver from that of gold rather than taking a ratio. Equal moves of 10% in gold from $300 to $330 and silver from $6.00 to $6.60 would result in a spread price change from $294.00 to $323.40, effectively mirroring the gold change rather than maintaining an unchanged spread.

Spread Ratio

The markets which offer sound spread opportunities will vary in their absolute price range or volatility. For example, during 1984, the price of spot live hog futures varied from 43.80¢ to 58.00¢ per pound, whereas pork bellies ranged from 54.70¢ to 74.10¢ per pound. Both appear to be consistent in volatility as seen from the ratios, yet more than a 50% difference occurred in the size of the price change.

Had the ratio been seen to drop to 1.15, a long bellies, short hogs spread would have been entered. If the ratio had moved to 1.35, a spread would have been entered to buy hogs and sell bellies. Assume that this distortion occurred at prices near the lows and that prices then adjusted to 1.27 at the highs shown in Table 13-2. There are two possible trades that might have occurred:

	Spread Price	High	P/L		Contract Size	Net P/L
Case 1: Long bellies	50.00	74.10	$24.10	×	38,000	$9,158
Short hogs	43.48	58.00	(14.52)	×	30,000	(4,356)
Ratio	1.15	1.27				$4,802
Case 2: Short bellies	54.70	74.10	(19.40)	×	38,000	($7,372)
Long hogs	40.52	58.00	17.48	×	30,000	5,244
Ratio	1.35	1.27				($2,128)

TABLE 13-2   Price Movement of Pork Bellies and Live Hogs in 1984

	Low	High	Average	Range	Mean Volatility
Pork bellies	54.70	74.10	64.40	19.40	30%
Live hogs	43.80	58.00	50.90	14.20	28%
Ratio	1.25	1.27	1.27		
Spread	10.90	16.10	13.50		

In Case 1, the trade produces a profit while the relationship adjusts to normal; in Case 2, there is a loss even though the same adjustment occurs. Two factors cause this: the different contract sizes and the absolute price range. If the contract sizes were adjusted to equal units, which can be done by trading four bellies and five hog contracts, the results would be:

	P/L per Contract	Number of Contracts	Total P/L
Case 1: Long bellies	$9,158	4	$36,632
Short hogs	(4,356)	5	21,780
Spread results			$14,852
Case 2: Short bellies	($7,372)	4	($29,488)
Long hogs	5,244	5	26,220
Spread results			($3,268)

This is slightly closer to the correct results but not yet right. Adjusting the number of contracts for volatility means attempting to equalize percentage moves per unit size. The range of 14.20 in hogs and 19.40 in bellies combined with their contract size gives:

	Range	Contract Size	Total	Ratio
Bellies	19.40	38,000	$737,200	
Hogs	14.20	30,000	$426,000	.5779 : 1

For convenience, the ratio will be taken as 1 : 2, which means trading two hog contracts for every one pork bellies contract. Then:

	P/L per Contract	Number of Contracts	Net P/L
Case 1: Long bellies	$9,158	1	$9,158
Short hogs	(4,356)	2	(8,712)
Spread results			$446
Case 2: Short bellies	($7,372)	1	($7,372)
Long hogs	5,244	2	10,488
Spread results			$3,116

Using the relative volatility and contract size to produce a *spread ratio* gives the correct results.

Metal Relationships

Most metals markets showed extreme volatility in early 1980 as a result of the silver crisis. Table 13-3 gives the comparable futures price moves of the four major metals markets and shows the spread ratios that should have been used.

TABLE 13-3   Metals Volatility and Spread Ratios

	Cash Prices			Contract Size	Range	Total	Ratio to Gold
	1978	1980	1985				
Gold ($/oz)	150	850	300	100 oz	700	70,000	—
Platinum ($/oz)	170	420	300	50 oz	250	12,500	.18
Silver ($/oz)	5.00	38.00	6.50	5,000 oz	33.00	165,000	2.36
Copper ($/lb)	.60	1.35	.65	25,000 lb	.75	18.750	.27

Gold is seen to be much more volatile than either platinum or copper but less than silver. During this volatile period, a spread of five platinum to one gold, four copper to one gold, and two silver to five gold would have been necessary. Unfortunately, this spread ratio represents an exceptionally volatile period. From the beginning of 1985 through June 1986, the monthly average spot gold price varied from $302 to $345 per ounce—silver prices ranged from $5.11 to $6.45 per ounce. This produces the following relationship:

	Range	Contract Size	Total	Ratio to Gold	Contracts in Spread
Gold	$43/oz	100 oz	$4,300		3
Silver	$1.34/oz	5,000 oz	$6,700	1.56	2

The ratio of three gold to two silver is normally most practical but is not safe enough when prices move above these levels.

Volatile Spreads

Trading a high-priced spread is always riskier than one where both legs are at normal levels for the following reasons:

1. If only one leg is at a high level, the profitability of the spread depends entirely on the profitable trading of the most volatile leg.
2. If both legs are volatile, specific events may cause them to move independently, creating unprecedented spread levels.
3. Highly volatile spreads are usually in nearby months and may not adjust to normal before the expiration of the contract. At expiration, extreme demand in the cash market may cause further unusual spread differences.
4. A highly volatile spread may have greater risk than a single outright position in one leg. This is not usually the purpose of a spread trade.

LEVERAGE IN SPREADS

Because a spread is the difference between two or more fundamentally related markets or delivery months of the same market, the risk is usually less than that of an outright long or short position. Interdelivery spreads within the same crop year, or in nonagricultural products, are recognized by the exchange as having lower risk. The result is that spread margins can be less than 20% of the margin required for a nonspread position. Because the margin on outright positions may be as low as 5% of the contract value (underlying asset), the spread market can be as low as 2%.

The profit potential is also less for a spread than for a net long or short position. You would expect that, if the margin requirement is 20% of the outright position, then both the risk and reward of the trade would be about 20% of an outright position. That is not necessarily the case. In agricultural products, the bull and bear spreads can be highly volatile; in contrast, the potential for an intramarket metals spread is equal to the change in interest caused by higher and lower contract values. Traders manage to compensate for the lower profits and risks by taking advantage of the smaller margins and entering more positions. With five contracts, the trader has managed to convert a conservative spread trade into the same risk and reward as a nonspread trade—perhaps with even higher risk—without added capital. The small trader, however, should not leverage spreads to their maximum.

Some trades that derive the benefit of spread margins are not always of proportionately less risk. For example, when the IMM began, any two currencies could be spread with reduced margin. A short position in the Deutschemark against a long position in the Mexican peso would hardly have been considered reduced risk when the first devaluation of the peso occurred. The trader must keep in mind that the decrease in margin, which accompanies spreads entered on the same exchange, will cause a substantial increase in leverage and may counteract the intrinsic risk reduction in a spread that was related to the smaller price movement. Spreads are not necessarily less speculative or safer than trading a single net long or short position.

14

Behavioral Techniques

There are some approaches to trading that are directly dependent on human behavior and cannot be represented by pure mathematics. When viewed in the short term, most systems will be more representative of behavior than economic factors because, over a few hours of one day, the long-term influence of the trend is very small. The concepts presented in this chapter deal specifically with human reactions. *Measuring the news* covers an area that has always been important to a floor trader, yet been greatly overlooked by technicians; it offers great opportunity for research. *Event trading,* which studies market reaction to price shocks, has become increasingly important for both proactive and reactive traders; *contrary opinion* takes the form of a poll or consensus of opinions of traders and market publications. It may help answer the question, "What is everyone else doing?", or at least, "What are they thinking of doing?"

The principal works of Elliott and Gann are included with a review of the Fibonacci series and ratios, which form a significant part of their technique. The way in which traders respond to market moves, and the remarkable similarity that can be found in Nature, give serious underlying substance to these methods. Because not all of the assumptions upon which these systems are based can be quantified, they are substantiated by the performance of the systems themselves. Both are fascinating and open areas of creativity essential to broad system development. They are grouped together with discussions of natural phenomena and the rapidly growing area of financial astrology, all of which should leave your grey matter stimulated.

MEASURING THE NEWS

> *If you can keep your head when all about you are losing theirs, maybe you haven't heard the news.*

Rudyard Kipling[1]

The news is one of the greatest single elements affecting free trade. As a medium, it carries both fundamental and technical information about all markets, directly or indirectly, and is indispensable. If not objective, the news services could materially alter any opinion by the inclusion or omission of relevant information. The impact of news is so great that a speculator holding a market position according to a purely technical system would do best not reading, listening to, watching, or in any sense being exposed to news that might be cause for deviating from the system. In a study commissioned by the *Wall Street Journal,* it was shown that 99% of the financial analysts polled read the paper regularly, and 92% considered it the "most valuable" publication they read.[2]

As an element of a trading program or as an indicator of its own, the news is invaluable. If we could measure the impact of unexpected news, the importance of the *Wall Street Journal* or the wire service articles, the USDA crop reports and the CFTC positions

---

[1] Adam Smith, *The Money Game* (Random House, New York, 1967, p. 48).

[2] Frederick C. Klein and John A. Prestbo, *News and the Market* (Henry Regnery, Chicago, 1974, p. 3).

reports,[3] and the anticipation of news, we would have a better view of the direction of the markets. But first we must be aware of the complications of analyzing the news. There is the problem of objectively selecting which items are relevant and which sources are most important. The most difficult problem is quantifying the news—how do you rank each item for measurement, and on what scale do you determine cumulative importance? Some news items are known to have a greater impact on the market—weather disasters, major trade agreements, key crop reports—but these must be ranked against themselves and other issues to produce a numerical system of analysis. On a single day, an address by the President about foreign trade may be ranked as a +6, a meeting of the Federal Reserve a +7, unemployment a +4, the NAFTA Agreement a +3, a continued lack of rain in the west as a +2, large grain stocks as a 4, and a key article in the *Wall Street Journal* on the improved Russian crude oil production as a 5, giving a net score of +4 to the news—interpreted as moderately bullish. Such a ranking scheme would be considered analytic in nature, because it tries to weigh relevance on a predetermined scale without knowledge of individual effects.

Klein and Prestbo attempted such a study by assigning values of 3, 2, and 1 to articles in the *Wall Street Journal* of decreasing importance. Their interest was the stock market, and their work was straightforward and some of the conclusions general in nature. They showed a direct correlation between the relevant positive and negative news articles and the direction of the stock market. As it was scored over 6-week intervals before and after major turning points in the Dow Jones Industrial Averages, the news would stay about 70% favoring the current market direction. Having eliminated the possibility of the market influencing the news, they could conclude that, in retrospect, the market reflected the nature of the news.

The focus of news that influences commodity prices is different from that which moves the stock market, because it is limited in scope and often specific to the particular physical market. News releases and economic reports are an implicit part of commodity pricing; newspaper releases become very important in the last phase of a long move, which is easily seen when weather is a primary factor, but also when trade agreements are being negotiated. For example, traders will watch the weather report beginning in June when there has been a shortage of rain. They will stay long while no rain is in sight and quickly sell if a thunderstorm develops over the Chicago Board of Trade building. They will also protect their positions going into the weekend, in the event of unexpected rain, then reset their net longs on Monday. The news items that affect prices the most are:

Release of economic statistics (inflation, sales, balance of trade, unemployment)

Action by the Federal Reserve or other central bank

News relating to the availability of funds

Government reports on production and stocks

Unexpected news (a potential price shock such as an assassination)

Trade negotiations, agreements, and legislation

Weather

In-depth studies by the *Wall Street Journal*

Front-page news articles (or lead television news) on high prices, strikes, and other topics with a direct economic impact

Market letters, research reports, and comments from accepted authorities and influential organizations

---

[3] A thorough analysis of the CFTC *Commitment of Traders* report can be found in Chapter 16. It should be noted that other government reports released on the same day may complicate the interpretation.

Ranking and Measuring

The problem of ranking and assigning values to news items requires a knowledge of how others see the news. Klein and Prestbo studied this problem for the stock market and concluded that about 90% of the *Wall Street Journal* readers perceived news in the same way (bullish, bearish, or neutral). The same relationship can be assumed for futures markets. A reason for the uniform interpretation of the news articles is the publicized analysis. Within minutes of the release of an economic report or Fed action, the wire services begin to quote independent and poll opinions of the meaning of the report, then transmit those interpretations over their news media to be relayed to most traders. The *professional analysis* is taken as correct, and later discussions based on that interpretation serve to solidify the opinion.

News can also be measured empirically, by studying the immediate impact of an expected or surprise news item. For statistical reports, such as the Producer Price Index, care must be taken to use the correct figures. Market reaction is a combination of expectations compared with actual figures, and corrections in the previous month's data. In some months it is difficult to know whether the jump in prices was due to a downward revision of the previous month, or current values that are lower than expectations. When testing these factors, the historic data must include the actual numbers released in the reports, and a separate value for the revision of the previous month. Industry expectations are also important, but they can be determined empirically from the market's reaction. Therefore, following the release of an economic report, we can expect the price change to be expressed as:

Price change = f(a(current value – expectations) + b(revision – previous value))

where *a* and *b* are weighting factors, *a > b* implying that the current value is more important than the previous one. It is necessary to make the assumption for this type of measurement that the effects of a news release are most important in the short term, and that their influence on the market is diluted daily. A starting point for representing the way in which the news decreases in value is to modify the standard physics formula:

$$I = \frac{1}{T^2}$$

where *I* is the net influence and *T* is the elapsed time since the release of the news. In science this relationship, which represents the physical impact declining with the square of the distance (or time), applies directly to sound and light.

Measured empirically, the impact of economic reports is worth studying. For futures markets, the CFTC releases its *Commitments of Traders* report each week (upgraded from monthly reports). It tells the distribution of holdings among large and small speculators and hedgers as a percent of total open interest. This report is watched with the idea that the small speculators are usually wrong and the large hedgers right (this is covered in a later section of this chapter).

It is important to understand the difference between the analytic and empirical approach to news. In the *analytic* method, the value of specific events is determined in advance, and when they occur their preassigned value is compared with the effects. Using the *empirical* method, the historic effects of each event are tabulated and measured, then applied to subsequent news items.

The analytic approach has the advantage of working in an environment where multiple events are occurring simultaneously, and only the sum of all news items can be calculated. When testing the empirical approach, the event of interest may not be clearly distinguished from other news of importance occurring at the same time. Finding situations that isolate a single type of event, from which you can measure its impact, may be impossible. The primary disadvantage of the analytic approach is that it does not account for the discounting or anticipation of the news. An event of modest importance may become neutral or more significant relative to other concurrent or anticipated events; the empirical method would not be subject to that problem since it measures reactions and not expectations.

Trading on the News

Even without a sophisticated method of measurement, there are many professional speculators who trade on the news. When a bullish news item or report is introduced and the market fails to respond upward, the experienced trader looks for a place to sell. It shows that expectations exceeded reality and prices had already anticipated the bullish interpretation of the news; there may be a large number of sellers above the market. Similarly, *opening calls,* available for most markets, are transmitted via wire services beginning about a half hour before the opening bell. Regardless of the means for determining the opening direction, an experienced trader may take advantage of a higher opening call to place a sell order. There are frequent cases of so many traders wanting to sell a higher opening that the influx of orders after a call, before the opening, has changed the direction from higher to sharply lower on the open.

Agricultural *weather markets* function purely on news. Traders with long positions wait for the 5-day forecast hoping for no rain; they anticipate a loss of a specific number of bushels per acre for every dry day once the rainfall is below a given level. Weather markets are nervous and are characterized by evening-up on weekends; they rely heavily on anticipation and emotion. It is said that a farmer loses his crop three times each year: once for drought, once for disease, and once for frost. In 1976, the news carried numerous articles on the desperate wheat crop in the western states, showing films of virtually barren fields, and yet the United States harvested one of their largest wheat crops on record. Weather markets have a history of volatile anticipation but are a risky way of making long-term price predictions.

The *discounting of news* is as important as the news itself. An old saying in the market, "Buy the rumor, sell the fact," implies that anticipation drives the price past the point where it would realistically adjust to news. When the actual figures are released, there is invariably an adjustment back to their proper level. The pattern of anticipation for each economic report or news event should be watched closely.

Market Selectivity

The market seems to focus on one news item at a time. Although the same factors are always there to affect prices, they must reach a point of newsworthiness before they become the primary driving force. For heating oil, the combination of unexpected, sustained cold weather compared with available inventories will activate a weather market. Interest rates, the U.S. dollar, and tension in the Middle East will either be magnified out of proportion or completely ignored, while the anticipation of demand rises sharply. A market analysis of shortages not supported by news may as well be discarded—it is more often that crowd behavior moves the market.

Media Indicators

In a delightful article,[4] the author Grant Noble argues that the news recognizes events when they are cresting, and most often provides a countertrend trading opportunity. First, the American media should be considered to provide signals in three major time frames:

[4] Grant Noble, "The best trading indicator—the media," *Technical Analysis of Stocks & Commodities* (October 1989).

- *Long-term*—as given by the large circulation news magazines such as *Time* and *Newsweek*. With the timeliness of a brontosaurus, they profile moves over many years.
- *Medium-term*—represented by *Barron's*, *Forbes*, and *Business Week*, cover a period of about 3 months.
- *Short-term*—held captive by the *Wall Street Journal* and the *New York Times*, which also provide intermediate prediction.

By reading these periodicals you find that the *Wall Street Journal* has run headlines on "killing drought," "dust bowl," and the *New York Times* on "Drought . . . imperils crucial wheat crop" just as the wheat price makes its highs for the current move. In another case, *Barron's* cover article asked "Is the bull leaving you behind?" in August 1987. It's not surprising that the media would highlight events only after they have become a popular concern. In that sense, we might say that there is a high public consensus, a topic addressed in the section "Contrary Opinion." It may be perfectly valid to construct a consensus indicator based on the number of square inches of news coverage given to an event in a combination of publications.

EVENT TRADING

The largest price moves and the greatest volatility are the result of reactions to unexpected news. These market events pose the greatest risks to all traders because they are unpredictable and of such great magnitude that they are out of proportion with normal trading risk. It may be possible to trade for a number of years without experiencing an adverse price shock; therefore, many traders do not plan properly for these situations. Those readers interested in price shocks and their effects should also refer to Chapter 21 ("Testing").

Not all price shocks are of such magnitude that they present an unmanageable problem. It may be that price moves are either the reaction to news or the anticipation of news. This news is most often a release of an economic report by a government agency or monetary authority, but can also be a natural disaster associated with weather or earthquakes, or a political event, such as an outbreak of war, a military coup, or an assassination. The U.S. government releases economic data on an announced schedule, many of them at 7:30 A.M. Chicago time, that create regular disruptions to price movements in world economic markets.

The frequency and size of these price moves, triggered by unexpected news, makes these events a natural candidate for a trading system.[5] The profit opportunity, however, does not lie in taking a position ahead of the anticipated market reaction, but in studying the systematic patterns that come after the initial price reaction to the news. Because the news is unexpected, you cannot predict the results nor the extent of the reaction; therefore, taking a market position in advance of a government report would have a 50% chance of success and often very high risk. Studies might show that there is a bias in the direction of the price shock due to the way the monetary authority plans economic growth and controls inflation; however, the risks would remain high. This section will only look at positions entered on the close of the *event day*, the day on which a sharp market reaction occurred.

Market Reactions to Reports

To determine whether there is ample opportunity to profit from the price move that follows an event, it is necessary to study the direction of the market move and the subsequent price changes that occur over the next few days. These lagged reactions are the results of market inefficiencies; it is unlikely that prices could immediately jump to the exact price

[5] Ben Warwick, *Event Trading* (Irwin, 1996).

that economic principles require, despite the Efficient Market Hypothesis. With large price shocks there is often an over- or underreaction that is corrected during the next few days. Sometimes prices jump one direction and immediately begin to go the other way until they have completely discounted the price shock.

Figure 14-1 illustrates the types of price movements that might follow an upward price shock. Where there is an underreaction the prices move higher over the next few days; when there is an overreaction prices move lower. Patterns are not as orderly as shown in Figure 14-1 because volatility is high and many traders react impulsively, or by financial necessity, to the move. To decide whether a market is a candidate for event trading, you must study the pattern of moves following the reaction to news and decide whether:

1. The size of the average move is enough to generate a profit.
2. The returns are worth the risk of loss associated with these volatile events.

When studying these events, there may be a direct relationship between the size of the reaction and the type of pattern that follows. For example, a small reaction to news may be followed by a steady continuation of the direction of the price shock. If unemployment jumps by ¼% in a month, there should be a reaction by the government to stimulate job growth. The same initial reaction would occur if unemployment jumped by 1 full percent, but the number would be so unexpectedly large that it may be considered an error in which case it is not clear to what extent the government would respond. The market may overreact to a large shock but underreact to a small one. The only way to discover this is by testing these events.

Fundamental to understanding price shocks is that the shock is based on the difference between the *expectations* and the actual reported data, not just the reported data. The market always discounts what it believes is its best guess at what the report will say; therefore, if bond prices rise in advance of an important unemployment report, we can say that the market expects unemployment to increase. If bond prices have moved up by ½% (equivalent yield) in expectation of a very bad report, and the report comes out neutral, then prices will drop sharply to offset the incorrect anticipation. When studying market reactions from historic records of economic data, you must have market expectations to

---

FIGURE 14-1   Price reaction to unexpected news, including delayed response. The upward price jump on the event day (0) may be followed by (a) a continuation move up or (b) a reverse move down over the next 3 days.

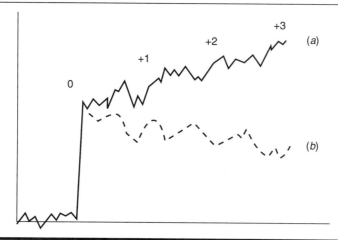

find consistent results; without those values, the best approach is to work backward from the reaction to infer the accuracy of expectations.

Measuring an Event

There are many economic statistics released each year, as well as special reports in the *Wall Street Journal* and other influential periodicals. To record the dates of each news item would be impractical for most traders; a simpler approach that might prove effective is to identify the importance of the event by the size of its reaction. This can be done by comparing the volatility of the current day with the average volatility of the recent past, using the *true range* calculation:

$$\text{volatility ratio} = \frac{\text{true range}_{\text{today}}}{\text{average true range}_{n\text{-days}}}$$

When the volatility ratio is below 1.0, current volatility is less than the average volatility over the past *n* days. When the ratio is greater than 3.0 we are likely to have identified a day in which a news event caused a price shock. The larger the ratio, the greater the surprise to the market. Note that the true range is used because the shock can occur overnight, causing an opening gap, or during the trading session, when the United States typically releases reports.

Key Government Reports

Even when there is public concern over the state of the economy, the market does not react in a similar way to all economic data. Some reports seem to be more important than others, and the market appears to focus on one report at a time. The most significant data seem to be unemployment and the Consumer Price Index (CPI). During a period of sustained low unemployment, as seen in 1997, even a modest increase will not cause much concern. A jump in the CPI, however, will always warn the market to expect a *preemptive strike* by the Fed, cutting off potential inflation by nudging rates up slightly. The *Trade Balance* report was particularly popular in the late 1980s when the deficit with Japan seemed to be at the root of the U.S. deficit. Sagging U.S. exports and overconsumption of foreign-made products by Americans looked as though the U.S. work force could not compete in the world market.

Other reports can also attract the attention of traders, but may be more difficult to interpret. Durable goods, retail sales, budget, and tax legislation all directly affect the economy and prices; however, it is not always clear how to relate the changes in durable goods orders with price change, or how the latest news on tax law will contribute to the economic well-being. More important, it is difficult to assess how the government will manipulate interest rates in reaction to these data.

Trading the Event Lag

Once you have studied the way prices move following an event day, or price shock, you can establish trading rules. For example, you find that a change in the Consumer Price Index of between 0 and ±.2% has no particular reaction, provided market expectations were similar to the data released. A change between +.2 and +.4 or −.2 and −.4 should give enough surprise for a noticeable market reaction, provided expectations were low, and data greater than a change of ±.4 should cause a price shock regardless of the anticipation. In addition, we might find that changes over ±.4 tended to react in the opposite direction to the normal government action because of overanticipation.

Based on the results of studying these patterns, Warwick established the following trading rules:

1. Buy on the close if the market closes in the upper 20% of the trading range on an event day (a price shock), if prices have shown a continuation pattern.
2. Hold for a predetermined number of days, based on the lag pattern of the market.
3. Use a stop-loss to limit risk.

In an older study by Arnold Larson[6] applied to the corn market, it was found that 81% of the price changes occurred on the event day, there was a typical price reversal of 8% over the next 4 days, and a net change in price of 27% in the original direction over 45 days. Although we should not expect those same numbers now, the pattern of a large move, a reaction, and a longer directional move may still be valid.

Results of Event Studies

In his book *Event Trading,* Warwick shows the test results of some of the major markets, allowing us to compare the effects of the systematic reaction of U.S. bonds with that of the S&P 500 and other markets. Unexpected news that causes bond prices to rally sharply (causing rates to decline) would result in a rise in the stock market, unless the news was particularly bad for the long-term economy of the country. Therefore, a drop in the consumption of durable goods should be followed by lower interest rates and a slightly lagged upward response in the stock market. This pattern is shown in Table 14-1 where the bond and S&P results are side-by-side.

In general, we expect a price shock to impact interest rates first, then currency and equities markets. Typically, the interest rates react in a way to compensate for the economic effects and stabilize the other two markets; this preempts the action that would be expected from the Central Bank. The exception is when the news is much more extreme than usual, and it affects the stock market first. Investors, because of a lack of confidence, will shift their funds from equities to interest rates in an effort to find a safe haven during uncertainty. This will cause a decline in the stock market and a corresponding rise in interest rate prices (lower yields), although normally the two will move in the same direction.

In Table 14-1 we can see the way the markets move after both the interest rates and stock market initially react with an upward price breakout. When both markets continue in the same direction, such as with retail sales, GDP, and employment data, then the full impact of the data takes longer to be assessed by the market, or there is expectation of

---

[6] Arnold Larson, "Measurement of a Random Process in Futures Pricing," *Food Research Institute Studies 1* (no. 3, November 1960, referenced in Warwick, *Event Trading*).

TABLE 14-1   Results of Upward Breakout of U.S. Bonds (left) and S&P 500 (right) for the Period 1989–1994

	U.S. Bonds			S&P 500		
	Holding Period	Buy or Sell	Confidence Level	Holding Period	Buy or Sell	Confidence Level
Durable goods	0–1	B	97	0–4	B	>99
Retail sales	0–1	B	90	0–2	B	96
Retail sales	1–5	S	95	2–4	S	96
CPI	Low confidence			0–3	B	92
PPI	0–5	S	95	0–1	B	97
NAPM	0–2	B	91	0–4	S	97
Industrial production	0–1	S	94	Low confidence		
GDP	0–3	B	90	0–4	B	96
Employment	0–2	B	91	0–1	B	93

some continued response by the government. The PPI and the National Association of Purchasing Managers (NAPM) do not show this consistency, indicating that the market takes this information differently. When the pattern of confidence is low, the market may do a good job of reaching the best price level in immediate response to the news; therefore, there is no consistency in the price move that follows.

Table 14-2 shows the side-by-side test results of reactions that cause a drop in bond prices and a corresponding drop in the S&P 500. The frequency of low-confidence results may represent the conflict between the normal upward bias of the stock market or the unusually bullish trend during the test period. The GDP results, which show the most confidence, indicate that the stock market moves higher even when the interest rates rise in reaction to positive GDP data. Trade balance data, which is not always the primary focus of the market, has a very consistent pattern, but is not clearly related to the interest rate move as are most of the other statistics.

Although this work concentrates on the short-term daily reaction to unexpected news, the long-term trend should not be overlooked. Economic data can exhibit consistency over long time periods, and the response by the Central Bank is usually moderate but consistent. If the CPI shows early signs of inflation, then the monetary authority will push rates up slightly; if this doesn't work, as seen by the next series of economic reports, they will move rates slightly higher again. This pattern allows for an underlying trend that can be used to filter the direction of trades and add confidence to the results.

Reaction to Unemployment Reports

Markets treat unemployment data seriously; because it is a direct reflection of how the population is faring, the government is sensitive to unexpected changes in the number of persons filing for unemployment benefits. Using LIM, it was found that when the market underestimated the unemployment figure by at least 0.2%, there was an average return of 4.5% in the S&P 500 during the following 27 days from the close of the report day. Similarly, U.S. 30-year Treasury bonds showed an average return (from a long position) in nearly all cases of 3.2% during the period from 3 to 28 days following the report.[7]

[7] Gibbons Burke, "Event-based Analysis," *Futures* (April 1995).

TABLE 14-2 Results of Downward Breakout of U.S. Bonds (left) and S&P 500 (right) for the Period 1989–1994

	U.S. Bonds			S&P 500		
	Holding Period	Buy or Sell	Confidence Level	Holding Period	Buy or Sell	Confidence Level
Durable goods		Low confidence		0–2	B	92
Retail sales		Low confidence		0–4	B	94
Retail sales		Low confidence			Low confidence	
CPI	0–4	S	97		Low confidence	
PPI		Low confidence			Low confidence	
NAPM		Low confidence			Low confidence	
Industrial production	0–4	S	93		Low confidence	
GDP	0–3	S	91	0–3	B	>99
Industrial production	3–4	B	>99	0–3	B	>99
Employment	0–1	S	93		Low confidence	
Trade balance	0–3	S	93	0–3	S	>99

Presidential Election Cycle

Of all the events that move the market, the Presidential elections have been the most consistent. The patterns stem from the motivation of the incumbent party to provide good economic news to the voters prior to the election year, and as far into the election year as possible. Stock market action during the election year is always more erratic, as parties battle over the value of each other's actions.

Studies of the 4-year patterns have all yielded very similar results to those shown in Table 14-3.[8] The year preceding the election (*year 3*) posts the strongest gains for the market, followed by a reasonably strong election year. The 2 years after the election show returns below average as the reality of politics reasserts itself.

There is the additional possibility that there is an 8-year cycle that should be watched; however, the 8-year period should be most informative if it represented only those years in which the same President was in office. Actions by a President who cannot be reelected are likely to be different from one who seeks another term; therefore, we should expect a different pattern. This can be made more intricate by studying the patterns preceding and following a change of party, all of which have a fundamental basis in the behavior of the political parties and the voters.

More sophisticated computer software, such as provided by Logical Information Machines, a Chicago firm, can produce a very interesting, closer view of how voters respond to election politics. Table 14-4 breaks the election year into periods between the key events for those years in which the stock market began the election year within 8% of its 2-year high price (*days* refer to business days):

1. The returns of the year preceding the election year
2. The first 10 days of the new year, typically a strong period (days 0–10)
3. Through the State-of-the-Union address and the primaries (days 10–83)
4. Waiting for the conventions (days 83–161)
5. Preelection blahs—the actual campaign (days 161–195)
6. The election to year-end reaction (days 195–253)
7. Combined periods (2) + (4) + (6)

Combining the three periods (2), (4), and (6), which have strong upward biases, gives consistently positive results. Even if the newly elected party fails to deliver on their campaign promises, traders could have already converted those marketing gimmicks into stock market profits.

---

[8] Articles by Adam White, "The Eight-Year Presidential Election Pattern," *Technical Analysis of Stocks & Commodities* (November 1994); Arthur A. Merrill, "The Presidential Election Cycle," *Technical Analysis of Stocks & Commodities* (March 1992); and Michael J. Carr, "Get out the vote and into stocks," *Futures* (February 1996), all show very similar results for the 4-year election pattern.

TABLE 14-3 The Presidential Election Cycle, 1912–1992, Based on the Percentage Returns of the Dow Jones Industrial Averages

Preelection year	11.0%
Election year	7.0
Postelection year	4.7
Midterm year	2.3
Average year	6.3%

Source: Adam White.

TABLE 14-4   Election Year Analysis for Years in Which the Stock Market Began the Year within 8% of the Previous Two-Year Highs

Year	1. Previous Year	2. First 2 weeks (1–10)	3. Primaries (10–83)	4. Preconvention (83–161)	5. Preelection (161–195)	6. Election to year-end (195–253)	7. (1) + (3) + (5)
1936	41.82	2.76	4.64	11.91	−0.62	5.85	20.52
1944	19.45	1.63	−.84	9.27	−.86	3.14	14.04
1952	16.15	1.60	−2.82	8.02	−2.49	5.47	15.10
1956	27.25	−1.78	5.42	3.16	−6.65	2.38	3.76
1960	8.48	−2.49	−5.75	2.94	−7.13	8.49	8.95
1964	18.89	1.79	4.44	3.03	2.52	0.06	4.88
1968	20.03	0.26	−0.10	1.44	4.39	4.25	5.95
1972	10.82	1.41	3.39	5.30	−1.78	4.88	11.59
1980	12.31	2.26	−5.42	18.57	−0.20	7.66	28.49
1984	17.53	1.27	−5.01	4.27	0.41	0.63	6.17
1992	26.30	0.80	−2.72	2.14	−0.23	5.87	8.82
Average	19.91	0.86	−0.44	6.37	−1.15	4.43	11.66

Source: Michael Carr, *Logical Information Machines.*

COMMITMENT OF TRADERS REPORT

Drawing from more than 20 years of experience in analyzing the CFTC's *Commitment of Traders Report,* William L. Jiler described a supplementary approach to identifying a major trend in his *1985 CRB Commodity Yearbook.*[9] With his usual thoroughness and clarity, Jiler presents material that had previously been unsuccessfully interpreted.

Originally released the 11th day of each month (biweekly since 1992), the *Commitment of Traders Report* summarizes the positions of *reporting* and *nonreporting* traders as of the last day of the previous month. Reported positions are those exceeding a minimum level determined for each futures market (e.g., 750,000 bushels for corn, 500,000 for soybeans, 500 contracts for 30-year Treasury bonds, and 300 contracts for the S&P 500). The report subdivides the open interest into positions held by hedgers (*commercials*) and speculators. By subtracting the reported positions from the total open interest, the total positions of small hedgers and speculators can be found. For grain reports (Figure 14-2), positions are further divided into *old crop* and *other* positions, which include new crop and intercrop spreading.

To analyze the shifts in position, Jiler has compiled tables of *normal* patterns, similar to a seasonal study (Figure 14-3). When the open interest of one group is significantly greater than their normal holdings, they express a definite opinion on the direction of the market. By tracking these changes for many years and observing the corresponding price changes, Jiler concludes that the large traders have the best forecasting record, with the large hedger better than the large speculator. The small traders were notably worse. Guidelines were stated as:

> The most bullish configuration would show large hedgers heavily net long more than normal, large speculators clearly net long, small traders heavily net short more than seasonal. The shades of bullishness are varied all the way to the most bearish configuration, which would have these groups in opposite positions— large hedgers heavily net short, and so forth. There are two caution flags when analyzing deviations from normal. Be wary of positions that are more than 40% from their long-term average and disregard deviations of less than 5%.

---

[9] William L. Jiler, "Analysis of the CFTC Commitments of Traders Reports Can Help You Forecast Futures Prices," *1985 CRB Commodity Year Book* (Commodity Research Bureau, Jersey City, NJ, 1985).

FIGURE 14-2   Commitment of Traders Report.

```
              SOYBEANS - CHICAGO BOARD OF TRADE
    COMMITMENTS OF TRADERS IN ALL FUTURES COMBINED AND INDICATED FUTURES, FEBRUARY 28, 1985
-----------------------------------------------------------------------------------------
        TOTAL  :                REPORTABLE POSITIONS
  F          :  --------------------------------------------------------- : NONREPORTABLE
  U          :          NON-COMMERCIAL                                     : POSITIONS
  T          :  --------------------------------------------             :
  U    OPEN   : LONG OR SHORT: LONG AND SHORT: COMMERCIAL    :   TOTAL     :
  R  INTEREST:   ONLY        :  (SPREADING)                                :
  E          :  ------------------------------------------------------------:
  S          :  LONG : SHORT:  LONG : SHORT:  LONG : SHORT:  LONG : SHORT:  LONG . SHORT
-----------------------------------------------------------------------------------------
                              (THOUSAND BUSHELS)
ALL  : 359,190  15,810  32,400  41,060  41,060 117,420 140,380 174,290 213,840: 184,900 145,350
OLD  : 302,170. 16,275  35,075  27,620  27,620 105,685 128,700 149,580 191,395: 152,590 110,775
OTHER:  57,020:  9,280   7,070   3,695   3,695  11,735  11,680  24,710  22,445:  32,310  34,575

                     CHANGES IN COMMITMENTS FROM JANUARY 31, 1985
ALL  :    -330   -9,240  15,575  18,280  18,280  16,560 -44,770  25,600 -10,915: -25,930  10,585

         :PERCENT OF OPEN INTEREST REPRESENTED BY EACH CATEGORY OF TRADERS:
ALL  : 100.0%      4.4     9.0    11.4    11.4    32.7    39.1    48.5    59.5:    51.5    40.5
OLD  : 100.0%      5.4    11.6     9.1     9.1    35.0    42.6    49.5    63.3:    50.5    36.7
OTHER: 100.0%     16.3    12.4     6.5     6.5    20.6    20.5    43.3    39.4:    56.7    60.6

       :NUMBER OF:
       :TRADERS         NUMBER OF TRADERS IN EACH CATEGORY
ALL  :   144           23      32      33      33      54      41     100     100:
OLD  :   134           23      32      23      23      51      39      88      90:
OTHER:    32            8       8       5       5       9       6      21      17:
-----------------------------------------------------------------------------------------
                     CONCENTRATION RATIOS
       PERCENT OF OPEN INTEREST HELD BY THE INDICATED NUMBER OF LARGEST TRADERS
-----------------------------------------------------------------------------------------
            BY GROSS POSITION              :              BY NET POSITION
-----------------------------------------------------------------------------------------
      4 OR LESS TRADERS  : 8 OR LESS TRADERS :  4 OR LESS TRADERS :  8 OR LESS TRADERS
      LONG : SHORT : LONG : SHORT : LONG : SHORT : LONG : SHORT
ALL    13.0    23.4    18.1    28.6    10.5    21.3    14.6    25.3
OLD    13.9    25.0    19.6    30.4    11.9    23.6    16.1    28.2
OTHER  18.6    20.6    27.4    28.7    18.6    20.2    27.3    26.8
```

FIGURE 14-3   Jiler's *normal* trader positions.

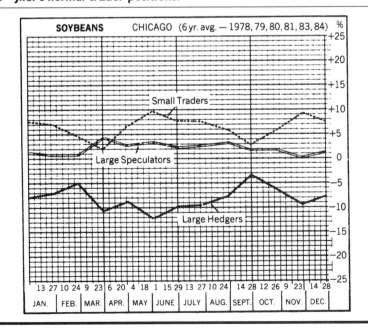

This result is confirmed by Curtis Arnold,[10] who compared positions of large and small speculators with commercials for a 1-year period spanning 1983–1984. Arnold shows (Figure 14-4) that the position of commercials and small speculators tend to be opposite, with the commercials positioned to profit from the subsequent price move.

Over a wider group of 36 markets from 1983 to 1989, a study conducted by Bullish Review[11] showed that a large weighting of long or short positions held by commercial hedgers correctly forecasts significant market moves 67% of the time. In retrospect it seems likely that a large commercial trader, bank, investment house, or other institution would take a longer-term view of the market, setting positions to take advantage, or avoid the risk, of a potential price move. Because of their size, institutions are not likely to change their positions on minor market variations. Analysts should be aware, however, that a qualified *hedger,* one that is registered with the CFTC to set large positions due to their ongoing risk of holding physicals, may also take large speculative positions under the same umbrella.

OPINION AND CONTRARY OPINION

Market sentiment seems to be a driving force in the market, yet it is very difficult to measure and even harder to deliver those results in a timely fashion. For that reason, analysts often substitute a combination of volume, open interest, and price for true sentiment, hoping that the recorded actions of traders closely relate to what they are thinking. Opinion, however, weighs on the marketplace and governs future actions in the same way the high volume may not move prices today, but provides a platform for a potentially large price move.

Public opinion is also fast to change. A prolonged bull market in stocks may show a gradual increase in bullish sentiment; however, the collapse of a bank, an increase in rates by the Central Bank, a sharp downturn in the economy of another region, or a single sharp drop in the stock index could quickly change the public's opinion. Oddly enough, sentiment indicators are most popular for trading in the direction opposite to the unified public opinion.

[10] Curtis Arnold, "Tracking 'Big Money' May Tip Off Trend Changes," *Futures* (February 1985).

[11] Steve Briese, "Tracking the big foot," *Futures* (March 1994).

FIGURE 14-4   Arnold's trader position study.

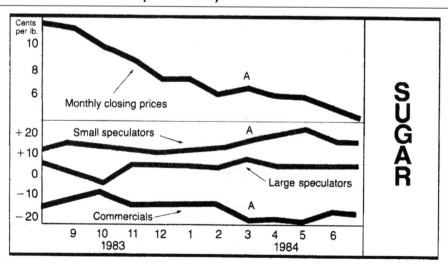

Contrary Opinion[12]

The contrarian lies somewhere between the fundamentalist and the technician, basing actions on the behavior of crowds, in this case the market participants. The contrarian sees the end of a bull market occurring when everyone is bullish. Once all long positions have been set, there is diminishing influence by the bulls; moreover, opportunities always lie in the reverse direction from crowd thinking.

Contrary opinion alone is not meant to signal a new entry into a position; it only identifies situations that qualify. It lacks the timing. It is more of a filter than a trading system, a means of avoiding risk and finding an opportunity. Consider the patterns that appear in every prolonged bull or bear move. First, there is a place where the direction is generally accepted as the major trend. After that, traders wait for a reversal to enter in the direction of the trend at a more favorable price. These price *corrections* become smaller or even disappear when everyone wants to *buy a lower open* or *sell a higher open* until you have the ultimate *blow-off* and a reversal of a major bull or bear market. The dynamic end of a prolonged move is generally credited to the entrance of the public; when the masses are unanimously convinced that prices are going higher, who is left to buy?

The other important ingredient for a contrarian is that all the facts cannot be known. The widely accepted belief that "prices will go higher" must be based on presumptions; if the final figures were out, the market would adjust to the proper level. This idea is older than *The Art of Contrary Thinking*. In 1930, Schabacker discussed cashing out of a long position if the market rallied on news that was general rather than specific.

The practical application of the theory of contrary opinion is the *Bullish Consensus*[13] and the *Market Sentiment Index*, created from a poll of market letters prepared by the research departments of brokerage firms and professional advisors. In the Bullish Consensus (see Figure 14-5), these opinions are weighted according to the estimated circulation of these letters until a final index value is determined.

$$\text{Bullish Consensus} = \frac{\text{Sum of (each source} \times \text{its relative weight} \times \text{opinion)}}{\text{Sum of (each source} \times \text{its relative weight} \times \text{bullish } \textit{opinion})}$$

The value of the Bullish Consensus will range from 0 to 100%, indicating an increasingly bullish attitude. Because of the bullish tendency of the novice trader, and the long-term upward bias of the stock market, the neutral consensus point is 55%. The normal range is considered from 30 to 80%, although each market must be individually evaluated.

Hadady also devised a simple mathematical way of displaying the bullishness of the market.[14] Using the formula below, he shows that when 80% of traders are bullish, then the average buyer will hold only ¼ the number of contracts as the average seller. This leads to a precipitous drop in prices once a decline begins.

$$N_t = \frac{20\% \, T \times N_s}{80\% \, T} = \frac{1}{4} \times N_s$$

where T = the number of traders in the market

N_t = average number of contracts held by a single bullish trader

N_s = average number of contracts held by a single bearish trader

[12] For the most definitive works, see Humphrey Neill, *The Art of Contrary Thinking* (Caxton Printers, Caldwell, OH, 1960), who is credited with having first formulated the concept, and R. Earl Hadady, *Contrary Opinion* (Hadady, Pasadena, CA, 1983).

[13] The Bullish Consensus is a product of Sibbett-Hadady, Pasadena, CA; a Market Sentiment Index is published in *Consensus*, Kansas City, MO.

[14] R. Earl Hadady, "Contrary Opinion," *Technical Analysis of Stocks & Commodities* (August 1988).

FIGURE 14-5   Interpretation of the Bullish Consensus.

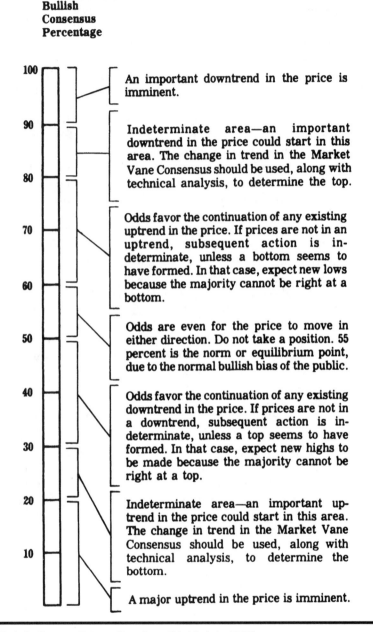

Bullish
Consensus
Percentage

100 — An important downtrend in the price is imminent.

90
80 — Indeterminate area—an important downtrend in the price could start in this area. The change in trend in the Market Vane Consensus should be used, along with technical analysis, to determine the top.

70
60 — Odds favor the continuation of any existing uptrend in the price. If prices are not in an uptrend, subsequent action is indeterminate, unless a bottom seems to have formed. In that case, expect new lows because the majority cannot be right at a bottom.

50 — Odds are even for the price to move in either direction. Do not take a position. 55 percent is the norm or equilibrium point, due to the normal bullish bias of the public.

40
30 — Odds favor the continuation of any existing downtrend in the price. If prices are not in a downtrend, subsequent action is indeterminate, unless a top seems to have formed. In that case, expect new highs to be made because the majority cannot be right at a top.

20
10 — Indeterminate area—an important uptrend in the price could start in this area. The change in trend in the Market Vane Consensus should be used, along with technical analysis, to determine the bottom.

A major uptrend in the price is imminent.

Source: R. Earl Hadady, *Contrary Opinion* (Pasadena, CA: Hadady, 1983).

The principle of contrary opinion does not require that trades only be entered in the direction opposite to the current price movement. Within the normal range, the contrarian will take a position in the direction of the trend. Frequently, the Bullish Consensus will begin increasing prior to the price turning higher, indicating that the attitude of the trader is becoming bullish. It is considered significant when the index changes 10% in a 2-week period. Once the Bullish Consensus reaches 90% during an upward move, or 20% during a bear move, the market is considered overbought or oversold, and the contrarian looks for a convenient point to exit from the current trade. Positions are not reversed until prices show that they are not continuing in the original direction. This could be identified using a moving average. Remembering Schabacker's advice, the occasion of a general news release that moves the market further in the direction of the general opinion would be an opportune moment to enter a contrary trade; specific news that fails to move prices would be a good indication of an exhausted trend when the consensus is overbought or oversold. A typical contrarian situation identified by Hadady is given in Figure 14-6.

R. Earl Hadady said: "The principle of contrary opinion, by definition, works 100% of the time. The problem is getting an accurate consensus."[15] Timeliness is a problem with this index; if 60 to 70 market letters are reviewed, read, and weighted to form an index, the results may be outdated before they can be used. The theory of contrary opinion also emphasized its use as a timing device for entering trades at an opportune moment and for filtering out the ambiguous trades; the theory is not readily applicable to exiting a position unless the reverse consensus occurs. Because a consensus does not have to switch uniformly from bullish to bearish, it is not always prudent to wait for an opposite confirmation before exiting a trade.

Commitment of Traders Sentiment Index[16]

The reported positions of traders, published in the CFTC's *Commitment of Traders Report,* may be considered a recording of market opinion into categories. By combining

[15] George Angell, "Thinking Contrarily," *Commodities* (November 1976).

[16] Stephen E. Briese, "Commitment of Traders as a sentiment index," *Technical Analysis of Stocks & Commodities* (May 1990).

FIGURE 14-6 Typical contrarian situation—wheat, 1978.

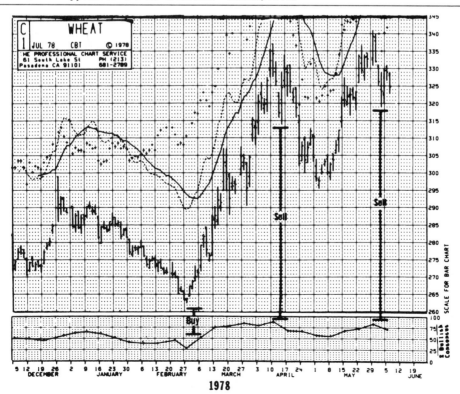

the idea behind the stochastic calculation with a method originally developed by Curtis Arnold, you can create an index:

$$\text{Commitment of Traders Index} = \frac{\text{current net} - \text{minimum net}}{\text{maximum net} - \text{minimum net}}$$

where: Net = Commercial net position (number of contracts) minus the total combined net position of large speculators and small traders
Maximum = Greatest net difference that occurred during the comparison period
Minimum = Smallest net difference that occurred during the comparison period

The intent of the Commitment of Traders Index is to rank the current spread between the commercial and speculative positions within the context of the historic range. There seems to be uniform agreement the commercials are the group that determines the direction of prices. A shift in the position of the commercials should be closely watched.

Put-Call Ratios

The ratio of put option volume to call option volume, called the *put-call ratio,* is the major sentiment index for listed options. It too is used for its contrary value. The interpretation of extreme levels of the put-call ratios (in particular, the index option) points out a problem that may reflect on the proper use of all contrary indicators.[17]

Prior to 1986, the market was considered ready for an upturn when the total put volume exceeded 65% of the total call volume. Similarly, when the put volume fell to 35% of the call volume it was a bearish indication. In the volatile markets of 1986 and 1987 these levels proved to be far too close, and as McMillan said, "Not surprisingly, the put-call ratios fell into some disfavor at that point." This could easily happen with a contrary indicator, or any indicator that rarely reaches its extreme values. Because contrary opinion is a valuable addition to analysis, use of these indicators now focuses on relative highs and lows. This can be accomplished by smoothing the ratio using a standard moving average or momentum indicator (a simple difference over *n*-days). When the ratio moves over 65% and turns down it is time to sell. Such an approach gives up a timing edge but greatly reduces risk and increases reliability.

FIBONACCI AND HUMAN BEHAVIOR

> *Even though we may not understand the cause underlying a particular phenomenon, we can, by observation, predict the phenomenon's recurrence.*
>
> R.N. Elliott[18]

History is a record of great achievement in the face of disbelief, as exhibited by the explorations of Columbus, Magellan, Marco Polo; the science of da Vinci, Galileo, Copernicus; and the philosophy of Socrates and other men now known to be great. We are more observant today and less apt to condemn those who delve into areas still unknown. Of these, astrology is the most popular, with a very large following, particularly in Asia. Its acceptance may be partly because of its strong basis in physical phenomena. It attempts to classify personality and behavioral traits based on positions of planets and stars at the time of birth, and to predict the actions of groups based on the relationships of planets, moons, and comets to one another. The science of physics confirms that the positions of our moon and planets, the energy given off, and the gravitational phenomenon are directly responsible for physical occurrences of tides and weather—should they not have a measurable effect on behavior? This will be considered in the following sections.

---

[17] Lawrence G. McMillan, "Put-Call Ratios," *Technical Analysis of Stocks & Commodities* (October 1995).

[18] R.N. Elliott, *Nature's Law: The Secret of the Universe* (Elliott, New York, 1946 p. 4).

Let us look first at the fascinating subject of symmetry in nature. Science is familiar with the symmetric shapes of crystalline substances, snowflakes, the spherical planets, and the human body. The periodicity of the universe—sun spots, eclipses, and other cyclic phenomena—is also understood, but its bearing on human behavior is not yet known. Work in biorhythms is only at the point of being a curiosity; the relationship of behavior to nonbiological functions, such as planetary positions, is too abstract.

In 1904, Arthur H. Church wrote about phyllotaxis, the leaf arrangement of plants,[19] showing its relationship to a mathematical series based on the works of Leonardo Pisano (Fibonacci).[20] This mathematical series of numbers has been attributed the quality of representing human behavior. Examples have been given that appear to be more than "interesting coincidences."

It is not certain how Fibonacci conceived his summation series. His greatest work, *Liber Abaci,* written in the early part of the thirteenth century, was not published until 1857.[21] It contained a description of a situation involving the reproduction of rabbits in which the following two conditions hold: Every month each pair produces a new pair, which, from the second month on become productive; deaths do not occur. This becomes the famous *Fibonacci summation series*

   1, 2, 3, 5, 8, 13, 21, 34, 55, 89, 144, . . .

(more currently written 1, 1, 2, 3, . . .). It can be easily seen that each element of the series is the sum of the two previous entries.

Those who have studied the life of Fibonacci often attribute the series to his observations of the Great Pyramid of Giza. This pyramid, dating from a preliterary, prehieroglyphic era, contains many features said to have been observed by Fibonacci. In the geometry of a pyramid there are 5 surfaces and 8 edges, for a total of 13 surfaces and edges; there are 3 edges visible from any one side. More specifically, the Great Pyramid of Giza is 5,813 inches high (5-8-13, and the inch is the standard Egyptian unit of measure); and the ratio of the elevation to the base is .618.[22] The coincidence of this ratio is that it is the same as the ratio that is approached by any two consecutive Fibonacci numbers; for example,

$$\frac{2}{3} = .667, \qquad \frac{3}{5} = .600, \qquad \frac{5}{8} = .625, \qquad \dots, \qquad \frac{89}{144} = .618$$

It is also true that the ratio of one side to a diagonal of a regular pentagon is .618.

Another phenomenon of the pyramid is that the total of the 4 edges of the base, measured in inches, is 36,524.22, which is exactly 100 times the length of the solar year. This permits interpretations of the Fibonacci summation series to be applied to time.

The Greeks showed a great fascination for the ratios of the Fibonacci series, noting that while $F_n/F_{n+1} = .618$, the reverse $F_{n+1}/F_n = 1.618$ was even more amazing. They expressed these relationships as *golden sections* and appear to have used them in the proportions of such works as the Parthenon, the sculpture of Phidias, and classic vases. Leonardo da Vinci consciously employed the ratio in his art. It has always been a curiosity that the great mathematician, Pythagoras, left behind a symbol of a triangle of Fibonacci proportions with the words "The Secret of the Universe" inscribed below.

---

[19] A.H. Church, *On the Relation of Phyllotaxis to Mechanical Laws* (Williams and Newgate, London, 1904).

[20] In the appendices to Jay Hambridge, *Dynamic Symmetry: The Greek Vase* (Yale University Press, New Haven, CT, 1931, pp. 141–161), there is a full discussion of the evolution of this number series within science and mathematics, together with further references.

[21] *Il Liber Abaci di Leonardo Pisano* (Baldassare Boncompagni, Rome, Italy, 1857).

[22] Jay Hambridge, *Dynamic Symmetry, The Greek Vase* (Yale University Press, New Haven, CT, 1931, pp. 27–38).

Church, in his work in phyllotaxis, studied the sunflower, noting that one of normal size (5 to 6 inches) has a total of 89 curves, 55 in one direction and 34 in another. In observing sunflowers of other sizes, he found that the total curves are Fibonacci numbers (up to 144) with the two previous numbers in the series describing the distribution of curves. The chambered nautilus is considered a natural representation of a *golden spiral,* based on the proportions of the Fibonacci ratio (see Figure 14-7) in which the logarithmic spiral passes diagonally through opposite corners of successive squares, such as DE, EG, GJ, and so forth. Nature also shows that the genealogical pattern of a beehive, and the stem (growth) structure of the Sneezewort (Achillea ptarmica) are perfect duplicates of the Fibonacci series.

Up to now, aspects of the Fibonacci series have been intriguing, but here it goes a step beyond. The numbers in the series represent frequent or coincidental occurrences:

> The human body has five major projections; both arms and legs have three sections; there are five fingers and toes, each with three sections (except the thumb and great toe). There are also five senses.
>
> In music an octave means eight, with 8 white keys and 5 black, totaling 13.
>
> There are three primary colors.
>
> The United States had 13 original states and 13 is an unlucky number.
>
> The legal age is 21 and the highest salute in the army is a 21-gun salute.
>
> The human emotional cycle has been determined at 33 to 36 days by Dr. R.B. Hersey.[23]
>
> The wholesale price index of all commodities is shown to have peaks of 50 to 55 years according to the Kondratieff wave: 1815 after the war of 1812, 1865 after the Civil War, 1920 after the World War I, and about 1975. . . .[24]

[23] R.N. Elliott, *Nature's Law* (p. 55). Elliott quotes other human emotional relationships.

[24] *Cycles* (January 1976, p. 21); see also *The Kondratieff Wave: The Future of America Until 1981 and Beyond* (Dell, New York, 1974), which is based on the theory developed by the Russian economist early in this century.

FIGURE 14-7   The golden spiral, also the logarithmic spiral, is a perfect representation of the chambered nautilus.

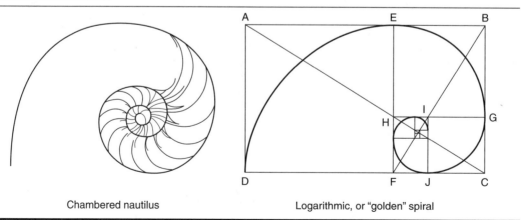

Chambered nautilus   Logarithmic, or "golden" spiral

Source: Robert Fischer, *Fibonacci Applications and Strategies for Traders* (John Wiley & Sons, 1993, p. 9). Original source: H.E. Huntley, *The Divine Proportion* (Dover, New York, 1970, pp. iv, 101). Reprinted with permission.

These examples are not meant to prove anything in the strict sense, but to open an area that may not have previously been considered. Human behavior is not yet a pure science and probes of this sort may lead the way to further understanding. The following sections deal with ideas such as these—sometimes reasonable and other times seeming to stretch the imagination.

ELLIOTT'S WAVE PRINCIPLE

R.N. Elliott was responsible for one of the more highly regarded and complex forms of market technical analysis. The *Elliott Wave Theory* is a sophisticated method of price motion analysis and has received careful study by A.H. Bolton (1960), and later by Charles Collins. His works are fully covered in two more recent publications by Robert Prechter; brief summaries of the analysis appear in some of the comprehensive books on market analysis.[25] This presentation of Elliott's technique will include both the original principles and extensions with examples.

The Wave Theory is an analysis of behavioral patterns based on mathematics and implemented using price charts; its original application was stocks and it is credited with predictive ability with respect to the Dow Jones Industrial Averages, which is second only to the occurrence of Haley's comet. It is understood that Elliott never intended to apply his principle to individual stocks, perhaps because the relatively low activity might distort those patterns that would have appeared as the result of mass behavior. If so, caution must be exercised when applying this method to individual stocks and futures markets.

The successes of the Elliott Wave Theory are fascinating and serve to reinforce the use of the technique; most summaries of Elliott's work recount them and the reader is encouraged to read these. The *waves* referred to in the theory are price peaks and valleys, not the formal oscillations of sound waves or harmonics described in the science of physics. The waves of price motion are overreactions to both supply and demand factors within major bull moves developed in five waves and corrected in three. His broad concept was related to *tidal wave bull markets* that have such large upward thrusts that each wave could be divided into five subwaves satisfying the same principle. After each primary wave of the major bull trend there was a major corrective move of three waves, which could be further divided into subwaves of three (see Figure 14-8).

The types of waves could be classified into the broad categories of *triangles* and *ABCs,* representing a main trend and a correction, respectively. The term triangle was taken from the consolidating or broadening shape that the waves form within trendlines, although in later works Elliott eliminated the expanding form of the triangle (see Figure 14-9).

An interesting aspect of the theory is its compound-complex nature, by which each sequence of triangles can occur in subwaves within waves (Figure 14-10). More recent work suggests that in futures markets, a three-wave development is more common than five waves. Prechter, a well-known interpreter of Elliott's principles, has shown many major stock index moves that conform to the ratio of 1.618. The stock index, which has great participation, is most likely to represent the generalized patterns of human behavior.[26]

---

[25] Robert R. Prechter, Jr., *The Major Works of R.N. Elliott* (New Classics Library, Chappaqua, NY (circa. 1980); and A.J. Frost and Robert R. Prechter, Jr., *Elliott Wave Principle* (New Classics Library, Chappaqua, NY, 1978); Merrill (1960) Appendices 5 and 6 contain one of the more thorough summaries and analyses of the basic Wave Theory, including performance.

[26] Robert R. Prechter, Jr., David Weiss, and David Allman, "Forecasting Prices with the Elliott Wave Principle," in *Trading Tactics: A Livestock Futures Anthology*, Todd Lofton (ed.) (Chicago Mercantile Exchange, 1986).

FIGURE 14-8   Basic Elliott wave.

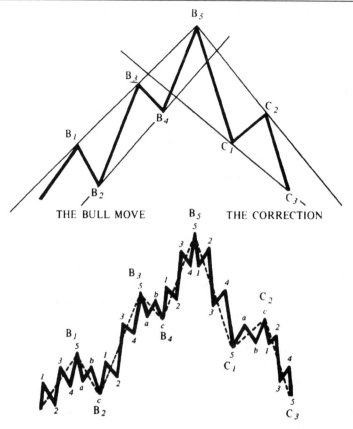

THE BULL MOVE   THE CORRECTION

Subwaves show 5 waves in the main move and 3 wave correction.

Elliott's Sideways Markets

Occasionally, the market pauses during a major move, or it may move sideways in a volatile pattern after completing the fifth leg of a wave. This has been described as "stock prices seen to be waiting for economic fundamentals to catch up with the market expectations."[27] These periods can be represented by a single *three,* a simple zigzag or flat formation, or by the more extended *double* or *triple three* (Figure 14-11).

A small variation of the single three has been noted to occur following the third wave, when the zigzag forms a minor swing reversal with *b* lower than its preceding top, and *c* lower than *a.* Elliott has also recognized this as a *descending zigzag* in an upward trend.[28]

Fitting the Market to the Patterns

One point to remember when applying an intricate set of rules is that an exact fit will not occur often. The best trading opportunities that will arise will be for those price patterns that fit best as the move is progressing; each successful step will serve as positive rein-

[27] See Robert R. Prechter, *Forecasting Prices* (1986).

[28] Robert R. Prechter, Jr., "Computerizing Elliott," *Technical Analysis of Stocks & Commodities* (July 1983), gives some general observations on how he would go about adapting Elliott's interpretations to a computer program.

FIGURE 14-9   Triangles and ABCs.

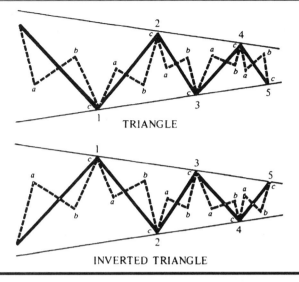

FIGURE 14-10   Compound correction waves.

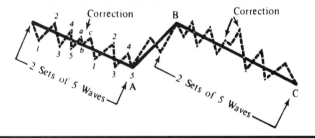

FIGURE 14-11   Elliott's threes.

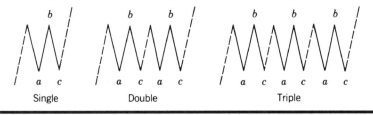

forcement for continuing. The critical period in the identification process is the fifth wave. The failure of the fifth wave to form indicates that the last correction of three waves will be retraced. In a bull market, an extension of the fifth wave is often followed by a corrective three-wave function. In addition, the recognition of a five-wave sequence should be followed by further analysis to determine whether that cycle was part of a more complex series. One of the difficulties in the method is the orientation of the current position to the wave formation; the multitude of primary and secondary waves makes some of the situations subjective until further developments clarify the position. Anyone interested in the further complexities of wave formation should refer directly to Bolton's work.

Elliott's Use of the Fibonacci Series

The application of the Elliott Wave Theory was unique in its use of the Fibonacci series. Besides the natural phenomena mentioned earlier, the summation series has the mathematical properties that

The ratio of any number to its successor (E_i/F_{i+1}) approaches .618.

The ratio of any number to its previous element (F_{i+1}/F_i) approaches 1.618.

The ratio of F_{i+2}/F_i is 2.618.

The two ratios (F_i/F_{i+1}) × (F_{i+1}/F_i) = .618 × 1.618 = 1

Elliott was also able to link certain measurements of the Great Pyramid to the Fibonacci series and connect the number of days in the year as well as the geometric figure of a circle to his theory. Both time and the circle will play a role in Elliott wave analysis.

While Elliott used the lower end of the Fibonacci series to describe the patterns in the stock market, it should be noted that there are increasingly larger gaps between successive entries as the series increases. To be consistent with the original principle, each gap could be subdivided into another Fibonacci series in the same manner that the waves take on a complex formation. Harahus offers an alternate approach to filling these spaces by use of Lucas numbers, formed in the same way as the Fibonacci summation beginning with (1, 3) and resulting in (1, 3, 4, 7, 11, 18, 29, 47, 76, 123, 199, . . .). The two sets are combined, eliminating common numbers, to form (*1, 2, 3,* 4, *5,* 7, *8, 13,* 18, *21,* 29, *34,* 47, *55,* 76, *89,* 123, *144,* 199, *233,* . . .). The Fibonacci numbers have been italicized since they will receive the most emphasis, whereas the Lucas numbers will serve as intermediate levels of less significance. The numbers themselves are applied to predict the length in days of a price move. A bull move that lasts for more than 34 days should meet major resistance or reverse on the 55th day or on the 89th day (considering Fibonacci numbers only). It is suggested that a penetration of the 89th day should permit the series to start again with the beginning of the series added to 89 (e.g., . . . , *94,* 96, *97,* 102, 107, *110,* 118, *123,* 136, . . .), including the more important Lucas and Fibonacci numbers from the original series. This effect is similar to the complex wave-within-a-wave motion.

The same numbers are used to express key levels in a trend reversal. For example, a bull move that carries prices up for about 47 days before a reversal should meet resistance at the price level on the 34th day. If that price does not stop the reversal, either the behavioral implications of the number series do not hold for this situation or prices are in a different part of the cycle.

With the introduction of Lucas numbers (L), there are some additional key ratios. In the combined Fibonacci-Lucas series (FL), denote an element with j if it is the first element of the other series following entry i; L_j is the first Lucas number entry following F_i that is a Fibonacci number. This results in the ratios $F_i/L_j = .72$, $L_i/F_j = .854$, and $F_i/F_{i+2} = L_i/L_{i+2} = .382$.

The important ratio of a Fibonacci number to its following entry can be represented by the ratio of successive numbers (1/2, 2/3, 3/5, 5/8, 8/13, 13/21, 21/144, . . .). When expressed in decimal, these ratios approach the number .618 in a convergent oscillating series (1.000, .500, .667, .625, .615, .619, . . .). These ratios, the key Fibonacci-Lucas ratios, and the alternate entry ratios, represent the potential resistance levels (in terms of percentage) for price adjustments within a well-defined move. For example, a price advance of $1.00 in silver to $5.00 might correct 100%, 50%, or 62%, to $4.00, $4.50, or $4.38, respectively, according to the most important ratios.

Trading Elliott

Elliott also knew that there was great variability in this adherence to waves and ratios. The appearance of the waves is not regular in either length or duration and should not be expected to continually increase as they develop, although the fifth wave is generally the longest. The waves must be identified by peaks only. Elliott introduced a channel into his theory to determine the direction of the wave being analyzed as well as to establish intermediate price objectives. Looking back at the diagram of the basic wave, note the channel drawn touching the peaks and bottoms of the bull move. For every two peaks, a channel can be drawn that will serve as a trendline for price objectives. This same technique is covered in detail in a later section of Chapter 12. A break of the lower trendline in the bull move will serve to tell when a correction has begun.

The Elliott Wave Theory is very intricate and should not be attempted without careful study of the original material, but some rules are presented here to help understand the nature of the method:

1. Identify a main trend.
2. Determine the current status of the main trend by locating the major peaks and bottoms that will form the five key waves.
3. Look for three wave corrections and five wave subtrends or extensions.
4. Draw trendlines to determine the direction.
5. Measure the length of the waves in days to determine its adherence to the Fibonacci-Lucas sequence; measure the size of reactions as compared with *FL* ratios.
6. Watch for reactions at points predicted by the *FL* sequence and corresponding to the patterns described by the five-wave main trend and three-wave correction.
7. Use the ratios, day counts, and trendlines as predictive devices to select price objectives.
8. Use the trendlines to determine changes of direction.

As can be seen below, much of this systematic identification of waves has been done using a computer.

The Supercycle

When the short-term patterns fail to fit the rules, the bigger formations are likely to work. This approach applies to all chart analysis, and Elliott's wave theory is not an exception. Shorter time periods include relatively more noise, which may be difficult to separate from the significant market movement. Robert Prechter, well known for his focus on Elliott, uses a *supercycle* to describe the fifth wave of the prolonged bull move, which is still intact in 1997 (see Figure 14-12), applying Fibonacci ratios to forecast targets and explain the past moves.[29]

When using a charting technique, it is best to look for markets that, in some time frame, conform to the type of patterns you are seeking. This is also true with Elliott, which requires that prices advance in proportion to the Fibonacci ratios. In the DJIA supercycle, shown in Figure 14-12,

---

[29] Robert R. Prechter, Jr., "Major sea change II," *Futures* (March 1996).

FIGURE 14-12   Price relationships in supercycle (V).

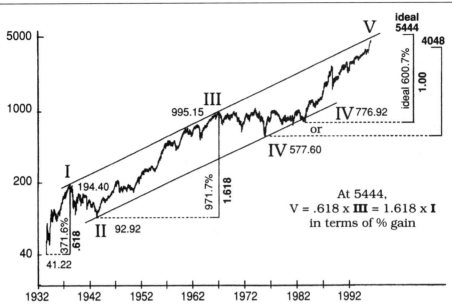

This chart includes the 1982 "orthodox" end-of-pattern low.

Source: Robert Prechter, Jr., *Futures* (March 1996). Copyrighted 1996 by Robert Prechter, Jr. Reprinted with permission of *Futures*.

1. Wave 1 begins at the 1932 low of 41.22, peaking in 1937 at the high of 194.40, a gain of 371.61%.
2. A wave 2 retracement follows.
3. Wave 3 starts in 1942 at the low of 92.29 and ends in 1966 at the high of 995.15, a gain of 970.975%. Note that when you divide the first gain by the second gain, 371.616/970.975, you get the classic Fibonacci ratio .3827.
4. The fifth wave should then follow the same pattern, and gain 600.692%. This target is found by solving for the value of wave 5, where

$$\text{wave } 1/\text{wave } 5 = \text{wave } 5/\text{wave } 3 = .618$$

This gain of 600% is based on the low of 776.92, and gives a target price of 5,444. Traders are cautioned that the high volatility and unusual extension of the current move is likely to cause very specific targets, such as this, to be violated by as much as 10%.

Automating Elliott's Wave Analysis

While analysts believe that there is substantial value in Elliott's method, it has been considered too subjective and cannot be evaluated with the rigorous historic testing that has become popular. Recent years, however, have shown that a talented analyst and much more computer power can combine to produce programs that can come close to a true version of what was once the exclusive domain of human interpretation. Elliott's wave theory has not been immune to this technology.[30]

---

[30] The content of this section is based on Murray A. Ruggiero, Jr., "Building the wave," *Futures* (April 1996). He credits Tom Joseph for the development of the computer software, which is the basis for the product, *Advanced GET.*

Murray Ruggiero has defined the trading opportunities for a basic Elliott wave pattern to be:

1. Enter wave 3 in the direction of the trend.
2. Stay out of the market during wave 4 (a retracement).
3. Enter wave 5 in the direction of the trend.
4. Take the countertrend trade at the top of wave 5.

When a wave appears in two time frames, such as both daily and weekly charts, the likelihood of the success of this formation increases. This concept is well accepted throughout technical analysis and can be found in many sections of this book, including Chapter 19 ("Multiple Time Frames"). Without confirmation of a pattern or trade, the risk increases.

The key to automating Elliott's technique is the creation of the *Elliott wave oscillator* (EWO). A series of extensions and pullbacks can be found using the EWO, combined with a method of counting waves that locates the current price within the standard Elliott wave pattern. The following steps present the bull move only, although the downside is treated as just the reverse set of rules.

1. Calculate the Elliott wave oscillator (EWO) as the difference between a 5-period and a 35-period simple moving average, applied to the average of the high and low prices,

```
mean = (high + low) / 2
EWO = @average(mean,5) - @average(mean,35)
```

2. A new upward trend begins when the EWO makes a new high for a period, n, determined by the user. This allows, for example, wave 3 to be identified when it goes above the high of wave 1.

3. A new upward trend also begins when the current value of EWO is below zero (the 5-day average is below the 35-day average), and the trend is down (Step 2), but the EWO has rallied by a percentage (called the *trigger*) of the lowest oscillator value of the past n periods (@lowest(EWO,n)). Then the trend is up if EWO is below zero, the previous trend value is down, and

```
EWO > trigger*@lowest(EWO,n)
```

This rule allows the next wave to be found based on the retracement that comes between each wave.

4. To relate this to Elliott, we must know where prices are located in the five-wave sequence. For an uptrend, this is done in the following order:

   a. When the trend turns from down to up we assume it is the beginning of wave 3 and save the current values of EWO and price.
   b. Continue to save the new high EWO value and new high price for wave 3.
   c. Wave 4 begins when EWO falls to zero.
   d. If wave 4 is currently active and the price is a 5-period high and EWO > 0, then wave 5 begins. Save the highest EWO value and highest price of wave 5 whenever they occur.
   e. If EWO in wave 5 becomes higher than the highest EWO value in wave 3, then we are still in wave 3. Label the current wave 5 values to indicate wave 3, and continue as in wave 3 with step b.
   f. If the trend turns from up to down in wave 5, then this is a *wave 3 down*. Reset all values and look for a new wave 3 up when step a is satisfied.

5. The trading rules needed are based on the values of n, the number of periods, and the trigger (the percentage retracement).

   a. Buy on open when wave 3 is first identified, whether on a new n-period high or a retracement of the previous downturn (step a).
   b. Buy on the open when wave 5 is first identified (step d).
   c. Buy on the open when wave 5 turns into wave 3 (step e).
   d. Close out any long position when EWO falls below zero.

With these rules, a long position is taken during the strongest parts of wave 3 and wave 5. As a guideline for selecting both the period and the trigger values, a test of the Deutschemark for 20 years from 1976 through 1995 showed robust results for periods n from 50 to 140 and for retracement trigger values of .70 or less.

```
{FUNCTION EWO}
{Find the Elliott Wave Oscillator (EWO)}
vars: mean(0);
mean = (high + low) / 2;
EWO = 0;
if @average(mean,35) <> 0 then EWO = @average(mean,5) - @average(mean,35);
{FUNCTION EWTREND}
{Find the trend using EWO}
inputs: period(numeric), trigger(numeric);
vars: trend(0), osc(0);

osc = EWO;
if osc = @highest(osc,period) and trend = 0 then trend = 1;
if osc = @lowest(osc, period) and trend = 0 then trend = -1;
if @lowest(osc,period) < 0 and trend = -1 and
        osc > -1*trigger*@lowest(osc,period) then trend = 1;
if @highest(osc,period) > 0 and trend = 1 and
        osc < -1*trigger*@highest(osc,period) then trend = -1;
EWTREND = trend;

{FUNCTION ELLIOTTWAVE}
{Find the current wave using EWTREND and EWO}
inputs: period(numeric), trigger(numeric)
vars: ET(0), mean(0), osc(0), wave(0), hiosc(-999), hiosc2(-999),hiprice(-999),
      hiprice2(-999);
osc = EWO;
mean = (high + low)/2;
{Is the current wave sequence up or down?}
ET = EWTREND(period,trigger);
{When the trend changes from down to up, label it wave 3 and save the current osc
and price}
if ET = 1 and ET[1] = -1 and osc > 0 then begin
        hiosc = osc;
        hiprice = mean;
        wave = 3;
        end;
{If wave 3 and the oscillator make new highs then save those values}
if wave = 3 then begin
        if mean > hiprice then hiprice = mean;
        if osc > hiosc then hiosc = osc;
{Test for the beginning of wave 4}
        if osc <= 0 and ET = 1 then wave = 4;
        end;
{Test for the beginning of wave 5}
if wave = 4 and mean = @highest(mean,5) and osc >= 0 then begin
        wave = 5;
        hiosc2 = osc;
```

```
        hiprice2 = mean;
        end;
if wave = 5 then begin
        if osc > hiosc2 then hiosc2 = osc;
        if mean > hiprice2 then hiprice2 = mean;
        end;
{Test for wave 5 becoming wave 3}
if wave = 5 and hiosc2 > hiosc and ET = 1 then begin
        wave = 3;
        hiosc = hiosc2;
        hiprice = hiprice2;
        hiosc2 = -999;
        hiprice2 = -999;
        end;
{Identify a wave 3 down while in wave 5}
if wave = 5 and ET = -1 then begin
        wave = 3;
        hiosc = -999;
        hiprice = -999;
        hiosc2 = -999;
        hiprice2 = -999;
        end;
{Return function value}
EWO = wave;
```

CONSTRUCTIONS USING THE FIBONACCI RATIO

Harahus shows interesting constructions using Fibonacci ratios; these are referred to as the *golden rectangle, golden triangle,* and *golden spiral.* Although there is no doubt of their importance, the application to markets can be complicated. As a behavioral model, any technique is subject to gross inaccuracy at times. In using a method as sophisticated as the Elliott Wave Theory, it is necessary to select situations that are representative examples of the phenomenon described by the *FL* sequence. Confirmation of such action can only be found by careful monitoring and development of an awareness of the nature of the price motion important to the system.

Harahus further introduced the regular pentagon as a tool for measuring corrections. This geometric figure has the property that any diagonal is 1.618 times the length of a side, exactly a Fibonacci ratio.

By constructing a regular pentagon so that the major trend falls along one diagonal (or one side), the other line connecting the corners of the pentagon will serve as support or resistance to price moves. In addition, the circumscribed and inscribed circle will serve as a measurement of support and/or resistance (Figure 14-13).

Harahus further extends the charting techniques of the Elliott Wave Theory using circles and arcs, a technique previously seen in measuring retracements. A circle drawn from the top or bottom of a wave, representing the 38%, 50%, or 62% levels serves as a convenient measurement of either elapsed time or a price adjustment, either of which could occur within the bounds of the rules. Prices are expected to meet resistance at any attempt to penetrate the key circles formed about either *A* or *B* in Figure 14-14.

The Elliott Wave Theory is highly regarded, although it is an odd combination of mathematics and chart interpretation bordering slightly on the mystic. Because it is primarily based on chart patterns it has been criticized as being too interpretive. The development of the fifth wave receives the most comment—sometimes it never develops; at other times, it must be extended into another subset of waves. In an analysis by Merrill, it is shown that the median stock market bull move has seven legs and the bear move has five legs; this may account for the need for the compound form of the Elliott wave. Those analysts who find

FIGURE 14-13 (*a*) Pentagon constructed from one diagonal. (*b*) Pentagon constructed from one side.

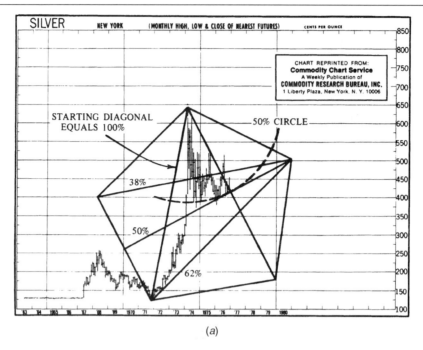

(*a*)

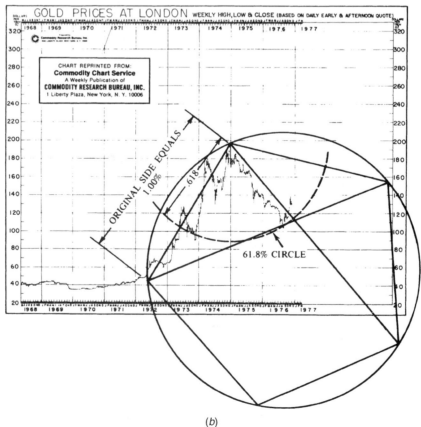

(*b*)

FIGURE 14-14   Using circles to find support and resistance.

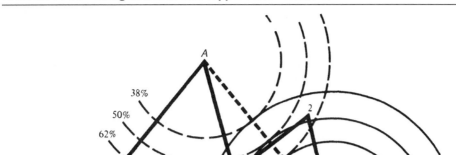

this study of interest should also read the works of W.D. Gann and Edson Gould, both of whom concentrated on mathematical approaches to charting.

Alternate Arc Measurement

In Chapter 12 ("Charting Systems"), it was noted that, for the purposes of finding retracement levels, Tom DeMark[31] identified the extent of a price move differently. In his approach, if the market is currently at a low, rather than judging the distance of this drop from the most recent swing high, he chooses to look for the highest point that has occurred since the last time the market traded at this low level. He then applies his choice of ratios to isolate key retracement levels. DeMark also uses this measurement from high to low to draw arcs identical to those shown in Figure 14-8 but limited to the Fibonacci ratio .618 and its complement .382.

FISCHER'S GOLDEN SECTION COMPASS SYSTEM

Although there are many systems that use the Fibonacci ratios, Fischer's *Golden Section Compass* (GSC) *System* is the only one based primarily on that concept.[32] The system is founded on the premise that human behavior reflects the Fibonacci ratios; the human decision-making process unconsciously selects points to act that appear to be the right time or the right price level. The behavior-based rules are combined with practical entry and stop-loss rules to eliminate those situations that do not properly develop.

Fischer is not alone in his observation of these patterns. Elliott, discussed in the previous sections, defined market cycles in five wave patterns with three wave corrections (Figure 14-15). In *Nature's Law*, Elliott shows the *complete* market cycle[33] as:

---

[31] Tom DeMark, "Retracing your steps," *Futures* (November 1995). Also see Chapter 2 of DeMark, *The New Science of Technical Analysis* (John Wiley & Sons, 1994).

[32] Robert Fischer, *The Golden Section Compass Seminar* (Fibonacci Trading, Ltd., Hamilton 5, Bermuda, 1984). Also see Robert Fischer, *Fibonacci Applications and Strategies for Traders* (John Wiley & Sons, 1993).

[33] Robert Fischer, *The Golden Section Compass Seminar* (Fibonacci Trading, 1984).

FIGURE 14-15   Elliott's complete wave cycle.

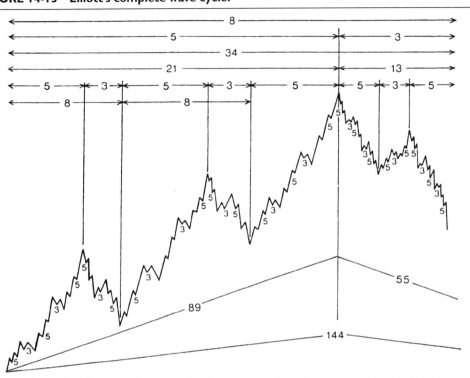

Source: Fischer, *Golden Section Compass Seminar* (1984, p. 28).

Number of	Bull Market	Bear Market	Total
Major waves	5	3	8 complete cycles
Intermediate waves	21	13	34 complete cycles
Minor waves	89	55	144 complete cycles

Time-Goal Days

The GSC System states that a new price direction will begin on, or shortly after, the day calculated as:

$$T_k = 1.618 \times (L_i - L_{i-1}) + L_i$$

or

$$T_{k+1} = 1.618 \times (H_i - H_{i-1}) + H_i$$

where L_i and H_i are the days on which lows and highs occurred, and L_i occurred before H_i.

For simplicity, an extreme may be used only twice—once as the first point and once as the second. Figure 14-16 shows the order in which the calculations occur. Time-goal day T_5 was calculated from lows L_3 and L_4 before time-goal day T_7 occurred. When more than one time-goal day occurs at the same point, or when the highs or lows that formed the time-goal days are more significant, the likelihood of a major reversal increases.

FIGURE 14-16 Calculation of time-goal days.

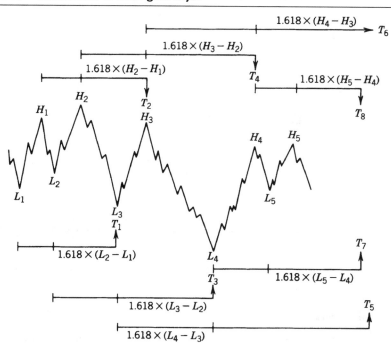

Specific entry signals occur on a 5-day price reversal. A long signal is given following a time-goal day when the closing price is higher than the high of the past 5 days. This is sufficient to identify a trend change and allows the stop-loss to be the recent low or a fixed point below the entry point.

Price Goals

Price objectives are determined using the same highs and lows. Elliott's wave theory is refined by Fischer, as shown in Figure 14-17. Once the low has been found, followed by wave 1, the price objectives for waves 3 and 5 can be calculated as a function of wave 1:

Wave 3 objective = $.618 \times$ (wave 1 − low) + low

Wave 5 objective = $1.618 \times$ (wave 1 − low) + low

The pullbacks to points 2 and 4 are not determined in this calculation, and the probability of the five-wave formation occurring is not confirmed unless the wave 3 objective is satisfied. Price goals are used for profit-taking rather than new entry points. The GSC System, however, does not require that markets move in five-wave patterns. Price objectives can be calculated from long-term lows as *1.618 × initial move up.* When price and time goals occur at the same point, there is greater reliance on the signal.[34]

In general, retracements from sustained moves can be expected to approximate or exceed 38.2% (1 − .618) of the initial move. Once a high-level objective has been reached and a reversal occurs, consistent profits may be taken using this goal. If prices fail to make

---

[34] Examples of time and price objectives can be found in Tucker J. Emmett, "Fibonacci Cycles," *Technical Analysis of Stocks & Commodities* (May 1983 and March/April 1984).

FIGURE 14-17   Price goals for standard five-wave moves.

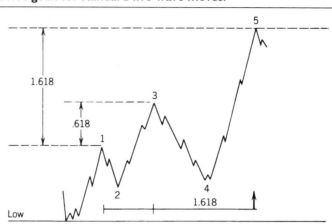

new highs following the first retracement, objectives for the next lower levels down can be set according to the inverted Elliott wave patterns, or *1.618 × initial downward move.*

Filtering Highs and Lows

The GSC System can be made to identify with more significant highs and lows by increasing the *selection filter.* For example, a sensitive system would select highs and lows in gold that are separated by a minimum swing of $10 per ounce. More significant points may be identified by swings of $20 per ounce. It can be demonstrated that a small filter will generate highs and lows that are produced by noise rather than significant behavioral actions. The system cannot be forced to produce more signals than the natural patterns allow.

The selection filter should be adjusted for market volatility. At higher price levels the noise also increases and will obscure the more important high and low points. Although Fischer only briefly touches on this, traders who apply this method should be prepared to adjust the selection filter from time to time.

W.D. GANN—TIME AND SPACE

The works of W.D. Gann cannot be explained with any thoroughness in a few words, but some of his main ideas have been selected and presented in this section. Gann was a pure technician using charts for all his analyses. His methods varied substantially from conventional charting techniques, but his philosophy was one of a professional trader: *Conserve your capital and wait for the right time.* Gann traded primarily grains for many years, and in his writings he attempted to summarize his most important observations; some of them are reminiscent of other well-known market lore.

Price moves are never exact. Gann was a believer in support and resistance lines, but expected some violation of the objectives because of *lost motion,* his way of accounting for the momentum that carries prices higher or lower than their likely goals. Nearly a cross between Elliott's *waves* and Angas's *cycles,* Gann classifies bull and bear moves into four *stages,* each one compared with a trending move and a subsequent reversal culminating in a major top or bottom. He observed that bull markets last longer than bear markets. He concluded that reversal patterns must reduce in magnitude as the move develops and persists. A similar argument is expressed in the *theory of contrary thinking.* Much of Gann's work is related in 1940 cents and requires an economic inflator close at hand to adjust prices to today's levels.

Gann's techniques combine mathematics and geometry with time and space; he finds duration as important as the size of the price change. One of his principles reflects the idea of a longer consolidation period resulting in a longer price move after a breakout. One popular approach to price objectives in bar charting is exactly this idea.

Time and Price

Gann proposed certain natural divisions for price swings expressed as percents. Zero and 100% are the most important of these. Based on behavioral awareness, he considered a potential resistance level at 100% of the original point of the move or 100% of the highest or lowest (the best guide) price of that market. In a reversal, 100% was a full retracement of the original move. The rationale for this theory is behavioral, as is his conclusion that most traders like even numbers; for this reason orders in grains are most often placed at 5 and 10¢ levels. Even now, traders will find more activity as prices attempt to cross whole number barriers, such as each 100 for the S&P, or each 1,000 for the DOW.

After the 100% level, decreased importance goes to increments of 50%, 25%, 12½%, and so on. For a grain, this would mean that major resistance could be expected at the even dollar levels with the next resistance at 50¢ intervals, then every 25¢, and so on; after a bull move of $1, the major support would be $1 lower, then 50¢, 25¢ and 75¢, and so on. The use of successive halving of intervals was also extended to time. A year is a full cycle of 360°, which makes one-half of a year equal to 26 weeks, one-quarter of a year 13 weeks, one-eighth of a year 45 days, and one-sixteenth of a year 22½ days. In cases of conflict, time always took precedence over price. The combination of a key price level (percentage move) occurring at a periodic time interval is the basis for much of Gann's work.

Geometric Angles

The most popular of Gann's methods is his use of geometric angles for relating price and time. By using square graph paper, it was not necessary to know the exact angle because the construction was based on the number of boxes up versus the number of boxes to the right. A 1×1 angle (45°) was drawn diagonally from the bottom of the lowest point of a price move through the intersection 1 box up and 1 box to the right. This is the primary bullish support line. A bearish resistance line is drawn down from left to right from the highest price using the 1×1 angle. The next most important angles in order of significance are 2×1, 4×1, and 8×1; for lower support areas there is also 1×2, 1×4, and 1×8. Places where the support and resistance lines cross are of special significance, indicating a major congestion area.

Figure 14-18 is taken from Gann's private papers and shows the use of geometric angles in an actual trading situation. Lines were first drawn where Gann expected a bottom, then redrawn. The initial upward move followed the primary 45° line; the second important support line, 1×2, met the primary downward line at the point of wide congestion at the center of the chart. The highest point on this congestion phase became the pivot point for the next 45° downward angle defining the next breakout. Traders have found the primary 1×1, or 45° line, an important tool for staying with the major trend. It is used to filter out small reversals in both standard charting techniques and point-and-figure.

Gann combined this method with a more remarkable technique, the *squaring of price and time.* It was fortunate to find a chart that complemented Figure 14-18, based on the lowest recorded cash price of soybeans, 44¢ per bushel. Figure 14-19 shows how Gann constructed this square, beginning with the lowest price at the center and moving one square to the right, circling counterclockwise and continuing the process. The basic geometric lines (horizontal, vertical, and diagonal) indicate the major support and resistance price levels; the most important one being 44, the junction of all lines.

FIGURE 14-18 Gann's soybean worksheet.

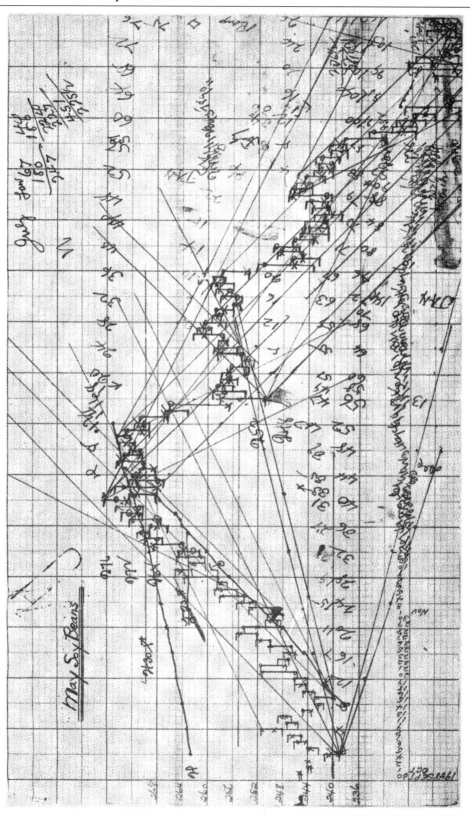

FIGURE 14-19　May soybean square.

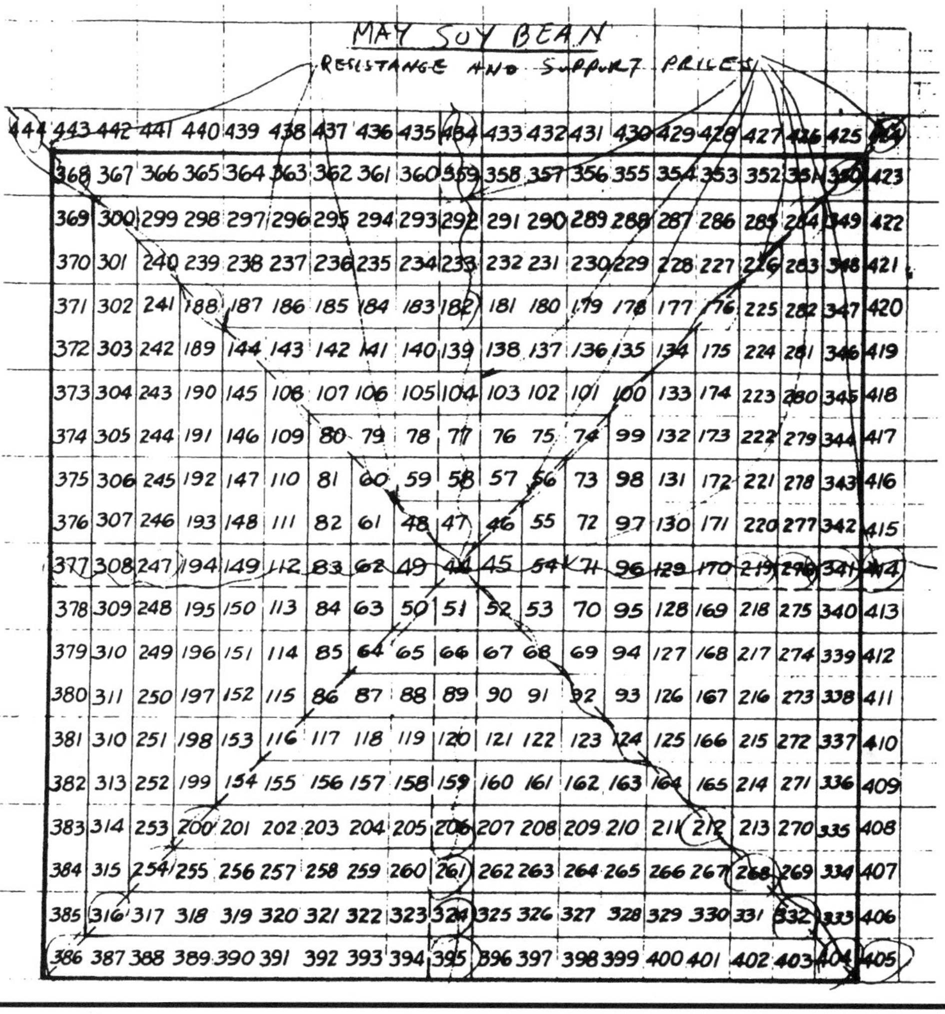

Relating the square to the price chart showing geometric lines, the first support level is seen to be exactly at 240 (upper left diagonal), the major resistance at 276 (right horizontal), the next minor support at 268 (lower right diagonal), congestion area support at 254 and 262 (1 box off), and back down to support at 240. Notice that the distance between the lines on the square becomes wider as prices increase, conforming to the notion of greater volatility at higher prices. It is also expected that soybeans at $10 will have some *lost motion* near these key support and resistance levels.

The Hexagon Chart

Gann generalized his squaring method to include both geometric angles and the main cyclic divisions of 360°. By combining these different behavioral concepts, the strongest levels of support and resistance are found where all three coincide. The generalized construction for this purpose is the *Master Calculator,* based on aligning the chart at a point representing a multiple of the lowest historic price for that market; crisscrossing angles will then designate support and resistance for the specific market. Other time charts of importance are the *Square of Twelve* (one corner of the Master Calculator), the *Hexagon Chart,* and the *Master Chart of 360°*. The Hexagon Chart can be used as an example of the combined effect.

As shown in Figure 14-20, the inner ring begins with six divisions, giving Gann the basis for the chart name. Each circle gains six additional numbers as it proceeds outward, which relates to the overall continuity of the construction. In using the hexagon, the degrees represent time and the numbers in the circle are price; a major support or resistance point exists when both time and price occur simultaneously.

For example, consider the 360° of the hexagon relating to the calendar year, or perhaps the crop year for grains. In his own work on grain, Gann equated 0° to March 20, near to the first day of spring when the sun crosses the equator going north. Then, the 45° line is on May 6, 90° on June 21 (the first day of summer), 180° on September 23 (fall), and 270° on December 21 (winter). These primary divisions also represent the most significant places for price support and resistance. The other lines represent secondary levels.

When looking at price and time together on the Hexagon Chart, the distance between the major degree lines becomes greater as prices increase showing the importance of

---

FIGURE 14-20   The Hexagon Chart.

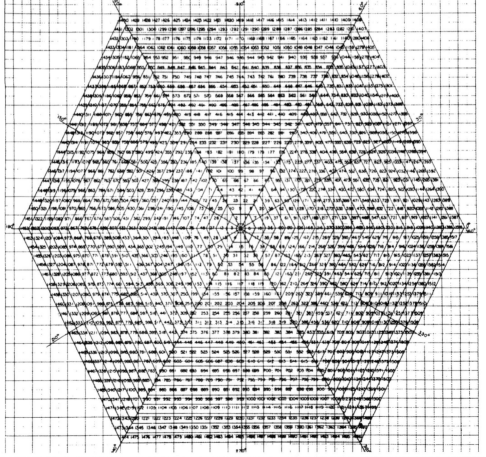

volatility. Using the price of November 77 soybeans, the chart shows that between 90° and 180°, or June 21 to September 23, 1977, the price of soybeans should have support at 567 and then move its major support level to 507 and its major resistance to 588 with next higher and lower support and resistance at 432 and 675, respectively. As it turned out, this was a very accurate prediction.

On many of Gann's charts there is notation showing planetary movement, not related to the cycles of seasonality, but what is believed to be the Jupiter-Saturn cycle, discussed in the next section. These techniques make Gann's work more difficult to reproduce than most methods; his tools are less conventional than others. If Gann were asked for a word of advice, there is no doubt that he would caution to patience, stating: *When price meets time, a change is imminent.*[35]

FINANCIAL ASTROLOGY

Astrology seeks a common bond in human behavior, similar to the work in biological rhythms and cycles. The impact of astrology on civilization has been great; observations of the periodicity of the moon is traced back 32,000 years. Star charts were known to have been in Egypt about 4200 B.C., and the earliest written ephemerides were in the seventh century B.C.[36] The pyramids at Giza are said to have sloping corridors leading from the faces to the interior that were used as sighting tubes for Egyptian astrologers for making accurate forecasts. The acceptance of astrology throughout history is widespread, including virtually all civilizations.

Even sophisticated analysts have been found to confuse astrology with the daily horoscope found in a local newspaper. *Astrology,* the interpretation of the effects of planets and stars on human affairs, is an art followed by a large portion of the world population and should not simply be discarded as mystical or occult. Interpretation of these effects can be complex and involves special skills. Most forecasts begin with a birth chart, which describes the position of the stars at the time of inception, then look at the current positions to identify the transitions. Over time, planets have taken on an association with specific raw goods, and constellations are associated with certain types of business; these relationships can now be verified using computer programs that check the intricate position of the planets with the financial statistics of companies to find a correlation. However, that task will be left for the more ambitious.

We must all agree that the positions of the planets and sun—those bodies with the largest gravitational pull on the Earth and each other—have clear physical effects. In the study of physics, this relationship is given as

$$\text{Force of attraction} = \frac{\text{Gravitational constant} \times \text{Mass}}{\text{Distance between centers}}$$

where the gravitational constant is 6.67×10^{-8}, the mass is found in Table 14-1, and the distance between the centers can also be calculated from Table 14-1.

Of these physical effects, the seasons and the tides are undeniable; and there is much more when you study astronomy, the science of motion of the stars and planets. In this section we will concentrate our attention on the physical phenomenon of planetary motion which can be identified and tested with the same confidence, and perhaps more, as other trading systems. Among these phenomena, eclipses and the lunar cycles are the most obvious, but there is one other combination that is important, the Jupiter-Saturn cycle.

---

[35] Computer software is available for calculating and plotting much of Gann's works. See "Ganntrader I," *Technical Analysis of Stocks & Commodities* (January/February 1984), or contact Gannsoft Publishing Co., 311 Benton St., Leavenworth, WA 98826, or Lambert-Gann, P.O. Box O, Pomeroy, WA 99347.

[36] Derek Parker and Julia Paricor, *The Compleat Astrologer* (McGraw-Hill, New York, 1971, p. 12).

The Jupiter-Saturn Cycle

Jupiter and Saturn combine to represent the overwhelmingly largest mass, other than the Sun, in our solar system (see Table 14-5). The two planets amount to about 95% of the total mass of all the planets and are about .7% of the mass of the Sun. Because they are in adjacent orbits, they have a very large gravitational pull on other planets when they are near one another, and very different effects when they move apart. They are so large that they cause the Sun to shift periodically based on their positions around the true center of mass of the solar system, called the *barycenter*. When Jupiter and Saturn are on opposite sides of the Sun, the center of mass is near the center of the Sun, but when the two large planets are together, the Sun is pulled away from this center. This positioning also has significant effects on the Earth's climate, which in turn affects agricultural production, supply and demand, and finally the economy.[37] The Greeks called the Jupiter-Saturn cycle "The Great Maker of Time," and it is said that every significant cycle in stocks, commodities, and interest rates is either a multiple or a harmonic or the Jupiter-Saturn cycle. The most well-known, the 59-year Kondratieff, is three times the Jupiter-Saturn cycle (3 × 19.859 = 59.577). Gann, who used a combination of time and price, based time expectations on seasonality and cycles. His work referred to a "Master Time Factor" that was never defined, but experts believe that the Jupiter-Saturn cycle satisfies his technique.

Charting the Saturn Line

Having decided that the movement of the largest planets affects the way markets move, you can create a *planetary envelope* based on Saturn's path with respect to the Dow Jones Industrials and find frequent concurrence. This requires converting the position of the planets into price.[38] When completed, this envelope is treated as support and resistance lines in a manner similar to the standard charting interpretation, in which penetration of a resistance line will become support; however, in appearance, the Saturn lines are curved to represent its cycle (see Figure 14-21).

---

[37] For a complete discussion of this topic, see Henry Weingarten, *Investing by the Stars* (McGraw-Hill, 1996). A section written by Richard Mogey, "Long Cycles and the Master Time Factor," is the basis for the next section.

[38] Jeanne Long, "Planetary Support and Resistance on the DJIA," *A Traders Astrological Almanac 1994* (Professional Astrology Service, 757 S.E. 17th St., Ft. Lauderdale, FL 33316).

TABLE 14-5   Size and Position of the Planets and Earth's Moon

	Equatorial Diameter (km)	Mass* (kg)	Distance from Sun (mil km)	Duration of Orbit (Earth years)
Sun	1,392,000	1.99×10^{30}	0	0
Mercury	4,880	3.34×10^{23}	57.9	0.24
Venus	12,102	4.87×10^{24}	108.0	0.62
Earth	12,756	5.98×10^{24}	149.6	1.00
Mars	6,794	7.35×10^{22}	227.9	1.86
Jupiter	142,800	8.39×10^{27}	778.3	11.86
Saturn	120,000	5.00×10^{27}	1,427	29.5
Uranus	52,000	3.77×10^{26}	2,870	84.
Neptune	47,500	3.29×10^{26}	4,497	165.
Pluto	2,500	5.98×10^{22}	5,893	248.
Earth's moon	3,476	7.34×10^{22}	384,400 km	0.075

* Note that *mass = volume × density* and, except for the Earth and the Earth's moon, the density of the planets can only be estimated.

FIGURE 14-21   Saturn lines drawn on the Dow Industrial.

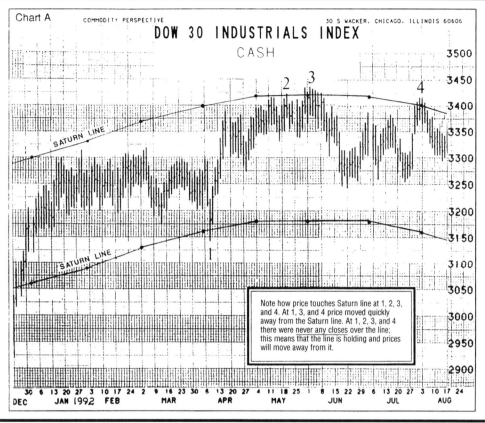

Source: Jeanne Long, *A Traders Astrological Almanac* (1994). Reprinted with permission from PAS, Inc. E-Mail: pas@bga.com Web Site: www.galacticinvestor.com.

Converting Planet Position to Price

Long transforms planetary position to price using two separate *wheels,* combined to form a *Universal Clock,* in a manner similar to W.D. Gann. Each wheel refers to a specific market. To create the Universal Clock for the DJIA, you begin above the right horizontal (at 3 o'clock) with the number 1 and move counterclockwise, placing 6 numbers per quarter and 24 for an entire cycle. You then move to the next outer circle and continue with the number 25 just outside the original number 1; therefore, each concentric circle contains the next 24 values, ending at 360 (a full cycle). The DJIA Clock is shown in Figure 14-22.

In the outer wheel of the clock, the DJIA is shown in increments of 10 points beginning at 1930 and continuing in circles of 24 values. Long does not explain the choice of the beginning price, but Gann uses a significant low, and astrologers tend to use the price at a key starting time, such as the beginning of a new Dow calculation, birth of an exchange, or transforming event.

To locate the planet on the time wheel, begin with the planet's position on a specific date. For example, on October 1, 1993, Saturn was at 24° (with respect to Aquarius) 14'. Aquarius falls between 300° and 330°; therefore, the position of Saturn is 300° + 24° + 14' = approximately 324°. By locating 324 on the inner part of the wheel, you can refer to the prices on the outer part of the wheel and find the two prices (each in adjacent circles) that

FIGURE 14-22   The DJIA Clock.

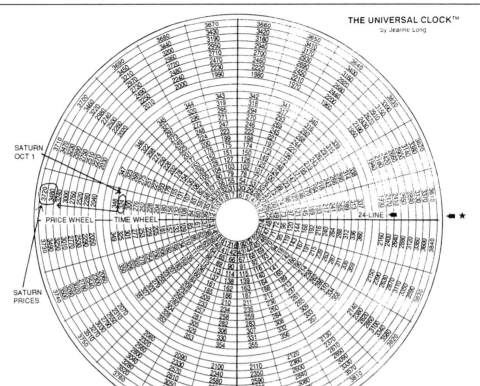

The price wheel of the DJIA

Source: Jeanne Long, *A Traders Astrological Almanac* (1994). Printed with permission from PAS, Inc. E-Mail: pas@bga.com Web Site: www.galacticinvestor.com.

span the current DJIA price. These values are the current support and resistance lines. New values are found monthly.

Major Physical Events

Of the major physical phenomena used in financial astrology, the most important are:

Solar eclipse—when the moon passes between the Earth and the Sun

Lunar eclipse—when the Earth passes between the moon and the Sun

Conjunction—when any two planets are on the same side of the Sun (and form a straight line with the Sun)

Opposition—when two planets are on opposite sides of the Sun (and form a straight line with the Sun)

The physical significance of an eclipse is said to be that it disrupts the flow of energy between two bodies by the interference of a third mass. In actuality, the gravitational forces of the two bodies are maximized when they are both on one side of the Earth, as in a solar eclipse, and minimized when they are on opposite sides, as in a lunar eclipse. Tables 14-6, 14-7, and 14-8 give the dates of the primary physical events for Jupiter and Saturn, lunar and solar eclipses, and new and full moon eclipses.

In astrology, the angles between planets are viewed from the position of the Earth; this is called a *geocentric system.* When a planet lies on the line between the Earth and Sun, it is in a *geocentric conjunction;* when it is aligned behind the Earth, it is in *geocentric opposition.* When a planet is at 90° to the Earth-Sun line, it is said to be *square.*[39] The angle that the planets form with the Earth-Sun line are called *aspects.* For the purposes of trading, squares are considered bearish while conjunctions and oppositions are bullish; however, there are other interpretations. Conjunction and opposition may not always conform to the strict definition of forming a straight line with the Sun, but may refer instead to close proximity. Both solar and lunar eclipses are conjunctions.

Trading on Aspects

Although the clearest physical phenomena combine the sun, moon, and largest planets when they are in conjunction and opposition, there are many other combinations of planetary positions that are considered important. It may also be necessary to follow a planet from the 90° to 270° position so that you track its effect on prices through the most extreme 180° path. The calculations for lunar and solar eclipses appear at the end of this chapter, but automatically calculating the aspect of combinations of planets would be beyond the ability of even the most computer-literate traders; commercial software is available for this level of detail and can calculate the number of occurrences that an aspect corresponds to a price move or price peak of a minimum size. The simplest method is to select days that represent swing highs or lows and record the major aspects. The larger the

[39] Hans Hannula, "Trading Planetary Eclipses," *Technical Analysis of Stocks & Commodities* (April 1992).

TABLE 14-6 Jupiter and Saturn Planet RX and Stations, 1996–2001*

	Jupiter (Retrograde)	Jupiter (Direct)	Saturn (Retrograde)	Saturn (Direct)
1996	May 4	Sep 3	Jul 18	Dec 3
1997	Jun 9	Oct 8	Aug 1	Dec 16
1998	Jul 18	Nov 13	Aug 15	Dec 29
1999	Aug 25	Dec 20	Aug 30	
2000	Sep 29		Sep 12	Jan 12 (Jupiter not in sequence)
2001	Nov 2	Jan 25	Jan 24, Sep 26	(Saturn not in sequence)
2002		Mar 1		Feb 8

Source: Weingarten, Investing by the Stars.

TABLE 14-7 Eclipses, 1996–2001*

	Lunar Eclipse	Solar Eclipse	Lunar Eclipse	Solar Eclipse
1996	Apr 4	Apr 17	Sep 27	Oct 12
1997	Mar 24	Mar 9	Sep 16	Sep 2
1998	Mar 13	Feb 26	Aug 8	Aug 22
	Sep 6			
1999	Jan 31	Feb 16	Jul 28	Aug 11
2000	Jan 21	Feb 5	Jul 16	Jul 1
		Jul 31		Dec 25
2001	Jan 9	Jun 21	Jul 5	Dec 14
	Dec 30			

Source: Weingarten, Investing by the Stars.

TABLE 14-8   New and Full Moons, Eclipses 1996–2001*

	New	Full	New	Full	New	Full	New	Full	New	Full	New	Full
1996		Jan 5	Jan 20	Feb 4	Feb 18	Mar 5	Mar 19	Apr 4	Apr 17	May 3	May 17	Jun 1
	Jun 16	Jul 1	Jul 15	Jul 30	Aug 14	Aug 28	Sep 12	Sep 27	Oct 12	Oct 26	Nov 11	Nov 25
	Dec 10	Dec 24										
1997	Jan 9	Jan 23	Feb 7	Feb 22	Mar 9	Mar 24	Apr 7	Apr 22	May 6	May 22	Jun 5	Jun 20
	Jul 4	Jul 20	Aug 3	Aug 18	Sep 1	Sep 16	Oct 1	Oct 16	Nov 14	Nov 30	Dec 14	Dec 19
1998		Jan 12	Jan 28	Feb 11	Feb 26	Mar 13	Mar 28	Apr 11	Apr 26	May 11	May 25	Jun 10
	Jun 24	Jul 9	Jul 23	Aug 8	Aug 22	Sep 9	Sep 20	Oct 5	Oct 20	Nov 4	Nov 19	Dec 3
	Dec 18											
1999		Jan 2	Jan 17	Jan 31	Feb 16	Mar 2	Mar 17	Mar 31	Apr 16	Apr 30	May 15	May 30
	Jun 13	Jun 28	Jul 13	Jul 28	Aug 11	Aug 26	Sep 9	Sep 25	Oct 9	Oct 24	Nov 23	Dec 7
	Dec 22											
2000	Jan 6	Jan 21	Feb 5	Feb 19	Mar 6	Mar 20	Apr 4	Apr 18	May 4	May 18	Jun 2	Jun 16
	Jul 1	Jul 31	Aug 15	Aug 29	Sep 13	Sep 27	Oct 13	Oct 27	Nov 11	Nov 25	Dec 11	Dec 25
2001		Jan 9	Jan 24	Feb 8	Feb 23	Mar 9	Mar 25	Apr 8	Apr 24	May 7	May 23	Jun 6
	Jun 21	Jul 5	Jul 20	Aug 4	Aug 19	Sep 2	Sep 17	Oct 2	Oct 16	Nov 1	Nov 15	Nov 30
	Dec 14	Dec 30										

*Source: Weingarten, *Investing by the Stars.*

swings, the more significant the results. By creating a table of key reversal levels, it may be possible to find those aspects that exert the greatest influence on the market. Once isolated, they may be used as a bias within a technical program.

The Moon: Buy Full, Sell New

It is known that the moon's effect on our planet is great—it is vitally connected with the movement of all fluids. The mass of the moon is about ⅛₁ that of the Earth and larger than the planet Pluto. It is remarkably large for a moon, with a diameter of 3,476 kilometers, 27% that of the Earth. Because of its large presence and close proximity to the Earth (about 230,000 miles), the moon is also believed to affect human behavior in strange ways, especially during a new or full moon.

In an experiment conducted on an arbitrary set of futures markets for the year 1972,[40] it was shown that short-term movements of prices react with some uniformity with respect to the phases of the moon. In fact, the markets chosen for observation—silver, wheat, cattle, cocoa, and sugar—showed an uncanny ability to form a rising market following a full moon and a falling market after a new moon.

To find the phases of the moon, you can refer to a number of books or any calendar; however, to perform any lengthy study of the moon's effect on prices, the moon's phases should be computerized. An *Easy Language* function that gives the dates of the new and full moon follow.

Calculation of a New Moon, Full Moon, Solar and Lunar Eclipse

Although a highly accurate calculation of planetary positions and eclipses requires consideration of many minor items, a good approximation can be found with far less difficulty.[41]

---

[40] Todd Lofton, "Moonlight Sonata," *Commodities* (July 1974).

[41] Jean Meeus, *Astonomical Algorithms* (Willmann-Bell, Inc., P.O. Box 35025, Richmond, VA 23235, 1991, Chapter 52). A shorter version appears in another volume, *Astronomical Formulae for Calculators, Fourth Ed.* (1988). For complete accuracy, the author refers readers to the *Astronomical Almanac,* or the *Canon* by Mucke and Meeus. The material in this section combines both versions of Meeus's work.

To calculate the exact time of the eclipses, it is first necessary to find the time of the new and full moons. The resulting times are expressed in Julian Ephemeris Days (JDE), also called *dynamic time* (DT).

Lunar Phases

The new and full moons are simply two of the four lunar phases, measuring when the excess of the apparent longitude of the moon over the apparent longitude of the Sun is $0°$, $90°$, $180°$, and $270°$. The times of these phases are given by the Julian date:

1. $JDE = 2451550.09765 + 29.530588853k + 0.0001337T^2$
$- 0.000000150T^3 + 0.00000000073T^4$

   where an integer value of k gives the new moon (i.e., 1, 2, 3, . . .), and an integer value increased by .25, .50, or .75 (e.g., 1.25, 1.50, 1.75) gives the three quarters, respectively. The value $k = 0$ corresponds to the new moon of January 6, 2000. Negative values indicate times prior to the year 2000. T is the time in Julian centuries since 2000, found by $T = k/1236.85$.

   To check your results, k is approximately equal to $(year - 2000) \times 12.3685$ and the year is expressed in decimal (e.g., the end of March 1997 is 1987.25)

   Using this formula, we can get a list of dates for the full moon from about 1995 through the year 2000 (approximately 62) by creating an array called JDE and finding the 62 dates of the new and full moons ending at the year 2000 using the *TradeStation* code as shown in Figure 14-23.

   For each value of k in the previous program, corrections must be made to find the exact time of maximum solar or lunar eclipse using the following values:

2. Eccentricity of the Earth's orbit around the Sun:

   $E = 1 - 0.002516T - 0.0000074T^2$

3. The Sun's mean anomaly at time JDE:

   $M = 2.5534 + 29.10535669k - 0.0000218T^2 - 0.000000011T^3$

FIGURE 14-23 *TradeStation* function to calculate the moon's phases.

```
{MOONPHASES
 Returns the mean phases of the moon, corrected for the sun's aberration}
     VARS: k(0), t(0), next(0), i(0);
     ARRAY fullmoon[62](0), newmoon[62](0);
     next = -62;
     for i = 1 to 62 begin
             k = 2000 + next; {newmoons relative to the year 2000}
             T = k / 1236.85; {time in Julian centuries}
             newmoon[i] = 2452550.09765 + 29.530588853*k
                 + 0.0001337*@power(T,2);
                 -0.000000150*@power(T,3) + 0.00000000073*@power(T,4);
             k = 2000 + next + .5; {full moons relative to the year 2000}
             T = k / 1236.85;
             fullmoon[i] = 2452550.09765 + 29.530588853*k
                 + 0.0001337*@power(T,2)
                 -0.000000150*@power(T,3) + 0.00000000073*@power(T,4);
             next = next + 1;
             end;
```

4. The moon's mean anomaly:

$$M' = 201.5643 + 385.81693528k + 0.0107438T^2$$

$$+ 0.00001239T^3 - 0.000000058T^4$$

5. The moon's argument of latitude:

$$F = 160.7108 + 390.67050274k - 0.0016341T^2$$

$$- 0.00000227T^3 + 0.000000011T^4$$

6. The ascending node of the lunar orbit:

$$\Omega \text{ (Omega)} = 124.7746 - 1.56375580k + 0.0020691T^2 + 0.00000215T^3$$

7. The eccentricity of the Earth's orbit around the Sun:

$$E = 1 - 0.002516T - 0.0000074T^2$$

8. The following calculation, based on F and Ω, gives the basis for the solar or lunar eclipse; and if F differs from $0°$, $180°$, or $360°$ by less than $13°.9$ then an eclipse is certain. If F is more than $21°$ from these phases, there is no eclipse. If F falls between these values then there is no eclipse if $|\sin F| > .36$.

The next components needed for corrections are:

$$F_1 = F - 0°.02665 \sin \Omega$$

$$A_1 = 299°.77 + 0°.107408k - 0.009173T^2$$

9. Then to find the exact time of the full solar (or lunar) eclipse, the following corrections (in days) should be added to the time of the mean conjunction given by JDE in the first formula above (smaller quantities have been omitted):

Time of maximum eclipse

$$= \text{JDE} + (\textit{lunar} \text{ or } \textit{solar} \text{ component below})$$

$$+ 0.0161 \sin 2M' - 0.0097 \sin 2F_1 + 0.0073 \times E \times \sin (M' - M)$$

$$- 0.0050 \times E \times \sin (M' + M) - 0.0023 \sin (M' - 2F_1) + 0.0021 \times E \times \sin 2M$$

$$+ 0.0012 \sin (M' + 2F_1) + 0.0006 \times E \times \sin (2M' + M) - 0.0004 \sin 3M'$$

$$- 0.0003 \times E \times \sin (M + 2F_1) + 0.0003 \sin A_1 - 0.0002 \times E \times \sin (M - 2F_1)$$

$$- 0.0002 \times E \times \sin (2M' - M) - 0.0002\Omega$$

$\textit{solar}$ component $= -0.4075 \sin M' + 0.1721 \times E \times \sin M$
$\textit{lunar}$ component $= -0.4065 \sin M' + 0.1727 \times E \times \sin M$

10. $P = 0.2070 \times E \times \sin M + 0.0024 \times E \times \sin 2M - 0.0392 \sin M' + 0.0116 \sin 2M'$
$- 0.0073 \times E \times \sin (M' + M) - 0.0067 \times E \times \sin (M' - M) + 0.0118 \sin 2F_1$

11. $Q = +5.2207 - 0.0048 \times E \times \cos M + 0.0020 \times E \times \cos 2M - 0.3399 \cos M'$
$- 0.0060 \times E \times \cos (M' + M) + 0.0041 \times E \times \cos (M' - M)$

12. $W = |\cos F_1|$

13. $\gamma \text{ (gamma)} = (P \cos F_1 + Q \sin F_1) \times (1 - 0.0048W)$

14. $u = 0.0059 + 0.0046 \cos M - 0.0182 \cos M' + 0.0004 \cos 2M' - 0.0005 \cos (M + M')$

Solar Eclipses

For a solar eclipse, γ represents the shortest distance from the axis of the moon's shadow to the center of the Earth in units of the equatorial radius of the Earth (the distance from the center to the surface of the Earth at the equator). Its value is positive if the axis of the shadow is passing north of the Earth's center, and negative if it is passing south. When γ is less than +.9972 and greater than −.9972, the solar eclipse is *central;* that is, there is a line of central eclipse on the surface of the Earth (see Figure 14-24).

The value u gives the radius of the moon's umbral cone on the fundamental plane, which passes through the center of the Earth perpendicular to the axis of the moon's shadow (in units of Earth's equatorial radius). The radius of the penumbral cone in the fundamental plane is $u + .5460$.

Based on these values, the following situations exist:

$\lvert \gamma \rvert$ is between 0.9972 and $1.5432 + u$	The eclipse is not central.
$\lvert \gamma \rvert$ is between 0.9972 and 1.0260	Part of the eclipse may touch the polar regions.
$0.9972 < \lvert \gamma \rvert < 0.9972 + \lvert u \rvert$	The combination of a noncentral total or annular eclipse.
$\lvert \gamma \rvert > 1.5432 + u$	No eclipse is visible from the Earth's surface.

For a central eclipse,

$u < 0$	The eclipse is total.
$u > 0.0047$	The eclipse is annular.
$0 < u < 0.0047$	The eclipse is either annular or annular-total.

To remove the ambiguity of this last situation, calculate

$$\omega = 0.00464 \cos W, \quad \text{where } \sin W = \gamma$$

If $u < \omega$ then the eclipse is annular-total; otherwise, it is annular.

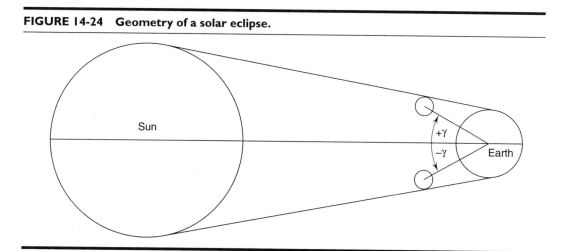

FIGURE 14-24 Geometry of a solar eclipse.

The greatest magnitude for a partial solar eclipse is reached at the point on the Earth's surface that comes closest to the axis of the shadow at

$$\text{Greatest magnitude of solar eclipse} = \frac{1.5433 + u - |\gamma|}{0.5461 + 2u}$$

Lunar Eclipses

For a lunar eclipse, γ is the least distance for the center of the moon to the Earth's shadow (see Figure 14-25). The value γ is positive if the moon's center is passing north of the axis of the shadow, and negative if it is passing south. At the distance of the moon, the penumbra radius $\rho = 1.2847 + u$ and the umbra radius $\sigma = 0.7404 - u$. The magnitude of the lunar eclipse is

penumbral eclipses: $(1.5572 + u - |\gamma|) / 0.5450$

umbral eclipses: $(1.0129 - u - |\gamma|) / 0.5450$

If the magnitude is less than zero, there is no eclipse. The *semidurations* of the partial and total phases in the *umbra* are calculated as

$P = 1.0129 - u$

$T = 0.4679 - u$

$n = 0.5458 + 0.0400 \cos M'$

and the semidurations in minutes are

$$\text{partial phase} = \frac{60}{n} \sqrt{P^2 - \gamma^2}$$

$$\text{total phase} = \frac{60}{n} \sqrt{T^2 - \gamma^2}$$

Example: Solar eclipse of May 21, 1993:
The following values can be used to verify your calculations:

May 21 is the 141st day of the year, therefore

$k = 1993 + 141/365 = 1993.38$

$T = 1993.38/1236.85 = 1.6116.$

$\text{JDE} = 2449128.5894$

FIGURE 14-25   Geometry of a lunar eclipse.

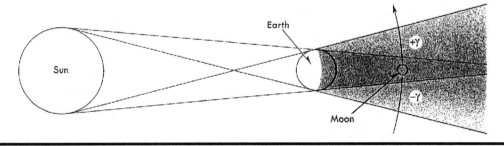

$M = 135°.9142$ $P = 0.1842$

$M' = 244°.5757$ $Q = 5.3589$

$F = 165°.7296$ $\gamma = 1.1348$

$\Omega = 253°.0026$ $u = 0.0097$

$F_1 = 165°.7551$

Because $180° - F$ is between $13°.9$ and $12°.0$ the eclipse is uncertain, and because $|\gamma|$ is between 0.9972 and $1.5433 + u = 1.553$, the eclipse is partial. By calculating the greatest magnitude of a solar eclipse, we get 0.740. Because F is near $180°$, the eclipse occurs near the moon's descending node, and because γ is positive, the eclipse is visible in the northern hemisphere of the Earth. By adding the corrections to JDE, the final time of maximum eclipse is 2449129.0979, which corresponds to May 21, 1993, at 14h21m0s TD. This differs from the exact value of 14h20m14s TD by less than 1 minute.

15

Pattern Recognition

Pattern recognition forms the basis for most trading systems. It is most obvious in traditional charting, which is entirely the identification of common formations; even moving averages attempt to isolate, using mathematical methods, what has been visually determined to be a trend. Traders have always looked for patterns in price movement. Because they were not equipped with computers, their conclusions are considered market lore rather than fact and are handed down from generation to generation as proverbs, such as "Up on Monday, down on Tuesday," "Locals even up on Fridays," and "Watch for key reversals." Because these three sayings have endured, they are candidates for analysis later in this chapter.[1]

The earliest technical systems based on patterns were of the form: "If after a sharp rise the market fails to advance for 3 days, then sell." As computers became more powerful, more complex approaches could be taken. For example, by observing the closing prices starting on an arbitrary day, *all* patterns of higher and lower closes can be recorded to find their tendency to repeat. A computer is well-equipped to perform this task. First, the 2- and 3-day patterns are eliminated because the recurrence of up-down or down-up and the equivalent 3-day patterns would be too frequent to be meaningful. Then, the closing prices are scanned for occurrences of predefined patterns. For example, if an up-up-down-up-down-up is to be matched, every six consecutive prices must be tested. From a table of occurrences we can conclude that these patterns can be predicted in advance or that they are leading indicators of other price moves. This approach, as well as the combination of events used to forecast profitable situations, are discussed later in this chapter.

Pattern recognition may appear to be more of a game than a business, but it is a source of many valuable ideas. Figure 15-1, a graph of the New York Stock Exchange (1854–1959), shows the simplification of patterns to the point where it is difficult not to count the recurrences of the more obvious patterns and look for the formations that precede them to see whether they could be predictive. For example, in 1922, 1924, and 1927, there were sharp advances in the market; the years preceding those showed an identical U pattern. It would be interesting to see whether another occurrence of a symmetric U was followed by a similar rise. Another pattern that stands out is that of two consecutive years of sharp rise, 1862–1863, 1908–1909, 1918–1919, and 1927–1928; in no case was there a third consecutive year, but neither the preceding nor following years seem consistent.

Patterns frequently provide the foundation for a trading method or the justification for beginning work in the development of a method. They have been applied in many ways to price analysis, from the time of day to place an order to the compound relationship of price, volume, and open interest. Daily trading opportunities may be a function of patterns based on the strength or weakness of the daily opening price. These are discussed in the next section. Weekly and weekend traits are studied, as well as types of reversals and their effects. These techniques can be considered complementary when used sequentially, or they can confirm the results of another test when used together. The end of this chapter discusses more general issues in pattern recognition.

---

[1] The only other known work that concerns similar patterns, although for the stock market, is by Arthur A. Merrill, *Behavior of Prices on Wall Street* (Analysis Press, Chappaqua, NY, 1966).

FIGURE 15-1 Graph of the New York Stock market.

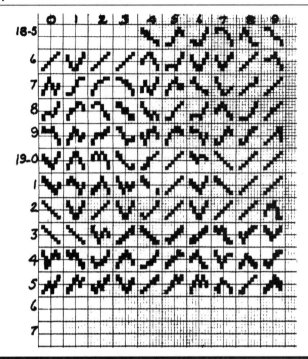

PROJECTING DAILY HIGHS AND LOWS

Statisticians claim that the best forecast of tomorrow's price is today's price; they state that no one has been able to reliably account for all the factors that would be needed to accurately project the changes that result in the high and low prices for tomorrow. Nevertheless, many traders project these values and seem to use them with success.

Pivot Technique

The simplest approach to projecting tomorrow's highs and lows is to base those figures on the average price of today plus or minus a value that somehow relies on the current trading range, or volatility. One technique, based on a pivot point,[2] projects two levels of support and resistance:

Pivot point	$P = (H + L + C)/2$
Resistance 1	$R1 = 2 \times P - L$
Support 1	$S1 = 2 \times P - H$
Resistance 2	$R2 = (P - S1) + R1$
Support 2	$S2 = P - (R1 - S1)$

DeMark's Projected Ranges

Another author and trader, Tom DeMark,[3] has based his projections on the positioning of today's opening price relative to yesterday's closing price, which gives him added timely

[2] Mark Etzkorn, "All in a day's work," *Futures* (January 95). This technique is attributed to William Greenspan.

[3] Tom DeMark, *The New Science of Technical Analysis* (John Wiley & Sons, New York, 1994).

information. If today's open is higher than the previous close, the projections are biased upward; if lower than the close, they are biased downward.

1. If today's close is below today's open, then
   Tomorrow's projected high = $(H + C + 2 \times L)/2 - L$
   Tomorrow's projected low = $(H + C + 2 \times L)/2 - H$
2. If today's close is above today's open, then
   Tomorrow's projected high = $(2 \times H + L + C)/2 - L$
   Tomorrow's projected low = $(2 \times H + L + C)/2 - H$
3. If today's close is the same as today's open, then
   Tomorrow's projected high = $(H + L + 2 \times C)/2 - L$
   Tomorrow's projected low = $(H + L + 2 \times C)/2 - H$

Once the basic formula is determined, biasing tomorrow's projection in the direction of today's close relative to today's open, then the projected high is found by removing two units of the low price, and the projected low is found by removing two units of the high price from the formula. This effectively shifts the projection in the direction of the new high by one-half the difference of today's close and today's low, $(C - L)/2$, and the new low by one-half the difference of today's close and today's high, $(H - C)/2$.

Comparing the Two Ranges

Because the two methods, the pivot point technique and projected ranges, use the same basic prices, combining them with simple multiples, it is not clear whether the results give values that are the same or different. For example, if the Deutschemark had a high, low, and close of 6600, 6450 and 6500, the first pivot method would give a projected first resistance level (high) of $2 \times (6600 + 6450 + 6500)/3 - 6450 = 6583$. DeMark's projected high is different based on how today's opening price relates to the previous close. If the open is lower than the previous close, we get $(6600 + 6500 + 2 \times 6450)/2 - 6450 = 6550$; if the open is higher, we have $(2 \times 6600 + 6450 + 6500)/2 - 6450 = 6625$; and if the open is about the same as the previous close, then the projected high is $(6600 + 6450 + 2 \times 6500)/2 - 6450 = 6575$. It seems reasonable that the pivot point method returns a value close to DeMark's neutral case, when the market opens unchanged from the previous close.

TIME OF DAY

Market participants, especially floor traders, are the cause of periodic movement during the day. Angas called these the "tides of the daily prices." Over the years, the great increase in participants has added liquidity to each pit but has not altered the intraday time patterns.

There are a number of reasons for the regular movement of prices. Because most of the daily volume is the result of day trades, those positions entered in the morning will be closed out by the afternoon to avoid the need for the margin required of positions held overnight. Orders that originate off the floor are the result of overnight analysis and are executed at the open. Scalpers and floor traders who hold trades for only a few minutes frequently have a midmorning coffee break together; this natural phenomenon causes liquidity to decline and may result in a temporary price reversal. All traders develop habits of trading at particular times. Some prefer the opening, others 10 minutes after the open. Large funds and managed accounts will have a specific procedure for entering the market, such as using close-only orders.

A day trader must watch certain key times. The opening moments of trading are normally used to assess the situation. A floor trader will sell a strong open and buy a weak one; this means the trade must be *evened-up* later and thus reinforces the opening direction. On a strong open without a downward reaction, all local selling is absorbed by the market and later attempts of the locals to liquidate will hold prices up. In any event, floor trades can be expected to take the opposite position to the opening direction, usually causing a reversal early in the session.

Tubbs' Stock Market Correspondence Lessons, Chapter 13, explains the dominant patterns in the stock market (given a 10:00 A.M.–to–3:00 P.M. session).

1. If a rally after the open has returned to the opening price by 1:00, the day is expected to close weaker.
2. If the market is strong from 11:00 to 12:00, it will continue from 12:00 to 1:00.
3. If a reversal from 1:00 to 1:30 finds support at 1:30, it will close strong.
4. If the market has been bullish until 2:00, it will probably continue until the close and into the next day.
5. A rally that continues for 2 or 3 days as in (4) will most likely end on an 11:00 reversal.
6. In general, a late afternoon reaction down after a strong day shows a pending reversal.

Putting these together, the following patterns (among others) can be expected:

1. A strong open with a reversal at 11:00 not reaching the opening price, then strength from 11:00 to 1:00, a short reversal until 1:30, and then a strong close; according to (5), another strong open the following day.
2. A strong open that reverses by 11:00, continuing lower until 1:00, reverses again until 1:30, and then closes weak.

Merrill's work shows the hourly pattern of the stock market in Table 15-1. The grid clearly indicates a bullish bias with 1963 the most obvious. The pattern is uniform and similar to what would be expected: early trending, an adjustment, then a wave of down-up-down. Contrary to commodities, these 4 years show extremely consistent strength on the opening with a sell-off on the close. Commodity prices may have regular patterns, but these patterns will occur with downward moves as well as upward ones. It is just as likely to see an opening sell-off with a rally on the close.

For commodities, the patterns are similar but may be compacted, as in the case of agricultural products, due to shorter, earlier hours (9:30 A.M. to 1:15 P.M. for most Chicago grains and livestock), or shifted as with currencies that open earlier. Knowing the daily time patterns would not only help a day trader but would also aid any speculator to enter an order at a better place. Figure 15-2 shows the time pattern for the Chicago Mercantile Exchange live cattle contract (open from 9:05 A.M. to 12:45 P.M.). Seventy-six consecutive trading days were tabulated for the June 75 contract from February 1 through May 31, 1975, an active period for cattle. The left scale of the chart shows the frequency of occurrences and the bottom shows the time of day. A line appearing in the top half of the chart indicates price movement in the direction of the opening price (from the prior close); the lower half shows a reversal trend. Measurements were first taken every 5 minutes and later every 15 minutes, due to a more variable price direction near the open.

TABLE 15-1 Merrill's Hourly Stock Market Patterns

	Time during Trading Session					
	10:00	11:00	12:00	1:00	2:00	3:00
1962	−	+	−	−	+	−
1963	+	+	+	+	+	−
1964	+	+	−	−	+	−
1965	+	+	−	−	−	−

Figure 15-2 shows that follow-through in the direction of the opening price slows down immediately and by 9:30, 25 minutes after the open, the price direction has usually reversed. There is a subsequent steady change in direction back and forth throughout the day. This pattern is remarkably similar to Merrill's stock market observations.

By showing two consecutive days of cattle price movement, Table 15-2 demonstrates how the data was accumulated. Although the table actually used 5-minute intervals from 9:00 to 10:15 and then 15-minute intervals from 10:15 until the close at 12:45, Table 15-2 is summarized in half-hour increments. If Friday's closing price was 45.00, Monday's open of 45.15 was indicated by a "+" for absolute direction and an O for opening direction. Any half-hour interval showing a price rise was marked with the relational symbol O and a reversal with an X. Tuesday opened lower, but the opening direction is still given as an O. Every interval that followed with lower prices is in the opening direction and is marked O. Adding the 76 test days together resulted in the scores shown in Table 15-3.

Knowing the direction of the price movement does not mean that trading these intervals will be profitable. To evaluate the potential, it is necessary to know the approximate size of the price move; the interval can then be selected with the greatest potential for movement in the direction of the time-of-day pattern. By observing Figure 15-2, the intervals to study can be picked from the tops and bottoms of the cycles:

Selected Time Intervals

a. Opening to 9:20
b. 9:20 to 10:00
c. 10:00 to 11:00
d. 9:20 to 11:00
e. 9:20 to 12:00
f. 12:00 to closing

FIGURE 15-2   Intraday time patterns, June 75 cattle.

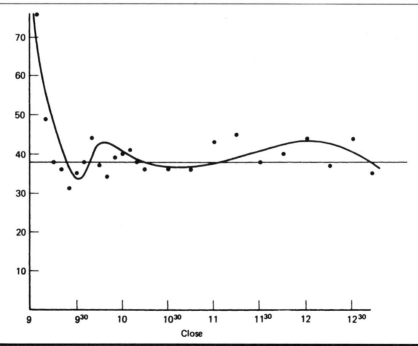

TABLE 15-2   Accumulating Time-of-Day Data

	Time	Price	Direction from Last	Direction from Open
		Monday		
9:05	(1)	45.15	+	O
9:30	(2)	45.25	+	O
10:00	(3)	45.10	−	X
10:30	(4)	45.05	−	X
11:00	(5)	45.20	+	O
11:30	(6)	45.30	+	O
12:00	(7)	45.40	+	O
12:30	(8)	45.30	−	X
		Tuesday		
9:05	(9)	45.25	−	O
9:30	(10)	45.35	+	X
10:00	(11)	45.45	+	X
10:30	(12)	45.40	−	O
11:00	(13)	45.50	+	X
11:30	(14)	45.40	−	O
12:00	(15)	45.20	−	O
12:30	(16)	45.05	−	O

For each interval, the average range from high to low (volatility) and the net result of this span (additive bias) were measured without considering the *relative direction* that was used to create the curve of time patterns. The results, shown in Table 15-4, indicate that the narrowest ranges, (b) and (c), were early in the day moving only a total of 14 points. The combined period (d) was 21.7 points, 50% greater than the individual periods (b) and (c). Figure 15-3 describes the likely combination of the intervals.

The results show a midmorning drift that nets a total of 4.6 points in the direction of the opening price, and a maximum potential profit of 21 points by entering a position between 9:20 and 10:00 and then liquidating between 10:00 and 11:00. During the test period, the magnitude of the cattle move did not appear worth the risk, but the same pattern might be profitably traded in a market with higher value per point.

When trying to find other market patterns, it might be best to observe only stronger or weaker openings. For example, a gap open of 5 to 20 points in cattle would indicate a potentially more volatile day allowing greater price reactions. More uniform results can be expected as seen in both the *reversal patterns* and *gap analysis,* which appear later in this

TABLE 15-3   Time Reversal Patterns*

9:05	76	9:35	38	10:05	35	11:15	31
9:10	27	9:40	32	10:10	38	11:30	38
9:15	38	9:45	39	10:15	40	11:45	36
9:20	40	9:50	42	10:30	40	12:00	32
9:25	45	9:55	37	10:45	40	12:15	39
9:30	41	10:00	36	11:00	33	12:30	32
						Close	41

*A more recent look at June 1976 cattle showed very similar results.

FIGURE 15-3   Cattle price ranges, 9:20–11:00 A.M.

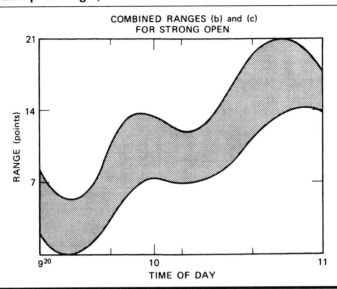

chapter. Restricting trading to days of higher volatility will reduce the trading opportunities but improve results.

Trading the Early Patterns

The best opportunity for trading against the trend would be 5 minutes after the open. The opening momentum that carries prices further in the opening direction can be used to advantage without waiting. After 20 or 30 minutes, the opening reversal should have occurred, and a trade may be entered in the same direction as the opening but at a more favorable price.

Relating the Opening Trade to the Prior Day

Another analysis performed on the time pattern chart was a correlation to determine whether the period from market open to 9:20 (15 minutes), related to the prior day's direction, could help predict the direction of the *tides* during the current day. The 15-minute interval was chosen as sufficient time to react to results and place an order. The two situations distinguished were the relationship of the first trade to the prior day's direction and the direction of the early trading, using the first 15 minutes. Because the same 76

TABLE 15-4   Summarized Time Data

Time	Average Volatility	Additive Bias	Points Moved in Direction of Open
a. Open–9:20	17.3	+4.9	+4.4
b. 9:20–10:00	14.3	+1.5	+.6
c. 10:00–11:00	14.2	+3.7	+3.9
d. 9:20–11:00	21.7	+5.3	+4.6
e. 9:20–12:00	25.8	+7.2	+3.3
f. 12:00–Close	19.6	+3.2	−1.2

days of cattle trading were used, it should be noted that the conclusions are based on a small sample. Even though they are believed to be valid, there should be some variation between these results and those based on a large sample.

Four cases were observed using the time intervals shown in Table 15-5. The percentages are calculated as the likelihood of movement in a specific direction relative to the conditions of the opening price and opening interval:

1. The opening price continued in the same direction as the prior day's open-to-close direction.
2. The opening 15-minute interval was consistent with the direction of the opening price as in (1).
3. The opening price and opening interval both continued the direction of the prior day.
4. The opening price and opening interval both continued opposite to the direction of the prior day.

Note that most of the intervals observed moved opposite to the opening price direction. This will support the more extensive work in the tables of reversal patterns and gap analysis. The two most extreme entries are the 39% in (1) and the 35% in (3). The first shows that by 9:20 there have been reversals 61% of the time, further supporting the previous conclusions. The second case, in (3), shows that an opening price and opening interval that continues in the direction of the prior close has reversed 65% of the time in the 10:00-to–11:00 A.M. interval.

Highs and Lows of the Day

In selecting a place to enter the market for a single-day trade, it would be a great advantage to know the time of day at which the highest or lowest price is likely to occur. To understand this, Figure 15-4 presents a combined tabulation of both the daily highs and lows positioned at the time they occurred. The pattern clearly indicates that the opening and closing ranges are most likely to be the highest or lowest price, with 11:00 as the only mid-day alternative. No attempt was made to determine whether a high at the open had a low at 11:00 or at the close, nor was any relative positioning of the high-low observed. Separate charts of only highs and only lows proved that there was no distinction in the patterns—highs were just as likely to occur at the three peaks as were lows.

There are simple ways in which this small piece of information could be of advantage. After the opening range has been formed, watch for the breakout of the range and assume the other direction is a high or low. In the example, the breakout will occur to the upside, and the bottom of the range will be considered the daily low. *Buy* the opening breakout

TABLE 15-5 Likelihood of Movement in the Same Direction as the Open

	Cases			
	(1)	*(2)*	*(3)*	*(4)*
Open–9:20	39%	—	—	—
9:20–10:00	52%	57%	58%	50%
10:00–11:00	43%	40%	35%	48%
9:00–11:00	45%	47%	43%	48%
9:20–12:00	43%	49%	43%	44%
12:00–Close	46%	53%	48%	42%

FIGURE 15-4   Combined occurrence of highs and lows.

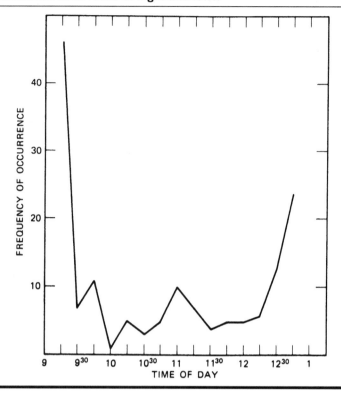

with a stop below the opening range. Look for the high of the day at 11:00. If there is a test of the highs at 11:00, liquidate the position assuming that the resistance will hold. If there is another upside breakout, buy again in anticipation of the highs of the day at the close. If no test of the highs occurs at 11:00, hold the position until the close; if support is broken, close out or reverse and expect the lows of the day at the close.

A Recent Look at the Timing of Intraday Highs and Lows

Since the timing of cattle was studied more than 20 years ago, we might expect the frequency of occurrence of highs and lows to have changed, but that is not so. The first 15 minutes of the day still account for a large percentage of the highs and lows, and the closing 15 minutes is the next most likely time, and somewhere around the middle of the day is the third most popular. But this is primarily a domestic market, compared with Eurodollars or the S&P 500, which attracts a significant world participation. In the case of currencies, most trading begins when the London markets open, at about 2:00 A.M., Chicago time, about 5 hours ahead of the CME's International Monetary Market open. By the time the United States makes its first trade, prices could have moved far from the previous U.S. settlement based on a half-day of business activity in Europe, and a gap opening simply puts U.S. prices in line with the rest of the world.

It should not be a surprise if price patterns have changed during the globalization of the past 10 years. With data more readily available, a selection of major markets could be sampled for 15-minute intervals and plotted to show the distribution of highs, lows, and the cumulative combination of highs and lows (see Figure 15-5) for the 3-year period from March 1992 through February 1994. The results are very similar although the markets are

FIGURE 15-5   Intraday distribution of highs and lows. (*a*) Eurodollars. (*b*) Japanese yen. (*c*) Deutschemarks. (*d*) U.S. Treasury bonds. (*e*) S&P 500. (*f*) Coffee.

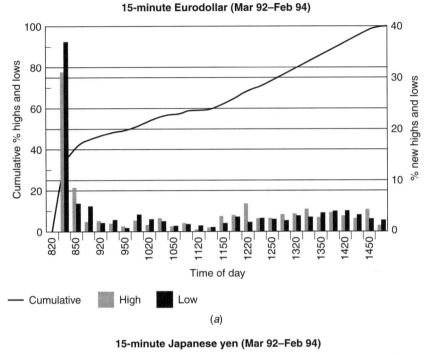

(*a*)

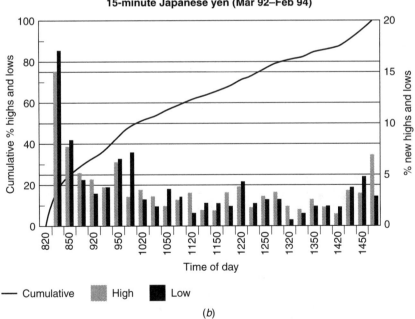

(*b*)

FIGURE 15-5 (*Continued*)

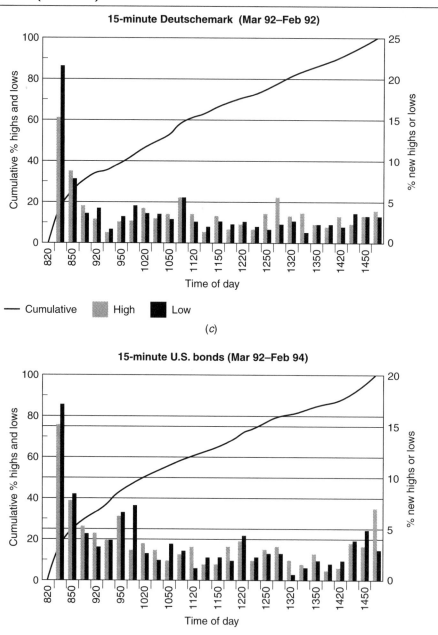

15-minute Deutschemark (Mar 92–Feb 92)

(*c*)

15-minute U.S. bonds (Mar 92–Feb 94)

(*d*)

quite different. They are also remarkably close to the pattern seen in 1976 cattle, except that the end of day is not as pronounced in the recent period.

In general, 25% to 40% of all highs and lows occur in the first 15 minutes of trading. Afterward, there seems to be an equal chance of a high or low occurring throughout the day. If we look closer, we can see a slightly larger increase just after 12:00 on most charts,

FIGURE 15-5 *(Continued)*

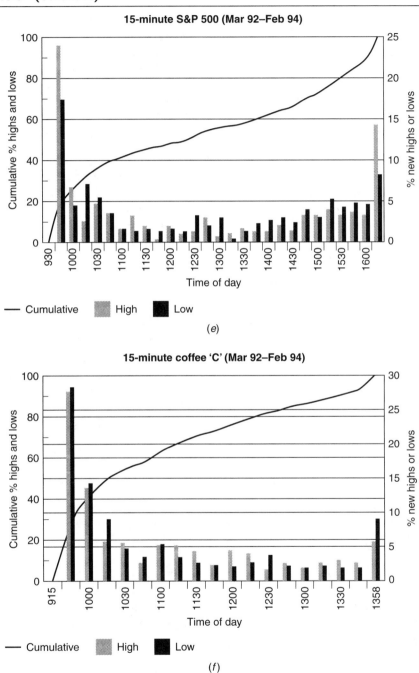

15-minute S&P 500 (Mar 92–Feb 94)

(e)

15-minute coffee 'C' (Mar 92–Feb 94)

(f)

and an additional increase in the frequency of highs and lows near the close. Eurodollars show the greatest chance of a high or a low occurring at the open, while coffee has the same 40% chance over the first 1 hour, 45 minutes of trading. The S&P futures makes 25% of its highs and lows in the last 1 hour, 15 minutes of trading, with 10% after the New York Stock Exchange closes at 3:00 P.M.

Trading Decisions

For markets such as the Deutschemark, which has a steady chance of posting a new high or low anytime after the first 15 minutes (remember that this interval includes any reaction to U.S. economic data that is released 10 minutes after the open), trading could be approached by deciding, after 15 minutes, whether the market has already made a high or a low for the day. For example, if an economic report indicates a weak dollar, and the price of the D-mark jumps 50 ticks, we could reasonably assume that we have seen the lows of the day. If prices make a new high during the next 15 minutes, we are even more likely to have seen the lows in the first 15 minutes. It is possible that we have seen both the lows and the highs, but it was the lows only that occurred at the most common time. If we assume that the high can occur anytime during the day, then buying sooner will give more opportunity to profit by the end of the day.

You can increase the confidence in your decision by waiting about 2 hours into the trading day, when most markets have a 50% chance of seeing a high or a low already established. While this may make it easier to identify the correct extreme, it reduces the opportunity for profit by the end of the trading day. A projection of volatility, which can be reasonably constant for many markets, could help decide whether there is enough opportunity to enter a trade.

OPENING GAPS AND INTRADAY PATTERNS

The daily price fluctuations and intraday patterns of a market may be related to the strength or weakness of the daily opening. A large *gap opening* implies greater volatility for the day, positions prices for a greater reaction, and may show more consistency in the subsequent intraday patterns than a market that opens nearly unchanged. A gap analysis was performed to study the combination of patterns that could be traded profitably. A strong open followed by a stronger close would allow a trader to buy on a pullback after the open, while a consistently weak close after a strong open would be an opportunity to set a short position. Specific entry timing can be improved by using the patterns discussed in the previous section.

The gap analyses for the six diverse markets shown in Table 15-6 are separated into two parts:

1. The position of the closing price following a gap opening.
    a. The close continued (extended the move) in the direction of the gap.
    b. The close was between the gap opening and the prior close.
    c. The close reversed the direction of the opening gap (that is, if the open was higher, the close was lower).
2. The type of trading range pattern that occurred.
    a. Prices crossed the prior closing price at least once during the trading session.
    b. Prices reversed from the open but did not cross the prior close.
    c. Prices continued in the direction of the open and never reversed.

In addition, a record is shown of the percentage of times that price *continued on the following open* in the same direction as the current gap.

Using the Deutschemark as an example, we see that the gaps ranged from +1.00 to −1.00 in IMM notation. The values in each of the columns, except for the far right column, are the percentage of occurrences based on the total cases, shown on the right. The number of cases show a typical price distribution, clustered near the smaller gaps, with an extended *tail* at the extremes. All gaps greater than +1.00 were included in the top row; all gaps less than −1.00 are included in the bottom row. The interesting patterns in the Deutschemark results are:

TABLE 15-6   Gap Analyses, January 1986–February 1996*

Gap	Closing Price			Trading Range			Cont Next Day	No. of Cases
	Cont Dir	Below Open	Rev Dir	Cross Prv Cls	Adj fr Open	Cont Only		
(a) Deutschemark								
1.000	60	40	0	0	100	0	50	10
0.900	60	40	0	0	100	0	40	5
0.800	64	27	9	18	73	9	36	11
0.700	58	38	4	8	88	4	58	26
0.600	64	24	6	6	91	3	48	33
0.500	58	34	5	15	82	2	37	62
0.400	54	30	15	28	65	6	58	102
0.300	55	23	16	34	61	5	50	173
0.200	45	20	28	58	37	4	48	285
0.100	51	5	38	81	10	6	45	448
0.000	0	0	0	0	0	0	0	79
−0.100	46	6	45	84	11	2	56	474
−0.200	44	21	33	63	32	2	52	339
−0.300	43	33	22	44	52	0	53	208
−0.400	45	41	8	21	77	1	51	103
−0.500	55	32	6	15	80	3	42	65
−0.600	43	45	13	18	78	5	45	40
−0.700	63	32	5	11	84	5	58	19
−0.800	70	20	10	10	80	10	50	10
−0.900	25	75	0	0	100	0	50	4
−1.000	47	53	0	6	88	6	53	17

Gap	Closing Price			Trading Range			Cont Next Day	No. of Cases
	Cont Dir	Below Open	Rev Dir	Cross Prv Cls	Adj fr Open	Cont Only		
(b) S&P 500								
5.000	58	37	5	16	84	0	53	19
4.500	20	40	40	60	40	0	20	5
4.000	57	14	14	43	57	0	43	7
3.500	55	45	0	18	82	0	36	11
3.000	44	22	33	33	56	0	11	9
2.500	59	29	12	29	71	0	59	17
2.000	42	27	31	56	44	0	52	85
1.500	57	18	21	58	36	6	57	150
1.000	51	10	36	78	16	5	47	311
0.500	51	4	43	90	5	3	45	481
0.000	0	0	0	0	0	0	0	185
−0.500	44	3	51	92	4	2	55	626
−1.000	46	10	41	76	18	3	51	300
−1.500	48	18	31	59	35	3	53	122
−2.000	45	23	31	55	34	9	55	74
−2.500	32	38	27	51	43	5	62	37
−3.000	35	35	30	50	35	15	45	20
−3.500	78	11	11	11	89	0	28	18
−4.000	13	38	50	63	25	13	50	8
−4.500	75	25	0	25	75	0	50	4
−5.000	46	21	25	42	42	17	50	24

* Values are shown as percentage of cases in each line category.

(continued)

TABLE 15-6 *(Continued)*

Gap	Closing Price			Trading Range			Cont Next Day	No. of Cases
	Cont Dir	Below Open	Rev Dir	Cross Prv Cls	Adj fr Open	Cont Only		
				*(c) U.S. Treasury bonds*				
1.250	54	46	0	8	85	8	38	13
1.125	0	100	0	0	100	0	100	2
1.000	50	17	33	50	33	17	67	6
0.875	40	30	20	40	60	0	30	10
0.750	29	24	47	71	24	6	47	17
0.625	53	29	18	35	65	0	53	17
0.500	35	29	32	65	29	6	47	34
0.375	43	25	26	70	21	4	46	84
0.250	50	12	34	69	20	6	55	235
0.125	52	2	38	86	4	6	53	724
0.000	0	0	0	0	0	0	0	321
−0.125	47	2	43	85	5	4	47	613
−0.250	51	8	37	75	14	8	49	245
−0.375	49	17	33	55	33	8	49	83
−0.500	36	33	28	61	36	0	53	36
−0.625	39	35	26	43	52	4	30	23
−0.750	30	50	20	30	70	0	50	10
−0.875	50	30	20	40	60	0	50	10
−1.000	67	17	17	33	67	0	42	12
−1.125	67	0	0	0	100	0	100	3
−1.250	30	60	10	10	90	0	60	10

Gap	Closing Price			Trading Range			Cont Next Day	No. of Cases
	Cont Dir	Below Open	Rev Dir	Cross Prv Cls	Adj fr Open	Cont Only		
				*(d) Heating oil*				
0.020	27	38	13	21	58	19	90	48
0.018	40	20	40	60	40	0	80	5
0.016	33	50	17	25	42	8	50	12
0.014	25	13	63	63	38	0	38	8
0.012	54	27	10	20	66	12	56	41
0.010	26	47	21	32	58	11	37	19
0.008	48	26	18	43	48	8	52	61
0.006	48	24	22	40	45	7	50	164
0.004	44	13	32	52	28	10	46	301
0.002	49	4	35	66	6	15	43	407
0.000	0	0	0	0	0	0	0	266
−0.002	41	3	40	78	4	4	55	462
−0.004	39	14	33	60	25	5	48	311
−0.006	41	28	24	46	41	4	55	184
−0.008	42	30	20	34	51	7	52	89
−0.010	50	29	17	29	63	4	42	24
−0.012	49	28	15	31	62	3	51	39
−0.014	50	50	0	13	75	13	63	8
−0.016	60	20	20	20	80	0	40	5
−0.018	67	0	33	33	67	0	0	3
−0.020	46	21	15	21	64	15	69	39

TABLE 15-6 *(Continued)*

Gap	Closing Price			Trading Range			Cont Next Day	No. of Cases
	Cont Dir	Below Open	Rev Dir	Cross Prv Cls	Adj fr Open	Cont Only		
				(e) Gold				
5.000	52	39	7	23	75	2	66	44
4.500	47	35	18	29	71	0	71	17
4.000	57	35	9	22	70	4	43	23
3.500	68	24	4	24	72	4	52	25
3.000	50	34	13	38	50	13	56	32
2.500	42	40	18	40	56	2	44	55
2.000	55	24	20	38	51	7	48	84
1.500	47	19	30	56	35	5	40	178
1.000	52	14	30	61	27	9	44	308
0.500	49	4	43	80	7	8	39	334
0.000	0	0	0	0	0	0	0	108
−0.500	41	3	48	92	4	1	52	358
−1.000	45	17	33	66	27	1	53	326
−1.500	42	29	25	53	41	3	49	197
−2.000	37	34	26	45	51	1	55	128
−2.500	31	52	14	37	57	1	41	86
−3.000	43	43	15	25	74	2	54	61
−3.500	38	43	17	38	55	2	64	42
−4.000	25	63	13	38	63	0	44	16
−4.500	44	39	17	28	72	0	61	18
−5.000	44	53	3	7	90	3	53	59

Gap	Closing Price			Trading Range			Cont Next Day	No. of Cases
	Cont Dir	Below Open	Rev Dir	Cross Prv Cls	Adj fr Open	Cont Only		
				(f) Soybeans				
10.000	37	30	14	23	60	17	59	70
9.000	63	19	13	25	63	13	56	16
8.000	41	35	24	41	41	18	41	17
7.000	53	29	18	35	41	12	41	17
6.000	52	18	25	34	52	14	48	44
5.000	52	15	27	38	47	13	53	60
4.000	52	25	20	49	40	8	42	103
3.000	48	22	25	64	24	8	46	158
2.000	44	9	40	72	16	7	45	295
1.000	53	2	39	86	2	7	49	347
0.000	0	0	0	0	0	0	0	192
−1.000	49	3	44	85	3	8	53	355
−2.000	50	9	35	71	14	9	50	359
−3.000	49	16	31	60	24	10	54	182
−4.000	53	23	21	49	36	12	46	103
−5.000	51	18	26	46	33	15	31	39
−6.000	53	28	19	50	31	14	33	36
−7.000	58	27	15	42	42	15	46	26
−8.000	35	59	6	29	59	6	35	17
−9.000	45	27	18	27	64	9	55	11
−10.000	62	17	13	19	59	22	57	63

1. "Cont Only" shows that the chance of the market continuing in the same direction, without a pullback, is extremely small; therefore, a market that gaps up and continues higher should be sold, expecting prices to fall below the open.
2. Except for sharply lower opens and quiet opens, there is a greater chance that the closing price will continue the direction of the opening gap and a relatively small chance that prices will reverse and close through the level of the prior closing price. This presents an opportunity to buy after a gap and a pullback. For example, a higher gap of 60 points has a 91% chance of a pullback, only a 6% chance of a closing reversal, and a 64% chance of a stronger close. A lower gap of 40 points has a 77% chance of a rally above the open, a small chance of a close above yesterday's close, but only an equal chance of a weak close for the day.
3. The most extreme gaps, both higher and lower, are always interesting. For the Deutschemark there seems to be no bias in the pattern over the past 10 years. None of the extreme moves shows a tendency to continue in a predictable direction, but none of them reversed on the close. This would indicate that extreme gaps do not mark the end of a move.

Some of the interesting features of the other markets in Table 15-6 are:

S&P 500

The percentage of time that S&P prices cross the previous closing price, or reverse direction on the close, indicates that it has much more noise than Deutschemarks and most other markets. A unique pattern of the S&P is that large upward gaps always trade lower while large downward gaps have occasions when prices just keep falling.

Treasury Bonds

This market, as with the S&P, has had an upward bias during the past 10 years; therefore, the symmetry of the patterns may be affected. For bonds it is interesting to view the small gap open, for example .125 equal to $\frac{4}{32}$. There is an 86% chance that prices will cross the prior close during trading, but a much smaller chance (38%) that prices will close lower. The 52% chance that prices will close above the open creates an opportunity for buying, provided risk can be controlled.

Heating Oil

Expressed in cents per gallon (.020 is 2 cents), this study shows a large number of extreme gaps exceeding 2 cents. When those gaps are higher there is a strong tendency to continue on the next open.

Soybeans

The extremes of soybeans, as with some other markets, show a tendency to continue the next day. Large gaps down are more likely to be consistently lower, while upward gaps are less consistent during the day.

Gap Study Program

The following Omega *Easy Language* program is easily converted to other programming languages. It can be used to evaluate gap opening of any market based on daily prices. The results are printed to a flat file called "gapout" stored in the Windows directory. Note that the results are given as the number of cases satisfying each condition rather than the percentages seen in Table 15-6. To print the percentages, simply multiple the value by 100 and divide by the number of total cases (`nitems`) in the print statement.

```
{SYSTEM: Gap Study}
{Copyright 1978-1998. PJ Kaufman. All rights reserved.}
      Inputs: gapincr(0), nbars(20);
      vars:   ix(0), n(0), n2(0), min(0), gap(0), ngap(0), middle(0);
      arrays: maxmin[50](0), ccont[50](0), cbelow[50](0), crev[50](0), trcross[50](0),
              tradj[50](0), trcont[50](0), ncont[50](0), nitems[50](0);
{Initialize increments}
        if currentbar <= 1 then begin
                n = nbars + 1;
                n2 = @intportion(n/2);
                middle = n2 + 1;
                min = -n2*gapincr;
                for ix = 1 to n begin
                        maxmin[ix] = min;
                        min = min + gapincr;
                        end;
                end;
{Process gap}
      if open <> close[1] then begin
              gap = (open - close[1])/gapincr;
              if gap > 0 then begin
                      ngap = @intportion(gap) + middle + 1;
                      if ngap > n then ngap = n;
                      end;
              if gap < 0 then begin
                      ngap = middle - 1 + @intportion(gap);{gap is negative}
                      if ngap < 1 then ngap = 1;
                      end;
              nitems[ngap] = nitems[ngap] + 1;
{Relative position of today's close}
                if (gap > 0 and close > open) or (gap < 0 and close < open) then
                        ccont[ngap] = ccont[ngap] + 1;
                if (gap > 0 and close > close[1] and close < open) or
                        (gap < 0 and close < close[1] and close > open) then
                        cbelow[ngap] = cbelow[ngap] + 1;
                if (gap > 0 and close < close[1]) or (gap < 0 and close > close[1]) then
                        crev[ngap] = crev[ngap] + 1;
{Pattern of entire trading range}
                if (gap > 0 and low < close[1]) or (gap < 0 and high > close[1]) then
                        trcross[ngap] = trcross[ngap] + 1;
                if (gap > 0 and low > close[1] and low < open) or
                        (gap < 0 and high < close[1] and high > open) then
                        tradj[ngap] = tradj[ngap] + 1;
                if (gap > 0 and low >= open) or (gap < 0 and high <= open) then
                        trcont[ngap] = trcont[ngap] + 1;
{Continue next day}
                if(gap[1] > 0 and open > close[1]) or
                        (gap[1] < 0 and open < close[1]) then
                        ncont[ngap] = ncont[ngap] + 1;
                end
        else
                nitems[middle] = nitems[middle] + 1;
        if lastcalcdate = date then begin
                for ix = n downto 1 begin
                        print (file("C:\windows\gapout"), maxmin[ix]:4:3, nitems[ix]:5:0,
                        ccont[ix]:5:0, cbelow[ix]:4:0, crev[ix]:4:0, trcross[ix]:5:0,
                        tradj[ix]:4:0, trcont[ix]:4:0, ncont[ix]:5:0);
                        end;
                end;
```

THREE STUDIES IN MARKET MOVEMENT—WEEKDAY, WEEKEND, AND REVERSAL PATTERNS

The next three sections are concerned with longer periods of time. The first, *weekday patterns,* looks only at the closing prices during a 5-day week from Monday through Friday to find recurring close-only patterns. A week is often considered to have integrity as a single unit of time, and participants are accused of acting in the same way each week. This study attempts to isolate predictive patterns; for example, if Monday through Thursday were all higher, what is the possibility of Friday being higher? If the weekly trend can be clearly identified, should a correction on Friday be expected due to evening-up (closing out positions before the weekend)? Because patterns represent human behavior, the results could prove interesting.

Weekend patterns are considered independently in the second study. The opening direction on Monday could restore the trend of the prior week, if those traders who liquidate on Friday intend to reset their positions. The weekend is also an extended period for unexpected news or a buildup of public interest. The study will attempt to relate the direction of the Monday opening price to some pattern or trend of the preceding week.

Reversal patterns are not based on a day of the week but have often been discussed as a leading indicator. They may also be used as a filtering or timing device.

Weekday Patterns

During their constant exposure to the market, professional traders often observe patterns in weekly price movement; their acceptance of these patterns is as old as the market itself. In *Reminiscences of a Stock Operator,* the fictional character Larry Livingston (assumed to be Jesse Livermore) begins his career recording prices on a chalkboard above the floor of the New York Stock Exchange, eventually becoming aware of patterns within these prices. The most accepted occurrence of a pattern is the Tuesday reversal, which is taken as commonplace by close observers of the market. When questioned why a strong soybean market on the first of the week is followed by a weak day, a member of the Board of Trade would shrug his shoulders and quote: "Up on Monday, down on Tuesday." If this is true, there is a trading opportunity.

If a commonly accepted idea is not enough to be convincing, consider the additional rationalization about human behavior: The weekend allows a buildup of sentiment, which should result in greater activity on Monday. Coupled with adding back positions that were liquidated prior to the weekend, this may cause a disproportionate move on Monday, especially early in the session. This pattern may be further exaggerated when a clear trend exists. With this overbought or oversold condition, it is likely that Tuesday would show an adjustment. So much for hypothesizing.

The first aspect of the test was to define the weekday pattern. This was done in terms of the Friday-to-Monday move (close-to-close). Monday always received the value X, regardless of whether its direction from Friday was up or down. For each day that closed in the same direction as the Friday-to-Monday move, another X is used; when the close reversed direction, an O is recorded. Therefore, XOXXO means that Tuesday and Friday, represented by O, closed in the opposite direction from the prior Friday-to-Monday move, while Wednesday and Thursday were in the same direction. This could have meant either of the situations:

		(1)	*(2)*
Monday	X	Up	Down
Tuesday	O	Down	Up
Wednesday	X	Up	Down
Thursday	X	Up	Down
Friday	O	Down	Up

It might be that there is a distinction between the weeks that begin with an upward move on Monday rather than a lower price, but both cases were combined. This assumes that the pattern, rather than the direction, is most important. It would also be reasonable to have assumed that the upward bias of the stock and interest rate markets during the past 10 years would justify a separation of patterns according to their initial direction.

Daily Sequences

Figure 15-6 shows the aggregate results of the weekday patterns for a sampling of 23 futures markets tested during the period 1976 through 1985, appearing in the previous edition of this book. The numbers next to the corresponding patterns indicate the percentage of occurrences of each new day's pattern. For example, if the Monday-Tuesday pattern was XX, indicating that prices moved the same direction, then there was a 58% chance that an O followed, indicating a reversal.

Returning to the original premise for studying weekday patterns, we can use the broad set of market to see if any dominant behavior exists. We see that there was a 58% chance of a reversal on Tuesday (XO) and a 53% chance of that reversal continuing into Wednesday (XOO). If a reversal did not occur on Tuesday, there was a 58% chance that it would occur on Wednesday (XOO). For a large number of tests, 58% shows a definite pattern that confirms the original view. There are very few significant values that appear on Thursday, but three patterns of interest appear on Friday—XOXXX, XOOXX, and XXOOX—showing 57%, 64%, and 60%, respectively. These three patterns are important because they all show midweek reversal and a continuation of the trend by the end of the week.

The weekday patterns for the same six markets studied in the previous section ("Opening Gaps") were also tested for the period January 1986 through February 1996 and appear

---

FIGURE 15-6 23 futures markets, 1976–1985.

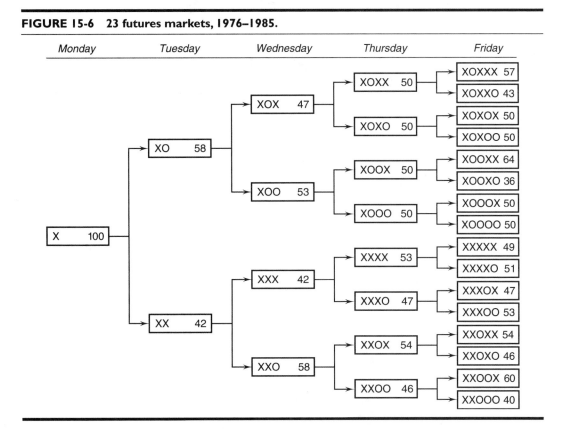

in Figure 15-7*a–f.* To understand the accuracy of these tests, each one includes approximately 480 complete weeks of information used to compile the patterns; therefore, each of the two combinations appearing on Tuesday have 240 entries, each pattern on Wednesday represents 120 weeks, Thursday 60, and Friday 30, assuming an equal distribution of patterns. All of these markets are actively traded.

Looking first at the Deutschemarks (Figure 15-7*a*), we see the same pattern as in the 10 years prior. There is a 55% chance of a Tuesday reversal (XO) and a 58% chance of a Wednesday reversal (XXO). If a reversal does not occur by Wednesday, there is a 57% chance of a reversal on Thursday (XXXO), but only a 28% chance that a reversal will occur on Friday (XXXXO), if it hasn't yet happened. The reverse situation shows that, if prices moved in the same direction Monday through Thursday, then there was a 72% chance they would move in that direction on Friday.

The same pattern seen in Deutschemarks is also apparent in the S&P (Figure 15-7*b*), where the chance of a reversal is 56%, 54%, 62%, and 38%. The most dominant Friday pattern is a trend continuation following a similar day on Thursday (XXXXX and XXOXX). Treasury bonds (Figure 15-7*c*) show a slightly greater consistency for reversal—57%, 59%, 55%, and 53%. For bonds, the chance of continuing in the same direction for the entire week is small. Gold (Figure 15-7*e*) also reflects similar reversal patterns—59%, 55%, 58%, and 38%. In view of the steady downtrend in gold prices during this 10-year period, this pattern appears to show a consistent method in the behavior of the traders. Soybeans (Fig-

FIGURE 15-7   Weekday study results. (*a*) Deutschemarks. (*b*) S&P 500. (*c*) Treasury bonds. (*d*) Heating oil. (*e*) Gold. (*f*) Soybeans.

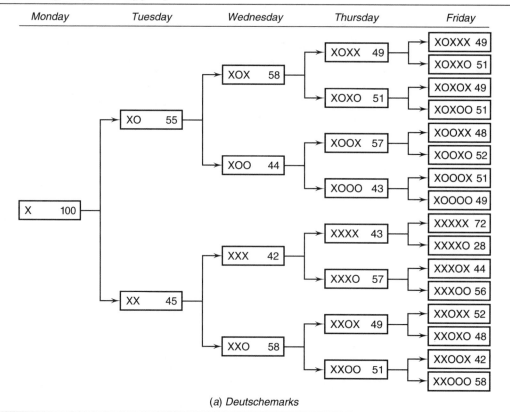

(*a*) *Deutschemarks*

FIGURE 15-7 *(Continued)*

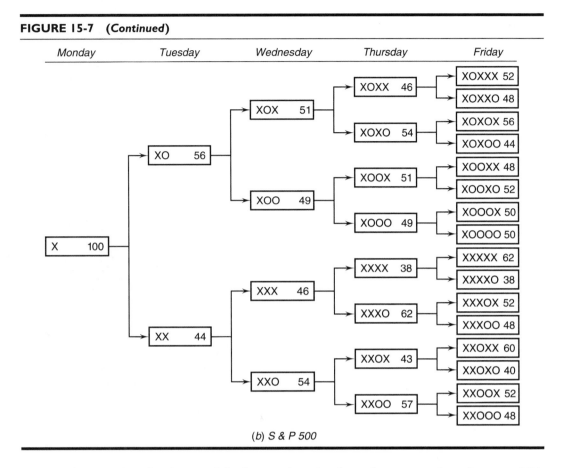

(b) S & P 500

ure 15-7*f*), a market clearly out of the financial circle, show their reversal tendency as 56%, 58%, 59%, and 58%. This variation on Friday does not change the uniform market reversal pattern seen early in the week.

Heating oil patterns (Figure 15-7*d*) are noticeably different from the other five markets. There seems to be no dominant pattern on Tuesdays and Wednesdays and only minor separation on Thursday. The three best patterns on Thursday, XOXO, XXXO, and XXOO, all show that Thursday moves in the direction opposite to Monday. The three best patterns on Friday, XOOXO, XXXOO, and XXOXO, also show that Fridays reverse from the opening Monday direction. After seeing the consistency of the other markets, these patterns indicate a very different participation. We might speculate that midweek release of oil stocks by the API, combined with weekend news about OPEC, have a tendency to create different reactions from traders.

Trading Weekday Patterns

The persistence of the weekday reversal over the past 20 years appears to be based on the nature of market participation. The patterns span nearly all markets with very similar results. To trade these weekday patterns, positions must be entered on the close of the prior day. Therefore, if soybeans move higher on Monday and Tuesday, we set a short on Tuesday's close with a 58% chance of a profit on Wednesday. If that does not occur, we can hold that short with a 59% chance of recovering at least some of that loss on Thursday. If Wednesday proved profitable, neither Thursday nor Friday have interesting patterns and we would close out the trade.

FIGURE 15-7 *(Continued)*

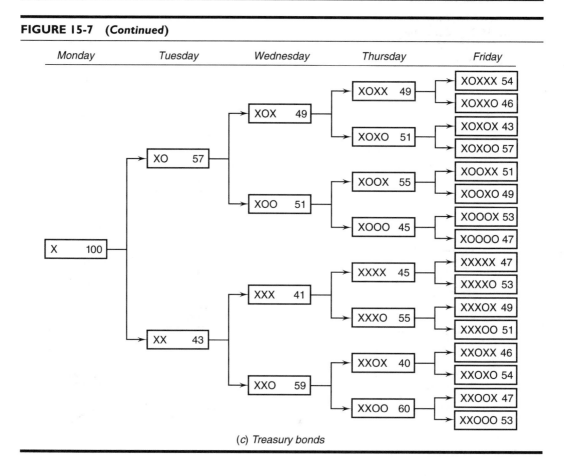

(c) Treasury bonds

In many cases, if you are trading the reversal pattern and it does not occur on the first day, it is best to hold that position at least one more day. This study may be taken further by looking at whether the open of the next day is a better point to enter a reversal trade than the previous close. Therefore, if Monday and Tuesday were both lower, a long entered on the open Wednesday may prove more profitable and less risky.

Programming the Weekday Study

The following program will produce results for the weekday study in the Printer Log window of *TradeStation.* There are a number of different methods that could be used to find these patterns; this approach is shown because it is transparent without using an excessive amount of programming code.

```
{SYSTEM: Weekday Study}
{Copyright 1985-1998. PJ Kaufman. All rights reserved.}
{Update weekday study in "Trading Systems and Methods"}
    vars:  dow(0), dir(0), ix(0),iy(0), error(0), Mon(0), day2(0), day3(0), day4(0),
               day5(0),div(0), pc(0);
    arrays:Tues[2](0), Wed[4](0), Thurs[8](0), Fri[16](0), pattern[5](0),
               n2[2](0), n3[4](0), n4[8](0), n5[16](0);
{create full pattern for week before entered values in case incomplete}
        dow = @dayofweek(date);
        if currentbar = 1 then begin
               Tues[1] = 10; Tues[2] = 11;
```

FIGURE 15-7 *(Continued)*

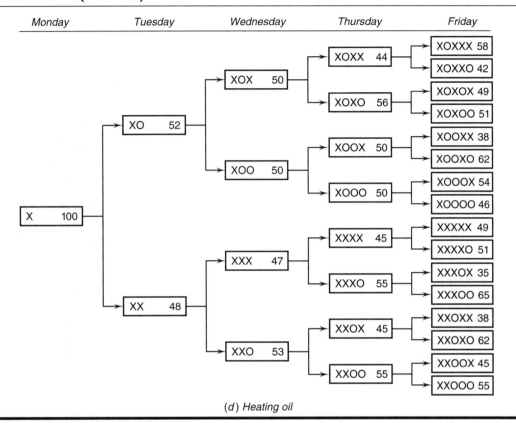

(*d*) Heating oil

```
            Wed[1] = 101; Wed[2] = 100; Wed[3] = 111; Wed[4] = 110;
            Thurs[1] = 1011; Thurs[2] = 1010; Thurs[3] = 1001; Thurs[4] = 1000;
            Thurs[5] = 1111; Thurs[6] = 1110; Thurs[7] = 1101; Thurs[8] = 1100;
            Fri[1] = 10111; Fri[2] = 10110; Fri[3] = 10101; Fri[4] = 10100;
            Fri[5] = 10011; Fri[6] = 10010; Fri[7] = 10001; Fri[8] = 10000;
            Fri[9] = 11111; Fri[10] = 11110; Fri[11] = 11101; Fri[12] = 11100;
            Fri[13] = 11011; Fri[14] = 11010; Fri[15] = 11001; Fri[16] = 11000;
            end;
{Monday}
    if dow = 1 then begin
            for ix = 1 to 5 begin
                    pattern[ix] = 0;
                    end;
            if close > close[1] then pattern[1] = 1 else pattern[1] = -1;
            end;
{Tuesday}
    if dow = 2 then begin
            if close > close[1] then pattern[2] = 1 else pattern[2] = -1;
            end;
{Wednesday}
    if dow = 3 then begin
            if close > close[1] then pattern[3] = 1 else pattern[3] = -1;
            end;
{Thursday}
    if dow = 4 then begin
```

FIGURE 15-7 (*Continued*)

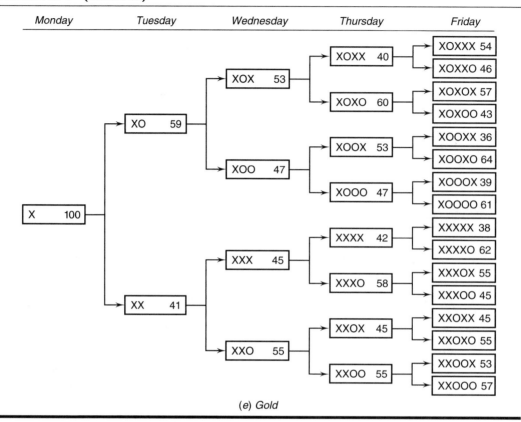

(*e*) *Gold*

```
            if close > close[1] then pattern[4] = 1 else pattern[4] = -1;
            end;
{Friday}
      if dow = 5 then begin
            if close > close[1] then pattern[5] = 1 else pattern[5] = -1;
            error = 0;
{process pattern for entire week, convert to pattern beginning with 1}
            for ix = 2 to 5 begin
                   if pattern[ix] = 0 then error = 1;
                   if error = 0 then begin
                         if pattern[ix] * pattern[1] > 0 then pattern[ix] = 1 else
                         pattern[ix] = 0;
                         end;
                   end;
            pattern[1] = 1;
            if error = 0 then begin
{create a value for each day}
                   Mon = Mon + 1;
                   day2 = 10 + pattern[2];
                   day3 = 100 + pattern[2]*10 + pattern[3];
                   day4 = 1000 + pattern[2]*100 + pattern[3]*10 + pattern[4];
                   day5 = 10000 + pattern[2]*1000 + pattern[3]*100 + pattern[4]*10 +
                   pattern[5];
{match each pattern and add to number of cases}
                   if day2 = Tues[1] then n2[1] = n2[1] + 1 else n2[2] = n2[2] + 1;
                   for ix = 1 to 4 begin
```

FIGURE 15-7 (*Continued*)

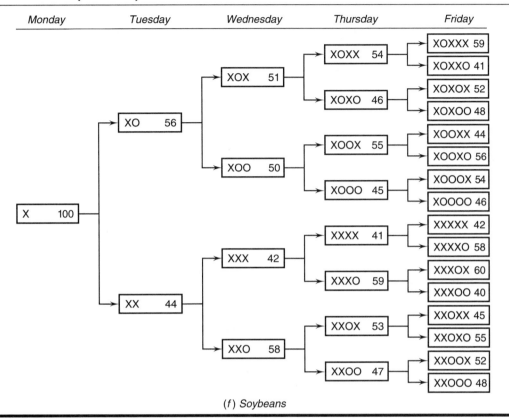

(*f*) Soybeans

```
                if day3 = Wed[ix] then n3[ix] = n3[ix] + 1;
                end;
        for ix = 1 to 8 begin
                if day4 = Thurs[ix] then n4[ix] = n4[ix] + 1;
                end;
        for ix = 1 to 16 begin
                if day5 = Fri[ix] then n5[ix] = n5[ix] + 1;
                end;
        end;
    end;
if lastcalcdate = date then begin
        print ("Monday = 1 100%, cases =", mon:5:0);
        print ("Tuesday");
        for ix = 1 to 2 begin
                div = @intportion((ix+1)/2);
                pc = n2[ix]*100/Mon;
                print (Tues[ix]:5:0, n2[ix]:4:0, pc:4:0);
                end;
        print ("Wednesday");
        for ix = 1 to 4 begin
                div = @intportion((ix+1)/2);
                pc = n3[ix]*100/n2[div];
                print (Wed[ix]:5:0, n3[ix]:4:0, pc:4:0);
                end;
        print ("Thursday");
        for ix = 1 to 8 begin
```

```
                    div = @intportion((ix+1)/2);
                    pc = n4[ix]*100/n3[div];
                    print (Thurs[ix]:5:0, n4[ix]:4:0, pc:4:0);
                    end;
            print ("Friday");
            for ix = 1 to 16 begin
                    div = @intportion((ix+1)/2);
                    pc = n5[ix]*100/n4[div];
                    print (Fri[ix]:5:0, n5[ix]:4:0, pc:4:0);
                    end;
        end;
```

Weekend Patterns

Of all patterns studied, this test was expected to be the most promising. Two factors lead to the anticipation of strong weekend patterns:

1. *Friday liquidation*—the aversion of traders to hold a market position over the weekend.
2. Setting of new positions and resetting of old ones on Monday, especially during a trending market.

If the patterns can be identified, the 2-day weekend delay should result in large price jumps and good profits for those willing to take the weekend risk. Not knowing what to expect but anticipating combining the results with the study of weekday patterns, a number of different trend indicators and patterns were tested. These were limited to closing price relationships.

Trend indicators

Prior Thursday-to-Friday direction

Friday-to-Friday direction

Most frequent direction last week

Following each of the trends or patterns, the prices on Monday were tabulated to determine the frequency and consistency of the opening price, closing price, and high or low prices that were in the same direction as each of the trends or patterns. Table 15-7 lists the results for the six markets studied for the 10 years from 1986 through February 1996. Based on the three trend patterns, none of the markets show any significant tendency to carry the trend over the weekend reflected in the open or close of the following Monday. The *extreme* on Monday, that is, the high or low price, normally provides an opportunity to exit at a profit from a *trend* position taken on Friday's close sometime on Monday.

It seems surprising that the price pattern on Monday no longer reflects the direction of the previous Thursday-to-Friday move, nor the trend of the previous week. In the same study performed in the prior 10 years, there was a clear pattern based on Thursday to Friday. Considering the fact that there have been dominant trends in the equities markets and interest rates, the only reasonable conclusion is that markets are more complex, based on greater participation. It will be necessary to look at longer trends or other patterns to find high-probability cases.

Combining Weekend and Weekday Patterns

The direction of Monday's prices is more interesting when viewed in terms of the previous weekday patterns. Seen side by side, the frequency of each pattern and the way the six sample markets react with respect to the following Monday closing price give insight into mar-

TABLE 15-7   Weekend Pattern Based on Possible Trends during the Prior Week, January 1986–February 1996

Market	Trend	Continued Direction Monday (%)		
		Open	Close	Extreme
Deutschemark	Thurs to Fri	55	51	74
	Fri to Fri	56	55	78
	Most frequent direction	54	51	99
S&P 500	Thurs to Fri	49	49	87
	Fri to Fri	46	51	88
	Most frequent direction	47	50	98
U.S. T-bonds	Thurs to Fri	46	47	87
	Fri to Fri	46	51	89
	Most frequent direction	46	49	96
Heating oil	Thurs to Fri	49	49	77
	Fri to Fri	49	48	80
	Most frequent direction	50	49	96
Gold	Thurs to Fri	53	47	76
	Fri to Fri	50	46	76
	Most frequent direction	51	47	97
Soybeans	Thurs to Fri	53	45	76
	Fri to Fri	52	46	77
	Most frequent direction	51	45	97

ket behavior. Table 15-8 shows the percentage of total cases for each weekday pattern (based on about 480 weeks) and the percentage of days for which Monday's price closed in the X direction, continuing the direction of the previous Monday.

In Table 15-8 there are two interesting items to observe, the frequency of patterns and the percentage of cases that Monday follows specific patterns. The most consistent pattern seems to be the low percentage associated with XXXXX, the case in which the market moves the same direction every day. While it appears most often in the Deutschemark, considered the most trending of these markets, it is not a common pattern in the other markets. When it does occur, the D-mark and heating oil are most likely to reverse direction on Monday, while the U.S. Treasury bonds and soybeans are likely to continue the trend.

Overall, the fluctuating patterns are more common than persistent direction. For example, XOXOX and XOOXO are among the most common patterns. These both show Tuesday reversals and the results can be compared with the weekday study. While there is consistency in the reaction of the financial markets, soybeans tend to move in the opposite direction.

Specific market patterns, such as weekday and weekend, can provide an edge for traders in a very different and more complex market environment. By finding patterns that are more likely, or even less likely, to occur over groups of similar markets, with 10% greater frequency, traders can vary their position size based on expectations and thereby gain a market advantage.

Programming the Weekend Study

The following Omega *Easy Language* program prints the results used in the weekend study to the Print Log. Some of the techniques used are the same as those used in the weekday study.

```
{SYSTEM: Weekend Study}
{Copyright 1985-1998. PJ Kaufman. All rights reserved.}
```

TABLE 15-8 Combining Weekend and Weekday Patterns, January 1986–February 1996*

Pattern	D-marks		S&P 500		U.S. T-Bonds		Heating Oil		Gold		Soybeans	
	%Total	%X	%Total	%X	%Total	%X	%Total	%X	%Total	%X	%Total	%X
XOXXX	6.3	60	6.3	57	6.5	35	5.7	37	6.8	53	7.5	42
XOXXO	8.6	44	6.5	48	4.9	39	4.0	32	5.9	50	5.9	32
XOXOX	6.9	58	7.5	53	5.7	70	6.1	55	10.5	52	6.1	38
XOXOO	7.7	38	7.1	44	7.2	44	6.6	39	7.6	56	6.3	53
XOOXX	6.1	52	6.5	61	7.2	47	4.4	52	4.4	62	6.1	48
XOOXO	7.1	44	6.7	44	7.2	41	7.6	47	9.9	51	7.1	56
XOOOX	4.8	52	5.2	56	6.3	43	7.2	56	3.8	50	6.1	45
XOOOO	3.8	44	6.1	55	6.5	32	5.3	40	7.2	47	4.4	62
XXXXX	5.6	41	4.6	55	3.0	71	4.4	38	2.5	50	3.1	60
XXXXO	2.3	64	3.1	40	4.2	55	4.2	45	4.2	55	4.8	57
XXXOX	4.4	71	6.7	44	5.3	32	5.1	58	4.6	36	6.1	45
XXXOO	6.5	58	5.4	58	4.0	63	7.6	50	5.1	42	4.6	45
XXOXX	6.1	45	6.1	31	4.2	45	4.4	57	4.2	50	6.1	34
XXOXO	5.6	44	3.6	53	5.5	65	6.6	58	5.5	35	7.1	50
XXOOX	5.4	54	6.3	50	7.0	42	6.6	48	6.5	45	5.9	57
XXOOO	6.9	61	6.1	48	7.2	56	7.6	47	5.9	54	5.7	41

*For each market, the first column shows the percentage of total cases and the second column gives the percentage that Monday's close was in the X direction.

```
{Update weekend study in "Trading Systems and Methods"}
     vars:  dow(0), ix(0), nx(0), error(0), Mon(0), weekly(0), cases(0),
                 div(0), pc(0), prevfri(0), savedir(0), start(0), change(0),
                 TFopen(0), TFclose(0), TFext(0), FFopen(0),
                 FFclose(0), FFext(0), Frqopen(0), Frqclose(0), Frqext(0);
     arrays: week[16](0), oweek[16](0), xweek[16](0), pattern[5](0), cprice[5](0);

     dow = @dayofweek(date);
     if currentbar = 1 then begin
             week[1] = 10111; week[2] = 10110; week[3] = 10101; week[4] = 10100;
             week[5] = 10011; week[6] = 10010; week[7] = 10001; week[8] = 10000;
             week[9] = 11111; week[10] = 11110; week[11] = 11101; week[12] = 11100;
             week[13] = 11011; week[14] = 11010; week[15] = 11001; week[16] = 11000;
             end;
{Monday}
     if dow = 1 then begin
{Process weekend pattern}
             if start = 1 then begin
                     cases = cases + 1;
{Thursday to Friday direction}
                     change = close[1] - close[2];
                     if (open - close[1]) * change > 0 then TFopen = TFopen + 1;
                     if (close - close[1]) * change > 0 then TFclose = TFclose + 1;
                     if (change > 0 and high > close[1]) or (change < 0 and low < close[1])
                     then
                             TFext = TFext + 1;
{Friday to Friday direction}
                     change = close[1] - prevfri;
                     if (open - close[1]) * change > 0 then FFopen = FFopen + 1;
                     if (close - close[1]) * change > 0 then FFclose = FFclose + 1;
                     if (change > 0 and high > close[1]) or (change < 0 and low <
                     close[1]) then
                             FFext = FFext + 1;
```

```
{Most common direction}
                    change = close - close[1];
                    nx = 0;
                    for ix = 1 to 5 begin
                            if pattern[ix] = 1 then nx = nx + 1;
                            end;
                    if (nx >= 3 and (open - close[1])*savedir > 0) or
                            (nx < 3 and (open - close[1])*savedir < 0) then Frqopen =
                            Frqopen + 1;
                    if (nx >= 3 and (close - close[1])*savedir > 0) or
                            (nx < 3 and (close - close[1])*savedir < 0) then Frqclose =
                            Frqclose + 1;
                    if (nx >= 3 and ((change > 0 and high > close[1]) or
                            (change < 0 and low < close[1]))) or
                            (nx < 3 and ((change < 0 and low < close[1]) or
                            (change > 0 and high > close[1]))) then Frqext = Frqext + 1;
{Pattern match}
                    for ix = 1 to 16 begin
                            if weekly = week[ix] then begin
                                    if (close - close[1])*savedir > 0 then xweek[ix] =
                                    xweek[ix] + 1;
                                    if (close - close[1])*savedir < 0 then oweek[ix] =
                                    oweek[ix] + 1;
                                    end;
                            end;
                    end;
            for ix = 1 to 5 begin
                    pattern[ix] = 0;
                    end;
            if close > close[1] then pattern[1] = 1 else pattern[1] = -1;
            cprice[1] = close;
            prevfri = close[1];
            savedir = pattern[1];
            end;
{Tuesday}
      if dow = 2 then begin
            if close > close[1] then pattern[2] = 1 else pattern[2] = -1;
            cprice[2] = close;
            end;
{Wednesday}
      if dow = 3 then begin
            if close > close[1] then pattern[3] = 1 else pattern[3] = -1;
            cprice[3] = close;
            end;
{Thursday}
      if dow = 4 then begin
            if close > close[1] then pattern[4] = 1 else pattern[4] = -1;
            cprice[4] = close;
            end;
{weekday}
      if dow = 5 then begin
            if close > close[1] then pattern[5] = 1 else pattern[5] = -1;
            cprice[5] = close;
            error = 0;
{process pattern for entire week, convert to pattern beginning with 1}
            for ix = 2 to 5 begin
                    if pattern[ix] = 0 then error = 1;
                    if error = 0 then begin
                            if pattern[ix] * pattern[1] > 0 then pattern[ix] = 1 else
                            pattern[ix] = 0;
```

```
                                        end;
                        end;
            pattern[1] = 1;
            weekly = 0;
            if error = 0 then begin
{create a weekly pattern}
                        weekly = 10000 + pattern[2]*1000 + pattern[3]*100 + pattern[4]*10 +
                        pattern[5];
                        end;
            start = 1;
            end;

    if lastcalcdate = date then begin
            print ("Thursday to Friday", cases:4:0, TFopen:4:0, TFclose:4:0, TFext:4:0,
                        TFopen*100/cases:4:0, TFclose*100/cases:4:0,
                        TFext*100/cases:4:0);
            print ("Friday to Friday", cases:4:0, FFopen:4:0, FFclose:4:0, FFext:4:0,
                        FFopen*100/cases:4:0, FFclose*100/cases:4:0,
                        FFext*100/cases:4:0);
            print ("Most frequent direction", cases:4:0, Frqopen:4:0, Frqclose:4:0,
                        Frqext:4:0, Frqopen*100/cases:4:0, Frqclose*100/cases:4:0,
                        Frqext*100/cases:4:0);
            print ("All patterns:");
            for ix = 1 to 16 begin
                        print week[ix]:6:0, xweek[ix] + oweek[ix]:4:0,
                                    (xweek[ix] + oweek[ix])*100/cases:4:1," %1=",
                                    xweek[ix]*100/(xweek[ix]+oweek[ix]):4:0);
                        end;
            end;
```

A Comment on Testing and Holidays

The weekday and weekend tests did not include any weeks in which there was a holiday or long holiday weekends. It would have been perfectly reasonable to view the opening of the first day of the following week as a "Monday," even though it occurred on a Tuesday following a Monday holiday. In fact, those special cases may have proved very consistent. Similarly, a holiday on Friday could have been worked out to fit the weekday patterns and allow the Monday direction to be added into the total results. These tests shown here only used complete 5-day trading weeks.

A well-known work that studies price movement prior to holidays is by Merrill, whose results are based on the stock market and demonstrate a strong bullish tendency before a holiday with a weak day immediately after. Remembering the bullish bias of the stock market (about 54% of all days were higher from 1897 to January 1964), Merrill's results are shown in Table 15-9. In relation to trading, this would indicate the possibility of a sharp trending move prior to or throughout a holiday season.

TABLE 15-9   Merrill's Holiday Results

Period Tested	Holiday or Holiday Period	% Upward Moves
1897–1964	Day prior to all holidays	67.9%
1897–1964	Day after all holidays	50.8
1897–1964	Thanksgiving to New Year	74
1897–1964	July 4th to Labor Day	69
1931–1965	Before Christmas	74
1931–1965	Before New Year	75

The January Effect

Another bias in the pattern of prices may be seen in the action of the stock market during the month of January. There are many investors who are not as anxious to trade in and out of the market as professional managers and speculators. It is perfectly sensible to look for a pattern in the way many of the long-term investors set positions at the beginning of the year, the result of a reallocation of their portfolios, or resetting positions liquidated before the end of the year for tax reasons.

If January is a leading indicator of stock market movement throughout the rest of the year, there is a combination of patterns that should be considered based on the few days immediately after the year begins, and the net market direction for the month of January.[4] Using the Dow Industrials as a stock market indicator, the January pattern was viewed from 1900 to 1989 in two parts, 1900 to 1937 and 1938 to 1989. The results are shown in Figure 15-8 for all years and Table 15-10 for the past 52 years.

Figure 15-8 shows that the early part of the century had no significant pattern. There were nearly the same number of bullish and bearish indications resulting in a larger number of incorrect predictions. The past 52 years are very different, with a much larger number of correct moves. One should note, however, that the ratio of up to down moves is more than 7 : 1. During the past 10 years it is likely that this pattern would continue to be successful if the prognosis was a bull market. To offset the market bias, it should be noted that the patterns shown in Table 15-10 are very logical. The direction of the first 5 days, confirmed by a continuation in that pattern for the balance of January, is then followed by the same pattern for the year. In the case in which the market changes direction after the first 5 days and nets a loss for the month, the pattern conforms to the new direction for the balance of the year.

Reversal Patterns

The last of the three studies looks at reversal patterns. The intention is to find a pattern in the open, high, low, and closing prices of the day that will help predict the next day's pattern or direction. Three combinations are tabulated here:

[4] Jay Kaeppel, "The January Barometer: Myth and Reality," *Technical Analysis of Stocks & Commodities* (July 1990).

FIGURE 15-8   Results of January patterns.

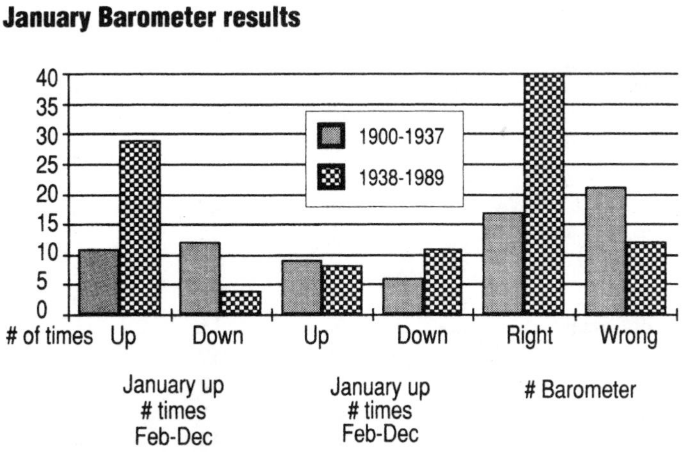

January Barometer results

Source: Jay Kaeppel, "The January Barometer: Myth and Reality," *Technical Analysis of Stocks & Commodities,* 8, no. 7 (July 1990). ©1990 Technical Analysis, Inc. Used with permission.

TABLE 15-10   The January Barometer Patterns, 1938–1989

| | S&P 500 | | |
Pattern	During First 5 Days of the Year	By the End of January	Expectations for Feb–Dec
1	Declines	Further decline	Bearish
2	Declines	Less decline, but loss for the month	Bearish
3	Declines	Gain for the month	Bullish
4	Advances	Further gains	Bullish
5	Advances	Less gain, but gain for the month	Bullish
6	Advances	Loss for the month	Bearish

Intraday trend continued ("Trend"). A continued upward trend is set up when yesterday's high is greater than the previous high and yesterday's close is greater than the previous close. We then find the percentage of days that open higher or close higher than yesterday. Continued downtrends are the opposite pattern.

Reversal day ("Reversal"). Beginning with yesterday's pattern of a higher high but a close below the prior close, a reversal day opens lower or closes lower than the previous close. An upward reversal starts with a lower trend day.

Extreme reversal ("Extreme"). Yesterday's high was greater than the prior high, but yesterday's close was below the prior low. The reversal from up to down is continued if today's open or close is lower than yesterday's close.

Results for these trend and reversal combinations are shown in Table 15-11 for the same six markets tested in the previous studies. In general, the financial markets show few extreme values, while gold and soybeans show a tendency for continued reversals following an upward move. An unusual and very consistent result that appears for all markets is

TABLE 15-11   Reversal Analysis for Six Sample Markets, January 1986–February 1996

Market	Pattern	Higher High		Lower Low		No. of Cases	
		Open	Close	Open	Close	Up	Down
Deutschemark	Trend	46	48	50	45	948	907
	Reversal	55	45	16	15	268	261
	Extreme	48	41	51	45	79	74
S&P 500	Trend	42	51	46	42	940	791
	Reversal	49	42	20	22	375	342
	Extreme	43	46	35	48	82	81
U.S. T-bonds	Trend	49	48	47	44	882	778
	Reversal	51	44	25	22	347	366
	Extreme	46	42	41	42	92	114
Heating oil	Trend	45	46	49	46	869	818
	Reversal	53	45	16	16	247	283
	Extreme	50	45	58	39	42	62
Gold	Trend	44	40	52	45	833	830
	Reversal	57	44	15	14	320	267
	Extreme	57	39	36	34	70	76
Soybeans	Trend	46	43	47	45	874	831
	Reversal	57	45	21	20	289	344
	Extreme	53	47	52	45	74	99

the low percentage of reversal follow-through after a lower price move. Readers are encouraged to verify the program printed at the end of this section, to be certain that there are no errors. This unusually persistent pattern may be either a special trading pattern or a program error. If valid, whenever today's low is below the prior low and today's close is greater than yesterday's close, a short sale should prove profitable about 80% of the time.

Programming the Reversal Study

```
{SYSTEM: Reversal Study}
{Copyright 1985-1998. PJ Kaufman. All rights reserved.}
{New reversal study for "Trading Systems and Methods"
        Each of the following based on direction of current pattern:
        1. Continued trend (higher high, higher close, then next open and close
        2. Reversal: Higher high, lower close, then next open and close
        3. Outside Reversal: Higher high, close below prior low, then next open and close}

        vars:   trend(0), TUopen(0), TUclose(0), TDopen(0), TDclose(0),
                    RUopen(0), RUclose(0), RDopen(0), RDclose(0),
                    EUopen(0), EUclose(0), EDopen(0), EDclose(0),
                    nTU(0), nTD(0), nRU(0), nRD(0), nEU(0), nED(0);

        trend = close - close[5];
{Continued trend}
        if high[1] > high[2] and close[1] > close[2] then begin
                    nTU = nTU + 1;
                    if open > close[1] then TUopen = TUopen + 1;
                    if close > close[1] then TUclose = TUclose + 1;
                    end;
        if low[1] < low[2] and close[1] < close[2] then begin
                    nTD = nTD + 1;
                    if open < close[1] then TDopen = TDopen + 1;
                    if close < close[1] then TDclose = TDclose + 1;
                    end;
{Reversal}
        if high[1] > high[2] and close [1] < close[2] then begin
                    nRU = nRU + 1;
                    if open < close[1] then RUopen = RUopen + 1;
                    if close < close[1] then RUclose = RUclose + 1;
                    end;
        if low[1] < low[2] and close[1] > close[2] then begin
                    nRD = nRD + 1;
                    if open > close[1] then RDopen = RDopen + 1;
                    if close > close[1] then RDclose = RDclose + 1;
                    end;
{Extreme Reversal}
        if high[1] > high[2] and close[1] < low[2] then begin
                    nEU = nEU + 1;
                    if open < close[1] then EUopen = EUopen + 1;
                    if close < close[1] then EUclose = EUclose + 1;
                    end;
        if low[1] < low[2] and close[1] > high[2] then begin
                    nED = nED + 1;
                    if open > close[1] then EDopen = EDopen + 1;
                    if close > close[1] then EDclose = EDclose + 1;
                    end;

        if lastcalcdate = date then begin
                    print ("Total cases:", currentbar:5:0);
                    print ("          open close open close");
                    print ("Trend  ", TUopen*100/nTU:4:0, TUclose*100/nTU:4:0,
                            TDopen*100/nTD:4:0, TDclose*100/nTD:4:0, " (", nTU:4:0, nTD:4:0,
```

```
                            ")");
          print ("Reversal", RUopen*100/nRU:4:0, RUclose*100/nRU:4:0,
                 RDopen*100/nTD:4:0, RDclose*100/nTD:4:0, " (", nRU:4:0, nRD:4:0,
                 ")");
          print ("Extreme", EUopen*100/nEU:4:0, EUclose*100/nEU:4:0,
                 EDopen*100/nED:4:0, EDclose*100/nED:4:0, " (", nEU:4:0, nED:4:0,
                 ")");
      end;
```

COMPUTER-BASED PATTERN RECOGNITION

The methods previously discussed were based on patterns familiar to traders. The weekly and weekend studies, as well as the intraday time patterns shown in the previous sections, were originally verified by hand and later recalculated using a computer. There is a type of pattern recognition, however, that would hardly be considered without the availability of a computer.

Rather than the conventional price patterns in which recurring sequences of higher and lower days are found within certain qualified intervals, *computer-based pattern recognition* refers to *sets of descriptors* and *classes of interest*. For example, Aronson[5] describes the sets and values that must be satisfied by a professional jockey as:

Descriptor	Value-Range
Height	Under 5'5"
Weight	Under 120 lbs.
Age	16 to 35
Years riding horses	Over 10

The *set* of people who satisfy all four conditions are said to *contain* all professional jockeys. The converse, that all people satisfying these conditions *are* professional jockeys, is not true. It will be necessary to qualify this set further to create a set that contains *only* professional jockeys; however, these four conditions go a long way toward reducing the field.

How can this tool be applied toward the development of a trading strategy? If the system is defined in terms of the *trade profile,* it becomes obvious. Consider the following characteristics of a trade:

1. The price moves higher or lower by at least 3% of the starting price.
2. The price move occurs within 20 days.
3. There is no loss exceeding .5%.

Either a computer or an analyst can locate all price moves that satisfy these conditions within a price series. Each of the 5 days preceding an upward move, which satisfies these conditions, can be marked as *buy* days, and the 5 days preceding a downward movement can be designated *sell* days (see Figure 15-9).

The computer now contains the set of all buy and sell days—those days on which it would be good to get a buy or sell signal. Next, some likely indicators must be specified to be used for identifying that these trades are about to begin. The following might be used:

1. The moving average direction
2. An overbought/oversold indicator such as a relative strength indicator (RSI) or contrary opinion

---

[5] David R. Aronson, *Artificial Intelligence Methods* (privately published). Also see David R. Aronson, "Artificial Intelligence/Pattern Recognition Applied to Forecasting Financial Market Trends," *Market Technicians Association Journal* (May 1985, pp. 91–131).

FIGURE 15-9 Specific buying and selling days.

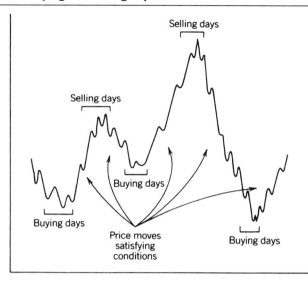

3. The direction of changes in trading volume
4. A 10-day momentum

By entering a broad selection of indicators and trying to avoid duplication, the computer can find unique values for combinations of indicators that primarily occur during the days selected as buy and sell periods. Ideally, all buy signals should occur when one indicator, or the value of combining indicators, exceeds a specific value. For example, all buy signals occur when the average value of the RSI and the market sentiment (contrary opinion) is below the 10% level. However, having all buy signals occur here is not enough. Poor signals may appear at this level, which cause large losses. The perfect system will have *no losing signals* occur in this zone.

Unfortunately, in the real world there are no perfect solutions. The trades that are signaled by the combinations of indicators will have to be studied for net return, risk, and other performance criteria. However, the technique of setting up classes of indicators, buy and sell days, is a new and valid approach to system development. It is analogous to the multiple regression method used by econometricians to find the relationship between statistics and prices. Although the econometricians use inflation, supply, interest rates, and so forth, pattern recognition can employ technical indicators and discrete patterns to forecast a buy or sell day.

ARTIFICIAL INTELLIGENCE METHODS

Artificial intelligence refers to a computer process that performs an operation corresponding to, or approaching, human thinking. This is intended to distinguish it from simple pattern recognition, with which it is often confused. The state of the art in artificial intelligence is the separation of two ideas. The collection of information that is stored in the brain has been termed the *knowledge base*. This is distinguished from reason, rules, and logic, called the *inference engine*. These ideas are not very different from the database and trading strategies that are discussed here.

The closest practical approach to artificial intelligence is *heuristic* programming. This refers to computer learning in very much the same way as finding the way out of a maze. The computer starts with rules relevant to the problem, then records the successful and unsuccessful experiences. Eventually, it has a complete table of what to do for each situation, or at least a table of probable solutions. This is a realistic, intelligent approach when the same events can be expected to recur in the same way. It does not help in new situations without the added complication of incorporating extrapolation, basic relationships (e.g., price level to volatility), and other forms of expectations.

The danger of the heuristic approach to pattern recognition is that it may continue to define extensions of combinations of patterns that have already produced inconsistent or poor results. Allowing the computer to identify a limitless collection of patterns is just another case of overfitting, but this time at a highly sophisticated level.

Heuristic programs have improved current technology in searching, optimization, and game-playing strategies; however, they are not readily available. There is no doubt that this technique will be quickly absorbed into trading strategies as it develops.[6] Those readers interested in the types of methods considered to be in the category of artificial intelligence, such as neural networks and genetic algorithms, should refer to Chapter 20 ("Advanced Techniques").

---

[6] Two books of interest that represent the state of the art in heuristics and game playing are Judea Pearl, *Heuristics* (Addison-Wesley, Reading, MA, 1984), and M.A. Bramer, *Computer Game-Playing: Theory and Practice* (Halsted Press, New York, 1983).

16

Day Trading

day trade is a position entered and liquidated during a single trading day. The techniques of *time of day* and *daily patterns,* discussed in such rigid form in Chapter 15, are put to use by the day trader. Day trading requires extreme discipline, excellent planning, anticipation, and concentration. The need for a fast response to changing situations tends to exaggerate any bad trading habits; as in other fields, the shorter the response time, the greater the chance for error. In this chapter, we will extend the idea of day trading to systems and methods that may also be held overnight, but expect to limit the trade to about 24 hours.

To keep mistakes to a minimum, each day's strategy must be planned in advance. It should focus on the most likely situations that might occur based on the nature of the current price movement. There should also be a contingency plan for the extreme unexpected moves in either direction. Making spot decisions during market hours will cause more frequent errors.

Computers have caused the number of day traders who rely on systems to increase, and have created an entire class of *screen traders.* The steady increase in automated exchanges, led by Germany's DTB and followed by France's conversion of Matif, is sending a strong message that electronic trading will dominate the future. The availability of intraday price feeds and system development platforms, such as Omega's *TradeStation,* have greatly increased the number of day-trading participants. Only 10 years ago the best one could expect was to display standard indicators and moving averages on a real-time price chart. Now you can fully program complex trading strategies that combine more than one market and more than one time frame into a single package and display buy and sell signals on the screen as well as record a historic log of trades. All of these tools have greatly increased competition among individual and commercial traders.

For the arbitrageur, computers have had an even stronger impact. Sophisticated systems at banks and large financial institutions consolidate data feeds that bring current transactions on every type of interest rate vehicle in every maturity and major currency. Analytic programs can find issues that are outliers and show which combinations (called strips) can produce a riskless profit. For the individual trader, few of these opportunities are available, although they add liquidity to the market. Individuals, however, find it much easier to create spreads of different deliveries within the same market as well as spread between two related products. Stock traders can create sector baskets or look for performance differences within a sector. Spread trading and formulated values, such as the energy crack or soybean crush, can be improved using similar displays. Many of the opportunities that now seem so easy to see would previously have been missed. This faster, more systematic response to the market allows traders to improve profits and reduce risk in any day-trading method.

IMPACT OF TRANSACTION COSTS

Transaction costs are the greatest deterrent to day-trading profits. The failure to execute near the intended price, plus the commission costs, can remove a large part of potential profitability and even turn expected profits into losses. An aspiring day trader has two ways of improving performance: by paying lower commissions and by careful selection of opportunities. Table 16-1 presents the percentage relationship of moderate transaction costs to the maximum daily price move. The average dollar volatility for the years 1990 through 1996 is shown next to the percentage represented by a $100 transaction cost. In general, $100 is a modest value for the combination of commissions and slippage, and traders would be very pleased to extract an average profit of one-half the daily volatility. A practical approach would therefore use twice the percentage effect of a $100 cost shown here.

Realistically, a day trader would choose the index markets, more volatile currencies, and long-term interest rates as their best opportunity for profits. Corn represents the least desirable market because very low volatility leaves more risk than opportunity. Although a $100 transaction cost may seem high for this market, a $20 commission and slippage equal to a minimum move of ¼¢, or $12.50, totaling $45, would be the smallest possible costs. An occasional fast move in the market, based on unexpected economic news, or large orders entering at one time, must result in a larger number, raising the average.

To keep dollar volatility of a futures contract to a level acceptable by most traders, exchanges have been forced to resize contracts, specifically stock index markets, as overall share values have climbed. During 1997, the S&P was reduced from $500 per basis point to $250, and the FTSE-100 from £25 to £10. In 1998, the French CAC40 contract was cut to 25% of its previous size. This increases the relative size of transaction costs.

Liquidity

The importance of liquidity is magnified in day trading. Execution slippage of $100, measured as the difference between the system price, or Market Order price, and the actual filled price, will have little impact on a month-long trade netting $2,000; however, it will be critical for a day trade with a profit objective of under $300. The selection of day-trading candidates begins with those markets of greater volume. Whether one contract or 1,000, a

TABLE 16-1 Volatility and Liquidity, U.S. Markets, 1990–1996

Market	$Volatility	%$100
Cotton	540	18.5
Corn	163	61.3
Soybeans	405	24.7
Australian dollar	353	28.3
British pound	848	11.8
Canadian dollar	291	34.4
Deutschemark	703	14.2
Japanese yen	869	11.5
Swiss franc	975	10.3
Gold	311	32.2
High-grade copper	421	23.8
Crude oil	454	22.0
Heating oil	518	19.3
S&P 500	2,154	4.6
NYSE Composite	1,144	8.7
Treasury bills	160	62.5
Treasury notes	568	17.6
Treasury bonds	764	13.1

thinly traded market produces slippage that will cut sharply into profits. In choosing among index markets that usually offer the greatest volatility and profit potential, you are always safest with the markets that combine the highest volume and highest volatility.

Occasionally, markets with light volume show larger price moves than similar markets traded on other exchanges. Traders will be tempted to profit from these moves but will consistently find that the execution of an order at the posted price is elusive. The reality of trading these markets is that a Market Order is not advisable due to the thinness of the trading, a Limit Order may not get filled, and a spread is not quoted at anything resembling the apparent price relationships that you see on a quote screen; there is no real way to take advantage of these perceived profits. If an execution succeeds, exiting the position still has the same problems plus some added urgency.

Missed Orders

Because the profit objective, projected daily range, holding time, and end-of-day constraints all put limits on a day trade, there are situations in which the market jumps after a news release and you cannot get filled anywhere close to your intended price. With most of the potential profit gone before you enter the order, it would not be surprising to simply skip that trade. These missed orders, called *unables,* can add up to a large part of your profits; at the same time they never reduce your losses.

Some markets are prone to more unables. For the energy complex, heated military or political activity in the Mid-East can cause a prolonged period of very erratic price movement, resulting in as much as 20% unexecuted trades during a 1-month period. If we consider the normal profile of a short-term trading system as having an average net profit of $250, an average loss of $150, and a 50% frequency of profits, we expect a profit of $5,000 for every 100 trades and a reasonable profit-to-loss ratio of 1.66. If, however, there are 10% unables, that missed opportunity must come from the profits; if the market was moving in the opposite way, you would get all of your positions filled. Then 10% of the profitable trades means 5 trades out of every 100 for a total of $1,250 missed. This reduces the total profits to $4,750 and the profit factor to 1.50. It may turn a marginal trading strategy, or one with small profits per trade, from a profit to a loss.

Price Ranges

The average *daily range* (not the *true range*) shows the maximum potential for a single day-trading profit. Some markets, such as gold and corn, combine a lack of liquidity with a narrow daily range and are easily disqualified from a day trade opportunity. Eurodollars have extremely high volume but very little movement; therefore, they are also not a good candidate for day trading. When volume is combined with volatility, the world index markets, followed by the currencies and long-term interest rates, are shown to be the best choices. Energy markets represent the next tier, grains remain active, and other markets have far lower volume.

Day traders may find that those markets with traditional daily trading limits present a problem during high-volatility periods. Day trading does best in markets that have wide swings not deterred by exchange limits; a single locked-limit move can generate a loss that offsets many profitable day trades. High volatility and locked-limit moves present a contradiction for day trading. Rules that provide for expanding limits have greatly helped reduce the frequency of locked-limit days; however, traders must always be on guard for this situation.

Estimating Slippage Costs

If you know the cost of slippage, you can do a much better job selecting the markets to trade and have a realistic appraisal of your trading expectations. The factors that make up slippage are volatility, overall market volume, current market activity, and the size of the order being placed. Of these items, current market activity is the most difficult to record, because it requires some estimation of volume as it accumulates throughout the day. While actual volume is not available for most markets, a reasonable approximation can be made using tick volume, the number of price changes during a fixed interval. In general, tick volume is directly proportional to actual trading volume; during periods of greater activity, both contract or share volume will increase along with the number of price changes.

If you have carefully recorded the order price, execution price, volatility (*daily high − low*), daily volume, time of day, and tick volume, you can find the importance of each factor and estimate the slippage for any trade by applying the model:

$$\text{Actual slippage at time } T = a_0 + a_1 \times \text{volatility} + a_2 \times \text{daily volume} +$$

$$a_3 \times \text{current activity at time } T + a_4 \times \text{size of order}$$

By creating a spreadsheet of values for all trades, you can solve for $a_0, a_1, a_2, a_3,$ and $a_4,$ and then estimate future slippage at any time T during the day, given the current volume and order size. This approach was taken in 1992[1] for large Stop orders using a ratio of order size to current market activity. The results, shown in Table 16-2, show that slippage was very modest for most markets. The far right column gives the slippage likely at the 5% level; that is, there is only a 5% chance of having slippage greater than $135 per contract for sugar, combining both entry and exit. Commissions were not included. The unusually large "worst" loss in Treasury bills was confirmed as correct.

Price Level

Continuing volatility is most common in markets that are at abnormally high price levels. Bull markets are followed by bear markets, and the combination creates sustained activity. Prices that are volatile at low levels are most likely to be at the end of a decline and can be returning to previous, less volatile patterns. The agricultural markets, when carryover

---

[1] Thomas V. Greer, B. Wade Brorsen, and Shi-Miin Liu, "Slippage Costs of a Large Technical Trader," *Technical Analysis of Stocks & Commodities* (January 1992).

TABLE 16-2   Slippage (Loss) for Stop Orders (Slippage in Dollars per Contract)*

Market	Average	Best	Worst	St Dev	5% Chance of Worse than on Entire Trade
World sugar	13.63	−11.20	200.20	33.71	135
Coffee	48.13	−22.50	168.75	48.44	194
Pork bellies	38.49	−12.00	168.00	42.22	169
Soybean meal	14.34	0.00	60.00	21.46	86
Heating oil	37.35	−17.50	109.39	33.58	134
Japanese yen	18.53	−12.50	112.50	28.86	115
Deutschemark	18.06	0.00	162.50	33.67	135
Treasury bills	62.86	0.00	700.00	139.51	558
Copper	25.70	−11.36	62.50	24.15	97
Platinum	77.92	−17.86	280.00	85.68	343
Gold	65.80	0.00	410.00	91.72	367

*Source: Thomas V. Greer, B. Wade Brorsen, and Shi-Miin Liu, "Slippage Costs of a Large Technical Trader," *Technical Analysis of Stocks & Commodities* (January 1992).

stocks are increasing, show reduced volatility. Many experts have theorized that the high interest rate yields seen in the 1980s, as well as the high precious metals prices, are a very unusual event not to be repeated often.

Some markets do not have a high or low price in the normal sense of a physical commodity; therefore, they do not contain volatility patterns directly proportional to price level. For example, foreign exchange markets have low volatility when they are at levels perceived as the fair value or equilibrium. Prices increase in volatility when they move either up or down from this level, because any change away from the norm is considered unstable.

Crude oil represents a different phenomenon because it is a controlled market. While currencies may become volatile as they move away from equilibrium, they will become quiet at a new price if that is perceived as reasonable by the market. This is not the case with oil, because the producing countries continue to drive prices back to their target levels by controlling the supply. Therefore, the farther prices decline from the producers' desired price, the more of a struggle exists between fair value and controlled price, resulting in higher volatility. The dynamics of higher oil prices are similar to other physical commodities. The day trader must always seek opportunities in potential volatility.

APPLICABILITY OF TRADING TECHNIQUES

Most traditional methods of technical analysis, in particular trend-following systems, are not used for trading intervals of less than 3 days; however, the price fluctuations during these shorter periods are nearly all *technical*. An economic analysis of supply and demand cannot be relevant over such a short time span; that approach can only be used for establishing longer-term trading policy. Other than the immediate reactions to overnight cash market movement, anticipated daily price changes based on political events and weather have not been successfully measured; however, techniques used for day trading can be applied to slightly longer periods of a few days. The principles used in these time frames are very different, and the number of data points used in the calculations reflect on the final reliability. For example, a 3-day daily moving average relies on only three data points for its decision of the direction of the trend; therefore, it will be very erratic.

Both day trading and short-term trading are concerned with timing to improve entry and exit points. The most common way to accomplish this is by a simple form of pattern recognition based on values relevant to the short time frame. From the floor trader's viewpoint, only the most obvious recent key levels are important. Today's price movements are compared with today's opening price, high and low, yesterday's closing price, yesterday's high and low, last week's high and low, very memorable older support and resistance points, and finally, life-of-contract high and low. When the same price satisfies more than one condition, there is greater confidence in the importance of that point.

The importance of noise is also very different for the day trader and the trend follower. Noise, the underlying erratic movement of prices, is not a significant issue for the position trader looking to follow interest rates to high levels over the next year. But it is very important for the day trader, because the trend component of price movement is very small over a 24-hour period compared with the noise. This makes it impossible, using the ordinary trend-following tools, to decide whether a move up over 15 minutes will begin a trend or whether it is simply part of the more common market noise.

Time-of-Day Patterns

Time-of-day and *short-term patterns* are combined in the most popular forms of day trading; the types of patterns have been discussed in Chapter 15. There are natural occurrences during the trading day that make certain times more important than others. The opening gap and the continuation of that direction usually take the first 15 to 20 minutes of the trading day, as does the reaction to the U.S. economic reports that are released at 7:30 A.M. in Chicago. After that, a price reversal occurs and a trading range is established, which lasts until the middle of the session. The midmorning period, which may marginally expand the initial trading range, tends to include low volume because many of the orders originating off the floor (called *paper*) are exhausted near the open; floor traders take this opportunity for a break, further reducing liquidity.

Following midday, activity steadily increases and the existing daily range is tested. It is common for most day traders to buy the bottom of the range and sell the top. A break of either support or resistance after midday is considered a major directional change; traders quickly shift to the direction of the breakout with the expectation of holding that position for the balance of the day. A more thorough analysis of time is shown in Figure 16-1. This chart, created by Walt Bressert, uses the important recent highs and lows and is very specific about relationships between the developing range, the previous day's range, and the time of day. Readers may want to compare Bressert's relationship with those found in Chapter 15. Intraday highs and lows that correspond to key levels found on charts—such as channel support and resistance, and head-and-shoulders objectives—are also likely to have increased importance.

Intraday versus Overnight Price Ranges

Holding a position overnight involves margin and, above all else, greater risk. It also increases the opportunity for larger profits. In moderately active markets, the opening gap, the difference between the prior close and the next open, can be one-third to one-half the size of the normal trading range. Markets that are traded in one time zone but reflect the business of a completely different geographic region, have larger systematic gap openings. For example, the Nikkei 225 is traded at the Chicago Mercantile Exchange, but the Nikkei reflects the value of the Japanese stock market. While the day session in Chicago is open from about 7:00 A.M. to 3:00 P.M. local time, the time in Japan is 10 hours earlier, 9:00 P.M. to 5:00 A.M., a period when there is no business activity in Asia. When Chicago opens, it must immediately reflect the price of the previous closing session in Japan; therefore, it gaps to that level. This same situation happens to a lesser degree for European currencies, which are actively traded on Chicago's IMM. When those markets open at 7:20 A.M., Europe is coming back from lunch and all local economic news has already been absorbed into the market.

In Table 16-3 and Figure 16-2 we see that the currencies and metals, representing markets actively traded 24 hours, have the largest *overnight* gaps. Viewing world markets only during the U.S. business hours can put a trader at a disadvantage and force him to deal with unpredictable, uncontrollable risks. This has prompted many traders to watch the markets through both day and night. Most computerized systems have no trouble continuing their calculation through various sessions.

Point-and-Figure for Short-Term Trading

Point-and-figure charting has been a primary tool of day traders for many years. Using the minimum price movement as the box size and a 3-box reversal, many traders will keep a continuous, although lengthy, chart of day-to-day price movement. Buy and sell signals can be taken in the standard manner, but day traders are most likely to use these charts for identifying countertrend support and resistance levels. Intraday point-and-figure, as well as moving averages, often show frequent changes of direction before a new buy or sell signal occurs, even when the minimum box size is used. Trend methods are best applied to short-term overnight positions in which the size of the move is much larger.

FIGURE 16-1 Intraday timing of market movement.

KEY

H — High
L — Low
C — Close
R — Range (H minus L) for Entry Day
Y — Yesterday
E — Day of entry/exit — "today"

B — Buy
S — Sell

$H_E < H_Y$ — high of entry is lower than yesterday's high
$H_E > H_Y$ — high of entry is higher than yesterday's high
$R > C$ — range of entry day extends above yesterday's close
$R < C$ — range of entry day extends below yesterday's close
$L_E < L_Y$ — low of entry day is lower than yesterday's low
$L_E > L_Y$ — low of entry day is higher than yesterday's low

Source: Walt Bressert.

TABLE 16-3   Percentage of Overnight Price Gap Compared with Subsequent Trading Range, for Selected U.S. Markets

| | % Change Overnight | |
Market	1985–1989	1990–1995
Cotton	29.6	27.5
Corn	26.3	26.5
Soybeans	25.5	23.8
Australian dollar	51.9	43.5
British pound	39.1	28.1
Canadian dollar	39.0	31.9
Deutschemark	37.9	30.9
Japanese yen	43.0	35.8
Swiss franc	38.4	25.5
Gold	28.7	31.5
High grade copper	na	30.9
Crude oil	32.4	26.6
Heating oil	33.8	29.0
S&P 500	19.3	16.3
NYSE Composite	22.0	19.9
Treasury bills	27.2	25.6
Treasury notes	26.6	13.6
Treasury bonds	22.6	11.6

Price reversals that occur during the day can be plotted using a smaller point-and-figure box size than is common for daily charting. The more frequent reversals due to the combination of more data and smaller box size will define the trend sooner or bring the protective stop closer. Remember, stop-loss levels advance only when there are reversals. In this way, day traders' improvements are transparent to the point-and-figure users who work only with the daily high, low, and closing prices. In general, when there is a choice of plotting a point-and-figure trend continuation or reversal, the reversal should be plotted. This allows the chart to reflect the reversal sooner and bring the stop-loss closer—both are an improvement over the standard rules.

Moving Averages

The intrinsic dependency on time makes a moving average less adaptable to day trading. To be used properly, a moving average must be recalculated at fixed intervals. Two philosophic questions must be answered with regard to intraday moving averages. Do trends exist in this short time interval, and does it make sense to apply a moving average to all intraday prices unevenly spaced with respect to time? In a previous section of this chapter, the conflict between noise and trends was discussed. Markets with a large noise component require more time to identify a trend, or a larger price move; therefore, it may not be possible to enter a trend trade and still have enough profit potential before the end of the trading session. It is likely that there will not be more than 25% of the daily range remaining after the trend has been identified, making the profit opportunity too small.

The versatility of computers allows all intraday prices to be used in a moving average rather than the traditional 5-minute bar; furthermore, you can create a price bar based on every 5 or 10 prices, regardless of time. In a liquid market, prices might be posted every

FIGURE 16-2   Opening gap as a percentage of daily move.

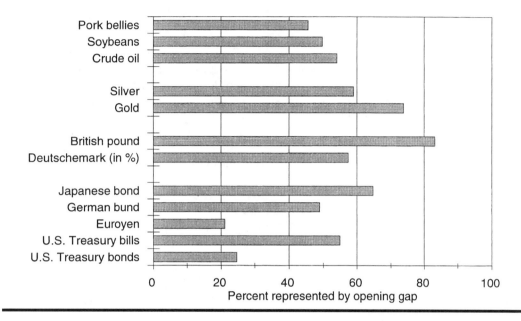

few seconds even though volume may vary. For practical purposes, prices might be considered equally spaced. But consider an extreme example. The price of a less liquid market changes every 15 seconds during more active times, then quiets to 5-minute intervals; at one time, there is a lull of 15 minutes followed by a jump in price. Is there a difference in the way we would interpret the following two patterns? Is there a difference in the way a moving average would calculate the trend?

Time A	Price	Time B
10:00	5005	10:00
10:01	5010	10:05
10:02	5005	10:06
10:03	5015	10:16
10:04	5025	10:26
10:05	5020	10:28
10:06	5015	10:29
10:07	5025	10:44

Pattern *A* shows a gradual upward movement over equal time intervals; pattern *B* shows slow rallies and fast drops. When interpreted by a trader, pattern *B* is often considered *toppy;* it is a market struggling to go higher with anxious sellers. Moving averages of pattern *A*, taken as shown, and pattern *B*, interpolated to equal intervals, will have the same trend direction at each point. There is not enough information to know which is best, but it is clear that the patterns can be interpreted differently.

More on Choosing the Length of the Intraday Bar

While there is no *right* bar length, traders most often choose 5-, 10-, 15-, 30-minute, and 1-hour periods to chart. Most of the commercial software packages require that the interval be evenly divided into 1 hour; therefore, a 6½-minute interval is not allowed. When using longer bars, such as 1 hour, it is important to consider the length of the last bar of the day. A 1-hour bar will post its first price at the end of the first actual hour, rather than 1 hour after the open; the last bar will be the interval from the last whole hour to the close. In the case of oil, this may only be 10 minutes. When bars are uneven in this way, the price ranges and corresponding volume are no longer comparable with one another.

There is a difference in opinion between analysts over the choice of intraday intervals. One group prefers to pick a standard number because it conforms to the way others trade; for example, you can expect orders to flow more actively every hour. This approach may be particularly valuable if you plan to take the opposite position. The other group of traders are constantly seeking their own time interval, avoiding uneven order flow and price distortion caused by most other traders. If you are part of this group, you may choose your interval by dividing the total number of minutes in the trading session by a value that gives you equal-length bars. You may also want to find a bar length, such as 21 minutes, that represents a Fibonacci number and comes close to dividing the day equally.

MARKET PATTERNS

A trade that lasts from 1 to 3 days can be improved if short-term patterns or cycles can be found. For example, in a trending market there are outstanding weekly and weekend patterns. It is most common to find that the price movements from Thursday to Friday (close-to-close) are in the direction of the major trend and that the movement on Monday is a continuation of that trend. By Tuesday (or sometimes Wednesday), the strength of new buyers or sellers has faded, and the market reverses due to lack of activity and some profit taking. It often stays in this state through Wednesday or early Thursday when it again resumes the trend. In a sideways market, the Friday and Monday directions differ from the direction during the prior week and often differ from each other.

Support and Resistance

Support and resistance levels are important to the short-term trader. If prices start to move higher, slow down, and finally reverse, it is natural to consider the top price as a resistance point. Prices are thought to have been stretched to their extreme at that level. Any subsequent attempt to approach the previous high price will be met with professional selling in anticipation of prices stopping again at the same point. In addition, it is common for the same traders and others to place orders above the previous high prices to take new long positions or close out shorts in the event of a breakout.

This method, very popular among floor traders and active speculators, tends to create and emphasize the support and resistance price levels until they define a clear *trading range*. Within a 1- to 3-day period, these ranges can be narrow and yet effectively contain price movement. During the life of the trading range, it will continue to narrow as the levels become clear to more traders and the anticipation of a reversal at those levels becomes imminent.

To take advantage of the smaller ranges caused in this manner, it is necessary to enter positions during the middle of a trading session, frequently holding that trade until the middle of the next session. An example using the Chicago Board of Trade December 75 Silver contract, during August 1975, will help to illustrate this. Prices on 4 consecutive days are seen in Table 16-4. The opening and closing prices for the first 3 days do not indicate

TABLE 16-4 December 75 CBT Silver

	Open	High	Low	Close
August 21	500.50	505.00	493.00	498.20
22	501.00	504.00	494.50	500.00
25	501.00	594.50	496.00	503.80
26	502.50	504.00	483.80	483.80

any opportunity for trading. Prices were generally in the middle of the daily range. By using the high and low of the previous day, this situation can be traded either of two ways.

Thursday, August 21, forms a range of 505 to 493, closing near the center of the range. After the next open, buy just above 493 and sell just below 505 to be certain of entering and exiting the position. For protection, a stop can be entered at about 506 and 492 to reverse the position on a breakout. Had this procedure been followed, entering 2¢ (200 points) before the bounds of the range, Table 16-5 shows how trades would have been executed.

In each case, the entry was 200 points before the level at which prices had reversed on the prior day. The Stop-Loss order was placed to limit losses to a 100-point penetration. Although this is an ideal situation, professional traders frequently use this method. It can be seen that the support levels did actually rise from 493.00 to 494.50, and then to 496.00. When support was penetrated, prices rapidly broke to new lows of 483.80, down to the permissible limit. Similarly, the resistance level remained intact going from 505.00 to 504.00, 504.50, and finally, 504.00. It is generally accepted that the resistance level represents a more volatile area that must be watched closely for false breakouts.

Support and resistance levels gain importance the more time they remain intact. The high and low of the prior day are not as significant as the weekly or the monthly range. Each can be traded using the same technique. The major support and resistance levels are contract highs and lows, which rarely allow breakouts with less than one attempt. Longer-term price objectives can be identified using a continuation chart. This chart plots only the nearest (spot) futures contract of a specific market to allow the location of support and resistance levels when the current contracts are in a new high or low area.

Before 1990 there were very few published day-trading systems. The more recent ones have had the benefit of sophisticated computer programs and large historical databases. The following method precedes this era and remains unique and a valuable part of our literature.

TABLE 16-5 Trading December 75 Silver Using Support and Resistance

		Profit/Loss
August 22	Sold at 503.00	
	Closed-out short and bought at 495.00	+8.00
August 25	Closed-out long and sold at 502.00	+7.00
	Closed-out short and bought at 496.50	+5.50
August 26	Closed-out long and sold at 502.00	+5.50
	Closed-out short and bought at 498.00	+4.00
	Closed-out long and sold at 495.00	−3.00
	Open position	+11.20

The Taylor Trading Technique

In 1950, George Douglass Taylor published his *book method* of day trading, which he had been using for many years in both the stock and grain markets.[2] The method is based on the experience of discipline and timing, but is carefully set down and can be implemented in either a sophisticated or simplified state. The system is intrinsically cyclic, anticipating 3-day movements in the grains. These 3 days can vary in pattern when they are within an uptrend or downtrend. Taylor's explanation of his method is thorough and includes many valuable thoughts for traders interested in working with the market full-time. The summary and analysis presented here cannot replace a reading of the original material.

Taylor developed his approach to trading through experience and a belief that there is a basic rhythm in the market. The dominant pattern is seen to be a 3-day repetition with occasional, although regular, intervals of 4- to 5-day patterns. Taylor's cycles are based on continuous trading days without regard to weekends and holidays. The 3-day cycle varies slightly if prices are in an uptrend or downtrend. The uptrend is defined as having higher tops and bottoms over some selected time period such as a week, month, or season. A downtrend is the reverse. During an uptrend the following sequence can be expected:

1. A *buying day objective,* where prices stop declining and a purchase can be made before a rally begins
2. A *selling day objective,* at which the long position is closed out
3. A *short sale day objective,* where prices meet resistance and can be sold prior to a reversal.

Following the third day, after a short position is entered, the cycle begins again with a *buying day objective.* Because an uptrend is identified, Taylor has given extra latitude to the long position with part of the day between the liquidation of the long (2), and entering a new short (3) reserved to allow the upward momentum to exhaust itself. Downtrends are the opposite, expecting some added time for the downward move to finish before the rally begins.

The actual *objectives* are extremely short-term support and resistance levels, usually only the prior day's high and low prices or occasionally the high and low of the 3-day cycle, which may be the same prices. On a buying day, the objective is a test or penetration of the prior day's low price, but only if it occurs first, before a test of the prior highs. Taylor's method is then a short-term countertrend technique, which looks for prices to reverse direction continuously. His belief was that speculation caused these erratic, sometimes large, cyclic variations above and below the long-term trend.

Taylor placed great emphasis on the order of occurrence of the high and low on each day. To buy, the low must occur first. If this is a buying day in an uptrend, a long position is entered after any lower opening whether or not the prior low is reached. Taylor reasoned that because an uptrend is generally stronger toward the close, the first opportunity must be taken on a buying day. However, if a high occurs first and prices then decline nearing the lows toward the end of the trading day, no long position is entered. This pattern indicates a lower open the following day, which will provide a better opportunity to buy. During a downtrend, the violations of the lows, or penetrations toward the close, are more common. By waiting until the next day to purchase, the 3-day cycle is shifted to favor the short sale.

Consider the same problems with regard to closing out a long and entering a new short during an uptrend. If on the same day that the long was entered prices rallied sharply, touching or penetrating prior highs, a higher opening would be expected the next day, at which time the long position would be closed out. Because of the uptrend, a small

[2] *The Taylor Trading Technique,* by George Douglass Taylor (1950) (reprinted by Traders Press, P.O. Box 6206, Greenville, SC 29606, in 1994).

setback and another test of the highs might be expected. It would then require another day to ensure that the strength was exhausted. If the highs of the *selling day* were tested on the open of the *short sale day,* a new short would be entered immediately. If the short sale day opened lower and finished higher, no position would be taken.

Shorter reactions to price moves are expected when a long position is entered on a buy day, or on the next open, when a downtrend exists. If prices rally sharply on the same day, the position is closed out at a profit. This is important to remember, because trading against the trend does not offer the latitude of waiting for the best moment; time is working against the position.

Taylor called this his *book method* because he recorded all the information necessary for trading in a small 3" × 5" spiral notebook that he carried. The organization of the book is shown in Table 16-6, an example that uses the November 75 soybean contract. Of course, in Taylor's book, there would be only 1 month per page due to its size. The first five columns contain the date and day, followed by the open, high, low, and closing prices. The

TABLE 16-6 November 1975 Soybeans

1975		Open	High	Low	Close	D	R	BH	BU	Net
					March					
M	10	540	(x542)	535	540½					
T	11	435	560¼	(x535)	560¼	7		18¾	0	
W	12	560	(x572)	552	571½		37			
H	13	568	(x577)	559	560½					
F	14	553	559	(✓549)	549½	28		0	10	+2¾
M	17	548	(✓560)	548	548		11			
T	18	555	(x558)	538	538½					
W	19	530	546	(x529)	545¼	29		0	9	
H	20	543	(✓555)	540	547½		26			
F	21	547½	(✓567½)	547½	567½				-1½	
M	24	573	581	(✓561)	573	6½		13½	0	
T	25	573	(x575)	564	574		14			
W	26	577	(✓594)	574	594					
H	27	587	590	(✓579)	585	15		0	0	+31½
M	31	592	(✓603½)	589	595½	24½				
					April					
T	1	599	(x599)	584	591½					
W	2	589	591½	(✓575)	575¾	24		0	9	
H	3	570	(✓573)	565	566¾		0			
F	4	570	(✓578)	567	576¾				-12	
M	7	577	577	(✓562)	565¾	16		0	5	
T	8	566	(✓579½)	563	568¼		17½			
W	9	565	(✓574)	561½	573½					
H	10	571	575	(✓556)	561¾	18		1	5½	
F	11	560	(x564½)	558	563½		8½			-9
M	14	561	(x568)	555½	561½					
T	15	565	569½	(✓560½)	563½	7½		1½	0	
W	16	562	(x566)	553	559¼		5½			
H	17	560	(✓565)	558	563½					
F	18	563	563	(✓557)	559	8		0	1	-1

first 10 days are used to determine where the cycle begins. Scanning the daily lows, circle the lowest of the first 10 days, in this case March 19. Then work backward and forward, circling every third low price. These are buying days. The sequences of two in-between days are circled in the high column and indicate the selling day and the short sale day, respectively. This example is especially simple because it assumes a consistent uptrend and shows no variation from the 3-day cycle.

To judge the opportunities for buying and selling, the next columns, marked *D* and *R,* indicate the number of points in the *decline* from the short sale to the buying day, and the number of points in the *rally* from the buying day to the selling day. In both columns, the differences are taken using the highs and lows only. These values represent the maximum number of points that could have been made in those trades, provided the highs and lows occurred in the proper order. An "x" or a "✓" in the circle next to the high or low means that the opportunity to buy or sell occurred first (if an x) or last (if a ✓). In the case of the first, the trade would have been entered that day and in the other case, Taylor would have waited.

The next two columns, BH and BU, show the adversity and opportunity of that day's prices to the buying objective. BH means a *buying day high* and is entered with the number of points that the day traded above the prior day's high (the *short sale day*); BU shows the opportunity to *buy under,* by recording the number of points by which the day sold under the low of the prior day—the area to buy if the low occurred first. If neither situation occurred, zeros were entered.

A wide column on the right is used to indicate the net weekly change in direction by taking the difference between the prior Friday's closing price and the current Friday's price. This should be used to compare with the trading performance.

By observing columns *D* and *R* in Table 16-6, it can be seen that there was ample opportunity for profits on both the long positions and short sales, with only one case of a zero entry on April 3. The trades that would have been entered or liquidated can be approximated using the BH and BU columns and the x and ✓ notations. For consistency, it might be assumed that the ✓ indicates that a position was taken on the next open. In either case, the results would have been good.

Taylor's daily method requires care in monitoring the market, which only a full-time trader can provide. The order of the highs and lows must be observed, as well as whether the new low is going to penetrate or fail to penetrate the prior lows. The trades must be timed carefully for maximum profit. In addition, it would be helpful to combine this method with a good trend identification technique as well as observe seasonal patterns to improve the choice of the overriding market direction.

For those who cannot watch the market constantly, Taylor offers a rigid *3-Day Trading Method,* which is a modification of his overall daily method. The cycles remain the same, but the buying and selling objectives are entered into the market in advance. This method is expected to work on balance, as are other well-defined systems. What is primarily lost by this approach is the order of occurrence of the highs and lows; otherwise, the concept of the system remains intact.

It is interesting that this technique profits from penetration of support and resistance levels. Most other methods consider a breakout of prior highs and lows as a major trend change indication, but Taylor views it as a better opportunity to do the opposite. It is one of the few examples of such an approach and could only succeed in the short term, where the behavioral aspects of trading are dominant.

Intraday Breakout Systems

As discussed earlier in this chapter, there are unique intraday price patterns caused by an uneven distribution of volume throughout the day. By far, the most popular systematic approach to day trading is the *N*-day breakout applied to intraday data; this transforms it into the *N-bar breakout.* Entry and exit signals occur during the trading session instead of only at the close; in addition, there may be more than one buy or sell during the day if prices have wide swings.

A variation of this technique intended for intraday data is the *opening range breakout,*[3] which gives the underlying entry and exit signals based on how far prices move from the open of the day. The trader is then buying when prices move up from the open by, for example, 8 ticks in bonds, in the same manner as a trend follower. If prices then decline to 8 ticks below the open, the long position would be reversed to a short. This approach uses the opening price as the *pivot point* for the day, claiming that price direction, relative to that point, is important. Tests exited all trades on the close of the day.

It is also reasonable to use the close of the previous day as the pivot point. Most traders watch today's prices to see if they are higher or lower than the prior close, which connects today's price patterns to the previous day. In its basic form, the opening range breakout treats one day as independent to previous price movements. This seems unnecessarily restrictive. Crabel, in his extensive study of intraday patterns, has found that combinations of inside days, low volatility, bull and bear hooks, and other patterns that precede the current day, all contribute to a selection process that improves trading. Table 16-7 shows a comparison of an opening range breakout with and without a preceding inside day.[4] The improvement due to selection is significant.

If you consider that intraday trading may give one new signal each day, any method that helps select the better trades is welcome. The intraday trading profile of many small profits and losses allows you to be more selective without fear of missing the one big trade of the year, which is a problem typical of a long-term trend-following system. Skipping as

[3] See Toby Crabel, *Day Trading With Short Term Price Patterns and Opening Range Breakout* (Traders Press, Greenville, SC 29603).

[4] Toby Crabel, "Opening Range Breakout, Part 4," *Technical Analysis of Stocks & Commodities* (February 1989).

TABLE 16-7 Opening Range Breakout, % Profitable Trades*

		Any Day (%)	Inside Day (%)
Bonds	Open plus 16 ticks	60	76
	Open plus 8 ticks	55	74
	Open minus 8 ticks	56	62
	Open minus 16 ticks	56	66
S&P 500	Open plus 160 points	68	61
	Open plus 80 points	55	57
	Open minus 80 points	49	48
	Open minus 160 points	49	45
Soybeans	Open plus 10 cents	60	70
	Open plus 5 cents	56	67
	Open minus 5 cents	58	69
	Open minus 10 cents	63	76
Cattle	Open plus 50 points	65	55
	Open plus 25 points	58	55
	Open minus 25 points	58	60
	Open minus 50 points	63	73

*Source: Toby Crabel.

FIGURE 16-3 (*a*) Omega *TradeStation* code for first-hour breakout system. (*b*) Omega *TradeStation* code for first-hour breakout indicator.

```
{ System: 1st hour Breakout (adapted from M. McNutt, 1994) }

     [10] MaxBarsBack
     [*] Generate Realtime Orders
     [*] Do not allow multiple entries in the same direction

System uses ten minute bars of S&P futures for data 1 and 60 minute bars for data
2 [daily data is held in data 3] }

vars: Sess1FirstBarDAte(9, data2, Sess1FirstBarHigh(0, data2),
     Sess1FirstBarLow(0, data2), avedayrange(0,data3);
input: RanLn(10);

avedayrange = @average(high of data3 - low of data3), RanLn) of data3;

if (time of data2 = Sess1FirstBarTime of data2) or
   (date of data2 > date[1] of data2) then begin
       Sess1FirstBarDate = Date of data2;
       Sess1FirstBarHigh = high of data2;
       Sess1FirstBarLow = Low of data2;
       end;
If (Sess1FirstBarDate = Date of data2) and
   (time of data2 < Sess1EndTime of data2) then begin
       if close[1] < Sess1FirstBarHigh then buy at
            Sess1FirstBarHigh + 20 point stop;
       if close[1] > Sess1FirstBarLow then sell at
            Sess1FirstBarLow - 20 point stop;
       end;

if low <= Sess1FirstBarHigh - avedayrange then exitshort at market;
if high >= Sess1FirstBarLow[1] + avedayrange then exitlong at market;
```
(*a*)

```
{Indicator: 1st hour Breakout (adapted from M. McNutt, 1994) }

vars: Sess1FirstBarDAte(9, data2, Sess1FirstBarHigh(0, data2),
     Sess1FirstBarLow(0, data2), avedayrange(0,data3);

avedayrange = @average(high of data3 - low of data3, 10) of data3;

if (time of data2 = Sess1FirstBarTime of data2) or
     (Date of data2 > date[1] of data2) then begin
       Sess1FirstBarDate = date of data2;
       Sess1FirstBarHigh = high of data2;
       Sess1FirstBarLow = low of data2;
       end;
if (Sess1FirstBarDate = date of data2) and
     (Time of data2 < Sess1EndTime of data2) then begin
       Plot1(Sess1FirstBarHigh, "1st Buy");
       Plot2(Sess1FirstBarLow,"1st Sell");
       Plot3(Sess1FirstBarLow + avedayrange,"Buy stop");
       Plot4(Sess1FirstBarHigh - avedayrange,"Sell stop");
       end;
```
(*b*)

many as 50% of the trades should not limit your profit potential; you should be able to stand aside and start again without much concern about continuity.

Breakout Ranges Based on Time

Instead of a breakout that occurs when prices move a fixed number of points away from the opening price, you can establish an opening range based on the first 60 minutes of trading.[5] After this time, a new high or low would be a signal to enter a long or short position. This is a trade-off between avoiding the erratic movements of early trading and missing the beginning of a price move to start early and continue in the same direction.

Combined with the first-hour breakout is a calculation of the day's trading range to be used for reversing your position or taking profits. The projected range high is calculated as the average daily range added to today's low price after the first hour of trading; the low is that same range calculation subtracted from the high of the first hour. The Omega *Easy Language* code for this system involves the use of multiple time frame data and can be found in Figure 16-3*a;* an indicator that shows the signal on a chart page is given in Figure 16-3*b.* In the practical application of this method, the first-hour range must be penetrated by at least 20 points for the S&P. If the first-hour range is nearly as large as the average 10-day range (used for the exit targets), use the anticipated high and low for buy and sell signals, rather than a breakout of the first-hour range. Other risk controls, such as a trailing stop (in addition to a reversal if the opposite signal is given) and a fixed stop, are also recommended.

---

[5] Malcolm McNutt, "First-Hour Breakout System," *Technical Analysis of Stocks & Commodities* (July 1994).

17

Adaptive Techniques

An *adaptive* technique is one that changes with market conditions. It could be as simple as using a percentage stop-loss; however, technicians have begun to associate the idea of "adaptive" with a broader scope, although the purpose remains the same—to handle more changing conditions without manual intervention. The trends and indicators that are discussed in this chapter are able to change the calculation period. Under some conditions, such as sideways markets, it may be best to use a slow trend or momentum, and during explosive intervals those same methods are expected to work better if they respond quickly.

ADAPTIVE TREND CALCULATIONS

We begin by looking at techniques that vary the length of the trend. These techniques are based on a common premise that it is better to use a longer-term trend, one that is slower to react to price change, when the market is either in a "sideways" pattern, has low volatility or, in the case of Kaufman, has high relative noise. This may seem a reasonable assumption, but identifying a sideways market is very difficult. A price may be unchanged from a week ago, yet during those 5 days it rose quickly for 3 days, then reversed sharply and, coincidently, was at the same level on the 5th day, as it continued to plunge. In many ways these adaptive techniques improve the basic performance of standard trend calculations, but they cannot solve all of the problems.

Kaufman's *Adaptive Moving Average*

Kaufman's *Adaptive Moving Average* (KAMA),[1] which began taking form in 1972, is based on the concept that a noisy market requires a slower trend than one with less noise. That is, the trendline must lag further behind in a relatively noisy market to avoid being penetrated by the price, which would cause a trend change. When prices move consistently in one direction, any trend speed may be used because there are no false changes of direction. The KAMA is intended to use the fastest trend possible, based on the smallest calculation period for the existing market conditions. It varies the speed of the trend by using an exponential smoothing formula, changing the smoothing constant each period. The use of a smoothing constant was selected because it allows for a full range of trends, compared with the simple moving average that uses integer values and is limited in the selection of the fast-end speeds (see the discussion of exponential smoothing in Chapter 4, "Trend Calculations").

$$KAMA_t = KAMA_{t-1} + sc_t \times (\text{Price} - KAMA_{t-1})$$

where $KAMA_t$ is the new adaptive moving average value
   $KAMA_{t-1}$ is the previous adaptive moving average value
   Price is the current price (for period t)
   sc_t is the smoothing constant, calculated each period as follows:

[1] See Perry J. Kaufman, *Smarter Trading* (McGraw-Hill, New York, 1995, pp. 129–153) for a complete discussion of this method.

$$\text{sc}_t = [\text{ER}_t \times (\text{fastest} - \text{slowest}) + \text{slowest}]^2$$

and

fastest = 2 / (fastest moving average period + 1)

slowest = 2 / (slowest moving average period + 1)

$$ER_t = \frac{|\text{price}_i - \text{price}_{i-n}|}{\sum_{t}^{t-n} |\text{price}_i - \text{price}_{i-1}|}$$

The *fastest* and *slowest* values represent the range of periods over which KAMA can vary, each converted to its exponential smoothing constant equivalent. Nominally, these values are set to 2 and 30. By squaring the smoothing constant components, the slow end becomes 30×30, equal to an extremely unresponsive 900-period trend. The effect of this is to stop the movement of the trendline when the market becomes very noisy. On the other end, when the market goes up steadily, without a reversal for n days, the speed of the trend can reach a very fast 4-period equivalent.

The *efficiency ratio, ER,* has more recently been called *fractal efficiency.* It has the value of 1 when prices move in the same direction for the full n periods, and a value of 0 when prices are unchanged over the n periods. When prices move in wide swings within the interval, the sum of the denominator becomes very large compared with the numerator and *ER* approaches 0. Smaller values of *ER* result in a smaller smoothing constant and a slower trend.

If you choose to use the default values for KAMA, where *ER* is calculated over 10 periods and the smoothing constant ranges from 2 to 30 (squared), its calculation can be expressed in Omega code as

```
KAMA = KAMA[1] + ((@absvalue(close-close[10])/
       @summation(@absvalue(close-close[1]),.10)* .6022) + .0645)^2*(close-KAMA[1])
```

Time Period for ER

In Kaufman's Adaptive Moving Average, the time period only affects the calculation of the efficiency ratio. The purpose is to keep that period, n, as small as possible so that the evaluation of a few days will allow the speed of the trend to change from fast to slow and back again. User's may begin testing in the range of 8 to 10 days.

Choice of Volatility

The use of the volatility function, `@summation(@absvalue(close-close[1]),10))` in Omega code, adds all the individual price changes rather than looking only at the high-low range. Noise is considered more active when prices jump up and down. It is not as important that prices moved from a particular low to a certain high, but the pattern of how it was done. A market in which prices moved from low to high then back to the low and high again is clearly more volatile and noisier than one that made a single move from low to high.

Small Moves in One Direction

Occasionally there will be a series of price moves that progress in very small increments in one direction without a reversal, causing *ER* = 1. Although this is theoretically correct, it may prove best to include a filter for those cases where the direction, $D = |\text{price}_i - \text{price}_{i-n}|$ < *min,* or a scaling function that does not allow the smoothing constant to produce the usual fast trend as the direction D moves below *min.*

Trading KAMA

The Adaptive Moving Average can be traded as any trend, and has the same characteristics of exponential smoothing. That is, when prices cross the trendline from up to down, the trendline must turn down. Although KAMA may use a trend with the equivalent of 900 days, the value of the current KAMA will still turn down a very small amount. Trading rules that base signals on the direction of the trendline should include a small band around the KAMA to prevent price penetrations during a sideways market to cause a change in the trading signal. Without this band, the benefit of a *sideways* KAMA trendline is eliminated.

When applying KAMA to a trading program, it can be seen that higher values of the efficiency ratio, *ER*, are rarely reached using a calculation period greater than 14. This would require an extremely directional move for 2 weeks of daily data. As longer periods are used, the pattern of *ER* becomes very uniform, based on the underlying level of noise in each market. Because peak levels in the *ER* cannot be sustained, they are valuable candidates for profit taking.

Programming KAMA

The following *Easy Language* user function can be used by a system or indicator to calculate Kaufman's Adaptive Moving Average.

```
{KAMA : Kaufman's Adaptive Moving Average
 Copyright 1990-1998, PJ Kaufman. All rights reserved}

        inputs: period(numericsimple);
        vars:           efratio(0), smooth(1), fastend(.666), slowend(.0645),
                        AMA(0), diff(0), signal(0), noise(0);

        {calculate efficiency ratio}
        efratio = 1;
        diff = @absvalue(close - close[1]);
        if currentbar > period then begin
                signal = @absvalue(close - close[period]);
                noise = @summation(diff,period);
                if noise <> 0 then efratio = signal / noise;
                end;
        if currentbar <= period then AMA = close;
        smooth = @power(efratio*(fastend - slowend) + slowend,2);
        AMA = AMA[1] + smooth*(close - AMA[1]);
        KAMA = AMA;
```

Chande's Variable Index Dynamic Average (VIDYA)[2]

Tushar Chande's *Variable Index Dynamic Average* (VIDYA) first appeared in *Technical Analysis of Stocks & Commodities* in March 1992. Both VIDYA and Kaufman's KAMA use an exponential smoothing as a base for varying the speed of the trend each day. VIDYA, however, uses a pivotal smoothing constant, which is fixed, and varies the speed by using a factor based on the relative volatility to increase or decrease the value of *s*.

$$VIDYA_t = k \times s \times C_t + (1 - k \times s) \times VIDYA_{t-1}$$

where   *s* is a fixed smoothing constant, suggested as a 9-day equivalent
            (i.e., $s = 2/(9 + 1) = .20$)
        C is the closing price

---

[2] Tushar S. Chande and Stanley Kroll, *The New Technical Trader* (John Wiley & Sons, New York, 1994).

t and $t - 1$ represent the current and previous periods
k is the relative volatility, calculated as

$$k = @\text{stdev}(C, n) \ / \ @\text{stdev}(C, m)$$

where   @stdev is the standard deviation function
n is the recent past n days
m is a longer historic interval in days, $m > n$

Volatility

Chande uses a very practical relative volatility measure based on the standard deviation, or distribution of price moves over the past n days, compared with a longer historic pattern, taken over b days. When $k > 1$ the current volatility is greater than the historic volatility; when $k < 1$ the current volatility is lower. VIDYA can be written as an indicator in Omega code as

```
{VIDYA : Variable Index Dynamic Average by Tushar Chande
 Copyright 1997-1998, PJ Kaufman. All rights reserved.
 Period suggested at 9, histper suggested at > 9}
        input:  period(9), histper(30);
        var:    k(0), sc(0), VIDYA(0);
{relative volatility}
        k = @stddev(close, period) / @stddev(close,histper);
{smoothing constant}
      sc = 2 / (period + 1);
{VIDYA}
      VIDYA = k*sc*close + (1 - k*sc)*VIDYA[1];
      plot1 (VIDYA, "VIDYA");
```

Alternate Choices for Varying the Trend Period

The use of an exponential formula, either the simplified one shown by Kaufman or the traditional one of Chande, allows the smoothing constant to vary according to the design of the user. There are indicators with which we are already familiar that might be substituted for the smoothing constant.

Correlation Coefficient, r^2

The most likely choice, suggested by Chande, is the correlation coefficient, r^2. This value is the result of measuring the residuals from a linear regression calculation. When the regression fit is very strong, the value of r^2 is near 1; when there is no apparent market direction, r^2 is near 0. This fits neatly into the same pattern of smoothing constants as the KAMA and VIDYA.

When programming this technique, the calculation of the correlation of the residuals, r, requires the use of arrays and your own code for the correlation. This can be done using the formulas found in Chapter 3. To avoid that complication, the following program calculates a similar technique (Method 1) by evaluating the correlation of the closing prices and a time series containing the sequential values 1, 2, 3, ... It then calculates the current value of the residual based on a linear regression of closing prices (Method 2) and finds the correlation coefficient, r^2, of the series of current residuals. In the following programming code Method 2 is plotted, and the result of Method 1 is commented out.

```
{Adaptive R2 : Adaptive Correlation Coefficient Indicator
 Copyright 1997-1998, PJ Kaufman. All rights reserved.
 Plot smoothing function based on linear regression residuals and
 on simple time series function}
```

```
        input:  period(9);
        var:    R2(0), AR2(0), timeseries(0), resid(0), RR2(0), ARR2(0);

        timeseries = currentbar;
{Method 1: correlation of price and timeseries}
        if currentbar <= period then AR2 = close
                else begin
                        R2 = (@correlation(close, timeseries, period) + 1) / 2;
                        AR2 = AR2[1] + R2*(close - AR2[1]);
                end;
{       plot1 (AR2,"R2");}
{Method 2: correlation with current regression residual }
        resid = close - @linearregvalue(close,period,0);
        RR2 = (@correlation(resid, timeseries, period) + 1) / 2;
        ARR2 = ARR2[1] + RR2*(close - ARR2[1]);
        plot2 (ARR2,"ARR2");
```

Momentum Calculations

There are many momentum calculations, such as RSI, that vary from 0 to 1, or from −1 to +1. In most cases the trend is considered strongest when the momentum value is closest to the extremes. The momentum values can easily be changed to fit the 0-to-1 pattern of the smoothing constant by using the transformations

(1) For a range of 0 to 1   `sc = @absvalue(M-.5)*2`
(2) For a range of −1 to +1   `sc = @absvalue(M)`

where `sc` is the smoothing constant to be used for the current period
`M` is the current momentum value

By reflecting the lower extreme around the midpoint of the calculation, then taking the absolute value, the transformed indicator shows a stronger trend near 1 and less direction near 0.

Programming the Adaptive RSI

The following Omega code adapts the RSI to a smoothing constant:

```
{Adaptive RSI : Adaptive Relative Strength Indicator
 Smoothing function based on RSI}

        input:  period(20);
        var:    sc(0), ARSI(0);

        if currentbar <= period then ARSI = close
                else begin
                        sc = (@absvalue(@RSI(close, period) / 100 - .5)*2);
                        ARSI = ARSI[1] + sc*(close - ARSI[1]);
                        end;
        plot1 (ARSI, "ARSI");
```

Comparison of Adaptive Trends

Figure 17-1 shows three of the adaptive trending methods compared with a moving average, all based on a base calculation period of 20. Kaufman's KAMA appears to be slightly closer to prices than Chande's VIDYA and flattens out faster during sideways periods; otherwise, they have similar characteristics because they both use the structure of the exponential smoothing calculation. The adaptive RSI (ARSI), used as a substitute for the smoothing constant, is most responsive to price and appears as though it moves through the center of many of the sideways periods. Because the ARSI is much faster, it tends to get caught with a false signal at the end of each sustained price move. The 20-period moving average is reasonably smooth during this market segment and shows typical characteristics of lag. When constructing trading rules for any of these methods, the buy and sell signals are best if taken as the direction of the trendline and not a price penetration of the trendline.

McGinley Dynamics[3]

Among the work produced by John McGinley is a list of popular adaptive methods. His own *New McGinley Dynamics* is included:

```
MD = MD[1] + (close - MD[1]) / (k*p*@power((close/MD[1]),4))
```

where MD is the current McGinley Dynamic

　　　　MD[1] is the previous McGinley Dynamic

　　　　k is a constant = .60 (60% of a selected moving average period p)

　　　　p is the moving average period

　　　　close is the closing price

The Parabolic Time/Price System

The first well-known adaptive technique was the Parabolic Time/Price System,[4] which attempts to reduce the lag intrinsic to a trend system. To do this, Wilder increased the speed of the trend by shortening the number of days in the calculation, whenever prices reached new profit levels. The philosophy of the Parabolic System is that time is an enemy. Once a position is entered, it must continue to be profitable or it will be liquidated.

[3] John McGinley writes *Technical Trends* (P.O. Box 792, Wilton, CT 06897), and has compiled a selection of adaptive techniques as well as developed the ones discussed here.

[4] J. Welles Wilder, Jr., *New Concepts in Technical Trading Systems* (Trend Research, Greensboro, NC, 1978).

FIGURE 17-1   Comparison of moving average, KAMA, VIDYA, AR2, and ARSI.

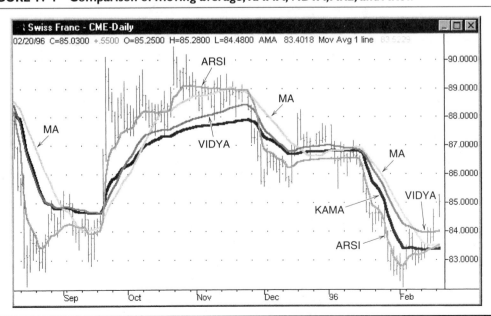

Source: Chart created with *TradeStation®* by Omega Research, Inc.

The Parabolic Time/Price System is always in the market; whenever a position is closed out, it is also reversed. The point at which this occurs is called the *Stop and Reverse* (SAR). When plotted, the Stop and Reverse point seems similar to a trendline, although it has a decreasing lag (the distance between the current price and the trendline, or SAR point, get closer each period), as shown in Figure 17-2. During periods of short, consistent trending, the Parabolic SAR converges on the price trend, extracting excellent profits.

To calculate the SAR value, first assume a long or short position. If the market has recently moved lower and is now above the lows of that move, assume a long. Call the lowest point of the previous trade the SAR initial point (SIP) because it will be the starting point for the SAR calculation (SARI = SIP). Calculate each following SAR as

$$SAR(today) = SAR(prior) + AF(today) \times [High(today) - SAR(prior)]$$

This is an exponential smoothing formula using the high price for a long position and the low when a short is held. For this method the smoothing constant is called the acceleration factor (AF), and it is initially set to .02 at the beginning of each trade. After a day in which a new extreme occurs (a new high when long, or a new low when short), the AF is increased by .02. In terms of moving average days, the AF begins at 99 days and increases speed to a maximum of a 9-day moving average, but not in a linear fashion. The acceleration factor, AF, cannot be increased above the value .20.

In the SAR calculation, the highest high of the current move is used when a long position is held, and the lowest low is used when a short is held. This feature keeps the SAR at its highest possible level during an upward move. An additional rule compensates for this strength and prevents premature reversal by not allowing the SAR to get any closer than the price range of the most recent 2 days:

> If long, the SAR may never be greater than the low of today or the prior day. If it is greater than this low, set the SAR to that low value. A reversal will occur on a new intraday low that penetrates the SAR.

FIGURE 17-2   Parabolic Time/Price System, Feb 96 S&P 500, 60-minute chart.

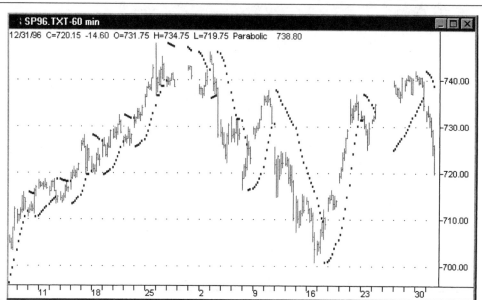

Source: Chart created with *TradeStation*® by Omega Research, Inc.

For short positions, the SAR is initialized as the high of the recent move, AF = .02, and the daily calculation uses the lowest low of the current price move. To allow some price fluctuation, the SAR may never be below the high of today or the prior day.

Wilder's Parabolic Time/Price System was unique in varying the smoothing constant to satisfy the notion that time worked against the trade. The idea of increasing the speed of the trend as the trade becomes more profitable is still a concept that has validity and has not been adopted in other adaptive methods. One weak point may be that AF always begins at .02. Although this allows the trade latitude to develop without being stopped out, a market that is moving quickly through the buy or sell signal would be better traded with a faster trend. This method also requires fairly consistent price swings to produce profits.

A strong point is that the initial Stop and Reversal is the market extreme high or low rather than an arbitrary, computer-generated point. Also, the SAR does not get closer than the previous day's high or low, which prevents a reversal when the market is moving strongly in a profitable direction. For those readers interested in the further development of this method, the Parabolic Time/Price System is combined with Directional Movement (described in Chapter 23) to form the Directional Parabolic System discussed in Chapter 6.

The following *Easy Language* user function allows the user to specify the starting value of the smoothing constant AFmin, the increment AFinc, and the maximum value AFmax. This provides for more flexible testing. Optimization of these values has been reported to produce good results.

```
{Parabolic.VRT
 This version of the Parabolic system was written by
 Sam Tennis, VISTA Research and Trading, Inc.,
 8103 Camino Real, South Miami, FL 33143, Email: skt@vista.com
 and reformatted by PJ Kaufman}

{Input values were formerly AFmin = AFactor, AFinc = AFactor, and AFmax = ALimit}
{Sample usage: Plot1 (Parabolic.VRT (0.02, 0.02, 0.20)[1], "Parabolic");
 Function returns SAR (stop & reverse) price objective}

        input:  AFmin(numericsimple), AFinc(numericsimple), AFmax(numericsimple);
        vars:   Position(1), AF(AFmin), SAR(low[0]), Hi(high[0]), Lo(Low[0]);

        if @currentbar <= 1 then Position = 1;
        if @currentbar > 1 then begin
                if High > Hi then Hi = High;
                if Low < Lo then Lo = Low;

                if Position = 1 then begin
                        if Low <= SAR[1] then begin
                                Position = -1;
                                SAR = Hi;
                                AF + 3 = AFmin;
                                Lo = Low;
                                Hi = High;
                                end; {Reverse position long to short}
                        end
                else begin
                        if High >= SAR[1] then begin
                                Position = 1;
                                SAR = Lo;
                                AF = AFmin;
                                Lo = Low;
                                Hi = High;
                                end; {Reverse position short to long}
```

```
                    end;
            end;
    if Position = 1 then begin
            if Position[1] = 1 then begin
                    SAR = SAR[1] + AF * (High[1] - SAR[1]);
                    if Hi > Hi[1] and AF < AFmax then AF = AF + AFinc;
                    end; {we have been "long" for at least one bar}
            if SAR > Low then SAR = Low;
            if SAR > Low[1] then SAR = Low[1];
            end {long}
            else begin
                    if Position[1] = -1 then begin
                        SAR = SAR[1] + AF * (Low[1] - SAR[1]);
                        if Lo < Lo[1] and AF < AFmax then AF = AF + AFinc;
                        end; {we have been "short" for at least one bar}
            if SAR < High then SAR = High;
            if SAR < High[1] then SAR = High[1];
            end; {short}
    Parabolic.VRT = SAR;
```

The Master Trading Formula

Another landmark method of creating a variable-speed approach is Mart's *Master Trading Formula*.[5] It is also based on an exponential smoothing formula where the smoothing constant and band around the trendline are calculated daily, based on market volatility. Mart's general technique is to combine the average *true range* (the maximum of yesterday's close and today's high or low) for the past 15 days with the net change over the same time period. Each of these volatility elements is ranked from 1 to 21 by defining a maximum value for each one and dividing that maximum into 20 equal zones (the 21st being anything higher). The two rankings are then averaged to get a *correlated volatility factor* (CVF). Another ranking of 21 zones is created by dividing the highest CVF into 20 equal parts. The CVF then relates linearly to a range of smoothing constants from .084 to .330, representing the approximate exponential equivalents of the moving average days from 5 to 23. The trendline value is then created daily using the formula

$$TREND(today) = TREND(prior) + CVF(today) \times [HLC(today) - TREND(prior)]$$

where HLC(today) is the average of the high, low, and closing price. As with the other adaptive methods, the speed of the trend increases as volatility increases.

A band is also placed around the trendline, based on an inverse relationship to the correlated volatility factor. The band is widest when there is low volatility and the smoothing constant produces a slow trend; it is narrowest in fast, highly volatile markets. Rules for trading Mart's Master Formula follow the basic band-trading rules. The system is always in the market, taking long positions when the upper band is broken and short positions when the lower band is crossed.

ADAPTIVE MOMENTUM CALCULATIONS

Varying the period of calculation does not have to be limited to a trend formula. The period for any technique can also be adaptive. The following techniques apply the same concept to indicators.

---

[5] Donald Mart, *The Master Trading Formula* (Winsor Books, Brightwaters, NY, 1981).

Variable-Length Stochastic

Written by Frank Key,[6] this adaptive technique uses Kaufman's efficiency ratio, *ER*. It changes the stochastic period within the default range of 5 to 30, using only integer values. The effect is that, when prices are trending with respect to the stochastic, the stochastic period is lengthened to allow the trading signal to stay with the trade. At turning points in the market, the stochastic period is shortened causing the reversal signal to be more responsive.

Stochastic period

```
NSP = @IntPortion(ER × (Maxperiod - Minperiod) + Minperiod)
```

Adaptive stochastic

```
ASTOK = @slowK(NSP)
```

where `ASTOK` is the adaptive stochastic value today (based on `NSP` days)
  `Maxperiod` is the maximum period, suggested as 30
  `Minperiod` is minimum period, suggested as 5
  `ER` is Kaufman's efficiency ratio

The variable-length stochastic uses the efficiency ratio in a manner opposite to Kaufman's AMA. While the AMA increases in speed when the trend gets stronger, Key's variable-length stochastic decreases in speed. This technique gives price more room to fluctuate during periods in which a strong trend is also associated with high volatility.

Trend-Adjusted Oscillator

One problem that confronts many traders who use stochastics or other oscillators is that the oscillator values tend to cluster at the bottom of the chart when the trend is down, and at the top when the trend is up. For a countertrend trader, this results in many oversold conditions during a downtrend, which can give false buy signals. A trend-adjusted oscillator[7] can help this bias by correcting the value of the oscillator by the amount that the trend of the oscillator varies from its midpoint (usually 50%). Therefore, if a 10-day oscillator has been steadily declining and its 5-day moving average has a value of 40, then the current oscillator value is raised by 10% (the midpoint of 50 minus the oscillator moving average of 40). The calculations for this are:

$$n\text{-}day\ oscillator = O = \frac{\sum_{i=t-n+1}^{t} (Close_i - Low_i)/(High_i - Low_i)}{n}$$

$$N\text{-}day\ moving\ average\ of\ oscillator = MA_O = \frac{\sum_{i=t-N+1}^{t} O_i}{N}$$

$$Trend\text{-}adjusted\ oscillator = Midpoint - (MA_O - O)$$

[6] Frank Key, Structured Software Systems, Mt. Holly, NJ. Copyright 1996.
[7] E. Marshall Wall, "Rolling with the punches," *Futures* (July 1996).

Dynamic Momentum Index

This approach to creating a dynamic, variable-length RSI, which changes the number of days based on market volatility, can be used to change the calculation period of any technique.[8] In the Dynamic Momentum Index (DMI), the length of the calculation period increases as the volatility declines. You may also select a pivotal period, one around which the calculation period will vary; for the RSI this will be 14 days. When the volatility increases, the periods will be less than 14 days and when volatility declines it will be greater. Based on this,

$$DMI = @Int\left(\frac{14}{volatility_t}\right)$$

$$volatility_t = \frac{@stdev(close,5)}{@avg(@stdev(close,5),10)}$$

The DMI is 14, the pivotal value, when the volatility is normal; that is, when the current 5-day standard deviation is the same as the 10-day average of the 5-day standard deviation. When the current volatility increases, the ratio is greater than 1 and the value of the DMI becomes larger than 14. The function @Int takes the integer value of the calculation to be used as the number of days in the RSI calculation.

A few changes in the DMI approach may improve results and should be considered when generalizing this technique. First, the standard deviation should always be applied to the *changes* in price, rather than the prices themselves. This removes the trend component. Alternately, the volatility ratio may be more robust if the sum of the absolute value of the price changes is simply compared against the average of that sum,

$$volatility_t = \frac{@sum(@absvalue(close_t - close_{t-1}),5)}{@avg(@sum(@absvalue(close_t - close_{t-1}),5),10)}$$

AN ADAPTIVE PROCESS

An adaptive method can be a process as well as a formula. Rather than using an index or ratio to change the smoothing constant, which in turn alters the trend speed to be in tune with the current market, you can retest your system regularly using more recent data. The period being retested can always be a fixed number of days, or it can be selected visually, beginning when the market changed its pattern, became more volatile, underwent a price shock, or moved to new highs or lows. The problem is having enough data to be satisfied that the results are dependable; the faster you react, the less data there is to make a decision. This approach, along with other testing methods, are covered in detail in Chapter 21 ("Testing").

A Development Example

The size of price changes can also be used to vary the period of a moving average. When prices become more volatile, as measured by the standard deviation of the price changes, a shorter period can be used to follow the market more closely. When there are smaller price changes, or stable volatility, the preference is to slow the trend by increasing the calculation period.[9] The following steps can be used to build and personalize a variable-speed moving average:

---

[8] Tushar Chande and Stanley Kroll, *The New Market Technician* (John Wiley & Sons, New York, 1994).

[9] George R. Arrington, "Building a Variable-Length Moving Average," *Technical Analysis of Stocks & Commodities* (June 1991).

1. Select the range over which the period of the moving average may fluctuate. For example, a medium to fast program might range from 5 to 30 days.
2. Calculate the mean and standard deviation of price changes over a separate, fixed time period, recommended as the length of the longest trend period (in this case, 30 days), but enough days to have a reasonable sample (no less than 10 days). Using a smaller period reduces the response time needed to switch from one moving average speed to another, but causes the results to be more erratic.
3. Select zones, or threshhold levels, at which the market is seen to be relatively more active or less active. For example, within the boundary of the mean $\pm$ .25 standard deviations, we will define a low-volatility, less active area where the longest period would be used. Outside the boundary of the mean $\pm$ 1.75 standard deviations would be an unusual, highly active market requiring a fast trend.
4. Establish the rate at which the moving average period would change as volatility (price change) increases from the inside to outside boundary. This could be the linear relationship

$$n_t = (30 - 5) * ((P_t - P_{t-1})/\text{stdev} - .25)/(1.75 - .25) + 5,$$
$$\text{for } 1.75 > (P_t - P_{t-1})/\text{stdev} > .25$$

when $(P_t - P_{t-1})/stdev$ is between 1.75 and .25. Otherwise, it is the max and min values, 30 and 5, respectively. The general form is

today's moving average period = (max ma period – min ma period) * (today's change/stdev of changes – min stdev boundary) / (max stdev boundary – min stdev boundary) + min moving average period

CONSIDERING ADAPTIVE METHODS

At first glance, there appears to be a conflict between the sound statistical approach that encourages the choice of a simple set of rules applied to a long period of test data and adaptive methods. The classic result is a statistically robust model, but one that might show considerable variation in performance over the test period. To stabilize returns we move away from fixed values in trading systems, such as a $500 stop-loss, or a 50-point breakout, and substitute risk and entry criteria that are based on volatility. The simplest of these methods uses a percentage of price; the most complex can be very intricate functions of volatility and cycles.

When a variable feature is incorporated into the strategy, the values should smoothly adjust to the market patterns, but each case, such as extreme high or low volatility, has fewer occurrences; therefore, we are not as certain that the *sliding scale* works at all levels. The best we can expect is that the technique has a sound premise, is well defined, and the profile of performance is improved.

If we follow that logic further, we eventually come to the adaptive, or self-adjusting method, in which the most fundamental elements of a calculation can vary based on price level, volatility, or a broad choice of patterns. The methods in this chapter focused on two areas that have not been presented elsewhere in a collected manner. The first is the variation of the trend period itself. The choice of a single trend does not serve us best for prolonged periods in the market. Slower trends are reliable, but give back much of their profits before ending; faster trends work only during periods when prices move quickly and uniformly. The obvious solution is that the calculation period should change, speeding up when there is a short-term, fast-moving price pattern. At other times, it should focus on the long-term direction. This concept is perfectly reasonable, although formulating the rules to vary the period has not been perfected. The methods shown here may work better than a static period, but should only be the beginning of a road on which to move forward.

The other adaptive method is the centering of an oscillator to avoid prolonged periods in which the value of the indicator loses significance by pushing against the upper or lower limits. By recording the high and low values of a past time interval, the oscillator values can be continually readjusted to provide a more useful tool. Analysts are encouraged to look further into these methods as an excellent way to improve system robustness.

18

Price Distribution Systems

Price movement is usually viewed as a chart on which each new time period is seen as a new bar or point recorded to the right of the previous prices. There are many applications that need to look at the way prices cluster, or *distribute,* rather than sequences of patterns. In options, it is important to evaluate the current market volatility to decide the chances of prices remaining in a specific range for a specific amount of time. To get that value, we use the standard deviation calculation first introduced in Chapter 2. The standard deviation gives the most basic measure of price distribution. From the value of 1 standard deviation we can estimate the chances of a price remaining within a range over time. The key values to remember are that 1 standard deviation defines 68% of the price movement (both up and down), 2 standard deviations contain 95%, and 3 standard deviations contain 99% of all price movement *based on the sample of data used to calculate the standard deviation value.*

USING THE STANDARD DEVIATION

The data used to determine the standard deviation is very important. Because it is a statistical measure, it is most accurate when a large amount of data is applied. For example, you might find that 1 standard deviation of the crude oil daily price move is only $0.25 per barrel when measured over the past 10 years, but during the 6 months of the Gulf War the same measurement yielded $.50, twice as large.

Most trading applications using the standard deviation tend to apply short data intervals to its calculation, such as 20 days. This short period is not likely to represent the same price distribution as a 10-year calculation; therefore, the probabilities given by the resulting standard deviation value must be interpreted differently. While it is less likely that the price will make a move of 3 standard deviations compared with 1 standard deviation, the probabilities can be misleading. Statistics tell us that there is only a 1% chance that prices will move a distance of 3 standard deviations higher or lower; however, that value is reliable only when measured over a long data period. If you selected 20 days of unusually low volatility, the chance of a 3–standard deviation move would be very high.

The frequency distribution is another very practical approach to measuring price distributions. This was also described in Chapter 2. It has the advantage of having a much clearer visual interpretation. While the standard deviation gives us what appears to be a highly mathematical probability, the large error factor that is caused by small amounts of data may make its usefulness about the same as the frequency distribution. In the following sections, both techniques will be used.

Standard Deviation Bands

Bollinger bands, discussed in Chapter 5 ("Trend Systems"), are a very popular application of price distributions. They do not detrend price, but calculate the standard deviation of prices over a period of 20 days and form a band of 2 standard deviations around the trendline. It is common for traders to vary both the period and the number of standard deviations used to construct the band. Once calculated, Bollinger bands can be displayed on any price chart and used to generate buy and sell signals, much the same as any other channel breakout system. Using a smaller Bollinger band, for example, 1 standard deviation, will give many more signals than using one of 3 standard deviations. At the same time, a band of 3 standard deviations translates into risk that is 3 times greater than 1 standard deviation. Signals produced with a larger band tend to be more reliable, but have greater risk.

Bollinger bands also describe market volatility. A relatively narrow band translates into low volatility. By comparing a 21-period Bollinger band with a 65-period band, you can see the relative difference between shorter-term and longer-term market volatility in Figure 18-1. The thicker lines, representing the 65-period calculation, cross the short-term band at points that show relative overbought and oversold situations. If this was a daily rather than a 15-minute chart, the 21-period band would give monthly volatility and the 65-period band would be quarterly volatility, useful values for options traders.

Problems in Using Moving Standard Deviations

Applying any technique to a rolling time interval of the most recent N bars is a common method of keeping in tune with current market conditions. In the case of a simple moving average, we should be very familiar with the lag that is introduced. For trends, when prices are moving steadily higher, the lag causes the trendline to be much lower.

There is a similar lag when using the most recent N bars to calculate a standard deviation, even when the data has been detrended. If we are measuring the volatility of the market, and prices rally quickly, the volatility rises. This will be seen in the larger value of 1 standard deviation measured over a fixed number of days, or bars. If we are looking for a confirmation of a buy signal based on an increase in volatility, we should get it.

However, the volatility represented by the standard deviation will not decline as fast as we expect because of the same lag. Once higher volatility has occurred on a single day, it

---

FIGURE 18-1   Comparison of 21- and 65-period Bollinger bands.

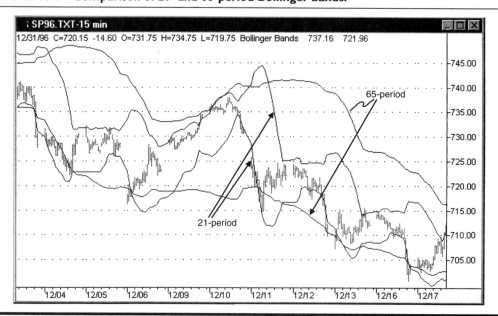

Source: Chart created with *TradeStation®* by Omega Research, Inc.

will remain part of the standard deviation value until it passes completely out of the calculation window. That will prevent a new volatility event from being recognized soon after a short decline in volatility. It will also make it difficult, if not impossible, to get a timely exit signal on reduced volatility, because the lag keeps the volatility appearing high until at least part of this new, more active price movement begins to pass out of the end of the calculation window. This can also be seen in Figure 18-1, where the 65-period bands expand quickly and narrow slowly.

USE OF PRICE DISTRIBUTIONS AND PATTERNS TO ANTICIPATE MOVES

Prices often form patterns that can be evaluated using probability methods, or simply viewed in much the same way as a frequency distribution, or histogram. Because the concepts are sound, but the statistical analysis is often difficult because of limited amounts of data or changing conditions, analysts have taken a much more empirical approach toward studying price distributions. The following section will look at some innovative ways to look at price distributions and how they are interpreted into trading opportunities.

Analysis of Zones

Rather than using standard deviations to identify the chance of a price move above or below yesterday's closing level, Bruce Gould observed that historic prices could be divided into five zones, each 20% of the price range over the previous 3 years. Using this long-term approach, it is easy to see that selling in zone 1 (the lowest price levels) would have less opportunity for profit than selling in zone 2, just above it. Similarly, buying in zone 5, the highest band, would carry both the greatest risk and the least opportunity of profit. This is likely to remain the case unless prices move to much higher levels and all zones need readjusting.

J.T. Jackson[1] has used this concept to define five short-term zones, based only on yesterday's prices, which can be associated with the strength or weakness of today's move. These daily zones, which are popular with floor traders, are calculated as:

Calculation	Zone	If Price Is Above Then
High2 = Average + High1 − Low1	6	Strong up
High1 = 2*Average − Low	5	Moderate up
Average = (High + Low + Close) / 3	4	Mildly up
Low1 = 2*Average − High	3	Mildly down
Low2 = Average + Low1 − High1	2	Moderately down
	1	Strongly down

where the High, Low, and Close are yesterday's prices. Note that there are five calculations but six zones needed to separate them. A test of how the S&P 500 falls into these relative rankings gives:

Zone	6	5	4	3	2	1
S&P frequency	20%	44%	83%	79%	42%	20%

[1] J.T. Jackson, *Detecting High Profit Day Trades In The Futures Markets* (Windsor Books, 1994).

which shows the slightly upward bias expected of the overall equities market. These distributions may vary depending on the interval used in their calculation and whether there is a dominant trend during that period. A longer interval that includes bull, bear, and sideways markets would be safest; otherwise, there is the chance that the calculations will create a bull market profile, while some trading will occur during a bear market reaction. Although you can avoid trend bias by using longer intervals for the calculations, the zones tend to get very large.

The strategies for trading price zones focus on short-term trends and holding periods. For example, you can sell when prices move into zone 4 (mildly up) with a stop in zone 5. If you consider zones 3, 4, and 5 as containing mostly market noise, then selling at the top of zone 4 and closing out that trade at about the average, or buying near the bottom of zone 3 and closing out at about the average, could capture the majority of price moves that have no direction.

Nonrandom Patterns

In evaluating the zone approach, the markets that offer the greatest potential for this strategy are those that show an abnormal distribution of prices within the six zones. For example, if the six zones were all equal in size, and the frequency of prices declined by one-half as they moved from the center to the extremes, there would be a perfectly random distribution and no profit potential:

Zone of Equal Size	6	5	4	3	2	1
Normal distribution	7%	14%	28%	28%	14%	7%

If the distribution is normal, but zones 3 and 4 are much wider than the outer zones, then the risk of selling at the top of zone 4 with a stop at the top of zone 5 and a profit target at the average (of zones 3 and 4) would result in an equal number of profits and losses, but the profits would be larger. If the zones are of equal size, the opportunities come when the distribution is clustered in the center:

Zone of Equal Size	6	5	4	3	2	1
Normal distribution	2%	8%	40%	40%	8%	2%

In this case, selling at the top of zone 4 would result in many more profits than losses, although profits and losses would be of equal size.

Applying a Moving Average Distribution

To extend the time frame and include trend bias within the zone values, the same zones may be created by using the moving average values applied to the close, high, and low separately. For example, if three separate 21-day moving averages are calculated on the high, low, and closing prices, the moving average values can be substituted for yesterday's high, low, and close to give new zones. In using this approach, a strong upward trend would cause all the zones to lag below today's prices, making current values strongly overbought. Zones created from the history of these averages will reflect the relative overbought and oversold price levels within trends. In a strong upward market, however, prices can remain in zone 6 while they are steadily moving higher in much the same way that an oscillator can remain over 80%.

Using moving average values is likely to change the way in which you trade these zones. For example, you might want to enter long positions only in zone 5 and look to exit in zone 6. You might find that, if prices close in zone 6 (very strong), they are likely to open in zone 4 (slightly higher).

Zones for Forecasting Range and Risk Control

Statistics have proved that, barring a superior forecasting method, the best estimate for tomorrow's price is today's price. That is, under most conditions, we cannot predict with any certainty that prices will go up or down tomorrow; therefore, the best estimate is to say that prices will be unchanged. However, if a trend system, such as a moving average, has been profitable, then its forecast for tomorrow is better than the mean. Market volatility, based on price changes, can be used with a directional forecast of tomorrow's price to create a set of zones used to control risk or project the probable trading range.[2]

Using a 10-day moving average of the daily price changes,

```
A = @Avg(@AbsValue(close - close[1]),10)
```

where `close[1]` represents the previous close. Taken as positive numbers, zones are created that center around the current price and expand according to the average price change (volatility) using the following calculations:

```
H2 = close[1] + 2 * A
H1 = close[1] + A
L1 = close[1] - A
L2 = close[1] - 2 * A
```

Five zones are then created by the areas above H2 and below L2, and the three ranges between H2, H1, L1, and L2, all of which change in proportion to the *n*-day volatility. These volatility levels, or bands, represent a very similar scenario to channel breakouts. The market often trades in a range defined by a normal or average level of volatility. When a new piece of information affects the price, it jumps to a new level, then trades with similar volatility (or slightly higher at first) at the new level. Most often, the first breakout of an existing trading range puts prices in a zone just above the old range, making the pattern appear to be divided into equal zones. This same philosophy is the reason that standard profit targets for a price breakout are equal to the previous trading range. Readers can find additional trading range projections in Chapter 15 ("Pattern Recognition").

DISTRIBUTION OF PRICES

In the search to understand how prices move, and what to expect, an analysis of price distributions can explain whether the market is trending, sideways, or unstable. Some of these patterns are clear and others need interpretation; in addition, the combination of patterns within patterns can become complex. The following is intended as a basic approach to interpreting price distributions, although each group of markets has special characteristics. Before engineering a systematic approach to trading, it is best to understand how prices are expected to distribute. This approach avoids surprises and the risk that goes with them.

Long-Term Price Distributions

A quick observation of price data for most tangible products, such as soybeans or gold, shows that we should expect a skewed long-term price distribution, with prices clustering at lower

---

[2] Based on Tushar Chande and Stanley Kroll, *The New Technical Trader* (John Wiley & Sons, New York, 1994, p. 172).

levels and a long tail representing extreme high prices. In the case of gold, we should remember that prices peaked briefly at $675 per ounce (New York cash price) in 1980, but have remained below $400 most of the time before and after. If we consider $375 as the approximate normal price of gold, then the rise to $800 is a gain of $425 per ounce. If $375 were the average price, and distributions were symmetric, then gold would be able to decline an equal amount, which would put the low price at negative $50 per ounce, which is not possible.

The process in which prices move up and down is not uniform. If the price of soybeans only gained a small percentage every year based on inflation, price forecasting would be very simple. Expectations, however, are based on carryover stocks (inventories), exports, weather, and government programs, all of which cause sharp price adjustments. These shifts up and down appear as steps on a price chart. Once a new step is reached, prices will fluctuate in a range with a new perceived base price. Within the period when the step is in transition, unexpected news will normally cause short-lived price peaks. Normally, prices trade at the lower end of the range.

Patterns of Market Groups

Those markets representing physical commodities, such as gold, soybeans, and coffee, have a cost of production that forms a practical lower bound to price movement. When there is ample supply, or low demand, prices decline to those cost levels, or slightly lower, volatility drops, and there is little price activity. This also applies to the interest rate market viewed in terms of yield. At low yields, volatility is proportionally low and prices move sideways with an occasional spike (downward for prices) in anticipation of change.

Currency markets are very different from physical commodities because they do not have a production cost, nor can you distinguish high from low. All currencies are quoted in terms of other currencies. What is high, relative to one country, might be low compared with another. A stable political situation, low inflation, and a controlled balance of trade puts a currency at equilibrium provided that it is quoted in terms of another stable currency. With no expectation of surprises, the currency will trade in a narrow range, showing low volatility. Unexpected economic news moves the foreign exchange rate sharply up or down; normalization of the problem allows prices to return to a quiet equilibrium. This pattern can appear to be similar to a normal distribution.

Frequency Distributions

If we remember the qualities of a standard deviation when measuring price distribution, it assumes a symmetric pattern; therefore, a simpler *frequency distribution* can be used to provide a more convenient representation of price distribution. The frequency distribution makes no assumptions about the shape of the curve, but records the amount of time that prices remained within a specified range. For example, if we look at the history of gold from 1976 through 1993 (see the bold line in Figure 18-2), prices have varied from $100 per ounce in 1976 to $675 per ounce in 1980. Because the first 3 years would lower the average, we will consider only the period from 1979 through 1993, which had a low of $228. Dividing the price range into 20 parts, we get bars of $23.60. Accumulating the history of monthly closing prices into the 20 slots from $227.60 to $251.20, $251.21 to $274.80, and so forth, we get a frequency distribution spanning the full range of gold prices, each bar indicating the number of months that the average monthly price fell in that bar. That distribution, seen in Figure 18-3, shows peak frequencies (gray bars) from $392 to $445, significantly below the midpoint price.

The total number of months from 1979 through 1993 is 228; therefore, we can find the approximate price that occurred at the 90% level by summing the frequency of the bars beginning at the highest price. Because 10% of 228 is 23, the bar that causes the total fre-

FIGURE 18-2 Cash gold prices, CPI, and deflated gold prices.

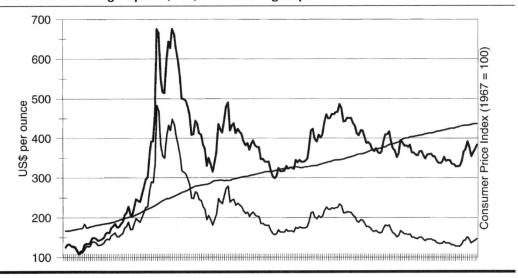

FIGURE 18-3 Frequency distribution of gold. Gray bars show the distribution of cash prices. The dark bars show the distribution of deflated cash prices. The deflated prices are skewed much further to the left.

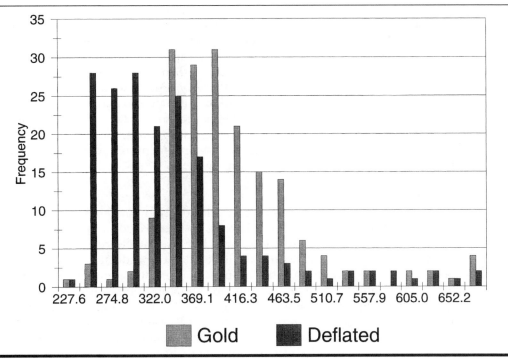

quency to exceed 23 will be the target price range for the 90% level. This works well for skewed distributions; the 90% level may be 3 bars from the top of distribution, while the 10% level may be the lowest bar of the distribution. For cash gold, the highest 10% of the prices span the highest 9 bars, while the lowest 10% are in the bottom 2 bars. This shows an extremely skewed distribution.

Adjusting for Inflation

One way of correcting for the apparent bias in the long-term charts is to adjust prices for inflation. That is, if we have a table of monthly Consumer Price Index values, all prices can be divided by the monthly percentage increase in the CPI. Therefore, if today's gold price is $400 per ounce, and inflation last year was 5%, today's price of $400 is divided by 1.05 to get $381. If the actual price of gold was $380 last year, it was very close to normal. In Figure 18-1 the CPI appears as a steady increase which, when used to adjust the cash gold prices, shows that 1993 prices had returned to 1979 levels on an inflation-adjusted basis. The frequency distribution of the adjusted prices, seen in Figure 18-3, shows a much broader frequency at lower levels and a smaller, longer tail at higher prices. These patterns are fundamental to understanding and using price distributions.

Structural Changes

Despite the need to correct for inflation, structural changes will affect the smooth pattern of the frequency distribution. For gold, cash prices below $100 per ounce are part of history that we can choose to ignore for now. By creating a new frequency distribution that reflects prices beginning in 1979, some of the price inconsistencies can be eliminated. For other markets this may not be as easy, because the structural changes may occur within the normal range of historic prices.

Medians and Means

Although the inflation-adjusted long-term distributions show that prices spend much more time at lower levels, there is a tendency to consider the average price of a market as the midpoint between the highest and lowest prices. Using the gold example, the midpoint for 1979 to 1993 was $451. The average of all monthly prices will give a reasonable approximation of a normal price; however, the best measure is the *median,* or middle, value when all monthly prices are sorted from high to low. The median value for gold over the same period was $381. If we look back at Chapter 2 ("Basic Concepts"), we find that skewness is measured as the difference between the mean and the median, as a percentage of the standard deviation. In this case, the difference of $70 is a very large value, indicating a distribution with a peak far to the left of center. For price distributions, the median is a much more useful value than the average, although not as convenient to calculate. The median naturally adjusts for the skewness in the price patterns.

Short-Term Distributions

Unlike the predictable patterns of the long-term price distributions, the distribution patterns of short intervals can vary widely and have been interpreted in many ways. Short-term distributions are not anchored to a base level because the entire period of analysis may be at prices that are significantly above intrinsic value or production costs, and away from equilibrium. Keeping in mind the normal shape of price distribution for each market group, a different configuration can be a strong indication of expected price movement.

Three distribution patterns are shown in Figure 18-4 (*b–d*), along with the larger, long-term distribution (*a*). The first short-term distribution (see Figure 18-4*b*) shows a pattern with a long tail toward the higher prices and a large accumulation near lower price levels in a manner very similar to a long-term chart, but with the extended tail much shorter and a little more extension on the bottom. This is most likely to occur at low price levels, where most activity is near the bottom with occasional short excursions up. This can be a small segment of a normal pattern or a temporarily higher level that is stable. Figure 18-4c is a bell-shaped, symmetric curve that could indicate a congestion area or short-term equilibrium. When prices trade equally within a range they do not exhibit any likelihood of favoring an immediate breakout either up or down.

The fourth distribution (see Figure 18-4d) is most interesting, because it is skewed in a pattern opposite to (b) and to the normal long-term distribution. For this pattern to have developed required a relatively short, quick move to a higher price level, then a congestion area formed at the higher level. You can be certain from this pattern that prices are higher than normal. By the very nature of the pattern, we can say that this price level is unstable, and that prices are more likely to go down than up. This last conclusion does not require statistics, because prices at high levels must not necessarily continue to rise, but they must eventually fall.

Identifying Potential Price Moves

From the patterns just described, the combination of a distribution of a long tail toward higher prices, but at a relatively low level, offers no promise of a potential price move.

FIGURE 18-4 Three short-term distribution patterns. (*a*) A traditional, long-term distribution. (*b*) A short-term distribution indicating stable prices at a temporarily higher level, or a permanent change. (*c*) A bell-shaped curve representing congestion but not indicating future direction; the market is in suspension or temporary equilibrium. (*d*) The tail points to lower prices with most activity at higher prices; the market is unstable and has substantial downside potential.

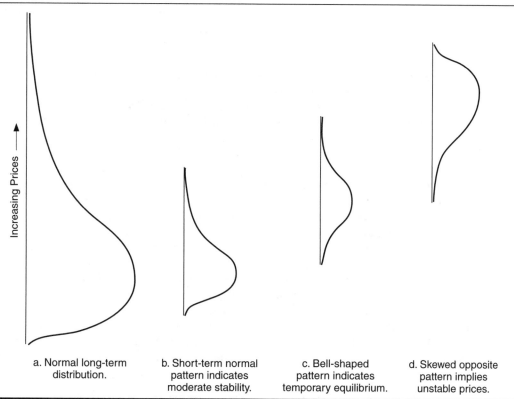

a. Normal long-term distribution.

b. Short-term normal pattern indicates moderate stability.

c. Bell-shaped pattern indicates temporary equilibrium.

d. Skewed opposite pattern implies unstable prices.

Prices that are not near the base level are always likely to move, and the farther they get from the base level, the more volatile they become. Three formations show that there is a greater chance for a move.

1. A broad, often erratic formation indicates volatile, current movement. Prices have not remained at one level and have not yet established a well-defined pattern or trading range.
2. A skewed distribution (with the tail toward higher prices), the mode well above the base level, and where the current price is at the extreme away from the tail (lower prices) indicates a likely move down.
3. A skewed distribution (with the tail toward lower prices), the mode well above the base level, and where the current price is in the tail (lower prices) indicates a likely move down.

Any time prices form a distribution that is not the same as a long-term distribution, and not at low levels, there is potential for movement and volatility.

STEIDLMAYER'S MARKET PROFILE

Market Profile, the effort of J. Peter Steidlmayer, appears to be a frequency distribution of intraday price movement but has used time, rather than volume, as its key element. Steidlmayer formalized this technique in 1985 while at the Chicago Board of Trade. The Board considered this such a unique insight that they copyrighted his work as *Market Profile* and *Liquidity Data Bank.* It was intended to provide detailed information to traders about how trading was facilitated. *Market Profile* offers much more than a count of how many times a price traded at one level. With proper studying, traders are able to separate participants by time frame and even identify their trading patterns. Figure 18-5 shows this technique as it originally appeared, with letters denoting sequential 30-minute time periods, and an analysis of who participated in the trade at each price.[3] Called a customer trade indicator (CTI), these categories are CTI 1, the local floor traders; CTI 2, the commercial clearing members; CTI 3, clearing members who fill for other members and nonclearing commercial traders; and CTI 4, clearing members who fill orders for the public or other customers not included in the previous groups (*outside paper*). This information, on whose behalf the trade was executed, is only available after the close of trading.

To understand what is described in *Market Profile* and the *Liquidity Data Bank,* you must know that the locals and commercial clearing members, CTI 1 and CTI 2, account for the largest part of volume (over 65%), and both have trading styles that are very different from the off-floor speculators who form groups 3 and 4. The locals take smaller positions, often counter to the current price moves and hold that trade for a period spanning seconds to a few hours. Most locals even up at the end of the day, which avoids the need to finance their positions. The commercials might be a bank that is hedging an existing currency exposure or arbitraging a gap between two or more short-term rates in the cash market. These positions may move the market but can be insensitive to current price direction and flow into the market at arbitrary times.

Outside paper, a term that refers to customer accounts, range from individual speculators to major fund managers. Because they trade from off the floor, their style of trading favors holding positions for more than 1 day, and a large majority will be trend followers. The style of CTI 3 is similar to CTI 4; that is, both tend to be directional, and the two can be combined for the purposes of evaluation. Although they account for a smaller portion of the volume, they are more influential in the short-term direction. Fig-

---

[3] F.M. "Doc" Haynie, "Stretching the 'profile' to cover 24-hour markets," *Futures* (February 1992).

FIGURE 18-5 Original Market Profile for T-bonds.

Market Profile
Analysis of a Trading Day

Price	Volume	% Volume by Type of Trader					Cnt	Participation		% Count		% Volume		Ratio (1+2)/(3+4)	
		Cti 1	Cti 2	Cti 3	Cti 4			Cti 1+2	Cti 3+4	%1+2	%3+4	%1+2	%3+4		
9609	736	54.6	8.8	0.0	36.5	LM	2	63.4	36.5	1.3	0.7	467	269	1.74	Buy 3+4
9608	8009	56.2	14.3	7.3	22.3	LM	2	70.5	29.6	1.4	0.6	5646	2371	2.38	
9607	7410	56.9	16.0	8.1	19.0	KLM	3	72.9	27.1	2.2	0.8	5402	2008	2.69	
9606	18142	62.1	13.0	3.5	21.4	KL	2	75.1	24.9	1.5	0.5	13625	4517	3.02	Sell 1+2
9605	31686	62.5	11.7	4.0	21.9	KL	2	74.2	25.9	1.5	0.5	23511	8207	2.86	
9604	13018	58.5	17.4	2.0	21.8	KL	2	75.9	23.8	1.5	0.5	9881	3098	3.19	
9603	14290	60.7	11.7	4.5	23.1	KL	2	72.4	27.6	1.4	0.6	10346	3944	2.62	
9602	5302	52.8	11.8	1.6	33.8	K	1	64.6	35.4	0.6	0.4	3425	1877	1.82	Buy 3+4
9601	3616	69.9	8.7	6.2	15.3	JK	2	78.6	21.5	1.6	0.4	2842	777	3.66	Sell 1+2
9600	4884	50.5	8.4	1.9	39.1	JK	2	58.9	41	1.2	0.8	2877	2002	1.44	Buy 3+4
9531	11828	60.4	12.5	1.2	25.8	J	1	72.9	27	0.7	0.3	8623	3194	2.70	
9530	13464	57.1	16.7	2.5	23.8	J	1	73.8	26.3	0.7	0.3	9936	3541	2.81	
9529	15878	59.7	12.7	3.5	24.1	J	1	72.4	27.6	0.7	0.3	11496	4382	2.62	
9528	4802	57.9	18.1	2.6	21.5			76	24.1	0.8	0.2	3650	1157	3.15	Buy 1+2
9527	4292	50.4	12.1	1.6	35.9	GJ	3	62.5	37.5	1.9	1.1	2683	1610	1.67	Buy 3+4
9526	23594	63.1	11.0	4.8	21.1	FGHIJ	5	74.1	25.9	3.7	1.3	17483	6111	2.86	
9525	27090	58.5	15.6	2.7	23.2	FGHIJ	5	74.1	25.9	3.7	1.3	20074	7016	2.86	
9524	20004	59.7	15.3	2.5	22.4	CEFGHIJ	7	75	24.9	5.3	1.7	15003	4981	3.01	
9523	13956	60.1	18.2	3.0	18.7	BCDEFGH	7	78.3	21.7	5.5	1.5	10928	3028	3.61	Sell 1+2
9522	11662	59.4	16.2	5.0	19.3	ABCDEF	6	75.6	24.3	4.5	1.5	8816	2834	3.11	
9521	23390	58.5	14.8	4.5	22.2	$ABCDEF	7	73.3	26.7	5.1	1.9	17145	6245	2.75	
9520	46184	63.5	14.4	5.1	16.9	$ABCD	5	77.9	22	3.9	1.1	35977	10160	3.54	
9519	16018	72.0	9.6	3.7	14.7	$ABC	4	81.6	18.4	3.3	0.7	13071	2947	4.43	Buy 1+2
9518	8750	59.4	12.8	2.3	25.5	$A	2	72.2	27.8	1.4	0.6	6318	2433	2.60	
9517	5912	64.6	12.3	3.9	19.2	Z$A	3	76.9	23.1	2.3	0.7	4546	1366	3.33	
9516	13896	62.9	15.7	4.9	16.5	Z$	2	78.6	21.4	1.6	0.4	10922	2974	3.67	Buy 1+2
9515	5234	62.0	10.1	1.8	26.1	Z$	2	72.1	27.9	1.4	0.6	3774	1460	2.58	
9514	1745	52.9	12.7	0.2	34.3	$	1	65.6	34.5	0.7	0.3	1145	602	1.90	Sell 3+4

Total	374792	51555
15%	56219	34297
		65983

R34-29 51555
R7-10   34297
R7-11   65983

Total volume 9528–9518   199742
15% of total   29961.3
Value area (70%) from 9525 to 9520 (inclusive)

459

ure 18-5 combines CTI 1 with CTI 2 and CTI 3 with CTI 4 to simplify the patterns attributed to each group. During the period shown in the figure, the combined categories 3 and 4 cause the market to move when their participation was greater than 30%. Observation shows that these trading points occur as prices move out of a previous area of sustained trading.

Steidlmayer was said to have first developed this information for his own trading. He taught a course on how to apply his evaluation technique, and there were a number of books written on the subject by himself and others.[4] He spent considerable time studying and classifying formations and separating days into three primary categories: *normal, trending,* and *nontrending.* A normal day forms a standard bell-shaped curve with the widest point, positioned near the center, called the *value area.* On a trending day, the value area is not as wide and appears closer to one end of the distribution. A nontrending day has neither of the two recognizable patterns.

There is an important philosophic basis for Steidlmayer's work. It is a very credible attempt to explain how the market functions. He says, "The market probes high prices to attract sellers and low prices to attract buyers." This creates a value area. By observing the patterns of intraday price distribution, you can know whether there are countertrend opportunities, when prices reach the extremes of perceived value on a normal day, or trend positions in the direction of current price movement.

Construction of *Market Profile*

The *Market Profile* is created in a manner very similar to a point-and-figure chart. You can list every price on the left scale or create boxes that represent a price range. This latter technique will make the distribution look more uniform by clustering the price activity in exactly the same way as a frequency distribution.

The most common way of plotting intraday data is to begin by placing the letter A in the boxes alongside the price at which the market traded. If we use half-hour intervals, called *time/price opportunities* (TPOs), then all prices that were traded during the first half hour are marked with the letter A. The letter B is used for the second half-hour period, the letter C for the third period, and so on. At the end of the day we have a chart that looks similar to Figure 18-5.

Market Profile is also intended to be used over many days, identifying long-term patterns as congestion areas or trending markets. To the extent that it accomplishes this distinction it can be very valuable. The ability to determine whether the market is directional or not is the greatest problem of the trader. In Figure 18-6, the *Market Profile* is constructed by using numbers instead of letters to represent the range of prices traded over each day. The entire chart covers a period of 9 days. Other than the substitution of days for half-hour periods, the chart is created in the same way.

Time/Price Opportunities

Time/Price Opportunities (TPOs) are the 30-minute blocks assigned letters on the *Market Profile* diagram. It is worth noting that the largest occurrence of TPOs at a single price does

---

[4] Three books on *Market Profile* appeared in 1989: J. Peter Steidlmayer, *Steidlmayer on Markets* (John Wiley & Sons); Kevin Koy, *Markets 101* (MLS Publishing, 401 S. LaSalle St., Chicago, IL 60605); and Donald Jones, *Applications of the Market Profile* (CISCO, 32 S. LaSalle St., Chicago, IL 60604). The most complete material, however, comes from the original course taught by Steidlmayer, called the *Market Logic School.* Readers may also want to study the original publication, *CBOT Market Profile* (1984, available from the Chicago Board of Trade); also J. Peter Steidlmayer and Shera Buyer, *Taking The Data Forward* (Market Logic Inc., Chicago, IL, 1986), and J. Peter Steidlmayer and Kevin Koy, *Markets & Market Logic* (The Porcupine Press, Chicago, IL, 1986).

FIGURE 18-6   Daily Market Profile.

Value Area Using Daily Data		
Price	Day Traded	
10228	1	
10224	12	
10220	120	
10216	120	
10212	120	
10208	245790	
10204	2456790	36 day counts
10200	245679	
10228	2345679	
10224	2345679	
10220	23589	
10216	589	
10212	58	

Source: Jones, Figure 2, "Locating value with auction market data," *Technical Analysis of Stocks & Commodities* (July 1989).

not necessarily correspond to the price at which the highest volume occurred, as seen by referring back to Figure 18-5. This distinction is at the root of *Market Profile,* because it emphasizes the amount of time that traders accepted a price, rather than the volume traded at that price, which could have occurred during a single period. In the bond example given in Figure 18-5, the greatest volume was transacted at 9520, although the center of the value area, where there is the largest record of TPOs, is at 9523, three points higher. Clearly, the *Market Profile* analysis is seeking out a different way of observing the actions of traders. In the formation of a value area, if the market moves between two prices, such as 9520 and 9523, because those values bracket the current trading range, each traverse will cause the prices in between to be marked with the same TPO letter, regardless of whether any volume occurred at those prices.

TPOs allow us to judge the potential direction for a move out of the current value area. This can tell a trader to buy strength or sell weakness. The market is said to favor the direction indicated by the upper or lower part of the value area that has the highest TPO count. When performing the TPO count, you must have a well-defined value area and limit the count to within that range. Using Figure 18-5, with the mode at 9523, count the TPOs prior to the interval that begins *J.* There were 16 TPOs above 9523 and 21 below (not including 8$ and 3Z). During time interval *J,* the balance shifted to the upside when it touched 9529, at which point there was a large increase in volume. This could be attributed to CTI 1 and CTI 2 exiting shorts and, to a lesser degree, going long. The locals were finally joined by groups 3 and 4, taking a long position at 9600. An imbalance in the TPO count expresses a willingness for the market to favor the direction given by the largest count, but applies to a normally distributed value area only.

Typical Patterns

It is generally accepted that the market spends the greatest time in a sideways, or congestion area, and a relatively small amount of time trending. The sideways period may be defined as an *extended time/price relationship* and the trending period as a *brief time/price relationship.* The extended period creates a value area where traders are willing to buy and sell, and this activity is reflected in higher volume. According to *Market Profile,*[5]

Value = price × time = volume

In this analysis, called *auction theory,* the value area is the place that the market is willing to trade, and is seen in the time value. The value area represents about 70% of the market volume. The center of this time value area is the price at which there are the most TPOs. Because market activity spends at least 80% of the time in this value area, prices tend to rotate about the center. *Rotation* is the term given to price action that moves back and forth above and below this central value, building the pattern of normal distribution similar to a bell-shaped curve.

What Are the Buyers and Sellers Doing?

The interpretation of the *Market Profile* is based on the concept that, under normal market conditions, prices rise to attract sellers and fall to attract buyers. There is a very active area of trading at a point called *equilibrium* where commercial buyers and sellers exchange freely, because they consider the price *at value* (Figure 18-7, panel *a*). If there are more buyers than sellers, the price rises to attract additional sellers who feel as though they are getting a price that is above value. However, as prices continue to rise there are fewer buyers, because they perceive the market as overpriced. In Figure 18-7, Day 1 (panel *b*) shows a buyer's curve and a seller's curve drawn on the frequency distribution of a normal trading day.[6]

In this way the market is said to *facilitate* trade. When there are not enough buyers, the price falls; when the sellers are scarce, prices rise. Constructing the buyer's and seller's curves for a sequence of days can help understand the dynamics of trading in terms of both price expectations and volume. For convenience, the *curves* will be shown as straight lines, similar to supply and demand lines, in the following examples.

On Day 2 in Figure 18-7 (panel *c*), the buyers disappear faster than the sellers; therefore, the buyer's curve is more horizontal and the seller's curve more vertical. On Day 2 (panel *c*), the sellers have held their position and the buyers are willing to move higher, retreating from their previous objective. This results in higher volume. Had the buyers moved lower and the sellers remained steady, the volume would be expected to decline. If on Day 2 (panel *d*) the volume increased while prices traded in the same range and at about the same peak price level (value level), the buyer's and seller's curves would have become more horizontal, indicating that both sides of the trade were holding firmly at the current level.

Quantifying the Value Area

The idea of a value area that is shaped as a bell curve, or an extended formation to represent a trending day, seems clear; unfortunately, patterns are rarely as clear as these examples. To help this process, Jones has applied *overlays* to these patterns, using a standard deviation to measure them. In Chapter 2, we explained that, for a normal distribution, the value of 1 standard deviation represents a clustering of 68% of all values around the mean; therefore, 34% are on either side. Similarly, 2 standard deviations contain 95% of all activity, 42.5% on either side of center. In his analysis, Jones has defined a value area as one contained within 2 standard deviations of the center using the TPO count to isolate the range. For example, if the entire chart contains 100 filled boxes, the price range is from 6615 to 6655, the center is right at 6635 and contains 10 filled boxes, then 2 standard deviations contain 90 × .425 = 38 boxes on each side of the center. This defines the value area.

[5] Donald L. Jones, "Locating value with auction market data," *Technical Analysis of Stocks & Commodities* (July 1989).

[6] The following discussion is based on Robert Pisani, "How market structure helps you analyze price behavior," *Futures* (October 1987).

FIGURE 18-7 Buyer's and seller's curves for a sequence of days.

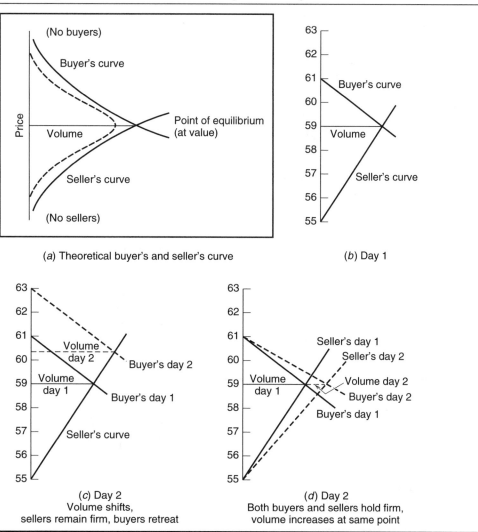

(a) Theoretical buyer's and seller's curve

(b) Day 1

(c) Day 2
Volume shifts,
sellers remain firm, buyers retreat

(d) Day 2
Both buyers and sellers hold firm,
volume increases at same point

Trending Markets

Trends spread volume out over price and are relatively easy to see. In the previous discussions, there is an early warning of a trend when prices move out of the value area or when there is a larger number of TPOs on one side of the center of the value area. Trends develop when the market attempts to probe a new price level causing the current price to diverge from the value area. The participants may reject this divergence and the price will return to the previous area causing a broadening formation, or they may accept the new price as fair value and generate a new value area by attracting volume (see Figure 18-8). The initial move that fails to find a new value area is called *price trend;* it usually begins and ends within a single time period (one TPO, which could be a half hour or a day). A price move that attracts volume over a longer time period is called a *value trend.* Daily charts, or a sequence of intraday 30-minute charts, are easier to use than a single 30-minute chart when looking for a trend.

When comparing the *Market Profile* of successive days, it is helpful to watch the activity of the recent day compared with the value area of the previous day. When trading within

FIGURE 18-8   *Market Profile* **for a trending market.**

	Beginning of a Trend		
	Price	Day Traded	
	10228	I	
	10224	I2	
	10220	I20A	
	10216	I20A	
	10212	I20AB	
	10208	245790AB	
	10204	2456790ABC	
	10200	245679ABC	
	10228	2345679ABC	
	10224	2345679C	
	10220	23589C	
	10216	589C	
	10212	58C	
	10208	CD	**Breakout at 10208**
	10204	CD	
	10200	DEH	
	10128	DEGH	**Consolidation or new**
	10124	DEGHJ	**value area being formed**
	10120	DEGIJ	**around center of 10124**
	10116	DEFIJ	
	10112	FI	
	10108	F	

the previous value area, both buyers and sellers are considered equal. A move above the value area is considered as motivated by the buyer and reactive by the seller, and trading below the prior value is initiated by the seller and reactive by the buyer.

Trends do not move in a fast, straight line to their *correct* new level; instead, they move in steps, pausing to test whether a new value area can be formed that facilitates price. The trend continues in this way until prices retrace to the previous consolidation area, where the TPO volume is expanded and the area is broadened, resulting in a value area.

Some Points to Remember about *Market Profile*

One great advantage of using the TPO count, rather than traditional volume, is that the *Market Profile* can be created at any time on any market. All the necessary information is available. The method is very different from traditional trending approaches and offers insight into the current status of price action, whether it is in a consolidation phase or trending. Although the evaluation of *Market Profile* has been very interpretive, there have been important steps toward defining value areas and trends in a more objective way. Using the overlay method proposed by Jones, a very simple trend filter could be constructed so that new trend trades, based on traditional moving averages, are not set until prices move out of the value area. During the past few years, there seems to be less interest in this technique; however, its underlying simplicity and clear distinction between other methods of analysis should keep its standing as a tool worth studying.

19

Multiple Time Frames

Although the use of multiple time periods for analyzing markets has been popular for decades, few professionals have talked about it. It is only since better quote equipment has allowed this technique to be accessed by a wider audience that this approach has begun to appear in the public domain. The combination of multiple time periods allows the trader to time entries into the market using very short-term data, such as 10-minute bars, while watching the longer-term picture for the daily or weekly trend. Because it is agreed that most trends are best identified over a longer time period, while choosing the entry point requires a much faster response, the combination of two, or even three time intervals is very sensible. If the trend can be identified profitably, then the trader can filter or select short-term trades that have a better-than-average chance of becoming winners.

For most traders, the use of any one time frame presents special problems. The very short term contains a high percentage of noise and obscures the market direction. The attempt to isolate patterns within charts of 5-minute bars can divert your efforts away from the big picture. Use of only weekly charts, although they clearly show the direction of prices, present higher risk and little opportunity for a good entry point. The obvious solution is to combine both charts into a program that uses each to its best advantage.

TUNING TWO TIME FRAMES TO WORK TOGETHER

Throughout most of this book, the individual systems and methods have been discussed for their own merits. An analyst would look for the specific RSI or stochastic that somehow generated the most profits by showing a trend change or an overbought/oversold condition. That is not the optimal use of an indicator when it is expected to tell you the best time to enter a trend. Instead, you will want the time period for the indicator to be much shorter than the time period used to calculate the trend. For example, if your trend system has a typical holding period of 1 month (about 23 business days), you may want your timing oscillator to have a good chance of giving you a better entry point within the first 5 days (20%) of that trade.

To get an indicator to reach overbought and oversold levels an average of every 5 days, you will need to use less than 5 days to calculate the indicator value. It doesn't matter if the indicator returns a loss when the results of all its buys and sells are totaled, because the profitable part of the program comes from the longer-term trend component. It is most likely that the oscillator will generate five overbought or oversold conditions during the typical holding period for the trend trade, but only one of them will be used—the first one after the new entry signal. It is only important to see how the timing helps to improve overall profits and risk.

Figure 19-1 gives a *TradeStation* program that uses two time frames, a shorter one called `data1` and a longer one, `data2`. These could be daily and weekly, hourly and daily, or any combination of shorter and longer time frames. The shorter one is used to calculate a fast stochastic (actually %*K*-slow), and the longer interval applies to the weekly data. This use of multiple time frames is at the root of the techniques in this chapter.

FIGURE 19-1   Program combining daily stochastic with weekly trend.

```
{Multiple time periods : Linear Regression Slope + Stochastic}

{period = length of exponential trend
 data1 = shorter time period of stochastic
 data2 = longer time period of linear regression slope}

        input:  fast(5), slow(50);
        vars:   slope(0), overbot(80), oversold(20), stoch(0);

{calculate stochastic over shorter data period}
        stoch = @slowk(fast) of data1;

{Linear regression slope}
        slope = LinearRegSlope(close of data2,slow);

        if slope > 0 then exitshort on close;
        if slope < 0 then exitlong on close;

{long signal : slope must be up and stochastic below low threshhold}
        if slope > 0 and stoch < oversold then buy on close;

{short signal : slope must be down and stochastic above upper threshhold}
        if slope < 0 and stoch > overbot then sell on close;
```

ELDER'S TRIPLE-SCREEN TRADING SYSTEM[1]

The *Triple-Screen* method combines three time frames to remove the disadvantages of each one. It combines indicators that are both trend-following with oscillators (normally associated with a countertrend direction). Dr. Elder has observed that each time frame relates to the next by a factor of 5. That is, if you are using daily data as the middle time period, then the shorter interval will be divided into five parts, and the longer period will be 5 days, or 1 week.

To be practical, it is not necessary to divide a 6-hour trading day into five intervals of 1 hour and 12 minutes. Rounding to 1 hour is close enough. If, for example, you want to focus on trading a 10-minute chart, then the middle interval is 10 minutes, the short-term is 2 minutes, and the long-term is 1 hour (not 50 minutes).

In the following description, screen 1 holds the longest time frame while screen 3 shows the shortest one.

Screen 1: The Major Movement

The long-term view gives the *market tide,* a clear perspective of the major market trend, or sometimes lack of trend. Weekly data is used for this example, which is consistent with most experience that less frequent data (i.e., weekly or monthly) smooths the price movement by eliminating interim noise. Although there are many other choices for a long-term trend, the Triple-Screen approach uses the slope of the weekly MACD, where the histogram that represents the MACD value is very smooth, equivalent to, for example, a 13-week exponential smoothing. The trend is up when the MACD bar, or 13-week exponential value is higher than that of the previous week; the trend is down when this week's value is lower.

[1] From Dr. Alexander Elder, *Trading for a Living* (John Wiley & Sons, 1993).

Screen 2: The Intermediate Movement

Using an oscillator, the Screen 2 identifies the time period in which we would trade. Again, the specific oscillator is not as important as the time frame and the ability to identify *market waves* in the major movement of Screen 1. Two oscillators are suggested, the Force Index and Elder-ray, both described below. A stochastic can also be used.

1. Force Index

$$\text{Force Index} = \text{volume(today)} \times [\text{close(today)} - \text{close(yesterday)}]$$

The Force Index is then smoothed using a 2-day exponential smoothing, which has a smoothing constant of .333, and the resulting value is used to determine the overbought and oversold levels.

Entering a long position using the Force Index is not as clear as when using the Elder-ray; however, the following steps are necessary:

Step 1. The trend in Screen 1 is up.

Step 2. The 2-day exponential of the Force Index falls below its centerline and does not fall below the multiweek low. When using a stochastic instead of the Force Index, buy when the stochastic falls below 30.

2. Elder-Ray

The Elder-ray is a technique for separating bullish and bearish movement.

Bull power = high − 13-day exponential smoothing

Bear power = low − 13-day exponential smoothing

To determine when to buy using the Elder-ray and Screen 1, the following two steps are necessary:

Step 1. The trend in Screen 1 is up.

Step 2. Bear power is negative but rising; bear power must not be positive.

Two additional steps may be used to filter trades and improve performance, but are not required:

Step 3. The last peak in bull power is higher than the previous peak (the most recent bull power should not be significantly lower than the previous peak).

Step 4. Bear power is rising from a bullish divergence.

The opposite rules apply for sell signals.

Screen 3: Timing

The final screen is for fastest response, primarily for identifying *intraday breakouts*. To improve the point of entry, Screen 3 can be used to set long positions when the current price moves above the previous day's high. There is no calculation involved, simply a Buy Stop order using the shortest time period. For this example, where Screen 1 is weekly and Screen 2 is daily, Screen 3 would be hourly. Then to get a new buy signal, the hourly bar must move above the highest hourly bar of the previous day.

Stop-Loss

Every system needs risk control, and that most often comes as a Stop-Loss order. The Triple-Screen approach positions the stop as a three-step process. For a long position,

Step 1. First, place the stop below the low of the day of entry, or the previous day's low, whichever is lower.

Step 2. Move the stop to the break-even level as soon as possible. Naturally, there must be some room between the stop-loss level and the current price; otherwise, the stop will always be hit.

Step 3. Move the stop to protect 50% of the highest profits. In addition, you may consider taking profits when the stochastic or Force Index moves above the 70% level.

ROBERT KRAUSZ'S MULTIPLE TIME FRAMES

Although multiple time frame techniques have become more visible, the most robust approach has been taken by Robert Krausz. To understand the importance of first arriving at a sound theory before implementing and testing a trading program, we need to briefly review the characteristics of performance that indicate a robust method.

When testing a trend-following system, we should expect that a trend of 100 days, compared with a trend of 50 days, will produce larger profits per trade, greater reliability, and proportionally fewer trades. As you increase the calculation period, this pattern continues; when you reduce the calculation period this pattern reverses. You are prevented from using very short calculation intervals because slippage and commissions become too large; the longest periods are undesirable because of large equity swings. There must be a clear, profitable pattern when plotting returns per trade versus the average holding period.

The sophistication in Krausz's work lies in his understanding of this pattern, and its incorporation into the structure of his program, *The Fibonacci Trader.*[2] Krausz works in three time frames rather than two. Each time frame has a logical purpose and is said to be modeled after Gann's concept that the markets are essentially geometric. The shortest time frame is the one in which you will trade; in addition, there are two longer time frames to put each one into proper perspective. The patterns common to time frames are easily compared with fractals; within each time frame is another time frame with very similar patterns, reacting in much the same way. You cannot have an hourly chart without a 15-minute chart, because the longer time period is composed of shorter periods; and, if the geometry holds, then characteristics that work in one time frame, such as support and resistance, should work in shorter and longer time frames. Within each time frame there are unique levels of support and resistance; when they converge, the chance of success is increased. In Krausz's work, the relationships between price levels and profit targets are woven with Fibonacci ratios and the principles of Gann.

One primary advantage of using multiple time frames is that you can see a pattern develop sooner. A trend that appears on a weekly chart could have been seen first on the daily chart. The same logic follows for other chart formations. Similarly, the application of patterns, such as support and resistance, is the same within each time frame. When a support line appears at about the same price level in hourly, daily, and weekly charts, it gains importance.

As a well-known trader,[3] Krausz brings more than just three time frames and some unique strategies to one display screen. He endows the program with six rules:

Laws of Multiple Time Frames[4]

1. Every time frame has its own structure.
2. The higher time frames overrule the lower time frames.
3. Prices in the lower time frame structure tend to respect the energy points of the higher time frame structure.

---

[2] Robert Krausz, *W.D. Gann Treasure Discovered* (Geometric Traders Institute, 757 SE 17th Street, Suite 272, Ft. Lauderdale, FL 33316). Also see references in the section "Fibonacci and Human Behavior," Chapter 14.

[3] See Jack Schwager, *The New Market Wizards* (John Wiley & Sons, New York, NY, 1992).

[4] Copyright, Robert Krausz.

4. The energy points of support/resistance created by the higher time frame's vibration (prices) can be validated by the action of the lower time periods.

5. The trend created by the next time period enables us to define the tradable trend.

6. What appears to be chaos in one time period can be order in another time period.

Using three time frames of about the same ratio to one another (10-minute, 50-minute, and daily), with daily being the longest, Figure 19-2 shows the June 98 contract of U.S. bonds with a number of techniques applied over multiple time frames. Figure 19-2a uses only daily bars, while Figure 19-2b has 10-minute bars, both charts drawn on the same price scale to facilitate comparison.

FIGURE 19-2   Krausz's multiple time frames, Jun 98 U.S. bonds. (a) Daily chart with Gann swings and a stepped moving average. (b) Multiple time frame structure for the corresponding 4 days.

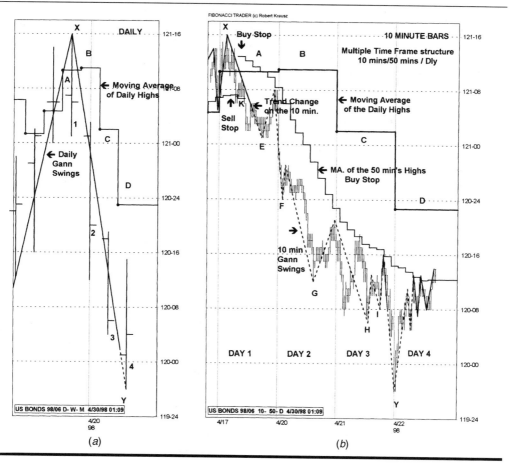

Source: Chart created using *The Fibonacci Trader.* Used with permission from Fibonacci Trader Corporation, 757 SE 17th Street, Suite 272, Ft. Lauderdale, FL 33316. www.fibonaccitrader.com

To understand the application of these techniques, it is necessary to identify the following features:[5]

1. The *Daily HiLo Activator* (in this case, it is the moving average of the daily highs) is presented as a stepped line. The 4 days of interest are marked by the letters *A, B, C,* and *D* and appear on both (*a*) and (*b*) of Figure 19-2.

2. The *50-minute HiLo Activator* (seen in Figure 19-2*b*) is the moving average of the 50-minute highs, used as a Buy Stop, or the moving average of the 50-minute lows, used as a Sell Stop.

3. The *10-minute Gann swings,* based on 10-minute bars (in Figure 19-2*b*). The solid line shows when the Gann swing represents an upward trend, and the broken line when it shows a downtrend.

The interpretation of these techniques relies on the faster response provided by the 10-minute bars, combined with the direction given by the longer time frames.

1. Based on the 10-minute Gann swings, the trend turned from up to down at about 121-00, while the daily Gann swings place the trend change much later, near 120-00.

2. The slope of the daily Gann swing, measured from point *X* to point *Y* on both charts, was down, defining the dominant trend. Short trades can be entered using the downtrend of the 10-minute time frame. The process of coordinating the trend of the higher time period with that of the lower time period, and acting in only that direction, seems to be the most advantageous approach. The low of each 10-minute swing, marked *E, F, G, H,* and *I* on the 10-minute bar chart, provides opportunities to add to the original position.

3. At the top left of the 10-minute chart, the 10-minute close falls below the Sell Stop of the 50-minute HiLo Activator at point *K* (about 120-06). The Buy Stop then applies and follows declining prices for 3 days. These changes occur in the same area where the Gann swing indicates a trend change from up to down.

4. The 50-minute moving average of the highs, shown in a step formation on the 10-minute chart, tracks the highs of the market rallies on days 1, 3, and 4. The daily moving average of the highs (the Daily HiLo Activator) remained level on day 2 and turned down on day 3. The trend can only change to up when the Daily HiLo Activator turns up again.

A COMMENT ON MULTIPLE TIME FRAMES

In thinking out the use of multiple time frames it is necessary to understand that you cannot substitute a 10-period moving average of 1-hour bars with a 40-period moving average of 15-minute bars. Similarly, you cannot substitute a 10-week average with a 50-day average. It seems natural to think that any two trends covering the same time span will give the same result, but that is not the case. Although we can average many data points, we cannot get rid of all the noise; fewer data points over the same time span will always yield a smoother result. Therefore, the use of hourly, daily, and weekly time periods—multiple time frames—gives a much different picture of the market than simply using three different moving averages based on the same data. It is much easier to see the major trend using weekly data, find the short-term direction based on daily data, and time your entry using hourly bars.

---

[5] This chart analysis was provided by Robert Krausz.

20

Advanced Techniques

Volatility is an essential ingredient in many calculations, from Wilder's RSI to variable stop-loss points and point-and-figure box sizes. But volatility is more uniform than its short-term measurement would imply; it is a more predictable component of a price series than the trend. Volatility is usually the main ingredient in risk; the more volatile the market, the greater the risk. As systematic programs mature, there seems to be a greater, justifiable concentration on how to manage volatility.

MEASURING VOLATILITY

In general, the volatility of most price series, whether stocks, financial markets, commodities, or the spread between two series, is directly proportional to the increase and decrease in the price level. This *price-volatility relationship* has been described as *lognormal* in the stock market and is very similar to a percentage-growth relationship. In Chapter 11 ("Point-and-Figure Charting"), it was shown that soybeans increased in volatility at an average rate of 2.38% relative to price, very much the same as a logarithmic increase.

$$(\textit{n-day volatility}) \ V(n) = c \times \ln \ (P_{today} - P_{base})$$

where $V(n)$ is the n-day volatility

P_{today} is today's price

P_{base} is the base price of the commodity, somewhere below the cost of production

c is a scaling factor, near 1

This shows that, beginning at its base price, the volatility of a market increases in proportion to its price increase. To express this relationship for interest rate markets, it is necessary to use yield rather than price. In addition, as we have discussed from time to time throughout this book, that currency volatility cannot be expressed this way because it has no base price; instead, it has a point of equilibrium. Prices become more volatile as they move away from equilibrium in either direction.

Shifting the Volatility Base

It follows that prices are more volatile at higher levels and that most trading systems must cope with this change by adjusting their parameters. For example, a stop-loss in gold might be $2 per ounce when the price is under $350 per ounce, $4 per ounce at about $400, and $10 per ounce at $500. A point-and-figure box size might vary in the same way as the stop-loss; as prices become higher, it requires a larger box size to maintain the same frequency of trend changes and signals. Similarly, a swing chart will need a larger reversal criterion.

Using the stop-loss as an example, most traders are willing to take a fixed amount of risk (for example, $500), regardless of whether this risk is too large or too small for market conditions; for many traders, it is only a matter of how much they can afford to lose. A stop-loss that is based on margin offers some improvement because margins are set according to market risk and contract size; however, the lag time needed for the exchange to change the margin is far too long to keep this relationship current. A percentage stop is a popular solution for analysts who realize that volatility increases with price, but it falls far behind during major bull and bear markets. A reasonable representation of long-term or underlying risk is the adjusted, lognormal price-volatility relationship. Although volatility may vary greatly at any price level, this relationship establishes a foundation for the normal level.

Base Price

The volatility relationship must include the price level at which volatility is essentially zero. Of course, we cannot find that level on a chart because no trading would have occurred. Although we do not know the price now, we call the level at which volatility is zero the *base price*. All interest rates, stock indices, and commodities have a base price. Certainly, if Treasury bills were to decline to a point at which the yield was near zero, most investors would choose to place their money elsewhere, causing activity (and volatility) to disappear. Similarly, when the price of corn falls to $1.75 per bushel, below the cost of production, farmers are not inclined to sell; they will wait until prices rise. This wait-and-see approach reduces volatility.

Figure 20-1*a* shows that the base price can be found by detrending the data and formulating the volatility based on the detrended values. Although Figure 20-1*b* does not indicate a time period, volatility only makes sense when measured over some interval. Once detrended, a scatter diagram of price versus volatility should show a relationship similar to Figure 20-1*b*. Figure 20-1*c* is a reminder that the magnitude of the volatility, and the price-volatility relationship, is directly proportional to the time interval over which the volatility is measured.

Considering the price-volatility relationship of gold since 1976 gives a typical example of how to find the base price. Figure 20-2*a* is a scatter diagram of monthly gold prices versus the monthly change in price, taken as positive numbers. A more sophisticated study would look at the price range over the month, rather than the net price change. The range will approach zero a little more slowly than the price change. Note that there is a cluster of dots in the price range from $100 to $175 per ounce and then at $300 to $450 per ounce. The lower values can be related to the pre-1980 price levels, while the higher grouping shows low volatility during periods of higher prices since 1980. Again, the use of monthly price changes can yield a value of zero even if there was significant volatility during the month, simply because prices ended at the same place at they began. Using a price range will show a smoother pattern of price versus volatility.

Detrending the price of gold using the Consumer Price Index, a technique applied to gold in Chapter 3, improves the uniformity of the results, seen in Figure 20-2*b*. Instead of two separate clusters of dots at low-volatility levels, there is only one cluster in the range from $110 to $250 per ounce. A curved line has been drawn to represent the pattern of declining volatility in relationship to declining price. This line could be straight if prices were further adjusted using a log or exponential function. According to this curve, volatility approaches zero at a slower rate as prices drop below $200 per ounce.

The time period over which volatility is measured is also a significant factor in the price-volatility relationship. Longer measurement periods give higher volatility values. Regardless of the number of days used to determine volatility, volatility will increase as price increases. This direct relationship will be very uniform for exchange-traded markets except when prices are very high. Exchange rules may limit trading when prices move too quickly; therefore, charts of real market prices will show that volatility stops expanding when it collides with these artificial constraints.

The magnitude of price movement will also increase as the period of measurement gets longer. During a volatile interval, prices will move farther in one direction during 3 or 4 days than they will in 1 or 2 days. As this interval gets very long, the volatility does not keep increasing at the same rate; it tends to slow, as shown in Figure 20-1*c*. The flattening

FIGURE 20-1 Measuring volatility from a relative base price. (*a*) Prices become less volatile relative to a long-term deflator (detrending line). (*b*) Volatility as a function of the detrended price. (*c*) Change in volatility relative to the interval over which it is measured.

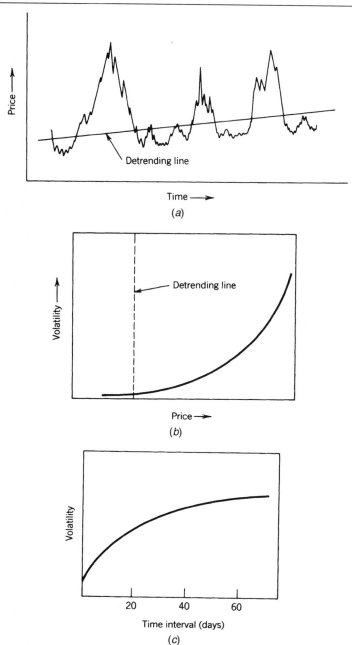

FIGURE 20-2   Finding the base price where volatility is zero, gold 1976–1993. (a) Volatility versus price. (b) Volatility versus deflated prices.

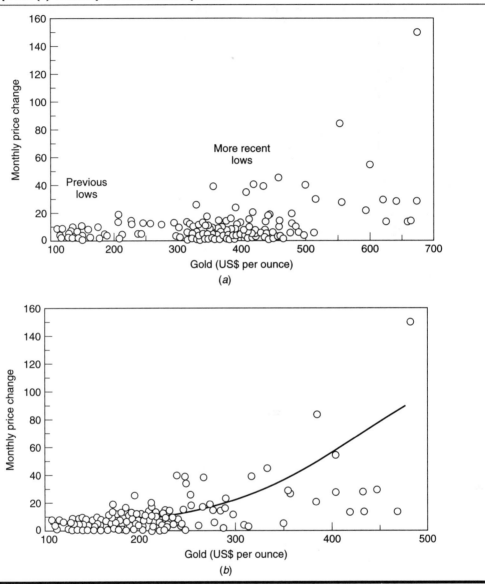

(a)

(b)

of the curve occurs at the point equal to the duration of the maximum sustained price move.

Alternate Measures

The three most used measures of volatility all satisfy the previous lognormal relationship; that is, they all expand at an increasing rate as prices rise. The one discussed so far has been *net price change over time*. This is equivalent to a momentum calculation $@abs(P_t - P_{t-n+1})$, where volatility is calculated over n days. This measure is most useful for establishing the probability of a price change at different levels.

Markets that do not have a significant price change may also be volatile. Many systems use the daily or weekly high-low range to define risk and volatility. This technique can work, although it does not always capture a full measure of activity. The *sum of the absolute price changes* is a more descriptive value. Using Figure 20-3, the three measures can be shown as:

1. Price change over time interval n:

$$V_t = P_t - P_{t-n+1}$$

2. The maximum fluctuation during the interval n:

$$V_t = \max (P_t, P_{t-n+1}) - \min (P_t, P_{t-n+1})$$

3. The sum of the absolute price changes over the interval n:

$$V_t = \sum_{i=t-n+1}^{t} |P_i - P_{i-1}|$$

In (1), the volatility is entirely dependent on the value of the two endpoints P_t and P_{t-n+1}, regardless of the price activity that occurred during the days between them. Over longer time periods, a predictable change can be expected, but in the short term this approach is not as good as either (2) or (3).

The maximum range (2) corrects for the dependence on only two points and will produce a more consistent measure of volatility, which may be used as an estimate of risk. This method may be effective as the basis for a stop-loss, because it defines the extent of the price fluctuation at each price level. Because prices end near where they began in Figure 20-2b, the close-to-close method (1) would show little or no volatility.

The sum of the absolute price changes (3) is the most descriptive measurement of volatility, although it is nondirectional. It clearly shows that prices are more or less active in cases that are not apparent to either (1) or (2). A price sequence that moves from highs to lows alternately each day is much more volatile than one in which prices move slowly to the highs and then back to the lows only once during the same time period. This measure is useful for indicating a change in market character, an increase or decrease in activity.

Ratio Measurements

Bookstaber[1] presents a volatility measurement V, which is a ratio of successive closing prices, the high and low, or a combination of the two as follows,

where C_t is the closing price on day t
H_t is the high price on day t
L_t is the low on day t
V_t is the volatility on day t

(a) *Close-to-close volatility*

$$R_t = \frac{C_t}{C_{t-1}}$$

and

$$A = \frac{1}{n} \sum_{i=1}^{n} \ln R_{t-i}$$

---

[1] Richard Bookstaber, *The Complete Investment Book* (Scott, Foresman, Glenview, IL, 1985, p. 349).

FIGURE 20-3   Three ways of measuring volatility.

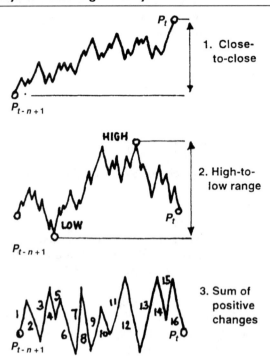

then

$$V_t^2 = \frac{1}{n-1} \sum_{i=1}^{n} (\ln R_{t-1} - A)^2$$

and

$$V_t = \sqrt{V_t^2}$$

(b) *High-low volatility*

$$V_t = \frac{.601}{n} \sum_{i=1}^{n} \ln \left(\frac{C_t}{C_{t-1}} \right)^2$$

(c) *High-low-close volatility*

$$S_t^2 = .5 \ln \left(\frac{H_t}{L_t} \right)^2 - .39 \ln \left(\frac{C_t}{C_{t-1}} \right)^2$$

$$V_t^2 = \frac{1}{n} \sum_{i=1}^{n} S_{t-i}^2$$

$$V_t = \sqrt{V_t^2}$$

Note that the current t may be a time interval rather than a single day. Then, C_t is the last price of the period, and H_t and L_t are the highest and lowest prices of the interval.

In the close-to-close estimation, the volatility V_t is the standard deviation of the closing price ratios. Bookstaber states that this measurement will follow a χ^2 distribution and that the actual volatility during the current period t can be set within the error bounds defined by the distribution.

Volatility System

The daily volatility can be used in a trading strategy, presented by Bookstaber,[2] as follows:

$$V_t(n) = \frac{1}{n} \sum_{i=1}^{n} D_{t-i+1}$$

where D_t is the maximum of:

    a. $|H_t - C_{t-1}|$

    b. $H_t - L_t$

    c. $|L_t - C_{t-1}|$

and H_t is the high on day t
             L_t is the low on day t
             C_t is the close on day t

Note that D_t is the *extended range* ("true range") concept that appears in many other works. V_t is the average extended range over the n-day interval. The trading strategy presented with this is

Buy if the close C_{t+1} rises by more than $k * V_t(n)$ from the previous close C_t.

Sell if the close C_{t+1} falls by more than $k * V_t(n)$ from the previous close C_t.

The volatility constant k is given as approximately 3, but it can be varied higher or lower to make the trading signals less or more frequent, respectively.

Volatility Filters

High volatility is clearly related to greater risk, but low volatility may also mean that there is no chance of profits. This is especially true for trend-following systems. The following are reasonable expectations for selecting trades based on volatility:

Entering on very high volatility will increase risk. It may be best to simply avoid those trades.

Entering on low volatility seems safe, but prices often have no direction and produce losses. Waiting for an increase in activity before entering might improve returns.

Exiting a position when prices become very volatile should reduce both profits and risk, but may come after-the-fact. This is an issue best resolved by testing.

Filter or Delay

Whenever a high- or low-volatility situation occurs at the time of an entry signal, there are two choices. The trade can be completely eliminated by *filtering*, or it can be delayed until the high volatility drops or the low volatility increases to an acceptable level. If the trade ends during the waiting period, the trade is eliminated. Both of these cases have been studied and the results follow.

Constructing a Volatility Filter

Calculating the volatility is simple to program using any spreadsheet or strategy-testing software. The following steps were used here:

---

[2] Ibid., pp. 224–236.

1. Calculate a moving average trend.
2. Calculate the volatility, using any one of the methods described early in this chapter, but not including the volatility of the current day.
3. Enter a new trade if the volatility is (a) above the low-filter level or (b) below the high-filter level.
4. Exit a current position if the volatility is above the high-filter level *and* (a) the current price change is a profit or (b) the current price change is a loss.

To give these choices a chance to show which are robust, five different markets were tested, each for more than 10 years ending in 1993: Eurodollars, Japanese yen, crude oil, IBM, and the S&P 500. Futures market prices were gap-adjusted and indexed, using the nearest delivery month. Results from these tests are shown as percentage changes; IBM was quoted in share price. The trend speed (a simple moving average) was the same as the period over which the volatility was calculated. Periods of 35 days and 10 days were the only ones tested; 35 days was arbitrarily chosen as about one-eighth of a trading year. The 10-day period (2 weeks) was included as a short-term contrast.

Standard Deviation Measurement

A standard deviation was used to determine the volatility threshold level. For example, for a high-volatility filter, a *1–standard deviation threshold* means that no trades were taken if the volatility was above the average volatility plus 1 standard deviation, the top 16%. A *2–standard deviation threshold* puts volatility in the top 2.5%, and a *3–standard deviation threshold* means the top .5%. A 0 standard deviation would filter all trades above the average volatility. Because only 35 days are used, actual volatility can jump well beyond the normal 3–standard deviation maximum. Filter values above 3 standard deviations (up to 7 standard deviations in these tests) must be used to isolate the most extreme volatile price movements.

Entry Filter Results

Table 20-1 shows the results for both high- and low-volatility entry options, expressed as rate of return based on maximum drawdown. The case where the standard deviation value is zero indicates no filtering; tests were run for a calculation period of 35 days. In part (*a*), the high-volatility filter causes a delay until volatility drops below the designated standard deviation level; in part (*b*), volatility must increase to be above the standard deviation level.

Results for the high-volatility filter are not impressive. The Eurodollar improves for lower levels while the Japanese yen and crude oil do not. Both IBM and the S&P improve by waiting for lower volatility, but both have underlying losing strategies; therefore, omitting trades is likely to improve results. Because these results are a function of both returns and risk, the elimination of high volatility does not clearly improve either component of performance.

The low-volatility filter is much clearer. In all cases except the S&P, taking only those trades that occur with conditions of higher volatility shows improvements for all markets. Because of the few cases that would have occurred with volatility greater than 6.0 standard deviations, the large return shown by IBM is not realistic. A standard deviation between −1 and +1, indicating the practical elimination of 16% to 84% of all trades, shows the most consistency.

High-Volatility Exits: Distinguishing a Volatile Good Move from a Bad One

It may be that exiting due to high volatility is acting after-the-fact; then, it would be ineffective for reducing risk. If a market is noisy then price jumps are short-lived, in which case you should close out positions when a volatile move is profitable because profits will soon disappear. Or, if the volatile move is an immediate loss, then waiting should recover at least

TABLE 20-1   High- and Low-Volatility Filter Results*

StDev	Euro$	Yen	Crude	IBM	S&P
(a) High-Volatility Entry Filter with Delayed Entry					
none	835	340	218	13	−6
6.0	886	340	182	7	−4
5.0	876	340	183	9	−4
4.0	884	361	183	18	−4
3.0	932	399	176	19	−17
2.0	948	401	197	12	−17
1.0	988	410	198	20	−22
0	923	425	323	−35	−27
(b) Low-Volatility Entry Filter with Trade Elimination					
6.0	109	266	139	3,181	−40
4.0	457	47	94	308	−55
2.0	1,172	85	−20	816	−85
0	491	340	83	214	−95
−1.0	860	337	156	−19	−67
−2.0	882	320	219	19	−36
none	835	320	84	13	−36

*Thirty-five days' calculation period, rate of return based on maximum drawdown.

part of the loss. The opposite is true for a trending market. A good price move should be followed by more profits, and a bad move by further losses.

Tests of exit filters were separated into *positive* and *negative* price moves. When the positive option was elected, exits occurred when the high-volatility level was reached *and* prices generated a profit for the day. When the negative was used, prices must have produced a loss for the day. For the Eurodollar, returns improve when volatile losing moves are liquidated, and returns decline when profitable moves are closed out. We can conclude that the Eurodollar is a trending market, and cutting a trade short due to increased volatility is not a good strategy. That is not true with the S&P, which has a high degree of noise over short time periods. It was also not the case for the yen, which has erratic price behavior. Both of these markets improved when profits were taken on a positive move.

Because shorter-term analysis operates in an environment of greater noise, the exit filters will generally be an improvement. For markets with significant long-term trends and systems that are intended to capitalize on those trends, exiting a trade for almost any reason, other than a change of trend, is going to adversely affect the performance.

Creating Your Own Filters

A volatility filter is a simple calculation. Deciding which volatility filter to use is more complex because it requires a number of different testing programs. The following Omega program and the spreadsheet program (Table 20-2) combine all of these features into one testing program. An option is used to select each feature.

```
OMEGA Easy Language Code.

{High and Low Volatility Filters
 Copyright 1994-1998, P.J. Kaufman. All rights reserved.

 Do not enter trades on high volatility and price in trend direction. Exit on high volatility
 and price change of direction option.
```

TABLE 20-2   Spreadsheet Sample

Corel Quattro Spreadsheet Code

Col	Description	Begin Row	Calculations
L3	Low-filter limit factor		[Constant]
M3	High-filter limit factor		[Constant]
A	Date	5	[Input]
B–D	Open, High, Low prices	5	[Input]
E	Closing price	5	[Input]
F–G	Vol, OpInt data	5	[Input]
H	Positive value of price changes	6	@ABS(E6..E5)
I	35-day moving average	39	@AVG(E5..E39)
J	Average volatility	39	@AVG(H5..H39)
K	Standard deviation of volatility	39	@STD(H5..H39)
L	Low-filter limit	39	+J39-$L$2*K39
M	High-filter limit	39	+J39+$M$2*K39
N	Position	40	@IF(I40<I39,-1,1)
O	Low-volatility indicator	40	@IF(H40<L39,1,0)
P	High-volatility indicator	40	@IF(H40>M39,1,0)
Q	Buy/sell with low filter	40	@IF($N40=1#AND#N39=-1, @IF($H40>$L39,"buy","c/o"), @IF($N40=-1#AND#N39=1, @IF($H40>$L39,"sell","c/o")," "))
R	Buy/sell with low delay	40	@IF($N40=1,@IF($H40>$L39,"buy", @IF($N39=-1,"c/o"," ")), @IF($H40>$L39,"sell",@IF($N39=1,"c/o"," "))," "))
S	Buy/sell with high filter	40	@IF(N40=1#AND#$N39=-1, @IF($H40<$M39,"buy","c/o"), @IF($N40=-1#AND#P39=1, @IF($H40<$M39,"sell","c/o")," "))
T	Buy/sell with high delay	40	@IF($N40=1,@IF($H40<$M39,"buy", @IF($N39=-1,"c/o"," ")),@IF($N40=-1, @IF($H40<$M39,"sell",@IF($N39=1,"c/o"," "))," "))
U	Exit on high volatility	40	@IF($H40>$M39,"c/o"," ")

```
Option 0 = No entry or exit filter
Option 1 = Entry filter only
Option 2 = Exit filter only - no price direction
Option 3 = Exit filter only - profitable move
Option 4 = Exit filter only - contrary move
Option 5 = Both entry and exit filters (options 1 and 2)}

input:  option(2), length(35), Efactor(1.0),ELfactor(1.0), Xfactor(1.0), prndate(0);
vars:   vavg(0), vsd(0), lowlimit(0), Euplimit(0), Xuplimit(0), mavg(0), aror(0), deltapl(0),
        totalpl(0),
        risk(0), ratio(0), position(0), variance(0), change(0), ELuplimit(0);
{Volatility = average + standard deviation of price changes.
 Calculate average and sd before new prices}
 change = @AbsValue(close - close[1]);
 vavg = @Average(change[1],length);
 vsd = @StdDev(change[1],length);

{Extreme volatility limits}
 lowlimit = vavg - vsd;
 Euplimit = vavg + 2*Efactor*vsd;
```

```
ELuplimit = vavg + 2*ELfactor*vsd;
Xuplimit = vavg + 2*Xfactor*vsd;

{System rules based on moving average trend}
 mavg = @average(close,length);
 if mavg>mavg[1] and position = -1 then position = 0;
 if mavg<mavg[1] and position = 1 then position = 0;

{Enter on new trend signals below high volatility:
 Efilter or new trend signals above low volatility: ELfilter}
 if option=1 or option=5 then begin
{High volatility delay}
{ if mavg>mavg[1] and position <> 1 and change<Euplimit then begin}
{Low volatility filter}
{ if mavg>mavg[1] and mavg[1]<=mavg[2] and change<Euplimit and change>ELuplimit then begin}
{Low volatility delay}
   if mavg>mavg[1] and position <> 1 and change<Euplimit and change>ELuplimit then begin
     buy on close;
     position = 1;
     end;
{High volatility delay}
{ if mavg<mavg[1] and position <> -1 and change<Euplimit then begin}
{Low volatility filter}
{ if mavg<mavg[1] and mavg[1]>=mavg[2] and change<Euplimit and change>ELuplimit then begin}

{Low volatility delay}
   if mavg<mavg[1] and position <> -1 and change<Euplimit and change>ELuplimit then begin
     sell on close;
     position = -1;
     end;
   end;

{Normal entry only once in the same direction}
 if option<>1 and option<>5 then begin
   if mavg>mavg[1] and position <> 1 then begin
     buy on close;
     position = 1;
     end;
   if mavg>mavg[1] and position <> -1 then begin
     sell on close;
     position = -1;
     end;
   end;

{Don't reenter after high volatility exit}
 if option>1 then begin
   if mavg>mavg[1] and change<Xuplimit and position <>1 then begin
     buy on close;
     position = 1;
     end;
   if mavg<mavg[1] and change<Xuplimit and position <> -1 then begin
     sell on close;
     position = -1;
     end;
   end;

{Exit without volatility}
 if option=0 or option=1 then begin
   if mavg<mavg[1] then exitlong on close;
   if mavg>mavg[1] then exitshort on close;
   end;
{Exit on high volatility and profitable direction}
 if option=2 or option=3 then begin
```

```
   if mavg<mavg[1] or (close>close[1] and change>Xuplimit) then exitlong on close;
   if mavg>mavg[1] or (close<close[1] and change>Xuplimit) then exitshort on close;
   end;
{Exit on high volatility and not a profitable direction}
 if option=2 or option=4 or option=5 then begin
   if mavg<mavg[1] or (close<=close[1] and change>Xuplimit) then exitlong on close;
   if mavg>mavg[1] or (close>=close[1] and change>Xuplimit) then exitshort on close;
   end;

{Replace high volatility days because they distort standard deviation}
{ if change > vavg+2*factor*vsd then change = vavg;}
```

Note that parts of the program have comment braces around one or more lines. These represent other options that may be tested. It will be necessary to remove the comment braces from one section and add them to another.

TRADE SELECTION

Once you have a basic system, the next step is to decide whether you can eliminate some of the losing trades without eliminating the profitable ones. In the extreme, we want to eliminate *all* of the losing trades, even if we reduce some of the profits; of course, that is impossible. Every system has a risk, even so-called "riskless" trades. Arbitrage, when done properly, has virtually no risk; however, it may be so competitive that the opportunities are rare and the margin of profit small. You might find, after months of trading a guaranteed arbitrage, that your returns are disappointing compared with the cost of doing business. Putting your money into U.S. bonds would have been nearly as good with a lot less work.

Nothing is free. Good trading is not a matter of hitting it rich on a single short position; it is grinding out a profit day by day and week by week. Occasionally, if you follow new markets, you might find an opportunity that others have not yet seen. If you act fast, you can capitalize on this for a short time, until others see the same situation. Then bigger players come in and push you out. In turn, they are followed by other investors who combine to remove all the profit opportunity, even for themselves.

When selecting trades to eliminate, the easiest place to begin is by associating performance with volatility or price level. While some systems perform better in an environment of higher volatility, it may be that the best return relative to risk occurs when there is less volatility. In general, markets with extremely low volatility do not perform well because they have less direction. Under moderate-volatility conditions, systems will return both lower profits and smaller losses; with high volatility we can expect large profits and high risk.

Predicting Volatility with Trading Ranges

William Brower[3] performed a thorough study of trading ranges, looking to find a higher range for tomorrow. This would be important for day traders and for any system in which higher volatility is an advantage. Specifically, high volatility is desirable for breakout systems. A summary of his results is shown in Table 20-3 for the S&P from 12/23/87 through 12/15/95.

Thomas Bierovic, On-Balance True Range

To visualize the change in volatility, Thomas Bierovic has created On-Balance True Range by following the same rules as On-Balance Volume, but using the True Range calculation instead of Volume. He then calculates a 9-day exponential smoothing of the On-Balance True Range and uses the crossovers of the oscillator and smoothed oscillator to confirm signals. Although the highs and lows may come at nearly the same time as other oscillators,

---

[3] William Brower, *Inside Edge* (Inside Edge Systems, 10 Fresenius Road, Westport, CT 06880, March/April 96).

TABLE 20-3 Predicting the Trading Range of the S&P 500*

Rule	Conditions Tested	Conclusion
1	$O < L[1] - x$	Very good predictor, but few cases (161 at $x = -.10$)
2	$O > H[1] + x$	Modest predictor, but few cases (101 at $x = .60$)
3	$C[1] + x > O > C[1]$	Range got smaller when $x = .35$
4	$C[1] - x < O < C[1]$	Range got smaller when $x = .30$
5	$O < C[1] - x$	Range tended to increase as x increased
6	$H[2] <= H[1]$ and $L[2] >= L[1]$	No significance
7	$H[2] > H[1]$ and $L[2] < L[1]$	Modest predictor of lower volatility
8	Day of week	Monday had lowest volatility, Tuesday and Friday the highest
9	Average(TrueRange,3)[1] $> x$	Higher avg true range for 3 days was a very good predictor of higher volatility
10	RSI(close,3)[1] $< x$	When RSI < 40 good predictor of higher volatility

* *Source:* William Brower.

the positioning of the relative peaks and valleys may offer new patterns. For many traders, this simple interpretation can help separate high- and low-volatility conditions.

PRICE-VOLUME DISTRIBUTION

Many systems that have excellent historic simulations fail when they are actually traded. These include models based on both intraday and daily data. One reason for this disappointing performance is the lack of understanding of market liquidity. Consider two systems:

A *trend-following method,* which signals a buy or sell order when prices rise or fall relative to a specific price during the day

A *countertrend system,* which sells and buys at relative intraday highs or lows

Although each system intends to profit with their opposing philosophies, both act when prices make a relatively unusual move. Figure 20-4 shows the normal distribution of intraday volume and the profitability associated with this distribution.[4]

[4] Gary Ginter and Joseph J. Ritchie, "Data Errors and Profit Distortions," in Perry J. Kaufman (Ed.), *Technical Analysis in Commodities* (John Wiley & Sons, New York, 1980).

FIGURE 20-4 Daily price/volume distribution.

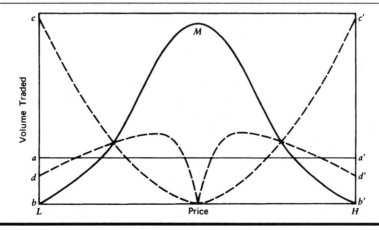

The solid line bb' is the actual volume on a theoretically normal day in which prices remained in a trading range. Volume is greatest at the median M and declines sharply to the high and low endpoints H and L, where only one trade may have occurred. The dotted line cc' represents the apparent profit for a countertrend system that makes the assumption of a straight-line volume distribution, aa'. The endpoints are shown to contribute the largest part of the profits when, in reality, no executions may have been possible near those levels. Assuming the ability to execute at all points on the distribution bb', the approximate profit contribution is shown as dd'. Trades are most likely to be filled at points that limit immediate profits.

For trend-following systems, no profits should be expected when buy or sell orders are placed at the extremes of the day. The actual price distribution bb' is the maximum that could be expected from such a system; in reality, the first day is usually a loss.

TRENDS AND NOISE

Throughout this book there are techniques that try to find the underlying trend when the price direction is not clear. The investor who buys sooner is more profitable, but only if the market moves higher. What makes it so difficult to identify the trend is *noise*. Noise is the erratic movement of price; by definition it is unpredictable, yet it has very definite statistical attributes.

Noise is the product of the market participants buying and selling at different times for different purposes. Each has their own objectives and time frame. Noise can also be a price shock—an unexpected event that may or may not cause a lasting price change. Noise has most of the qualities of a sequence of random numbers. Nearly half of all price moves change direction from the previous move; about 25% of all price moves continue in the same direction for two periods, and so on. These patterns should already be familiar to analysts. The size of a price move, or price shock, also appears to be random; that is, 50% are quite small, 25% are twice as large, 12.5% are four times as large, and a few are very large.

Then how can you tell if a price move up is an indication of a new direction or simply more noise? The answer is that you can't tell by studying only price until after the direction has continued. There are situations, of course, where the news will give us information to show that the price jump was a structural change (for example, when the Federal Reserve lowers interest rates). But price alone won't tell us.

We can improve our chances of selecting the trend direction based on a net price move by choosing only the largest moves. This is the reason why a long-term trend is more reliable than a short one. To see this clearly, consider Figure 20-5 to be random numbers, or market noise. Most of the time prices remain below the level P1, but a price move that reaches P2 (twice as large) is still fairly common. Less often, price will jump to level P3 but only rarely will it reach P8. Let's say that, out of 1,000 price moves, P1 is reached 500 times, P2 occurs 250 times, P4 occurs 64½ times and P8 about 4 times. If we use a breakout system to decide the price trend, and our breakout criteria is less than P2, then there would have been 250 total signals (both long and short) in which to find the right trend direction. If there were 10 confirmed trends during this period, you needed to reject or filter 240, or 96%, of all moves. Suppose your criteria was P8 instead of P2, and because the size of the subsequent price trend must be bigger due to the larger entry criteria, there was only one good trend during this period. Then you have a 1-in-4 chance of being correct, far better than the 1-in-25 using a very small trend criteria.

It is the magnitude of the market noise that determines the criteria needed for entering a trend. For a broadly traded market, the noise pattern is very predictable, while markets that have low volume might not conform closely to a traditional statistical profile.

FIGURE 20-5   Random occurrence of price levels.

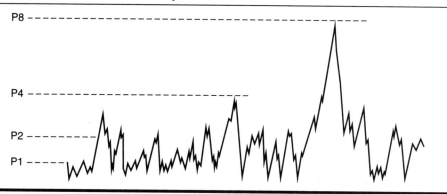

Noise can be measured using the same calculations as volatility, given at the beginning of this chapter, or as Kaufman's efficiency ratio found in Chapter 17 ("Adaptive Techniques").

EXPERT SYSTEMS

An *expert system* is one in which you draw conclusions based on an accumulated *knowledge base,* which has been stored as data, facts, and relationships in the form of *if-then-else* rules. For our purposes, these would include price and economic data as well as the knowledge that, for example, *highly correlated markets move together,* and *high volatility means high risk.* When the first expert systems were developed, the core information was actually gathered by interviewing experts, which is how the name *expert system* was derived. The success of this method depends upon the quality and completeness of the knowledge base.

The knowledge base is used by an *inference engine,* which is able to draw conclusions from the facts stored in the knowledge base. Therefore, if we have the following information,

FACT   1:   U.S. bonds are more volatile than Eurodollars.

FACT   2:   The S&P 500 is more volatile than U.S. bonds.

FACT   3:   Volatility is directly proportional to risk.

then the inference engine can create the new fact

FACT   4:   The S&P is riskier than Eurodollars.

The inference engine provides a straightforward, logical process; however, there may be many relationships to resolve, not all of which may apply to the problem you would like to solve. For example, if we also have the following facts:

FACT   5:   The S&P has a high degree of noise.

FACT   6:   Eurodollars have a low degree of noise.

FACT   7:   The S&P is currently trading below its 200-day moving average.

FACT   8:   The S&P is currently trading above its 20-day moving average.

FACT   9:   The S&P has been above its 200-day moving average for 80% of the past 20 years.

FACT 10:   Eurodollar rates are driven by monetary bank policy.

FACT 11:   Current monetary policy is dominated by concerns of inflation.

FACT 12:   Inflation results in higher interest rates.

FACT 13:   Net trading returns for the S&P have been 40% per annum.

FACT 14:   Net trading returns for the Eurodollar have been 20% per annum.

then human logic might conclude that Eurodollar yields are likely to rise because of concerns over inflation. In addition, the S&P has greater risk, erratic behavior, and is currently not as strong as it has been on average over the past 20 years, although it is now rising. Compared with Eurodollars, there is greater risk trading the S&P, but its returns have been higher.

How can this expert conclusion be duplicated by a computer? By adding a set of rules that parallels the thinking of experts, a computer can theoretically arrive at the same conclusions. For example,

RULE 1a: IF the Producer Price Index rises by more than the annualized rate of 4%, THEN we have inflation.

RULE 2a: IF there is high noise, THEN there is less chance of a trend.

RULE 3a: IF there is high noise, THEN there is greater risk.

RULE 4a: IF the faster trend is above the slower trend, THEN prices are trending up.

For each positive rule 1 through 4, there should also be a negative rule:

RULE 1b: IF the Producer Price Index does not rise by more than 4% annualized, THEN we do not have inflation.

RULE 2b: IF there is low noise, THEN there is a greater chance of a trend.

RULE 3b: IF there is low noise, THEN there is lower risk.

RULE 4b: IF the faster trend is below the slower trend, THEN prices are trending down.

Even with the negative rules there are some ambiguous cases. For example, in Rule 4 there is the case in which the two trends are in conflict. In other situations, the positive rule might be true, but the negative rule may not be as strong. In Rule 1b, we see that the effect is that "we do not have inflation" rather than "we have deflation."

Forward Chaining

The process of combining the rules and facts to yield an expert opinion is called *forward chaining.* For example, beginning with FACT 6, "Eurodollars have a low degree of noise," we find the relevant rule, RULE 3b: "IF there is low noise, THEN there is lower risk," and create a new fact: "Eurodollars have (relatively) low risk." Note that in each case, the terms *low, high,* and *faster* are all relative.

Once we have this new fact, that Eurodollars have relatively low risk, and we similarly conclude that the S&P has *relatively high risk,* we can also conclude that Eurodollars have lower risk than the S&P. The process of following the path of each fact as it is handled by various rules is called *forward chaining.* It will lead to other rules and other facts; it may be that the expert opinion will be found along this route, or that the combination of new facts, such as the relative risk between the Eurodollars and the S&P, will provide the expert opinion.

This example shows only a few facts that can be easily summarized; however, there are thousands of pieces of information about performance characteristics, relationships to other markets, and fundamental factors that might alter expectations. If accumulated by asking experts, it is also likely that there will be conflicting information. While the human brain has a remarkable ability to sort through these items and select the information it considers most relevant, some important items can be overlooked when there is too much to consider. An expert system is expected to use all of the data and reduce it to a single decision. In doing this, it must also select the most significant facts and resolve conflicts associated with the proper order of events and the time horizon of the investor.

A Technical Expert System

An expert system can treat indicator values as expert opinions and create systems without the fundamental relationships shown in the previous section. An example by Fishman, Barr, and Loick,[5] applied to the DJIA, defines *rules* as the relationships between the various indicators and calculations, and the *facts* as the values of those items. The purpose of this expert system is to inspect trending and nontrending characteristics of price movement to give the probability of a continued trend. The following example is adapted from their article:

Rule 1: IF ADX > 18 AND ADX >= ADX[2]
(AND nontrending is false or undefined),
THEN there is a 95% chance the market is trending.

Rule 2: IF ADX < 30 AND ADX <= ADX[2]
(AND trending is false or undefined),
THEN there is a 90% chance the market is nontrending.

Rule 3: IF the market is trending,
THEN MACD = probability of .8 AND SD = probability of .5 (85%).

Rule 4: IF the market is nontrending,
THEN MACD = probability of .55 AND SD = probability of .75 (75%).

Rule 5: IF stochastic AND SK[1] < 30 AND SD[1] < 30 AND SK[1] < SD[1]
AND SK < SD, THEN sell with 80% confidence.

Rule 6: IF stochastic AND SK[1] > 70 AND SD[1] > 70 AND SK[1] > SD[1]
AND SK > SD, THEN buy with 80% confidence.

Rule 7: IF MACD AND MACD value > signal line value,
THEN buy with 75% confidence.

Rule 8: IF MACD AND MACD value < signal line value,
THEN sell with 75% confidence.

where the following periods are assumed:

ADX	is an 18-period ADX calculation
ADX[2]	is the ADX 2 periods ago
MACD	is the Moving Average Convergence/Divergence with smoothing constants .15 and .075
SK	is a 9-period, %*K* fast stochastic
SD	is a 9-period, %*D* slow stochastic

and *undefined* means that there is no information about the values. The *facts* are the actual values to be used in the evaluation:

FACT 1: ADX = 19

FACT 2: ADX[2] = 19

FACT 3: SK = 90

FACT 4: SD = 80

[5] Mark B. Fishman, Dean S. Barr, and Walter J. Loick, "Artificial Intelligence And Market Analysis," *Technical Analysis of Stocks & Commodities* (Bonus Issue 1993).

FACT 5:   SK[1] − SK = 68

FACT 6:   SD[1] − SD = 92

FACT 7:   signal line value = −70

FACT 8:   MACD value = −68

FACT 9:   the market is trending

The results, expressed as probabilities, offer greater insight into the likelihood of success using this method. Arriving at these probabilities, however, requires additional decisions. Without any further information, we can assume that there is only a 50% chance that the stochastic is a correct trend indicator. If we were to test the number of times the stochastic indicated an upward move with the number of days that the subsequent price moved higher, we could get a much better indication of the chance of success.

FUZZY LOGIC[6]

In the second example of expert systems, the results were expressed as probabilities. Because trend and indicator calculations are estimations of market movement, very little is strictly true or false; therefore, probabilities are a more realistic way to view the results. The probability of being right can be represented by the *reliability* (percentage of profitable trades) of a system using these calculations. When right, the average payout is the *average profits per trade,* and when wrong, the loss is the *average loss per trade.* When you can assign a probability to results, the variable has often been called *fuzzy.* But this way of looking at values is really a twist on basic probability analysis.

The idea of *fuzziness* is intended to describe the lack of precision in normal human conversation and thought. In its pure form, the use of fuzziness allows human uncertainty to be introduced into methods of artificial intelligence. For example, we often say,

"There were a lot of people in line at the show."

"I had to wait a long time."

"It was really cold while I was waiting."

"The stock market was strong yesterday."

"Unemployment dropped sharply."

In all these cases, we understand what is being said although there are no specific values associated with "a lot of people," "a long time," "cold," "strong," and "sharply." In fuzzy logic, all is not *true* or *false, 0* or *1, there* or *not there.* True fuzzy logic will answer the question "If a half-eaten apple is still an apple, how much do you have to eat before it stops being an apple?"

The concept of fuzziness includes *fuzzy numbers,* such as "small," "about 8," "close to 5," and "much larger than 10," as well as *fuzzy quantifiers,* such as "almost," "several," and "most." Phrases such as "Unexpected results of Government reports cause big moves" is a common fuzzy expression.

Fuzzy Reasoning

Fuzzy events and fuzzy statistics are combined into *fuzzy reasoning.* It is a remarkable phenomenon that the answers to the following examples are clear to the human brain, but not to a machine (the answers can be found at the bottom of this page).[7]

---

[6] Parts of this section are drawn from Perry Kaufman, *Smarter Trading* (McGraw-Hill, NY, 1995).

[7] The answers to the examples are: (1) *very small,* (2) *most,* and (3) *bad.*

Example 1:   *X* is a small price move.
             Y is much smaller than *X*.
             How small is *Y?*

Example 2:   Most price moves are small.
             Most small price moves are up.
             How many price moves are up?

Example 3:   It is not quite true that the quarterly earnings were very bad.
             It is not true that the quarterly earnings were good.
             How bad were the quarterly earnings?

Common Approach to Fuzzy Solutions

In the terminology of fuzzy logic, there are three aspects of problem solving: *membership*, to show how the data are related to each other; *fuzzy rules*, to draw conclusions; and *defuzzifiers*, to turn the fuzzy answers back into useable results.[8]

For example, we would like to predict whether a price move will be big enough to capture a profit needed by our trading system. To have a robust system, we always use a 20-day trend but would like to predict which price moves will be above our minimum needs before we enter the trade. In general, we have found that, given commissions and slippage, we need to net $500 per trade. Because we are using a trend-following system that gives up profits before exiting, we would like to see an $800 profit to capture a net of $500. Based on our needs, we can define our limits as:

1. Average peak move between $300 and $800 is acceptable
2. Average peak move over $800 is desirable.
3. Average peak move under $300 is unacceptable.

To decide whether current price movement is likely to give us enough profit to enter a trade, we measure the average price move over every 20-day period for the past 1 year (long-term) and for the past 1 month (short-term). Based on this approach, we create the rules:

1. If both the long-term and short-term profit potentials are unacceptable, then the current profit potential is unacceptable.
2. If both the long-term and short-term profit potentials are desirable, then the current profit potential is desirable.
3. If both the long-term and short-term profit potentials are acceptable, then the current profit potential is acceptable.

These three cases are very clear, but what if the long-term and short-term expectations are different? For example, if the long-term average peak profits are $250 and the short-term are $600, what can be expected from the current move? In the current application of fuzzy logic, this converts to a problem in probability for which we need more information about the history of these price moves. Through testing, we find that the 1-year average price move has a standard deviation of $75 and the past 1 month has a standard deviation of $200. We could then construct a diagram that shows the expected results from combining the two measurements (see Figure 20-6). The average returns are shown with descending lines based on their standard deviations. These cross at about $350 per trade, giving a reasonable answer to how to combine the two values.

One additional measurement that cannot be overlooked is the potential error in each statistic. The longer-term measure used 250 trading days, while the short-term used only

---

[8] Murray A. Ruggiero, Jr., "Artificial trader jumps candlesticks," *Futures* (February 1995), and "Lighting candlesticks with fuzzy logic," *Futures* (March 1996).

FIGURE 20-6   Expectations of a price move using two time periods.

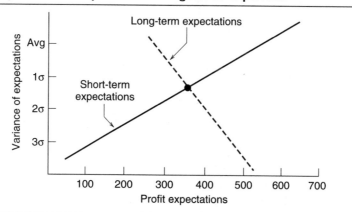

about 20 days. The standard error for each calculation is 6.3% and 22.3%, respectively. In the final interpretation of results, we can say that the longer-term data are more important than the short-term values by about 3.5 : 1. Then we could write additional rules:

4. If the long-term potential is unacceptable and the short-term is acceptable, then the current potential is unacceptable.
5. If the long-term potential is unacceptable and the short-term is desirable, then the current potential is acceptable.

Using just the rules, we can claim that we are applying fuzzy logic to our trading; however, the state of the art indicates that fuzzy logic is still hanging onto the coattails of simple probability. When it lets go, it is likely to be the most significant breakthrough in market analysis.

FRACTALS AND CHAOS

Another new area that has captured the interest of market analysts is chaos. *Chaos theory* is a way to describe the behavior of nonlinear systems, those that cannot be described by a straight line. Chaotic systems are not necessarily without any form or method, as the expression is commonly used, but those phenomena that are not a simple variation of a linear relationship. Some examples of this behavior will be given later in this section.

One method of measuring chaotic systems is with various geometric shapes. This effort has resulted in an area of mathematics now called *fractal geometry;* its approach strikes a true note about how the real world of numbers actually works.[9] All of us have been taught Euclidean geometry in school; it is the world of straight lines and clean edges in which we can measure the length of a line or the area of a rectangle very easily. In the real world, however, there are no straight lines; if you look closely enough, they all have ragged edges and all may be described as chaotic.

Fractal Dimension

In fractal geometry we find that there is a way of representing the irregularity of numbers, and the formations seen in nature. We first must accept the notion that there are no *whole* numbers in nature, that real-world objects are more likely to be described as fractional, or having a *fractal dimension.* The classic example of this is the algebra of coastline dimen-

---

[9] An excellent discussion of this topic can be found in Edgar Peters, *Chaos and Order in the Capital Markets* (John Wiley & Sons, New York, 1991). The coastline example is originally credited to Benoit Mandelbrot.

sion. We will see that the questions "How long is the coastline?" and "How far did prices move?" are very similar.

The answer to both these questions is "That depends on how it is measured." Consider the problem of measuring the coastline of Australia using a large wall map. If we take a 12-inch ruler, we might find that the coastline is about 10 feet (perhaps 10,000 miles according to the scale). Had we taken a slightly smaller ruler we would have been more accurate and perhaps have found the coastline to be 11,000 miles; even a smaller ruler would have followed the contours better and found 12,000 miles of coast. As the ruler gets smaller the coastline appears to get longer. If we had an infinitely smaller ruler, the coast would be infinitely long. There is really no correct answer to the question, "How long is the coastline?"

Fractal dimension is the degree of roughness or irregularity of a structure or system. In many chaotic systems, there is a constant fractal dimension; that is, the interval used for measuring will have a predictable impact on the resulting values in a manner similar to a normal distribution. Therefore, using a 12-inch ruler, we measure the coastline and get 10,000 miles:

24-inch ruler	5,000-mile coastline
12-inch ruler	10,000-mile coastline
6-inch ruler	20,000-mile coastline

Note that the large 24-inch ruler returns a value that is actually smaller than what we believe is a reasonable answer. This is because, when you place a long ruler from one point to another on the map, it cuts across part of the land mass.

Using Fractal Efficiency

In Chapter 17 ("Adaptive Techniques"), there is a discussion of Kaufman's efficiency ratio. This ratio is formed by dividing the net change in price movement over *n* periods by the sum of all component moves, taken as positive numbers, over the same *n* periods. If the ratio approaches the value 1.0, then the movement is smooth (not chaotic); if the ratio approaches 0, then there is great inefficiency or chaos. This same measurement has more recently been called *fractal efficiency*.

Fractal efficiency measures the amount of chaotic movement in prices; this can also be considered similar to market noise. In Chapter 17, Kaufman related this to trending and nontrending patterns, when the ratio approached 1.0 and 0, respectively. While each market has its unique underlying level of noise, the measurement of fractal efficiency is consistent over all markets. Markets may vary in volatility, although their chaotic behavior is technically the same; therefore, the characteristics of one market may be compared with others by matching both the fractal efficiency and volatility.

Interpreting fractal efficiency as noise allows other trading rules to develop. For example, a market with less noise should be entered quickly using a trending system, while it may be best to wait for a better price if the market is classified as having high noise. A noisy market is one that continues to change direction, while an efficient market is smooth. These characteristics are important in choosing trading rules and in turning a theoretical model into a profitable trading system.

Chaotic Patterns and Market Behavior

Chaotic patterns are easy to imagine in the behavior of prices, but very difficult to measure. There would be no problem in predicting price direction if every participant reacted in the same way to the same event, much the way a single planet would smoothly orbit a single sun. In the real world nothing is quite as simple. Consider the pattern of prices represented as planets that are affected equally by two events, E1 and E2. We will get a wobbly pattern whenever the planet passes across the midpoint where one *attractor* is stronger than the other, shown in Figure 20-7*a*. At point *a*, the object is most affected by the nearest attractor, E1, but as it circles it becomes closer to E2 and tries to form an orbit around it. The possible patterns are too complex and they vary based on the distance between E1 and E2 and the size of E2 compared with E1. If attractor E2 is much larger than E1, there will simply be a distortion in the orbit around E2; if E1 and E2 are the same size, objects *a* and *b* will switch orbits, forming figure eights.

As complex as these patterns might get, they are simple when compared with reality. Each day brings events of various importance into the market, acting as attractors. Each attractor has an initial importance that loses value over time. To make matters worse, we cannot predict when a new attractor, or news event, will appear. This makes the chaotic pattern very similar to raindrops falling on a pond. Each new drop, equivalent to a new event, hits at an unpredictable time and place, with variable size, and forms circular ripples. These ripples dissipate as they get further away from the point of contact in the same way that the importance of an event fades away over time. The interesting aspect of the raindrop analogy is that, while we cannot predict where the next raindrop will fall, once it has landed we can completely determine its effects—until the next drop hits. This is remarkably similar to the market. Less often there is a significant event, a price shock, that overwhelms the smaller events, the market noise, for a short time.

NEURAL NETWORKS[10]

Another area of analysis that has continued to grow rapidly is *neural networks*. During the past 5 years there has been a deluge of material on the advantages of using neural net-

[10] Parts of this section are based on Perry Kaufman, *Smarter Trading* (McGraw-Hill, 1995, pp 164–171).

FIGURE 20-7 (*a*) Equal attractors cause a symmetric pattern that switches between E1 and E2. (*b*) Very unequal attractors show only a small disturbance in a regular orbit.

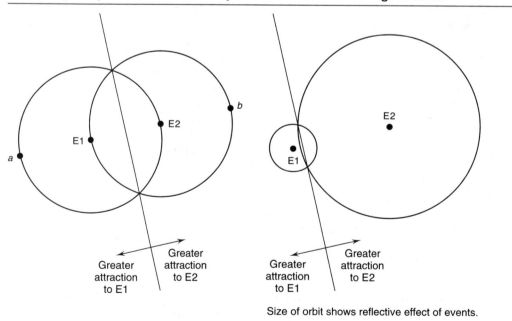

Size of orbit shows reflective effect of events.

(*a*) (*b*)

works as a tool for uncovering market relationships and finding better systems. Most of what has been said is true. This technique offers unparalleled power for discovering nonlinear relationships between any combination of fundamental information, technical indicators, and price data. Its disadvantage is that it is potentially so powerful that, without proper control, it will find relationships that exist only by chance.[11]

Although the idea and words for the computerized neural network are based on the biological functions of the human brain, an *artificial neural network* is not a model of a brain, nor does it learn in the human sense. It is simply very good at finding patterns, whether they are continuous or appear at different times.

The operation of an artificial neural network can be thought of as a *feedback process,* similar to Pavlov's approach to training a dog:

1. A bell rings.
2. The dog runs to one of three bowls.
3. If right, the dog gets a treat; if wrong, the dog gets a shock.
4. If trained, stop; if not trained, continue at step 1.

Terminology of Neural Networks

The terminology used in the computerized neural network is drawn from the human biological counterpart, shown in Figure 20-8. The principal elements are:

Neurons, the cells that compose the brain, process and store information.

Networks, groups of neurons.

Dendrites, receivers of information, passing it directly to the neurons.

Axons, which come out of the neuron and allow information to pass from one neuron to another.

Synapses, which exist on the path between neurons and may inhibit or enhance the flow of information between neurons. They can be considered *selectors.*

---

[11] Readers are referred to E. Michael Azoff, *Neural Network Time Series Forecasting of Financial Markets* (John Wiley & Sons, 1994), for a thorough treatment of this subject, and Edward Gately, *Neural Networks for Financial Forecasting* (John Wiley & Sons, 1996), for a more introductory approach.

FIGURE 20-8 A biological neural network. Information is received through dendrites and passed to a neuron for storage. Data are shared by other cells by moving through the output connector, called an axon. A synapse may be located on the path between some individual neurons or neural networks; it selects the relevant data by inhibiting or enhancing the flow.

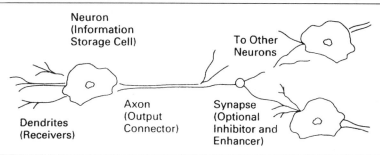

Source: Perry Kaufman, *Smarter Trading* (McGraw-Hill, 1995, p. 165).

Artificial Neural Networks

Using essentially the same structure as a biological neural network, the computerized, or artificial neural network (ANN), can generate a decision on the direction of the stock market. It relies heavily on the synapses, which are interpreted as weighting factors in this process. To achieve its result, it will also combine inputs that interact with one another into a single, more complex piece of data using layers of neurons, as shown in Figure 20-9, a classic 3-layer neural network.

To be most efficient, the inputs to the ANN should be those factors considered most relevant to the direction of stock prices. The five items chosen here were the Gross Domestic Product, unemployment, inventories, interest rates, and the value of the U.S. dollar—all readily available data. Each of these items is input and stored in separate neurons. Changing values may have a positive or negative effect on the final output, which is the direction of stocks. An improved GDP, lower unemployment, higher inventories, and a lower U.S. dollar are all good signs for the economy and result in the possibility of higher interest rates (defensive action by the Federal Reserve to prevent inflation) and a likely decline in stock prices. Interest rates themselves have a direct effect on stock prices, improving profits as rates decline.

Each neuron in layer 1, which receives the data from the dendrites, is connected to a second layer of neurons through a synapse. Each synapse can be used to filter or enhance information by assigning a weighting factor. For example, if changes in unemployment have a greater impact than changes in the GDP, then it may receive a weight of 1.5 compared with .9 for the GDP. If very small changes in any of the data is considered unimportant to the result, then the synapse can act as a threshold and only allows data to pass if it exceeds a minimum value.

The second layer of neurons is used to combine initial data into significant subgroups. In Figure 20-9, the GDP, unemployment, and inventories are combined into a single item

FIGURE 20-9   A 3-layer artificial neural network to determine the direction of stock prices.

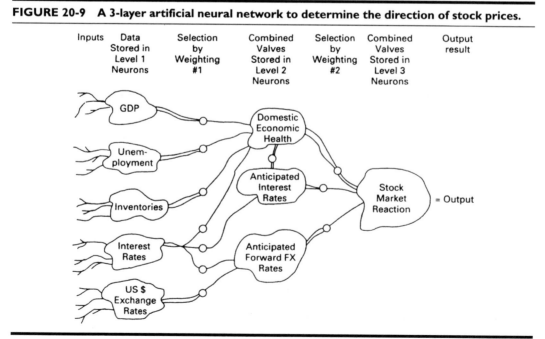

Source: Perry Kaufman, *Smarter Trading* (McGraw-Hill, 1995, p. 166).

called Domestic Economic Health. The synapses allow each element to be assigned a specific level of importance using a weighting factor. Also note that this neuron is altered by anticipated interest rates, which is the result of data flowing to another neuron in layer 2. Finally, the three neurons in layer 2 are combined according to importance, giving the net stock market reaction to the input data.

The human brain works in a way very similar to the artificial neural network shown in Figure 20-9. It groups and weighs the data, combining them into subgroups and finally producing a decision. The human process of weighting the data is complex and not necessarily transparent; that is, we may never know the precise flow of data, how many layers exist, and how weights are assigned and reassigned before the final decision.

A computerized neural network is not as complex. Because it cannot know whether its answer is correct, you must tell it. This is done by giving the computer the historic data and the corresponding answers. By giving the artificial neural network a long history of information, it can determine, using feedback, the weighting factors that would have given the correct results most often. The more history that is given to the computer, the more likely it will find a robust answer. Figure 20-10 shows the results of using five different inputs to predict the direction of the stock market. Two of the inputs, the Academy Award Winners and the Number of NASA Launches are not likely to be useful in the long term, but may appear to provide valuable information for short intervals. By using enough comparisons, the weighting factors are found to show that unemployment has a strong negative effect on prices, the GDP a strong positive effect, and inventories have a weak positive effect. The other items had no consistent predictive ability and received a weight of zero. This feedback process is called *training*.

Selecting and Preprocessing the Inputs

There is considerable debate over the inputs needed to find a successful solution using a neural network; however, everyone agrees that the selection of inputs is critical. These inputs must be presented in the most direct form because, unlike an expert system, the

FIGURE 20-10 Learning by feedback.

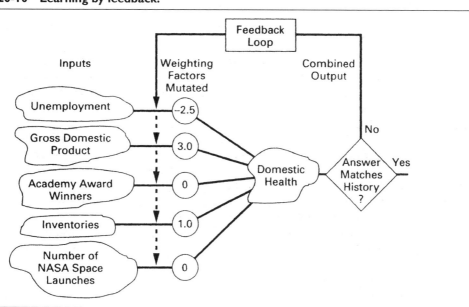

Source: Perry Kaufman, *Smarter Trading* (McGraw-Hill, 1995, p. 166).

neural network will not be able to change them. This step is called *preprocessing*. We must decide what factors affect the direction of stocks and the ability to anticipate that direction, then prepare data that contains information with these qualities. For example, we may want to know the short-term and long-term trends; the direction of interest rates and the Dow Utility Index; the ratio of interest rates to gold; economic data such as the GDP and balance of trade; technical indicators such as the RSI, stochastic, and ADX; and a 20-day moving correlation between the U.S. stock market and other major markets. There are countless factors that might influence the direction of stocks; the more you choose, the slower the solution and the greater the chance of a less robust model. If you choose too few, they may not contain all of the information necessary; therefore, the preprocessing problem requires practice. You may also construct a number of systems that produce profits and include their basic components as inputs to the neural network. You might create a performance series for a specific system that has only values −1, 0, and 1, representing short, neutral, and long market positions. In that way the neural net may be used to enhance an existing trading strategy.

Selecting the Output

In a manner similar to evaluating optimization results, it is necessary to select the success criteria. This should be based on a combination of frequency of trading, the size of the profits per trade, a reward/risk criterion, and a frequency of profitability. According to Ruggiero,[12] neural networks can be used to predict price direction, such as the percentage change 5 days into the future; however, they are much better at predicting *forward-shifted technical indicators,* because these tend to have smoother results.

Most technical indicators, such as trend and momentum calculations, smooth the input data, which is most often the price. The longer the time period used in the calculation, the greater the smoothing. Ruggiero suggests an output function such as

```
@Average((close[-5] - @Lowest(Close[-5],5))/(@Highest(close[-5],5) -
    @Lowest(close [-5],5)),5)
```

which is similar to a smoothed 5-period stochastic shifted forward by 5 periods. In this notation, the bracketed value [-5] represents 5 periods into the future.

The Training Process

At the heart of the neural network approach is the feedback process used for training, shown in Figure 20-10. To observe sound statistical practice, it is advised that only about 70% of the data be used for training. As the neural net refines the weighting factors for each of the inputs and combinations of inputs (in the layers between the input and output), it will need more data to test these results. Of the remaining 30% of the data, 20% should be designated for *testing*. The success or failure of the method to find a solution is based on the performance of the test data. The remaining 10% is saved for out-of-sample validation.

Weighting factors are found using a method called a *genetic algorithm,* discussed in the next section. For now, we need to know that the training process begins with an arbitrary or random value assigned to the weighting factors of each input. As the training proceeds, these weighting factors are randomly mutated, or changed, until the best combination is found. The genetic algorithm changes and combines weighting factors in a manner referred to as "survival of the fittest," giving preference to the best and discarding the worst.

---

[12] Murray A. Ruggiero, Jr., "Build a real neural net," *Futures* (June 1996), the first of a series of excellent articles on this subject.

Testing is completed when the results of the test data converge to a single value. That is, after a number of feedback loops, the test data is used with the new weighting factors. If the results are improving the process continues. If the results are improving at a very slow rate, or have become stable at one level, the neural network process is considered completed. Sometimes the results get worse, rather than better. This can be fixed by beginning again using new random weighting factors. If this doesn't work, then the inputs must be reevaluated for relevance.

Because the genetic algorithm is a trial-and-error process, rather than an analytic approach, the best results could be found by coincidence, rather than by cause and effect. With enough data series it is always possible that two series of events will appear related, although they are not. It is necessary to review the results to avoid simple mistakes.

A Training Example

We would like to train a neural net to tell us whether we should buy or sell stocks. As inputs, we select what we believe to be the five most relevant fundamental factors: GNP, unemployment, inventories, U.S. dollar index, and short-term interest rates. This test does not use any preprocessed data, such as trends or indicators. To simplify the process, the following approach is taken:

1. Each input is normalized so that it has values between +100 and −100, indicating strength to weakness, with 0 as neutral.
2. When the combined values of the five indicators exceed +125, we will enter a long position; when the combined value is below −125, we will enter a short.
3. Combined values between +125 and −125 are considered neutral.

To show how the training process works, two events are shown in Tables 20-4 and Table 20-5 as Case 1 and Case 2. Table 20-4 is the initial state of the neural network, where we have chosen to set all of the weighting factors to 1.0. In actual training, the network might require that the sum of all weights total to 1.0. The actual values of the normalized inputs are shown in the columns marked "relative value," and the correct historic answer is at the bottom, marked as "strong" and "weak" stock market reactions to these values. For the neural network to return the correct answers, it must produce a result greater than +125 for Case 1 and below −125 for Case 2. By assigning initial weights of 1.0 to all inputs, the value of Case 1 is +75 and the value of Case 2 is +40; both fail and testing continues searching for better weighting factors.

TABLE 20-4   Two Training Cases (Initial State)

	Case 1			Case 2		
Input	Relative Value	Weight	Net	Relative Value	Weight	Net
GNP	Strong	50	1.0	50	Weak	−60	1.0	−60
Unemployment	Low	−25	1.0	−25	High	40	1.0	40
Inventories	Low	−50	1.0	−50	Neutral	15	1.0	15
U.S. dollar	Vry Strg	75	1.0	75	Neutral	0	1.0	0
Interest rates	Falling	−25	1.0	−25	Rising	45	1.0	45
Total value		75				40	
Threshold		+/−125				+/−125	
Current response		None				None	
Actual market reaction		Strong				Weak	

Source: Perry Kaufman, *Smarter Trading* (McGraw-Hill, 1995)

TABLE 20-5   Two Training Cases (After Mutated Weighting Factors)

Input	Case 1 Relative Value		Weight	Net	Case 2 Relative Value		Weight	Net
GNP	Strong	50	1.0	50	Weak	−60	1.0	−60
Unemployment	Low	−25	−1.0	25	High	40	−1.0	−40
Inventories	Low	−50	1.0	−50	Neutral	15	1.0	15
U.S. dollar	Vry Strg	75	1.0	75	Neutral	0	1.0	0
Interest rates	Falling	−25	−1.0	25	Rising	45	−1.0	−45
Total value		125				−130		
Threshold		+/−125				+/−125		
Current response		None				None		
Actual market reaction		Strong				Weak		

Source: Perry Kaufman, *Smarter Trading* (McGraw-Hill, 1995).

In Table 20-5, the weighting factors have undergone mutation using a genetic algorithm. This example attempts to use only weighting factors of +1.0, 0, and −1.0. By reversing the effect of unemployment and interest rates on the direction of the stock market, and by random selection of weighting factors, the results now match the historic pattern of stock movement. Using fractional values for weighting factors, and many more training cases, the ANN method should find the current underlying relationship between these inputs and stock market movement.

Reducing the Number of Decision Levels and Neurons

The robustness of a neural network solution is directly related to the number of decision levels, the number of neurons in each level, and the total number of inputs. Fewer elements produce more generalized and, therefore, more robust solutions. When there are many decision layers and many neurons, then the inputs can be combined and recombined in many different ways allowing very specific patterns to be found. The more specific, the greater the chance that the final solution will be overfitted, or that the neural network program will fail because it cannot converge on a satisfactory result.

The trade-offs using a neural network are the same as most other optimization methods. Too many inputs and combinations require lengthy testing and a greater chance of a solution that is overfit. Too few values can produce a result that is too general and not practical. It is best to begin with the most general and proceed in clear steps toward a more specific solution. In this way you will understand the process better, ultimately save time, and be able to stop when you have reached the practical limitations of this method.

GENETIC ALGORITHMS

The concept of a *genetic algorithm* is based on Darwin's theory of survival of the fittest. In the real world, a mutation with traits that improve its ability to survive will continue to procreate. This has been applied to the process of finding the best system parameters. Although a genetic algorithm[13] is actually a sophisticated search method that replaces the standard optimization, it uses a technique that parallels the survival of the fittest. It is particularly valuable when the number of viables is so large that a test of all combinations is impractical. Instead of the typical sequential search, it is a process of random seeding,

[13] This technique is attributed to John H. Holland, *Adaptations in Natural Language and Artificial Systems* (University of Michigan Press, 1975).

selection, and combination to find the best set of trading rules. Standard statistical criteria are used in the selection process to qualify the results.

Representation of a Genetic Algorithm

Using the words common to this methodology, the most basic component of a genetic algorithm is a *gene;* a number of genes will comprise an *individual,* and a combination of individuals (and therefore genes) is a *chromosome.* Each chromosome represents a potential solution, a set of trading rules in which the genes are the specific values and calculation expressions, and these form individuals that represent rules and ultimately form a trading strategy. For example, Chromosome 1 might be a rule to buy on strength:

If a 10-day moving average is less than yesterday's close and a 5-day stochastic is greater than 50, then buy.

Chromosome 2 could be a rule that buys on weakness:

If a 20-day exponential is less than yesterday's low and a 10-day RSI is less than 50, then buy.

If we rewrite these two chromosomes in a notational form, the genes and individuals in its structure become more apparent:

Chromosome 1:   MA, 10, <, C, [0], &, Stoch, 5, >, 50, 1

Chromosome 2:   Exp, 20, <, L, [1], &, RSI, 10, <, 50, 1

Each of these chromosomes has 11 genes, any one of which can be changed. In addition, each chromosome has two individuals, separated by an "&" operator. In Table 20-6, the description of the genes indicates other values that can replace the current ones. Table 20-6 is a way to represent the chromosomes and individuals in a general form. It is easy to see that each gene can be changed, and each change will represent a new trading rule. A combination of trading rules, or chromosomes, will create a trading strategy. Before continuing, the following steps will be needed to use the genetic algorithm to find the best results:

1. A clear way of representing the chromosomes, or individuals
2. A criterion to decide that one chromosome is better than another
3. A selection procedure that determines which chromosomes will survive, and in what manner
4. A process for mutation (introducing new characteristics) and crossover (combining genes) to procreate chromosomes with greater potential

TABLE 20-6   Functional Description of the Genes in Chromosomes 1 and 2

Gene	Chr 1	Chr 2	Function
1	MA	Exp	A trend calculation (moving average, linear regression, breakout)
2	10	20	The calculation period for the trend calculation
3	<	<	Relational operator (<, <=, >)
4	C	L	Price used in trend calculation ((H + L + C)/3, indexed value)
5	0	1	Reference data ([0] = current day, [1] = previous day)
6	&	&	Method of combining individuals (and, or)
7	Stoch	RSI	Indicator calculation
8	5	10	Indicator calculation period
9	>	<	Relational operator
10	50	50	Comparison value for relational operator
11	1	1	Market action (1 = Buy, −1 = Sell)

Fitness

Having represented the chromosome in Table 20-6, we next must define a fitness criterion, which ranks the results. Because fitness will lead to survival, it is very important to decide which chromosomes should be discarded and which should be used further. A fitness criterion must combine the most important features associated with a successful trading strategy:

1. Net profits, or profits per trade
2. The number of trades, or an error criteria
3. The smoothness of the results

Ideally, we prefer systems that have large profits, lots of trades, and very consistent performance. To measure that result, the following might be used:

Rank = Profit per trade * (1 − (1/sqrt(number of trades) * (gross profits/gross losses)

If the profits per trade are larger, the rank is also higher; if there are more trades, the rank is higher, and if ratio of gross profits to losses is greater, the rank is higher. These factors are not weighted, but they serve as a simple criterion for comparing or measuring the fitness of a chromosome. For example, a trading method that returned $500 per trade for 10 trades, with a gross profit/loss ratio of .5 would have a rank of 170.75. Another system that returned only $250 per trade over 100 trades with a profit/loss ratio of 1.4 would rank 315.00. Therefore, the system with the smaller returns has a much more agreeable trading profile according to the fitness criteria. Each analyst must create a criterion that allows those strategies with a personally desirable profile to survive.

Mutation and Crossover

Remembering that a genetic algorithm is a sophisticated search method, it needs a way to introduce new rules (genes), combine genes into individuals that have passed the fitness criteria, and discard genes and individuals that are less promising. This is done through *mutation* and *crossover.* Mutation is the process of introducing new genes, or combinations of genes, from a gene pool, which we have defined as a set of rules and relational operators, similar to those in Table 20-6. For example, the first gene, which represents a trend-following calculation, could be a moving average, exponential smoothing, linear regression, or breakout. In mutating the gene, one of these four techniques is chosen randomly. Similarly, the calculation period and the way in which rules are combined are selected randomly. Typically, only one of the individuals in the chromosome is mutated in each step; therefore, in Chromosome 1,

Chromosome 1:   MA, 10, <, C, [0], &, Stoch, 5, >, 50, 1

the genes in the second individual (Stoch, 5, >, 50, 1) might be mutated to (RSI, 10, >, 40, 1).

Crossover is a way of combining two chromosomes by exchanging their individuals. The result is called an *offspring.* Using chromosomes 1 and 2, we can switch the first individuals to get

Offspring 1:   Exp, 20, <, L, [1], &, Stoch, 5, >, 50, 1
Offspring 2:   MA, 10, <, C, [0], &, RSI, 10, <, 50, 1

The two methods of mutation and crossover provide the only tools needed to introduce new features to the optimization and to combine features in all ways. If you could continue this process indefinitely, you can study every possible mutation and combination.

Selection

The process of *natural selection* is to allow only the best individuals to survive. A strong selection criterion chooses only those individuals with the highest ranking, as determined by the fitness test. A weak criterion allows lower rankings to survive. The implementation of the selection process is also drawn from evolution. When an individual has a high fitness score, it becomes a larger part of the population; when it has a low score, it is removed or reduced from the population. This can be done by modifying the list of conditions, which is used to create new genes and individuals randomly. For example, in the first gene we have the possibility of four trend criteria:

1. Moving average
2. Exponential smoothing
3. Linear regression
4. Breakout

Using random selection, each one has an equal chance of being picked. Let us say that we perform the first 10 tests without removing any of the possibilities, but only measure the average ranking of the results. On the 11th test, we select linear regression and compare the results of its fitness with the average fitness of the first 10 tests. If the fitness is greater, we make a number of copies of this linear regression gene and add it to the list of trending methods. One popular way to calculate the number of copies is to divide the current fitness, f, by the average fitness, F, of previous tests. Therefore,

Number of copies = current fitness/average fitness

This method works best when there are a large number of choices rather than only four possibilities. However, if the fitness of the linear regression was 4, and the average fitness of previous tests was 2, we would make two copies, replacing the original entry. The new list would then have

1. Moving average
2. Exponential smoothing
3. Linear regression
4. Breakout
5. Linear regression

When a trend criterion is mutated, that is, another criterion is selected randomly from the list, there is now a 40% chance that a linear regression will be selected, and a 20% chance that another method will be used. Natural selection has resulted in the linear regression being more desirable because its fitness ranks higher. In the initial tests that formed the average fitness, there were other conditions that were mutated other than the trend criteria. It could be that these conditions were the reason for the higher score, and not the trend method. At the same time the first gene is copied, other genes that were part of the same chromosome were also copied, so that all of these genes have a better chance of appearing. Because we have not eliminated any of the other trend criteria, each one should appear from time to time. If the breakout method is actually better than the linear regression, it should have a higher fitness when it is mutated; it will then be copied and, theoretically, displace the linear regression as the survivor. Eliminating a choice may speed up the genetic algorithm, but introduces the possibility of removing a good technique on the basis that it only appeared in combination with other genes that were not strong.

Putting It into Practice: Training, Tuning, and Testing

The technique for a successful search using a genetic algorithm requires that the data be divided into three subsets—training, tuning, and testing—in a manner similar to a neural network and using a procedure of step-forward testing. Beginning with the first 1,000 data points, the system is trained; it is then tuned on the next 500 data points, and finally the performance using a test set of only 10 points is recorded. The process is then continued by shifting the data forward by 10 points. In this way, the performance is recorded for disjoint tests of 10 points. This process implies that new parameters must be found every 10 data points for trading to duplicate the training method.

CONSIDERING GENETIC ALGORITHMS, NEURAL NETWORKS, AND FEEDBACK

Stumbling onto the perfect solution, or even a better solution, is always acceptable. Recognizing a good solution, by hard work or by chance, still requires talent; many discoveries that seem to have occurred by chance are really the product of hard work that provides the opportunities for discovery. A genetic algorithm is a way of recognizing a situation that may be an improvement or a brilliant new method—but not always. Unlike real-life genetic mutations in which you can relate the change to the environmental need, this genetic algorithm may simply apply an isolated rule because of a single situation that may never occur again in the same way. To follow the path of a mutation, we need to confirm that this new rule is statistically and logically sound—that there are enough cases to make it appear to be the right choice. Don't accept the results without careful thought and validation.

The large number of possible tests that make the genetic algorithm valuable also requires that you understand the concept of local versus global solutions. When you start with a random set of rules and parameters, then vary some and combine others, it is possible that you will find a *local maxima,* that is, a good solution but not the best. It is possible that a combination of trends and indicators that would have produced the perfect system was never seeded by the random process, nor was it found by changing some of the values during the process. One solution is to run the genetic algorithm a number of times to see if it arrives at the same solution starting with different random values. While it is not a guarantee that you will cover all major combinations, especially when there are a massive number of variations, it is the simplest way to avoid serious oversights.

Feedback is the basis for successful solutions using advanced searching methods, but it also creates uncertainty. For example, a neural network may be trained on 70% of the data and tested on 20%. When the test data is used to evaluate the weighting factors found using the training data, it provides feedback, which biases the selection of weighting factors in the training data. Although these data sets are separated, the constant feedback between the two provides a connecting tunnel that requires them to be considered as one data set. The testing data is no longer *out-of-sample;* therefore, another 10% of the data is withheld for scientific out-of-sample testing when the final solution is found. If that 10% data does not produce results consistent with the training and testing, then the inputs must be changed and the process begins again. There is now a dilemma as to whether there is any out-of-sample data at all because the 10% held aside has been used as feedback for the entire process.

This problem is not unique to neural networks and genetic algorithms, but to all testing processes beginning with basic serial optimization. How do you test your results on current data without being guilty of feedback? There is really no answer. Statisticians claim that the best solutions use the most data; you can't overfit a solution when you test a large number of situations. The results are forced into being generalized. Holding a small amount of data aside for out-of-sample testing may not prove anything unless the results are exceptionally bad. If the out-of-sample results are poor, they may still be representative of one or two small periods during a long historic test. The final decision rests with the trader and not the computer. If the results seem reasonable, there was sufficient test data, the inputs were relevant, and the performance was monitored before trading begins, then the solution is likely to be good.

21

Testing

Testing a trading system was once a very simple process. Not so long ago it was difficult to get data, you needed to apply your rules manually to each price, you kept a handwritten record of your trades, and it took a long time. You were careful not to begin unless you were reasonably sure that the method had a good chance of success; this was based on an understanding of the fundamentals or market experience.

During the past 20 years that process has changed, not always for the better. Those who have applied the same diligence and selectivity to the automation of systems are likely to have gotten better results and more useful information than ever before. Others who have become careless because of the power and convenience of trading strategy development software are not having much success. Bigger and faster computers do not mean better results.

Computers give back as much as you put in. The tools alone do not result in a successful trading program. The thought process and creativity are needed to be competitive in today's market, although thoroughness and focus are qualities that can never be underestimated. Certainly, computers allow us to solve problems of magnitude and complexity that we could never have considered before, and do it in a way that is easy to understand. We can manipulate incredible amounts of data and find out not only whether our ideas are sound, but the risks associated with various events.

One of the most interesting techniques to develop from computerization is *optimization.* It is not the mathematical process of finding a *local maximum* in a field of continuous contours; instead, it is the iterative process of repeatedly testing data to find the single best moving average speed, point-and-figure box size, stop-loss size, or other information. That is not to imply that it could not be more. Optimization is an irresistible method when a computer is available, and, in an indiscriminate way, it has replaced logical selection. It is frequently the means of creating strategies referred to as *black box* methods, and often results in *fine tuning,* which produces systems that invariably generate high expectations but poor actual performance.

Computers present a serious, often futile, dilemma for the analyst. If a trend-following system is the objective and some form of smoothing technique is selected (a simple or step-weighted moving average, exponential smoothing), how do you select the right speed? Twenty years ago, the 5-, 10-, and 20-day moving averages were most popular because they represented a 1-week, 2-week, and 1-month time interval. They were also easy to calculate. In fact, the 10-day moving average was the most common because no division was necessary to arrive at the average. Unfortunately, that simple approach no longer works.

Consider what is necessary to create a trading strategy. For a trend system, once the trend period has been logically selected (e.g., 10-day) and the trading rules determined (such as a stop-loss), you will want to know the performance of that choice over past markets. If it proves successful, you may trade using that method; however, if it does not meet expectations using the test data, what do you do? With a computer, the answer is easy: try another trend speed and see if the results are better. This follows a perfectly natural progression; after all, who would use a system today that has failed to be profitable in the past?

It is obvious that a trader with a talent for computers who has purchased a *Trade-Station, MetaStock,* or another software package for testing, will take an organized approach to experimenting with a broad selection of trend speeds, box sizes, stop-loss points, and trading rules to arrive at a system with an excellent trading profile. When no satisfactory combination can be found for a specific market, that market will not be traded. This method of optimization has become a dominant factor in the development of trading systems; it is entirely dependent on having a computer.

The following sections will discuss various aspects of testing and optimization. Performed properly, testing can teach a great deal; done incorrectly, it can be misleading and completely illogical. It is not always easy to know which case has just been satisfied.

EXPECTATIONS

Expectations are an underrated part of system development. It forces you to define your ideas in advance and put substance into those plans. You need to decide the rules, time period over which the system should work, the relative risk, the proportion of profitable trades, and other characteristics. The importance of this comes when you see actual test results.

Testing should be the process of validating your ideas. That first requires that you define those ideas in a clear plan and decide whether it should work for hourly, daily, or weekly intervals. If the test results confirm your ideas, then you can have confidence in the strategy. If they differ, you know that something is wrong, either with your plan or the way it was entered into the computer. Without expectations, there can be no validation or confirmation; therefore, if you indiscriminately test all indicators combined together, you have no idea whether you have found a good idea or simply overfit the data.

Setting Your Objective

There are a number of steps that must be carefully performed before testing can begin. These steps are more important than the actual testing and will decide what you are looking for and how you will use the results. Correctly defined, the final system will have realistic goals and predictive qualities. Incorrectly done, it will look successful but fail in actual trading.

First, define the test objective. What results should the test present so that you can determine its success? Is it the highest profits possible from the test strategy, the frequency of profitable trades, or the average-profit to average-loss ratio? Testing software gives you a choice, but doesn't allow a combination of these items; most likely, it will be a combination that you want. For example, if maximum profits are used as the performance criteria, which is most often the default case, the resulting system may have one or two large profits (as Iraq's invasion of Kuwait in 1989 and the U.S. retaliation in January 1991) and an overwhelming number of small losses before and after it. The same performance would also show a very impressive average-profit to average-loss ratio. The highest frequency of profitable trades can also be inadequate if there are very small profits and large losses.

A popular way to view results is to look for a test profile with high profits and low risk. If we simply choose the largest equity drop as a measure of risk and net profits as a reward, a measurement function for best results could be

Test function = net profits × (100 − percentage equity drop)

which will reduce profits according to the size of the equity drop. The larger the losses, the smaller the test function value. A higher test function value should yield a smoother performance.

IDENTIFYING THE PARAMETERS

Once the test strategy is known, the *parameters* to be tested must be identified. A parameter is a value within the strategy that can be changed to vary the timing of the system. For example, parameters include:

1. Moving average speed (in hours, days, weeks)
2. Exponential smoothing constant (in percentage)
3. Band width around a moving average (number of standard deviations)
4. Stop-loss values (in points or percentages)
5. Size of a point-and-figure box (in points)

The simplest optimization would be a test of the number of days in a moving average system, where all other values are fixed. The test would then simulate the results of the trading strategy by stepping through the possible range of moving average days: 1, 2, 3, and so forth, until a satisfactory range has been covered. This is called a *1-dimensional optimization*.

Most systems have more than one important parameter. In the moving average system that is being used as an example, both the moving average period and the stop-loss value are important. One test procedure selects the first moving average value, then tests all of the stop-loss values; the second moving average value is then set and all of the stop-loss values are retested. The process is repeated until all of the moving average values have been tested. This is a *2-dimensional optimization*.

Distribution of Values to Be Tested

When more than two parameters are tested, the test time for the optimization may increase dramatically. For example, a test of 100 moving average values, 20 combinations of entry/exit bands, and 20 stop-loss values gives $100 \times 20 \times 20 = 40,000$ tests. Even with today's faster computers, that's going to take more than 50 hours if each test takes 5 seconds. It may be necessary to select fewer values to test for each parameter and choose them more carefully. For a moving average trend, it is best to use all of the smaller values for the number of days and then fewer values as the numbers become larger. For example,

1, 2, 3, 4, 5, 6, 8, 10, 12, 15, 20, 25, 30, 40, 50

would be a better set of values than using all numbers between 1 and 50. If you observe that the difference between a 49- and 50-day period is only 2%, while the difference between the 2- and 3-period test is 50%, you realize that the set of tests at the two ends of the test series represents very different situations. If you expect to judge overall performance by the average of all tests, then using equal increments will weight this set of tests heavily toward the long end. By reducing the tests using percentage increments, you not only improve the test time but you improve the results. The moving average example shows that it is not possible to equalize the percentages due to the restriction of integer values at the low end, but by replacing this method with a smoothing constant used in an exponential smoothing, the problem can be fixed. The need to distribute results evenly over a set of tests will be important for comparing two systems and finding robust results, topics discussed later in this chapter.

Types of Test Variables

Test variables can be of three forms: *continuous, discrete,* or *coded* (alphabetic). To interpret and display test results properly, it is important to identify these forms in advance.

Continuous parameters refer to values, such as percentages, which can take on any fractional number within a well-defined range. If a stop-loss level is defined as a percentage, it may be tested beginning with the fractional value .02% and increasing in steps of .005% until 2.0% is reached.

Discrete parameters are whole numbers, or integer values, such as the number of days in a moving average.

Coded parameters represent a category of operations, also called a *regime*. For example, when the parameter value is *A*, a single moving average is used; when the value is *B*, a double moving average system is tested; and when the value is *C*, a moving average and a breakout are used.

It is important to distinguish between the first two parameter types, continuous and discrete, and the last one. The analyst can expect some pattern in the results when testing parameters that take on progressively larger or smaller values. The coded parameter, however, usually causes rule changes. There is no reason why a change of rules, which causes the system to switch from one regime to another, would result in any performance pattern that makes sense across these regimes. The first rule may be profitable, the second losing, and the third profitable. The display of results, discussed later, is only valid for continuous and discrete parameters tested in an incrementally ascending or descending manner.

SELECTING THE TEST DATA

Testing a trading strategy on a computer is different from verifying a charting technique or taking prices from the *Wall Street Journal* to check results manually. If a computer is to be used for testing, there must be a complete database of price history and, if more ambitious recently, of economic statistics as well. This is readily available from numerous vendors and normally includes daily price data on U.S. and major European markets. When you purchase software to test your strategies, a database of daily prices is usually included. Intraday (tick) data is limited to only a few vendors, the most well-known being CQG and Tick Data, Inc. A complete database is an important asset. It should be kept current by automatic downloading at the end of each day.

Some computer systems, which are designed for trading strategies, have created special *continuous test series* specifically for optimization. While stock data or cash market prices are always continuous (except, of course, for stock splits), futures and options data present problems resulting from their limited contract life. To make this easier for testing, some vendors provide special features for combining shorter data periods into a single series. This gives the user the following choices:

1. *Individual full contracts.* The entire futures contract, or more than one contract, are tested. Using full contracts is a tedious process and can result in overlapping test periods and duplications of results. Individual tables of results must be combined in a spreadsheet to be evaluated. Figure 21-1 gives an example of the test bias resulting from carelessly using all contracts within the range December 1992 through December 1996. Once the number of tests being performed at any one time is seen, it is easy to construct a distribution (Figure 21-1b) by counting the horizontal bars at specific points. This distribution will show the testing bias due to duplication. Because of the 18-month life of the contracts, there was only 1 delivery month tested in the last half of 1991, compared with six contracts tested during the middle period, falling off to two contracts at the end of 1996.

2. *Selected parts of contracts.* Segments can be selected that include the last 30 to 90 days of a contract. By limiting a test to the period you are planning to trade, you have a good representation of expected performance, although there are a lot of little pieces to evaluate. When operating this way, you must remember to allow a *windup* period for your trend calculations prior to when you begin taking trading signals.

**FIGURE 21-1   Testing using full contracts from December 1992 through December 1996.
(a) Test intervals. (b) Distribution of testing.**

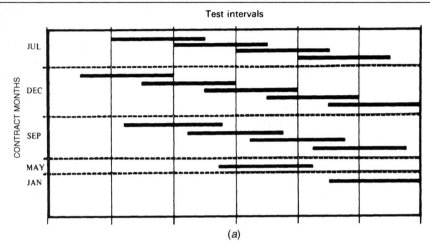

Test intervals

(a)

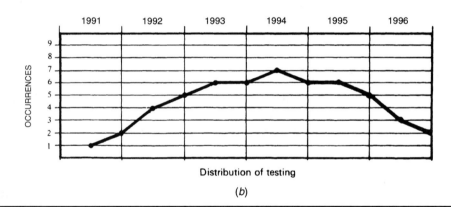

Distribution of testing

(b)

3. *Backward (or forward) adjusted data.* The data segments in item 2 are combined
   on a specific *roll* date by adjusting all the prices in that one contract by the difference between the closing prices of the new and old contract on the roll date. In a
   backward adjustment, all data prior to the adjustment date are changed by the dif-
   ferential on the roll date. This technique has become popular and works well for
   trend systems. The adjustments will cause large distortions in the oldest data, especially if the data go back more than 10 years. In the extreme case, the adjusted price
   can even become negative. If the strategy uses a percentage value, this series will
   not give the right numbers; or, if you expect to compare various high and low prices
   over time, it is best to use another type of series.
4. *Indexed data series.* A continuous series is constructed by adding the price
   change each day to the prior index value. When there is a change of contract, the
   price change is that of the new contract compared with its prior price. The conversion into an indexed series is useful for comparing two markets and for con-

structing portfolios, but has most of the same problems as its raw counterpart in item 3.

5. *Constant forward series.* In the same manner as the London metals contracts are quoted (*n*-days out), an artificial price is calculated by interpolating the prices of the delivery months on both sides of the date needed for this price series. This type of data series has also been called a *perpetual* contract and presents its own set of problems. Deferred contracts are not as volatile as the nearby contract, and formulated values create a series that is much smoother than the one you are likely to trade. This means less risk, probably less profits, and greater reliability in identifying trends. More important, you would be testing your ideas on a data series in which none of the prices actually occurred.

If all five methods have problems, which is best? If you use a trend calculation and do not rely on a percentage or compare the absolute levels of past prices, then you can use backward adjusted data (item 3). Although it requires more work, the safest choice is always to use the individual contracts, provided you take care not to duplicate performance over the same dates in different contracts unless you plan to trade that way.

In a seasonal or cyclic commodity, there is good reason for selecting more than one delivery month during each year—new and old crops or production cycles can cause substantially unique price patterns during the same time period for different deferred deliveries. Even the proper overlapping of a traditionally nonseasonal product may pick up deviations due to anticipation or extreme short-term demand or surplus. But the market shown in Figure 21-1*a* was not seasonal or cyclic, and the 18-month contract duration caused the overlapping time intervals that simply distorted the test results.

SEARCHING FOR THE OPTIMAL RESULT

There are many complex techniques for optimizing; the two most basic will be discussed here. The first, and the only simple method, is to test all combinations of parameters. A single moving average system with a stop-loss might have the following tests:

1. All moving average days from 1 to 50
2. Stop-loss values from 0 to $1,000 (or equivalent in points), in steps of $10

The total number of tests would then be $50 \times 100 = 5,000$. When three parameters are tested, the number of tests increase rapidly. Taking care to use the best parameter distribution, as discussed earlier, is a simple way to reduce the test time and improve the usefulness of the results. When there are too many tests, even with selected values, a wider spacing of values can be used to locate the general pattern of performance. Once the approximate range of parameter values is known, more detailed retesting can be done.

Calculate the number of tests you will run before beginning an optimization. Although the time may not be a problem, your test software may not be set up to hold the number of test results that you are creating. All computers have limits. If you generate as many as 1,000 combinations, remember that you will need to evaluate them using a spreadsheet. Large numbers of rows and columns, combined with numerous markets, can create an unmanageably large spreadsheet.

Sequential Testing

If you have created a system on a grand scale and the number of tests and the number of parameters are too great, then *mathematical optimization* offers some solutions in the form of testing procedures. One caveat is that they only apply to continuous results, that is, performance that increases and decreases somewhat smoothly based on parameter values. You cannot use this method to test coded variables that cause an abrupt shift in the methodology. In the simplest example, the procedure is:

1. Test one parameter, such as the moving average period.
2. Find the best result, and fix that value for the remaining tests.
3. Select the next parameter and test.
4. Go back to step 2.

This is called a *sequential optimization*. It has the advantage of reducing a 3-parameter test case from $n_1 \times n_2 \times n_3$ total tests to $n_1 + n_2 + n_3$. It has the disadvantage, however, of not always finding the best combination of parameter values when the test is very large. Figure 21-2 shows a 2-dimensional map of test results, a good way of visualizing the relationships between parameter sets. By testing all the combinations, the best choice was seen to be a 20-day moving average with a 30-point stop-loss, netting 400. Using sequential testing, beginning with the moving average days, the best result is 15 days. Fixing that value and testing the stop-loss values, we find that the best stop-loss is at 30 points. While this result is good, it is not the peak result nor the next best 350. If the tests begin with the stop-loss value, it ends at the same point; there, the best results cannot be found, whether the test begins with the rows or columns. Even though the area of greatest profitability is clear, the best choices in the first row and column do not peak at values consistent with the overall best result.

There are two ways that traditionally avoid this problem. One method is to list the parameters in order of importance, that is, those that would have the greatest impact on profitability, although you might choose this by its fundamental importance to the strategy. In this example, the number of days in the moving average is most likely to be the primary parameter. This doesn't work in Figure 21-2; however, mathematicians are prepared for this problem.

The final alternative is to choose a series of random starting values for each parameter and proceed to test a row or column beginning with those values. The object is to find the best results with as few of these tests as possible. Although each 3-parameter test is only $n_1 + n_2 + n_3$, the total number of tests will accumulate steadily. When you have performed a number of searches beginning with a random seed, and found the same results,

FIGURE 21-2 Visualizing the results of a 2-dimensional optimization.

Moving average days

		5	10	15	20	25
	10	100	150	200	150	150
	20	200	150	250	300	300
Stop-loss (points)	30	250	200	300	400	350
	40	200	150	200	300	300
	50	100	100	150	250	250

you can conclude with some certainty that you have located the peak. For example, if you begin searching in Figure 21-2 in four places, one row and one column inside the four corners (moving average of 10, stop of 20, 20 × 20, 10 × 40, and 20 × 40), you will always find the peak value. For a test of this size, if these were random seeds, three values that gave the same results would be enough. For larger tests, more seed values would be needed.

More on Test Continuity

Any system can be tested using a computer, but automatic selection of the best results only makes sense when they are continuous. A moving average system with stops is continuous in all directions. Adding a third dimension, an entry or exit delay (0, 1, or 2 days) will produce continuous results in the three directions. But not all tests satisfy this principle. It has already been briefly mentioned that rule changes are the most likely cause of discontinuity. Consider a test in which one variable is the speed of the trend and the other is a set of rules, *L*, *S*, and *B*, where *L* only takes long positions, *S* only takes short positions, and *B* takes both long and short positions. Although there may be interesting patterns and relationships, averaging these results does not make sense.

If each parameter tested has values that result in a continuous profit/loss curve, there are mathematical techniques available to locate the point of maximum profit with the minimum steps. One method, *optimization by steepest descent,*[1] uses both the profit and the rate of change of profitability to determine the size of the steps taken during the optimization process. This method can be suboptimal, however, if there is more than one profit peak.

VISUALIZING AND INTERPRETING THE RESULTS

Visualizing the test results properly can make interpretation far easier. Figure 21-2 has already given a preview of how results might be presented in a way that shows continuity, rather than a simple list of one test result after the other. For example, if a 1-parameter optimization is run in which all values are fixed except for the number of days in a moving average, then three possible results are shown in Figure 21-3.

In all three cases, the resulting profit or loss is shown on the left, and the number of moving average days is shown along the bottom. Figure 21-3*a* is a simple curve, indicating that both fast and slow parameters generate losses, although the midrange is profitable. It may be reasonable to select the number of moving average days that produced the highest profit due to the good continuity around that point.

Figure 21-3*b* shows two possible areas of success. Because both are about equal in size, there is no reason for choosing one over the other. One possibility is to trade one moving average from each peak. If you must choose only one, then it is most likely that the longer-term results are more stable, and considered a more conservative selection. A fast trading system can result in errors, poor execution prices, and large transaction costs. Unless these factors have been carefully incorporated into the trading strategy, a highly profitable simulation will result in large, real losses.

The preceding case is exaggerated in Figure 21-3*c,* where the fast system has much higher profits in a very narrow range, and the long-term trend has a wide range of success. The spike in the area of the 3-day moving average is surrounded by losses, indicating that the high profits may have been caused by a short-lived price shock, or a pattern in the data that was perfect by chance.

---

[1] F.R. Ruckdeschel, *BASIC Scientific Subroutines, Vol. II* (Byte/McGraw-Hill, Peterborough, NH, 1983).

FIGURE 21-3   Possible resulting patterns from a test that varies only the moving average days.

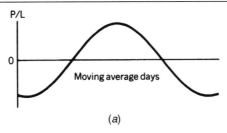

(a)

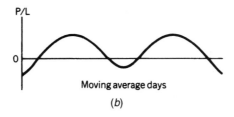

(b)

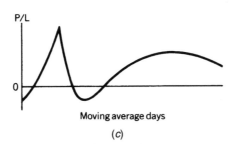

(c)

Two-Parameter Tests

The most popular tests are those that have two parameters, either two trends of different periods or a trend and a stop-loss value. Considering a moving average and stop-loss, the best visualization is a *grid* (a 2-dimensional table), with the moving average days along the left (rows) and the stop-loss values at the bottom (columns). Figure 21-4 shows that the lowest number of days and the smallest stop-loss value will give the profit/loss value in the top left corner box.

By presenting the results as shown in Figure 21-4, there is a continuity of performance in all directions. The upper left corner represents the fastest system—the one with the most trades; the bottom right corner shows the results of the slowest strategy. The patterns of the upper right may be similar to those of the lower left if the system displays some symmetry. A faster trend speed with a large stop (top right) and a slow trend with a small stop (bottom left) are likely to have the same number of trades and similar profitability.

Depending on the data used for testing as well as the trading rules, three patterns are most likely to appear in the results of a 2-dimensional display. Figure 21-5*a* shows the simplest case of a single area of successful performance gradually tapering off. This is analogous to the single-parameter test shown in Figure 21-3*a*. Selecting the parameters that

FIGURE 21-4   Standard configuration for a 2-dimensional optimization.

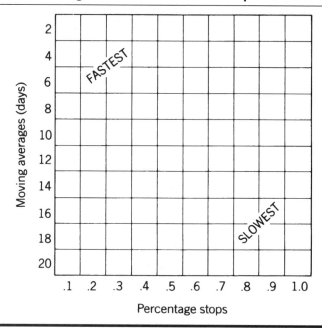

gave the center of the best performance area is the most reasonable, because moderate shifts in price patterns are still likely to be profitable.

The appearance of two areas of profitability are usually the results of a highly volatile market (Figure 21-5b). Prices that are moving quickly and sustain a major trend can be traded using a fast or slow model. The fast model is often more profitable because it captures more of the rising trend; it reacts faster and also profits from the decline. The slower trend-following approach captures less of the price move but keeps clear of the sharp reactions that stop out the middle-speed trends. The selection of parameters to use in real trading follows the same reasoning applied to Figures 21-3b and c. The third case, shown in Figure 21-5c, is one of erratic profits and losses. The absence of a consistent pattern in the performance indicates that the trading strategy does not apply to the data.

Alternate Ways of Visualizing Results

With software such as *MathCad,* you can see the 2-parameter test as a *contour* or *topological relief map.* For some users this form can make it much easier to see the peaks and valleys of performance and is highly recommended. Any spreadsheet program will allow a surface plot, which will give you a rough look at the continuity of a 2-parameter test, as shown in Figure 21-6. This 3-dimensional graph gives the net profits of a moving average crossover system applied to the Swiss franc. The slower trend is shown along the front scale and the faster one along the right. There is a ridge running from the front to the back, indicating that a slow trend of about 50 to 60 days dominates the results. Other than the fastest trends of 3 days, it is easy to see that there are many combinations of fast and slow moving averages that are historically profitable.

Visualizing with Scatter Diagrams

To see the performance of more than two variables, you can plot the results of all tests against each parameter (see Figure 21-7) using a scatter diagram (also called an *XY Plot*).

FIGURE 21-5   Patterns resulting from a 2-dimensional optimization. (*a*) Single profitable area. (*b*) Two distinct profitable areas. (c) No obvious pattern.

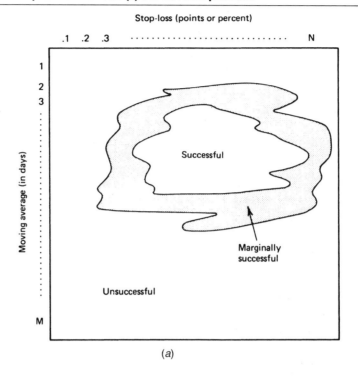

(*a*)

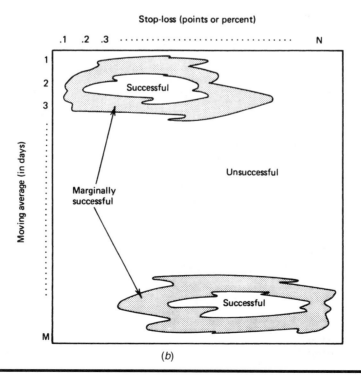

(*b*)

FIGURE 21-5 *(Continued)*

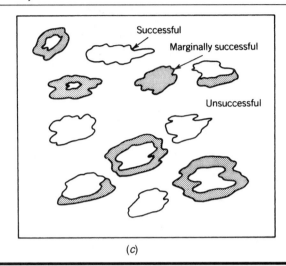

(c)

This will give you a better understanding of how each value affects the total picture and allow you a way to visualize the robustness of each variable. Using a 2-variable example, a range of fast and slow moving averages were tested for the Swiss franc based on a crossover strategy. The results of the slow moving averages are plotted for all combinations of the fast moving average in Figure 21-7; the fast average is shown in Figure 21-7*b*.

The individual test results are shown as circles above the slow or fast moving average period in Figure 21-7. For the slow moving average, it is clear that profits are greatest when 50 and 60 days are used for the calculation period; however, it is not as clear which of those two values is the best choice. The 60-day moving average posted profits higher than the 50-day average, but also showed profits below the lowest 50-day returns. A closer look shows that the average returns of the moving averages over those periods is about the same, but the 60-day moving average has a higher variance. Normally, the best choice is the result that is most stable (the 50-day calculation), although in this example we must be cautious that the small number of tests do not make the 50-day results look stable just by chance.

The results of the faster moving average, seen in Figure 21-7*b*, show much greater variance. The 7-period results have a very wide range including the highest returns; however, the averages of the 7th through 15th periods are very similar. With variance in mind, the 13-day calculation seems to be the best candidate. We can be confident that this method is robust, because nearly all combinations of fast and slow moving averages gave profitable returns, net of a $50 commission.

Standardizing Test Results

When testing a single system, the results of one set of parameters can easily be compared with other sets because the test period, commissions, and other basic values are all the same. However, over time you will test many different systems and variations of those systems, and you will want to compare them to decide which strategy is best. This requires some advanced planning.

Standardizing test results is the best way to increase the usefulness of extensive testing. This should include:

FIGURE 21-6   Three-dimensional map of crossover model.

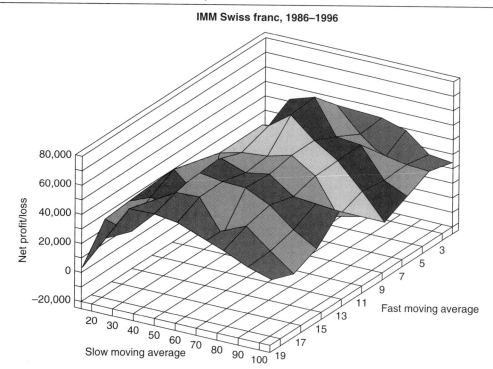

IMM Swiss franc, 1986–1996

1. *Annualizing all values.* Tests that you perform 6 months or 1 year apart are likely to use different time periods. Annualizing the results will make comparisons easier.
2. *Risk adjusting.* A profit of $10,000 with a drawdown of $5,000 is effectively the same as a profit of $20,000 and a drawdown of $10,000, given adequate reserves. Expressing the results as profits divided by risk can be useful.
3. *Adjusting for standard error.* The important difference between two tests that yield the same results, one with 2 trades and one with 50 trades, is that the one with only 2 trades is a less reliable result. If both posted 50% profitable trades, another losing trade would make the reliability of the second test drop to 49%, while the first case would drop to 33%. Instead, results should be presented at the same confidence level, which means subtracting the standard error from the current result. Analysts developing relatively slow trading systems will find that this procedure has a startling effect on expectations.

Averaging the Results

Because the testing process is computer dependent, it is desirable to make the selection of the best parameters automatic. This can usually be done effectively by averaging either the profits or other results displayed in the test map. In the case of a moving average system, first determine how broad the area of success must be so that it is not a spike, an anomaly in the results. For example, the results of a 3-, 4-, 5-, and 6-day test show profits of 1,000, 8,000, 3,000, and 4,000, respectively. The 4-day case is clearly a profit spike and could be minimized by replacing its value with the average of the three other values or by the interpolated value of the two adjacent points (Figure 21-8). In general, the substitution process in which $\overline{PL_i}$ replaces PL_i,

FIGURE 21-7   Visualizing the performance of multiple parameters. (a) The slow moving average peaks at 50–60 days. (b) The fast average may be best at any value from 7 through 15.

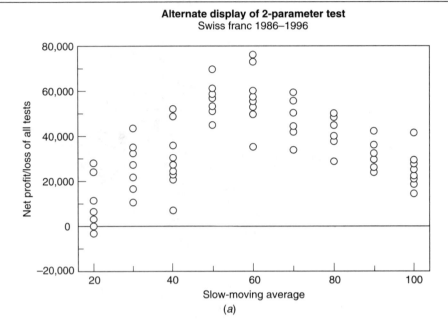

(a)

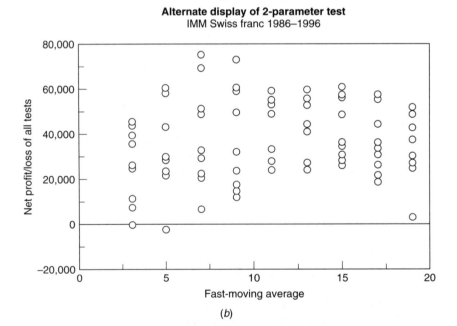

(b)

FIGURE 21-8 Replacing a spike with the average A or an interpolation B.

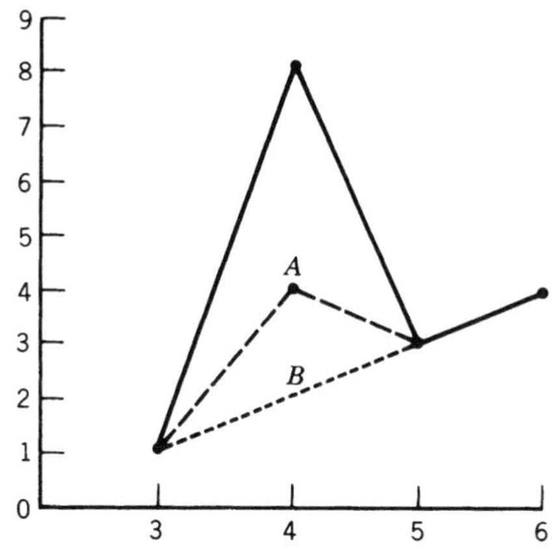

$$\overline{PL_i} = \frac{PL_{i-1} + PL_i + PL_{i+1}}{3}$$

will smooth the performance. The best parameter set is the highest value of $\overline{PL_i}$ once all averages have been substituted for the raw test results.

It is more likely that a spike or erratic results will appear in areas that test shorter periods than in those that test longer trends. The difference between the results of a 2- and 3-day moving average is greater than that of a 30- or 31-day average or even a 30- or 40-day test. If the optimization was scaled properly, leaving more space between tests of higher value in the manner of a percent difference, the simple averaging technique will be a good substitute for testing every value.

Two-Parameter Averaging.

The results of a 2-parameter test may also be averaged. Using the form discussed earlier (Figure 21-9), the results of each test will be denoted as PL_{ij}, the profit/loss associated with row i and column j of a 2-dimensional display. The object is to replace each PL_{ij} with $\overline{PL_{ij}}$, the average value of its surroundings. This is done, as seen in Figure 21-9a, by taking an average of the eight test results adjacent to the ijth value as well as the center value. There are special cases when the ijth result is not fully surrounded but on the perimeter of the test map. Figure 21-9b–d shows the averaging technique used when the ijth box is a top, side, or corner value. The 9-box average shown here is comparable to the 3-point average in the 1-parameter test. If the test has relatively small increments between calculation values and more test cases, an average of a larger area would be appropriate.

STEP-FORWARD TESTING AND OUT-OF-SAMPLE DATA

The correct procedure for testing always includes reserving some data to be used afterward to validate the results. The data used during testing is called *in-sample data,* and the reserved portion for validation is called *out-of-sample data.* This concept should be familiar to everyone involved in the design or development of a system.

Traditionally, analysts use as much data as possible to determine whether their proposed strategy is sound. The use of long test periods assures a good sample of price patterns, including long periods of sideways movement, bull and bear markets, and a good

FIGURE 21-9   Averaging of map output results. (*a*) Center average (9-box). (*b*) Top-edge average (6-box). (*c*) Left-edge average (6-box). (*d*) Upper left corner average (4-box).

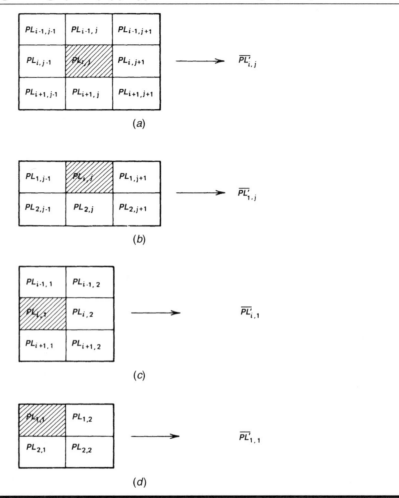

number of price shocks of various sizes. When more data are used, it is most likely that the results will show larger profits and larger losses.

When there is, for example, 10 years of data available for testing, a standard approach would be to test the oldest 9 years, find the best set of parameters, then test the system on the most recent year using the selected values. If the results of the out-of-sample period are similar to the in-sample performance, the system is considered validated.

One serious problem occurs when the results of out-of-sample testing fail to perform as expected. The results are inspected closely to find how this period differed from the past, and if successful, a rule change is incorporated into the program and the in-sample data retested. This repeated use of out-of-sample data is called a *feedback process.* Unfortunately, there is no longer any out-of-sample data to be used for validation. The improved results are the product of fitting the data and you are left uncertain about the ability to produce profits in the future. This is a problem that can only be resolved by a broad view of robust testing procedures discussed throughout this chapter.

Step-Forward Testing Procedure

The concept of choosing a parameter set from a test of in-sample data, then applying the results to out-of-sample data, has been developed into a test process called *step-forward testing*[2] (also *walk-forward testing*). This process goes as follows:

1. Select the total test period, for example 10 years of daily data from 1988 through 1997.
2. Select the size of the individual test intervals, for example 2 years.
3. Begin testing with 1988 and 1989 data.
4. Select the best parameters from those results.
5. Find the performance of the next 6 months of data (the first half of 1990) using the parameters selected in step 4. Accumulate this out-of-sample performance throughout the test process.
6. If there is more data to test, move the test period forward by 6 months (the second test will be from the second half of 1988 through the first half of 1990) and test the data; otherwise, go to step 8.
7. Go to step 4.
8. The results of the step-forward test are the accumulated results of the individual out-of-sample tests in step 5.

This process clearly simulates the traditional approach to test design, using in-sample and out-of-sample data in its proper order. Unfortunately, it does not correct the problems of reusing the out-of-sample data, which transforms that step to another piece of in-sample data.

Step-forward testing can introduce a bias that favors faster trading models. Because the in-sample test has only 2 years of data in our example, a long-term trading model may only post a few trades during this period, and one of the longer trades may be interrupted by the end of the data window and discarded. This makes the results of the longer-term models unreliable. In addition, these slower trading approaches will often start a trade at the beginning of the test data window at a point that is abnormal, that is, one that would not occur if the data were continuous.

The problem of short-term bias can be identified by the optimum parameters switching from short-term to long-term in successive test periods. For example, if you test moving averages from 5 to 50 days, you will find one period shows 10 days as the best followed by a period in which 50 days is best, followed again by a period in which 15 days is best. This erratic behavior is a sign that the testing specifications are too limited. It can be corrected by extending the test intervals from 2 years to 5 years and making the out-of-sample period 1 year. None of these solutions, however, correct for the use of out-of-sample data more than once. More on this problem can be found in the following section "Retesting Procedure."

CHANGING RULES

As testing progresses, it is inevitable that the analyst will want to modify a rule in the trading strategy. This is usually the result of inspecting the results of tests and noting that a specific pattern was not treated properly (or profitably). After some work, the analyst introduces a special rule, which turns a previously losing situation into a profit. Figure 21-10 shows two possible patterns in the test performance pattern based on this change.

If the rule change improves one price pattern at the cost of others, the complete test results will appear as shown in Figure 21-10*a*. Higher profits at the previous peak and greater losses at the ends result in the same cumulative test profitability. Because the new

[2] A thorough presentation of both step-forward testing and optimum search techniques can be found in Robert Pardo, *Design, Testing and Optimization of Trading Systems* (John Wiley & Sons, 1992).

FIGURE 21-10 Patterns resulting from changing rules. (*a*) A rule change that improves one situation at the cost of others. (*b*) A rule change resulting in general improvement.

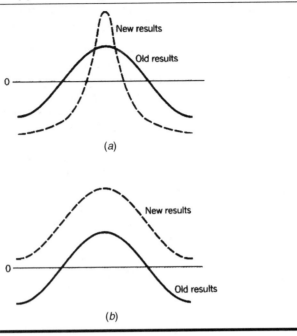

rule caused the fitting of a specific pattern at the cost of added losses in other patterns, it should not be considered an improvement.

In Figure 21-10*b*, the new rule improves performance in all cases. This type of pattern is desirable in optimizations. It is possible, of course, that the improvement was caused by a rule that corrects one case only in a way that is so specific that it does not affect any other trade. That type of rule fitting, on a sample of one pattern, is likely to harm results in the long run.

ARRIVING AT VALID TEST RESULTS

It is not unusual for the results of an optimization, especially one with many parameters, to appear perfect. All the trades could be profitable, the equity drops might be small, and the strategy might perform in changing markets, and yet, the final system might have no real expectation of profit. To create a system with predictive qualities, rather than one that is historically fitted, requires preparation in advance of testing.

You Can't Prove a System (or Indicator) Works by One Case

You can always select a moving average or indicator gave a sell signal in the S&P just before the 1987 crash. That's not difficult when there are thousands (or millions) of combinations of trend speeds, filters, momentum indicators, divergence rules, and so on. However, what works in a specific case, and often an unusual one, is not likely to work in general. Manipulating the rules is only a waste of time. Showing that a combination of technical indicators would have profited from the last market crash has no bearing on the next drop.

The addage that "there are lies, half lies, and statistics" is too true. Statistics can prove a point or prove just the opposite, depending on how the numbers are presented. A market can be in an uptrend and a downtrend at the same time, based on the time interval over which you view it. You must be constantly aware of those problems that you cannot see— the omissions.

It will be necessary for you to draw your own picture of system performance. What is the chance of a big profit this year or this week? What is the worst-case scenario? Will the method survive a sharp change in market volatility? Can I choose a long-term or short-term horizon with more confidence? Is an 8-day moving average really better than a 10-day breakout? The following guidelines will get you started by giving you one way to look at test results. From this you will be able to develop, over time, your own method of evaluation. As Jack Schwager has stated, "The mistake is extrapolating probable future performance on the basis of an isolated and well-chosen example from the past."[3]

Searching for Robustness

A *robust* system is one that performs consistently in a wide variety of situations, including patterns that are still unforeseen. From a practical view, this translates into a method that has the fewest parameters and is tested over the most data. In a test by *Futures Truth*, the best performing systems commonly have four or less optimized variables.[4] The characteristics of a system with forecasting ability are:

1. *It must be logical.* Each rule and formula must be designed to capitalize on a real fundamental or price phenomenon. *Discovering* a price pattern or cycle through optimization may seem to be a revelation, but it is more likely to be an illusion. By testing enough patterns, it is statistically probable that one of them will seem to fit. Without a fundamental reason for the existence of that pattern, it is not safe to use it.
2. *It must adjust to changing market conditions.* A system that assumes that markets don't change, or that everything has been seen in past data, will suffer large equity swings. Self-adjusting features might include an inflator or deflator, stop-loss values that change with volatility, and rule shifts based on seasonal or nonseasonal years.
3. *It must be tested properly.* The principles of statistics state that the best tests use the most data. More data includes bull, bear, and sideways markets; large and small price shocks; and periods of instability and doldrums. There is no substitute for more data. Proper test procedures also suggest that you reserve some unseen data until the very end, so that you can validate your work on an out-of-sample period. If that is not available, you can always paper trade until you can compare the accumulated trading profile with the expectations defined by your tests.

Some analysts prefer a technique called *blind simulation,* commonly known as stepforward testing. In this procedure, discussed in a previous section, a series of fixed-length tests are defined and the parameters found to be optimal are used to trade using data in the next period forward. The process then moves forward by dropping off old data and adding an equal amount of new data. The results of this second test are again traded on forward data. The method is continued until the out-of-sample results include all of the available test data. This is an important concept and is also discussed in the section "Reoptimization" later in this chapter.

From time to time each of the three characteristics above will seem to be the most important. In the long run they must all be satisfied to have a robust program.

---

[3] Jack D. Schwager, *Schwager on Futures: Technical Analysis* (John Wiley & Sons, 1996, p. 673).

[4] John Hill, "Simple vs. complex," *Futures* (March 1996, p. 57).

Performance Criteria

Assuming that the proper principles have been followed, are the test results good enough? Although the strategy shows steady profits with a low equity drawdown, could a naive system have done better? Did the famous skeptic on television throw darts at buy and sell signals on a board and show a 75% return while your system only netted 25%?

Benchmarks

It is necessary to have a benchmark that provides a way of measuring success. It is best if this is a well-documented indicator, such as the S&P Index, the Lehman Brothers Treasury Index, a class of Fund Managers, or the Commodity Trading Advisor Index. Newspaper articles that highlight the spectacular profits or losses of one manager is not a good benchmark, but simply *ex post selection* (hindsight).

It may seem desirable to have achieved the recognition for having the largest gain during a single month, but you should focus on having very good gain over each year. The largest gain can only come with high risk. You should not be surprised if those investment advisors posting remarkably high returns in one month have had very erratic performance overall.

Measuring Test Results

A number of performance criteria are needed to evaluate any trading strategy during the test phase and to compare results under actual market conditions.

1. *Net profits or losses.* Although not the most interesting statistic, the net profit is the motivation for trading. While you would not select a system that produces a net loss, it is the other statistics that will tell which of the better results, if any, are realistic.
2. *Number of trades.* This simple value indicates whether your test was long enough to depend on the results. A few trades can appear very profitable, but the trading profile is not yet clear.
3. *Percentage of profitable trades.* Also called *reliability,* a high value of 60% tells you that the method captures profits regularly. A trend system will be working correctly if its reliability is near 40%.
4. *Average net return per trade.* With or without commissions and slippage costs, the average return per trade gives you an indication of how difficult it will be to realize the system returns. A theoretical average of $50 per trade for a currency is likely to net less than one-half after slippage in normal markets, and when a U.S. economic report is released, slippage alone could be $500 on a single trade.
5. *Maximum drawdown.* The largest equity swing from peak to valley, this measurement can be very erratic and is not likely to be the largest drawdown seen in the future; however, it gives you some idea of the minimum capital needed to trade this market. If the value is very small, it is likely to be based on a small amount of data, too many specific rules, or a narrow range of test parameters.
6. *Annualized rate of return.* The rate of return is the profit for a predetermined investment. The investment can be calculated in reverse by knowing the funds-at-risk to equity ratio, the maximum drawdown, or standard deviation of expected returns. These returns should be annualized to compare one test, market, or benchmark with another.
7. *Total profits to total losses.* This simple ratio gives a reasonable measure of the smoothness of the equity curve. As the ratio increases, the proportion of losses declines and the equity curve becomes smoother. Any value over 2.0 is very good.
8. *Time to recovery.* A large drawdown may be inevitable in a realistic system, but a shorter time to recovery is most desirable. A larger drawdown with a much faster recovery seems to be a better trade-off for most investors.

9. *Time in the market.* All else being equal, a trading system that is in the market less than another system is preferable. If two systems have approximately the same returns and risk, then the one that has more time out of the market is actually exposed to less risk.
10. *Smoothness of returns.* In addition to the individual measurements described above, some form of traditional equity smoothness is desirable. This can be the standard deviation of the residuals when the linear regression of the returns is calculated, or it can be some weighted combination of the previous measurement. This measurement should reflect the type of equity profile you seek.

Having decided the measurements needed to evaluate the results of the testing, some other procedural issues must be resolved before testing begins. This will help to avoid bending the rules to fit the results.

Defining the test range. Each optimization run should represent a broad sampling of tests over a wide range of parameter values. This range should be established in advance based on expectations of what is reasonable. If the returns in this range are not profitable, you must first understand why your ideas have not worked before looking for other periods in which the system might show profits. A thorough review of your trading rules may show that you have defined them wrong, not limited them to the best situations, or simply programmed them incorrectly.

Use the average of all test results. Most tests will show both profits and losses, with some areas of very attractive profits. If you tested 100 cases and 30 showed profits of about 30% per year, 30 showed break-even results, and the last 40 showed various losses, you might say that the 30 profits represented a successful system. That assumes that the market will continue to perform in a way that allows those 30 parameter combinations to generate profits during the next year. It is better to assume that market changes will make it difficult to tell which combination of parameters will be the best in the future. Then you want a system that can generate profits with any parameter set, not just 30 out of 100. Perhaps that's too ambitious; nevertheless, one system is better than the other if the average of all tests is higher than the average of all tests in the other system. To be more precise, we could say that the best system is the one in which:

Adjusted Returns = Average of all tests − 1 standard deviation of all test returns

is greatest. From the discussion of standard deviations in Chapter 2, we know that a return greater than the adjusted returns will occur 68% of the time.

Set aside data for final validation. To give yourself a way of knowing whether you have overfitted the data, do not use all the data in your tests. This is needed for out-of-sample verification at the end. If the results of using this data are not good, you will need to reassess the performance. If it is good, you have some assurance that your testing was done correctly, but there are no guarantees other than time.

Stability over time. Be sure that the test data was long enough to have included a substantial change in price, a major bull and bear market, and an extended sideways period at low volatility. By viewing performance over a number of smaller time intervals, instead of only one average or total figure, it is possible to assess the stability of the strategy.

Elimination of outlier periods. Realistically, a system should not base its profitability on a single major market move over the test interval. In particular, if the move that generated the profit was actually a price shock, the system had only a 50% chance of posting that profit, and has an equal chance of a loss in the future. It may be practical to remove the profits generated on the first day or two of a move that began with a price shock, allowing for the possibility of holding the wrong position in the future.

Concentrate on large profits and large losses. The largest profits and losses are critical to the net performance of any system; therefore, you should make a special effort to study those trades. In doing that, you may find that the largest profits were the results of price shocks, as discussed in the preceding point, or that there is an odd piece of data that was not obvious before. If there are a number of large profits and no large losses, you may have excellent risk control, but more likely you have overfit the data. There is an unfortunate tendency to look for problems when results are bad, but to accept them when they are good.

Reading between the Lines

It is easy to show specific examples of rules that produce large profits, while the overall strategy is bad. Many books base intuitive proof or justification on specific examples. This can work if the general theory is sound, when there is fundamental or economic substantiation, such as expecting a seasonal low in the U.S. crops at harvest. For patterns and many purely technical indicators, such as those using momentum, this is not as clear. Results are likely to show that the situations that fail greatly outnumber the fewer exceptionally good examples.

Systems That Work in Only One Market

From time to time, all traders receive mail offers for a highly specialized system called "The Cattle Trader," the "Silver Day-Trading System," or "Easy Profits through Stock Index Trading." It is most likely that each of these systems has been finely tuned with rules unique to this one market. Once aware of the optimization process and its results, these offers must be viewed more critically; after all, with optimization techniques able to test combinations of indicators and rules, *you* could just as easily create a system that seemed to make as much on a single market. To prove that you have actually found something that works requires an understanding of the rules and the way it was tested, or time to watch the system operate in the real market. If possible, a comparison of the real trading profile compared with the expected performance based on testing should be available.

Student *t*-Test

Among tests that help determine whether the results are significant, the student *t*-test is one of the most useful. It tells you whether there is a systematic bias in the data by showing whether the mean of the data is significantly different from zero. This is a useful piece of information when you try to decide whether the results of only a few trades represent a good system, or whether a series of losing trades implies that a system has no value. For a single set of trades produced by computer testing or by actual trading, the *t*-test is:[5]

$$t = \frac{\text{average trade results}}{1 \text{ standard deviation of trade results}} \times \sqrt{\text{number of trades}}$$

The critical value of *t*, which can be found in Appendix A, depends on the number of trades in the sample. For the case of a series of trades produced from the same market and same system, the *degrees of freedom = number of trades* − 1. Using the table in Appendix A, if there were only 10 trades, the degrees of freedom would be 9, and the value of *t* must be greater than 1.833 to reach the 95% confidence level.

Where you want to know if two systems are producing results that are significantly different from each other, the technique is more complicated. It requires comparing the

---

[5] Ben Warwick, *Event Trading* (Irwin, 1996).

mean, variance, and number of trades of the two systems; most important is the approximation for the degrees of freedom, which allows you to determine the confidence level of the results:

$$t = \frac{\bar{x}_1 - \bar{x}_2}{\sqrt{\dfrac{s_1^2}{n_1} + \dfrac{s_2^2}{n_2}}}$$

where $\bar{x}_1$ = the average of method 1 trades
$\bar{x}_2$ = the average of method 2 trades
s_1 = variance of method 1 trades
s_2 = variance of method 2 trades
n_1 = number of trades in method 1
n_2 = number of trades in method 2

The calculation of degrees of freedom uses Satterthwaite's approximation:

$$df = \frac{\left(\dfrac{s_1^2}{n_1} + \dfrac{s_2^2}{n_2}\right)^2}{\dfrac{\left(\dfrac{s_1^2}{n_1}\right)^2}{(n_1 - n_2)} + \dfrac{\left(\dfrac{s_2^2}{n_2}\right)^2}{(n_2 - n_1)}}$$

POINT-AND-FIGURE TESTING

The point-and-figure system is representative of the group of swing systems. Buy and sell signals occur when prices move above or below previous highs and lows, respectively. The current market direction changes when a price reversal exceeds a specified cumulative price change, designated in points. Because it is a charting method, the reversal is shown in terms of boxes; the reversal criterion traditionally is expressed as a "3-box reversal" (for a complete explanation, see Chapter 11).

The size of the box and the number of boxes that define a reversal are the two variables that make up the reversal criteria. If silver were the object of the test, the box size might start as low as 10 points (1/10th of one cent, the minimum move) and increase in increments of 10 points; the number of boxes in a reversal would be the integer values 1,2,3, ... Figure 21-11a shows that the expected pattern of test results is symmetric, extending across the diagonal drawn from the top left to the bottom right corners. This example followed the convention of putting the fastest trend change in the upper left (smallest box size and a 1-box reversal) and the slowest in the lower right corners.

The symmetry is the result of very similar performance for equal reversal values, the product of the box size, and the number of boxes in a reversal. For example, a trend change of 40 points for the Swiss franc could have occurred using combinations of 40 points × 1 box, 20 points × 2 boxes, 10 points × 4 boxes, 4 points × 10 boxes, 2 points × 20 boxes, and 1 point × 40 boxes (among others). The difference in profitability occurs because the selection with the smallest box size will satisfy the penetration criteria sooner, giving slightly faster signals and more trades. The average profitability of all combinations of reversal size will appear as in Figure 21-11b. This representation can be used with the 2-dimensional map to find the most consistent set of parameters.

When tested over long periods, most markets have increasingly wide price ranges, as clearly seen in the S&P. Testing for fixed combinations of box size and number of reversal

FIGURE 21-11   Point-and-figure mapping strategy. (*a*) Reversal number of boxes. (*b*) Reversal (box size × number of boxes).

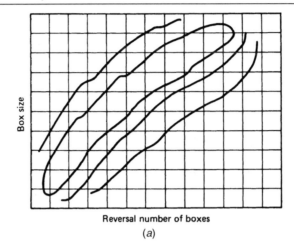

Reversal number of boxes

(*a*)

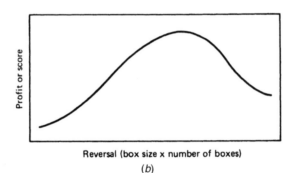

Reversal (box size x number of boxes)

(*b*)

boxes for the past 10 years would find the single parameter set that performed best over this period; however, the increasing volatility would result in much larger profits and losses in recent years. This change of risk will force the optimized results to favor parameters that performed best in the last few years and might ignore the profits and losses of the earlier period, which would be relatively small. To put it in perspective, a 10% move in the S&P in 1987 would only be about 25 points, equal to a total of $12,500, while it would be 90 points in 1997, or $45,000. If prices moved 1% per day (3.00 points) in 1987, a reasonable reversal combination would be from .45 points for fast trading (.15-point box with 3-box reversal) to a full day's move of 3.00 (1.00-point box with a 3-box reversal). In 1997, either combination is likely to produce a new trade every few hours, creating a very different performance profile than prior years.

The problem of volatility was discussed in Chapter 11. The alternative to a fixed box over time was to vary the box size as a percentage of price. Therefore, if the best reversal in 1987 was .45 for the S&P at a value of 300, it would be 1.35 in 1997 at 900. However, this may not have increased enough, and many market analysts treat volatility as an exponential function with respect to price. This can be approximated using a square root function or log function, both readily available in a spreadsheet or testing program:

$$\text{Box size} = p \times \sqrt{\text{price}}$$

$$\text{Box size} = p \times \ln \text{(price)}$$

where p is the percentage that is varied as a parameter in the optimization. This last method would be similar to the technique of using point-and-figure on a log chart.

COMPARING THE RESULTS OF TWO SYSTEMS

The easiest way to understand the use of testing is by example. Using daily IMM Swiss franc data from January 1986 through February 1996, we compare the results of two trend systems, one based on a moving average and the other on exponential smoothing. These calculations can be found in Chapter 4 ("Trend Calculations"). In both cases, the system generates a buy signal or a sell signal when the trendline turns up or down, respectively. Table 21-1 shows the results of varying the calculation interval from 10 to 250 days in steps of 10 days. Parts *a* and *b* give the results using a commission of $25 per trade, and parts *c* and *d* use $100 per trade.

Which System Is Better?

If we scan the results of the net profit (NetPrft) in column two of parts *a* and *b*, we can find that the largest profit was $52,125 for the exponential smoothing at 120 days, the largest return on account (ROA) was 376% for exponential smoothing at 160 days, and the highest profit factor was 3.47 for the moving average at 250 days. However, looking at individual values can be confusing and misleading. Choosing the one best performer is only sensible if you can guarantee that those parameters will be the ones that perform best in the *next* period—an impossible request.

At the bottom of each part of Table 21-1 are the average and standard deviation of each set of tests. For parts *a* and *b*, the average net profits for the moving average system were slightly better than exponential smoothing; however, looking at all the averages and variance of the two systems show that the results are nearly identical. From a practical point of view there is really no difference between the performance of the two systems. One might profit from one particular situation in one system, but over the long run they will be extremely close. This may be easier to see in Figure 21-12, which shows the net profits of the two methods on the same chart. It may seem that the moving average technique performs slightly better with shorter intervals (30 to 100 days) and the exponential at longer ones (120 to 170 days), but these distinctions are very small. The overall picture is that a trending system produces profits based on the time interval used in the calculation, and is not dependent upon the specific method of calculation. This observation allows us to view the robustness of trend following as a trading approach.

A comparison of optimization results usually selects the one with the highest profits, but that may not be the best choice. Comparisons should account for the following minimum criteria:

1. A good sample of parameter combinations were tested. This will include those variables that cause frequent, as well as slow, trading. The distribution of fast and slow test results should be similar, which may involve scaling the calculation periods in different ways. One simple way of knowing if you have succeeded in this distribution is by observing the average number of trades per test on each system.
2. The average results of all tests and the variance of results should be compared. Significantly higher and more consistent overall results is a strong argument for a fundamentally sound approach.

TABLE 21-1 Comparison of Swiss Franc Trend Tests
Swiss Franc 1986–1995, 10 years

			(a) Moving Average with $25 Commission				
Period	NetPrft	PFact	ROA	MaxDD	#Trds	%Prft	AvgTrd
250	39063	3.47	354	−11038	36	39	1085
240	3900	1.07	12	−31700	61	28	64
230	22350	1.48	129	−17263	47	36	476
220	25950	1.54	136	−19088	57	25	455
210	25900	1.46	87	−29725	65	37	398
200	20213	1.44	68	−29575	47	36	430
190	7388	1.16	20	−37113	51	27	145
180	28438	1.74	106	−26825	41	34	694
170	38150	2.26	283	−13463	51	33	748
160	34363	1.82	110	−31238	69	29	498
150	30475	1.62	150	−20375	69	26	442
140	37363	1.79	180	−20738	67	31	558
130	40988	1.88	200	−20488	64	31	640
120	39488	1.65	133	−29750	76	37	520
110	17725	1.24	62	−28463	90	37	197
100	44513	1.68	294	−15138	109	36	408
90	21088	1.25	73	−28988	113	35	187
80	40988	1.60	330	−12425	101	31	406
70	33050	1.44	171	−19313	105	37	315
60	34300	1.39	150	−22850	115	34	298
50	22488	1.23	79	−28413	111	33	203
40	46563	1.49	317	−14700	139	36	335
30	46175	1.40	269	−17163	177	36	261
20	16850	1.10	47	−35963	238	31	71
10	5763	1.03	23	−25150	340	33	17
Average	28941	1.57	151	−23478	98	33	394
Stdev	12213	0.48	101	7333	67	4	236

			(b) Exponential Smoothing with $25 Commission				
Period	NetPrft	PFact	ROA	MaxDD	#Trds	%Prft	AvgTrd
250	37363	2.81	339	−11038	42	38	890
240	11013	1.26	38	−28763	51	22	216
230	26150	1.67	170	−15388	45	40	581
220	20963	1.41	99	−21163	61	31	344
210	27400	1.57	89	−30725	51	33	537
200	9300	1.17	23	−39988	49	29	190
190	18600	1.42	55	−33863	55	35	338
180	23088	1.56	91	−25238	41	32	563
170	45388	3.06	336	−13500	41	44	1107
160	45863	2.42	376	−12188	61	38	752
150	39338	1.89	181	−21788	67	36	587
140	38313	1.82	174	−22063	65	28	589
130	36113	1.71	179	−20163	73	29	495
120	52125	1.95	272	−19138	80	45	652
110	12250	1.15	29	−42050	100	28	123
100	35800	1.48	254	−14088	113	38	317
90	30163	1.40	117	−25788	111	38	272
80	29875	1.37	199	−15000	103	27	290
70	7725	1.08	24	−31588	125	30	62
60	37538	1.44	124	−30363	107	30	351
50	26563	1.29	128	−20788	123	31	216
40	37538	1.37	193	−19400	151	32	249
30	30813	1.24	116	−26600	185	33	167
20	23938	1.15	81	−29638	234	32	102
10	−8975	0.96	−20	−44325	362	33	−25
Average	27770	1.58	147	−24585	100	33	399
Stdev	13709	0.51	104	9056	71	5	267

TABLE 21-1 (Continued)

(c) Moving Average with $100 Commission

Period	NetPrft	PFact	ROA	MaxDD	#Trds	%Prft	AvgTrd
250	36363	3.07	325	−11188	36	36	1010
240	−675	0.99	−2	−35525	61	28	−11
230	18825	1.38	92	−20488	47	34	401
220	21675	1.42	100	−21775	57	25	380
210	21025	1.36	66	−31900	65	37	323
200	16688	1.34	51	−32725	47	32	355
190	3563	1.07	9	−39888	51	25	70
180	25363	1.63	89	−28475	41	29	619
170	34325	2.04	227	−15150	51	29	673
160	29188	1.64	85	−34463	69	25	423
150	25300	1.48	110	−23000	69	26	367
140	32338	1.64	141	−22913	67	30	483
130	36188	1.72	161	−22438	64	27	565
120	33788	1.53	104	−32600	76	34	445
110	10975	1.14	35	−31163	90	33	122
100	36338	1.51	209	−17350	109	33	333
90	12613	1.14	40	−31763	113	32	112
80	33413	1.45	260	−12875	101	28	331
70	25175	1.31	112	−22463	105	33	240
60	25675	1.28	96	−26675	115	33	223
50	14163	1.14	48	−29763	111	32	128
40	36138	1.36	224	−16125	139	33	260
30	32900	1.27	176	−18738	177	31	186
20	−1000	1.00	−2	−42563	238	28	−4
10	−19738	0.92	−57	−34575	340	31	−58
Average	21624	1.43	108	−26263	98	31	319
Stdev	14127	0.42	89	8323	67	3	236

(d) Exponential Smoothing with $100 Commission

Period	NetPrft	PFact	ROA	MaxDD	#Trds	%Prft	AvgTrd
250	34213	2.51	306	−11188	42	36	815
240	7188	1.16	23	−31538	51	22	141
230	22775	1.56	142	−15988	45	36	506
220	16388	1.30	71	−23088	61	28	269
210	23575	1.46	73	−32450	51	29	462
200	5625	1.10	13	−42763	49	29	115
190	14475	1.31	40	−36413	55	33	263
180	20013	1.46	74	−26888	41	32	488
170	42313	2.77	284	−14875	41	41	1032
160	41288	2.17	286	−14450	61	31	677
150	34313	1.72	142	−24100	67	36	512
140	33438	1.66	138	−24313	65	26	514
130	30638	1.56	129	−23675	73	27	420
120	46125	1.79	219	−21025	80	39	577
110	4750	1.05	10	−45650	100	24	48
100	27325	1.34	162	−16863	113	33	242
90	21838	1.27	77	−28488	111	34	197
80	22150	1.25	125	−17700	103	27	215
70	−1650	0.98	−5	−36088	125	27	−13
60	29513	1.32	88	−33663	107	29	276
50	17338	1.18	72	−24088	123	30	141
40	26213	1.24	126	−20825	151	30	174
30	16938	1.12	60	−28100	185	29	92
20	6388	1.04	18	−35250	234	30	27
10	−36125	0.85	−62	−58600	362	30	−100
Average	20282	1.45	105	−27523	100	31	324
Stdev	16746	0.45	92	10798	71	4	267

FIGURE 21-12   Comparison of Swiss franc trend-following techniques.

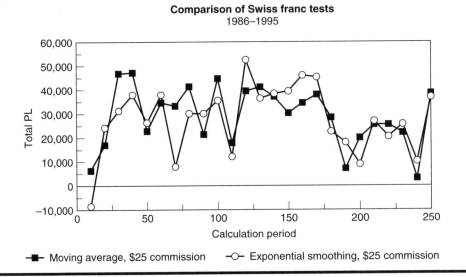

3. Results should be scored in some way to include profitability and risk. Other measurements can be used, but stability is of great importance.
4. Results, or scores, should be averaged to avoid spikes or unusual distortions.
5. Execution costs, including liquidity factors, must be included in the manner appropriate to each system. A trend-following system with entries and exits in the direction of the trend should have greater slippage than a countertrend entry method.
6. Make mistakes in the direction of being conservative. If two systems have comparable returns, select the one with the lower risk. If they have similar returns and risk, choose the one with fewer trades.

Choosing the speed of the trading system is often the most critical decision in the performance profile. Parameters that cause a trend method to trade faster are most desirable, because the higher number of trades adds confidence to the validity of the test results. You might also find that there is more consistency in the performance of a faster trading program compared with a slower one that generates the same net profits. To compensate for its advantages, faster trading is more susceptible to execution problems, so that performance will deteriorate quickly if slippage increases. Figure 21-13 shows the change in performance of all test intervals from 10 to 250 days for the moving average method when transaction costs are increased from $25 to $100 per trade. Note that the shortest interval turns from a small profit to a large loss and profits for intervals through 40 days are halved. Some areas of particularly poor performance, such as at 70 and 110 days, are magnified by the increased costs. In general, there is very little impact on the performance of slower parameter selections.

PROFITING FROM THE WORST RESULTS

Under the right conditions, the worst results of an optimization or test sequence may hold valuable information; it presents the worst-case scenario that should be carefully reviewed for system problems, in particular with regard to risk control. If the area of poor results is broad and continuous, it may also show a way to improve entry and exit timing. Figure 21-14a and b shows the continuous results of 1- and 2-variable tests. Both identify faster trading areas as having maximum loss and slower trends as having best performance.

FIGURE 21-13   Impact of increased transaction costs on performance.

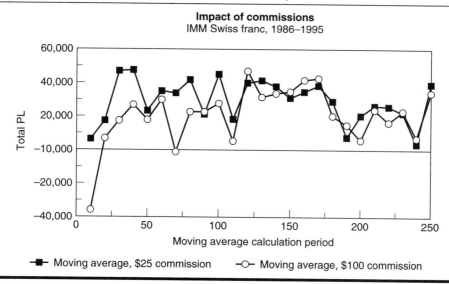

The worst results are only useful if there is a net profit from taking the opposite position. This is the case only if the net loss is greater than the transaction costs, including commissions and slippage. But even if the worst score has a near-zero return before transaction costs, it can be used profitably. Unprofitable results of a fast trend mean that a long or short position taken at that point lasts only a few days and does not indicate a sustained trend. Use the following rules:

1. Trade a system of two moving averages, a long-term, designated by the best score *D2,* and the short-term, selected as the worst score *D1.*
2. When prices cross the long-term moving average, a long position becomes eligible. A long position is entered when the short-term moving average signals a short signal. Positions may be entered on a 1-day delay.
3. Short positions may be closed out when prices cross above the long-term trendline; they *must* be closed out when a long position is entered.
4. Short positions and exits from long positions are the opposite of rules 2 and 3.

Because the short-term signals are not good indicators of trends, they can be used as a countertrend entries. That allows for better execution when trading larger positions or in less liquid markets. The choice of immediate exit or delayed exit is the trader's preference. Once a position is held, there is greater risk waiting to exit, yet most exits would be improved by better timing.

RETESTING PROCEDURE

One optimization is never the end of the testing process. If you have successfully finished the development of a system, and have retained the most recent data for out-of-sample verification, then you should retest the system including the out-of-sample data before beginning to trade the program. Any additional data adds robustness to the system. The impact of adding data will depend on the nature of the market during the new period and the amount of data originally used in the testing.

As in step-forward testing, some analysts prefer to test a fixed amount of data, dropping off the oldest. This does not mean that they test only 6 months, or 1 year of data and

FIGURE 21-14   Dual use of test map. (a) Single-variable test. (b) Two-variable test.

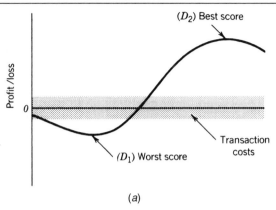

(a)

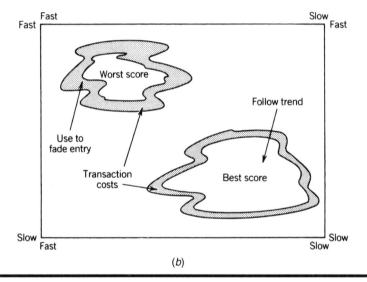

(b)

retest every month. You may decide that data before a particular date is no longer relevant. In some cases, there are structural changes that support that approach, such as the formation of a unified European currency, which would put controls on the variance in exchange rates between the participating countries even before the inception date. You might also consider a new market with low liquidity during its earlier years as different from more active, current market conditions. Retesting remains an important way to adjust the system to characteristics of new data. You might decide that retesting is necessary when time representing 5% to 10% of the test period has elapsed. Using the 2-variable test as an example, a shift may be expected in the area of best performance as shown in Figure 21-15.

Because only a small amount of data was added, the size of the shift in Figure 21-15 should be small. If a large shift actually occurs, then two possibilities should be considered:

1. The data was unusually volatile and introduced patterns not previously seen in the data. In this case, the shift in parameters is justified.
2. The data period for the original tests was short and did not include enough patterns to make the parameter choice robust. With a small amount of test data, there is a

FIGURE 21-15   Consecutive tests.

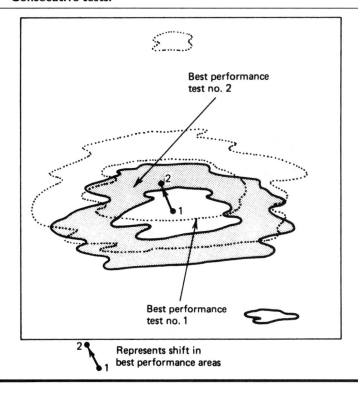

greater likelihood that a faster trading model will be selected. As the data shifts and that faster model is no longer good, the parameters may jump to a very slow model. This erratic pattern of shifting from fast to slow is indicative of too little test data.

Optimizing after a Major Move

When your system fails to produce the right amount of profit from a major move, or when the stock market takes an uncomfortably large plunge, it is natural to question whether the system has the right parameters. Is the trend fast enough? Is the stop-loss too close? This is the same process as retesting. If you have used enough data for your original tests, then it is very likely that the new tests won't change anything. If you make up new rules to fix this one problem, you are overfitting and accomplish nothing. If you have doubts about the test period, use more data rather than less. The new patterns will only give you a more realistic idea of the market risk than you had before. A major move that contains a *price shock* is a special situation discussed later in this chapter, as well as Chapters 22 and 23.

COMPREHENSIVE STUDIES[6]

A comprehensive study points out the robustness of a trading strategy. When a system performs well in many markets using similar calculation intervals, it is fair to assume that the method is sound. If a technique works in the Swiss franc but not the Deutschemark, or in Euroyen but not Eurodollars, you must be able to understand the significant differences

---

[6] Readers with an interest in performing optimizations such as these should read the basic material in Chapter 4 and the additional systems in Chapter 5.

before accepting the method. Markets have individual characteristics that might justify differences in performance; however, a strategy that can generate profits in a broad range of markets is robust. In addition to the studies that follow, Chapter 5 ("Trend Systems") includes a section "Comparison of Major Trend Systems," which will be helpful to anyone interested in viewing the results of different systems side by side.

Colby and Meyers, in *The Encyclopedia of Technical Market Indicators* (Dow Jones-Irwin, 1988), have given a very useful comparison of major market indicators simply by presenting all of their test results in a common form. Any one of the methods may have proved good or bad during the past 10 or 20 years, but taken as a whole, the consistency of various techniques adds to the robustness of that approach. For example, if one volume-based indicator was profitable, while four others generated consistent losses, you would need to understand why that one method worked before it could be used; the evidence of the four poor indicators argues that the use of volume in this way is not robust.

There are three previous, well-known comprehensive studies of moving average systems by Maxwell, Davis and Thiel, and Hochheimer. In addition, optimizations of Wilder's *Directional Movement* and *RSI* will be found in the sections that discuss those techniques. Although dated, these studies are very similar in structure to the way anyone would begin to test a trading idea; they emphasize different features of trading that were important to the authors and give us useful insight. By virtue of hindsight, we can see that along with completeness in one area often comes a deficiency in another. Davis and Thiel analyze the greatest variety of markets, covering virtually all of the U.S. crops as well as cattle, eggs, and the soybean complex. They include about 5 years of data and use relatively fast moving averages (up to 10 days); they introduce variations in lead-oriented plotting and in testing nonconsecutive days; the data used are only the closing prices. The results are clearly presented in both detail and summary, and yield generally good returns.

The authors R.E. Davis and C.C. Thiel, Jr., present excellent credentials and experience in systems testing. Their study of moving averages uses combinations of simple buy and sell signals, leading plots, and skips in the selection of sequential prices used (e.g., a skip of two uses every other price). They test a total of 100 combinations of the three factors:

A skip from 1 day (none) to 5 days (1 week)

An average of 5, 6, 7, 8, or 10 days

A leap of 0 or 2 days

Markets tested were soybeans, bellies, cattle, cocoa, copper, corn, eggs, soybean meal, oats, soybean oil, potatoes, rye, sugar, and wheat.

Maxwell's study is extremely comprehensive but limited by its application to only pork bellies. His idea was to apply combinations of features and test the results. The first feature was the choice of trend and included the possibilities of a simple mean, or a moving average of 3, 5, or 10 days, of either a conventional, average-modified, or weighted type. The second feature was the delay factor, used to improve timing of both entry or exit. Some of the possibilities were: (1) act without delay; (2) act if the signal condition persists for one additional day; (3) enter if the signal condition persists for 2 additional days, but liquidate without delay; and others. Combinations of two types of moving averages and a delay factor were tested, with and without fixed or moving stops. With 10 types of averages, 6 delay factors, and different stops, Maxwell has a lot of combinations to examine.

The study is then expanded to 3-factor systems with a list of 18 combinations of rules to generate 324 systems, of which the results of 285 are recorded, with 49% profitable and 51% losers. The *largest loss* was generated by a system with the rules:

1. Enter a new position when both the weighted 3-day and weighted 10-day moving averages cross the price-mean, as long as the signal condition persists for 2 additional days (buy if averages cross moving down, sell if up).

2. Liquidate positions when the 3-day average reverses its direction through the price-mean as long as it continues for 1 additional day.
3. No fixed stops are used.

The best profits in the 3-factor system required both a 5-day average-modified and a 10-day weighted average to move across the price-mean, provided the 5-day average lagged behind the 10-day. The current position was liquidated when the shorter-term average crossed the longer term. No fixed stops were used.

Maxwell's study represents a great amount of work and some simple and sound philosophy, but does not cover an adequate sampling of data to justify most of his conclusions. Conclusions were drawn based on a selected 50-day test period using May 72 pork bellies, leaving many questions regarding the success of this system or any other system when applied to this short test interval. Maxwell does test four other selected 50-day periods, but the reader cannot know how these periods were chosen. Considering the effort in outlining a testing program and establishing rules, the extent of the system testing is disappointing.

Comparing Methods of Calculation

Hochheimer[7] performs two interesting studies: a comparison of three types of *moving average calculations* and a test of the use of *channels* and *crossovers*. In the first analysis, Hochheimer compares *simple, exponentially smoothed,* and *linearly weighted* moving averages, tested on a good sampling of markets (without financials and currencies, which did not exist during the 1970 through 1976 test period). The simple moving average and exponentially smoothed calculations are covered in Chapter 4 ("Trend Calculations"), and the *linearly weighted* refers to *step-weighting,* in which integer values are used and each successive day is incremented by one, the most recent day having the highest weighting factor.

The rules that apply regardless of which calculation was performed, were:

1. The trend calculation used the closing price only.
2. A *buy* signal occurred on an upward penetration of the moving average by the closing price; a *sell* signal occurred under the opposite conditions.
3. The model is always in the market.
4. A trade cannot be executed when the day's high and low prices are the same. It is assumed to be a *locked-limit* day.

The test covered 7 years of data from 1970 through 1976 and moving average days (or equivalent smoothing constant converted as $2/(days + 1)$), which appear to range from 2 to 70. The results shown in Table 21-2 are interesting and logical, considering the rules. The longer trends (using more days) were consistently better than shorter ones, regardless of which technique was used. This would imply that the longer trends are more reliable. With a few exceptions, the best selection of days ranged from 40 to 70.

A more careful look at the results proves interesting. During the 7 years of test data, soybeans had 728 trades using a 55-day simple moving average. That is more than 100 trades each year, one every 2 or 3 days. Hogs had 1,093 trades during the same period, and other commodities were similarly high. That seems to be an unusually large number of trades for the time interval used, indicating that there must have been many false trends that resulted in small losses. This is confirmed by the very low percentage of profitable trades, only 21% for soybeans. Nothing is indicated about transaction costs, and 728 trades costing $50 per trade in commissions and slippage would generate $36,400 in costs, about 15% of the Net

[7] Frank Hochheimer, "Moving Averages," and "Channels and Crossovers," in *Technical Analysis in Commodities,* Perry J. Kaufman (ed.) (John Wiley & Sons, New York, NY, 1980).

TABLE 21-2   Results of a Simple Moving Average Model

	Best Day	Best Range	Net P/L	Max. Run of Losses	Trades		
					Total	Profit	% Prof
Cocoa	54	53–59	$87,957	$–14,155	600	157	26
Corn	43	43–46	24,646	–6,537	565	126	22
Sugar	60	55–60	270,402	–15,563	492	99	20
Cotton	57	52–57	68,685	–11,330	641	121	19
Silver	19	—	42,920	–15,285	1,393	429	31
Copper	59	54–59	165,143	–7,687	432	158	37
Soybeans	55	55–60	222,195	–10,800	728	151	21
Soy meal	68	65–70	22,506	–20,900	704	148	21
Wheat	41	40–45	65,806	–12,550	480	124	26
Pork bellies	19	16–25	97,925	–9,498	774	281	36
Soy oil	69	65–70	89,920	–8,920	586	122	21
Plywood	68	65–70	1,622	–3,929	372	98	26
Hogs	16	16–20	35,595	–7,190	1,093	318	29

P/L shown in the table. The total soybean profit of $222,195 was equal to $305 per trade profit over the test period, a very good net return and one that might have been unusual because of the exceptional volatility of the agricultural markets during the early 1970s.

Comparing the Hochheimer results with the same system applied to the 10 years from 1986 to 1996, we see a very different picture (see Table 21-3). Many of the markets that produced large profits now show losses. The currencies stand out as uniformly successful; however, the time periods for calculations vary from 40 to 75 days. The appearance of large calculation periods for the "Best Day" column indicates either a very successful long trend, as in the T-bonds, or an attempt to minimize the losses of markets without profitable trends.

In most cases, you will find that the shorter trend periods are unstable. Because consistent short-term trends are rare over long test intervals, such as 10 years, profitable results for a 15-day moving average are usually caused by one or two very large profits, or a sustained move in one direction. The choice of a short-term trend rarely produces profits in the future.

The ease of new computerized testing platforms allows a convenient look at robustness. For the single moving average, 20 periods from 5 to 100 days were tested in steps of 5 days. The last column of Table 21-3 gives the number of profitable tests. Six of the 15 markets tested had no profitable results using any calculation period. Overall, 45% of all tests were profitable. The interest rates show very erratic results with a wide range of best days, even for the T-notes and T-bonds, which had a large number of profitable combinations. Only the currencies appear to be robust within a framework of moderate performance.

Channels and Crossovers

This Hochheimer study consisted of two tests. The first is a *crossover of two simple moving averages*. The short-term average (fast trend) ranged from 3 to 25 days and the long-term from 5 to 50 days. The objective was to eliminate the whipsaws that were evident in the first study. The rules for this system were:

1. Each moving average used closing prices only; the long-term number of days was always greater than the short-term days.

TABLE 21-3   Results of a Simple Moving Average Model (1986–1996), $50 Transaction Costs

Market	Best Day	Net P/L	Max Loss	Trades Total	Trades Prof	% Prof	Robust-ness
Corn	80	–937	–8,462	98	23	23	0/20
Cotton	60	62,060	–76,640	99	38	41	18/20
Soybeans	95	–1,825	–11,175	124	33	27	0/20
Silver*	40	–485	–12,720	112	24	21	0/20
Copper*	45	18,987	–9,000	89	34	38	9/20
Gold	45	–3,240	–16,500	146	44	30	0/20
Swiss franc	45	76,025	–15,000	125	54	43	18/20
German mark	75	46,462	–13,462	91	29	32	20/20
Japanese yen	60	85,475	–13,737	169	61	36	18/20
British pound	40	61,825	–33,237	158	54	34	14/20
S&P 500	35	–4,650	–75,750	200	68	34	0/20
NYSE Index*	90	–7,100	–21,350	88	29	33	0/20
T-Bills	30	8,350	–6,325	156	49	31	8/20
T-Notes	15	52,215	–9,235	267	102	38	16/20
T-Bonds	100	51,084	–14,036	74	33	45	15/20

*Test data began in 1987 or 1988.

2. A *buy* signal occurred when the short-term average moved above the long-term average; a *sell* signal occurred when the short-term average moved below the long-term average.
3. The model was always in the market.
4. If the high and low prices of the day were equal, a *locked-limit* day was assumed and no execution occurred.

The use of a longer and shorter trend introduces the ability to identify a trend bias in the market and trade only in that direction. Theoretically, this should apply to the interest rates and to the index markets, which have either sustained trends or an upward bias. During the period of the original tests, it may be the seasonality of the agricultural markets that dominate the trend. Using two moving averages, the faster one can be considered a timing mechanism, while the slower one tracks the underlying market direction. In Table 21-4, the number of trades are less than the simple moving average model, and the percentage of profitable trades was increased, the type of results that indicate a more robust method.

Retesting

The testing performed to find the best set of parameters is never the last test. It is always important to monitor performance and compare the out-of-sample results with a new optimization to determine the success of the system rules and the testing process. A 1982 publication of Hochheimer[8] provides a rare opportunity to see how the original tests fared and how parameter selection would have changed based on both additional data and changes in price patterns. We can do this ourselves by testing 5- or 10-year periods and comparing the results of the same portfolio. From these results we can visualize an overall change in

[8] Frank L. Hochheimer and Richard J. Vaughn, *Computerized Trading Techniques 1982* (Merrill Lynch Commodities, New York, 1982).

TABLE 21-4   Results of Two Simple Moving Average Crossovers

	Best Days	Net P/L	Max. Run of Losses	Trades Total	Trades Profit	% Prof
Cocoa	7 25	$176,940	$–4,436	468	199	43
Corn	11 47	69,275	–2,697	225	93	35
Sugar	5 50	335,843	–13,851	311	109	35
Cotton	16 25	304,485	–4,755	485	233	48
Silver	3 26	100,790	–8,610	661	262	40
Copper	17 33	212,939	–3,057	354	177	50
Soybeans	16 50	286,440	–15,665	311	148	48
Soybean meal	18 50	117,155	–8,155	272	118	43
Wheat	11 47	113,118	–2,660	209	87	42
Pork bellies	25 46	13,124	–21,538	226	100	42
Soybean oil	14 50	121,749	–6,585	327	128	39
Plywood	24 42	18,505	–3,184	219	100	46
Hogs	3 14	97,448	–7,805	793	321	40

which the market moves. We may find that noise has increased, causing a shift to longer trends, or that risk is much greater and the returns are proportionally smaller.

Crossovers Retested

In the 1982 update of the Crossover System optimization using data through 1979, it is interesting to note that 11 out of 17 markets selected two moving average speeds either identical (in six cases) or nearly identical to the previous test. Five of the remaining six tests showed new selections that traded slower than the previous test. Only gold resulted in a faster selection, but the original test in 1976 could have had only one year of data.

Because the results of using the parameters selected in 1976 were not shown in the new study, their performance could not be assessed. Eleven cases, however, in which the new parameters were either identical or had very small changes, can be used as a conservative estimate. Their out-of-sample performance is shown in Table 21-5. If the parameters are not identical, the 1979 test must show results that are higher than the actual out-of-sample would have been.

The first reaction to the update of the 1976 crossover test should be very positive. Almost identical parameters for 11 out of 17 products originally tested were selected. This means that the traders who used this system were using the *optimum* parameters during the 3-year period from 1977 through 1979. How did they do?

Table 21-6 is a comparison of the out-of-sample period, 1977 through 1979. In the cases in which the parameter selection was slightly different, it must be assumed that the total performance, 1970 through 1979, was better than the performance using the original parameters. Therefore, the out-of-sample period should be at least as good as the results actually achieved. Total profits were $201,649, trading one contract of each market.

Two additional factors should be considered. Although only 3 of the 11 showed losses, the fast nature of this system results in very low profits per trade in 4 of the remaining 8 markets. This may not seem serious until the realities of trading are considered, where the exact execution price is rarely achieved. A trend-following system, with orders entered as intraday stops, must always allow for slippage caused by lack of liquidity and directly related to the size of the order being executed (see the discussion of liquidity in Chapter 18). In a fast market, this slippage can be large, often hundreds of dollars (in contract

TABLE 21-5   Retesting of the Crossover System

| | Through 1976 | | | | | Through 1979 | | |
	Best Days	Net P/L	Trades Profitable/ Total	%	Profits/ Trade	Best Days	Net P/L	Trades Profitable/ Total
Corn	11 47	$ 69,275	93/225	41	$ 308	12 48	$ 83,586	129/332
Sugar	5 50	335,843	109/311	35	1080	6 50	348,833	160/449
Cotton	16 25	304,485	223/485	46	628	16 25	378,440	329/697
Silver	3 26	100,790	262/661	40	152	3 26	96,995	385/1098
Copper	17 33	212,939	177/354	50	602	17 32	218,790	245/571
Wheat	11 47	133,118	87/209	42	637	12 48	151,871	130/305
Pork bellies	25 46	13,124	100/226	44	58	25 46	78,207	137/312
Soy oil	14 50	121,749	128/327	39	372	14 50	125,848	190/488
Plywood	24 42	18,505	100/219	46	84	20 46	2,667	132/351
Cattle	7 13	147,540	337/792	43	186	7 13	162,280	490/1186
T-Bills	6 18	39,710	69/148	47	268	6 18	28,210	148/388

value) away from the intended price. Even Market-on-Close orders are subject to slippage. A buyer using a Close-Only order should expect to get the high of the closing range; a seller will get the low.

In Table 21-6, the furthest right column assumes a conservative slippage, one that should be included in any test program. In some cases, such as copper and bellies, the slippage is small and does not seem to impact on profits; even the large profits of cotton survive well. But in the fastest trading commodities, even the smallest slippage will severely reduce large profits, frequently turning them into losses. The final total shows that those small costs, when applied to every product, were greater than the profits. Instead of making a killing in the market, these traders netted a loss.

TABLE 21-6   Out-of-Sample Results for the Crossover System

	Net P/L	Trades Profitable/ Total	%	Profits/ Trade		1-Way Slippage (5% Daily Range)		
Corn	$ 14,311	36/107	34	$ 133*	½¢	=	25 × 250	=	$ −5,350
Sugar	12,990	51/138	37	94*	10 pts	=	112	=	−34,500
Cotton	73,995	106/212	50	349	10 pts	=	50	=	−21,200
Silver	−3,795	123/437	28	−9	½¢	=	50	=	−43,700
Copper	5,851	68/217	31	27*	20 pts	=	50	=	−21,700
Wheat	18,753	43/96	45	195*	½¢	=	25	=	−2,400
Pork bellies	65,083	37/86	43	757	10¢	=	42	=	−7,224
Soy oil	4,099	62/161	39	25	5¢	=	30	=	−9,660
Plywood	−15,838	32/132	24	−120*	20 pts	=	15	=	−3,960
Cattle	14,740	153/394	39	37	10 pts	=	40	=	−31,520
T-Bills	−11,500	79/240	33	−48	2 pts	=	50	=	−24,000
Totals	$201,649							−$205,214

*Best case (could have been no better, possibly worse).

Crossover System, 1986 to 1996

Bringing this technique forward to current markets, seen in Table 21-7, there is again a tendency to select longer calculation periods, especially for the short-term trend; therefore, there has been a shift from the optimum trend speeds of 5 to 10 years earlier. The number of total trades has dropped significantly across all markets, and may be attributed to more market noise and less definitive trends. Because the use of two trends greatly increases the chance of overfitting the data, it should not be surprising that all of the markets show profits for some combination of fast and slow moving averages. The last column, indicating the number of profitable combinations, is needed to get a picture of the robustness.

Taking a closer look at Table 21-7, it appears at first that the S&P would be highly profitable; however, the profit of $194,750, drawdown of $63,650, and 63% profitable trades is deceiving because only 8 of 120 combinations were profitable. As a group, the currencies and interest rates performed well, and the total of all profitable combinations was 56%, showing that the technique of using two moving averages is likely to be more robust than the 45% given by the simple moving average. When making these system comparisons, you must be cautious that these tests represent a comparable range of test speeds.

Channels

The next model relies on trends but are very different from the moving averages used in the previous optimizations. Originally called a *price channel,* it is now more familiar as an *N-day breakout,* the penetration of the high and low of the past *N* days. The penetration, which causes a *buy* or *sell* signal, occurs if the closing price penetrates the high-low band.

Table 21-8 shows the results of the *interday* test. A common variation of this method is to buy when the intraday high penetrates the upper band; however, this can cause ambiguities when both the high and low of the day exceed both bands. It is not possible to know which one occurred first. Intuitively, the closing price is expected to be a more reliable indicator of direction than the intraday high or low.

TABLE 21-7   Results of a Two–Moving Average Crossover Model (1986–1996), $50 Transaction Costs*

Market	Best Day	Net P/L	Max Loss	Trades Total	Trades Prof	Trades % Prof	Robustness
Corn	17 × 60	3,775	−5,375	44	17	39	21/120
Cotton	11 × 60	66,725	−5,390	40	18	45	105/120
Soybeans	20 × 25	73,450	−44,100	131	80	61	28/120
Silver[†]	15 × 19	18,230	−10,180	155	98	63	18/120
Copper[†]	15 × 25	17,337	−15,087	81	46	57	29/120
Gold	11 × 25	27,990	−8,900	93	43	46	78/120
Swiss franc	7 × 55	79,600	−13,912	54	20	37	109/120
German mark	25 × 50	52,387	−10,750	44	19	43	103/120
Japanese yen	11 × 20	121,362	−14,112	113	53	47	110/120
British pound	25 × 45	61,612	−19,025	62	31	50	99/120
S&P 500	20 × 23	194,750	−63,650	199	126	63	8/120
NYSE Index[†]	20 × 23	58,400	−31,475	179	96	54	27/120
T-Bills	19 × 45	12,100	−4,975	55	23	42	83/120
T-Notes	11 × 30	58,643	−7,368	79	34	43	103/120
T-Bonds	11 × 35	45,305	−14,513	67	28	42	88/120

*Fast trend tested from 3 to 25 in steps of 2; slow trend tested from 15 to 60 in steps of 5.
[†]Test data began in 1987 or 1988.

TABLE 21-8   Results of Interday Closing Price Channel

	Best Day	Net P/L	Max. Run of Losses	Trades Total	Trades Profit	% Prof
Cocoa	53	$147,913	$ −6,248	110	60	55%
Corn	49	39,533	−5,048	118	50	42
Sugar	40	296,027	−20,758	133	57	43
Cotton	62	206,575	−6,870	89	48	54
Silver	14	27,690	−12,365	552	212	38
Copper	27	151,671	−7,225	217	115	53
Soybeans	51	244,839	−11,325	120	68	57
Soybean meal	49	104,690	−7,000	166	71	43
Wheat	23	111,087	−6,900	205	80	39
Pork bellies	52	60,263	−9,892	94	51	54
Soybean oil	51	8,646	−3,622	109	48	44
Plywood	49	8,632	−4,432	120	57	48
Hogs	9	83,702	−9,854	606	253	42

In the original tests shown in Table 21-8, the channel method has much lower profits and proportionally greater risk than the crossovers; results tend to be more erratic as well. This method is clearly better than the single moving average, with more consistent profits, fewer trades, greater reliability, and even smaller drawdowns.

Testing the breakout strategy for 1986 to 1996 (Table 21-9), we see a different pattern than the update of the moving average method. The number of trades have dropped, the maximum drawdown has increased, while only one market showed all

TABLE 21-9   Results of an *N*-Day Breakout (1986–1996), $50 Transaction Costs*

Market	Best Day	Net P/L	Max Loss	Trades Total	Trades Prof	% Prof	Robustness
Corn	55	5,275	−3,375	23	10	43	9/20
Cotton	35	54,605	−10,700	34	16	47	19/20
Soybeans	95	13,225	−6,150	12	7	58	4/20
Silver[†]	85	−2,685	−13,250	13	6	46	0/20
Copper[†]	40	9,400	−6,887	23	9	39	10/20
Gold	95	1,310	−14,430	14	5	36	1/20
Swiss franc	40	67,862	−16,600	31	16	52	19/20
German mark	40	42,775	−9,137	31	16	52	17/20
Japanese yen	25	76,062	−17,062	44	20	45	17/20
British pound	35	62,012	−13,625	36	15	42	18/20
S&P 500	85	15,025	−36,750	16	7	44	3/20
NYSE Index[†]	55	950	−21,200	17	7	41	2/20
T-Bills	30	10,875	−3,825	41	17	41	15/20
T-Notes	25	42,600	−9,087	53	27	51	20/20
T-Bonds	70	41,302	−20,323	19	10	53	17/20

*Breakout tested from 5 to 100 days in steps of 5.
[†]Test data began in 1987 or 1988.

losses. Of the 300 total tests, 57% were profitable, greater than either the moving average or crossover methods.

Modified Three-Crossover Model

The use of one or more slow-moving averages may result in a buy or sell signal at a time when the prices are actually moving opposite to the position that is about to be entered. This may happen when:

1. The rules consider the crossover of the moving average, rather than a penetration of the price.
2. The change in a simple moving average value based on the new price is less than the change in the oldest price that was dropped.

For example, if a long signal occurs and the oldest price showed a decline of 50 points while today's price declined 40 points, the new moving average value will rise by the difference, +10, divided by the number of days in the moving average. This may also occur using exponential smoothing under the special conditions

$$E_{t-1} - P_t > P_{t-1} - E_{t-1}$$

By using a third, faster-moving average, the slope can be used as a confirmation of direction to avoid entry into a trade that is going the wrong way. This filter can be added to any moving average or multiple moving average system with the following rule:

Do not enter a new long (or short) position unless the slope of the confirming moving average (the change in the moving average value from the prior day to today) was up (or down).

The speed of this third, confirming moving average only makes sense if it is equal to or faster than the faster of the trends used in the Crossover System.

Test Results

Fortunately, the results of both the Crossover System as well as the Modified Three-Crossover System were available for the same commodities and the same years. Because the crossovers used in the latter model are exactly those of the first system, the comparison will show whether the confirming feature improved overall results. From the 22 markets tested, plywood was removed because its poor results on both systems tended to distort the comparison. The important statistics are shown in Table 21-10.

The difference in using the Modified Three-Crossover System versus the simpler Crossover System are:

Average change in profits	−15.3%
Average change in equity drop	−15.5%
Average change in percentage of profitable trades	.9%
Average change in number of trades	−26.1%

A decline in profits equal to a decline in equity drop (or risk) is the same as using the original Crossover System with a 15.4% smaller investment. The percentage of profitable trades increased negligibly, indicating that the confirmation filter did not eliminate more losing trades as was expected. The last point, however, shows a larger decline in the total number of trades, indicating that the profit per trade has increased. The new filter appears to catch the entries at a better point, and eliminate some trades with smaller profits. This type of improvement means that there is more latitude for trading error,

TABLE 21-10   Comparison of Systems 1970–1979

	Crossovers				Modified Three-Crossover				Change	
	P/L	No. Trades	% Drop	% Profitable Trades	P/L	No. Trades	% Drop	% Profitable Trades	% P/L	% Trades
Deutschemark	$ 96,510	259	7.6	54	$ 97,698	226	3.4	52	1.2	−12.7
Japanese yen	94,575	131	3.1	51	92,287	111	2.9	58	− 2.4	−15.3
Canadian dollar	71,940	158	7.0	52	69,690	116	5.2	60	− 3.1	−26.6
British pound	80,262	113	8.2	46	69,808	81	8.3	53	−13.0	−28.3
Swiss franc	120,674	121	4.8	48	100,891	91	4.6	46	−16.4	−24.8
Cocoa	408,262	353	2.4	46	282,453	291	7.6	43	−30.8	−17.6
Coffee	83,586	332	3.9	39	56,338	231	5.8	35	−32.6	−30.4
Sugar	348,833	449	3.8	36	331,526	322	4.1	41	−5.0	−28.3
Cotton	378,440	697	2.8	47	282,460	483	3.3	41	−25.4	−30.7
Silver	96,995	1098	13.9	35	89,165	990	15.7	37	−8.1	−9.8
Copper	218,790	571	2.7	43	217,689	408	2.9	43	−.5	−28.5
Soybeans	386,137	483	4.8	47	308,233	317	5.7	48	−20.2	−34.4
Soybean meal	165,294	429	5.3	43	135,643	316	5.9	39	−17.9	−26.3
Wheat	151,871	305	2.7	43	90,093	207	6.9	44	−40.7	−32.1
Pork bellies	78,207	312	27.5	44	76,363	246	14.2	43	−2.4	−21.2
Soybean oil	125,848	488	5.2	39	89,834	346	9.3	40	−28.6	−29.1
Hogs	88,097	853	9.2	39	94,634	647	7.9	41	7.4	−24.2
Cattle	162,280	1186	4.8	41	155,135	875	3.3	40	−4.4	−26.2
GNMAs	76,291	197	4.4	52	56,217	133	6.5	47	−26.3	−32.5
T-bills	28,210	388	27.0	38	20,436	284	3.4	37	−27.6	−26.8
Gold	131,325	275	1.6	53	98,030	158	2.2	57	−25.4	−42.5
Average			7.3	45			6.1	45	−15.3	−26.1

such as slippage. Although the overall profile of the Modified Three-Crossover is not much better than the Crossover System, it would be the preferred choice based on this information.

4-9-18 Crossover Model Results

This model, using the same rules as the Modified Three-Crossover System, was well known before Hochheimer's studies. It can be assumed that the selection of 4, 9, and 18 days was a conscious effort to be slightly ahead of the 5, 10, and 20 days frequently used in moving average systems. It is likely that the system was not developed by extensive testing, since all markets are traded with these same speeds.

As simple as it seems, there are a few very sound concepts in this approach:

1. Each moving average is twice the speed of the prior, enhancing their independence in recognizing different trends.
2. They are slightly faster than the conventional 5-, 10-, and 20-day moving averages.
3. They are the same for all products, implying an attempt at robustness.

It would not be possible for either the profits or the equity drops to be better in this model than an optimized strategy, such as the Modified Three-Crossover Method; yet, out of 17 commodity markets simulated during the 1970 through 1976 period, only two lost money. That is a very impressive record. There should be a greater degree of confidence in this performance than in an optimized program.

Importance of Failed Tests

When the period from 1986 to 1996 is tested, as seen in Table 21-11, we see much lower profits, large losses in the index markets, and uniformly high risk. Net results are worse than other methods tested. This certainly means that this technique is no longer good. Perhaps it means that a rigid set of trends cannot survive over the long term; the lengths of the underlying trends have changed; they are no longer uniform because of changing market participation; or there is more noise in the market, making it difficult to identify the trend in a timely fashion.

These results should make us rethink the conclusions drawn from the previous tests. We have looked at the best days and the robustness of the technique. Because we are no longer confident that the best day of the past will be the best day of the future, we need to depend on the robustness of the system even more. If a large percentage of all tests are profitable, then there is a much greater chance that any parameter selected will be profitable. Our goal is to find the most robust system.

To remove the dependence upon specific fixed parameters that might return unstable performance over many years, it is necessary to generalize many of the features in a system. For example, instead of a fixed stop-loss at 10 points or $500, it will be necessary to allow that stop to vary based on market volatility. Even the calculation period of the trend may change according to volatility, market noise, volume, or some other factors. This approach is discussed further in Chapter 17 ("Adaptive Techniques").

Test Criteria

The method used in these tests is not bad, but real market factors must be included or the results are deceiving. Although the researchers may have been pleased with the out-of-sample profits, they were only paper profits. In real trading, the chances greatly favor losses.

Testing should closely approximate trading. If there is doubt about the costs, make them larger. A system that can profit under testing *penalties* should make money when actually traded. Even when using prepackaged computer optimization software, the slippage

	Net	Max	Trades		
Market	P/L	Loss	Total	Prof	% Prof
Corn	−425	−12,087	114	38	33
Cotton	28,110	−21,000	119	46	39
Soybeans	−19,087	−33,987	139	51	37
Silver*	−20,740	−21,640	94	28	30
Copper*	6,862	−10,062	86	28	33
Gold	2,250	−12,910	130	43	33
Swiss franc	3,325	−43,350	124	48	39
German mark	11,562	−31,525	119	47	39
Japanese yen	86,412	−17,075	104	41	39
British pound	45,512	27,362	122	44	36
S&P 500	−76,650	−110,350	136	48	35
NYSE Index*	−31,475	−51,075	98	36	37
T-Bills	−7,025	14,400	125	40	32
T-Notes	15,674	−11,406	116	42	36
T-Bonds	−14,668	−44,013	130	38	29

TABLE 21-11   Results of a 4-9-18 Crossover (1986–1996), $50 Transaction Costs

*Test data began in 1987 or 1988.

can be added by making the commission costs high; both are per trade costs. If a mistake is to be made, do it by being too conservative; however, it is always best to be realistic.

Getting the Big Picture through Testing

As mentioned throughout this chapter, the key to robustness is to test more data, more markets, more of everything, and then to observe the results looking for a common pattern of overall consistency. There is no better way to tell if a market has trends than to test it for a variety of trending methods. A market that performs well using an interday breakout, but fails with a dual-trend crossover, is not a good candidate for trending profits in the future.

A comprehensive look at 12 trading methods applied to 12 futures markets gives us a chance to see generalized performance.[9] The annualized percentage returns for a variety of U.S. markets are shown for 12 well-defined technical methods in Table 21-12. These trading systems are:

CHL   *Channel breakout,* using the closing price penetration of the N-day high and low

PAR   Wilder's *Parabolic System,* in which the stop and reverse gets closer each day

DRM   *Directional Movement,* a Wilder method that averages the ups and downs separately

RNQ   *Range Quotient,* basing a breakout on a ratio of current change to past change

DRP   *Directional Parabolic,* combining DRM and PAR systems

MII   *MII Price Channel,* a breakout system using only the oldest and most recent prices

LSO   *L-S-O Price Channel,* using two parameters, including an interval of oldest prices, to decide a channel breakout

REF   *Reference Deviation,* determining a volatility breakout based on a standard deviation of past closing price changes

[9] Louis P. Lukac, B. Wade Brorsen, and Scott H. Irwin, "How to test profitability of technical trading systems," *Futures* (October 1987).

TABLE 21-12   Percentage Returns by System and Market, 1978–1984*

	CHL	PAR	DRM	RNQ	DRP	MII	LSO	REF	DMC	DRI	MAB	ALX	Average
Corn	22.4	3.8	29.8	−6.2	30.1	43.3	10.7	4.6	37.9	−2.9	−4.7	22.9	16.0
Cocoa	10.0	−101.7	−121.9	−345.0	−112.1	−73.6	−256.9	−120.5	−72.9	−281.8	−219.2	−35.2	−144.2
Copper	−15.4	2.9	−46.1	−78.4	−4.2	−31.4	−83.0	−66.2	−39.8	−94.3	−118.4	−16.8	−49.3
Cattle	−12.2	−28.4	−12.4	−72.5	−16.5	−34.8	−44.9	−56.3	−11.4	−70.0	−58.9	−5.5	−35.3
Pork bellies	−30.8	22.0	−6.8	−134.4	4.8	20.6	−117.4	−145.3	−6.5	−127.6	−112.0	−12.1	−53.8
Lumber	38.7	−43.6	−0.4	−19.2	−40.6	31.3	−46.3	−18.4	36.6	−19.1	−47.1	24.6	−8.6
Soybeans	7.7	−19.1	25.8	−57.9	−10.0	13.3	−21.5	−45.6	2.6	−10.7	−22.5	13.1	−10.4
Silver	60.5	54.4	0.2	−15.9	82.3	−19.1	12.5	−72.4	34.2	−76.2	−18.0	55.9	8.2
Sugar	103.4	46.2	61.2	−42.1	63.4	72.6	−0.8	−47.3	82.3	17.6	15.2	71.6	36.9
British pound	−3.5	8.1	20.7	−36.1	30.3	1.9	−7.8	3.5	25.9	−10.2	−65.8	−39.8	−6.1
German mark	66.5	35.4	68.2	18.8	78.0	63.3	19.2	−17.8	46.3	24.6	6.6	−50.0	29.9
T-bills	108.7	48.5	132.7	−40.1	225.5	189.9	221.8	239.8	127.8	39.2	−12.0	32.9	109.6
Average	29.7	2.4	12.6	−69.1	27.6	23.1	−26.2	−28.5	21.9	−51.0	−54.7	5.1	−8.9

*Calculation of annual percent returns assumes that 30% of the initial investment is used for initial margin, in which margin is estimated as 10% of contract value.

DMC   *Dual Moving Average Crossover,* holding a trend position when both moving averages have the same trend

DRI   *Directional Indicator,* a ratio of current price change to total past price change

MAB   *Moving Average with % Price Band,* giving a signal when prices penetrate the band

ALX   *Alexander's Filter Rule,* generating signals when prices reverse from a previous swing high or low by a percentage amount

To create the results in Table 21-12, each market was tested for 3 years and the best parameters used to generate the returns for the next years, in a step-forward approach. It is easy to see that some markets are not profitable for any strategy and that some strategies are generally poor. Unless you were creating a strategy for a specific group of markets, you would not want to trade a system that was not profitable in less than 50% of the markets, nor would you want to trade a market that failed in most of the trend strategies. For example, cattle lost in every system, and the RNQ, REF, and MAB systems were consistently unprofitable; therefore, none of those would be good candidates for trading. The most consistent systems were CHL, PAR, MII, and DMC, each posting 8 of 12 winning markets; yet, each has a noticeably different technique. T-bills present an interesting choice because the highest profit, 239.8%, occurred in one of the least reliable systems, REF; choosing DRP is likely to be a better choice.

Displaying the system results by year for all markets is another way to look at robustness. In Table 21-13, we see that RNQ and MAB net losses over all markets in all years, while CHL, MII, and DMC stand out as very consistent. The combined presentation of results across all markets and systems is a clear way of avoiding overfitting by looking at the big picture.

PRICE SHOCKS

Price shocks are large changes in price caused by unexpected, unpredictable events. The impact of price shocks on historic tests can change the results from profits to losses, and vary the risk from small to extremely large and, unfortunately, not enough thought is given to how these moves affect test results and future performance. A discussion of price shocks could easily fill an entire book, but the concepts that are important can be explained

---

TABLE 21-13   Percentage Returns by System and Year*

System	1978	1979	1980	1981	1982	1983	1984
CHL	6.1	47.9	81.6	21.8	28.3	19.9	28.0
PAR	18.5	16.4	54.5	29.9	−31.7	−43.2	−19.4
DRM	29.3	21.7	92.2	−31.6	−22.7	7.8	−7.3
RNQ	−57.2	−69.0	−9.6	−152.1	−31.2	−135.5	−100.1
DRP	34.8	63.8	88.7	31.0	−13.4	−20.0	38.5
MII	12.9	41.6	87.8	54.6	−30.7	3.1	7.1
LSO	−47.1	−4.0	39.1	−55.1	−55.1	−37.6	−59.5
REF	−13.5	23.3	53.2	−85.2	2.0	−109.6	−69.2
DMC	17.6	26.8	85.4	5.9	22.9	1.9	−1.6
DRI	−60.7	−15.4	46.3	−108.1	−114.4	−105.3	−34.0
MAB	−38.0	−44.3	−7.7	−114.4	−91.1	−81.8	−45.7
ALX	28.3	38.6	82.6	−34.4	−8.2	−2.0	−14.4
Average	−5.8	12.3	57.8	−36.5	−28.8	−41.9	−23.1

*Equal percentage amounts of margin are assumed to be invested in each market.

briefly. When it comes to actual trading, the difference between your expected results and actual performance (not attributed to slippage) is entirely dependent on the number of price shocks.

By its very nature, a price shock must be unexpected. However, not all events cause shocks. An assassination, abduction, or political coup is likely to be a surprise, while a crop freeze can be anticipated as weather turns unusually cold. Some economic reports, such as a .5% increase in the Producer Price Index or jump in the balance of trade, will come as a shock, but a low carryover supply of soybeans or a tightening of the money supply after steady economic growth can be anticipated. When a change is anticipated, the market adjusts to the correct level before the news is announced; when it is wrong, prices react in proportion to how poorly it was anticipated.

The problem comes when you test historic data. We know at the time of a price shock that we could not have anticipated the event; at best we have an even chance of being on the right side of the price move. But the computer doesn't know that, and the best results from a large series of tests often include profiting from the largest price shocks—a situation that would be impossible in actual trading. For example, if there were 10 price shocks in 10 years of data, and your historic tests profited from 8 of those shocks, then you have overestimated your profits. Even worse, you have underestimated your risk by believing that a price shock produced a profit and not a loss.

How can you correct this problem? First, you can look at the pattern of profits and losses from a series of tests. If a 20-day and 30-day moving average each showed a maximum drawdown of $10,000, but the 25-day average only lost $5,000 you should assume that the 25-day results could have had the same drawdown as the nearby tests. By some quirk of timing one test was able to avoid a loss while the normal test was not. It would be risky to assume such good fortune in trading.

If you have a record of major price shocks, such as a chart published by the exchanges showing key events, you can verify how many of these events produced profits or losses in your final system. If you have profited from more than 50% then you should reassess your risk based on losses rather than profits from some of those trades. Also check to see that there is an even distribution with regard to the size of the price shocks. You may have selected parameters that took small losses on minor shocks and large profits on major ones.

If you do not treat price shocks as a serious risk, you may overleverage and undercapitalize your trading account. This is the most common cause of catastrophic loss. Any price shock that causes a windfall profit could have, just as easily, produced a devastating loss. The example that follows, "Anatomy of an Optimization," shows how expectations and reality are often quite different. Further examples can be found in Chapter 22 ("Practical Considerations").

ANATOMY OF AN OPTIMIZATION[10]

Using the Iraqi invasion of Kuwait on August 6, 1990, and the U.S. retaliation on January 17, 1991, we optimized a simple moving average strategy for crude oil. The test period began January 2, 1990, but 100 days were needed to initialize the calculations; therefore, the first trade was entered May 24, 1990 (see Tables 21-14, 21-15, and 21-16). In both Test 1 and Test 2, the optimization selects moving averages that produced the highest profits. By accepting these choices, the trader would have held a short position before the invasion of Kuwait, and a long position before the U.S. retaliation. In reality, there would have been a large loss rather than an exceptional profit. When a price shock is an important part of the data being tested, the best system is the one that took the most profits out of that move, even at the cost of other trades.

---

[10] Perry Kaufman, "Price Shocks: Reevaluating Risk/Return Expectations," *Futures Industry* (June/July 1995).

TABLE 21.14   Test 1: Optimizing Crude Oil, January 2, 1990, through August 3, 1990*

Period	NetPrft	ROA	MaxDD	Trds
5	2615	82.9	−3155	11
10	6765	959.6	−705	5
15	6975	989.4	−705	3
20	4975	705.7	−705	3
25	6975	989.4	−705	3
30	4635	657.5	−705	3
35	3635	313.4	−1160	3
40	3215	276.0	−1165	3
45	3255	187.6	−1735	3
50	255	10.6	−2415	3
55	−715	−21.1	−3385	5
60	2625	156.7	−1675	5
65	2785	239.1	−1165	5
70	−385	−12.6	−3055	7
75	1955	112.7	−1735	3
80	−5040	−100.0	−5040	2
85	−5040	−100.0	−5040	2
90	−5040	−100.0	−5040	2
95	−5040	−100.0	−5040	2
100	−5040	−100.0	−5040	2

		Trade Detail from Testing		
Trade Date	B/S	Price	Profit/ Loss	Cum P/L
May 24, 90	Buy	23.58		
May 25, 90	Sell	23.55	−55	−55
Jul 11, 90	Buy	22.49	1035	980
Aug 3, 90	Sell	28.51	5995	6975

* Testing stopped the day before the invasion of Kuwait.
  Test selects 15-day moving average.
  Holding short on August 6, 1990, when Iraq invades Kuwait.

In Test 2, although there were large profits from the first price shock, the trader would have still held the wrong position when the second shock occurred. This method of testing hides the real trading risk, focuses on profits that cannot be predicted, and does it all at the expense of consistent trading profits.

DATA MINING AND OVEROPTIMIZATION

Advances in computing power and testing software have made it very easy to test trading strategies using historic data. It is only logical that you should prove that your ideas would have worked in the past. It is also sensible that you understand the amount of risk that you must take to gain the results. For more sophisticated analysts, a relationship may be found between fundamental factors, volatility, and risk. For fundamental analysts, the expected price of oil is greatly dependent upon the crude inventories; for many stock issues, the per capita disposable income is the key element in predicting revenues; and, the anticipated volatility of soybeans is often found in the size of the carryover stocks. Although past prices

TABLE 21-15 Test 2: January 2, 1990, through January 16, 1991*

Period	NetPrft	ROA	MaxDD	Trds
5	−6010	−32.3	−18610	32
10	3660	22.3	−16430	20
15	12350	103.8	−11895	14
20	19810	345.4	−5735	10
25	8410	105.5	−7970	10
30	8420	86.8	−9705	8
35	18075	1348.9	−1340	5
40	11150	308.9	−3610	6
45	9335	304.1	−3070	5
50	8265	246.7	−3350	3
55	2485	55.0	−4515	7
60	9075	184.8	−4910	5
65	7155	100.4	−7130	7
70	3815	53.3	−7160	7
75	7195	83.9	−8580	9
80	−8540	−82.6	−10340	12
85	−3860	−54.2	−7125	8
90	1960	35.7	−5485	4
95	440	9.5	−4615	4
100	−3950	−85.6	−4615	2

Trade Detail from Testing

Trade Date	B/S	Price	Profit/ Loss	Cum P/L
May 24, 90	Buy	23.58		
May 25, 90	Sell	23.55	−55	−55
Jul 12, 90	Buy	23.49	35	−20
Oct 19, 90	Sell	40.10	16585	16565
Oct 30, 90	Buy	41.23	−1155	15410
Oct 31, 90	Sell	41.92	665	16075
Nov 19, 90	Buy	38.39	3505	19580
Nov 21, 90	Sell	37.30	−1115	18465
Nov 26, 90	Buy	40.62	−3345	15120
Nov 27, 90	Sell	40.53	−115	15005
Jan 7, 91	Buy	35.70	4805	19810

* Testing stopped the day before the U.S. retaliation.
Test selects 20-day moving average.
Total profits are $3,225 without price shock.
Holding long when U.S. attacks Iraq.

and their relationships to economic data cannot be ignored, they can also be misleading, or even erroneous, if used carelessly.

The most important factor in the success of a trading program is a sound premise; that is, you must find a real-life relationship between the price and the way participants react. For example, when the monetary authority of any country raises interest rates, the price of equities tends to fall. Or, when there is bad news for the economy, investors shift from equities to guaranteed interest rates, driving the stock market lower and the bond market higher. Once these relationships have been identified, it is perfectly sensible to look

TABLE 21-16   Test 3: January 2, 1990, through March 28, 1991*

Period	NetPrft	ROA	MaxDD	Trds
5	−17255	64.0	−26975	45
10	−13195	−45.0	−29295	31
15	4480	26.6	−16840	20
20	8430	67.6	−12475	16
25	−4690	−22.6	−20725	20
30	−1395	−6.4	−21775	17
35	28335	2114.6	−1340	9
40	−360	−2.5	−14420	12
45	18245	594.3	−3070	7
50	8265	246.7	−3350	3
55	2485	55.0	−4515	7
60	9075	184.8	−4910	5
65	7155	100.4	−7130	7
70	3815	53.3	−7160	7
75	7195	83.9	−8580	9
80	−18225	−81.3	−22410	13
85	−12945	−70.4	−18390	9
90	−4065	−40.3	−10080	5
95	−8645	−56.0	−15430	5
100	−3485	−75.5	−4615	5

| | | Trade Detail from Testing | | |

Trade Date	B/S	Price	Profit/ Loss	Cum P/L
May 24, 90	Buy	23.58		
May 25, 90	Sell	23.55	−55	−55
Jul 16, 90	Buy	24.16	−635	−690
Nov 9, 90	Sell	40.58	16395	15705
Jan 14, 91	Buy	38.76	1795	17500
Jan 16, 91	Sell	39.36	575	18075
Mar 8, 91	Buy	29.89	9445	27520
Mar 13, 90	Sell	30.89	975	28495
Mar 19, 90	Buy	30.75	115	28610
Mar 28, 90	Sell	30.50	−275	28335

* Test period includes both price shocks.
  Test selects 35-day moving average.
  Total profits are $2,495 without price shocks.
  Optimization profits include both Iraqi invasion of Kuwait and the U.S. attack on Iraq.

through historic data to uncover the size of the interest rate increase needed to move the market, or the type of pattern shift from equities to bonds that could yield a profitable trade.

When we begin looking for a relationship between inventories and price we are reasonably confident that there is a solution, and we can even identify those elements that form the solution. The process is one of careful reasoning and a small amount of testing, or validation. However, when we test a set of trading rules on historic data, we do not actually know that this method will yield a profitable result.

For example, take the simplest case of a trading system that only uses a moving aver-age trendline. A long position is signaled when the trendline turns up, and a short is gen-erated when the trendline turns down. Is this a sound premise? How do you decide that a profitable test result will become profitable real-time trading? The process for understand-ing this is far from trivial.

Realistic Assumptions

After you have decided on your underlying strategy, and before you begin testing, there are a number of decisions to make. These must be made without the benefit of hindsight, but according to your own reasoning. They include:

1. The amount of data to be tested
2. The commission cost per unit traded
3. The slippage cost per unit traded
4. The range of each parameter (variable) to be tested

This last item, the range of each parameter, means that you must decide, in advance, which moving average periods will be tested. If this is to be a long-term program trying to capitalize on the way governments manipulate interest rates or money supply, then you might choose periods beginning with 50 days, up to 300 days. If you believe that the long-term is too risky and most trends are medium-term, then a range of 20 to 100 days might be best. The very fast day trader, looking to downplay the trend, would want to test peri-ods from 5 minutes to 1 day. It is important that the periods chosen for testing correspond to how you perceive the price movement. It is not enough to say, "I'll trade anything that makes money."

Commissions and slippage are also vital to the results, but more significant for the short-term trader. As a system focuses on shorter holding periods, the profits per trade must become smaller; therefore, the commissions and slippage can become the difference between profits and losses. Because a computer assumes that orders can be executed per-fectly (at the signal price), even during a 5-minute bar where prices jumped 1% with virtu-ally no trading, it takes some effort to decide on a realistic level of slippage. Normally, it is safe to overestimate the cost of entering and exiting the market, but for a short-term trader, even a small overestimation could eliminate a potentially profitable trading technique. Accuracy, as near as possible, is the best approach.

By making clear assumptions in advance, you gain the advantage of validating your ideas. You thought that medium-speed trends were likely to be best, but test results show that only a narrow range of speeds are profitable. You must now rethink why this occurred. Using negative feedback to learn more about the market is a very healthy process.

Statistics Can Say Whatever You Want

Most computer software that allow historic testing give results that emphasize the highest returns. Given a choice, most users of these programs want to see the highest returns. A single test result, however, should not be considered representative of the worth of the sys-tem being tested.

If we test the same 10-year period of historic data for 1,000 different parameter values, spread over a wide range, we are likely to be pleased if 50 of those test results were very attractive. Statistically, we might say that 50 are significant at the 5% level. But that is not necessarily true. In a well-distribution, or random, set of results, we can expect 5% to be statistically significant. If the trading system is truly sound, then we would like to see much more than 5% successes.

Robustness

Practically speaking, *robustness* translates into getting the most realistic results by using the fewest parameters and the most data. Robustness is a term used to describe a system or method that works under many market conditions, one in which we have confidence; it is associated with a successful result using an arbitrary set of parameters for a system. This is most likely to occur when only a few parameters are tested over a long time period. For example, if you claim that a long-term moving average system is robust, then someone unfamiliar with the system should be able to choose the moving average period of 130 days and have reasonable expectations of a profit. This would be most likely if a large percentage of all time intervals in the long-term test were profitable.

When first testing a system, it is best to avoid looking at the largest profits, but instead, study only the average values of all tests, that is, the average net profit, average number of trades, average drawdown, and average profit per trade. In addition, looking at the standard deviation of profits for all tests will give a very good idea of the consistency of returns over the range of tests.

The following is a checklist along with a brief explanation that might help when trying to follow a procedure to get robust test results:[11]

1. *Deciding what to test.* Testing should be used for validation of an existing idea, not for discovery.

   a. *Is the strategy logical?* It should be based on careful observation of the market, or an awareness of relationships between different factors that drive the market, or between different markets themselves.

   b. *Can you program all the rules?* Programming a system guarantees that all of the contingencies have been thought out. While not everything can be programmed, in particular situations requiring crisis intervention, these cases are few.

   c. *Does the strategy make sense only under certain conditions?* A trading program can be limited to a specific situation, and testing should reflect those limitations.

   d. *Take a guess as to the expected results.* It is important to know if your estimate of the system success is correct. Getting a good result for the wrong reason requires just as much rethinking of the problem as getting bad test results.

2. *Deciding how to test.* There are a number of steps necessary before you can actually begin the test process.

   a. *Choose the testing tools and methods.* Select a test platform, such as *TradeStation* or *MetaStock,* which can speed up the test process and keep it objective.

   b. *Do you have enough of the right data?* More data is best, but if there is less data available, it should have a wide range of market conditions, such as bull and bear markets, price shocks, and sustained sideways periods.

   c. *Will you test a full range of parameters?* The nature of your trading strategy, for example, long-term or short-term breakouts, may determine the parameters that are tested. Test only the range that makes sense for the strategy. This serves to validate the concept and avoids discovering better techniques.

   d. *In what order will the parameters be tested?* Test the most important parameters first, such as the time period. More subtle parameters are often used for refining the results, and may not be helpful at all. You can usually tell the most important parameters because they cause the widest range of results.

   e. *Are the parameters distributed properly?* Testing equal intervals of trend periods can be misleading. The difference between a 3- and 4-day moving average is

---

[11] A more detailed explanation of testing robustness can be found in Perry Kaufman, *Smarter Trading* (McGraw-Hill, 1995).

33%, while the difference between a 99- and 100-day average is only 1%. When you test periods from 1 to 100 days, your average results are heavily weighted toward the slow end, which has similar performance.

   f. *Have you defined the evaluation criteria?* You must know whether highest profits, highest reliability, or some other combination will be used to evaluate the results. Risk-adjusted performance can be a very good objective criteria.

   g. *How will the output be presented?* Results can look very different when presented in a plain table. Two- and 3-dimensional contour maps can give a better view of the way performance varies when two parameters change.

3. *Evaluating the results.* Careful review of the test results can avoid many hours of unnecessary work. Looking at the detail of the performance, and even the individual trades of a few selected results, will give you insight into the good and bad aspects of your program.

   a. *Are the calculations correct?* Just because calculations were done by a computer doesn't mean they are always correct. A person had to tell the computer what to do, and people make mistakes.

   b. *Were there enough trades to be significant?* We have uncertainty when the results show excellent performance on only a few trades. When there is not enough data, there is no way to be sure that the results are robust. The system can only be used if you have complete confidence in the underlying premise, and the sparse results simply confirm that logic.

   c. *Does the trading system produce profits for most combinations of parameters?* The best assurance of robustness is when most parameter combinations produce profitable results, even though they vary.

   d. *Did logic changes improve overall test performance?* When you improve the results by adding a special rule, the average of all tests must increase, while the standard deviation remains unchanged. Otherwise, you may have simply overfit part of the data.

   e. *How did it perform on out-of-sample data?*

4. *Choosing the specific parameters to trade.* Choosing the parameters to be used in trading is another unique and difficult problem. Does the system that showed the peak historic profits give you the best chance of getting the peak future profits, or was it just chance?

   a. *Did the last test include the most recent data?* If you have left out data to perform an out-of-sample test, then respecify the parameters using the most recent data. You must be as current as possible before trading.

   b. *Did you choose from a broad area of success?* Parameters should be chosen from an area that showed consistent profits, but should not be determined by the one that had peak profits. It is best to look for average returns using average parameters.

   c. *Are profits distributed relatively evenly over the tested history?* Although there may be attractive total profits, sustained periods of loss would not survive real trading. Returns should be reasonably steady.

   d. *Did the historic results show any large losses due to price shocks?* It is not possible to avoid large price shocks in real trading because you never know when they will come. Historic results that do not show large equity jumps due to price shocks are not realistic, and result from overfitting. Even worse, those results that only profit from price shocks are benefiting from hindsight. In real trading, 50% of the price shocks should produce a windfall profit, while the other 50% will give equal losses.

    e. *Have you risk-adjusted the returns to your acceptable risk level?* The best comparison between tests is to annualize all returns, to avoid comparing unequal time periods, and to risk-adjust the results. Risk adjusting changes each result so that it has the same unit risk as every other test.

5. *Trading and performance monitoring.* The development of a system is never complete. There is a continuous evolution in the markets, seen in the changing participation, volatility, interrelationships between markets, and the introduction of new markets. The only way to see how these changes affect your trading program is to carefully monitor the system signals and the corresponding fills. From this evaluation you can reallocate funds, change the way you execute signals, and even find better rules. Without monitoring your trading, and comparing the results with your expectations, there is no basis for saying that your system is performing correctly.

    a. *Are you following the same rules that were tested?* It is often convenient to program a simple version of your ideas, but trade a more complex set of rules. If so, you have no basis for comparison.

    b. *Are you trading the same data that was tested?* The use of an artificial, continuous contract for testing futures will not give you the same results as testing each contract, beginning at the time it becomes the most active of the delivery months. Normally, artificial continuous prices are smoother than real prices and appear to perform better.

    c. *Are you monitoring the difference between the system and actual entries and exits?* Slippage, the difference between the system price and the actual market execution, can change performance from theoretically profitable to a real trading loss. Monitoring this difference will tell you the realistic execution costs, the maximum volume that can be traded, and the best time of day to trade.

SUMMARY

This chapter has covered a lot of material vital to the successful development of a trading program. Because there are so many issues, the following is a brief summary of the most important concepts:

1. Select a trading strategy with a sound underlying premise; complexity is not necessary.
2. Reserve out-of-sample data for validation.
3. Select the range of parameters to test that is logical, favoring the faster or slower trading approach.
4. Perform the longest reasonable test to include as many market situations as possible.
5. Test as many different markets as possible looking for a common pattern in the results.
6. Standardize the results to facilitate comparisons between systems and test periods.
7. Evaluate the robustness of the method rather than the peak performance; avoid fine tuning.
8. Assess the effects of past price shocks on profits and risk.
9. Beta-test (paper trade) the system until you are certain that it is working properly.

You might also keep in mind that testing uses historic data and works best in real trading when the current market has the same patterns seen during the test data. The premise of optimization is that the markets will continue to behave in the future as they have in the past. This may be why the index markets traditionally have been among the poorest system performers—because they are trading at price levels and volatility that have never been seen before.

    Other areas of interest to readers actively testing and evaluating test performance will be *genetic algorithms,* a new search technique, discussed in Chapter 20, and most of Chapter 23, especially the section "Measuring Risk."

22

Practical Considerations

This chapter discusses areas of technical and mathematical analysis that are not systems by themselves, yet essential to the successful development of a system. The first part concerns the use of the computer. Technical analysis and computers have become synonymous with each other and, with the simple steps provided by development software such as *TradeStation, MetaStock,* and spreadsheets, it would be rare to trade a new technical system without first running it through a computer to simulate its past performance. Those who do not use a computer directly are strongly influenced by the computer systems of others.

The second section, "Price Shocks," is the most underestimated deterrent in finding the right system and generating trading profits. This idea has been discussed in different places during this book, specifically in Chapter 21 in the section "Anatomy of an Optimization"; yet it cannot be overstated. Unpredictable events, once they become part of price history, are often treated as though they could be anticipated. This can inflate performance returns and minimize risk during strategy testing with serious consequences to actual trading. This section will try to explain how to close the gap between testing and trading.

The Theory of Runs is actually an application of gambling techniques, primarily Martingales, to trading. What would seem more reasonable than assuming that the odds are against you in the futures market or as a short-term trader and treating it as a gambling situation? The third section is about combining systems together that focus on different market characteristics, and the understanding of the trade-offs inherent in each type of analytic method. There is also a short analysis of trading limits to show some of the problems and flaws of moving from a test to an operating environment. The last section reviews the similarity of systems and the impact of technical systems on futures markets.

USE AND ABUSE OF THE COMPUTER

Make sure your present report system is reasonably clean and effective before you automate. Otherwise your new computer will just speed up the mess.

Robert Townsend[1]

Computers are not a substitute for thinking. They excel in performing the same tedious task, over and over again, quickly and accurately—provided, of course, that correct information was entered. But even though technology has not yet reached the stage depicted in *Star Wars,* the computer is the only practical tool for evaluating trading ideas. This section will consider both good and bad ways to approach a computer problem, none of which can be credited to or blamed on the machine. As a powerful tool, a computer can't be beat; many of the systems, advancements, and refinements presented in this book could not have been considered without it.

Computers come in many shapes and sizes, and can be purchased, leased, and borrowed. Their packaging has become second only to the car. During the 1980s, the average life of a computer *generation* was about 10 years; however, advances in technology have

---

[1] Robert Townsend, *Up the Organization* (Knopf, New York, 1970, p. 36).

reduced that to about 3 years, if you don't mind a year when you feel obsolete. The past few years have seen a remarkable evolution in the computer industry. From an acceptance of the personal computer (PC) to the point at which some households would rather give up their television than their computer, the PC has revolutionized data processing and brought the Internet into tens of millions of homes. Because not everyone knows how to program a computer, software companies have developed *turn-key* packages, programs that are *user-friendly,* operated primarily by menu selection. The combination of these two factors, cheap hardware and sophisticated software, has reached far into the realm of individual and institution investors.

One of the first and foremost organizations to provide convenient computer research tools for the trader was the Technical Analysis Group (TAG), which began in 1975 as a user's group. It provided menu-driven capabilities for analysis of daily price data and programming capability similar to a spreadsheet using its *CompuTrac* software. It provided daily automatic updates of data at a time when that luxury was the state of the art. The company that breaks ground is not always the one that survives the race, and those analysts developing systems now expect much more. Generally, development software falls into two groups:

1. Daily market analysis, with price updates at the end of the day
2. Intraday trading platform, providing users with on-line data feeds to execute their strategies

Both types of software provide the ability to enter your trading strategies and test them on historic data. The software that operates on daily data is considered "off-line" and is used by traders who prefer to evaluate the market after it closes and prepare orders that can be executed the next day without having to constantly watch the market. The intraday trading platform is much more complex and more expensive. It requires active data feeds and provides both real-time graphics and generates trading signals at the close of each price tick or *bar,* as defined by the user.

Acquiring Data

Daily historic data, essential to the development of trading systems, is readily available and most often comes with the purchase of the software. It is common to see 25 years of historic data on all U.S. markets, but not as common to have European and Asian data provided as well. Intraday data is available from a few major vendors and can be easily obtained for at least 15 years on U.S. markets, but is also much more difficult to get on markets outside the United States. Occasionally, there are sales on this data, and it can be purchased at a reasonable price. The Chicago Mercantile Exchange has made most of its tick data available on compact disk, but it is necessary to convert their form into one that can be read by your trading strategy software.

Of the non-U.S. firms, London's LIFFE has been providing tick data for the longest time, and 10 to 15 years is available for their oldest markets. France's MATIF is just now providing tick data, as is Germany's DTB, Singapore's SIMEX, and many other exchanges. The form of the data provided is very similar, but all of them are incompatible with the trading strategy software and require what is called *data reduction.* Because the exchanges have taken the policy that providing data facilitates trading on their markets, there is usually no cost for it; this gives you some latitude to pay a programmer to write a program to convert this into your own format.

Cleaning the Data

Occasionally, you will find that your strategy was immensely profitable, or lost much more than you expected. When you test 20 years of data, you may not look at each trade but accept the results as correct and rationalize the outcome as a sequence of bad or good trades. You might be surprised to learn that there can be many erroneous prices in your data. It is an incredible waste of time to use data without first reviewing it to find errors.

Tick data is notorious for including bad data with the good, simply because of the magnitude of the problem. Most daily data is already clean. The easiest approach to checking your data is to display it as a chart and scan through all of the markets that you plan to use. Bad data points are obvious once seen on a screen. A low price of zero will show up as a vertical line going to the bottom of the chart; this will result in the correct data points being scaled down to look as though they are just a horizontal line. You can then find the date of this point and correct it (provided your software has a correction feature).

If you can program the computer yourself, you will want to scan the data looking for *outliers,* those data points that are at least 10% away from the previous data points. The data provider should have prescanned the data to be sure that there are no intraday prices that were outside the end-of-day high and low prices transmitted by the exchanges, but this is not usually the case, and you will find that the most obvious errors have been overlooked. There are more subtle errors that can be found and corrected, but the largest ones must be fixed before you use the data. For testing, even one error per year is enough to make all of the tests useless. Don't forget that, if you remove a price instead of correcting it, you must reduce the tick volume as well.

Data Updates

It is not difficult to remember when all traders kept a copy of the *Wall Street Journal* and clipped the price pages so that data could be entered into their computer. These pages, kept in a file drawer, became their historic database and absolute reference. This doesn't make sense any more. Automatic end-of-day updates are available to anyone at very little cost. They provide complete and accurate data as well as correcting any past data that might have been wrong. Some exchanges post daily prices on their Web sites and can be retrieved for free, but this requires added effort to convert that data into a form acceptable by your database. Most data providers will accommodate a number of different formats so that data received each day simply gets added to your historic data and is immediately ready to use. Don't do it manually. Your time is best spent finding a profitable trading strategy rather than fiddling with data.

Archiving Data

Not only must you have a complete database of accurate, historic data, but you must keep that data current. Even if you have a live data feed, the data management of your system cannot store an unlimited amount of ticks or days before it begins to discard the oldest values. Most software will have a specific number of data points that it will hold for intraday data, and much more for daily data. For example, it is common to have only 3 months of tick or 15-minute data, or the computer may hold 4,000 entries each of 1-minute, 5-minute, 15-minute, and daily data, which mean about 16 years of daily data but only 4 months of 15-minute data. This design may be important when you choose the system you use. By being aware of how much data is held, you will need to remember to archive the 15-minute data before each 4-month period elapses; otherwise, you will lose the data and your history will not be continuous.

Combining Standard Techniques into a System

Strategy development programs provide a wide assortment of standard techniques in the form of indicators and systems. You can pick a stochastic oscillator, a moving average, or an N-day breakout and combine them in various ways to evaluate markets over different time horizons, such as a 10-day and 40-day smoothing, or even vary the frequency of data using 30-minute, 1-hour, and daily bars. In most cases, you can write your own formulas to create customized indicators. If you experiment with these software features, you might find that they provide the ability to create a trading strategy that matches the time frame and risk profile that you want. For example, a long-term trend can be found with a standard moving average, weighted average, exponential smoothing, N-day breakout, or linear regression. All of these techniques are already available. You may want to combine that with a band to avoid whipsaws. That is also easily done. If you want to alter your timing so that you enter on a pullback after a trend signal, then you can add a stochastic or RSI to your rules. Before you begin specialized programming, there is a lot to be learned by using these standard tools. It is not at all clear that you can create a trend that is any better than the ones provided in your system. It may be that the choice of trend period is much more important than the trend technique.

Choosing Hardware

In an era of remarkable advances in technology, the hardware costs no longer seem an obstacle. As each new, faster chip is introduced, the previous model computers are reduced in price. This process seems to be happening at least once each year. The cost of a computer with a maximum configuration is small compared with your objectives, and not much greater than one trading loss. Because hardware has a shorter shelf life than only a few years ago, buying the biggest and best equipment is the only way to extend the life of your purchase.

The process of testing your strategies by optimization is a computationally intensive method for the computer. You'll want to have the fastest processor. In addition, testing may still take one or more uninterrupted hours of data crunching; therefore, you'll want to have a large RAM to allow that process to go on in the background while you use the computer to do some other tasks. Institutional users will find it more practical to have one or more machines dedicated to testing. This will allow the calculations to continue at a predictable pace, rather than being interrupted by demands from other programs.

Programming the System

Computer programming talent is no longer rare, but in high demand. In addition, understanding a trading strategy is a special talent that requires training. Fortunately, the most arcane parts of system development are already part of any trading development software you buy; therefore, it is only necessary to code the actual strategy, rather than how to retrieve and store prices from the exchange data feed.

The prevailing philosophy about software development is to try to use as much third-party software as possible. If you need to see the results of a *TradeStation* optimization, save the results to a spreadsheet, then sort, organize, analyze, and graph the results using your favorite spreadsheet. You can compare one set of tests with another if you save them all in the same format. For the more popular platforms, such as *TradeStation* and *Meta-Stock,* there are a number of user's groups, support groups, and newsletters that can be of great help. Some companies provide alternate statistical measurements for your tests, while others have an add-in portfolio program. It is a good idea to check to see if these services satisfy your needs before attacking the programming yourself.

Selecting a Programmer

If you are not going to program the computer yourself, try to find someone with experience in a language similar to the one you'll be using. It would be helpful if the programmer had some knowledge of trading, which might avoid errors caused by misunderstanding concepts, but that is not likely to happen. Given a choice, a scientific background is better than business programming experience.

Getting a programmer to say how much it will cost or how long it will take to solve a problem is going to be difficult—they just don't know. Programmers are incurable optimists, always thinking that the problem will be done at any moment. Even competent managers of programmers have difficulty in scheduling a project, based on the uncertainty of the debugging, or checking-out process. If it is necessary to contract the work or hire a programmer, try to get a fixed-price quote and avoid the problems that will occur later.

Define the Steps

To keep the work on schedule, you will need to know what you want to do in advance. You can take a chart and mark the places where you believe the system will buy and sell. It is important that you have an actual example of what is expected so that you can verify the programmed results against the example.

Write down all the rules in outline form. You must be able to be precise about every rule. The computer cannot deal with ambiguities. It is very likely that a programmer can work directly from your rules to create the final strategy. This is also an opportunity to be sure that your rules are clear and complete. Using your rules, select a price series and mark the trading signals that will be used to verify the program output. Check the results carefully. If one trade doesn't match your expectations, don't stop until you find the reason.

Looking into the Past

We have already thoroughly discussed the advantages of using as much data as possible—the results reflect a broader variety of market conditions and are, therefore, more representative. There is often a concern that older data does not represent current conditions. While there may be some truth in that, there is usually more to be gained with a system that can survive those years and still perform well in current markets. Unless there has been a structural change that makes the old data invalid, you should always favor longer tests and more data. Even if you are convinced that the older years represent a period of low volatility that will never be seen again, your system should, at the very least, not post losses for that period.

Paper Trading

With all good intentions, when you develop a new strategy you plan to hold the most recent data aside for out-of-sample testing. Somehow, before you're done, that data has been used a number of times. Therefore, as careful as you have tried to be, it is possible that you have overfitted the data by fine tuning the rules and parameters.

The only alternative is some period of *paper trading*. By monitoring the program daily, you can see how it is performing under real market conditions. Before doing that, however, you should write down the system expectations, for example, the size and frequency of the profits and losses. It is always a relief when the system posts its first profit, but it is the overall profile that is most important. When paper trading, assume that your fill is the worst price of the 5-minute period immediately following an intraday signal, or the highest price of the closing range if your trades come at the end of the day. A touch of reality can start you thinking and save a lot of money. Don't start trading a new system without monitoring its performance first.

Dealing with the Unexpected

By the time a computer and database have been acquired and installed, you have programmed or had a programmer implement your ideas, debugged and tested the programs, and finally analyzed the results, there has been a substantial investment made. Hard work has resulted in proving one of four things:

1. The system is profitable.
2. The system is not profitable.
3. The system cannot be implemented effectively.
4. The whole process is too expensive.

If you've gotten to the end and your result is not satisfactory, you might want to reexamine the process that you used. Trading strategies should be built slowly; each piece must be proved to be sound before you go on to the next step. You should never have gotten to the end without knowing that the final product was going to be profitable. If the performance was deteriorating as you added new rules and features, you should have stopped and reconsidered these features and modified each step to be more robust.

You may also find that your rules were too subjective, that you substituted a rule that was not well thought out, because you were not able to clearly define one part of your strategy. Knowing that you have been subjective about a trading decision is a valuable discovery. Many speculators believe that they are very clinical about their trading policies; they know exactly what will be done in every circumstance and, therefore, think that their approach can be well defined in writing. But computerization cannot be done successfully if there are any "maybes," "wait and see," or any other exceptions.

One common problem is that the system does not work using either the rules or the variables imposed by the program. If moving average periods ranging from 20 through 50 were first used unsuccessfully, it is likely that you would test intervals of less than 20. If stop-loss points were too big or too small (judging by the size of frequency of the losses), you'll try other sizes. Systems do not always work as expected and perhaps only a slight change to the rules is necessary. Negative results are important feedback. They can help create a better strategy before it is too late. After all, if the answers were known in advance, this would all be unnecessary. If the results are good, but different from what was expected, you should take the time to understand why. Don't accept the results without careful review. This is an opportunity to either increase your understanding of how the market works, or find that you have been making a mistake all along.

A common result is that the system works in some markets but not in others. This can be the product of using fixed values rather than a rule. For example, a stop-loss of 4 ticks would make sense for Eurodollars trading at 4% yield, but not the S&P at 1100. Try to locate the problem and make the rules more adaptable to changing conditions. Once this is done, if the problem persists, you must face the issue of robustness.

Expectations

In some work, defining your expectations can bias the process and give poor results. For the development of a trading system, you must first have a sound idea before you start. Along with this idea is whether it works best in the short or long term, the frequency of profitable trades, and even the size of the expected profits and losses. By defining your expectations you can apply special rules and techniques that seem consistent with the philosophy of the method. These expectations of the profit profile are particularly important to keep you focused throughout the development and testing of the strategy. If you expect to trade one each day and capture about 50% of the trading range, then signals that occur only once each week should immediately cause you to look for an error. If profits are too small or losses too big, then you can carefully study how the rules apply to a series of prices and understand whether you have omitted some rules, applied the rules incorrectly, or have made a mistake in your thinking. Without setting down clear expectations in advance, you have no benchmark to help you through the development process.

A Winner in Disguise

One important twist on performance should not be overlooked: A consistently bad performer can become a consistent winner by doing just the opposite. Finding a profitable trend system in the range of shorter time intervals may seem to be a hopeless effort. On the other hand, systematic losses mean that the price movement fails to trend, and every buy signal and sell signal is actually an overbought and oversold condition, predictive of price change. This can happen in markets that are heavily traded using systems; what appears at first to be a trend change is a temporary distortion due to massive buy and sell orders.

Consistent losses do not always mean that the reverse trade will work. The net losses may be less than the total transaction costs; therefore, the opposite action will show even larger losses. The successful reverse system is one in which the net losses far exceed the transaction costs.

Simple or Complex?

It is not necessary to create or acquire a system that is exceptionally complex to be successful. Simple systems, such as a dual moving average crossover, can be profitable as well. The difference between the performance of a simple system and a well-developed, complex method is the risk/reward ratio and the magnitude of the equity swings.

Simple systems will catch the trends and take as much profit from the big moves as the more sophisticated approaches. It is the other patterns that make distinctions. Added features should reduce the losses and modify the trading patterns during nontrending periods. This may be accomplished by identifying a trading range, using positions of varying size, or by the inclusion of economic data. Sometimes, more complex systems are just more complex, without improving results. In that case, use the simple system, but retain larger reserves than normal.

Just Because It Doesn't Work in Practice Doesn't Mean It Won't Work in Theory

You thought that you followed all the rules by

1. Precisely defining the system
2. Using enough test data
3. Evaluating performance by forward extrapolation
4. Investing enough to survive the worst losing streak
5. Trading a diversified portfolio
6. Following every signal

And still you lost all your money. . . . What happened?

Most likely you skipped some part of the well-planned development process. Careful reassessment will usually show that some corners were cut. For example, new traders often only test their ideas in general by spot checking a few selected markets during years that seem to have interesting or typical movement. They assume that these shortcuts do not affect the results of the system. The advantage of computerized testing is that *all* years can be tested easily—the procedure necessary to produce a robust system that works in most markets.

There is always the temptation to force a system to work if it failed because of one or two large losses. An analyst can find something unique about these losing trades and create a rule that eliminates just those items. Some traders may just assume that circumstances would have caused them to pass the trade rather than buy or sell in an obviously adverse market. This type of tampering doesn't work and the reason for many of these problems is explained in the next section on price shocks.

Suppose you are not guilty of any of these infractions, that the system was developed without making exceptions, and all the rules were followed. Then, the most common problem is to misjudge the volatility of the market or some systematic change that has occurred. You might see that the program was more profitable in the earlier years, and that the average profit has been declining and the average loss rising. This might be due to increased participation and more market noise. As this occurs, it is necessary to increase the period of calculation to compensate for the noise. For example, in the early 1980s, the energy markets were very smooth, and a 3-day moving average generated good profits. As volume increased, the market appeared more erratic, and a 10- to 20-day moving average would have been needed. In the early 1990s, the trend speed would have increase to 30 to 40 days, all due to changing market noise. When there is higher noise, it takes longer to identify the trend. Even when you sit still, the market will continue to change.

Start Slowly

After paper trading, to begin trading with an exceptionally small portfolio, one that can be lost 10 times over, will not hurt at the beginning. There must be a chance to see if the system performs the way it appeared in testing. This will be the first opportunity to find out the cost of execution. The slippage may be the factor that separates profits from losses. You may find that, during quiet periods, when the market is moving sideways, there is small slippage but no profits; during fast market, when you expect the largest profits, the slippage also increases. The size and frequency of the losses should be checked as well as the equity cycle. When everything passes inspection, the investment can be increased slowly. Patience and thoroughness are important ingredients for success.

Once the system has been checked out, it is even safer to turn the day-to-day executions over to someone else. It may be the only certain way to follow the rules precisely. Try to stay detached and objective, but monitor the results carefully to be sure there are no surprises. Even a large profit may be an early warning of a problem. Large losses often follow large profits.

PRICE SHOCKS

Price shocks represent the most significant obstacle in the effort to close the gap between test results and actual trading, or expectations and reality. A *price shock* is, by circumstance, an unexpected event. Exceptionally volatile price moves are caused by actual news that differs from expectations, such as the Fed raising rates by 1% when only ¼% was anticipated; or, it may be a significant, unexpected political event, such as the abduction of Gorbachev in 1991. The key word to remember is "unexpected."

If an event was expected, then there would be no price change. The market would have already moved to the anticipated level. Therefore, we cannot expect to profit from a price shock by clever planning, but only by chance. We should never assume that we would be on the right side of a large, unexpected move in more than 50% of those events. Unfortunately, when we back-test a trading system using historic data, we tend not to identify specific price shocks and treat them as normal, predictable events. We choose systems that perform best over a set of parameters, without regard to specific trades that may have been the result of shocks. We judge results by higher profits, lower risk, or a combination of statistical values. The results chosen as the *best* performance often have been the greatest beneficiary of these unpredictable price shocks.

Making Money with Hindsight

We should already be aware of the problems of back-testing. While there are no other alternatives for validating a proposed trading strategy, it is necessary to look at the problems more carefully to see a solution. No market is more evident than crude oil during the Gulf War, discussed in the previous chapter (see Figures 22-1, 22-2, and 22-3). From August 1, 1990, through the end of the War in February 1991, oil prices were driven by news. But not all news is a surprise. In the agricultural markets, a crop freeze in orange juice or coffee is often anticipated by a change in weather. Before a freeze can occur, the temperature must drop. And that low temperature must be sustained to cause damage. This weather change causes processors to protect themselves by buying forward contracts or futures. In turn, prices move up.

Because Iraq had been moving troops near the Kuwait border, their intentions were not a surprise; however, diplomacy failed. The threat of an oil supply disruption caused oil prices to slowly rise. Many systematic traders and commercials would have been long on August 7, 1990, when Iraq invaded Kuwait.

Identifying Price Shocks

If we can't predict price shocks, and they seriously impact our historic tests, then we must identify those shocks so that we can correct for their effects. In the end, this may mean that we need to look at the individual trades, compare them against a list of price shocks of which we are aware, and decide which of the profits were realistic. Even more important, we must decide which risk was understated. There may not be a safe way of changing this final process. It may always be necessary to manually review the results for credibility. Some analysts may find it comforting to think that the computer may not be able to do everything on its own!

FIGURE 22-1 **A far-reaching price shock. A vivid reminder of price shocks occurred on August 16, 1991, and again 3 days later when Russian premier Gorbachev was abducted and then released. Most financial markets were affected simultaneously, as were the energy markets. In the case of the currency markets, many traders profited from the first shock, which occurred on a Sunday, then gave it all back on the following Wednesday.**

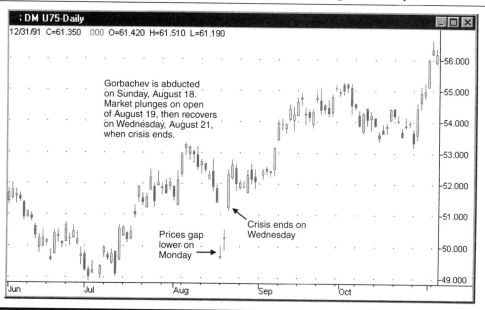

Source: Chart created with *TradeStation*® by Omega Research, Inc.

FIGURE 22-2   A more common shock. The election of conservatives in Britain in January 1992 was a surprise, but the effect was relatively local.

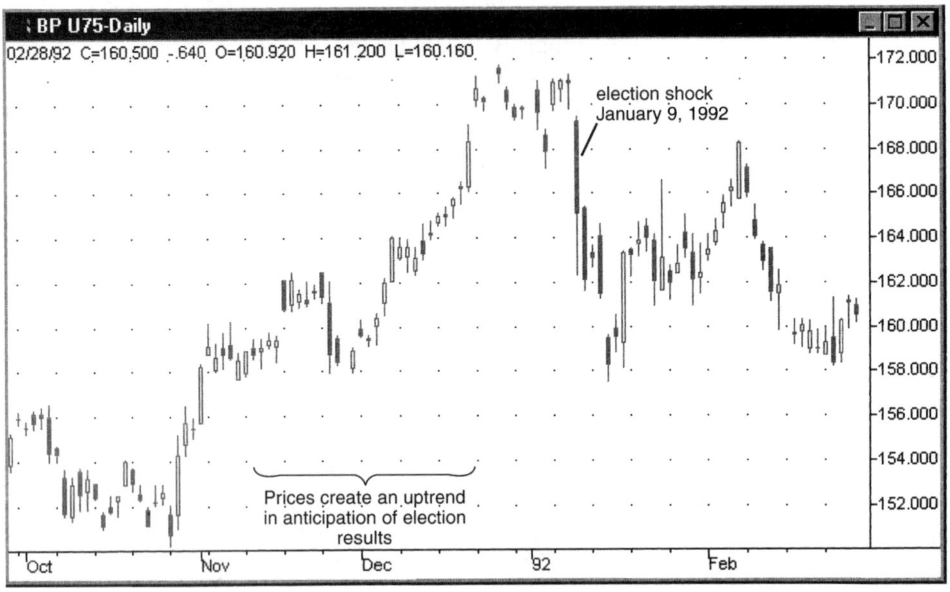

Source: Chart created with *TradeStation*® by Omega Research, Inc.

The process of identifying price shocks can be speeded up with a small amount of automation. A price shock will be defined as a day with a true range greater than the average true range by a multiplier, called the *shock factor.* This would be coded as

```
shock = 0;
truerange = high - low;
if high - close[1]> truerange then truerange = high - close[1];
if close[1] - low > truerange then truerange = close[1] - low;
volatility = @average(truerange[1],vperiod);
if truerange > volatility*shockfactor then shock = truerange;
```

Having coded the identification of a price shock, we can write a record to a file or print log to create a list of all price shocks, the date they occurred, and the size of the initial shock. It might also be useful to count the number of periods until prices return to a relatively normal level. It may be unrealistic to assume that the volatility resulting from a price shock will completely disappear; therefore, the point at which some degree of normal might begin could be when volatility declines to one-half the level of the initial price shock. This would be found using the code

```
if truerange < shock/2 then shock = 0;
```

With this simple method of identifying both the beginning and end of a price shock, we can study the effects of price shocks on testing performance. A simple test was performed in which an optimized trend system was inspected for periods of price shocks, where a shock was defined as a price move of three times normal volatility. The profits and losses from these periods was removed from the net performance over a 10-year period, with the results shown in Table 22-1. The reduction in profits was more than 50% when price shocks were eliminated. This means that the selection of parameters heavily favored profits that were generated by large, probably unpredictable, price jumps.

FIGURE 22-3 **The invasion of Kuwait by Iraq. News of massing armies and troop movements near the Kuwait border helped the market anticipate the August 7, 1990, price jump in oil. At the beginning, many traders were on the right side of the market, although the move was not very dramatic.**

Source: Chart created with *TradeStation®* by Omega Research, Inc.

How can we use these results if we cannot see the price shock until after it's happened? The only way is to correct the optimization process so that the parameter selection is not based on which calculation period is best tuned to get the most profit from these events. If you remove the profits or losses during the initial price shock from the historic test results, as shown in Table 22-1, the optimization would then show the best performers, net of price shocks. Because price shocks are unpredictable, selecting from a shock-adjusted result should yield a better trading system. Some traders might also prefer to use the identification of a price shock period to change the current trading strategy to one of *crisis management.*

GAMBLING TECHNIQUE—THE THEORY OF RUNS

The application of Gambling Theory to high-leveraged or short-term trading satisfies two important conditions. First, it presumes no statistical advantage in the occurrence of profits

TABLE 22-1 Results of Removing Price Shocks from 10-Year Historic Performance

	Trend System	Adjusted for Shocks	Percent Change
Crude oil	17.12	7.88	−52%
U.S. Treasury bonds	9.85	4.21	−57%
Deutschemark	14.92	5.97	−60%
British pound	20.56	10.85	−47%
S&P 500	−3.50	−4.25	n/a

and losses but concerns itself with the probable patterns. Each trade could be treated as an occurrence of red or black—up or down price moves or profits. Second, Gambling Theory stresses money management under adverse conditions. A successful professional gambler and an active trader must both be highly disciplined and conserve capital. This section will look at a gambler's approach to money management and risk, using the *Theory of Runs*.

If the assumption is made that each trade is unrelated to the previous trade or that each successive price has an equal chance of going up or down, the situation closely resembles roulette. In Monte Carlo, the roulette wheel has 37 compartments: 18 black, 18 red, and 1 white, assuring a loss of 2.7% in the same way that transaction costs are a handicap to trading. Continuously betting on only red or black will break even, less 2.7%, over long betting periods. The only way to change the odds is by money management—varying the size of the bets. Although the variables in trading are more complex, we will look at this first.

The most well-known method for winning in a gambling situation is based on the probability of successive wins, the Theory of Runs. On each spin of the wheel, the likelihood of the same color (red or black) reoccurring is 50%, or ½ (ignoring the white slot). To define a run of 3 reds, it is necessary to show a black on each side, that is,

Black-Red-Red-Red-Black

otherwise, the run may not be complete. If each color had a 50% chance of occurring, the probability of a run of 3 is

$$\frac{1}{2} \times \frac{1}{2} \times \frac{1}{2} \times \frac{1}{2} \times \frac{1}{2} = \left(\frac{1}{2}\right)^5$$

One run of 3 can be expected for every 32 spins of the wheel (called *coups*). Extending that to runs of n consecutive reds gives $(\frac{1}{2})^{n+2}$. For 256 coups, which is both a power of two and the approximate number of trading days in a year (if you consider daily closing prices rather than intraday trades), there are the following possibilities for runs of red:

Run of Length	Probability of Occurrence	Expected Number of Occurrences	Total Appearances of Red
1	$\frac{1}{8}$	32	32
2	$\frac{1}{18}$	16	32
3	$\frac{1}{32}$	8	24
4	$\frac{1}{64}$	4	16
5	$\frac{1}{128}$	2	10
6	$\frac{1}{256}$	1	6
			Total appearances: 120

A run of greater than 6 is not expected to occur. Notice, however, that the total appearances of red is only 120, short by 8. These 8 appearances could increase any of the runs from 1 through 6, or become a run of 7 or 8. The likelihood of a run greater than 6 is calculated using a geometric progression to get the sum of all probabilities greater than 6, or $(\frac{1}{2})^{n+2}$, where $256 \geq n \geq 7$:

$$P = (\frac{1}{2})^9 + (\frac{1}{2})^{10} + \cdots + (\frac{1}{2})^{256}$$

$$= \frac{(\frac{1}{2})^9}{1 - (\frac{1}{2})} = \frac{1}{256}$$

There is a single chance that there will be a run greater than 6 in 256 tries. The average length of a run greater than 6 turns out to be 8, based on the decreasing probability of occurrences of longer runs. The average length of all runs greater than n will be $n + 2$. That makes the table of runs complete, with the number of occurrences of red equal to 128.

Martingales and Anti-Martingales

The classic application of the Theory of Runs is called *Martingales*. In the simple version of this approach, an initial bet is doubled each time a loss occurs; whenever there is a win, the betting begins again at the initial size. To demonstrate how this works, it is necessary to use a table of uniform random numbers (which can be found in Appendix 1). These numbers vary from 0 through 9. Let all those numbers beginning with digits 0 through 4 be assigned to red and 5 through 9 to black. Figure 22-4, read left to right, where open squares are red and solid squares are black, shows the first 257 assignments according to Appendix 1. Assuming that we bet on black, losses will depend on the longest run of red. We must decide the size of the initial bet in advance, which should be as large as possible and still withstand the longest run of red that is likely to occur. By using the results from the analysis of the length of runs, we find that for every 256 coups, it is likely that only one run greater than 6 will occur, and that run would most probably be 8 in length. The probability of a run of 9 is $(\frac{1}{2})^{11}$, or 1 in 1,024. In 256 coups, the odds are about 3 to 1 against a run of 9 occurring.

Having decided that capitalization must withstand a run of 8, we calculate that a bet of $1 doubled 8 times is $128. Divide the maximum amount of money to be risked by 128 and the result is the size of the initial bet. Each $1,000 divided by 128 gives 7.8125, which must be rounded down to $7; therefore, on the eighth consecutive occurrence of red, the bet will be $897. Counting the occurrences of runs on the simulated roulette table (Table 22-2), it is interesting to see that a run of 8, but not 7, appears.

The results are within expectations, and no runs greater than 8 occurred in either red or black. For the purposes of this example, the betting would then proceed as shown in Figure 22-5, using an initial bet of $1. The numbers in the squares represent winning bets.

FIGURE 22-4 Sequence of random numbers representing occurrences of red and black.

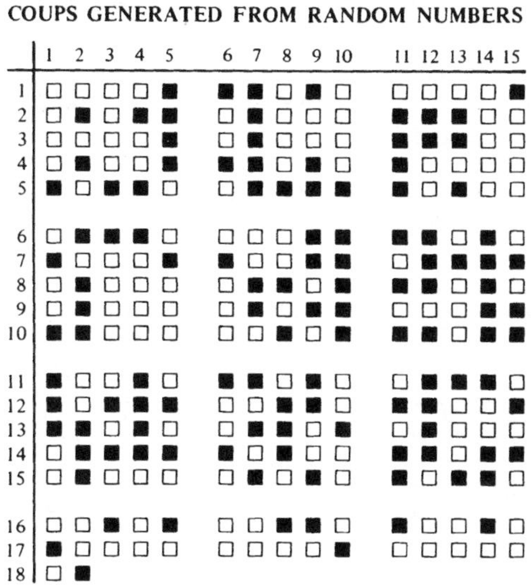

COUPS GENERATED FROM RANDOM NUMBERS

TABLE 22-2   Simulated Runs

Red	Black
35 runs of 1	35 runs of 1
12 runs of 2	14 runs of 2
7 runs of 3	11 runs of 3
7 runs of 4	3 runs of 4
2 runs of 5	2 runs of 5
2 runs of 6	
1 run of 8	
138 total occurrences	118 total occurrences

Every occurrence of black is a winner. Although $64 is actually won on a single black coup, each sequence of runs nets only the initial bet because of the accumulated losses during that sequence. For the 256 coups shown in Table 22-2, there were a total of 65 distinct runs resulting in a profit of $65 (or $455 based on a $7 initial bet), or about one-half of the initial capitalization ($128 or $1,000, respectively). Instead of using Martingales, if we had used the benchmark strategy of betting equal amounts on black to win on every coup, we would have lost $20 on a $1 bet. The Martingales method, therefore, has a good chance of winning a reasonable amount.[2]

Anti-Martingales

The *anti-Martingales* approach offers a smaller chance of winning a large amount; it is exactly the opposite of applying Martingales. Instead of doubling each losing bet, the winners are doubled until a goal is reached. Because there is an excellent chance of 1 run of 6 in 256 coups and a similar chance of a longer run, this method wins if the long run occurs in the first half of the number of coups to be played (256 in this case). Once a run of 6 occurs, you must immediately stop playing.

We already know that a run of 6 returns $32 on a bet of $1, and a run of 8 nets $128. This method would have lost if it had been applied to black in the test sequence; because there were 138 red coups with no black runs greater than 5, there would have been a loss of $138. If the bet had been on red, looking for a run of 6, there would have been three wins, each for $94, and a loss of $118 for that many appearances of black. Waiting for a run of 8 would have won $128 and lost $117 on black by stopping right after the win. The success of anti-Martingales depends on how soon the long run appears. In 4,096 coups, a run of 11 will occur once, returning $1,024 on a bet of $1. In the same 4,096 spins, there will

---

[2] The Martingales approach is likely to work if the player could withstand adverse runs of 11, but casinos tend to limit bets to amounts significantly less than 2^{10} times the minimum bet.

FIGURE 22-5   Betting pattern.

	1	2	3	4	5		6	7	8	9	10		11	12	13	14	15
1	1	2	4	8	[16]		[1]	[1]	1	[2]	1			2	4	8	16	[32]
2	1	[2]	1	[2]	[1]		1	[2]	1	2	4		[8]	[1]	[1]	1	2
3	4	8	16	32	[64]		1	[2]	1	2	4		[8]	[1]	[1]	1	2
4	4	[8]	1	2	[4]		[1]	[1]	1	[2]	1		[2]	1	2	4	8
5	[16]	1	[2]	[1]	1		2	[4]	[1]	[1]	[1]		[1]	1	[2]	1	2

be 2,048 losses, showing that if the long run happens in the middle of play, the method breaks even; if it occurs sooner, you win.

The Theory of Runs Applied to Trading

Before applying either Martingales or anti-Martingales to the markets, it must be determined whether the movement of prices up or down is as uniform as in the case of roulette. A simple test was performed on a combined set of 21 diverse futures markets. The combined results of all up and down runs are shown in Table 22-3. The expected occurrences of both up and down were twice the probability of either a red or black coup occurring.

Some differences between the random pattern previously used and actual results can be seen in Table 22-3. These futures markets show fewer runs of 1 and more frequent runs of 2; their tendency to fluctuate in a narrowing pattern around the expected (random) length of a run (Figure 22-6) may be due to the smaller sample of longer runs. The probabilities found here might be used to decide the chances of the next trading day continuing in the direction of the prior day's trend, noting that a 3- to 4-day run is as long as might be expected. The most interesting applications are in the betting strategies of the Martingales and anti-Martingales methods, applied to futures markets. The following sections show two possibilities.

Trading Daily Sequences

By combining the Theory of Runs with the direction of the trend, the chances of being on the correct side of the longest run are increased; and, the size of the price move in the direction of the trend may also tend to be larger. To give yourself the best chance of identifying the trend, it should be long-term. Assuming that the trend is up as determined from a chart or moving average, enter a long position on the close of a day in which the price moves lower.

If Martingales is used, double the position each day that prices move adversely. A single day in which prices move up should recoup all losses and net a reasonable profit. If the trend is sustained, there should be fewer days down and more days up, thereby yielding a better return to capitalization ratio. A variation on Martingales might include holding the trade for 2 consecutive days in the profitable direction because of the bias shown in the distribution of runs. Another variation would take profits while prices are moving in a favor-

TABLE 22-3 Expected Occurrences of Ups and Downs for a Diverse Set of Markets

Length of Run	Expected Probability of Occurrence	21 Markets Combined	
		Expected	Actual
1	1/2	1,225	1,214
2	1/4	612	620
3	1/8	306	311
4	1/16	153	167
5	1/32	77	67
6	1/64	38	41
7	1/128	19	16
8	1/256	10	5
9	1/512	5	3
>=10	1/1,024	4	5
Total tested			2,449

FIGURE 22-6   Actual futures movement compared with random movement.

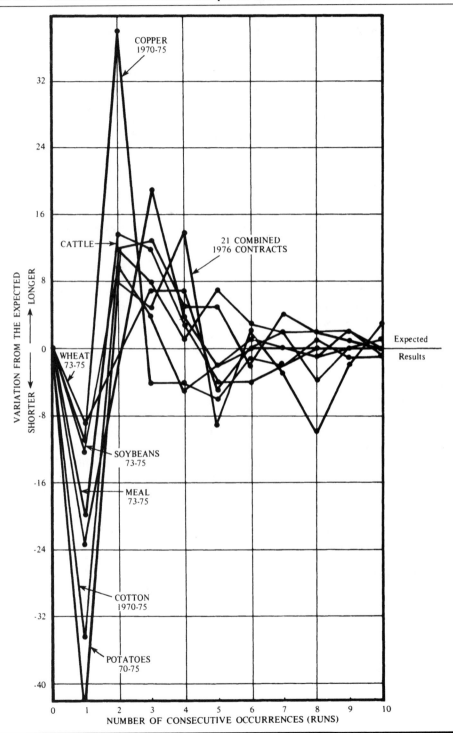

able direction and set new trend positions after 1 or even 2 days of price reversal. Either variation might improve the return ratio after a random occurrence of runs.

For the anti-Martingales approach, double the position after each profitable day, take profits after runs of 3, and begin again after a reversal day. By trading with the trend, profit sequences may be increased to 4 days; it may also be expected that, on average, the price change will be smaller on days that move counter to the trend.

System Trading

A standard trend-following system can expect 30% to 40% successful trades (called its *reliability*) of varying profitability, which can be defined in terms of a profit/loss ratio. In considering the Martingales or anti-Martingales methods, it should be noted that the lower probability of profitable trades would make the wait for a long run of profits less attractive. If a system has a profile of 35% successful trades and a profit/loss ratio of 3 : 1, then trading equal amounts on each signal results in the following, assuming $750 each profit and $250 each loss:

Total trades	$100 \times \$25$ (commission) = $-2,500
Profitable trades	$35 \times \$750 = \$26,250$
Losing trades	$65 \times \$250 = \$-16,250$
Net ($75 per trade)	$7,500

Taking these same figures and applying Martingales to a uniform sequence of two losses and one profit gives $275 as the first loss ($250 plus a $25 commission), $550 for the second loss, then $2,175 for the profit, netting $1,375 for three trades, which would return $229 per contract traded.

The disadvantage of applying Martingales to the irregular returns of high-leverage markets is that a long run of losing trades requires a large amount of capital. If it is necessary to keep a large reserve in the event of a long run of losses, why not simply trade equal amounts of a larger position on each signal, without using Martingales? A sound trading strategy should differ from a pure gambling situation because a specific system will win in the long term, while you will lose at roulette. The results show that trading the same larger position on each signal will return a higher profit than an application of Martingales, which requires the same available capital; however, a less aggressive betting method that assumes favorable odds can improve the return on investment.

In another study of applying Martingales, an actual trading system based on Wilder's RSI was used to create buy and sell signals.[3] During the test, a total of 277 contracts were held at one point, which is far beyond the realm of the normal speculator. That means an investment of 277 times the initial margin, plus any accumulated loss, just to recover one unit of your initial margin! It should not be surprising that the risk-to-reward ratio of this betting method was found to be unacceptably large.

Complex Martingales

The simple Martingales discussed do not present an attractive way of managing risk; however, a slightly more complex form is far more practical and has very different results. Instead of doubling the bet each time there is a loss, as in the case of simple Martingales, increase the bet by a smaller amount, for example, 40%.[4] This slows down the process and avoids the risk of ruin, or table limits. You may even choose to divide one bet into more than

---

[3] Roger Altman, "Tactical Trading Revisited," *Technical Analysis of Stocks & Commodities* (September 1993).

[4] James William Furguson, "Martingales," *Technical Analysis of Stocks & Commodities* (February 1990); and "Reverse Martingales," *Technical Analysis of Stocks & Commodities* (March 1990).

one, so that a situation in which you would trade 8 contracts may be traded in two trades of 4 each. You must simply remember to stop the sequence and begin again when your profits have exceeded your losses. In the following example, each loss is followed by increasing the bet by an equal amount. When a profit occurs, the bet size is reduced by one unit and the sequence ends when there is a net profit. Profits and losses are equal to the bet size.

EXAMPLE 1   Equal-Size Bets with Equal Payoff

Bet	Amount	Result	Net Profit or Loss
#1	$500	Loss	−$500
#2	$1,000	Loss	−$1,500
#3	$1,500	Loss	−$3,000
#4	$2,000	Profit	−$1,000
#5	$1,500	Profit	$500

In Example 1, it was necessary to win twice to realize a profit the size of the original investment; however, that profit could be achieved with 40% winning trades and 60% losing trades.

Applying this strategy to a more realistic trading profile, consider a system with an average loss of $1,000, an average profit of $2,000, and a win to loss ratio of 1 to 3. This means that there are 2 losses and 1 profit in every 3 trades, a net system result of zero, equivalent to a gambling situation. Example 2 shows another sequence of trades. Even though there are 3 losses to start, a single win nets a profit for the sequence.

EXAMPLE 2   Equal-Size Bets with a Trading System Profile

Bet	No. of Units Bet	Result	Net Profit or Loss
#1	1	Loss	−$1,000
#2	2	Loss	−$3,000
#3	3	Loss	−$6,000
#4	4	Profit	$2,000

When applying a more complex form to reverse Martingales, it is best to target sequences of profitable runs that are likely to occur with reasonable frequency. Instead of betting the entire accumulated profit on the next trade, bet a fixed percentage of those profits. Alternatively, if you are looking for profitable runs of 4, remove the amount of the initial bet from the total bet after the system has returned two profits in sequence. This tends to conserve capital but slows down the process.

SELECTIVE TRADING

It may be unrealistic to think that you can always follow a technical, fully automatic system without manual intervention. Overriding system signals may occur for reasons of sound risk management during a crisis period when you feel that the system is not programmed to deal with the current volatility and that a conservative action is the best business policy.

The beginning system trader often has concerns that the impersonal buy and sell orders will not react properly to the underlying forces that are driving prices. This can cause the trader to override the system signals. For example, if the program is geared to take profits after a move of 2%, the trader might judge that the current price move is going to continue; therefore, he will hold the trade rather than take profits. The application of this special *intuitive* filter generally favors holding a position through ups and downs until it shows a profit, rather than applying consistently good risk management. Judgment tends to interpret all news in favor of the position being held until it shows a profit. A trader who will survive must learn not to take a loss personally, to keep losses small, to establish and stay with a trading plan, and to filter out unsupported opinions. Trading is a business, and business principles must apply.

Technical systems can be taken to extremes in an effort to automatically select only profitable trades. Two approaches to this are most common. The use of more than one trend indicator, such as two moving averages, is one method of isolating the best trend. It is intended to find a smaller piece of a trend that is more reliable or one that performs better than a single, longer trend. In principle, it is no different from using three, four, or more trends of different periods to isolate the one point of a price move that always generates profits. As you become more and more selective, you will find that your opportunities have disappeared, you have used your capital poorly, and the performance profile has actually deteriorated. Using multiple trends, just as any system with many rules, is another attempt at perfection, but only succeeds at overfitting the problem.

There are many systems that can be bought that promise profits. Trying to incorporate a black-box approach, a method that does not disclose its exact rules, to improve the performance of your own program is not a good idea. Without knowing everything about the other system, there may be inadvertent duplication of a faster trend, a 3-day cycle, or some other feature. You may think that an analysis of the correlation of results between the black-box system and your own method will show if the methods work well together, but there are still too many uncertainties. The unknown system may have been overfitted and will not show its real risk, or it may have a particular weakness to a market pattern that has not occurred during your testing period. You must understand every method that you trade. It's your risk.

The best way to create a successful trading system is to look for unique elements, each with a sound basis, and combine them one at a time, testing each to be sure they successfully stand on their own. The selection of the speed of a moving average will be more important than either the smoothing technique or the number of moving averages to be used. There may be an advantage to the double moving average approach, but a third, fourth, and so on, lose their significance. A momentum indicator bears a close resemblance to a moving average when its rules are to buy or sell in the direction of the price move, especially when it crosses the zero line. Both have great similarities and will not offer much diversification when applied to the same data. Each system building block should be fundamentally different. A technique, such as a breakout method, that does not depend on time would be a sensible complement to a moving average, which is driven by time. The more complicated cycle and wave theories, contrary opinion, and other methods all view price movement in a completely different way than a moving average, even when applied to the same data. The same moving averages may make the most sense when you apply the same period to different types of data, such as volume and open interest, or compare two related series, such as the Swiss franc and German bund exchange rates.

Filtering is a tool not restricted to price analysis, but applicable to money management, reliability, risk, portfolio selection, and other aspects of a trading program. Selection of which markets to trade and position size is as important as the buy and sell signals. If the system itself corrects for high-volatility markets by decreasing the distance of the stop-loss point (keeping the risk constant), it would be redundant to trade fewer positions of that market, thereby reducing the effects of any profits or losses relative to other items in a portfolio.

SYSTEM TRADE-OFFS

Although traders are continually searching for a system that has no losses, they are realistic enough to know that most profit, loss, and risk decisions are dependent on one another. Just as in Gambling Theory, a system can be structured to have frequent small losses and occasional large profits—or frequent small profits with some large losses. It is simply not possible to create a system with such small losses that these losses are essentially zero without increasing the frequency of the losses to the point at which profits rarely occur. In short-term or high-leveraged trading, the *cost of doing business* prevents such an approach from working.

The basic principles of systematic trading require that the trader choose between the frequency of profits to losses, the relative size of those profits and losses, and the number of opportunities that will be available to trade. These interrelationships will be different for various types of systems.

Trend-Following Systems

The relative risks and rewards of a trend-following system are based primarily on the selection of the trend speed. As an example, using a simple moving average system applied to closing prices, Figure 22-7 shows that a faster moving average (smaller number of days) will stay closer to the current price than a moving average that uses a larger number of days. The maximum risk is equal to the largest lag, as measured from the current price to the corresponding moving average value. This lag is limited by:

$$M = P - (L \times N)/2$$

where P is the current closing price, L is the limit move or 3 standard deviations of the average daily true range, and N is the number of days in the moving average.

The smaller losses of the faster trend system are kept in proportion to the profits because of the relative system sensitivity. The price changes of smaller magnitude, which cause the moving average to change direction and hold losses to a minimum, also break the sustained trends into shorter movements. The net results are more frequent trades with relatively small losses and modest profits. Longer-term trends cause fewer trades by

---

FIGURE 22-7   Relative risk of a moving average system.

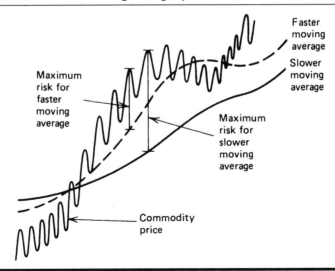

holding to the market direction for a longer time. This results in larger profits and correspondingly larger losses.

The risk of a single trade being small or large is not a complete measure of trading risk. Because there are more losses than profits in normal trend-following systems, it is important to consider the sequence of losses as part of the ultimate risk of trading. It is the aggregation of these losses that provides a reasonable comparison in determining whether a slow or fast moving average system has the best profit to loss ratio.

The feature of a trend system that is most appealing is the small losses relative to large profits. This feature also causes frequent small losses during sideways markets, and the number of these false signals cannot be significantly reduced simply by using a longer-term trend. Testing will show that there is always some sideways price movement that coincides with the trendline, resulting in a high percentage of whipsaw losses. It is unrealistic to expect a smoothing technique to produce more than 40% to 45% profitable trades.

Countertrend Systems

The risk and reward structure of a countertrend method is different from that of a trend-following approach. Although the size of your profits and losses relates to the time period of analysis in a manner similar to trend following, positions must be set in advance of an expected price reversal. This clearly introduces more risk and makes the success of the method dependent upon good timing. When countertrend methods are discussed here, those techniques that require a confirmation (i.e., they wait until prices reverse their direction) are not included as countertrend systems.

Due to the greater risk of a countertrend system, its objectives are generally well defined. In a trend system you let the profits run until prices reverse; however, most countertrend methods rely on an oscillator, contrary opinion, or an overbought/oversold analysis, and set goals for exiting when the overbought or oversold condition disappears. This results in a profile that limits profits; therefore, it should not also limit losses.

Trade-Offs

The selection of a performance profile goes together with particular trading styles. Some combinations are entirely incompatible. Ideally, you would want very large profits, high reliability, and small losses. Unfortunately, these combinations are not possible. The trade-offs that are readily available are:

1. A few large profits and frequent small losses
2. Many small profits and a few large losses
3. More opportunities with greater risk
4. Fewer opportunities with less risk

It is easy to identify the first combination with trend following. To have fewer losses you must allow greater risk. Keeping losses small means being stopped out because of market noise rather than underlying trend; therefore, you can expect many more losses than profits. In the case of a countertrend system you might profit from market noise, which accounts for a large percentage of the price variability. The moves caused by market noise are also much smaller and more frequent than trend moves. To profit from noise you must enter the market while prices are going in the opposite direction, as in a countertrend technique, and allow more risk. This causes the profile in option 2, many small profits and a few large losses.

The last two choices are the result of a random distribution of price moves. If you look back at the study of runs, you will remember that price changes exhibit a pattern very similar to random movement. For every 100 days of prices, there will be 50 days in which prices reversed after only 1 day of up or down movement, 25 days of price movement in the same direction for 2 consecutive days, 12.5 days for 3 consecutive days, and so on. Although real price patterns may vary slightly from that distribution, they are very close. For any fixed time period, these patterns remain the same; that is, there are always more opportunities for smaller moves than larger ones. To hold a trade for the long term, you must be able to withstand all of the market noise that might occur during that period. The longer you hold a trade, the greater chance you will see larger market noise, or adverse price moves.

You can see how this applies to a countertrend trading using a typical price oscillator. Figure 22-8 shows the fluctuations of a sideways market, one that has no trend bias. Assuming that there is a normal distribution of prices, there is a clustering near the center and less frequent peaks and valleys as prices move further away from the middle. Construct an overbought/oversold indicator, which can be categorized as *slightly* (S), *moderately* (M), or *extremely* (E) overbought or oversold, by drawing lines on Figure 22-8.

It can be seen that there are more opportunities to buy a *slightly oversold* market and sell a *slightly overbought* market; all prices must pass through the area closest to the center before reaching a more overbought or oversold condition. Therefore, the *opportunities* must increase as profit goals decrease. But what about the risk? If profits are limited, risk must be restricted to a small part of the potential profits, or not limited by a dollar amount but by a patterned condition. In this countertrend system example, an attempt to make losses small relative to profits entered during the slightly oversold zone would cause the number of losses to increase dramatically, overwhelming the potential profits (seen in Figure 22-8). If losses are not restricted, they will be larger when there are more opportunities with smaller price objectives, and smaller for the fewer cases when prices are in the *extreme* zone. The minimum risk occurs on a single trade taken at the absolute extreme points. Figure 22-9 shows the relationships that exist in a standard countertrend system.

All systems have trade-offs. To reduce the losses, either the profits or the frequency of opportunities must be reduced whether the trading approach favors the trend or countertrend. A trend follower looking for the big move must also take a big risk. In the development of a system or trading philosophy, personal preference determines the combination of risk, reward, and opportunity.

The Commodex Method of Combining Elements

The *Commodex* system was first presented in 1959 and is still active, published daily by *Commodity Futures Forecast* in New York. Commodex combines the components most acceptable to the experienced trader in a unique weighting method. It includes moving averages, price momentum, and open interest to calculate a trend index.

The most interesting aspect of the Commodex system is its ranking process, intended to produce a relative strength value for each trend. Using a 10- and 20-day double moving

FIGURE 22-8   Countertrend alternatives using detrended price series.

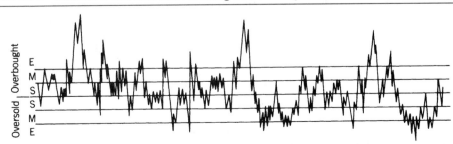

FIGURE 22-9   Relationship of profits to risk per trade based on opportunities.

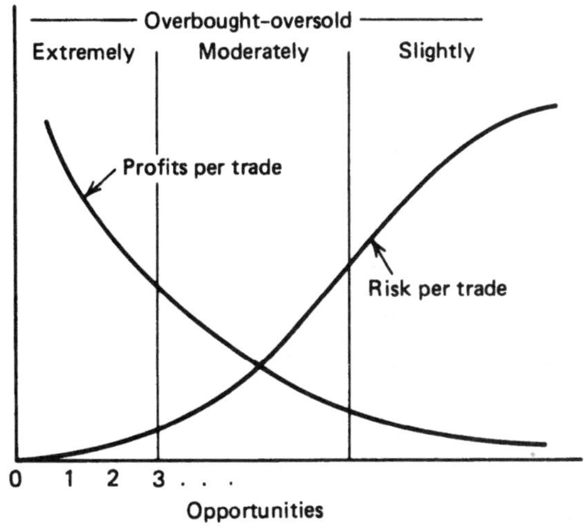

average, the system scores the current market performance to establish the value of the trending component. Bullish and bearish values are calculated by looking at three situations independently: the simple moving average signals derived from both the long- and short-term trends, and the double moving average signal generated by combining the two trends. The two techniques of single and double moving averages are exactly as treated in Chapter 5. The most important of the three factors is the long-term trend; second is the short-term trend, and last the relative position of the fast to the slow moving average. The strongest upward-moving trend is generated when current prices are above both the faster- and slower-moving averages and the faster average is below the slower. The opposite positions would result in the strongest downward-trending component. Trends are considered neutral if the most important element, the long-term moving average, conflicts with the other two factors.

The rate of change in open interest is considered a secondary reinforcement of the trend. Using a concept different from the usual charting techniques, Commodex considers it a bullish sign if there is an increasing *growth momentum* in open interest combined with rising prices. The growth momentum is the difference between the rate of increase of the open interest and the 20-day moving average of the open interest. Continuing a bull move with rising prices and rising open interest is a classic concept of charting. The bear move is confirmed with rising open interest and falling prices. Commodex also considers a drop in open interest along with falling prices to be a bullish factor. The movement of volume is treated in the same manner as open interest and can confirm a bull or bear trend. An increasing volume momentum with rising prices is support of an upward move; other combinations indicate bear trends.

Added together, the signals are ranked from a strong *buy* to a strong *sell* with lesser degrees in between. The system must be given credit for the quantification and balancing of these elements, which are generally treated as highly interpretive charting techniques. The rules for applying the daily signals to trading combine both the individual strength of the signal with the movement of the Commodex trend index. The trend index itself acts as an overbought-oversold indicator, encouraging profits at specified levels and considering a position reversal in more extreme situations; stops are placed using the 20-day moving average with predetermined band penetrations. Additional objectives are based on the profits accrued from a trade, with a 50% return justifying a protective stop on part of the positions, and a 100% profit requiring the liquidation of half the position. These money management concepts are an important aspect of any system and tend to round out Commodex.

The Commodex system has been used as an example of combining techniques that have been studied individually in previous sections. It is important to see that each element is simple to understand and avoids duplication; it has single and double moving averages (with and without bands), momentum indicators derived from volume and open interest, an overbought-oversold indicator formed from a combination of all elements, trading stops, and liquidation based on money management and inverse pyramiding.

Combining Trends and Trading Ranges

Trends and trading ranges account for most price movement; a small percentage cannot be identified. Most traders must decide whether they intend to profit from trend moves or sideways markets and then develop techniques that target that objective. A trend is concerned with the periodic tendency of prices to move in one direction without a limiting objective, and a trading range is a definition of price containment. The role of time is different for the two approaches. The trend is expected to advance with some regularity over time, while prices within a trading range can move in any direction with varying speed, providing the upper and lower bounds are not violated.

Trading ranges and trends take turns dominating price movement, with the trading range most common. Long-term trends are easy to see, as for example, represented in the buying power of the U.S. dollar and the Consumer Price Index. When there is no actual or anticipated change in fundamental factors, prices fluctuate in a restricted range, bounded by *support* and *resistance* levels. The top of a trading range is often wider than the bottom because of the inherently greater volatility at higher prices; but even with the broader formation, there is a clear point at which prices have gone higher and are no longer within the trading range.

It often happens that the two techniques of price trend and trading ranges are in conflict: The trend is up and a resistance level is encountered, or the downtrend is stopped by a support level. Established support and resistance levels cannot be ignored, neither can a major trend; it makes sense to combine both features. The simplest way is to use the trading range while prices are within that area and follow the trend when prices break out either above or below (Figure 22-10).

The exact rules depend on the size of the trading range, the speed of the trend, and whether the support and resistance levels have been established over time. Recent range formations offer less of an obstacle than those that have survived for some time. If the range is narrow, a moving average buy or sell signal invariably occurs at the resistance or support level and is met with an initial reversal. For a larger range, a medium-speed moving average signal may occur closer to the center of the range and allow some opportunity for trend profit before resistance is encountered. For very wide ranges, there may be ample latitude for a moving average to signal entry and closeout without the interference of support and resistance levels. One method of combining the two techniques is to use whichever signal is generated, regardless of the system. The following combinations of short position entry and exit are possible for medium to wide ranges:

1. Enter a new short position when the moving average turns down.
2. Enter a new short position when prices enter the sell zone around the resistance level.
3. Enter a new short position when prices fall below the support area, then close out the short position when the moving average turns up.

FIGURE 22-10   Combining trends and trading ranges.

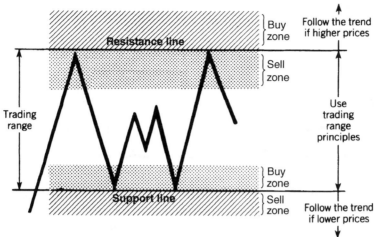

4. Close out a short position when prices enter the buy zone above the support level.
5. Close out a short position when prices break through a resistance level moving up.

The same rules apply in reverse for long positions. The advantage of this filtering method is that new short trades are not entered at support levels, which causes immediate losses or prolonged trades of little result.

TRADING LIMITS—A DAMPENING EFFECT

The existence of trading limits in some of the U.S. markets has always been the concern of novice speculators who seem convinced that their first entry into the market will result in an adverse locked-limit move, stripping them of their future and happiness overnight. There is no doubt that many people have suffered from being caught on the wrong side of a move, but trading limits would tend to protect rather than harm them. The limits established by the exchanges are intended to allow free trading within the normal range of price fluctuation. While the agricultural markets still have traditional daily limits, the financial markets have gone to a system of suspending trading for a short period, then reopening with larger limits. If properly established, these limits should rarely be reached. As prices rise, the volatility of the market increases, and so the limits must be expanded to correspond to the new price range. At this point, trading risks become proportionately greater and margins are raised.

The purpose of limits is to prevent an immediate reaction to unexpected news from moving prices to unjustifiable levels. The first reaction to bad news is usually more extreme than is realistic, and when proper assessment of the problem is completed, the results are rarely as bad as initially thought. Limits also serve to give the losing trader more time to capitalize the position, or meet a margin call, rather than be forced to liquidate.

Frequency of Limit Moves

Sugar prices, which had a spectacular rise in 1974, can serve as an extreme case of changing volatility. Beginning in 1969, Table 22-4 shows the remarkable price move seen in the frequency of limit moves. The contracts shown have no duplicate dates and do not include the actual delivery month.

TABLE 22-4   Frequency of Limit Moves

	Total Days Examined	Days Closing at Limit	Percentage of Limit Closes	Range of Closing Prices	Exchange Limits (¢/lb)
Sep 70	248	0	.0	2.91–4.01	.50
Sep 71	249	0	.0	2.74–5.08	.50
Sep 72	240	18	7.5	4.26–9.17	.50
Sep 73	239	9	3.8	5.44–10.50	.50
Sep 74	239	40	16.7	7.56–28.15	.50–2.00
Sep 75	239	54	22.6	11.51–50.82	1.00–2.00
Sep 76	238	3	1.3	12.07–18.65	1.00

The obvious conclusion to be drawn from the pattern of the sugar market is that limits did not expand quickly enough at higher price levels. In 1975, 22.6% of all trading days closed at the limit; at low price levels, the limits were of no consequence. The 1974 price of sugar increased by 15 times its 1969 price, while the limits only expanded from 50 to 200 points, a factor of four. Limits present a problem for a trading system because they artificially alter the volatility of the market. The consolation is that a trading system is useless in a market that is locked-limit for a week. You might find it enlightening to test your system on a market and period where limit moves were evident to see their effect on signals and performance.

The only realistic way of comparing the effects of limit moves against a limitless market is to compare the U.S. and London exchanges. Using the May 77 Coffee contract for the month of February 1977, we can show three separate examples of limit moves in the U.S. contracts and the corresponding London action. Figure 22-11 illustrates the closing prices of the two markets on the same day. Two problems must be considered: the conversion of sterling to U.S. dollars, which was fixed at $1.70 for the entire comparison, and the overlapping hours of the New York Coffee and Sugar Exchange and the London Sugar Exchange. The exchange hours may have some difference in the daily price but should not appreciably affect the comparison.

The first U.S. locked-limit day was on February 7, when the New York coffee prices for the May 77 contract moved to 230.82 (up 300 points). On the same day, London prices for the May 77 contract moved from 218.80 to 230.56 (actually 2883 to 3038 sterling). A trader who closed out his position on the open in the London market would have taken a fill of 2850 and a loss of 12.67 cents per pound relative to the U.S. market. The traders locked into their New York position could have gotten out on the open on February 8 at 233.50, a loss of 568 points. Had both the U.S. and London traders waited for the closing prices as shown in Figure 22-9, the corresponding losses would have been reduced to 1176 points in London and 318 points in New York.

The second case was on February 17 and 18 when the U.S. market stayed locked at the limit for 2 days. A trader entering the market in London on the prior day at 241.91 (3187.50 sterling) could have gotten out on the next day at 247.07 (3255.07) for a loss of 516 points. The corresponding New York trader would have entered at 246.00 and exited at 254.50 for a loss of 810 points.

Remarkably, the London coffee prices had moved to 252.04 by the time the New York market was trading again. London prices had gained 1013 points during the time that a locked-limit U.S. market gained only 850 points. In both cases, the volatility of the London market with no limits was much greater than the U.S. equivalent, and the results do not show any disadvantage to trading limits.

FIGURE 22-11 Comparing limit moves in U.S. and London coffee markets.

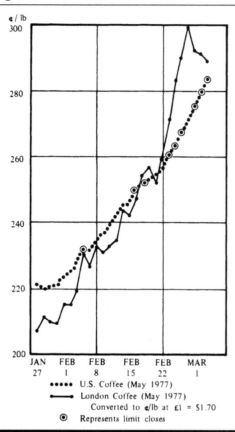

¢ / lb

U.S. Coffee (May 1977)
London Coffee (May 1977)
Converted to ¢/lb at £1 = $1.70
Represents limit closes

The third case of locked-limit moves began on February 24. On the day prior to the first locked-limit day, the U.S. market traded actively even after the London Exchange moved up an equivalent of 698 points. There should have been ample time that day or even the prior day, when the U.S. market traded at the limit but closed lower, for any trader to exit an undesirable position. Figure 22-11 shows the larger moves of the London market peaking and starting down to meet the plodding U.S. prices. The market with no limits has overreacted to the bullish news by at least 1,000 points. Of course, for traders who didn't get out of New York coffee soon enough, the overreaction of the London market was not very gratifying.

Changing the Rules

Due to the frequency of locked-limit moves during the exceptional periods, and the need to keep changing them as inflation forced prices higher, most exchanges have changed the way daily trading limits are established. At one time, an exchange committee was convened to review limits; now, limits automatically expand to meet conditions. The S&P, along with some other financial markets, have *circuit breakers* that cause the market to halt when specific limits are reached. After a short pause they reopen and can trade to new levels before another circuit breaker is activated. At an extreme level, however, the S&P will also stop trading, putting it in the same situation as New York coffee versus London coffee. The years have changed but the problems remain the same.

The normal policy for agricultural markets is that, following a trading day in which prices closed at the limit, limits expand to 1½ their initial value. They may remain at this level for 1 or 2 days, provided prices continue to close at either limit (higher or lower). Limits will then expand to twice the initial range; if a locked-limit move persists, limits are entirely removed for 1 day. After this, or after any day that prices do not close at the limit, the pattern begins again with the initial limit value. Occasionally, the initial value may be altered by the exchange.

GOING TO EXTREMES

In 1974, public awareness of inflation caused an overwhelming interest in all forms of hedging, with large numbers of naive investors purchasing silver and gold as currency protection. Many sophisticated investors turned to the futures markets, which offered leverage on their purchases; some learned how to use the markets themselves and others relied on advice.

One investment system that was sold at this time was more of a leveraged substitute for the purchase of bouillon than a trading strategy. At the time it was published, it had always worked—the sponsor of the system stood behind it with his reputation. The rules of the system were:

1. Trade silver futures because of their intrinsic value, historic performance, potential, and fundamental demand with short supply.
2. Use the futures contract between 3 and 7 months from delivery to combine the advantages of liquidity and duration.
3. Always buy, never sell, because it is always successful.
4. Buy whenever you like. Although any sophisticated method can be used, it won't matter in the long run—any guess will do just as well. Follow the same method for adding to positions or reentering after closing out a trade.
5. Close out the position when there is a profit, not before.
6. Meet all margin calls—don't let the market beat you.
7. Invest $5,000 per contract (5,000 troy ounces). This will allow a $1-per-ounce adverse move (silver was at $4.50 per ounce).
8. Whenever you need reinforcement, reread the reasoning behind this system.
9. Do not let anyone or anything interfere with following this system.

How did the investors do? It depended on when they started. Entering in the first half of 1975, shortly after the system was released, showed individual contract returns ranging from profits of 51¢ to losses of 18¢ per ounce. A drop in silver prices then produced losses of up to $1.02 per ounce for the next 9 months (slightly over 100%), followed by a 2-month rally, and losses again. This system would have worked from 1979 to February 1980 and then lost for the next 15 years. An investor following these rules, entering at a chance place would have had more than a 10 : 1 likelihood of losing. Any profit made would have been given back if the investor persisted in following the method.

In trying to understand how a system such as this can have a chance of reaching the public, remember the time in which it was introduced. With prices increasing drastically, food shortages, and publicity over the devaluing U.S. dollar, the rationale of the system seemed justifiable. There was serious talk about leveraged *inflation funds* using futures. These systems fill an immediate need, without regard to long-term consequences. There is no doubt that, if high inflation returns, systems just like this one will reappear. Given the bull market in stocks for the past 20 years, it is surprising that more of these systems are not in evidence. With only small changes in the nine rules for trading silver, we could create a scenario that would be very believable to many people looking to enter the stock market.

SIMILARITY OF SYSTEMS

A primary concern of both the government regulatory agency (CFTC) and individual traders is the similarity of computer-based systems that are used to manage large positions. If the propagation of technical trading systems has similar foundation and testing methods, it is possible that many of them will produce buy and sell signals on nearly the same day. That is, these systems may appear different in their rules and parameters, but they could be essentially quite similar—too many people looking at the same markets and using the same tools.

First, consider the extreme case in which two systems with the same trend-following philosophy have the same profit over the same period of time. Will the signals occur on the same day? Are they on the same side of the market most of the time? Figure 22-12 shows one combination that has a low correlation given this situation.

System *A* is a slow trend-following method, which avoids the choppy markets but nets only a small profit. System *B* jumps in and out, capturing profits quickly but with frequent losses. They both return the same profits. System *B* is on the same side of the market as *A* about 50% of the time because the overall trend was up; therefore, it cannot be negatively correlated, but it could have a low positive correlation. If system *B* were not as fast as in this illustration, the positive correlation would be greater. As the time periods used for calculation become closer, the correlation increases.

If computer-based, trend-following systems with different calculation periods are not highly correlated, then it is possible to reduce portfolio risk by trading a variety of different techniques and time periods; however, the reality of the issue may be different from the theory. Lukac, Brorsen, and Irvin[5] performed such a study. They compared 12 popular trading techniques (mostly trend-following) over 12 varied futures markets for the years 1978 to 1984. Each system was optimized, using 3 years of data, and the best parameters used to trade the next year. The systems selected were

1. *Channel systems*
    a. Closing price channel (CHL)
    b. MII price channel (MII)
    c. L-S-O price channel (LSO)

---

[5] Louis P. Lukac, G. Wade Brorsen, and Scott H. Irwin, *Similarity of Computer Guided Technical Trading Systems* (CSFM-124, Working Paper Series, Columbia Futures Center, Columbia University Business School, New York, March 1986). Also by the same authors, "Do similar signals from trading systems move prices?" *Futures* (November 1987).

FIGURE 22-12   Two trend-following systems with low correlation.

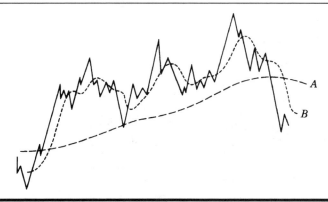

   2. *Momentum/oscillators*

      a. Directional indicator (DRI)
      b. Directional movement (DRM)
      c. Range quotient (RNQ)
      d. Reference deviation (REF)

   3. *Moving averages*

      a. Moving average with percent band (MAB)
      b. Dual moving average (DMC)

   4. *Systems with trailing stops*

      a. Parabolic Time/Price System (PAR)
      b. Alexander's Filter Rule (ALX)
      c. Combined Directional Movement and Parabolic Time/Price System (DRP)

The study used three measures to test system similarity:

   1. The percentage of the time that systems are on the same side of the market (long or short)
   2. The percentage of buy or sell signals that occurred on the same day, or within a few days of one another
   3. The correlation of aggregate monthly portfolio returns

The results show a significant positive correlation in the system profitability (Table 22-5). However, there is no pattern that shows that one particular type of system is notably more correlated than others. The Parabolic and Directional Parabolic systems are most similar because one is based on the other.

Only four of the systems were significantly profitable: CHL, MII, DRP, and DMC. The correlations of those systems do not seem any more significant than others that were not profitable. In Table 22-6, the percentage of trades that occur on the same day is very low. A more informative comparison is seen in Table 22-7, which tallies the percentage of days that each system held the same position. This last table is a practical way of finding the performance correlations.

TABLE 22-5 Correlations of Aggregate Monthly Returns from 12 Systems

System	Trading System										
	CHL	PAR	DRM	RNQ	DRP	MII	LSO	REF	DMC	DRI	MAB
PAR	0.57										
DRM	0.72	0.61									
RNQ	0.70	0.41	0.70								
DRP	0.65	0.81	0.79	0.57							
MII	0.75	0.54	0.67	0.73	0.67						
LSO	0.59	0.43	0.53	0.68	0.54	0.70					
REF	0.55	0.37	0.57	0.66	0.52	0.54	0.60				
DMC	0.72	0.41	0.68	0.78	0.55	0.74	0.58	0.57			
DRI	0.71	0.42	0.69	0.77	0.55	0.70	0.59	0.66	0.64		
MAB	0.72	0.55	0.75	0.74	0.69	0.69	0.63	0.60	0.78	0.72	
ALX	0.58	0.55	0.62	0.55	0.57	0.57	0.58	0.51	0.52	0.56	0.57

All coefficients significant at the 0.01% level with the exception of REF and PAR coefficient, which is significant at the 0.05% level.

Source: Reprinted with permission of *Futures Magazine*, 250 S. Wacker Drive, #1150, Chicago, IL 60606, (November 1987).

TABLE 22-6   Percent of Trades That Occur on the Same Day

System		Trading System									
	CHL	PAR	DRM	RNQ	DRP	MII	LSO	REF	DMC	DRI	MAB
PAR	19*										
DRM	25**	21**									
RNQ	22**	9	15								
DRP	30**	93**	48**	10							
MII	20*	15	10	28**	17						
LSO	22**	13	17	27**	18	23**					
REF	12	7	7	11	9	12	14				
DMC	16	6	8	28**	6	12	18	19*			
DRI	18	9	14	38**	10	32**	22**	15	25**		
MAB	28**	18	23**	23**	27**	18	25**	11	19*	23**	
ALX	12	20*	12	19*	20*	9	17	10	10	16	17

Percent of trades that occur on the same day by each pair of systems. Significance assuming a binomial distribution with * denoting 95% confidence limits and ** denoting 99% confidence limits.

Source: Reprinted with permission of *Futures Magazine,* 250 S. Wacker Drive, #1150, Chicago, IL 60606 (November 1987).

The study concludes that computer-based systems *trade on the same day significantly more often than would randomly be expected, but the actual percentage of trades that occur on the same day is small.* These systems have the potential to move market prices, but the trades do not often occur at the same time. One must be concerned, however, if trend-following systems are holding the same position 75% of the time, they must compete with each other when they exit, even if that occurs over a period of a few days. Trading signals that occur at the exact same time may not be necessary to push the market.

Correlation When You Don't Need It

There is often a theoretical answer and a practical one to the same question. There is no doubt that a variety of trend-following systems generate trading signals at different price

TABLE 22-7   Percent of Trading Days Systems Hold the Same Positions

System		Trading System									
	CHL	PAR	DRM	RNQ	DRP	MII	LSO	REF	DMC	DRI	MAB
PAR	70										
DRM	82	76									
RNQ	75	61	73								
DRP	68	83	75	59							
MII	82	69	80	75	65						
LSO	73	58	71	73	57	73					
REF	72	57	69	69	55	72	69				
DMC	81	62	77	79	61	79	76	78			
DRI	70	56	68	72	54	71	69	67	73		
MAB	65	54	66	62	53	63	61	57	65	59	
ALX	72	64	71	68	59	73	65	67	73	63	58

Percent of the trading days each pair of systems is on the same side of the market (long or short) at the same time. All coefficients are significant, assuming a binomial distribution with 99% confidence limits.

Source: Reprinted with permission of *Futures Magazine,* 250 S. Wacker Drive, #1150, Chicago, IL 60606 (November 1987).

levels, some nearer to each other and some farther away. During active, high-volume trading periods, a few of these systems can give buy signals without causing prices to move and other trending systems to be triggered. During sessions with light volume, it is more likely that a system traded with a large position will cause piggy-backing by others, resulting in a price spike that disappears once all the systems have kicked in.

The worst case is a price shock. Although not caused by systems, all trend systems not holding a position in the direction of the shock will get signals to enter at the same time, the result of a large price jump. The correlations mean very little and only diversification using different trading philosophies, rather than time periods, would help. Although relatively infrequent, large price shocks can be fatal. When designing your trading strategy, keep the practical issues of diversification and risk management always in sight.

Risk Control

A trading system alone will not assure success without proper risk control beginning with each trade and continuing until a portfolio of different trading methods is created. Systems have losing streaks that will ruin any investor with inadequate resources and poor timing; a speculator must decide the initial capitalization, the markets to trade, and when to increase or decrease leverage. There are risks that can be controlled or reduced, called *systematic risk,* and another called *market risk,* that can take the form of a price shock and can never be eliminated.

This chapter tries to cover a broad range of topics relating to risk, including individual trade risk, leverage, portfolio diversification and allocation, price shocks, and catastrophic risk. It is not possible to say that one is more important than another. In a specific situation, any one of the areas discussed may be the answer to preventing substantial loss. The first part of this chapter discusses capitalization and shows why many traders will be successful for months and then lose everything in only a few days. It will explain the choices in leveraging and offer alternatives of less risk. The last section analyzes when a system is performing properly and when it is not living up to its expectations.

Risk control begins with a trading philosophy; the most common is called *conservation of capital.* It is the assurance that the investor has been given the most opportunities for success, which usually translates into keeping losses small. This is often accomplished by allowing only small losses per trade or using a trend-following system. Once a trend position is established, it is held as long as prices continue in the direction of the position; it is closed out when the trend changes. The resulting performance profile is one of more frequent small losses and fewer large profits.

RISK AVERSION

Daniel Bernoulli, a famous mathematician, proposed a theory of utility in 1738 that distinguished between price and value, where price is equal for everyone, but value (*utility*) depends on the individual making the estimate and their circumstances.[1]

Bernoulli's approach defined a concept of *diminishing marginal utility,* shown in Figure 23-1, which indicates that as wealth becomes greater, then the preference for more wealth diminishes. In the lower left part of the chart, where the investor has a small net worth, the likelihood of accepting risk is much higher, although the magnitude of the risk is still small. When risk becomes greater, even proportional to reward, all investors become cautious. Bernoulli's graph shows the curve beginning at zero and moving up and to the right in a perfect ¼ circle, ending horizontally where risk is no longer attractive. This implies that people are risk-averse. Most people are not interested in an even chance of gaining or losing an equal amount. Other theories that have been proposed are that the market maximizes the amount of money lost, and the market maximizes the number of losing participants. All of these concepts appear to be true and are very significant in developing an understanding of how the market functions.

---

[1] Peter L. Bernstein, ed., *The Portable MBA in Investment* (John Wiley & Sons, 1995, p. 37).

FIGURE 23-1   Changes in utility versus changes in wealth.

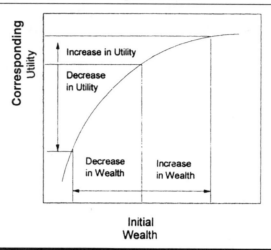

Source: Peter Bernstein, *The Portable MBA in Investment* 1995, p. 38. © 1995 Peter Bernstein. Reprinted by permission of John Wiley & Sons, Inc.

Risk Preference

The Bernoulli theory of utility is general, but each investor has their own unique objectives and attitudes toward risk. Some of the participants in futures markets would like to keep risks low and returns steady; others would like to risk all of their capital for a chance at the "big move." This trait is called the investor's *risk preference.* The risk preference or utility of an investor for a specific venture (in this case a trade) can be found by adding the expected value of the investor's utilities or preferences for the various outcomes of that event,

$$P = w_1 p_1 + w_2 p_2 + \cdots + w_n p_n, \qquad \text{where } \sum w_i = 1$$

where there are n possible outcomes. The weighting factors may be the results of personal bias or may be the calculated probabilities of each outcome. For example, a gold trade has a likely profit of $4,000, with a risk of $1,500. Adjust the reward values by dividing by 1,000. If the probability of success is 60%, the total utility of the trade is:

$$P(\text{trade}) = 0.60 \times 4 + 0.40 \times (-1.5) = 1.8$$

If the probability of success were increased, the utility P would increase linearly. But investors do not feel the same about different rewards. Given a scale of 0 to 100 (negative to positive reaction), an investor may rank the 60% chance of a $4,000 profit and a 40% chance of a $1,500 loss as a 65. If the reward is increased to $8,000 while the risk remains at $1,500, the investor might raise the preference of the trade to 80, although the utility would be 4.2, more than twice as large.

The various patterns of a curve drawn through the computed utilities represent the risk preference of the individual. Figure 23-2 shows the curve formations progressing from extreme risk aversion to extreme risk seeking. As the risk increases in (1), the trader is less likely to participate in the trade; in (3), there is equal chance of taking the trade at all risk levels; and in (5), the trader is more likely to enter a trade that has higher risk.

FIGURE 23-2   Investor utility curves.

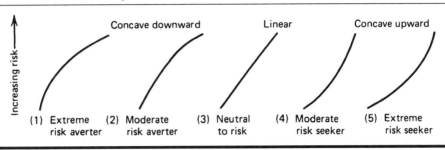

Increasing risk →

Concave downward   Linear   Concave upward

(1) Extreme   (2) Moderate   (3) Neutral   (4) Moderate   (5) Extreme
risk averter   risk averter   to risk   risk seeker   risk seeker

Source: R.J. Teweles, C.V. Harlow, and H.L. Stone, *The Commodity Futures Game: Who Wins, Who Loses, Why?* (McGraw-Hill, New York, 1974, p. 133). © 1974. Reprinted by permission of The McGraw-Hill Companies.

Common Sense

Risk control is as much an issue of common sense as it is complex rules and mathematics. Most of the chapter that follows shows how various measurements, diversification, and leveraging techniques can reduce risk; however, successful traders have applied common sense, without complex formulas, for a long time. Some of these principles are:

1. Don't risk very much of your total capital on any one trade. The total risked should allow you to comfortably survive more losses than you would normally expect.
2. With whatever method you use, determine the maximum loss for the current trade in advance. Many floor traders believe that their survival is the result of being the first to exit a trade. ("I didn't pay to get in, but where do I pay to get out?")
3. Exiting a trade is more difficult than entering because the timing is not always yours. Exiting quickly is often safer than being clever.
4. Stay with your trading philosophy. If you are a trend follower, then keep losses small and let profits run. You can't be a trend follower by taking many small losses and a few small profits.
5. Every system has a trading profile. Be sure that profile is agreeable to you.
6. Plan for contingencies. Not everything goes as planned, and you must be prepared for infrequent, but important exceptions.

LIQUIDITY

The realities of trading are directly related to the liquidity of the market. Even though liquidity can have more than one meaning, lack of liquidity has only one trading result: poor execution. A *liquid* market does not necessarily mean good fills, but an *illiquid* market assures bad ones. Two types of illiquidity are most often encountered in the markets:

1. Fast-moving markets, in which there are mostly buyers or sellers, and few traders are willing to take the other side of the position.
2. Inactive markets, usually in the deferred months in which there is less interest in either hedging or speculating.

The fast market is the result of a supply-demand imbalance, or perceived imbalance, where everyone is in agreement on the direction the market should move. The few hedgers and traders willing to take a position do little to offset the vast number of orders that flood the floor, pushing the price in the direction of the trend. In the inactive market, a premium must be paid to attract another trader to take the opposite trade. This will only succeed in an inactive market when the bid or offered price clearly appears to give the other trader a guaranteed short-term profit.

The illiquidity of a market produces the most important execution cost, often greater than a sizable commission and sometimes unreasonably large. Ginter and Richie[2] have described this as a function of the order size, volume, and the speed of the market, in a single formula:

$$C = K \times \frac{Q \times V}{L_c \times L_o}$$

where C = cost of execution due to liquidity
   Q = size of the order entered
   V = volatility of the market
   L_c = volume of the market (all deliveries)
   L_o = volume of the specific option (delivery month)
   K = constant factor

The volatility V might be the daily range (high minus low), or a factor of the standard deviation of the range. This would provide a measure of how much volume would move the market a specified number of points. The total volume (liquidity) L_c is important because it implies liquidity due to interdelivery spreading. Volume also serves as a measurement of the general interest in the product. More active trading in other contract months opens the possibility for trading in all months given the right circumstances.

The constant factor K will vary according to the nature of the order being placed and the current direction of the price with regard to that order. If prices are moving higher and a buy order is placed, K will be large; if prices are moving higher and a sell order is placed, K will be smaller. The investor can see that trading overhead, including both commissions and other execution costs, will have considerably greater impact on systems that trade more often, have smaller average profits, and trade in the direction of the trend. Given a choice between systems of equal gross profits, the investor should favor the method of fewest trades in the most liquid markets.

CAPITAL

Success does not depend on having enough capital, but in using it properly.

Dixon G. Watts

Every type of system has its own profit-and-loss cycle, depending on what price patterns or behavior it is measuring. A simple moving average will be profitable in a trending market and will lose in a nontrending one; a system that operates within a trading range will profit from nontrending situations. It has been estimated that prices spend 70% to 80% of their total time in a nontrending movement; therefore, when using a trend-following system, it is likely that trading will begin in a nontrending period. Because the risk of the system during a sustained trendless market may be unknown, it is best to start small. Find the minimum amount that can be used to follow the system in a representative manner. During the start-up period, it is best to profit on 10% or 20% of capital than lose on 100%. Always begin slowly—actual trading performance is rarely as good as expected.

Establish the maximum margin based on the experiences of nontrending markets. If uncertain, keep the total margin well under 50% of available capital. The following sections review ways of increasing margin and compounding profits.

Diversification reduces both risk and reward; done properly, the risk is reduced more than the reward. Using a well-distributed portfolio for a system whose risks are known, a

[2] G. Ginter and J. Richie, "Data Errors and Price Distortions," in *Technical Analysis in Commodities,* Perry J. Kaufman (ed.) (John Wiley & Sons, New York, 1980).

larger portion of the total capital can be allocated to margin. Advantages of statistics become apparent in the netting out of profits and losses daily; the majority of trades will move in a favorable direction a majority of the time. The volatility of a portfolio will be dampened by this netting effect; a trade with a slow upward trend and a distant stop-loss will be offset by a slow downward trending position in another commodity.

An undercapitalized account cannot be traded safely by selecting a system with a favorable risk-reward profile. Because there is very little *staying power,* the trader must accept the fact that there is a small chance of success. There are two choices, based on the personality of the trader:

1. Try for the maximum profit possible on a single trade with the capital available. If it loses, trading is halted. If it profits, there may be enough capital for a diversified approach.
2. Take a low-risk approach, which allows the most losses for the given capital. This increases the time in the market, with comparably reduced profits. It is necessary to have an unusually long run of small profits to reach a point of success.

There are two important rules in managing an account: (1) *Don't meet margin calls,* which implies that a margin call represents an objective identification of a bad trade, or a system that is not meeting expectations. A margin call is a time to review trading performance. (2) *Liquidate your worst position when lightening up.* The profitable trades have proved that they are trending or performing properly; the losing ones have proved they are not. Stay with the good positions and liquidate the worst.

The management of capital is especially important at the beginning stages of trading, although it continually affects results. At some point, every trader wants to compound profits—a system that is profitable can be more profitable. This philosophy most often leads to disastrous results. The next sections present methods for measuring risk, followed by a traditional and a conservative approach to compounding and increasing leverage.

MEASURING RISK

An important part of both system development and money management is the recognition, measurement, and ultimately, the limiting of risk. Broadly speaking, money management is the art of limiting the risk of a portfolio while maximizing its return. To perform these tasks, it is first necessary to select, or develop, profitable trading strategies to be used for each commodity. It is the results of these strategies, both simulated and real, that will be used to structure a risk-controlled trading program (see the discussion of "System Trade-Offs" in Chapter 22).

Selecting a Trading Model

A trading model is a set of rules and formulas that, when applied to a price series, yields trading signals. These signals might be as simple as buy and sell Market on Close or complex contingent orders involving multiple delivery months and markets. To *simulate* results, the model must be well defined; that is, all the rules must be logically stated and programmable. Interpretive methods, such as many charting techniques, cannot be simulated; they depend on patterns that cannot be defined in advance. The use of actual trading results for later analysis is always preferable and is not limited to computerized systems.

Suppose there is a choice of systems to trade, and the daily equity of each is available. If only one can be selected, which should it be? There are some characteristics of performance that are universal:[3]

[3] Norm Strahm, "Preference Space Evaluation of Trading System Performance," in *Handbook of Futures Markets,* Perry J. Kaufman (ed.) (John Wiley & Sons, New York, 1984).

1. Larger profits are better than smaller profits.
2. Small, short-term fluctuations are better than large, short-term fluctuations.
3. Upward equity surges (profits) are better than downward surges (losses).

Naive Performance Criteria

The use of a single piece of information is not sufficient to satisfy the basic criteria stated previously. The system with the *maximum profit* is not necessarily a good choice. There might have been a run of losses greater than the investment before profitability was achieved. Similarly, the risk alone is not sensible. The system with the smallest risk is one that never trades. A valid performance measurement technique must include a comparison of risk and reward.

The Sharpe Ratio

The classic measurement of performance is the *Sharpe Ratio* (SR), expressed as

$$SR = \frac{E - I}{\sigma}$$

where E is the expected return, I is the risk-free interest rate, and σ is the standard deviation, or fluctuation, of the periodic returns (for example, the yearly returns). For practical purposes, E should be an annualized rate of return in percent, if you expect that return to continue, and I is often omitted. The inclusion of I is important when a large part of the performance is a contribution of interest on the investment, or when the equity streams being compared are inconsistent in their use of interest income. The standard deviation of the equity is a standard way of measuring risk.

The Sharpe Ratio satisfies the first criterion, that all else being equal, higher profits are better. It does not satisfy either of the other requirements, because it cannot distinguish between:

1. Consecutive small losses (System B) and alternating small losses (System A)
2. Large surges of profits and large losses (Figure 23-3)

Clearly, System A is best in both cases.

Average Maximum Retracement

Schwager[4] has presented a comprehensive study of evaluation techniques. Although each method may emphasize a particular equity trait, he seems to favor the *average maximum retracement* (AMR). This method answers the question: "For each day, what would be the retracement if one had started trading the system on the worst possible trade entry date?" The AMR is the average of the daily maximum retracement values.

$$AMR = \frac{1}{N} \sum_{i=1}^{N} POS(MCE_i - TE_i)$$

where

$$POS(X) = \begin{bmatrix} x \text{ if } x > 0 \\ 0 \text{ if } x < 0 \end{bmatrix}$$

and MCE = closed-out equity (realized profits) on any trade entry date prior to i
        TE_i = total equity on day i
         N = total number of days of equity data

---

[4] Jack D. Schwager, *A Complete Guide to the Futures Markets* (John Wiley & Sons, New York, 1984).

FIGURE 23-3 Two cases in which the Sharpe Ratio fails. (*a*) The order in which profits and losses occur. (*b*) Surges in profits versus evenly distributed losses.

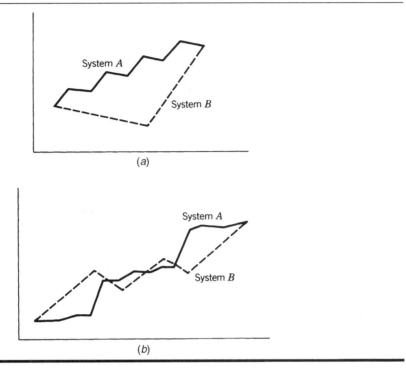

When $TE_i > MCE$, all traders will have a profit on day i, regardless of when they began. Schwager suggests that a much simpler computation would use only the low total equity day of each month; it would give a rough but good approximation.

Largest Loss

Measurements such as Schwager's AMR, and even the basic standard deviation, are good techniques for comparing the long-term performance of one system against another; they lack a certain reality of simply looking at the largest loss seen over the test periods. John Sweeney calls this the *maximum adverse excursion*,[5] claiming that traders should minimize the size of their largest loss.

Consider the standard deviation of equity changes, showing that in any month there is a 68% chance that your returns will be between 15% and −5% (a mean of 5% and a standard deviation of 10%). There is only a 2.5% chance that you will lose more than 15% in 1 month (2 standard deviations); therefore, there is a 50% chance you will lose that 15% in 1 of the first 20 months (20 ÷ 2.5). Yet probability shows that you should lose more, if you keep trading, or less if you stop sooner.

The largest historic loss, called the *maximum drawdown*, is a practical alternative. It simply states that the trading program *did*, for example, lose 15% during 1 month of a 3-year test. While it is possible, and even likely, that the program will have a larger loss in the future, you must be prepared for a 15% loss in a single month.

---

[5] John Sweeney, "Maximum Adverse Excursions for Stops," *Technical Analysis of Stocks & Commodities* (April 1987).

Potential Risk

The measurement of risk may include other safety factors. Once a large loss has occurred, it is likely that a larger one may follow. It is unreasonable to think that all future losses will be smaller than the maximum already experienced. This *potential for loss* can be expressed as a probability by calculating the standard deviation of all equity drops, measured from lows to previous high equity points, and creating an *equity drop ratio* (EDR):

$$EDR = \frac{E}{\sigma(ED)} = E/@stdev(ED)$$

where E is the annualized return (equity), and $\sigma(ED)$ is the standard deviation of the equity drops. Although this is not far from Schwager's approach, it satisfies all three of the original criteria: higher profits are favored, the order of profits and losses will result in larger and smaller net equity drops, and large gains are not penalized because only the drops are used to measure risk.

The conservative investors may want to include some additional simple considerations of potential risk. All else being equal, systems with greater risk will be:

1. Those tested with samples that are too small
2. Those that have not shown any (or few) equity drops
3. Those that concentrate on fewer product groups (not properly diversified)
4. Those that compound positions

Efficient Frontier

It is always helpful to visualize the relative risk of how one system performs with respect to others. A plot of each system using its return and risk as coordinates will appear as in Figure 23-4.

Clearly, the best system would be the one that had the highest returns (*C*) if all of them had the same risk; or *A*, the one with the lowest risk, if it also had the highest profit. The three systems, *A*, *B*, and *C*, are similar because they have the highest returns for their level of risk. However, each used a different degree of leverage, or reserves, and therefore had close to the same profit to risk ratio but in different magnitudes. The choice between systems *A*, *B*, and *C* is a personal preference discussed earlier in this chapter. Theoretically, the best choice is found by drawing a straight line from the risk-free rate of return (on the left scale) to the tangent point on the efficient frontier. This selection avoids the combinations in which risk increases more quickly than reward.

FIGURE 23-4   Efficient frontier.

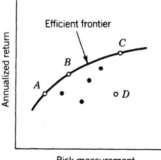

Risk Characteristics of Systems

The selection of a type of trading approach implies the type of risk you are willing to take on each trade. The difference between trend and countertrend systems was discussed in the section System Trade-Offs in Chapter 22 ("Practical Considerations"). In general, a trend system has many smaller losses and fewer larger profits; a countertrend system has the opposite, many smaller profits and fewer larger losses. This is similar to the choices available with gambling strategies.

Even among trending systems there are enormous differences in trading risk. A typical moving average system, which qualifies under *conservation of capital,* keeps individual trade losses small compared with individual profits, but may have a series of losses that add up to one very large continuous loss. In addition, trend systems fail when they encounter a sideways period, and frequently reverse from long to short and back again until prices finally pick a direction. Tests show that you cannot reduce the number of trend trades below a threshold level, even if you make the trend period very long. It always gets caught in a sideways price pattern that generates a series of small losses.

A breakout system, the other very popular trending technique, exchanges a much larger risk for much greater reliability than the moving average or exponential smoothing. When a new long position is entered based on a new high price for a specific time period, the risk is defined as the price needed to make a new low for the same period. Therefore, the trade risk at the time of entry is the difference between the high and low for the period,

```
trade_risk = @highest(close,period) - @lowest(close,period)
```

If the highest high and lowest low are used, the risk can be much greater.

The advantage of the moving average or smoothing method is that individual losses are small. Using the breakout approach, the advantage is that the method does not demand as much of price movement; that is, prices may be very erratic, and take as long as needed to move to a new level, as long as they do not make a new low. It seems illogical that, if prices had given a buy signal by moving to new high levels because something fundamental was affecting the market, prices could turn around and make a new low. That would indicate that the reason behind this move has disappeared.

Risk-Adjusted Returns

The decision whether to choose one trading approach with higher returns and higher risk, or another with smaller returns and lower risk can be resolved by converting performance to an annualized, risk-adjusted return. Using any method for measuring risk—a standard deviation of monthly equity changes, average maximum retracement, or even largest drawdown—divide the annualized rate of return by the risk to get the risk-adjusted rate of return. The highest value is the better choice.

Time to Recovery

A trading program that recovers quickly from losses is more desirable than a program that lingers at its lowest level of loss. The fact that the first program recovers quickly does not change its level of risk, only its practical appeal.

How Much Bigger Could the Risk Really Be?

Many of the risk measurements described in this section attempt to express the probability of a future loss. Within reason, many of them succeed. An investor must distinguish between the calculated probability and the effects of a real loss. If there was only a 1% chance of a 50% loss in a single month, then by the 50th month there would have been a 50% chance of a 50% loss. There is also a large error factor in most of these calculations because the amount of data used to find the statistics was too small. If 100 cases were used there is still a 10% chance of error in the results. The value of the measurement is also dependent upon the period in the market that was used to create these values; the risk in crude oil was exceptionally high during the Gulf War. If that period is not included, the risk of trading crude oil might seem very low.

LEVERAGE

The consequences of leverage are readily seen in a risk/reward analysis, but it also plays a crucial role in the trading strategy itself. Futures markets offer exceptionally high leverage opportunity, and most traders and analysts act as though they are obligated to take advantage of the maximum allowable. Without leverage, futures prices show no more risk than stocks.

Consider the case of an investor with the substantial sum of $50,000 allocated to futures trading. If the price of soybeans is $6.00 per bushel and silver is $7.00 per ounce, a 5,000-bushel contract of soybeans is worth $30,000 and a 5,000-ounce contract of silver is valued at $35,000. With no leverage, the investor could only purchase one contract with the certainty of being able to hold that contract as long as necessary to achieve a profit. Let us assume that, because of fundamental reasons, the investor believes that soybean prices will move to $8 per bushel and silver to $11 per ounce within the next 6 months. The nonannualized gross return on investment will be 33% for soybeans and 57% for silver, equivalent to a 20% and 40% return on $50,000, respectively. With no leverage and not enough money to invest in both, the choice must be silver, which has the highest return; in neither case could their be any *risk of ruin*. In both cases there would be surplus capital.

But 100% capitalization is hardly necessary. Even the most conservative investor would agree that the price of either commodity would not drop to 30% of the current value; therefore, there is no significant risk in capitalizing 70%, rather than 100%, of the contract values. By reducing the individual capitalizations, the investor can then purchase both silver and soybeans, thus adding diversification and a much higher return on the available investment. Table 23-1 shows that 30% leverage would increase the return on investment from 40% to 60%, in addition to the way in which the investment could be allocated, given different levels of capitalization.

As the capitalization is lowered and the leverage increased, both risk and return get rapidly larger. In Table 23-1, there are certain levels which are more significant than others:

TABLE 23-1   Varying the Leverage of an Investment

	Soybeans			Silver			Total Return		
Leverage (%)	Qty	Needed ($)	Profit ($)	Qty	Needed ($)	Profit ($)	Profit ($)	Needed ($)	%P/L
0	0	30,000		1	35,000	20,000	20,000	35,000	40
10	0	27,000		1	31,500	20,000	31,500	31,500	40
20	0	24,000		1	28,000	20,000	28,000	28,000	40
30	1	21,000	10,000	1	24,500	20,000	30,000	45,500	60
40	1	18,000	10,000	1	21,000	20,000	30,000	39,000	60
50	1	15,000	10,000	2	17,500	40,000	50,000	50,000	100
60	1	12,000	10,000	2	14,000	40,000	50,000	40,000	100
70	2	9,000	20,000	3	10,500	60,000	80,000	49,500	160
80	3	6,000	30,000	4	7,000	80,000	110,000	46,000	220
90	7	3,000	70,000	8	3,500	160,000	230,000	49,000	460
95	15	1,500	150,000	15	1,750	300,000	450,000	48,750	900

30% leverage, the point at which there is added diversification, an increase in return, and a negligible increase in risk.

90% leverage, equivalent to *exchange minimum* margin levels.[6] It allows well-capitalized traders to have margins averaging about 10% of the contract value.

95% leverage, equivalent to the margin level given to hedgers and spreaders, based on owning the physical product as offsetting risk.

At 90% leverage, the investor is required to use $49,000 for margin. The positions may be maintained without an additional investment as long as the account does not show a loss in excess of $12,250[7] (with a total of 30 contracts, i.e., equivalent to a loss of $408 per contract, or 8¢ per ounce of silver and 8¢ per bushel of soybeans). Because the daily trading range of both commodities exceeds that value, it is very possible to have a margin call on the first day the position is established. It is not possible for an investor to hold this position for long.

Reserves

Most professional money managers use *reserves* to reduce the leverage and risk, thereby increasing their staying power. The size of the reserves usually averages about 60% of the capital; however, ranges of 10% to 80% have been known. The use of a 50% reserve effectively halves the returns and the risk (Figure 23-5).

Looking again at Table 23-1, there is now only $25,000 of capital available for margin. If exchange minimum margin rates are used, there is 90% leverage available; this means each contract of soybeans requires a $3,000 deposit and each contract of silver $3,500. The 80% leverage line, with one-half the margin shown, would require a total margin commitment of $23,000, slightly under our limits. The net effect of 90% leverage on one-half the total investment is the same as 45% leverage. Returns are:

[6] In futures trading, *initial margin* is the minimum amount required on deposit when the position is entered.

[7] *Maintenance margin* is the level of capitalization that must be maintained in the account. Losses that reduce equity to below 75% (the current maintenance margin level) of the initial margin level require the investor to reestablish the capitalization to the full initial level.

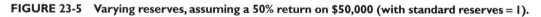

FIGURE 23-5   Varying reserves, assuming a 50% return on $50,000 (with standard reserves = 1).

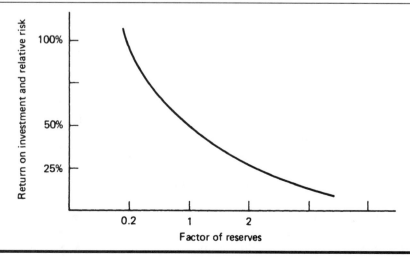

3 contracts of soybeans × $10,000 profit =	$30,000
4 contracts of silver × $20,000 profit =	$60,000
Total profit	$90,000
Net return on investment	180%

DIVERSIFICATION

Diversification means spreading risk; it is the well-established way of lowering systematic risk, and every investor is well advised to diversify. For the purposes of risk reduction, it is necessary to distinguish between *systematic risk,* which can be reduced by diversification, and *market risk,* which cannot be eliminated. The benefits of diversification are greatest when the markets traded are very different and the methods of making decisions are also unrelated. Typical investment portfolios contain a variety of fixed income, equities, real estate, art, as well as different investment philosophies, all intended to provide different rates of return with different patterns and not suffer losses all at the same time. Unfortunately, this is not always the case. Market risk, including *catastrophic risk,* is not predictable, and can surprise even the best investors. Avoiding market risk is the subject of this and other sections in this chapter.

Practical diversification can be implemented using a broad selection of markets within a single tactical system, a selection of different trading strategies for one product, or a combination of multiple systems and products. The objectives of diversification are:

1. *Lower daily risk* due to the offsetting of losses in some markets and systems with profits in others.
2. *Insure participation in major moves* by continuously trading those markets in various groups that are likely to reflect fundamental changes. This avoids the need to identify which market will perform the best.
3. *Offset unexpected losses* caused by a system failing to perform in the current market, or a single trade that generates a large loss. It may be only bad luck that one system gave a short signal in coffee the day before the freeze that moved prices limit-up for 21 days, but another system might have given an offsetting buy signal.
4. *Reduce exposure* in any one market or related group by having funds distributed over many groups. If there are 10 unique asset classes, then an equal allocation only risks one-tenth of the portfolio. The more groups, the less the risk.

Diversification is accomplished by applying as many of the following techniques as possible:

1. *Selecting individual markets from different groups.* Trying to trade those products with as little interrelationship (low *covariance* or *correlation,* discussed in Chapter 3, "Regression") as possible. Traditionally, futures markets have been categorized into sectors of interest rates, currencies, index, grains, livestock, metals (industrial and precious), foods, and miscellaneous. The last group accounts for fibers, woods, oil, and other products with little relationship to other markets.

   There is a larger category called *financials,* which encompasses interest rates, currencies, and index markets. While these sectors tend to move on their own most days, they are known to have very sympathetic, correlated reactions to unexpected economic news. This overriding similarity must be considered when allocating assets within a portfolio.

   Even without the close economic ties shown by the financials, there is considerable interaction between all of these groups. Without special news, agricultural markets have little to do with metals and each moves according to their own fundamentals; however, a radical change in the value of the U.S. dollar or interest rates could move all prices in the same direction. For example, rising interest rates are bad for commodities that must be stored, because it increases those costs. In turn, investors will sell gold and farmers will sell soybeans rather than pay a larger carrying charge.

Slow changes in the value of the U.S. dollar will affect export markets; changes in interest rates will directly impact the stock index. A crisis in the potato market, however, has little effect on other areas of the economy. When selecting those markets to be used in a diversified portfolio, it is necessary to check the historical similarity of equity patterns as well as consider the major forces that currently drive the market—both historic and predictive sides of the problem. When properly selected, diversification will reduce risk, as shown in Figure 23-6.

2. *Multiple systems.* Using more than one system will reduce risk, provided the systems are not similar. Techniques may appear different and yet be highly correlated. A moving average system, ARIMA model, and point-and-figure are very different methods, but all are trend-following. If the sensitivity of all three systems is similar (as determined by the number of trades per year), the equity patterns will also be similar. For system diversification, it is best to select strategies with different functional attributes. For example, the following list gives systems that are likely to be less correlated and techniques within each method that tend to be different.

   a. Trend-following (moving averages or point-and-figure)
   b. Countertrend (stochastic or contrary opinion)
   c. Spreading (interdelivery, intercommodity, arbitrage, product)
   d. Fundamental

   All four techniques are very different. Fundamentals may be trending in nature but should have a longer time perspective. The four types of spreads all offer excellent diversification.

3. *Balanced risk.* Equalizing risk is necessary if the selection of different commodities and systems is to offer proper diversification. Traditionally, price volatility or market value is used to equate risk; however, this method tends to concentrate trading in those products that are least active—and less likely to be profitable. For example, in early 1986, corn was trading at $3 per bushel and the S&P 500 Index at 200, making their contract values $15,000 and $100,000, respectively. Equalizing contract

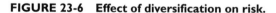

FIGURE 23-6   Effect of diversification on risk.

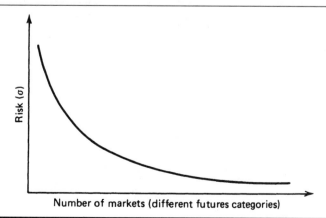

Number of markets (different futures categories)

values would mean trading seven corn to one S&P, even though the likelihood of profiting in corn is far less than that of the S&P.

Equalizing risk must account for the way the trading model performs in the selected markets; most systems do best in volatile periods. Because the most profitable strategies require some substantial price move, they concentrate on markets that have greater volatility. Therefore, it is both easier and better to diversify by distributing the investment among different systems and evaluating only the correlations in equity. A *dynamic capital allocation* will be necessary as one system becomes successful and its contribution to both profits and risk becomes disproportionately large. Withdrawing trading capital from the more successful systems at such times will maintain equal risk among systems and stabilize equity patterns.

These three justifications for diversification have their negative side as well. *Diversification can mean lower profits.* If there are equal returns from trading all markets and all systems, the diversified returns reduce risk and leave profits at the same high level. However, this never happens. It is not likely that silver and soybeans will be profitable at the same rate, nor is it to be expected that two systems will parallel themselves in performance using two distinctly different techniques.

A classic example is the use of a system that actually loses money but has such a negatively correlated performance to one with a high return that the results of using them together are obviously better than either of them alone (Figure 23-7). Because system *B* returns only a small loss, it does little to affect the profitability of System *A*. It will, however, sharply reduce the equity drops by being profitable during periods when System *A* is losing.

Portfolio Calculations

Deciding which systems and markets should be traded at the same time, in an effort to reduce risk through diversification, is an entire field of expertise called *portfolio management*. While markets have always changed, reflecting economic policy and the growth of participation, more recent years of globalization have made portfolio management much more difficult. As more institutions trade international markets as they do their own, they cause a higher correlation of price movements throughout the world. This increase in correlation between previously unrelated areas makes it more difficult to reduce risk through diversification, and makes previous asset allocations obsolete. One answer to this problem is simply to rebalance the portfolios more often, regrouping assets by their similar price movements.

FIGURE 23-7   Stabilizing equity using negatively correlated systems.

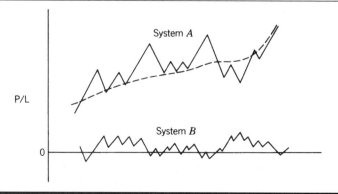

Traditionally, the analyst builds up a portfolio from the expectations of the individual items to be traded. Even more sophisticated portfolios are constructed by selecting markets from groups that have been chosen, in advance, after performing a correlation analysis. Those that show different performance patterns qualify as potential assets in the portfolio. Once selected, the expected return of the portfolio is the weighted average of the expected returns on the individual components of the portfolio,[8] assuming each component is invested with the same percentage of the total.

$$E(R) = w_1 E(R_1) + w_2 E(R_2) + \cdots w_n E(R_n)$$

$$= \sum_{i=1}^{n} w_i E(R_i)$$

The worth of a portfolio is not only its return, but its risk; therefore, the variance of the portfolio becomes an important criterion in deciding which combination of assets create the best results:

$$\sigma_R^2 = \sum_{i=1}^{n} w_i^2 \sigma_i^2 + \sum_{i=1}^{n} \sum_{j=1}^{n} w_i w_j C_{ij}$$

where σ_i^2 is the variance of the returns of market i, and C_{ij} is the covariance between the returns of market i and the returns of market j. The covariance, C, between two markets is the product of their standard deviations times the *correlation coefficient (corr)* between the same two markets:

$$C_{ij} = \text{corr}_{ij} \sigma_i \sigma_j$$

Given two portfolios with the same returns, the one with the smaller variance is more desirable; when the variances are the same, the portfolio with the highest return is best. For a portfolio of only two assets, the calculations needed for expected return and variance are:

$$E(R) = w_1 E(R_1) + w_2 E(R_2)$$

$$\sigma_R^2 = w_1^2 \sigma_1^2 + w_2^2 \sigma_2^2 + 2 w_1 w_2 C_{12}$$

It is important to compare portfolios using this basic comparison of return and risk; however, it is not the entire picture. When evaluating the relationship between a large number of data points, there may be only one case in which an extreme price movement would have caused a fatal loss of equity. That one case can be lost in the statistics, because the large number of normal cases overwhelm one extreme. For safety, it is necessary to also look at the maximum portfolio loss. In addition, we must assume that the largest historic loss will be exceeded sometime in the future, if only by chance (consider the number of heads or tails in a row based only on the number of coin flips). Ideally, we should try to imagine the worst-case scenario, in which globalization increases the correlations, and the past events are not fully representative of future events.

Spreadsheet Approach

A practical way of evaluating a portfolio without requiring special mathematical knowledge or expensive software is to use a spreadsheet program. Using a classic stock and bond mix, Table 23-2 shows the monthly returns of the S&P 500 (S&P) and the Lehman Brothers Treasury Index (LBTI) combined into a portfolio of 60% stocks and 40% bonds. Columns B and C show the monthly percentage returns of these two inputs and columns E and F have the corresponding cumulative returns. At the bottom of columns B and C are some basic calculations that describe the performance. The S&P has an annualized return of 16.41% with a monthly standard deviation of 3.32%; bonds have a 7.65% return with a 2.61% standard

---

[8] Peter L. Bernstein, *The Portable MBA in Investment* (John Wiley & Sons, 1995, p. 252).

TABLE 23-2 Portfolio Evaluation of Stocks and Bonds Using a Spreadsheet

(A)	(B) S&P	(C) LBTI	(D) Stk + Bnd	(E) S&P	(F) LBTI	(G) Stk + Bnd
	Percentage Change			*Cumulative Values*		
Jan 94	3.40	2.44	3.02	3.40	2.44	3.02
Feb 94	−2.71	−4.03	−3.24	0.69	−1.59	−0.22
Mar 94	−4.00	−4.22	−4.09	−3.31	−5.81	−4.31
Apr 94	1.28	−1.36	0.22	−2.03	−7.17	−4.09
May 94	1.64	−0.61	0.74	−0.39	−7.78	−3.35
Jun 94	−2.45	−0.09	−1.51	−2.84	−7.87	−4.85
Jul 94	3.60	3.03	3.37	0.76	−4.84	−1.48
Aug 94	4.10	−0.53	2.25	4.86	−5.37	0.77
Sep 94	−2.45	−3.09	−2.71	2.41	−8.46	−1.94
Oct 94	2.25	−0.43	1.18	4.66	−8.89	−0.76
Nov 94	−3.64	0.48	−1.99	1.02	−8.41	−2.75
Dec 94	1.48	2.42	1.86	2.50	−5.99	−0.90
Jan 95	2.59	2.68	2.63	5.09	−3.31	1.73
Feb 95	3.90	2.88	3.49	8.99	−0.43	5.22
Mar 95	2.95	0.64	2.03	11.94	0.21	7.25
Apr 95	2.94	1.78	2.48	14.88	1.99	9.72
May 95	4.00	7.90	5.56	18.88	9.89	15.28
Jun 95	2.32	1.06	1.82	21.20	10.95	17.10
Jul 95	3.32	−1.64	1.34	24.52	9.31	18.44
Aug 95	0.25	2.13	1.00	24.77	11.44	19.44
Sep 95	4.22	1.73	3.22	28.99	13.17	22.66
Oct 95	−0.36	2.93	0.96	28.63	16.10	23.62
Nov 95	4.39	2.57	3.66	33.02	18.67	27.28
Dec 95	1.93	2.67	2.23	34.95	21.34	29.51
Jan 96	3.26	−0.02	1.95	38.21	21.32	31.45
Feb 96	0.69	−4.82	−1.51	38.90	16.50	29.94
Mar 96	0.79	−1.85	−0.27	39.69	14.65	29.68
Apr 96	1.34	−1.72	0.12	41.03	12.93	29.79
May 96	2.28	−0.04	1.35	43.32	12.89	31.15
Jun 96	0.22	2.10	0.97	43.54	14.99	32.12
Jul 96	−4.57	0.00	−2.74	38.97	14.99	29.38
Aug 96	2.11	−1.34	0.73	41.08	13.65	30.11
Sep 96	5.63	2.74	4.47	46.71	16.39	34.58
Oct 96	2.76	3.94	3.23	49.47	20.33	37.81
Nov 96	7.56	3.32	5.86	57.03	23.65	43.68
Dec 96	−1.98	−2.34	−2.12	55.05	21.31	41.55
Jan 97	6.25	−0.84	3.41	61.30	20.47	44.97
Feb 97	0.78	−0.01	0.46	62.08	20.46	45.43
Mar 97	−4.10	−2.44	−3.44	57.98	18.02	42.00
Apr 97	5.97	2.34	4.52	63.95	20.36	46.51
May 97	6.09	1.14	4.11	70.04	21.50	50.62
Jun 97	4.48	1.94	3.46	74.52	23.44	54.09
Jul 97	7.96	5.89	7.13	82.48	29.33	61.22
Aug 97	−5.60	−2.87	−4.51	76.88	26.46	56.71
Sep 97	5.48	2.84	4.42	82.36	29.30	61.14
Oct 97	−3.34	3.34	−0.67	79.02	32.64	60.47
Cum	79.02	32.64	60.47			
AROR	16.41	7.65	13.13			
StDev	3.32	2.61	2.71			
Ratio	4.94	2.93	4.84			

deviation. The ratio of AROR to standard deviation shows that the stock market has been returning a much better reward to risk ratio during these 4 years.

Using the standard 60% stock and 40% bond portfolio, column D (row 5) becomes +B5*.6 + C5*.4 and column G becomes the cumulative value of that portfolio. When the same statistics are calculated for the mix, the *AROR* is 13.13% with a standard deviation of 2.71%. As expected, the return of 13.13% is about 60% of the difference between the bond and S&P returns; however, the standard deviation has increased only 14% (rather than 40%) of the difference between the two initial standard deviations. The ratio of 4.84 is very close to the S&P ratio, reflecting the sharp drop in risk due to combining these two assets. This easy method allows us to look for maximum drawdown, plot the original assets and final portfolio, and even apply a strategy to the new equity stream.

INDIVIDUAL TRADE RISK

The first line of defense in controlling risk is the individual trade, although sequences of trades are also an important consideration. Trades can be viewed as one continuous event for the purpose of assigning risk; alternately, a strategy may consider separating the trade into two or more parts, for example (1) from the time of entry until the trade becomes profitable, and (2) from the time it is profitable until the end of the trade.

Risk on Initial Positions

We associate the entry point of a trade with a period of greatest uncertainty. Depending on how quickly you anticipate the new trade, prices are either about to change direction or have just changed. Each type of trading method has its own intrinsic risk associated with initial entries. The trend philosophy will take small, frequent losses and reenter the trade as many times as necessary; the breakout technique will only limit losses by the size of the current trading range. It is not clear that the accumulated sequential losses of the trend method is less than a single loss in the breakout approach; and, in exchange for these two distinct approaches, the profit profile is also different.

Additional Risk Control

Most traders prefer specific risk controls added to the one that occurs naturally when the trading method reverses position. These are generally considered *stops,* because they are converted to price levels and subsequently into orders that will force the exit for a current position. Three of the more general approaches to determining the level of individual trade risk are:

1. *An estimate based on initial margin, for example, 50% to 70% of initial margin.* This is loosely related to long-term volatility and lags considerably.[9] An estimate of long-term volatility may be a more satisfactory alternative.
2. *A percentage of the portfolio, for example, 1.0% to 2.5%.* This concept of equalizing risk (and perhaps reward) across all markets is very popular; however, it is not sensitive to individual markets, and as with many stops, imposes artificial overrides. If the volatility becomes very high, as in the case of the S&P, then this risk level could be reached on every trade causing consistent losses. It is, therefore, necessary to determine when a market with exceptional volatility should be removed from the portfolio.
3. *The maximum adverse excursion determined by historic evaluation.*[10] A stop is placed just beyond the maximum adverse excursion for each trade, or 2.5%, whichever is smaller.

[9] Tushar Chande and Stanley Kroll, *The New Technical Trader* (John Wiley & Sons, 1994).

[10] John Sweeney, *Campaign Trading* (John Wiley & Sons, New York, 1997).

Stops

Stop orders provide the ability to control risk most of the time. The reason it is not "all the time" is that exchange-traded markets can gap open, leaving your stop far behind. When stops are placed very close to the market, they are hit with a frequency resembling a random distribution; this is not particularly helpful to performance unless you only want to remain with a trade if it performs properly from the beginning. When stops are placed much farther from the current price levels, they can serve to protect you from extreme losses, but not always. When a price shock occurs, stops are often filled far from their intended level and can actually be filled at the worst point of the move. A system should not be profitable because of stops, but must work before stops are introduced.

If stops are to work, they must be based on values other than an arbitrary financial limit. Some worthwhile possibilities that change with the market are:[11]

1. Advance the stop by a percentage of price, as in Wilder's parabolic system.
2. Use a swing high or low point, based on a percentage minimum swing.
3. Use the highest high or lowest low of the recent n periods.
4. Apply a method such as Kaufman's Adaptive Moving Average (KAMA) as a stop.
5. Adjust the stop by the volatility, such as three times a 10-day average true range.

Standard Deviation Stop

As a sound statistical measurement of risk, the standard deviation can be used to determine stop-loss levels.[12] In a method called the *Dev-stop*, Cynthia Kase uses the following steps to create stop-loss levels for both long and short positions:

1. Calculate the true range (*TR*) of the past 2 trading days using the highest high and lowest low of the 2-day period.
2. Calculate the moving average *ATR* of *TR* (in step 1), using 30 periods for intraday charts and 20 periods for daily charts.
3. Calculate the standard deviation of the true ranges in step 1 using the same period as in step 2.
4. The stop-loss values are $DDEV = ATR + (f*SDEV)$, where f = 1, 2.06 to 2.25, and 3.20 to 3.50, and where the larger values of the pairs correct for skew and the larger numbers allow for larger risk.
5. The dev-stop for long positions is *Trade high* − *DDEV*; the dev-stop for short positions is *Trade low* + *DDEV*.

This method adjusts for volatility using standard statistical measurement and is applied to the extreme profit of a trade to prevent unnecessary loss of equity.

Kaufman on Stops

As with many techniques, the use of stops has both good and bad features. The good aspects are summarized in the increased control of risk—in particular, the unexpected, extremely large risk. It is an added assurance that volatility will not cause losses that are out of proportion to system performance and expected returns.

Ideally, a Stop order entered into the market is expected to automatically get you out of a position when prices move against you. It has the advantage of forcing the trader to decide, in advance, the size of the maximum loss, so that risk is under control. It avoids

---

[11] Chande and Kroll (see footnote 9).

[12] Cynthia Kase, "Redefining Volatility and Position Risk," *Technical Analysis of Stocks & Commodities* (October 1993).

last-minute decisions and the temptation to hold a losing position with the hope that prices will recover.

Stops are normally *resting orders;* that is, they are held by the floor broker to be executed when the price is reached. For the purposes of discussion, a stop will be any form of an order that is intended to limit losses to a fixed amount, whether the order is placed in advance or monitored real-time.

Risk Protection or False Hope?

The use of stops, or the intent to limit losses to a predetermined, fixed amount may give a false sense of security. For example, a Stop order that is reached during an illiquid or quiet market will result in large slippage; during a fast market, or a price jump, it will often result in the worst fill. Large traders cannot enter stops because they will move the market and guarantee substantial slippage.

Market Noise and the Frequency of Stops

The use of small stops, or the trading practice of exiting a trade with a small loss, causes the total performance of a trend strategy to be worse. Small losses occur frequently due to market noise and are not an indication that the trading strategy, or the trend direction, is wrong.

Larger stop-losses offer some benefit for longer-term trading, when high volatility has caused the natural system stop to be very far away. Large stops may help reduce the risk of a price shock, but not always. Stops may reduce the performance volatility of a portfolio simply by causing more time out of the market.

Theoretically, the purpose of using a stop-loss order is to limit each loss to a controlled amount, and generate a performance profile with a reasonable ratio of average profits to average losses (for example, 2 : 1). In addition, a trader would like to have at least one-half of all trades profitable. Unfortunately, the market does not work this way. It is not possible to control both the reward/risk ratio and the percentage of profitable trades.

Noise is the term given to erratic and unpredictable price movements. It is most often associated with relatively small moves, but can actually be any size. Noise is caused by traders entering and exiting the market with different objectives and different time horizons. For example, an institutional investor adds positions because of new funds from its clients; Russia sells gold to pay for a wheat purchase; or, an auto company liquidates part of its stock portfolio to cover foreign exchange losses. Because each event is unrelated to the other, and there are so many of them, the total picture of this noise creates a random distribution. This pattern has many of the properties of a random number distribution, in particular, *erratic prices (noise) that are twice as large occur half as often.*

Total Losses Are Constant

If noise is very similar to a random distribution, then the number of occurrences times the size of the move will be very close to a constant value. The following is a typical result of setting stops of different sizes:

Size of Stop	No. of Occurrences	Size of Loss
5 pips	20	100 pips + slippage
10 pips	10	100 pips + slippage
20 pips	5	100 pips + slippage

In reality, this pattern may vary slightly from market to market; however, the cost of slippage will usually be large enough to cause the net losses to be similar. In addition, the more frequent trades must also have additional transaction costs, with a chance of larger slippage from time to time; therefore, the strategy that uses smaller stop-losses should perform worse than the strategy with larger stops.

A Stop-Loss Can Conflict with the Trading Strategy

Combining a small stop-loss with a trend-following system is very likely to conflict in purpose. If a trending system gives one new trend signal each month, but the stop-loss is so small that it would be reached once each week, it would be very difficult to stay with a system position. Once stopped-out, if the market turns and moves in the direction of the trend, the system is proved right but you have no position. It is necessary to create a reentry strategy that can be unnecessarily complex.

If every time you are stopped out of a trade, the price continues in the same direction until a reverse position is signaled, then it follows that the selection of the trend period is too slow. Rather than exit the trade when the stop is reached, the system should be reversing its position. By shortening the trend calculation period, the need for a stop is eliminated.

Testing Stops over Ten Years

Table 23-3 gives the pattern of performance for a simple moving average trading system with calculation periods from 5 to 300 days and stops from .02% to 10%. Four major markets were selected, two stocks and two futures markets. The smallest stop-loss of 2% appears on the left, and the largest of 10% and no stop ("NONE") appear on the far right. Overall, the performance of the trend program without a stop is most consistent for the range of trend periods, although specific stops can be better for some intervals. It may be noted that there is a pattern in Siemens, in which the best performance runs diagonally from the upper left toward the bottom right, indicating that the size of the optimum stop-loss may be related to the speed of the trend, but this pattern is not the same for the other markets tested and, therefore, it may be the result of a single trade, such as the crash of 1987, and not a robust relationship. Table 23-4 shows the same results for the Deutschemark and Eurodollars in terms of risk-adjusted returns, in which the returns are divided by one standard deviation of the equity changes. In general, these results were the same as the unadjusted ones in Table 23-3.

Managing Risk with and without Stops

Despite the conclusion that the placement of fixed-level stops causes a trade to be stopped out arbitrarily, it is difficult to trade without a clear idea of risk. For longer-term positions, a fixed stop-loss may help in the case of catastrophic risk. Before a stop-loss is used, it should be tested and compared with system performance that does not use a stop. Careful selection of the trading strategy may provide adequate risk control with a separate stop-loss.

While fixed stops do not seem to enhance a trading program, a stop based on support and resistance levels may be quite different. It is already known that a breakout system, which enters on a new high and reverses on a new low, assumes the risk of the range defined by the difference between the high and low. This is analogous to the size of a support-resistance range. Because this range varies with market volatility and offers a view of risk that contrasts with a trend system, the combination of the two may improve net performance.

The safest way to reduce risk is simply by reducing the size of your positions. Trading a smaller portfolio, a lower margin to equity ratio, is the simplest approach to risk reduction and does not conflict with the underlying trading strategy. In the final analysis, the one who can profit by trading the smallest amount will be hurt the least when a price shock hits the market.

TABLE 23-3   Results of Tests Comparing Trend Period and Size of Fixed Stops*

Annualized Rate of Return (Adjusted for 25% Drawdown)

					Stop-Loss in Whole Percent							
	.02	.05	.10	.15	.25	.50	1.00	2.00	4.00	7.00	10.00	NONE
a. Chrysler Motors: 2,329 Days (1/05/84 to 3/18/93)												
5	−2.8	−2.8	−2.7	−2.7	−2.7	−2.8	−2.8	−2.7	−2.8	−2.8	−2.8	−2.8
10	−2.8	−2.8	−2.8	−2.8	−2.8	−2.8	−2.8	−2.8	−2.8	−2.8	−2.8	−2.8
25	−2.8	−2.8	−2.8	−2.7	−2.8	−2.8	−2.6	−2.6	−2.6	−2.6	−2.6	−2.6
50	−2.6	−2.6	−2.6	−2.6	−2.6	−2.6	−2.2	−2.3	−2.2	−2.2	−2.2	−2.2
75	−1.2	−1.2	−1.2	−1.4	−1.4	−1.5	−1.5	−1.6	−1.4	−1.5	−1.5	−1.5
100	−1.5	−1.5	−1.5	−1.6	−1.7	−1.9	−.6	−.7	−.5	−.6	−.6	−.6
150	5.8	5.7	5.7	5.3	5.4	4.9	4.5	4.0	3.6	3.5	3.5	3.5
200	2.2	2.2	2.2	1.9	1.7	1.6	1.4	2.8	2.7	2.7	2.7	2.7
250	−2.5	−2.5	−2.5	−2.5	−2.5	−2.5	−2.5	−.4	−.1	2.0	2.0	2.0
300	3.6	3.6	3.4	3.4	3.2	3.1	3.0	2.5	2.4	2.4	2.4	2.4
b. Siemens: 1,452 Days (2/3/87 to 11/23/92)												
5	1.5	1.5	2.1	1.6	.9	1.4	1.9	1.5	1.2	1.2	1.2	1.2
10	11.8	11.7	12.0	11.4	10.6	8.5	8.2	7.5	6.7	6.0	6.0	6.0
25	10.1	10.1	9.4	8.8	7.4	6.8	5.0	3.7	3.5	3.0	3.0	3.0
50	6.3	6.3	6.1	5.6	8.9	6.7	6.7	8.4	8.8	7.7	7.7	7.7
75	9.8	9.4	11.4	11.6	12.1	11.1	8.3	10.0	9.7	8.7	8.7	8.7
100	5.2	5.2	4.8	4.9	4.1	3.1	4.8	5.9	5.9	5.3	5.3	5.3
150	5.0	4.9	4.9	5.0	5.0	4.2	3.0	4.7	7.8	7.7	7.0	7.0
200	3.6	3.6	3.6	3.2	2.9	2.2	2.9	1.8	2.9	2.8	2.8	2.8
250	4.5	4.4	4.4	4.3	3.9	3.3	4.4	5.2	4.9	4.9	4.9	4.9
300	4.4	4.4	4.4	4.2	5.4	4.9	4.1	2.7	2.4	2.4	2.4	2.4
c. Deutschemark: 2,570 Days (11/24/82 to 11/23/92)												
5	−1.9	−1.9	−1.9	−1.9	−1.9	−1.8	−1.8	−1.8	−1.8	−1.8	−1.8	−1.8
10	−1.4	−1.1	−1.0	−1.0	−1.1	−.7	−.6	−.6	−.6	−.6	−.6	−.6
25	1.7	2.6	3.6	2.9	3.8	3.8	5.5	5.7	5.3	5.2	4.9	5.4
50	5.2	6.9	6.8	6.4	3.7	12.8	11.0	11.5	10.8	10.8	10.8	10.8
75	3.4	4.8	6.1	5.6	8.5	13.4	10.0	8.7	7.8	7.6	7.6	7.6
100	5.3	7.2	8.5	8.3	4.5	10.8	11.5	7.4	9.1	7.5	7.5	7.5
150	.5	.3	.0	−.4	1.6	8.1	6.8	7.7	5.3	3.6	3.6	3.6
200	.7	2.0	1.7	1.1	10.1	11.7	7.7	9.6	6.9	7.6	7.0	7.0
250	8.0	9.1	8.1	8.1	6.5	5.5	7.2	8.8	5.4	11.0	9.1	10.4
300	.7	.4	.2	−.1	.5	5.1	5.1	5.6	4.3	12.3	10.7	10.4
d. Eurodollars: 2,556 Days (1/03/83 to 12/14/92)												
5	1.2	1.3	1.4	1.0	1.0	1.0	1.1	1.1	1.1	1.1	1.1	1.1
10	1.8	2.1	3.1	2.7	2.7	2.6	2.7	2.7	2.7	2.7	2.7	2.7
25	3.8	3.0	6.7	6.1	8.2	7.4	7.4	7.4	7.4	7.4	7.4	7.4
50	4.0	8.5	10.5	7.7	8.1	7.8	7.7	7.7	7.7	7.7	7.7	7.7
75	6.5	10.2	8.1	9.2	10.8	10.0	9.9	9.9	9.9	9.9	9.9	9.9
100	7.1	4.8	8.9	6.3	6.4	7.2	7.8	7.8	7.8	7.8	7.8	7.8
150	4.1	1.8	2.9	2.6	6.4	5.0	7.6	7.6	7.6	7.6	7.6	7.6
200	7.3	5.4	.8	.4	2.9	5.9	6.5	6.5	6.5	6.5	6.5	6.5
250	1.1	−.8	−.8	.1	4.1	3.8	6.9	5.6	5.6	5.6	5.6	5.6
300	.2	−.1	−.6	−.8	.3	6.7	5.6	5.4	5.4	5.4	5.4	5.4

* Exponential smoothing was used to create a trend with buy and sell signals given when the trendline turned up or down, respectively. Stops apply to absolute losses, all orders were executed at the close of the day, and there were no commissions or slippage charged. Although stops improve performance in specific cases, there does not seem to be a consistent pattern. Smaller stops are especially erratic, as the trends increase in length, often showing alternating better and worse performance.

TABLE 23-4   Comparison of 4-Year Results*

Comparison of Cash Return versus Risk-Adjusted Return

					Stop-Loss in Whole Percent							
	.02	.05	.10	.15	.25	.50	1.00	2.00	4.00	7.00	10.00	NONE

Deutschemark: 1,030 Days (11/22/88 to 11/23/92)

Annualized Rate of Return (on Cash, in Percent)

	.02	.05	.10	.15	.25	.50	1.00	2.00	4.00	7.00	10.00	NONE
5	−7.5	−7.1	−7.3	−8.3	−9.9	−8.5	−7.1	−7.1	−7.1	−7.1	−7.1	−7.1
10	−6.8	−5.0	−5.3	−6.2	−7.6	−7.0	−4.4	−4.3	−4.3	−4.3	−4.3	−4.3
25	2.8	5.5	5.4	5.4	5.4	4.2	6.5	7.4	7.4	7.4	7.4	7.4
50	5.6	10.2	9.9	10.1	9.6	8.3	8.3	8.7	8.0	8.0	8.0	8.0
75	2.8	2.2	1.6	1.6	5.0	7.0	5.1	5.0	3.6	3.4	3.4	3.4
100	1.3	4.2	3.6	3.5	7.4	5.4	8.7	8.6	9.3	9.1	9.1	9.1
150	1.2	.9	.7	.7	−1.1	7.6	9.3	11.2	8.8	7.5	7.2	7.2
200	5.3	9.1	8.9	8.7	8.2	6.4	7.9	9.7	7.0	5.2	4.6	4.6
250	5.9	8.3	8.1	8.0	7.7	6.7	6.1	7.9	5.2	5.6	4.9	4.7
300	2.0	1.8	1.5	1.2	.9	4.5	6.4	8.1	5.4	6.6	5.9	5.5

Annualized ROR (Adjusted for 25% Drawdown)

	.02	.05	.10	.15	.25	.50	1.00	2.00	4.00	7.00	10.00	NONE
5	−3.7	−3.6	−3.6	−3.8	−4.2	−4.0	−3.6	−3.6	−3.6	−3.6	−3.6	−3.6
10	−3.9	−2.8	−2.9	−3.2	−3.6	−3.5	−2.5	−2.4	−2.4	−2.4	−2.4	−2.4
25	2.7	4.8	4.6	4.6	4.6	3.3	7.1	10.9	10.9	10.9	10.9	10.9
50	12.7	23.3	22.5	25.2	21.7	17.3	16.0	16.8	15.5	15.5	15.5	15.5
75	4.4	3.6	2.2	2.2	7.8	14.5	7.5	6.6	4.4	4.2	4.2	4.2
100	2.8	8.7	7.0	6.8	18.1	9.5	18.1	11.3	19.1	18.6	18.6	18.6
150	3.7	2.4	1.7	1.7	−1.7	12.1	12.0	14.6	10.8	8.3	8.0	8.0
200	14.0	22.0	19.3	19.2	17.1	13.4	13.2	15.1	9.1	5.9	5.3	5.3
250	14.7	18.8	17.6	16.7	16.0	12.8	9.9	12.9	7.4	8.2	7.2	6.9
300	5.7	4.5	3.4	2.8	1.9	8.3	9.8	12.8	7.0	10.3	9.2	8.7

Eurodollars: 1,042 Days (11/22/88 to 12/14/92)

Annualized Rate of Return (on Cash, in Percent)

	.02	.05	.10	.15	.25	.50	1.00	2.00	4.00	7.00	10.00	NONE
5	.3	.3	.3	.3	.3	.3	.3	.3	.3	.3	.3	.3
10	.9	.9	1.0	1.1	1.0	1.0	1.0	1.0	1.0	1.0	1.0	1.0
25	.3	.4	.9	1.2	1.3	1.3	1.3	1.3	1.3	1.3	1.3	1.3
50	.3	.5	1.0	1.3	1.6	1.6	1.6	1.6	1.6	1.6	1.6	1.6
75	.7	.8	1.1	1.1	1.3	1.3	1.3	1.3	1.3	1.3	1.3	1.3
100	.9	.8	1.0	1.0	1.1	1.0	1.0	1.0	1.0	1.0	1.0	1.0
150	.0	.1	−.1	−.1	.6	.9	.9	.9	.9	.9	.9	.9
200	.1	.1	.1	.1	.7	1.1	1.1	1.1	1.1	1.1	1.1	1.1
250	.2	.2	.2	.2	.9	1.2	1.2	1.2	1.2	1.2	1.2	1.2
300	.2	.3	.2	−.3	.4	.6	.6	.6	.6	.6	.6	.6

Annualized ROR (Adjusted for 25% Drawdown)

	.02	.05	.10	.15	.25	.50	1.00	2.00	4.00	7.00	10.00	NONE
5	2.9	2.4	2.4	2.4	2.4	2.4	2.4	2.4	2.4	2.4	2.4	2.4
10	21.9	22.4	25.7	19.5	25.9	25.9	25.9	25.9	25.9	25.9	25.9	25.9
25	2.9	4.6	11.3	28.6	32.9	32.9	32.9	32.9	32.9	32.9	32.9	32.9
50	7.6	12.6	23.8	33.0	38.8	38.8	38.8	38.8	38.8	38.8	38.8	38.8
75	18.5	20.7	27.4	27.1	32.6	32.0	32.0	32.0	32.0	32.0	32.0	32.0
100	22.1	18.3	25.9	25.6	28.5	25.6	25.6	25.6	25.6	25.6	25.6	25.6
150	.7	1.4	−1.3	−1.3	7.3	11.4	10.9	10.9	10.9	10.9	10.9	10.9
200	3.5	1.7	1.2	1.0	9.1	13.8	14.1	14.1	14.1	14.1	14.1	14.1
250	4.4	5.9	4.9	4.4	16.8	14.8	15.1	15.1	15.1	15.1	15.1	15.1
300	4.3	6.5	5.6	−3.4	4.1	5.2	5.4	5.4	5.4	5.4	5.4	5.4

* The pattern in the "NONE" column (no stops) shows that the risk-adjusted results, in general, are more consistent than unadjusted returns.

RANKING OF MARKETS FOR SELECTION

Choosing the right market to trade at the right time would clearly improve performance. To accomplish this, there are a number of ways to measure the *trendiness* of a market, from standard statistical techniques to more complex rules. Each unique method will measure some special characteristic of price movement. To take advantage of this, it is necessary to trade using a system that targets this type of price pattern. For example, if you use a correlation coefficient, r^2, to rank the trend over 20 days, then a linear regression is probably the best choice of a trend-following system, using a period no greater than 20 days.

It may be interesting to list a number of trend-ranking approaches, then keep track of their values in a table over various time periods.[13] For example, the five measurements below can be calculated for periods of 5, 10, 20, and 40 days.

1. Correlation coefficient, but no less than .25
2. Sum of the net $ movement over n, $2 \times n$, and $4 \times n$ days
3. Slope of an n-day regression converted to 1-day $ change
4. Wilder's ADX, but no less than .20
5. Average absolute value of price changes

Each measurement will need to have threshold values that determine when they represent significant trends. For the correlation coefficient, anything below .25 is most likely to be a sideways market; similarly, Wilder's ADX would need to be above .20 to indicate a trend. If the results are erratic, it may be necessary to smooth the last 3 days of each value. In the case of item 5, higher volatility is often associated with greater profits and greater risk for a trend-following system; therefore, a careful look at how ranking affects performance is warranted.

Commodity Selection Index (CSI)

Among Wilder's trading tools is the *Commodity Selection Index* (CSI),[14] a calculation for determining which products are most likely to make the greatest move for each dollar invested. In this case, the movement measured is *directional* and, therefore, may apply more to trending models. The CSI combines directional movement, volatility, margin requirements, and commission costs into an index that allows for comparison and selection.

Directional Movement

The trending quality of the market, as defined by Wilder, begins with *directional movement*, the greater of either:

1. Plus DM (+DM), today's high minus yesterday's high, or
2. Minus DM (−DM), today's low minus yesterday's low.

The directional movement is either up or down, whichever is larger. It is the largest part of today's range which is outside yesterday's range. When an inside day occurs, the directional movement is zero (Figure 23-8).

DM is expressed relative to the daily range (high minus low), defined as today's *true range* (TR1), the larger of the following:

1. Today's high minus today's low
2. Today's high minus yesterday's close
3. Yesterday's close minus today's low

---

[13] Based on an idea suggested in Chande and Kroll, *The New Technical Trader* (John Wiley & Sons, 1994).

[14] J. Welles Wilder, "Selection and Direction" in *Technical Analysis in Commodities,* Perry J. Kaufman (ed.) (John Wiley & Sons, New York, 1980).

FIGURE 23-8   Defining the DM.

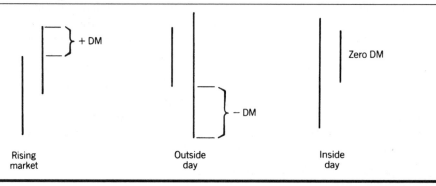

The true range is always positive.

The relationship of the directional movement to the true range is called the *Directional Indicator.* Today's directional indicator is calculated using either the plus DM or the minus DM, whichever is greater.

$$+DM14 = +\frac{DM14}{TR14} \quad \text{or} \quad -DM14 = -\frac{DM14}{TR14}$$

Once the first DM14 is calculated, an *average off* technique is used to find each successive DM14 as follows:

$$\text{Today's } +DM14 = \text{prior } +DM14 - \frac{\text{prior } +DM14}{14} + \text{today's } +DM14$$

The same procedure is followed for the true range:

$$\text{Today's } TR14 = \text{prior } TR14 - \frac{\text{prior} TR14}{14} + \text{today's } TR14$$

These results can also be produced using a smoothing constant of .93 as follows:

Today's $+DM14 = .93 \times (\text{ prior } +DM14) + \text{today's } +DM1$

Today's $-DM14 = .93 \times (\text{ prior } -DM14) + \text{today's } -DM1$

Today's $TR14 = .93 \times (\text{ prior } TR14) + \text{today's } TR1$

At this point, the Directional Indicator can be used as a trading indicator, and is the subject of the next section; however, Wilder's interest was to use this in a more complete concept. Once the +DM14, −DM14, and the TR14 are calculated, +DI14 and −DI14 follow, and the *true directional movement* is the difference between +DI14 and −DI14. When an upward trend is sustained, the +DI14 becomes larger, the −DI14 becomes smaller, and the true directional movement becomes greater. This is then *normalized* to allow it to be expressed as a value between 0 and 100.

$$DX = \frac{+DI14 \text{ minus } -DI14}{+DI14 \text{ plus } -DI14} \times 100 = \frac{DI \text{ difference}}{DI \text{ sum}} \times 100$$

where multiplying by 100 converts the percentage to a whole number. The DX is then smoothed out using a 14-day average (or 0.07 smoothing constant), and is called the *Average Directional Movement Index* (ADX).

$$ADX(\text{today}) = ADX(\text{prior}) + .07 \times [DX(\text{today}) - ADX(\text{prior})]$$

One last adjustment is made to the extreme variance of the ADX by taking the 14-day difference of ADXs. This final rating is called the *Average Directional Movement Index Rating* (ADXR),

$$\text{ADXR} = \frac{\text{ADX(today)} + \text{ADX(14 days ago)}}{2}$$

The ADX and ADXR are shown plotted together in Figure 23-9. The ADX is seen to oscillate about the ADXR. Measuring the amplitude of the ADX from the zero line, a higher amplitude means higher directional movement and a stronger trend, whether up or down. The peaks are always the extremes in the same direction as the trend. If the major trend was down, the peaks would be extremely low points and the valleys would be relatively high points. The greater the distance between the peaks and valleys, the greater are the reactions to the trend.

All this leads to the *Commodity Selection Index* (CSI), which is calculated as:

$$\text{CSI} = \text{ADXR} \times \text{ATR14} \times \left[\frac{V}{M} \times \frac{1}{150 + C} \right] \times 100$$

where   ADXR = average directional movement index rating
       ATR14 = 14-day average true range
            V = conversion factor; value of a 1¢ move (in dollars)
          M = margin (in dollars)
          C = commissions (in dollars)

Note that for a particular commodity, the values in brackets do not change. By calculating them once and calling that value K, the CSI can be expressed as:

$$\text{CSI} = \text{ADXR} \times \text{ATR14} \times \text{K}$$

A portfolio allocation can be chosen by calculating the CSI daily (or weekly) for each commodity. Simply select those products to trade that have the highest CSI or allocate multiple contracts in proportion to their CSI value.

Optimizing Directional Movement[15]

The +DI14 and −DI14 are indicators that can be used in a simple trading strategy. Hochheimer, known for other studies of moving averages, crossovers, and channels, has defined the rules of a *Directional Movement System* in two ways.[16] The first set of rules are:

[15] For a general discussion of this topic, see Chapter 21.

[16] Frank L. Hochheimer and Richard J. Vaughn, *Computerized Trading Techniques 1982* (Merrill Lynch Commodities, New York, 1982).

FIGURE 23-9   Appearance of the ADX and ADXR.

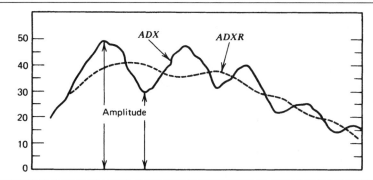

1. a. If the +DI crosses above the −DI, enter a *buy stop* on the next day using today's high price. This order remains as long as it is not executed and +DI remains higher than −DI.

   b. If the −DI crosses below the +DI, enter a *sell stop* on the next day using today's low price. Maintain this order until it is executed and while −DI remains below +DI.

Hochheimer calls the first case "directional movement with delay." The second case is an immediate market entry following the crossing of the directional indicators:

2. a. If the +DI crosses above the −DI, buy on the open of the next day.

   b. If the −DI crosses below the +DI, sell on the open of the next day.

In both cases the system is always in the market.

Before seeing the actual results, it is possible to generalize the expected performance.

1. Case 2 must have more trades than case 1 as a result of always taking a position when a crossing occurs.
2. Because there is no commitment to the trade (i.e., no channel), there could be frequent whipsaws in case 2.
3. Because case 1 uses the high and low of the prior day, its entry prices will always be equal to or worse than case 2.
4. If the Directional Indicator gives a highly reliable signal, it would be better to enter immediately, as in case 2.

Parameters Defined

The purpose of the optimization was to see if changes in the time intervals caused improvements in results. Hochheimer chose the following parameters to test:

1. The +DM was calculated from 7 to 20 days.
2. The −DM varied from 5 above to 5 below the +DM value.
3. Two *true ranges* (TR) were calculated, the first using the weight of the +DM, the other using the weight of the −DM.

The test data covered all information available from 1970 to 1981.

Results

Selected results are shown in Table 23-5. The patterns of the two cases are as expected. Case 2 has more trades, with a higher percentage of losses and higher risk. The profit/loss shown in case 1 is generally higher than case 2, indicating that, even under ideal conditions, the RSI generates many false signals using these rules.

It can also be seen that those markets with a small amount of available data, T-bills, T-bonds, currencies, and gold, had the shorter intervals selected for calculation. By observing the tendency for the products with more data to use longer intervals, a *standard set* of days should have been chosen rather than allowing an apparent overfitting of the data.

The philosophy of these tests, however, should be questioned. Although the independent varying of the number of days in the +DM, −DM, and TR accounts for all combinations, it seems illogical. The Directional Movement Indicator is intended to be a measurement of relative strength over a fixed time period; it produces a percentage from 0 to 100. In this study, the TR (the denominator) may have a time interval smaller than one of the +DM or −DM, generating a value greater than 100.

The independent varying of the up and down segments of the indicator also allowed a long-term directional bias to appear. This can be seen in the optimum selection of those commodities with the shortest amount of data: the financials markets and the currencies. In case 2, almost all of the products with 11 years of data produced interval selections that were nearly identical, in the area of either 14 or 20 days.

TABLE 23-5 Comparative Performance of Directional Movement Systems

	Case 1				Case 2			
	Days	P/L	Equity Drop	No. of Trades	Days	P/L	Equity Drop	No. of Trades
Cocoa	22 17	$43,083	$–13,019	723	23 18	$–4,117	$–17,152	1238
Corn	21 20	26,456	–7,072	613	21 20	26,456	–7,072	613
Cotton	18 21	37,495	–21,740	1256	24 19	29,765	–18,340	1462
Copper	18 20	219,639	–10,230	633	12 14	88,561	–13,390	1549
Deutschemark	8 13	140,538	–6,335	277	14 14	101,476	–7,290	423
Gold	15 10	827,980	–10,740	504	16 12	664,390	–13,810	1041
Cattle	22 19	–7,850	–11,710	474	20 20	–14,860	–27,920	808
Soybeans	16 20	254,495	–39,639	895	19 20	177,584	–29,759	1420
Silver	16 11	1,034,825	–82,870	788	22 17	351,360	–136,585	1161
T-Bills	3 7	37,840	–12,005	286	11 8	5,235	–17,545	369
T-Bonds	8 7	185,371	–11,326	436	9 8	118,256	–7,294	739

Kaufman's System Selection Indicator

A market's *personality* is in its price patterns. Some markets, such as the stock index, are very volatile with gradual sustained upward moves and fast, sharp drops. In contrast, Eurodollars are very steady, often trading high volume at the same price. Qualifying markets by *noise* allows you to decide which trading strategy is most likely to be successful. Lower noise favors trending systems and high noise makes countertrend techniques more appropriate.

The concept of noise has been discussed in numerous sections throughout this book, and it is again of great value when choosing which system to apply to a market, and identifying when a market is best treated as trending. In essence, noise is market movement that has no direction or one in which the amount of direction is overwhelmed by volatile erratic up and down movement. It is an undercurrent of unpredictable movement caused by a broad range of participants acting for their own individual objectives.

The calculation for noise can be found with examples in Chapter 17 ("Adaptive Techniques"). As a simple reminder, it is defined as the *efficiency ratio, ER:*

$$ER = \frac{\text{Net price change}}{\text{Sum of price changes as positive values}}$$

Time Frame

There always appears to be more noise over short time periods. That is because noise remains at about the same level, but price trends are not clear until they have persevered for at least a few days, and often for weeks. For a trend comparison we should avoid very short-term trends; therefore, a 16-day exponential smoothing will be used in the following comparison. To be certain that the efficiency ratio is stable, it will be calculated over a 65-day period.

Results of Efficiency Ratio Selection

Figure 23-10 shows that, when returns are compared using the efficiency ratio, profits are clearly greater when the ER is high; losses are larger when the ER is low. Based on a broad sampling of markets, this is a very useful pattern for classifying markets. The greatest profits are in the upper right part of the diagram where there is less noise; the greatest losses are in the lower left corner where there is the most noise. We can conclude that

FIGURE 23-10   Efficiency ratio and trend performance. A clear pattern can be seen when a long-term efficiency ratio (market noise) is plotted against the trend performance of a broad sampling of markets using a 16-day exponential smoothing.

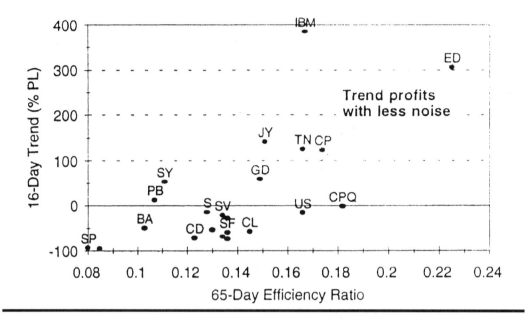

When the efficiency ratio is high, then a trend system is a better strategy.

When the efficiency ratio is low, then a countertrend system is best.

In the second case, a countertrend approach does not mean that you must set a short position when the market is moving up. It can also mean taking profits on a long position when there is a countertrend sell signal, or building a long position when a countertrend buy signal occurs on a price drop. While the efficiency ratio is not specifically a directional indicator, it does seem to classify markets as trending or nontrending.

PROBABILITY OF SUCCESS AND RUIN

The relative size of trading profits and losses, the frequency of the losses, and the sequence in which they occur comprise the equity profile of traders and systems. This profile can be used to determine the capitalization necessary to maintain trading during the losing periods and allow the system to return to its full potential. In investment terminology and probability theory, the level at which you no longer have enough money to continue trading is called the *point of ruin,* and the chance of getting there is the *risk of ruin.* The probability of the risk of ruin is normally expressed as

$$R = \left[\frac{1-A}{1+A} \right]^c$$

where $0 \leq R \leq 1$, 0 indicates no risk, and 1 certain ruin

$A = P - (1 - P)$, P is the proportion of winning trades, also considered the *trader's advantage*

c = the beginning units of trading capital

A system of trading that has 60% profitable trades and trading capital in $10,000 units will have a risk of ruin calculated as follows:

$$A = 0.60 - (1 - .060) = 0.20$$

$$R = \left(\frac{1 - 0.20}{1 + 0.20}\right)^c = \left(\frac{0.80}{1.20}\right)^c = \left(\frac{1}{3}\right)^c$$

When $c = 1$ ($10,000), $R = 0.33$, and when $c = 2$ ($20,000), $R = 0.11$. Therefore, the greater the trader's advantage or the greater the capital, the smaller the risk of ruin (Figure 23-11).

When using profit goals, the chance of ruin should decrease as the goal becomes smaller. The relationship can be expressed as:

$$R = \frac{[1 + A)/(1 - A)]^G - 1}{[(1 + A)/(1 - A)]^{c + G} - 1}, \qquad 0 \leq R \leq 1$$

where all terms are the same as above, and G is the goal in units of trading capital.

Wins Not Equal to Losses

The basic equations just presented are generally applied to gambling situations, where the size of profits and losses are the same. This requires that the percentage of winning events exceed the losing events to avoid ruin. Futures trading, however, often results in more losing trades than profitable ones and must, therefore, return much *larger* profits than losses. Such a structure is common to all conservation of capital, or trend-following, systems. This situation can be applied to the more complex form[17] where

C_T = the total capital available for trading (in units)
C_R = the cutoff point, where level of ruin is reached ($C_R < C_T$)
$C_A = C_T - C_R$, capital available to be risked
E = the expected mean return per trade, the probability-weighted sum of values that a trade might take

$$E = \sum_{i=1}^{N} (PL_i p_i)$$

[17] Fred Gehm, *Quantitative Trading & Money Management* (Revised Edition (Irwin, 1995)).

FIGURE 23-11   Risk of ruin based on capital.

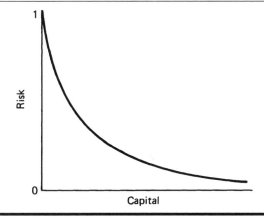

where PL_i is the possible profit or loss value, and p_i is the probability of PL_t occurring $(0 < p_i < 1)$.

E_2 is the expected squared mean return per trade, the probability-weighted sum of all the squared values of a trade,

$$E_2 = \sum_{i=1}^{N} (PL_i^2 p_i)$$

where PL_i and p_i are defined above.

$$D = C_A/\sqrt{E_2}$$

$$P = 0.5 + E/(2\sqrt{E_2})$$

and the risk of ruin is

$$R = \left(\frac{1-P}{P}\right)^D$$

Introducing an objective and a desired level of capital L, the risk of ruin R becomes

$$R = 1 - \frac{[(1-P)/P]^D - 1}{[(1-P)/P]^G - 1}$$

where

$$G = 1/\sqrt{E_2}$$

As in the first situation, using equal profits and losses, the risk increases as the objective L increases.

Ralph Vince, in *Portfolio Management Formulas* (Wiley, New York, 1990) derived similar results from P. Griffin's work, *The Theory of Blackjack* (Gamblers Press, Las Vegas, 1981), which claims to provide a "fair approximation" of risk. Vince's approach has been modified for convenience and given in a way that allows spreadsheet formulas:

Risk of Ruin = ((1 − P)/P)^(MaxRisk/A)

where the following terms are defined in the order needed for calculation:

AvgWin is the average winning trade (e.g., $400)

AvgLoss is the average losing trade (e.g., $200)

Investment is the amount invested (e.g., $10,000)

ProbWin is the probability (percentage) of a winning trade (e.g., .40)

ProbLoss is the probability (percentage) of a losing trade (e.g., .60)

MaxRisk is the maximum part of the investment that can be lost, in percent (e.g., .25)

AvgWin% is @ABS(AvgWin/Investment)

AvgLoss% is @ABS(AvgLoss/Investment)

Z is the sum of possible events, ProbWin*AvgWin% − ProbLoss*AvgLoss%

A is the square root of the sum of the squares of possible events, (ProbWin*AvgWin%^2 + ProbLoss*AvgLoss%^2)^(1/2)

P is .5*(1 + (Z/A))

This can be written as the following spreadsheet example:

Row		Col A	Description of value or calculation in column A
1	AvgWin	400.00	Enter average winning trade in $
2	AvgLoss	200.00	Enter average losing trade in $
3	Investment	10000.00	Enter initial capital invested in $
4	ProbWin	.40	Enter probability of a winning trade
5	ProbLoss	.60	(1 − A4)
6	MaxRisk	.25	Enter maximum part of investment that can be lost (in %)
7	AvgWin%	.040	@abs(A1/A3)
8	AvgLoss%	.020	@abs(A2/A3)
9	Z	.0040	A4*A7 + A5*A8
10	A	.0297	(A4*A7^2 + A5*A8^2)^(1/2)
11	P	.5674	0.9444
12	Risk of Ruin	.1016	((1 − A11)/A11)^(A6/A10)

In the above example, the risk of ruin is slightly greater than 10% based on historic data. The change in risk can be seen by varying the investment amount. Note that in row 11, when $P = 1$, the risk of ruin is 100%; therefore, P cannot be greater than 1.

COMPOUNDING A POSITION

At some point, all speculators find themselves adding to, or compounding, their position. Many traders view this as a means of concentrating on those commodities that have more potential. There are two lines of thinking among these traders. When a trade becomes more profitable, it is confirming its move and is thought to deserve more of a commitment than a trade that has not become profitable. On the other hand, by adding positions to a trade at preset intervals, the effect of a single poor entry point is reduced and a better average entry price is created. This latter technique is called *scaled-down buying* in the securities industry.

The following sections will assume that positions are added based on profitability as a means of increasing leverage. There are a number of techniques used by experienced traders, but the time to add must be carefully selected. The situation chosen must have potential for a long move with limited risk; the sustained consolidation period of a market that is priced near its historic lows would be a candidate. No matter how well chosen, each method will result in the largest holdings at the highest (or lowest) price; when the market reverses, losses occur on a larger base and profits will disappear quickly. Compounding a position is very fragile, hard work and must be watched cautiously for a changing market; there are enough stories of speculators who leveraged small capital into a large fortune in less than a year's time and then lost it all in a week. As in all investments, the risk balances the opportunities.

The Scaled-Down Pyramid

The patterns used to compound positions can be represented geometrically as pyramids. The standard pyramid, or *upright pyramid,* has a larger base than its top. The largest portion of profits are developed early and an adverse price move is not as likely to be disastrous. The profit-compounding effect of this technique is comparably reduced. A favorite scaling method of this type adds one-half of the prior position at each opportunity (Figure 23-12a). The maximum number of contracts to be held must be planned in advance. The total position, if followed to completion, will be about twice the number of contracts that were initially entered; starting with 20 lots, 10, 5, 2, and 1 would be added, respectively. An

FIGURE 23-12 Pyramid structure. (*a*) Scaled-down (upright) pyramid offers a small amount of compounding. (*b*) Adding equal amounts (inverted pyramid) gives maximum leverage. (*c*) Reflecting pyramid combines leverage and profit taking.

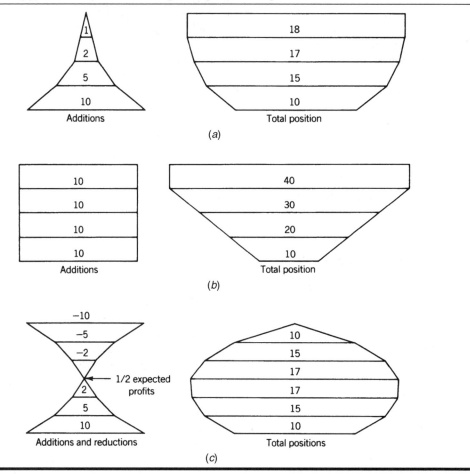

advantage of this or any other pyramiding method is that an initial loss will be based on a smaller number of contracts than the final commitment.

Adding Equal Positions

As larger commitments are added, an inverted pyramid is created (Figure 23-12*b*) in which the risk of an immediate loss due to a small reversal becomes greater.

Adding equal numbers of contracts reduces the proportion of the original commitment in the event the trend does not materialize but increases later exposure (when, hopefully, there are large profits). The shift of risk can only be determined by the trader. With this approach, as well as the other inverted pyramid formations, the speculator should follow the rule that *no unsuccessful secondary position should offset the entire profits of the prior positions.*

Adding Equal Amounts

To offset the effects of disproportionate risk, subsequent positions can be added based on the new value of the market being traded. Comparing this to the previous method of equal contracts, this would reduce the number of purchases in a rising market and increase them in a declining market. The effect of increased volatility at higher levels would substantiate this approach to adding as a means of maintaining the same relative effect of each new position to the prior ones.

Maximum-Leverage Compounding

The greatest risk and the most potential is in adding positions using all profits accumulated to date. To do this necessitates a close working arrangement with the margin department of a brokerage firm. They might even want to install a direct telephone line. Whenever possible, new positions are added, based on the assumption that profits are considered a confirmation of the trend. Being completely leveraged is a tenuous position, requiring constant monitoring of the market; there must be a well-defined stop-loss at all times in anticipation of a premature reversal.

Reflecting Pyramid

One way to reduce the extreme risks of compounding is to remove positions once a specific profit level has been reached. For example, if there is a reasonable expectation of an average profit of 60 points, a *reflecting pyramid* (Figure 23-12c) will add positions until the maximum commitment is reached at one-half the expected profit and then reduce positions until it is entirely closed out at 60. This technique can be modified to apply to any of the methods of adding positions by requiring that the full commitment be achieved at a level below the expected profit; full liquidation may be targeted for a point above the average profit.

Comparison of Compounding Methods

Table 23-6 and Figures 23-13a and 23-13b show the risks and rewards of three methods of compounding compared with holding a single position from trade entry to exit. All forms of pyramiding increase both profits and risk. Holding an unchanged position shows consistently lower returns with a mostly higher reward/risk ratio, especially at early equity levels. Scaled-down additions show an improved return and less attractive ratio; equal additions show much higher returns with a much lower reward/risk profile. The reflecting pyramid has both higher returns than the single position and an improved ratio. At one-half the expected return, it is clearly a better choice than the other methods. As expected profits are neared, the investor must choose between the extremely high leverage and profits of adding equal positions and the excellent reward/risk ratio of the reflecting pyramid.

EQUITY CYCLES

Every system has profit-loss cycles that can be seen clearly by plotting its daily or weekly equity. Trending techniques show that once or twice each year, there are major increases in profits corresponding to a trending market; at other times, there is a steady decline and a stabilizing pattern to the total equity. For a system to operate as it is expected, the positions must be kept constant. Increasing positions as equity increases in a trending cycle results in always being fully invested at the top of the cycle, when losses begin. Losses will be on a larger base than profits, and equity will drop much faster than it increased.

The same effect can occur at the bottom of an equity cycle after a nontrending market period. A sustained losing streak may cause a speculator to reduce the investment in proportion to dwindling capital. If this happens, the result will be entering into a profitable period with a smaller investment than the prior losing period. The system must have disproportionately larger profits to recover the losses and achieve a net gain. An example of a typical system is shown, using a 100% gain for each profitable cycle, followed by a 50% loss cycle. Assume this cycle is repeated twice each year; in one year, the following equity pattern will occur:

TABLE 23-6   Comparison of Compounding Methods*

| | | | | | | | Scaled to 10 | | |
Price	Add	Total	Equity	Liq Val	Risk	Equity/Risk	Equity	Liq Val	Risk
				No Pyramiding					
0	10	10	0	−100	100	0			
10	0	10	100	0	100	1.00			
20	0	10	200	100	100	2.00			
30	0	10	300	200	100	3.00			
40	0	10	400	300	100	4.00			
50	0	10	500	400	100	5.00			
60	0	10	600	500	100	6.00			
			Scaled-Down (Upright) Pyramid						
0	32	32	0	−320	320	0	0	−100	100
10	16	48	320	−160	480	.67	100	−50	150
20	8	56	800	240	560	1.42	250	75	175
30	4	60	1360	760	600	2.27	425	237	187
40	2	62	1960	1340	620	3.17	612	418	193
50	1	63	2580	1950	630	4.11	806	609	196
60	0	63	3210	2580			1003	806	
			Equal Positions						
0	10	10	0	−100	100	0			
10	10	20	100	−100	200	.50			
20	10	30	300	0	300	1.00			
30	10	40	600	200	400	1.50			
40	10	50	1000	500	500	2.00			
50	10	60	1500	900	600	2.50			
60	0	60	2100	1500					
			Reflecting Pyramid						
0	10	10	0	−100	100	0			
10	5	15	100	−50	150	.67			
20	2	17	250	80	170	1.47			
30	0	17	420	250	170	2.47			
40	−2	15	590	440	150	3.93			
50	−5	10	740	640	100	7.40			
60	−10	0	840	740					

* 1 point = $100.

	Change in Equity	Total Equity	
Original margin		$10,000	
Gain of 100%	+10,000	20,000	First 6 months
Loss of 50%	−5,000	15,000	
Gain of 100%	+10,000	25,000	Second 6 months
Loss of 50%	−5,000	20,000	

This leaves a net gain of 100% for the year. Each 100% profit was $10,000, and losses were $5,000—the rate of return is always based on the original margin. Had the cycle started

**FIGURE 23-13   Returns and risks from compounding. (a) Equity and liquidated value
(10-point reversal). (b) Reward to risk ratio.**

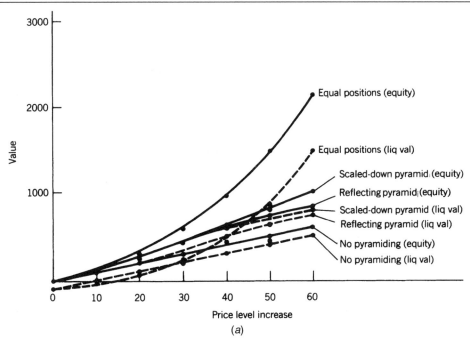

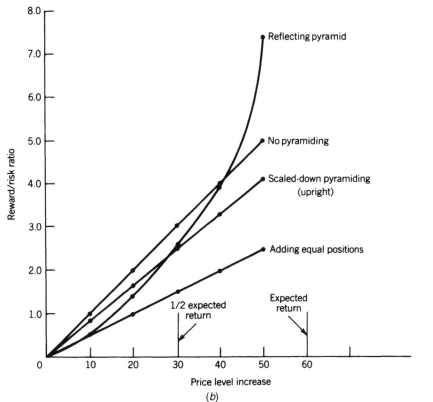

with the losing phase, there would be a profit of 50% for the first year and 100% for each subsequent year.

Many traders would not net 100% each year from a system that performs as the one in the example. As their profits increased, positions would be added so that at the time the total equity was worth $20,000, the margin requirements would also be $20,000. The 50% loss is then applied to the total equity:

	Change in Equity	Total Equity	
Original margin		$10,000	
Gain of 100%	+10,000	20,000	First 6 months
Loss of 50%	−10,000	10,000	
Gain of 100%	+10,000	20,000	Second 6 months
Loss of 50%	−10,000	10,000	

Trading futures would be a great deal of effort for no return.

Holding the investment constant as shown can also be viewed by studying the growth and decline of the account excess, called the *reserve*. The size of the reserve relative to total equity is the key to successful management. Starting with margin and reserves equal, reserves increase during profitable periods and decrease during losing ones. Proportionately more of the total equity is traded during losing phases. This pattern can be used to improve results safely, as follows:

	Change in Equity	Margin	Reserve	Total Equity	Reserve/ Equity
Original investment		10,000	10,000	20,000	50%
Gain of 100%	+10,000	10,000	20,000	30,000	67%
Loss of 50%	−5,000	10,000	15,000	25,000	60%
Gain of 100%	+10,000	10,000	25,000	35,000	71%
Loss of 50%	−5,000	10,000	20,000	30,000	67%

Using the natural equity cycles, hold the number of positions the same and allow the reserve to increase during profitable periods; maintain the same position size through the beginning of the next losing period. When the equity drop has slowed or stabilized, the total equity can be redistributed into margin and reserve according to the original 50% formula. In the next example, the total equity of $25,000 is distributed 40% to margin and 60% to reserve at the end of the first cycle. It is redistributed so that the next profit phase will be entered with a larger base than the previous losing cycle. The result is a gradual increase in profits:

	Change in Equity	Margin	Total Reserve	Reserve/ Equity	Equity
Original investment		10,000	10,000	20,000	50%
Gain of 100%	+10,000	10,000	20,000	30,000	67%
Loss of 50%	−5,000	10,000	15,000	25,000	60%
Redistribute		12,500	12,500	25,000	50%
Gain of 100%	+10,000	12,500	25,000	37,500	67%
Loss of 50%	−5,000	12,500	18,750	31,250	60%
Redistribute		15,625	15,625	31,250	50%

Trading on Equity Cycles

If a moving average technique is traded, the equity resulting from this strategy will fluctuate with the trending nature of the market. By applying a moving average analysis to the equity itself, the trending and nontrending periods are identified by *buy* and *sell* signals just as though the equity series was a price series.

An equity *buy* means that the market has begun trending; the length of this period depends on the calculation period of the trend. A *sell* signal means that the market is no longer trending. These signals can be taken as "buy the system" or "short the system"; that is, enter all positions that the system currently holds or liquidate the entire portfolio and hold cash. An equity buy could also be taken as the point to redistribute the equity into the original ratio of margin to reserves. If the normal profile of price movement is to spend a large proportion in a sideways pattern, then there should be sustained periods of downward equity trends; trading equity cycles can improve performance.

INVESTING AND REINVESTING: OPTIMAL *f*

Optimal f is the optimal fixed fraction of an account that should be invested at any one time, or the size of the bet to place on any one trade. The amount to be risked is measured as a percentage of the portfolio size. The objective is to maximize the amount invested (put at risk), yet avoid the possibility of total loss. Trading a very small part of assets can be a poor use of capital, while trading too much guarantees bankruptcy or ruin. Optimal *f* is the ideal portion of an investment that should be placed at risk at any one time. If you risk less than the optimal *f*, then you are not generating the peak profits; however, if you trade more than optimal *f*, you assure eventual ruin.

Investing generally has a two-level optimal *f*: the part of the total portfolio put at risk compared with that part held in cash equivalents, and the individual size of the commitment to each stock or futures market within that portfolio. This is particularly important for futures, where the high leverage of individual markets makes it very easy to risk too much on each trade.

Fixed Initial Investments

Then, how much should be invested? The optimal amount is difficult to pinpoint because you would have to know what risks lie ahead, and of course, that's not possible. However, based on a very small likelihood of losing 50% of the portfolio when 50% is invested, one might say that a portion under a 50% investment is best. To account for greater uncertainties in the future, you could increase your confidence by investing only 25% of the initial portfolio. This approach has negative effects, because a smaller relative investment reduces both risk and returns. When the investment becomes too small, the returns are no longer attractive.

The chance of a catastrophic risk is an important concern for any investor or portfolio manager. For practical purposes this is always figured on the historic profile of the data or trading results. This still leaves uncertainty in the final values. Nevertheless, the most extreme situation is often found by using the calculation for risk of ruin (in a previous section of this chapter), most often applied to gambling situations in which the bet sizes, payout, and odds are well defined. When there are enough test data and trades, this technique has been applied to trading systems (see the section "Wins Not Equal to Losses").

Some analysts have tried to deal with the uncertainties of price movements by using a *Monte Carlo* technique in testing, which shifts the sequence of blocks of data, or profit and loss results, so that they occur in random order. The worst results are considered the greatest risk. This approach may be unrealistically severe, yet even the real performance is not likely to reflect the size of the risk in the future. For those traders applying a long-term trend-following technique to capture moves that are based on economic or government policy, sustained profits are most often followed by a reversal before the trade is ended. In fact, the ending change of direction is directly related to the sustained move. To move this data around so that the loss comes at a different time may create a large loss without the offsetting profit, which is a situation that is unfair to the trading strategy. Before applying a Monte Carlo analysis, it is first necessary to identify the dominant period of sequential correlation to avoid segmenting the series incorrectly.

For an initial investment, the optimal f is simply the maximum part of that portfolio that can safely be traded without any significant risk of ruin. For those investors who take out profits when they occur and continue to trade based on the same assumed initial investment, nothing need be changed unless exceptionally high risk causes a reassessment and decrease in the amount of leverage. However, it is more common and more complicated for the investor to vary the amount committed to the market by either increasing or decreasing leverage. This involves (1) determining the right time to change the leverage, (2) calculating the amount to increase the investment when there are profits, and (3) figuring the size of the reduction when there are losses exceeding some designated amount. These are issues that are addressed by optimal f.

Finding Optimal f

Ralph Vince, in his popular book, *Portfolio Management Formulas*,[18] focuses on optimal f, risk of ruin, and other practical items. Optimal f is the ideal amount of an investment that should be put at risk at any one time. As background for this, we need to formulate the relationship where the percentage gain needed to recover a loss is larger than the percentage lost.

$$Required\ gain = \frac{1}{1 - percent\ loss} - 1$$

That is, a 50% loss requires a 100% gain to restore the original value. Because the amount risked on each trade depends on our expectations of loss, the results obtained from the optimal f calculation will be the size of the bet, invested amount, or the number of contracts to be traded, as a percentage of the maximum loss. As we already know, the value used as a maximum loss will be an estimate, because losses can always be greater than only those experienced in the market, whether theoretical or real. In addition, the optimal f will be different for each system, depending upon its performance profile.

The mathematics needed to determine optimal f is based on the Kelly Betting System.[19] Kelly states that the optimum bet is the one that maximizes the growth function $G(f)$:

$$G(f) = P * \ln(1 + B * f) + (1 - P) * \ln(1 - f)$$

where f is the optimum fixed fraction
         P is the probability of a winning bet or trade
         B is the ratio of the average winning return to the average losing return
         ln is the natural log function

The solution for finding the optimal fixed fraction to invest uses the geometric product and geometric mean, which represent the way in which profits and losses accrue.

$$Optimal\ f = \max\left(\prod_{i=1}^{N}\left(1 + \frac{f \times (-PL_i)}{largest\ loss}\right)\right)^{1/N}, \qquad for\ f = .01\ to\ 1.0$$

---

[18] Ralph Vince, *Portfolio Management Formulas* (John Wiley & Sons, 1990, pp. 79–86).

[19] John L. Kelly, Jr., "Kelly Betting System," *Bell System Technical Journal* (July 1956).

where max is the function that selects the maximum value

$\prod$ is the product

largest loss is the largest loss of any PL_i

PL_i is the profit or loss for trade i

N is the number of trades

By testing values of f between .01 and 1.0, and finding the geometric mean of all trades (each percentage profit or loss applied to the account value before the current trade), we find the value of f that gives the best return. That f-value is the optimal f, the amount of the total account that should be invested for each trade.

A simpler way of expressing optimal f, the amount invested on a single trade, is given as[20]

$$f = [p \times (R + 1) - 1] / R$$

where R = the ratio of average profit to average loss

p = the probability of a winning trade

Therefore, if $p = .50$, there is an equal chance of a profit or a loss, and the average profit is $400 while the average loss is $200 (giving $R = 2.0$), then $f = (.50(2 + 1) - 1)/2 = .5/2 = .25$ or 25% of the available capital. Given an equal chance of a profit or a loss, it is not likely that there would be four losses in a row, each of 25%; however, the theory of runs shows that, out of every 100 trades, there should be one run of six. Eventually, there will be a run of four or five losses in a row. Optimal f, however, invests a fraction of the current equity; therefore, after a loss of 25%, the next investment is 25% of the balance, or 18.75% of the initial equity. If there are further losses, that amount drops to 14.06%. After three losses in a row, instead of having lost 75% of the initial equity, the investment has only dropped by 57.81%. Over time, with profits twice as large as losses, and winning trades normally alternating with losing trades, the losses will be recovered.

Observations of Optimal f

According to Alex Elder,[21] there are some difficulties in using optimal f. Because the value is based on every historic trade, the ideal amount to invest on the next trade will keep changing. In addition, if you trade a position larger than the optimal f, with average results, you can expect to go broke eventually because you are overinvesting. On the other hand, if you invest less than the optimal amount, then your risk decreases arithmetically, but your profits decrease geometrically, which is another bad scenario. Because this process can become very complicated, the simple solution for most investors is to keep trading the same amount, leaving a large reserve so you are not caught short.

On the positive side, Dr. Elder concludes that the most useful results of optimal f is that it shows the important principles:

1. Never average down.
2. Never meet margin calls.
3. Liquidate your worst position first.

Practically Speaking

Evaluating the risk and reward of a trading program, even using a number of years of actual performance, rarely gives results that are statistically accurate. Markets change and the performance profile of any trading system can vary significantly over long time periods. Determining the amount to invest on a single trade based on the average risk and average return

[20] Robert P. Rotella, *The Elements of Successful Trading* (The New York Institute of Finance, 1992, pp. 549–550).

[21] Dr. Alexander Elder, *Trading for a Living* (John Wiley & Sons, 1993).

of past performance can lead to a tragic end. When investing 25% in each trade, a loss that is twice what is expected, followed by a smaller profit and another large loss (in a more volatile period), could exhaust your capital, regardless of the statistics.

In general, the less you risk, the safer you are. From time to time there are price shocks that produce profits and losses far greater than the averages show. Although the theory of an optimal fixed fraction may be correct, the numbers used in the calculation are not often reliable.

COMPARING EXPECTED AND ACTUAL RESULTS

In the development of an economic model or trading system, the final selection is usually the result of a performance comparison of the completed models. Often the results are given in terms of profit/loss ratios, annualized percentage profits, expected reliability (percentage of profitable trades to total trades), and potential risk. Although these statistics are common, their predictive qualities and sometimes their accuracy are not known. On occasion, these results are generated by a sample that is too small, and usually they are not the results of a predictive but an historic test. This does not mean that the model will be unsuccessful, but that the pattern of success might vary far from the expected profit/loss ratio, reliability, and risk. In actual trading, every speculator experiences a series of losses far exceeding anything that was expected; at that point, it is best to know whether this situation could occur within the realm of the system's profile or whether the system has failed. For example, a moving average system is expected to have 1 out of 3 profitable trades with a profit/loss ratio of 4 : 1. But the first 10 trades of the system are losers. Should trading be stopped?

Binomial Probability

Consider the application of a random-number sequence to the trading model. What is the probability of l losses in n tries when the probability of a loss is p? Most of the work in this area of probability is credited to Bernoulli, whose study of a random walk is called a *Bernoulli process*. A clear representation of a random walk is shown by the Pascal triangle (Figure 23-14), where each box represents the probability of being in a particular position at a specific time in a forward random walk. The result of this process is called a *binomial distribution*.

The forward random walk has an analogy to price movement, with the far edges of Pascal's triangle showing the probability of a continuous sequence of wins or losses using random numbers. The sequence $\frac{1}{2}, \frac{1}{4}, \frac{1}{8}, \ldots, (\frac{1}{2})^n$ is exactly the same as in the discussion of the Theory of Runs. The probability of successive losses can be calculated as the likelihood of a run of the same length, $(\frac{1}{2})^{n+2}$.

FIGURE 23-14   Pascal's triangle.

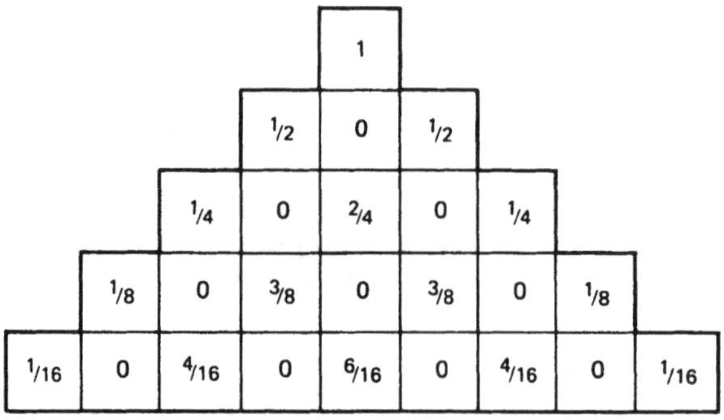

A binomial distribution is useful in considering the total number of losses that can occur in any order within a sequence of trades; it is the probability of getting to a specific point at the base of Pascal's triangle when there is a high probability of moving to the left (losses) rather than the right (profits). The formula for the binomial probability is:

$$B(l{:}p,n) = \frac{n!}{l!(n-l)!} p^l (1-p)^{n-l}$$

where l is the number of losses

   n is the total number of tries

   p is the probability of a loss

and the symbol "!" is the factorial (e.g., $5! = 5 \times 4 \times 3 \times 2 \times 1$).

Consider the first 5 trades of a system with a probability of success of ⅓. How many losses should be expected? To answer the question, find the binomial probability B for all possibilities and form a distribution function. Let $l = 4$. Then,

$$B(4{:}.667,5) = \frac{5!}{4!1!}(.667)^4 (.333)^1$$

$$= \frac{120}{24} \times (.19792)(.333)$$

$$= 5 \times .0659 = .32954$$

The binomial probability of having 4 losses out of the first 5 trades is about 33%. The following table shows the probability of losses for the first 5, 10, and 15 trades of a system, with a ⅓ predicted reliability. Results show the highest probability of occurrence of loss is at the ⅔ point (mean) for each sequence, but the standard deviation gives the range of variance about the mean, so that from 2.3 to 4.4, losses are expected in every 5 trades, 5.2 to 8.2 in 10 trades, and 8.2 to 11.8 losses in 15 trades (Table 23-7).

Note that in the 5-trade example, the chances of no losses is only 1%, and there is a 13% chance of all losses. For the purpose of evaluation, it is easier to look at the maximum rather than the minimum number of losses. For 15 trades, there is an 8% chance of 13 or more losses; if the system has produced more than 12 losses in that period, there is something wrong with the predicted reliability.

In addition to the Pascal distribution, the reader may find the Poisson and various skewed distribution functions have application to system evaluation.

χ^2—Chi-Square Test

Once a system has been traded and there is enough data to give a performance profile, the significance between these actual results and the expected results can be found using the *chi-square test*. First, there must be enough data for a relevant answer. From the section on sampling, the formula for error is $1/\sqrt{N}$, where N is the number of items sampled. If there are 25 trades, the expected error in the calculation is $1/\sqrt{25}$, or 20%; 100 trades would give results accurate to 10%.

Assume that the real trading results show a reliability of 20% (1 out of 5) as compared with the expected reliability of 35%. What are the chances of getting these results? The chi-square test is

$$\chi^2 = \frac{(O-E)^2}{E}$$

where O is the observed, or actual result, and E is the expected or theoretical result. Then,

TABLE 23-7   The Probability of a Specific Number of Losses

5 Trades		10 Trades		15 Trades	
Losses	Probability (%)	Losses	Probability (%)	Losses	Probability (%)
0	1	0	0	0	0
1	4	1	0	1	0
2	16	2	0	2	0
3	33	3	2	3	0
4	33	4	5	4	0
5	13	5	14	5	1
		6	23	6	2
		7	26	7	6
		8	19	8	11
		9	9	9	18
		10	2	10	21
				11	20
				12	13
				13	6
				14	2
				15	0
$m^* = 3\frac{1}{3}$		$m = 6\frac{2}{3}$		$m = 10$	
$sd^\dagger = 1.05$		$sd = 1.5$		$sd = 1.825$	

* Mean.
† Standard deviation.

$$\chi^2 = \frac{(20-35)^2}{35} + \frac{(80-65)^2}{65}$$

$$= \frac{(-15)^2}{35} + \frac{(-15)^2}{65}$$

$$= \frac{225}{35} + \frac{225}{65} = 6.428 + 3.46$$

$$= 9.89$$

The percentage of actual winning trades is compared with the anticipated winning trades and the losing trades with the expected losing trades. The answer must be found in the first row of Table 23-8, which gives the distribution of χ^2.

The probability is distributed unequally in the table because the results are only significant if the probability is small, showing less likelihood of the results occurring by chance. For this simple two-element test, the result P is classified as

Highly significant   if $P \geq 10.83$ (.1% or 1/1,000)

Significant: if $P \geq 6.64$ (1% or 1/100)

Probably significant   if $P \geq 3.84$ (5% or 1/20)

The answer $\chi^2 = 9.89$ is between .1% and 1% showing *significance*. For a large sample, the actual reliability should not have been 20% when 35% was expected.

The chi-square test can be used to compare actual price movement with random patterns to see whether there is appreciable variation. In the section on the Theory of Runs, Table 23-9 showed:

TABLE 23-8 Distribution of χ^2

Cases	Probability of Occurring by Chance								
Less 1	.70	.50	.30	.20	.10	.05	.02	.01	.001
1	.15	.46	1.07	1.64	2.71	3.84	5.41	6.64	10.83
2	.71	1.39	2.41	3.22	4.61	5.99	7.82	9.21	13.82
3	1.42	2.37	3.67	4.64	6.25	7.82	9.84	11.34	16.27
4	2.20	3.36	4.88	5.99	7.78	9.49	11.67	13.28	18.47
5	3.00	4.35	6.06	7.29	9.24	11.07	13.39	15.09	20.52
6	3.83	5.35	7.23	8.56	10.65	12.59	15.03	16.81	22.46
7	4.67	6.35	8.38	9.80	12.02	14.07	16.62	18.48	24.32
8	5.53	7.34	9.52	11.03	13.36	15.51	18.17	20.09	26.13
9	6.39	8.34	10.66	12.24	14.68	16.92	19.68	21.67	27.88
10	7.27	9.34	11.78	13.44	15.99	18.31	21.16	23.21	29.59

TABLE 23-9 Results from Analysis of Runs

Length of Run	Expected Results (E)	Actual Results (O)
1	1225	1214
2	612	620
3	306	311
4	153	167
5	77	67
6	38	41
7	19	16
8	10	5
9	5	3
≥10	4	5
≥ 8*	19	13

* The last groups were combined in order not to distort the results based on a small sample.

Applying the actual data for runs of one through eight against a random distribution,

$$\chi^2 = \sum_{n=1}^{8} \frac{(O_n - E_n)^2}{E_n}$$

$$= \frac{(1214 - 1225)^2}{1225} + \frac{(620 - 612)^2}{612} + \frac{(311 - 306)^6}{306} + \frac{(167 - 153)^2}{153}$$

$$+ \frac{(67 - 77)^2}{77} + \frac{(41 - 38)^2}{38} + \frac{(16 - 19)^2}{19} + \frac{(13 - 19)^2}{19}$$

$$\begin{array}{ccccc} (1) & (2) & (3) & (4) & (5) \end{array}$$
$$= .09877 + .10457 + .08169 + 1.2810 + 1.2987$$

$$\begin{array}{ccc} (6) & (7) & (8) \end{array}$$
$$.23684 + .47368 + 1.8947$$

$$= 5.470$$

Table 23-8 gives the probability of about 55% for 8 cases. The results are not significant; the Theory of Runs shows that all cases taken together give the same patterns as chance movement. Individual runs or sets of two or three adjacent runs can be inspected for distortion. In both cases, the results are further from normal but not mathematically significant. The two runs that differed the most were 4 to 5 days, which showed an 11% probability of occurring by chance.

Highly significant price runs can be found in the occurrence of extended runs, for example, 20 days, which is experienced occasionally in trending markets. By looking at the *asymmetry* of price movement, where a reverse run of 1 day is of negligible value, the significance of these runs will dramatically increase. Price movement is not a simple matter of random runs and equal payout.

Statistical Tables

PROBABILITY DISTRIBUTIONS TABLES

TABLE A1-1   Normal Curve Areas

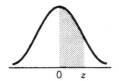

z	.00	.01	.02	.03	.04	.05	.06	.07	.08	.09
0.0	.0000	.0040	.0080	.0120	.0160	.0199	.0239	.0279	.0319	.0359
0.1	.0398	.0438	.0478	.0517	.0557	.0596	.0636	.0675	.0714	.0753
0.2	.0793	.0832	.0871	.0910	.0948	.0987	.1026	.1064	.1103	.1141
0.3	.1179	.1217	.1255	.1293	.1331	.1368	.1406	.1443	.1480	.1517
0.4	.1554	.1591	.1628	.1664	.1700	.1736	.1772	.1808	.1844	.1879
0.5	.1915	.1950	.1985	.2019	.2054	.2088	.2123	.2157	.2190	.2224
0.6	.2257	.2291	.2324	.2357	.2389	.2422	.2454	.2486	.2517	.2549
0.7	.2580	.2612	.2642	.2673	.2704	.2734	.2764	.2794	.2823	.2852
0.8	.2881	.2910	.2939	.2967	.2995	.3023	.3051	.3078	.3106	.3133
0.9	.3159	.3186	.3212	.3238	.3264	.3289	.3315	.3340	.3365	.3389
1.0	.3413	.3438	.3461	.3485	.3508	.3531	.3554	.3577	.3599	.3621
1.1	.3643	.3665	.3686	.3708	.3729	.3749	.3770	.3790	.3810	.3820
1.2	.3849	.3869	.3888	.3907	.3925	.3944	.3962	.3980	.3997	.4015
1.3	.4032	.4049	.4066	.4082	.4099	.4115	.4131	.4147	.4162	.4177
1.4	.4192	.4207	.4222	.4236	.4251	.4265	.4279	.4292	.4306	.4319
1.5	.4332	.4345	.4357	.4370	.4382	.4394	.4406	.4418	.4429	.4441
1.6	.4452	.4463	.4474	.4484	.4495	.4505	.4515	.4525	.4535	.4545
1.7	.4554	.4564	.4573	.4582	.4591	.4599	.4608	.4616	.4625	.4633
1.8	.4641	.4649	.4656	.4664	.4671	.4678	.4686	.4693	.4699	.4706
1.9	.4713	.4719	.4726	.4732	.4738	.4744	.4750	.4756	.4761	.4767
2.0	.4772	.4778	.4783	.4788	.4793	.4798	.4803	.4808	.4812	.4817
2.1	.4821	.4826	.4830	.4834	.4838	.4842	.4846	.4850	.4854	.4857
2.2	.4861	.4864	.4868	.4871	.4875	.4878	.4881	.4884	.4887	.4890
2.3	.4893	.4896	.4898	.4901	.4904	.4906	.4909	.4911	.4913	.4916
2.4	.4918	.4920	.4922	.4925	.4927	.4929	.4931	.4932	.4934	.4936
2.5	.4938	.4940	.4941	.4943	.4945	.4946	.4948	.4949	.4951	.4952
2.6	.4953	.4955	.4956	.4957	.4959	.4960	.4961	.4962	.4963	.4964
2.7	.4965	.4966	.4967	.4968	.4969	.4970	.4971	.4972	.4973	.4974
2.8	.4974	.4975	.4976	.4977	.4977	.4978	.4979	.4979	.4980	.4981
2.9	.4981	.4982	.4982	.4983	.4984	.4984	.4985	.4985	.4986	.4986
3.0	.4987	.4987	.4987	.4988	.4988	.4989	.4989	.4989	.4990	.4990

TABLE A1-2 *T*-Distribution

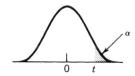

d.f \ α	.10	.05	.025	.01	.005
1	3.078	6.314	12.706	31.821	63.657
2	1.886	2.920	4.303	6.965	9.925
3	1.638	2.353	3.182	4.541	5.841
4	1.533	2.132	2.776	3.747	4.604
5	1.476	2.015	2.571	3.365	4.032
6	1.440	1.943	2.447	3.143	3.707
7	1.415	1.895	2.365	2.998	3.499
8	1.397	1.860	2.306	2.896	3.355
9	1.383	1.833	2.262	2.821	3.250
10	1.372	1.812	2.228	2.764	3.169
11	1.363	1.796	2.201	2.718	3.106
12	1.356	1.782	2.179	2.681	3.055
13	1.350	1.771	2.160	2.650	3.012
14	1.345	1.761	2.145	2.624	2.977
15	1.341	1.753	2.131	2.602	2.947
16	1.337	1.746	2.120	2.583	2.921
17	1.333	1.740	2.110	2.567	2.898
18	1.330	1.734	2.101	2.552	2.878
19	1.328	1.729	2.093	2.539	2.861
20	1.325	1.725	2.086	2.528	2.845
21	1.323	1.721	2.080	2.518	2.831
22	1.321	1.717	2.074	2.508	2.819
23	1.319	1.714	2.069	2.500	2.807
24	1.318	1.711	2.064	2.492	2.797
25	1.316	1.708	2.060	2.485	2.787
26	1.315	1.706	2.056	2.479	2.779
27	1.314	1.703	2.052	2.473	2.771
28	1.313	1.701	2.048	2.467	2.763
29	1.311	1.699	2.045	2.462	2.756
30	1.310	1.697	2.042	2.457	2.750
40	1.303	1.684	2.021	2.423	2.704
60	1.296	1.671	2.000	2.390	2.660
120	1.289	1.658	1.980	2.358	2.617
∞	1.282	1.645	1.960	2.326	2.576

Source: Hoel, *Elementary Statistics, 3d ed.* (John Wiley & Sons, New York, 1971).

TABLE OF UNIFORM RANDOM NUMBERS

	1	2	3	4	5	6	7	8	9	10	11
1	10480	15011	01536	02011	81647	91646	69179	14194	62590	36207	20969
2	22368	46573	25595	85393	30995	89198	27982	53402	93965	34095	52666
3	24130	48360	22527	97265	76393	64809	15179	24830	49340	32081	30680
4	42167	93093	06243	61680	07856	16376	39440	53537	71341	57004	00849
5	37570	39975	81837	16656	06121	91782	60468	81305	49684	60672	14110
6	77921	06907	11008	42751	27756	53498	18602	70659	90655	15033	21916
7	99562	72905	56420	69994	98872	31016	71194	18738	44013	44840	63213
8	96301	91977	05463	07972	18876	20922	94595	56869	69014	60045	18425
9	89579	14342	63661	10281	17453	18103	57740	84378	25331	12566	58678
10	85475	36857	53342	53988	53060	59533	38867	62300	08158	17893	16439
11	28918	69578	88231	33276	70997	79936	56865	05859	90106	31595	91547
12	63553	40961	48235	03427	49626	69445	18663	72695	52180	20847	12234
13	09429	93969	52636	92737	88974	33488	36320	17617	30015	07272	84115
14	10365	61129	87529	85689	48237	52267	67689	93394	01511	26358	85104
15	07119	97336	71048	08178	77233	13916	47564	81056	97735	85977	29372
16	51085	12765	51821	51259	77452	16308	60756	92144	49442	53900	70960
17	02368	21382	52404	60268	89368	19885	55322	44819	01188	65255	64835
18	01011	54092	33362	94904	31273	04146	18594	29852	71585	85030	51132
19	52162	53916	46369	58586	23216	14513	83149	98736	23495	64350	94738
20	07056	97628	33787	09998	42698	06691	76988	13602	51851	46104	88916
21	48663	91245	85828	14346	09172	30168	90229	04734	59193	22178	30421
22	54164	58492	22421	74103	47070	25306	76468	26384	58151	06646	21524
23	32639	32363	05597	24200	13363	38005	94342	28728	35806	06912	17012
24	29334	27001	87637	87308	58731	00256	45834	15398	46557	41135	10367
25	02488	33062	28834	07351	19731	92420	60952	61280	50001	67658	32586
26	81525	72295	04839	96423	25878	82651	66566	14778	76797	14780	13300
27	29676	20591	68086	26432	46901	20849	80768	81536	86645	12659	92259
28	00742	57392	39064	66432	84673	40027	32832	61362	98947	96067	64760
29	05366	04213	25669	26422	44407	44048	37937	63904	45766	66134	75470
30	91921	26418	64117	94305	26766	25940	39972	22209	71500	64568	91402
31	00582	04711	87917	77341	42206	35126	74087	99547	81817	42607	43808
32	00725	69884	62797	56170	86324	88072	76222	36086	84637	93161	76038
33	69011	65795	95876	55293	18988	27354	26575	08625	40801	59920	29841
34	25976	57948	29888	88604	67917	48708	18912	82271	65424	69774	33611
35	09763	83473	73577	12908	30883	10317	28290	35797	05998	41688	34952
36	91567	42595	27958	30134	04024	86385	29880	99730	55536	84855	29080
37	17955	56349	90999	49127	20044	59931	06115	20542	18059	02008	73708
38	46503	18584	18845	49618	02304	51038	20655	58727	28168	15475	56942
39	92157	89634	94824	78171	84610	82834	09922	25417	44137	48413	25555
40	14577	62765	35605	81263	39667	47358	56873	56307	61607	49518	89565

Source: Francis F. Martin, *Computer Modeling and Simulation* (John Wiley & Sons, 1968, p. 288 (reprinted by permission)).

Method of Least Squares

The following programs, written in Microsoft FORTRAN for the IBM PC,[1] solve the two-variable regression analysis using the *method of least squares*. The program allows for the regression of two series against one another, and the regression of one series against time.

OPERATING INSTRUCTIONS

In the following example, the user's entries are underlined:

```
LSTSQ
Enter data in sets of 2 (Y then X).
If second variable is omitted, sequential numbers will be used for x.
Extra <return> ends input.

Enter below:
YYYYYY XXXXXX
1.27    2.43
1.19    2.26
1.10    2.15
<RETURN>

Print data (Y/N)? Y
```

(Computer prints data and solutions)

```
Sample results (Y/N)?Y

Enter start, end and increments below
sssss eeeee iiiiii
1.00   7.00    .50
```

(Computer prints sample results)

```
Plot results (Y/N)?Y
Name for X-scale (9 chars)?
SOYBEANS
Name for Y-scale (9 chars)?
CORN

Which plot?
   1: Linear
   2: Logarithmic
   3: Exponential
   4: Curvilinear
Which number? 1

(Computer plots)

Another plot (Y/N)?Y

Which plot?
   1: Linear
```

(and so forth)

COMPUTER PROGRAMS

```
1 $TITLE: 'LSTSQ: LEAST SQUARES'
2 $SUBTITLE: 'COPYRIGHT 1986 P J KAUFMAN'
```

---

[1] BASIC programs for both plotting and least-squares regression can be found in F.R. Ruckdeschel, *BASIC Scientific Subroutines, Volume I* (Byte/McGraw-Hill, Peterborough, NH, 1981).

```
 3 $STORAGE:2
 4        PROGRAM LSTSQ
 5 C---- Least Squares Regression Analysis for 2 variables
 6
 7        CHARACTER*1 ANS
 8        DIMENSION X(100),Y(100)
 9
10        DATA MAX/100/
11
12        OPEN(6,FILE='PRN')
13
14 C---- Read data in sets of 2 variables
15        I = 1
16        WRITE(*,7000)
17 7000 FORMAT(' Enter data in sets of 2 (Y then X).'/
18      +        ' If second variable is omitted, sequential numbers',
19      +        ' will be used for X.'/' Extra <return> ends input.'//
20      +        ' Enter below:'/
21      +        ' YYYYYY XXXXXX')
22    10 READ(*,5000)Y(I),X(I)
23 5000 FORMAT(BN,F6.2,F7.2)
24        IF(Y(I).EQ.0)GOTO 30
25        IF(X(I).EQ.0)X(I)=I
26        IF(I.EQ.MAX)THEN
27          WRITE(*,7001)MAX
28 7001    FORMAT(' Data input reached max of',I5,'. Processing begins.')
29          GOTO 30
30          ENDIF
31        I =I+1
32        GOTO 10
33
34    30 N = I-1
35        WRITE(*,7002)
36 7002 FORMAT(' Print data (Y/N)?'\)
37        READ(*,5001)ANS
38 5001 FORMAT(A1)
39        IF(ANS.NE. 'Y')GOTO 50
40        WRITE(6,6000)
41 6000 FORMAT('1Least-Squares Regression Analysis',20X,'Data Input'\\
42      +        ' Y (dep)  X (ind)'\)
43        DO 40 J = 1,N
44          WRITE(6,6001)Y(J),X(J)
45 6001 FORMAT(2F8.2)
46    40 CONTINUE
47
48    50 CALL RA2V(Y,X,N)
49
50        CALL EXIT
51        END

 1 $TITLE: 'RA2V: Regression for 2 Variables'
 2 $SUBTITLE: 'Copypright 1986 PJ Kaufman'
 3 $STORAGE:2
 4        SUBROUTINE RA2V(Y,X,N)
 5
 6 C---- Regression Analysis for 2 Variables
 7 C----      With Linear, Power and Log Transformations
 8
 9 C---- Y = Dependent variable
10 C---- X = Independent variable
11 C---- N = Number of data entries
```

```
12
13        CHARACTER*1 ANS
14        CHARACTER*2 SIGN,SIGNC
15        CHARACTER*9 YNAME,XNAME
16
17        DIMENSION X(100),Y(100),ZA(4),ZB(4),ZR(4)
18
19        DATA MAX/100/
20
21 C---- Perform linear regression
22        ITYPE=1
23        CALL BSTFIT(Y,X,N,ZA(1),ZB(1),ZR(1),SD,ITYPE)
24        SIGN=' '
25        IF(ZB(1).GE.0)SIGN=' +'
26
27        WRITE(6,6000)ZA(1),SIGN,ZB(1),ZR(1),SD
28 6000 FORMAT(/54X, 'r2 St dev'//
29            + ' LINEAR Y=',F8.3,A2,F8.3,'*X',18X,F7.1,F9.3)
30
31        CALL LSTSQ2(Y,X,N,ZA(4),ZB(4),C,S4)
32
33        SIGN =' '
34        IF(ZB(4).GE.0)SIGN =' +'
35        SIGNC =' '
36        IF(C.GE.0)SIGNC =' +'
37        ITYPE = 4
38
39        WRITE(6,6004)ZA(4),SIGN,ZB(4),SIGNC,C,S4
40 6004 FORMAT(/' CURVI Y=',F8.3,A2,F8.3,'*X',A2,F8.3,'*X2',12X,F9.3)
41
42        ITYPE=2
43        CALL BSTFIT(Y,X,N,ZA(2),ZB(2),ZR(2),SD,ITYPE)
44        SIGN=' '
45        IF(ZB(2).GE.0)SIGN=' +'
46
47        WRITE(6,6001)ZA(2),SIGN,ZB(2),ZR(2),SD
48 6001 FORMAT(/' LOG   Ln(Y)=',F8.3,A2,F8.3,'*Ln(X)',10X,F7.1,F9.3)
49
50        ITYPE=3
51        CALL BSTFIT(Y,X,N,ZA(3),ZB(3),ZR(3),SD,ITYPE)
52        SIGN=' '
53        IF(ZB(3).GE.0)SIGN=' +'
54
55        WRITE(6,6002)ZA(3),SIGN,ZB(3),ZR(3),SD
56 6002 FORMAT(/' EXPON Ln(Y)=',F10.3,A2,F10.3,'*X',10X,F7.1,F9.3)
57
58        WRITE(*,7000)
59 7000 FORMAT('Sample results (Y/N)?'\)
60        READ(*,5000)ANS
61 5000 FORMAT(A1)
62        IF(ANS.NE.'N')THEN
63            WRITE(*,7001)
64 7001    FORMAT(/' Enter start, end and increments below'/
65     +            'sssss eeeee iiiiii')
66            READ(*,5001)P,END,STEPS
67 5001    FORMAT(BN,F6.2,2F7.2)
68
69            WRITE(6,6009)
70 6009    FORMAT(//12X, 'X LINEAR  CURVI    LOG   EXPON'/)
71
72 C---- Calculate all four fits at the same time
```

```
73    100      Y1 = ZA(1) + ZB(1)*P
74             Y2 = ZA(4) + ZB(4)*P + C*P*P
75             Y3 = ZA(2) + ZB(2)*ALOG(P)
76             Y3 = EXP(Y3)
77             Y4 = ZA(3) + ZB(3)*P
78             Y4 = EXP(Y4)
79
80             WRITE(6,6010)P,Y1,Y2,Y3,Y4
81    6010     FORMAT(5X,5F8.2)
82
83             IF(P.LT.END)THEN
84               P = P + STEPS
85               GOTO 100
86               ENDIF
87
88             ENDIF
89
90          WRITE(*,7002)
91    7002 FORMAT(/' Plot results (Y/N)?'\)
92         READ(*,5000)ANS
93         IF(ANS.NE.'N')THEN
94            WRITE(*,7003)
95    7003    FORMAT(' Name for x-scale (9 chars)?')
96            READ(*,5002)XNAME
97    5002    FORMAT(A)
98            WRITE(*,7004)
99    7004    FORMAT(' Name for y-scale (9 chars)?')
100           READ(*,5003)YNAME
101   5003    FORMAT(A9)
102    120    WRITE(*,7005)
103   7005    FORMAT(/' Which plot?'/' 1: Linear'/' 2: Logarithmic'/
104      +           '     3: Exponential'/' 4: Curvilinear'/
105      +           ' Which number?'\)
106           READ(*,5004)I
107   5004    FORMAT(BN,I4)
108           TC = C
109           IF(I.NE.4)TC = 0
110           CALL PLOTRA(N,X,Y,ZA(I),ZB(I),TC,I,XNAME,YNAME)
111           WRITE(*,7006)
112   7006    FORMAT(/' Another plot (Y/N)?'\)
113           READ(*,5000)ANS
114           IF(ANS.NE. 'N')GOTO 120
115           ENDIF
116
117       RETURN
118       END


  1 $TITLE: 'LSTSQ2: 2nd Order Least Squares'
  2 $SUBTITLE: 'P.J. Kaufman'
  3 $STORAGE:2
  4       SUBROUTINE LSTSQ2(Y,X,N,A,B,C,S)
  5
  6 C---- Second Order (Curvilinear) Regression for 2 variables
  7
  8 C---- Y = Dependent variable
  9 C---- X = Independent variable
 10 C---- N = Number of data entries
 11 C---- A = Constant term
 12 C---- B = Coefficient of X
 13 C---- C = Coefficient of X**2
 14 C---- S = Standard deviation of residuals
```

```
15
16          DIMENSION X(2),Y(2)
17
18          DOUBLE PRECISION SXX,SXY,SYY,SXX2,SX2X2,SYX2
19
20 C---- Find the mean of x and y
21          AX = 0
22          AY = 0
23          DO 10 I = 1,N
24             AX = AX + X(I)
25     10     AY = AY + Y(I)
26          AX = AX/N
27          AY = AY/N
28
29 C---- Initialize for summations
30          SXX = 0
31          SXY = 0
32          SYY = 0
33          SXX2 = 0
34          SX2X2 = 0
35          SYX2 = 0
36
37 C---- Sums
38          DO 20 I = 1,N
39             XI = X(I)
40             YI = Y(I)
41             XM = XI - AX
42             YM = YI - AY
43             XM2 = XI*XI - AX*AX
44             SXX = SXX + XM*XM
45             SXY = SXY + XM*YM
46             SYY = SYY + YM*YM
47             SXX2 = SXX2 + XM*XM2
48             SX2X2 = SX2X2 + XM2*XM2
49     20     SYX2 = SYX2 + YM*XM2
50
51          B = (SXY*SX2X2 - SYX2*SXX2) / (SXX*SX2X2 - SXX2*SXX2)
52          C = (SXX*SYX2 - SXX2*SXY) / (SXX*SX2X2 - SXX2*SXX2)
53          A = AY - B*AX - C*AX*AX
54
55 C---- Standard deviation of residuals
56          S = 0
57          DO 150 J = 1,N
58             TY = Y(J)
59             TX = X(J)
60             RV = A + B*TX + C*TX*TX
61             ERR = TY - RV
62             AVGY=AVGY+TY
63    150     S = S + ERR*ERR
64
65          S = SQRT(S/(N-1))
66
67          RETURN
68          END

 1 $TITLE: 'REGVAL: Get regression value'
 2 $SUBTITLE: 'Copyright 1986 PJ Kaufman'
 3 $STORAGE:2
 4      FUNCTION REGVAL(X,A,B,ITYPE)
 5
```

```
  6 C---- Transform data from log form to normal form based upon the
  7 C----     type of regression fit (transmitted via ITYPE)
  8
  9          GOTO (110,120,130),ITYPE
 10
 11 C----     Linear
 12    110    TY=A+B*X
 13          GOTO 140
 14
 15 C----     Log
 16    120    TY=A+B*ALOG(X)
 17          TY=EXP(TY)
 18          GOTO 140
 19
 20 C----     Exponential
 21    130    TY=A+B*X
 22          TY = EXP(TY)
 23
 24    140    REGVAL=TY
 25
 26          RETURN
 27          END

119
120          SUBROUTINE BSTFIT(Y,X,N,A,B,R,SD,ITYPE)
121
122 C---- Basic linear regression
123 C---- N      Number of input items
124 C---- X      Independent variable
125 C---- Y      Dependent variable
126 C---- A      Y-intercept
127 C---- B      Slope
128 C---- R      Correlation coefficient
129 C---- SD     Standard deviation of residuals
130 C----
131 C---- If ITYPE = 1 then linear (no prior x,y conversion)
132 C----        = 2 then log (x=log x,y=log y)
133 C----        = 3 then exponential (x=log x)
134
135          DIMENSION X(2), Y(2)
136
137          DOUBLE PRECISION SUMX2,SUMY2,XY
138
139          SUMX=0.
140          SUMX2=0.
141          SUMY=0.
142          SUMY2=0.
143          XY=0.
144
145          DO 100 I=1,N
146             TX=X(I)
147             IF(ITYPE.EQ.2)TX=ALOG(TX)
148             TY=Y(I)
149             IF(ITYPE.NE.1)TY=ALOG(TY)
150             SUMX=SUMX+TX
151             SUMX2=SUMX2+TX*TX
152             SUMY=SUMY+TY
153             SUMY2=SUMY2+TY*TY
154             XY=XY+TX*TY
155    100    CONTINUE
```

```
156
157        IF(N.LT.2)RETURN
158        B=(N*XY-SUMX*SUMY)/(N*SUMX2-SUMX*SUMX)
159        A=(SUMY-B*SUMX)/N
160
161 C---- Correlation coefficient
162        R1=N*XY-SUMX*SUMY
163        R2=(N*SUMX2-SUMX*SUMX)*(N*SUMY2-SUMY*SUMY)
164        R = ((R1**2)/R2)*100
165
166 C---- Standard deviation around fitted function
167        SD=0
168        DO 150 J=1,N
169           TY=Y(J)
170           TX=X(J)
171           RV=REGVAL(TX,A,B,ITYPE)
172           T=TY-RV
173 150       SD=SD+T*T
174        SD=SQRT(SD/(N-1))
175
176        RETURN
177        END
```

LEAST-SQUARES SOLUTION FOR CORN VERSUS SOYBEANS

Least-Squares Repression Analysis   Data Input

Y (dep)	X (ind)
1.27	2.43
1.19	2.26
1.10	2.15
1.10	2.07
1.05	2.03
1.00	2.45
.98	2.36
1.09	2.44
1.12	2.52
1.18	2.74
1.16	2.98
1.24	2.93
1.03	2.69
1.08	2.63
1.15	2.63
1.33	3.08
1.08	3.24
1.57	6.22
2.55	6.12
3.02	6.33
2.54	4.92
2.25	6.81
2.02	5.88
2.25	6.61
2.52	6.28
3.11	7.61
2.50	6.05

		r^2	St dev
LINEAR	Y= .274 + .339*X	84.2	.278
CURVI	Y= .310 + .323*X + .002*X2		.278
LOG	Ln(Y)= -.616 + .799*Ln(X)	86.3	.282
EXPON	Ln(Y)= -.373 + .195*X	87.3	.283

```
       X      LINEAR     CURVI      LOG      EXPON
    1.00       .61        .63       .54        .84
    1.50       .78        .80       .75        .92
    2.00       .95        .96       .94       1.02
    2.50      1.12       1.13      1.12       1.12
    3.00      1.29       1.29      1.30       1.24
    3.50      1.46       1.46      1.47       1.36
    4.00      1.63       1.63      1.64       1.50
    4.50      1.80       1.80      1.80       1.66
    5.00      1.97       1.97      1.95       1.83
    5.50      2.14       2.14      2.11       2.01
    6.00      2.31       2.31      2.26       2.22
    6.50      2.48       2.48      2.41       2.45
    7.00      2.65       2.66      2.56       2.70
```

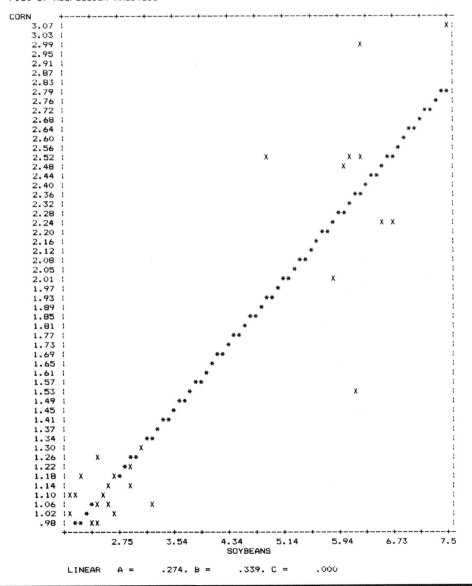

Plot of Regression Analysis

```
LINEAR    A =     .274. B =       .339. C =      .000
```

Plot of Regression Analysis

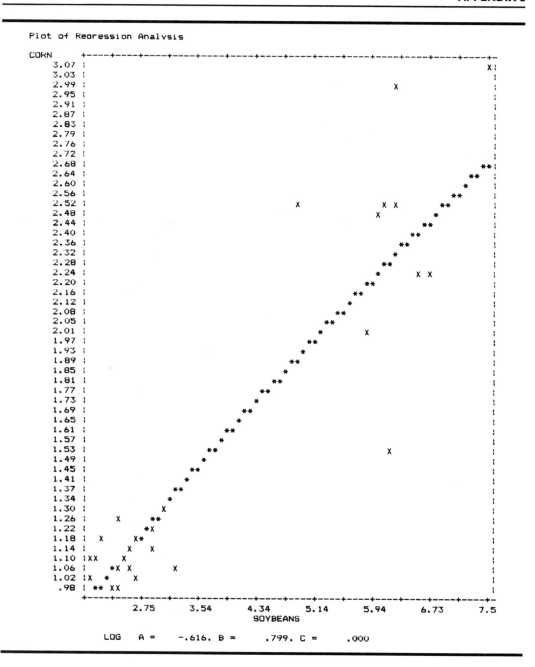

LOG   A =   -.616. B =   .799. C =   .000

Plot of Regression Analysis

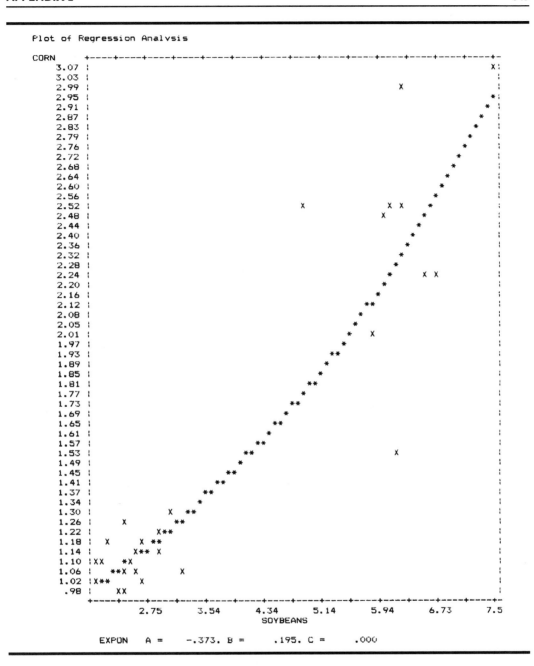

```
CORN      +----+----+----+----+----+----+----+----+----+----+----+----+----+-
    3.07 !                                                              X!
    3.03 !                                                               !
    2.99 !                                               X               !
    2.95 !                                                             *!
    2.91 !                                                           *  !
    2.87 !                                                         *    !
    2.83 !                                                       *      !
    2.79 !                                                     *        !
    2.76 !                                                   *          !
    2.72 !                                                 *            !
    2.68 !                                               *             !
    2.64 !                                             *              !
    2.60 !                                           *               !
    2.56 !                                         *                 !
    2.52 !                     X                X X                  !
    2.48 !                                  X      *                 !
    2.44 !                                       *                  !
    2.40 !                                     *                    !
    2.36 !                                   *                     !
    2.32 !                                 *                       !
    2.28 !                               *                         !
    2.24 !                             *       X X                 !
    2.20 !                           *                            !
    2.16 !                         *                              !
    2.12 !                       **                               !
    2.08 !                      *                                 !
    2.05 !                    *                                   !
    2.01 !                  *    X                                !
    1.97 !                *                                       !
    1.93 !              **                                        !
    1.89 !            *                                           !
    1.85 !          **                                            !
    1.81 !        **                                              !
    1.77 !      *                                                 !
    1.73 !     **                                                 !
    1.69 !    *                                                   !
    1.65 !   **                                                   !
    1.61 !  *                                                     !
    1.57 ! **                                                     !
    1.53 ! **              X                                       !
    1.49 !  *                                                      !
    1.45 ! **                                                      !
    1.41 !**                                                       !
    1.37 !**                                                       !
    1.34 !*                                                        !
    1.30 ! X   **                                                  !
    1.26 !  X    **                                                !
    1.22 !    X**                                                  !
    1.18 ! X     X **                                              !
    1.14 !     X** X                                               !
    1.10 !XX   *X                                                  !
    1.06 ! **X X      X                                            !
    1.02 !X**    X                                                 !
     .98 !   XX                                                    !
         +----+----+----+----+----+----+----+----+----+----+----+----+----+-
              2.75      3.54      4.34      5.14      5.94      6.73     7.5
                                  SOYBEANS

         EXPON   A =    -.373.  B =    .195.  C =     .000
```

Plot of Regression Analysis

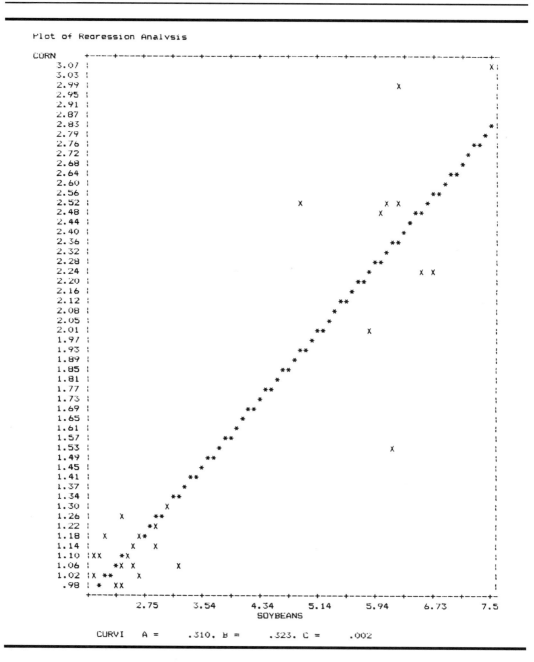

CURVI   A =   .310. B =   .323. C =   .002

LEAST-SQUARES SOLUTION FOR SOYBEANS ONLY

Least Squares Regression Analysis   Data Input

Y (dep)	X (ind)
2.43	1.00
2.26	2.00
2.15	3.00
2.07	4.00
2.03	5.00
2.45	6.00
2.36	7.00
2.44	8.00
2.52	9.00
2.74	10.00
2.98	11.00
2.93	12.00
2.69	13.00
2.63	14.00
2.63	15.00
3.08	16.00
3.24	17.00
6.22	18.00
6.12	19.00
6.33	20.00
4.92	21.00
6.81	22.00
5.88	23.00
6.61	24.00
6.28	25.00
7.61	26.00
6.05	27.00

		r2	St dev
LINEAR	$Y= .987 + .211*X$	78.3	.881
CURVI	$Y= 1.684 + .112*X + .004*X2$		.830
LOG	$Ln(Y)= .271 + .416*Ln(X)$	58.0	1.212
EXPON	$Ln(Y)= .527 + .053*X$	83.1	.806

X	LINEAR	CURVI	LOG	EXPON
1.00	1.20	1.80	1.31	1.79
2.00	1.41	1.92	1.75	1.88
3.00	1.62	2.05	2.07	1.99
4.00	1.83	2.19	2.34	2.09
5.00	2.04	2.33	2.56	2.21
6.00	2.25	2.48	2.77	2.33
7.00	2.47	2.64	2.95	2.45
8.00	2.68	2.80	3.12	2.59
9.00	2.89	2.98	3.27	2.73
10.00	3.10	3.16	3.42	2.87
11.00	3.31	3.34	3.56	3.03
12.00	3.52	3.53	3.69	3.19
13.00	3.73	3.74	3.82	3.37
14.00	3.94	3.94	3.93	3.55
15.00	4.15	4.16	4.05	3.74
16.00	4.37	4.38	4.16	3.94
17.00	4.58	4.61	4.27	4.16
18.00	4.79	4.84	4.37	4.38
19.00	5.00	5.09	4.47	4.62
20.00	5.21	5.34	4.56	4.87
21.00	5.42	5.59	4.66	5.14

22.00	5.63	5.86	4.75	5.41
23.00	5.84	6.13	4.84	5.71
24.00	6.05	6.41	4.92	6.02
25.00	6.27	6.70	5.01	6.34
26.00	6.48	6.99	5.09	6.69
27.00	6.69	7.29	5.17	7.05
28.00	6.90	7.60	5.25	7.43
29.00	7.11	7.91	5.33	7.83
30.00	7.32	8.23	5.40	8.26
31.00	7.53	8.56	5.48	8.71
32.00	7.74	8.89	5.55	9.18
33.00	7.95	9.24	5.62	9.68
34.00	8.17	9.59	5.69	10.20
35.00	8.38	9.94	5.76	10.75
36.00	8.59	10.31	5.83	11.34
37.00	8.80	10.68	5.90	11.95
38.00	9.01	11.06	5.96	12.60
39.00	9.22	11.44	6.03	13.28
40.00	9.43	11.83	6.09	14.00

Plot of Regression Analysis

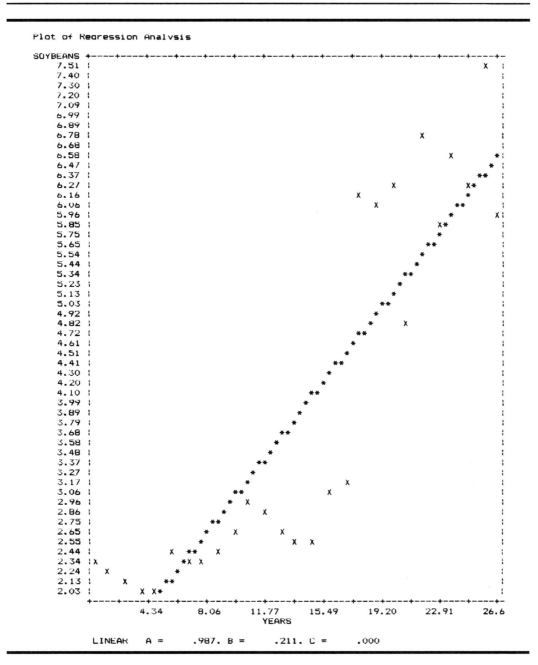

LINEAR   A =   .987. B =   .211. C =   .000

Plot of Regression Analysis

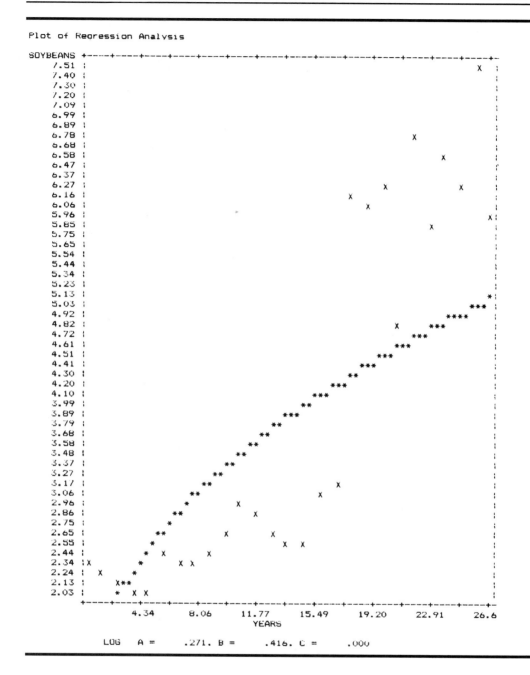

LOG   A =   .271. B =   .416. C =   .000

Plot of Regression Analysis

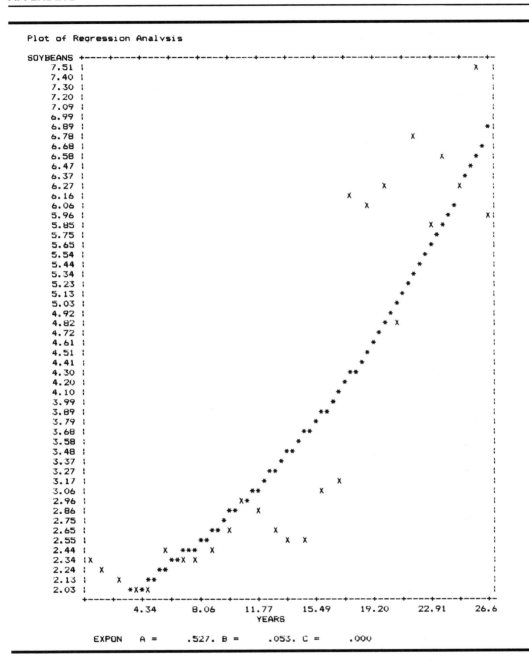

```
SOYBEANS +----+----+----+----+----+----+----+----+----+----+----+----+----+-
   7.51 |                                                              X  |
   7.40 |                                                                 |
   7.30 |                                                                 |
   7.20 |                                                                 |
   7.09 |                                                                 |
   6.99 |                                                                 |
   6.89 |                                                               *|
   6.78 |                                                    X            |
   6.68 |                                                           *  |
   6.58 |                                               X          *   |
   6.47 |                                                         *    |
   6.37 |                                                       *     |
   6.27 |                                        X             X      |
   6.16 |                                  X                          |
   6.06 |                                     X             *         |
   5.96 |                                               *           X|
   5.85 |                                          X *               |
   5.75 |                                           *               |
   5.65 |                                          *                |
   5.54 |                                         *                 |
   5.44 |                                        *                  |
   5.34 |                                       *                   |
   5.23 |                                      *                    |
   5.13 |                                     *                     |
   5.03 |                                    *                      |
   4.92 |                                  *                        |
   4.82 |                                *  X                       |
   4.72 |                               *                           |
   4.61 |                              *                            |
   4.51 |                             *                             |
   4.41 |                            *                              |
   4.30 |                          **                               |
   4.20 |                         *                                 |
   4.10 |                                                           |
   3.99 |                        *                                  |
   3.89 |                       **                                  |
   3.79 |                      *                                    |
   3.68 |                     **                                    |
   3.58 |                    *                                      |
   3.48 |                   **                                      |
   3.37 |                                                           |
   3.27 |                  **                                       |
   3.17 |                 *                   X                     |
   3.06 |                **                 X                       |
   2.96 |            X*                                             |
   2.86 |           **    X                                         |
   2.75 |          *                                                |
   2.65 |         ** X             X                                |
   2.55 |        **              X   X                              |
   2.44 |     X  ***  X                                             |
   2.34 |X      **X X                                               |
   2.24 |  X       **                                               |
   2.13 |     X    **                                               |
   2.03 |       *X*X                                                |
        +----+----+----+----+----+----+----+----+----+----+----+----+----+-
          4.34      8.06     11.77     15.49     19.20     22.91     26.6
                               YEARS

        EXPON   A =      .527, B =      .053, C =      .000
```

Plot of Regression Analysis

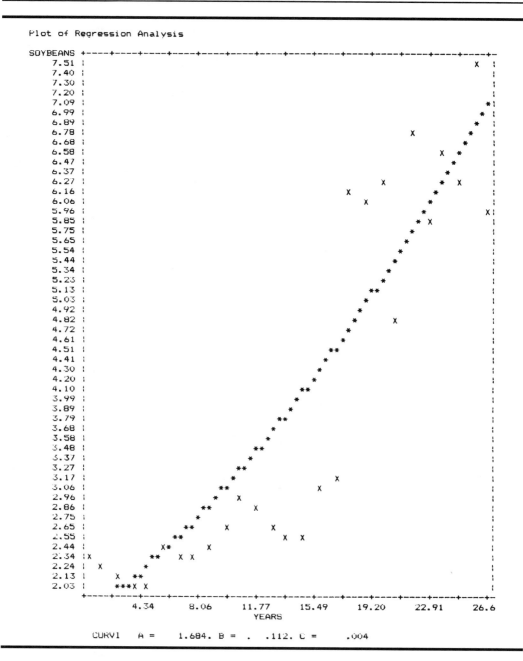

```
SOYBEANS +----+----+----+----+----+----+----+----+----+----+----+----+----+--
    7.51 |                                                                  X  |
    7.40 |                                                                     |
    7.30 |                                                                     |
    7.20 |                                                                     |
    7.09 |                                                                  * |
    6.99 |                                                                * |
    6.89 |                                                               * |
    6.78 |                                          X                  * |
    6.68 |                                                           * |
    6.58 |                                               X   * |
    6.47 |                                                       * |
    6.37 |                                                     * |
    6.27 |                                        X          *   X |
    6.16 |                              X                 * |
    6.06 |                                  X          * |
    5.96 |                                          *              X|
    5.85 |                                          * X |
    5.75 |                                        * |
    5.65 |                                      * |
    5.54 |                                    * |
    5.44 |                                  * |
    5.34 |                                * |
    5.23 |                              * |
    5.13 |                            ** |
    5.03 |                          * |
    4.92 |                        * |
    4.82 |                      *        X |
    4.72 |                    * |
    4.61 |                  * |
    4.51 |                ** |
    4.41 |              * |
    4.30 |            * |
    4.20 |          * |
    4.10 |        ** |
    3.99 |      * |
    3.89 |    * |
    3.79 |  ** |
    3.68 | * |
    3.58 | * |
    3.48 | ** |
    3.37 | * |
    3.27 | ** |
    3.17 | *          X |
    3.06 | **      X |
    2.96 | X |
    2.86 | **    X |
    2.75 | * |
    2.65 | **    X        X |
    2.55 | **          X   X |
    2.44 | X*    X |
    2.34 |X  **   X X |
    2.24 | X    * |
    2.13 | X  ** |
    2.03 | ***X X |
         +----+----+----+----+----+----+----+----+----+----+----+----+----+--
            4.34      8.06     11.77     15.49     19.20     22.91     26.6
                                        YEARS

            CURV1    A =    1.684.  B =  .    .112.  C =     .004
```

Matrix Solution to Linear Equations and Markov Chains

DIRECT SOLUTION AND CONVERGENCE METHOD

Before computer programs offered ready solutions, problems such as Markov chains were solved in a direct manner, by algebraically manipulating the equations. This direct solution requires an understanding of simple matrix arithmetic, and very careful attention to calculating the numbers correctly. The convergence method is now easier, although it requires many more calculations. Without the computer, we would never even consider using this approach—with a computer, it is the best choice.

GENERAL MATRIX FORM

A matrix is a rectangular arrangement of elements into rows and columns. A matrix A is said to be $m \times n$ (pronounced "m by n") if there are m rows and n columns in A.

$$a_{m \times n} = \begin{pmatrix} a_{11} & a_{12} & \cdots & a_{1n} \\ a_{21} & a_{22} & \cdots & a_{2n} \\ \vdots & \vdots & & \vdots \\ a_{m1} & a_{m2} & \cdots & a_{mn} \end{pmatrix}$$

Certain properties of a matrix make it a valuable tool for solving simultaneous linear equations. These elementary matrix operations, called transformations, allow you to alter the rows (which will represent equations) without changing the solution. There are three basic row operations:

1. Multiplication or division of all elements of the row by any number.
2. Interchanging of any two rows (and consequently of all rows).
3. The addition or subtraction of the elements of one row with the corresponding elements of another.

To relate the matrix to simultaneous linear equations, consider a three-equation example, where only the coefficients, a, remain as unknowns:

$$a_{11}x_1 + a_{12}x_2 + a_{13}x_3 = a_{14} \qquad (1)$$
$$a_{21}x_1 + a_{22}x_2 + a_{23}x_3 = a_{24} \qquad (2)$$
$$a_{31}x_1 + a_{32}x_2 + a_{33}x_3 = a_{34} \qquad (3)$$

The three elementary row operations can now be interpreted in terms of simple operations on an equation:

1. When both sides of an equation are multiplied or divided by the same value, the results are equal.
2. Any two equations in a system of equations can be interchanged with no effect.
3. When two equals are added or subtracted, the results are equal.

DIRECT SOLUTION

Putting these rules into use, write the coefficients of the three simultaneous linear equations as a 3×4 coefficient matrix,

$$\begin{pmatrix} a_{11} & a_{12} & a_{13} & a_{14} \\ a_{21} & a_{22} & a_{23} & a_{24} \\ a_{31} & a_{32} & a_{33} & a_{34} \end{pmatrix}$$

with the objective of reducing the matrix to the form

$$\begin{pmatrix} 1 & 0 & 0 & A_1 \\ 0 & 1 & 0 & A_2 \\ 0 & 0 & 1 & A_3 \end{pmatrix}$$

which would mean that $x_1 = A_1$, x_2, $= A_2$, and $x_3 = A_3$ since

$$1 \times x_1 + 0 \times x_2 + 0 \times x_3 = A_1$$

$$0 \times x_1 + 1 \times x_2 + 0 \times x_3 = A_2$$

$$0 \times x_1 + 0 \times x_2 + 1 \times x_3 = A_3$$

To achieve the results, divide the first equation by a_{11}, the first element, leaving

$$\begin{pmatrix} 1 & \dfrac{a_{12}}{a_{11}} & \dfrac{a_{13}}{a_{11}} & \dfrac{a_{14}}{a_{11}} \end{pmatrix} \qquad (1\text{-}1)$$

and then multiply by a_{21} to get the first elements in rows one and two the same:

$$\begin{pmatrix} a_{21} & \dfrac{a_{12} \times a_{21}}{a_{11}} & \dfrac{a_{13} \times a_{21}}{a_{11}} & \dfrac{a_{14} \times a_{21}}{a_{11}} \end{pmatrix} \qquad (1\text{-}2)$$

Now subtract (1-2) from (2) and get

$$\begin{pmatrix} 0 & a_{22} - \dfrac{a_{12} \times a_{21}}{a_{11}} & a_{23} - \dfrac{a_{13} \times a_{21}}{a_{11}} & a_{24} - \dfrac{a_{14} \times a_{21}}{a_{11}} \end{pmatrix} \qquad (2\text{-}1)$$

That successfully eliminates the first element a_{21} from the second equation. By going back and multiplying (1,1) by a_{31} and subtracting the resulting equation from (3), a_{31} can be eliminated from equation (3). Now column 1 looks like

$$\begin{pmatrix} 1 \\ 0 \\ 0 \end{pmatrix}$$

Column two or any column can be operated upon in the same manner as the first column:

1. Divide row n by the element in position n (for example, a_{nn}), thereby setting $a_{nn} = 1$.
2. Multiply row n by the corresponding element in row $i \neq n$, so that $a_{nn} \times a_{in} = a_{in}$.
3. Subtract row n from row i, resulting in $a_{in} = 0$, and all other elements reduced by the corresponding element in row n.

Continue this procedure for each row i until all elements

$$a_{1n}, a_{2n}, \ldots, a_{i-1n}, a_{1+1n}, \ldots, a_{mn} = 0 \qquad \text{and} \qquad a_{in} = 1.$$

For example, beginning with

$$\begin{pmatrix} 2 & 4 & 8 & 34 \\ 6 & 5 & 2 & 22 \\ 3 & 6 & 5 & 30 \end{pmatrix}$$

Divide row 1 by the value 2 (position a_{11}):

$$\begin{pmatrix} 1 & 2 & 4 & 17 \\ 6 & 5 & 2 & 22 \\ 3 & 6 & 5 & 30 \end{pmatrix}$$

Multiply row 1 by the value 6 to get (6   12   24   102) and subtract the new calculated row from row 2:

$$\begin{pmatrix} 1 & 2 & 4 & 17 \\ 0 & -7 & -22 & -80 \\ 3 & 6 & 5 & 30 \end{pmatrix}$$

Multiply row 1 by the number 3 to get (3   6   12   51), then subtract the calculated row from row 3:

$$\begin{pmatrix} 1 & 2 & 4 & 17 \\ 0 & -7 & -22 & -80 \\ 0 & 0 & -7 & -21 \end{pmatrix}$$

Column 1 is now completed. Divide row 2 by −7 and get:

$$\begin{pmatrix} 1 & 2 & 4 & 17 \\ 0 & 1 & +22/7 & +80/7 \\ 0 & 0 & -7 & -21 \end{pmatrix}$$

Multiply row 2 by 2 and subtract the result (0   2   44/7   160/7) from row 1 to eliminate position 2 in the first row:

$$\begin{pmatrix} 1 & 0 & -16/7 & -41/7 \\ 0 & 1 & +22/7 & +80/7 \\ 0 & 0 & -7 & -21 \end{pmatrix}$$

Because the element in row 3 and column 2 is already 0, move to row 3. Divide row 3 by −7 and get

$$\begin{pmatrix} 1 & 0 & -16/7 & -41/7 \\ 0 & 1 & +22/7 & +80/7 \\ 0 & 0 & 1 & 3 \end{pmatrix}$$

Multiply row 3 by −16/7 and subtract the result (0   0   −16/7   −48/7) from row 1:

$$\begin{pmatrix} 1 & 0 & 0 & 1 \\ 0 & 1 & +22/7 & +80/7 \\ 0 & 0 & 1 & 3 \end{pmatrix}$$

Multiply row 3 by +22/7 and subtract (0   0   +22/7   +66/7) from row 2:

$$\begin{pmatrix} 1 & 0 & 0 & 1 \\ 0 & 1 & 0 & 2 \\ 0 & 0 & 1 & 3 \end{pmatrix}$$

The results show that $x_1 = 1$, $x_2 = 2$, $x_3 = 3$.

There are other ways to reduce the matrix to the final representation, but this technique is well defined and lends itself to being programmed on a computer.

Solution to Weather Probabilities Expressed as a Markov Chain

$$\text{Let } A = P(\text{clear})_{i+1} = P(\text{clear})_i$$

$$B = P(\text{cloudy})_{i+1} = P(\text{cloudy})_i$$

$$C = P(\text{rainy})_{i+1} = P(\text{rainy})_i$$

because when they converge all ith elements will equal $(i + 1)$th elements. The equations are

$$A = .7A + .2B + .2C \qquad (1)$$

$$B = .25A + .6B + .4C \qquad (2)$$

$$C = .05A + .2B + .4C \qquad (3)$$

In addition

$$A + B + C = 1 \qquad (4)$$

To solve this system of equations using matrices, convert and add equation (3) to (4),

$$-.3A + .2B + .2C = 0 \qquad (1')$$

$$.25A - .4B + .4C = 0 \qquad (2')$$

$$1.05A + 1.2B + .4C = 1 \qquad (3')$$

which becomes the matrix

$$\begin{pmatrix} -.3 & .2 & .2 & 0 \\ .25 & -.4 & .4 & 0 \\ 1.05 & 1.2 & .4 & 1 \end{pmatrix} \quad \begin{matrix} (1') \\ (2') \\ (3') \end{matrix}$$

The following are key steps in the solution:

1. Reduce the first row,

$$\begin{pmatrix} 1 & -.6667 & -.6667 & 0 \\ .25 & -.4 & .4 & 0 \\ 1.05 & 1.2 & .4 & 1 \end{pmatrix}$$

and make the leading entries of rows 2 and 3 zero:

$$\begin{pmatrix} 1 & -.6667 & -.6667 & 0 \\ 0 & -.2333 & .5667 & 0 \\ 0 & 1.9000 & 1.1000 & 1 \end{pmatrix}$$

2. Reduce the second row,

$$\begin{pmatrix} 1 & -.6667 & -.6667 & 0 \\ 0 & 1 & -2.4291 & 0 \\ 0 & 1.9000 & 1.1000 & 1 \end{pmatrix}$$

and make the second entries of rows 1 and 3 zero

$$\begin{pmatrix} 1 & 0 & 2.2857 & 0 \\ 0 & 1 & -2.4291 & 0 \\ 0 & 0 & 5.7143 & 1 \end{pmatrix}$$

3. Reduce the third row,

$$\begin{pmatrix} 1 & 0 & 2.2862 & 0 \\ 0 & 1 & -2.4291 & 0 \\ 0 & 0 & 1 & .1750 \end{pmatrix}$$

and make the third entry of rows 1 and 2 zero:

$$\begin{pmatrix} 1 & 0 & 0 & .4000 \\ 0 & 1 & 0 & .4250 \\ 0 & 0 & 1 & .1750 \end{pmatrix}$$

Then $A = .4000$, $B = .4250$, and $C = .1750$.

Computer Program Direct Solution

The following FORTRAN program accepts a system of 10 equations in 10 variables (unknowns) and applies the matrix method of solution. This is done using the method of Gaussian elimination, discussed in the previous section.

```
      PROGRAM MATRIX
C---- Matrix solution to simultaneous linear equations
C---- Copyright 1986 PJ Kaufman
      DIMENSION A(10,10), C(10)
      OPEN(6,FILE='PRN')
      WRITE(*,7000)
7000  FORMAT(' Enter matrix size (n)>'\)
      READ(*,5000)N
5000  FORMAT(BN,I4)
      IF(N.GT.10)STOP 'Matrix limited to 10 x 10'
      WRITE(*,7001) (1,1=1,N)
7001  FORMAT(' Enter matrix elements row by row under headings
     +         ' do not include constant to right of
     +      7X,10(I2,'-xxxxx'))
      DO 20 I = 1,N
         WRITE(*,7003)1
7003     FORMAT(' Row',I2,':'\)
         READ(*,5003) (A(I,J), J=1,N)
5003     FORMAT(BN,10F8.0)
20       CONTINUE
      WRITE(*,7004) (J,J=1,N)
      WRITE(6,7004) (J,J=1,N)
7004  FORMAT(/' Input matrix is:'//9X,10(I2,'-col '))
```

```
        DO 30 I = 1,N
           WRITE(6,7005)I,(A(I,J),J=1,N)
  30       WRITE(*,7005)I,(A(I,J),J=1,N)
7005    FORMAT(/' Row',I2,':',10F8.3)
        WRITE(*,7008)(I,I=1,N)
7008 FORMAT(/' Enter constant vector under headings…'/
     +         1X,10(I1,'xxxxxx '))
        READ(*,5008)(C(I),I=1,N)
5008    FORMAT(BN,10F8.0)
        WRITE(*,7009)(C(I),I=1,N)
        WRITE(6,7009)(C(I),I=1,N)
7009    FORMAT(/' Constant vector is:'/10F8.3)
C----- Process row by row (Gaussian Elimination)
        DO 100 I = 1,N
           DIV = A(I,I)
           DO 40 J = 1,N
  40          A(I,J) = A(I,J)/DIV
           C(I) = C(I)/DIV
C----- Zero out column I for each row
           DO 60 J = 1,N
              IF(J.EQ.I)GOTO 60
              FACTOR = A(J,I)
              DO 50 K = 1,N
  50             A(J,K) = A(J,K) - A(I,K)*FACTOR
              C(J) = C(J) - C(I)*FACTOR
  60          CONTINUE
 100    CONTINUE
        WRITE(*,7007)(C(I),I = 1,N)
        WRITE(6,7007)(C(I),I = 1,N)
7007    FORMAT(/' Solution vector is: '/10F8.3)
        CALL EXIT
        END
```

Sample Computer Printout

```
MATRIX
Enter matrix size (N)>3
Enter matrix elements row by row under headings…
do not include constant to right of =
        1-xxxxx 2-xxxxx 3-xxxxx
Row 1:  2       4       8
Row 2:  6       5       2
Row 3:  3       6       5

Input matrix is:

        1-col      2-col      3-col
Row 1:  2.000      4.000      8.000
Row 2:  6.000      5.000      2.000
Row 3:  3.000      6.000      5.000

Enter constant vector under headings…
1xxxxxx 2xxxxxx 3xxxxxx
34      22      30

Constant vector is:
  34.000  22.000  30.000

Solution vector is:
   1.000   2.000   3.000
```

CONVERGENCE METHOD

This method performs a series of matrix multiplications until the difference between the new and previous matrix is very small.[1] Following the procedure in Chapter 2, "Basic Concepts," we can create a 3×3 frequency matrix by counting the number of up, down, and neutral days that follow other up, down, and neutral days. We use the term *neutral* to allow very small price changes to be considered in this group, rather than limit it to only those days with zero changes. For this example we will look at the number of up, down, and neutral days that follow a 5-day trend that was considered up, down, or neutral on the previous day. Suppose the results were those shown in the *frequency matrix F*:

		Next Day Price Change			
		Up	Neutral	Down	Total
Previous day trend	Up	70	40	30	140
	Neutral	50	30	45	125
	Down	35	45	65	145

Divide each item in F by the total given at the end of that row, and get the probability of each occurrence in a *transition matrix T*.

		Next Day Price Change		
		Up	Neutral	Down
Previous day trend	Up	.500	.285	.214
	Neutral	.400	.240	.360
	Down	.241	.310	.448

Now it is necessary to perform matrix multiplication. To multiply matrix B by matrix B, we multiply the corresponding items in row i of A by the corresponding item in column j of B, add those products together to get the item in row i, column j of the new matrix C. If we have two 3×3 matrices A and B, and we wanted to find the element in row 2, column 1 of the new product matrix C, we would multiply and add

$$c_{21} = a_{21} \times b_{11} + a_{22} \times b_{21} + a_{23} \times b_{31}$$

The general formula for this is

$$c_{ij} = \sum_{k=1}^{N} (a_{ik} \times b_{kj})$$

For spreadsheet users, there is no general formula to copy from one cell to another. For matrix A of 3 columns and 3 rows located in columns A, B, C, rows 1, 2, 3; matrix B in columns D, E, F, rows 1, 2, 3; and matrix C in rows G, H, I, columns 1, 2, 3, we enter the formula for c_{11} in cell $G1$ as

cell $G1 = A1*D1 + B1*D2 + C1*D3$

While this is clearly tedious, at least the arithmetic will be correct.

---

[1] George R. Arrington, "Markov Chains," *Technical Analysis of Stocks & Commodities* (December 1993).

Iterative Matrix

We can now find the solution to the Markov chain, the long-term probabilities, by performing a series of matrix multiplications beginning with the transition matrix.

1. Multiply the transition matrix T by itself to get the first iterative matrix I_1,

   $$I_1 = T \times T$$

2. Multiply the iterative matrix by the transition matrix to get the next iterative matrix,

   $$I_2 = I_1 \times T$$

3. Continue to multiply the last iterative matrix by the transition matrix until the new iterative matrix is unchanged (or very close) to the previous iterative matrix,

   $$I_n = I_{n-1} \times T$$

   When each element satisfies the condition

   $$@abs(I_{ij}(n) - I_{ij}(n-1)) < .001$$

   then the iterative matrix holds the final long-term probabilities of the Markov chain.

Trigonometric Regression
for Finding Cycles

The following computer programs and examples solve the cycle problems in Chapter 8.

SINGLE-FREQUENCY TRIGONOMETRIC REGRESSION

The FORTRAN program *TRIG1* and the subroutine *LINREG* are used to find the single-frequency representation of the copper cycle. The program output is clearly separated into the following information:

1. Input data, where each time period is the average cash price for a calendar quarter.
2. The solution to the linear regression, giving the detrending line. With $b = .267$, there is an inflationary bias of $+.267$¢ per quarter.
3. The detrended data resulting from subtracting the line values (2) from the original data (1).
4. Intermediate values for α, ω, and T.
5. The constant values a and b for the normal equations solving the single-frequency problem.
6. The cycle resulting from the detrended data.
7. The final cycle with the trend added back.

The results show a copper cycle of approximately 8.4 quarters, or slightly more than 2½ years.

An additional test was run on monthly cash corn prices from 1964 through 1983 to see if the seasonal cycle dominated the detrended pattern. The linear regression equation used for detrending was calculated as:

$$y = .939 + .01x$$

showing only a 1¢ per bushel per month rate of inflation, despite the bull markets in 1973 and 1980 through 1981. The cycle showed a period of 21.4 months, with the last highs in the cycle in August 1983 and the last lows in September 1982. Because this is clearly not a seasonal pattern, it must be either:

1. Dominated by other supply-demand characteristics, such as stocks, or,
2. Distorted by the nonseasonal rallies of 1973 and 1980, which each took three years to return to the traditional seasonal pattern.

```
      PROGRAM TRIG1
C---- Single Frequency Trigonometric Regression
C---- Copyright 1986 PJ Kaufman

      DIMENSION X(250), Y(250), D(250), R(250)
      DOUBLE PRECISION SC2,SCD

      DATA MAX/250/

      OPEN(6,FILE='PRN')

C---- Read data, set X to incremental time
      I = 1
      WRITE(*,7000)
```

```
7000 FORMAT(' SINGLE FREQUENCY TRIGONOMETRIC REGRESSION'/
    +          ' Enter data 1 per line'/' Extra <return> ends input'//
    +          ' Enter below:')

  10 WRITE(*,7001)I
7001 FORMAT(14,'>'\)
     READ(*,5000)Y(I)
5000 FORMAT(BN,F8.2)
     X(I) = I
     IF(Y(I).NE.0)THEN
       IF(I.GT.MAX)STOP 'Maximum data exceeded'
       I = I+1
       GOTO 10
       ENDIF
     N = I-1
     WRITE(6,6000)
6000 FORMAT('1Single Frequency Trigonometric Regression',20X,
    +          'Data Input'//' Time',16X,'Prices')
     DO 40 J = 1,N,4
  40    WRITE(6,6001)J,(Y(I),I=J,J+3)
6001    FORMAT(14,4F8.2)

C---- Linear regression analysis for detrending
     CALL LINREG(N,Y,A,B,SD)
     WRITE(6,6002)A,B
6002 FORMAT(/'Linear regression results: A =',F8.3,', B =',F8.3)
C---- Detrend data into D and computer sums for equation (4)
     DO 60 I = 1,N
  60    D(I) = Y(I) - (A+B*I)
C---- Print detrended data
     WRITE(6,6003)
6003 FORMAT(/' Detrended data'/)
     DO 65 I = 1,N,4
  65    WRITE(6,6001)I,(D(J),J=I,I+3)
     SC2 = 0
     SCD = 0
C---- Solve equation (4) using detrended data
     DO 70 I = 2,N-1
         DI = D(I)
         SC2 = SC2 + DI*DI
  70    SCD = SCD + DI*(D(I-1)+D(I+1))

     ALPHA = SCD/SC2
     WRITE(6,6004)SC2,SCD,ALPHA
6004 FORMAT(/'Sum C-squared =',F8.1,', Sum C x D =',F8.1,', Alpha =',
    +          F8.3)
C---- Solve for omega
     W = ACOS(ALPHA/2)
     T = 360/W
     WRITE(6,6014)W,T
6014 FORMAT(/'Omega (W) =',F5.1,' degrees, Period (T) =',F6.2,
    +          'time units')

C---- Sums for normal equations
     COS2 = 0
     COSSIN = 0
     YCOS = 0
     SINCOS = 0
     SIN2 = 0
     YSIN = 0
```

```
       DO 80 I = 1,N
           C = COS(W*I)
           S = SIN(W*I)
           COS2 = COS2 + C*C
           COSSIN = COSSIN + C*S
           YCOS = YCOS + Y(I)*C
           SINCOS = SINCOS + S*C
           SIN2 = SIN2 + S*S
   80      YSIN = YSIN + Y(I)*S

C---- Solve normal equations
       TB = (YSIN*COS2 - YCOS)/(SIN2*COS2 - COSSIN)
       TA = (YCOS - B*COSSIN)/COS2
       WRITE(6,6005)TA,TB
 6005 FORMAT(/' Solution to normal equations: A =',F8.3,',  B =',F8.3)

C---- Values of fitted curve using detrended data
       DO 90 I = 1,N
   90    R(I) = TA*COS(W*I) + TB*SIN(W*I)
       WRITE(6,6006)
 6006 FORMAT(/' Trigonometric regression results using detrended data',
      +        /)
       DO 100 I = 1,N,4
  100    WRITE(6,6001)I,(R(J),J=I,I+3)

C---- Add trend back to result
       DO 110 I = 1,N
  110    R(I) = R(I) + A + B*I

       WRITE(6,6007)
 6007 FORMAT(/' Final regression results with trend added back'/)
       DO 120 I = 1,N,4
  120    WRITE(6,6001)I, (R(J),J=I,I+3)

       CALL EXIT
       END

       SUBROUTINE LINREG(N,DATA,A,B,SD)
C---- Generalized simple linear regression

       DIMENSION DATA(2)

C---- Initialize sums
       SX=0.
       SY=0.
       SXY=0.
       SX2=0.
       A=0.
       B=0.
       SD=0.
       IF(N.LE.2)RETURN

       DO 100 I=2,N
           X = I
           Y = DATA(I)
           SX=SX+X
           SY=SY+Y
           SXY=SXY+Y*X
           SX2=SX2+X*X
  100    CONTINUE
       M=N-1
       B=(M*SXY-SX*SY) / (M*SX2-SX*SX)
       A=(SY-B*SX) / M
```

```
C----- Residuals
       SSR=0
       DO 200 I=2,N
          Y=DATA(I)
          R=Y-(A+B*I)
          SSR=SSR+R*R
  200    CONTINUE

       SD=SQRT(SSR/M)
       RETURN
       END
```

Single Frequency Trigonometric Regression

Time		Prices		
1	22.12	22.46	22.17	22.00
5	23.18	24.56	25.57	30.59
9	28.23	33.77	35.90	40.05
13	46.22	51.48	40.76	40.16
17	36.51	29.30	30.36	36.42
21	39.75	30.07	29.08	32.13
25	38.94	42.95	43.38	46.23
29	47.70	46.98	35.78	27.35
33	25.40	29.45	27.15	28.48
37	32.74	33.53	30.01	29.25
41	36.82	45.07	55.13	65.51
45	66.56	70.06	27.30	35.62
49	32.06	31.46	35.75	36.46
53	38.22	43.24	45.46	38.96
57	37.08	38.72	34.01	33.00
61	35.07	40.23	41.63	44.95
65	51.12	63.71	59.56	63.38

Linear regression results: A = 28.889, B = .267

Detrended data

1	-7.04	-6.96	-7.52	-7.96
5	-7.05	-5.93	-5.19	-.44
9	-3.06	2.21	4.07	7.95
13	13.86	18.85	7.86	7.00
17	3.08	-4.40	-3.61	2.19
21	5.25	-4.70	-5.96	-3.17
25	3.37	7.11	7.28	9.86
29	11.06	10.07	-1.39	-10.09
33	-12.31	-8.52	-11.09	-10.03
37	-6.04	-5.51	-9.30	-10.33
41	-3.02	4.96	14.75	24.86
45	25.65	28.88	-14.15	-6.10
49	-9.92	-10.79	-6.77	-6.32
53	-4.83	-.08	1.87	-4.89
57	-7.04	-5.67	-10.64	-11.92
61	-10.12	-5.23	-4.09	-1.04
65	4.86	17.19	12.77	16.32

Sum C-squared = 6338.4, Sum C x D = 9282.2, Alpha = 1.464

Omega (W) = .7 degrees, Period (T) =480.50 time units

Solution to normal equations: A = -.603, B = 1.831

```
Trigonometric regression results using detrended data
  1     .81    1.78    1.80     .86
  5    -.54   -1.66   -1.88   -1.10
  9     .27    1.50    1.92    1.32
 13     .01   -1.31   -1.92   -1.51
 17    -.28    1.09    1.88    1.66
 21     .56    -.85   -1.80   -1.79
 25    -.82     .59    1.68    1.87
 29    1.06    -.32   -1.53   -1.92
 33   -1.28     .04    1.34    1.92
 37    1.47     .23   -1.13   -1.89
 41   -1.64    -.51     .89    1.82
 45    1.77     .77    -.64   -1.71
 49   -1.86   -1.02     .37    1.56
 53    1.91    1.24    -.09   -1.38
 57   -1.93   -1.44    -.19    1.17
 61    1.90    1.61     .46    -.94
 65   -1.83   -1.75    -.72     .69

Final regression results with trend added back
  1   29.96   31.21   31.50   30.82
  5   29.68   28.83   28.88   29.93
  9   31.57   33.06   33.75   33.41
 13   32.37   31.32   30.98   31.66
 17   33.15   34.79   35.85   35.90
 21   35.06   33.92   33.23   33.52
 25   34.75   36.43   37.79   38.24
 29   37.70   36.58   35.64   35.52
 33   36.43   38.02   39.59   40.43
 37   40.25   39.28   38.18   37.69
 41   38.21   39.60   41.27   42.46
 45   42.68   41.95   40.81   40.01
 49   40.12   41.23   42.89   44.34
 53   44.96   44.56   43.49   42.47
 57   42.19   42.95   44.47   46.09
 61   47.09   47.07   46.18   45.05
 65   44.42   44.78   46.07   47.74
```

TWO-FREQUENCY TRIGONOMETRIC REGRESSION

The FORTRAN program *TRIG2* and its subroutines *LINREG* (found in Appendix 4) and MTX are used to find the two-frequency representation of the copper cycle. The program output is clearly separated into the following steps.

1. Input data, where each time period is the average cash price for a calendar quarter.
2. The solution to the linear regression, giving the detrending line.
3. The detrended data resulting from subtracting the line values (2) from the original data (1).
4. Intermediate values for α_1, α_2, ω_1, and ω_2.
5. Resulting values a_1, b_1, a_2, and b_2, which are derived from the matrix solution using Gaussian elimination.
6. The cycle resulting from the detrended data.
7. The final cycle with the trend added back.

```
      PROGRAM TRIG2
C---- 2-Frequency Trigonometric Regression
C---- Copyright 1986 PJ Kaufman
      DIMENSION X(250), Y(250), D(250), R(250), A(4,4), B(4)
      EQUIVALENCE (A(1,1),C2W1),(A(1,2),CW1SW1),(A(1,3),CW1CW2),
```

```
     +              (A(1,4),CW1SW2),(A(2,1),DUP1),(A(2,2),S2W1),
     +              (A(2,3),SW1CW2),(A(2,4),SW1SW2),(A(3,1),DUP2),
     +              (A(3,2),DUP3),(A(3,3),C2W2),(A(3,4),CW2SW2),
     +              (A(4,1),DUP4),(A(4,2),DUP5),(A(4,3),DUP6),
     +              (A(4,4),S2W2),(B(1),YCW1),(B(2),YSW1),(B(3),YCW2),
     +              (B(4),YSW2),(B(1),A1),(B(2),B1),(B(3),A2),(B(4),B2)
      DATA MAX/250/,NDIM/4/

      OPEN(6,FILE='PRN')
C---- Read data, set X to incremental time
      I = 1
      WRITE(*,7000)
 7000 FORMAT(' 2-FREQUENCY TRIGONOMETRIC REGRESSION'/
     +       ' Enter data 1 per line'/'Extra <return> end input'//
     +       ' Enter below:')

   10 WRITE(*,7001)I
 7001 FORMAT(14,'>'\)
      READ(*,5000)Y(I)
 5000 FORMAT(BN,F8.2)
      X(I) = I
      IF(Y(I).NE.0)THEN
         IF(I.GT.MAX)STOP 'Maximum data exceeded'
         I = I+1
         GOTO 10
         ENDIF
      N = I-1
      WRITE(6,6000)
 6000 FORMAT('12-Frequency Trigonometric Regression'//
     +       'Time',16X,'Prices')
      DO 40 J = 1,N,4
   40    WRITE(6,6001)J,(Y(I),I=J,J+3)
 6001    FORMAT(14,4F8.2)

C---- Linear regression analysis for detrending
      CALL LINREG(N,Y,ALIN,BLIN,SD)
      WRITE(6,6002)ALIN,BLIN
 6002 FORMAT(/' Linear regression results: A =',F8.3,', B =',F8.3)

C---- Detrend data into D and computer sums for equation (4)
      DO 60 I = 1,N
   60    D(I) = Y(I) - (ALIN+BLIN*I)
C---- Print detrended data
      WRITE(6,6003)
 6003 FORMAT(/' Detrended data'/)
      DO 65 I = 1,N,4
   65    WRITE(6,6001)I,(D(J),J=I,I+3)
      SC2 = 0
      SCD = 0
      SCP = 0
      SD2 = 0
      SDP = 0
C---- Solve for alpha1 and alpha2 using detrended data
      DO 70 I = 2,N-3
         C = D(I) + D(I+2)
         T = D(I+1)
         P = D(I-1) + D(I+3)
         SC2 = SC2 + C*C
         SCD = SCD + C*T
         SCP = SCP + C*P
         SD2 = SD2 + T*T
```

```
   70    SDP = SDP + T*P
         ALPHA2 = (SDP*SC2-SCP)/(SD2*SC2-SCD)
         ALPHA1 = (SCP-ALPHA2*SCD)/SC2
         T = SQRT(ALPHA1*ALPHA1+8*(1+ALPHA2/2))
         W1 = ACOS((ALPHA1+T)/4)
         W2 = ACOS((ALPHA1-T)/4)

         WRITE(6,6004)SC2,SCD,SCP,SD2,SDP,ALPHA1,ALPHA2,W1,W2
 6004 FORMAT(/' Intermediate values:'//
      +         ' SUMS C2 =', F8.1,', C*D =',F8.1,', C*P =',F8.1/
      +         '      D2 =', F8.1,', D*P =',F8.1//' Alpha1 = ',F8.3,
      +         '  Alpha2 =', F8.3,' Omega1 =',F5.2,', Omega2 =',F5.2)
C---- Sums for normal equations. . .to be used for matrix solution
         C2W1 = 0
         CW1SW1 = 0
         CW1CW2 = 0
         CW1SW2 = 0
         YCW1 = 0
         S2W1 = 0
         SW1CW2 = 0
         SW1SW2 = 0
         YSW1 = 0
         C2W2 = 0
         CW2SW2 = 0
         YCW2 = 0
         S2W2 = 0
         YSW2 = 0

         DO 100 I = 1,N
            DI = D(I)
            SW1 = SIN(W1*I)
            CW1 = COS(W1*I)
            SW2 = SIN(W2*I)
            CW2 = COS(W2*I)
            C2W1 = C2W1 + CW1*SW1
            CW1SW1 = CW1SW1 + CW1*SW1
            CW1CW2 = CW1CW2 + CW1*CW2
            CW1SW2 = CW1SW2 + CW1*SW2
            YCW1 = YCW1 + DI*CW1
            S2W1 = S2W1 + SW1*SW1
            SW1CW2 = SW1SW2 + SW1*CW2
            SW1SW2 = SW1SW2 + SW1*SW2
            YSW1 = YSW + DI
            C2W2 = C2W2 + CW2*CW2
            CW2SW2 = CW2SW2 + CW2*SW2
            YCW2 = YCW2 + DI*CW2
            S2W2 = S2W2 + SW2*SW2
  100       YSW2 = YSW2 + DI*SW2
C---- Duplicate calculations for matrix
         DUP1 = CW1SW1
         DUP2 = CW1CW2
         DUP3 = SW1CW2
         DUP4 = CW1SW2
         DUP5 = SW1SW2
         DUP6 = CW2SW2

         WRITE(6,6009)
 6009 FORMAT(/' Coefficient matrix:'/)
         DO 110 I = 1,NDIM
  110       WRITE(6,6010)(A(I,J),J=1,4),B(I)
 6010       FORMAT(5F8.3)
```

```
C---- Solve using matrix Gaussian Elimination
      CALL MTX(A,B,NDIM)

C---- Solution vector
      WRITE(6,6011)(B(I),I=1,NDIM)
 6011 FORMAT(/' Solution vector:'/4F8.3)
C---- Values of fitted curve using detrended data
      DO 90 I = 1,N
   90    R(I) = A1*COS(W1*I) + B1*SIN(W1*I) + A2*COS(W2*I) +
      +          B2*SIN(W2*I)
      WRITE(6,6006)
 6006 FORMAT(/' Trigonometric regression results using detrended data',
      +      /)
      DO 105 I = 1,N,4
  105    WRITE(6,6001)I,(R(J),J=I,I+3)

C---- Add trend back to result
      DO 115 I = 1,N
  115    R(I) = R(I) + ALIN + BLIN*I

      WRITE(6,6007)
 6007 FORMAT(/' Final results with trend added back'/)
      DO 120 I = 1,N,4
  120    WRITE(6,6001)I,(R(J),J=I,I+3)

      CALL EXIT
      END

      SUBROUTINE MTX(A,C,N)
C---- Matrix solution to simultaneous linear equations
C---- Copyright 1986 PJ Kaufman

      DIMENSION A(4,4), C(4), A1(4,4), C1(4)

C---- Process row by row (Gaussian Elimination)
      DO 100 I = 1,N
         DIV = A(I,I)

         DO 40 J = 1,N
   40       A(I,J) = A(I,J)/DIV
         C(I) = C(I)/DIV

C---- Zero out column I for each row
         DO 60 J = 1,N
            IF(J.EQ.I)GOTO 60
            FACTOR = A(J,I)
            DO 50 K = I,N
   50          A(J,K) = A(J,K) - A(I,K)*FACTOR
            C(J) = C(J) - C(I)*FACTOR
   60       CONTINUE

  100    CONTINUE

      RETURN
      END
```

2-Frequency Trigonometric Regression

Time	Prices			
1	22.12	22.46	22.17	22.00
5	23.18	24.56	25.57	30.59
9	28.23	33.77	35.90	40.05
13	46.22	51.48	40.76	40.16
17	36.51	29.30	30.36	36.42
21	39.75	30.07	29.08	32.13

```
25    38.94    42.95    43.38    46.23
29    47.70    46.98    35.78    27.35
33    25.40    29.45    27.15    28.48
37    32.74    33.53    30.01    29.25
41    36.82    45.07    55.13    65.51
45    66.56    70.06    27.30    35.62
49    32.06    31.46    35.75    36.46
53    38.22    43.24    45.46    38.96
57    37.08    38.72    34.01    33.00
61    35.07    40.23    41.63    44.95
65    51.12    63.71    59.56    63.38
```

Linear regression results: A = 28.889, B = .267

Detrended data
```
 1    -7.04    -6.96    -7.52    -7.96
 5    -7.05    -5.93    -5.19     -.44
 9    -3.06     2.21     4.07     7.95
13    13.86    18.85     7.86     7.00
17     3.08    -4.40    -3.61     2.19
21     5.25    -4.70    -5.96    -3.17
25     3.37     7.11     7.28     9.86
29    11.06    10.07    -1.39   -10.09
33   -12.31    -8.52   -11.09   -10.03
37    -6.04    -5.51    -9.30   -10.33
41    -3.02     4.96    14.75    24.86
45    25.65    28.88   -14.15    -6.10
49    -9.92   -10.79    -6.77    -6.32
53    -4.83     -.08     1.87    -4.89
57    -7.04    -5.67   -10.64   -11.92
61   -10.12    -5.23    -4.09    -1.04
65     4.86    17.19    12.77    16.32
```

Intermediate values:

SUMS C2 = 17396.7, C*D = 8753.0, C*P = 10475.1
     D2 = 6126.9, D*P = 5499.2

Alpha1 = .151, Alpha2 = .898, Omega1 = .47, Omega2 = 2.52

Coefficient matrix:

```
34.206      .790     -.461      .426    124.829
  .790    33.794     -.454      .479     -7.036
 -.461     -.454    33.742     -.781    -33.500
  .426      .479     -.781    34.258     28.219
```

Solution vector:
```
 3.635     -.317     -.930      .762
```

Trigonometric regression results using detrended data
```
 1     4.29      .84      .69    -1.20
 5    -3.72    -2.38    -4.57    -2.18
 9    -1.06     -.43     3.23     2.12
13     4.21     3.45     1.39     1.82
17    -2.17    -1.93    -3.36    -4.39
21    -1.80    -2.78      .67     1.72
25     2.23     4.76     2.31     3.24
29     1.05    -1.35    -1.09    -4.45
33    -2.90    -3.25    -2.67      .70
37      .12     3.49     3.41     2.97
41     3.91      .27      .59    -2.04
45    -3.65    -2.57    -4.56    -1.50
```

```
49    -1.06      .38     3.44     2.19
53     4.54     2.79     1.38     1.20
57    -2.70    -1.91    -3.91    -3.91
61    -1.68    -2.44     1.44     1.69
65     2.86     4.60     2.08     3.19

Final results with trend added back
 1    33.44    30.26    30.38    28.75
 5    26.50    28.12    26.19    28.85
 9    30.23    31.13    35.05    34.21
13    36.58    36.08    34.29    34.98
17    31.26    31.77    30.61    29.85
21    32.71    31.99    35.70    37.02
25    37.80    40.60    38.42    39.61
29    37.69    35.56    36.08    32.99
33    34.81    34.72    35.57    39.21
37    38.89    42.54    42.72    42.54
41    43.76    40.38    40.97    38.60
45    37.26    38.61    36.89    40.22
49    40.93    42.63    45.96    44.98
53    47.59    46.11    44.96    45.06
57    41.42    42.47    40.75    41.01
61    43.50    43.01    47.16    47.68
65    49.12    51.13    48.87    50.25
```

Fourier Transformation

The original computer program that solves the Fourier transformation as described by Jack Hutson and Anthony Warren (*Technical Analysis of Stocks & Commodities*) is based on the Cooley-Tukey Fast Fourier Transform Algorithm (1965), developed at the IBM Thomas J. Watson Research Center. A full explanation of this program and its interpretation can be found in the two articles that appeared in the January 1983 edition of *Technical Analysis of Stocks & Commodities*, then reprinted in the September 1986 issue.

The following program appeared in the September 1986 issue of *Technical Analysis of Stocks & Commodities*. It was written by John Ehlers and appended to the article "A Comparison of the Fourier and Maximum Entropy Methods."

FAST FOURIER TRANSFORM PROGRAM

```
10 REM "FAST FOURIER TRANSFORM"
20 REM FOR APPLE ][ WITH 2 DISKS USING
30 REM DATA IN CSI OR COMPU-TRAC FORMAT
40 REM BY JOHN F. EHLERS
45 REM COPYRIGHT (C) 1986 BY TECHNICAL ANALYSIS, INC.
50 HOME
60 DIM DF$(20)
70 HTAB 5: INVERSE : PRINT "* FAST FOURIER TRANSFORM *" :
   NORMAL
71 HTAB 19: PRINT "BY"
72 HTAB 14: PRINT "JOHN EHLERS"
73 HTAB 16: PRINT "BOX 1801"
74 HTAB 12: PRINT "GOLETA, CA 93116": PRINT
80 LET D$ = CHR$(4)
90 PRINT D$ + "OPEN MASTER,L40,D2"
100 FOR I = 1 TO 20
110     PRINT D$ + "READ MASTER,R";I
120     INPUT DF$(I)
130     IF LEFT$ (DF$(I),5) = "99999" GOTO 150
140     NEXT I
150 PRINT D$ + "CLOSE"
160 FOR J = 1 TO I-1
170     PRINT "<"; CHR$ (J + 64); ">"; MID$ (DF$(J),4,16)
180     NEXT J
190 PRINT "<V> VIEW NEW DATA DISK"
200 PRINT "<X> EXIT TO MENU": PRINT
210 PRINT "    SELECT <>": CHR$(8); CHR$(8);
220 POKE - 16368,0: GET X$: PRINT X$; ">"; CHR$(8); CHR$(8);
230 IF X$ = "V" THEN
        HOME : VTAB 10:
        PRINT "INSERT NEW DATA DISK IN DRIVE 2":
        PRINT: PRINT "PRESS";: INVERSE: PRINT "RETURN";:
        NORMAL: PRINT "TO CONTINUE": VTAB 22:
        POKE - 16368,0: GET S$: GOTO 30
240 IF X$ = "X" THEN HOME
250 LET SF = ASC (X$) - 64
260 IF SF > 1 AND SF <= J - 1 THEN 290
270 HTAB 13: PRINT "": CHR$(8);: GOTO 220
280 IF K < 120 OR K > LR THEN
        PRINT "OOPS - RUN AGAIN": END
```

```
290 HOME : VTAB 10: INVERSE: PRINT MID$ (DF$(SF),4,16):
    NORMAL: PRINT: PRINT
300 PRINT: PRINT D$ + "OPEN" + MID$ (DF$(SF),4,16) + ",L40":
    PRINT D$ + "READ" + MID$ (DF$(SF),4,16) +",R0":
    INPUT X$: LET LR = VAL (X$)
310 PRINT D$ + "CLOSE"
320 IF LR < 32 THEN 370
330 IF LR < 1024 THEN 410
340 PRINT "CONTAINS"; LR; " RECORDS"
350 PRINT "A MAXIMUM 1024 RECORDS ARE ALLOWED": PRINT
360 PRINT "PRESS";: INVERSE: PRINT "RETURN";: NORMAL:
    PRINT " TO CONTINUE": VTAB 22
370 PRINT "CONTAINS ONLY"; LR; "RECORDS"
380 PRINT "AT LEAST 32 RECORDS ARE REQUIRED": PRINT
390 PRINT "PRESS";: INVERSE: PRINT "RETURN";: NORMAL:
    PRINT "TO CONTINUE": VTAB 22
400 POKE - 16368,0: GET S$: HOME: CLEAR: GOTO 20
410 PRINT "CONTAINS "; LR; " RECORDS": PRINT
420 PRINT "ENTER ONLY 32, 64, 128, OR 256"
430 PRINT "FOR ANALYSIS. THIS NUMBER MUST BE"
440 PRINT "LESS THAN THE FILE LENGTH.": PRINT
450 INPUT "RECORDS FOR ANALYSIS? "; N
460 IF (N = 32 OR N = 64 OR N = 128 OR N = 256 OR N = 512)
        AND N < LR THEN 480
470 PRINT: PRINT "OOPS -- RUN PROGRAM AGAIN": END

480 DIM DA$(1024), F(1024), A(257,8)
490 PRINT: PRINT D$ + "OPEN" + MID$ (DF$(SF),4,16) + ",L40"
500 FOR I = 1 TO N:
        PRINT D$ + "READ " + MID$ (DF$(SF),4,16) + ",R";
        (LR - N + I): INPUT DA$(I):
        NEXT I
510 PRINT D$ + "CLOSE"
520 REM *** DATA CONVERTER ***
530 IF MID$ (DA$(1),23,5) <> "99999" THEN 550
540 LET DA$(1) = DA$(2)
550 FOR I = 1 TO N
560    LET F(I) = VAL (MID$ (DA$(I),23,5))
570    IF MID$ (DA$(I),23,5) = "99999" THEN
          LET F(I) = F(I - 1)
580    NEXT I

590 REM *** SPECTRUM ANALYSIS ***
600 LET PI = 3.1415926
610 LET P0 = INT (N / 4): LET S0 = 8
620 FOR I = 1 TO R0 + 1:
        FOR J = 1 TO 8: LET A(I,J) = 0: NEXT J:
        NEXT I
630 FOR I = 1 TO R0
640    FOR J = 1 TO S0 STEP 2
650        LET K = 4 * (I - 1) + .5 * (J + 1)
660        LET A(I,J) = F(K)
670        LET A(I,J + 1) = 0
680        NEXT J
690    NEXT I
700 LET M = LOG (N) / LOG (2): LET N2 = N / 2:
    LET N1 = N - 1:          LET J = 1
710 FOR I = 1 TO N1
720    IF I > J THEN 850
730    LET R  = INT ((J - 1) / 4)
740    LET S  = 2 * J - 8 * R
```

```
 750      LET R1 = INT ((I - 1) / 4)
 760      LET S1 = 2 * I - 8 * R1
 770      LET R1 = R1 + 1
 780      LET R  = R + 1
 790      LET T  = A(R,S)
 800      LET A(R,S)   = A(R1,S1)
 810      LET A(R1,S1) = T
 820      LET T  = A(R,S - 1)
 830      LET A(R,S - 1)   = A(R1,S1 - 1)
 840      LET A(R1,S1 - 1) = T
 850      LET K = N2
 860      IF K > J THEN 910
 870      LET J  = J - K
 880      LET K  = K / 2
 890      GOTO 860
 900      NEXT I
 910 LET J = J + K
 920 NEXT I
 930 LET L0 = 1
 940 FOR L = 1 TO M
 950      LET L1 = L0
 960      LET L0 = 2 * L0
 970      LET V  = 1
 980      LET W  = 0
 990      LET Z  = PI / L1
1000      LET W1 = COS (Z)
1010      LET W2 = SIN (Z)
1020      FOR J = 1 TO L1
1030          FOR I = J TO N STEP L0
1040              LET K  = I + L1
1050              LET R1 = INT ((K - 1) / 4)
1060              LET S1 = 2 * K - 8 * R1
1070              LET R1 = R1 + 1
1080              LET A1 = A(R1,S1 - 1)
1090              LET B1 = A(R1,S1)
1100              LET T  = A1 * V - B1 * W
1110              LET U  = A1 * W + B1 * V
1120              LET R  = INT ((I - 1)/ 4)
1130              LET S  = 2 * I - 8 * R
1140              LET R  = R + 1
1150              LET A(R1,S1 - 1) = A(R,S - 1) - T
1160              LET A(R1,S1)     = A(R,S) - U
1170              LET A(R,S - 1)   = A(R,S - 1) + T
1180              LET A(R,S)       = A(R,S) + U
1190              NEXT I
1200          LET U = V * W1 - W * W2
1210          LET W = V * W2 + W * W1
1220          LET V = U
1230          NEXT J
1240      NEXT L
1250 LET Z = - 1E6
1260 FOR I = 1 TO R0 / 2
1270      FOR J = 1 TO S0 STEP 2
1280          IF I = 1 AND J = 1 THEN 1310
1290          LET A(I,J) = SQR (A(I,J) * A(I,J) + A(I,J + 1) *
                  A(I,J + 1))
1300          IF A(I,J) > Z THEN LET Z = A(I,J)
1310          NEXT J
1320      NEXT I
1330 HOME: PRINT "SPECTRUM FOR" + MID$ (DF$(SF),4,16)
```

```
1340 PRINT
1350 PRINT "PERIOD  RELATIVE AMPLITUDE'
1360 PRINT "(DAYS)     (DB)": PRINT
1370 LET K = 0
1380 FOR I = 1 TO R0 / 2
1400     FOR J = 1 TO S0 STEP 2
1410         IF I = 1 AND J = 1 THEN 1460
1420         LET L = INT (N / K + .25)
1430         IF L + 1 > P THEN 1460
1440         LET P = L
1450         PRINT TAB( 2): L; TAB( 16);
                 INT (1000 * LOG (A(I,J) / Z) / LOG (10)) / 100
1460         LET K = K + 1
1470         NEXT J
1480     NEXT I

PROGRAM LENGTH: 152 LINES/3304 BYTES
```

Construction of a Pentagon

CONSTRUCTION OF A PENTAGON FROM ONE FIXED DIAGONAL

Establish the diagonal D by connecting the top and bottom of a major price move by a straight line. This diagonal will be toward the left and top of the pentagon to be constructed (see Figure A6-1).

1. Measure the length of the diagonal D. This diagonal connects two points of the pentagon.
2. With the point of a compass at one end of the diagonal and the tip on the other, draw a long arc to the right; placing the point on the other end of the diagonal, draw another arc to the right. These arcs should not cross to avoid confusion.
3. The length of a side of a regular pentagon is calculated from the diagonal by the formula

$$S = .618 \times D$$

Using a ruler, set the compass to the length of a side and place the point at one end of the diagonal. Draw an arc on both sides, crossing the arc on the right; do the same for the other end of the diagonal. The two new arcs will cross on the left. The three new crossings are the missing points of the pentagon.

FIGURE A6-1 Construction of a pentagon from one diagonal.

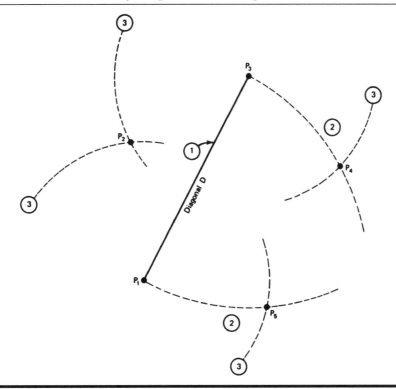

4. The center of the pentagon can be found by bisecting any two sides. The point at which the two bisecting lines cross is the center. Use this point to circumscribe a circle around the pentagon.

CONSTRUCTION OF A PENTAGON FROM ONE SIDE

Establish the side S by connecting the top and bottom of a major price move with a straight line. As in the previous example, this side will be toward the top and left of the pentagon, which will extend down and to the right (see Figure A6-2).

1. Calculate the length of the diagonal D by applying the formula $D = S/.618$. This will require a ruler to determine the length of S.
2. Using a ruler again, set your compass to the length of the diagonal calculated in the first step. Draw wide arcs of radius D from the endpoints of S crossing to the lower right of S. The place of crossing will be the third point of the pentagon P_4, opposite side S.
3. Set the compass back to length S and place the point at P_4. Cross the inner arcs drawn in step 2 with a small arc drawn on either side of P. The place of crossing will be the two remaining points of the pentagon.
4. The perpendicular bisectors of any two sides will cross at the center of the pentagon and allow you to circumscribe a circle around the pentagon.

FIGURE A6-2   Construction of a pentagon from one side.

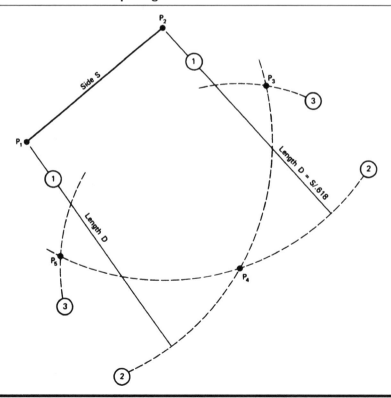

The perpendicular bisector of any side is constructed by setting the compass to any length greater than half of the line being bisected, then placing the point at one end of the line. Draw an arc on both sides of the line in the area above the center of the line. Do the same by placing the point of the compass at the other end and crossing the arcs already drawn. A line through the two crosses will be the perpendicular bisector of the original line.

Bibliography

Aan, Peter W. "How RSI Behaves." *Futures* (January 1985).

Abraham, Bovas, and Johannes Ledolter. *Statistical Methods for Forecasting.* New York, NY: John Wiley & Sons, 1983.

Achelis, Steven B. *Technical Analysis from A to Z.* Chicago, IL: Probus, 1995.

Ainsworth, Ralph M. *Profitable Grain Trading.* Greensville, SC: Traders Press, 1980 (originally 1933).

Altman, Roger. "Tactical Trading Revisited." *Technical Analysis of Stocks & Commodities,* (September 1993).

Andrews, W.S. *Magic Squares and Cubes.* New York, NY: Dover, 1960.

Angas, L.L.B. *Investment For Appreciation.* New York, NY: Somerset, 1936.

Angell, George. "Thinking Contrarily" (an interview with R. Earl Hadady). *Commodities Magazine* (November 1976).

Angell, George. *Winning in the Commodities Markets.* New York, NY: Doubleday, 1979.

Anon, Louis J. "Catch Short-Term Profits with ARIMA." *Commodities Magazine* (December 1981).

Appel, Gerald. *Winning Market Systems: 83 Ways to Beat the Market.* Great Neck, NY: Signalert, 1974.

———, and Martin E. Zweig. *New Directions in Technical Analysis.* Great Neck, NY: Signalert, 1976.

Arms, Richard W., Jr. "Equivolume—A New Method of Charting." *Commodities Magazine* (April 1973).

Arnold, Curtis M. *The Personal Computer Can Make You Rich in Stocks and Commodities.* West Palm Beach, FL: Weiss Research, 1980 (published in hardcover 1984).

———. "Tracking 'Big Money' May Tip Off Trend Changes." *Futures* (February 1985).

———. "Your Computer Can Take You Beyond Charting." *Futures* (May 1984).

Aronson, David R. "An Introduction to Computer-Based Pattern Recognition." *Financial and Investment Software Review* (January/February 1984).

———. "Artificial Intelligence/Pattern Recognition Applied to Forecasting Financial Market Trends." *Market Technicians Association Journal* (May 1985): pp. 91–131.

Arrington, George R. "Building a Variable-Length Moving Average." *Technical Analysis of Stocks & Commodities* (June 1991).

———. "Markov Chains." *Technical Analysis of Stocks & Commodities* (December 1993).

Aspray, Thomas. "Fine-tuning the Demand Index." *Technical Analysis of Stocks & Commodities* (June 1986).

———. "Demand Oscillator Momentum." *Technical Analysis of Stocks & Commodities* (September 1989).

Azoff, E. Michael. *Neural Network Time Series Forecasting of Financial Markets.* (New York, NY: John Wiley & Sons, 1994.

Barnett, Eugene H. *Programming Time-Shared Computers in BASIC.* New York, NY: Wiley-Interscience, 1972.

Becker, John D. "Value of oscillators in determining price action." *Futures* (May 1994).

Bernstein, Jacob. "Cyclic and Seasonal Price Tendencies in Meat and Livestock Markets." In Todd Lofton (Ed.), *Trading Tactics: A Livestock Futures Anthology.* Chicago, IL: Chicago Mercantile Exchange, 1986.

———. *Seasonal Concepts in Futures Trading.* New York, NY: John Wiley & Sons, 1986.

———. *The Handbook of Commodity Cycles.* New York, NY: John Wiley & Sons, 1982.

Bernstein, Peter L. *The Portable MBA in Investment.* New York, NY: John Wiley & Sons, 1995.

Beyer, William H. (Ed.). *Standard Mathematical Tables, 24th ed.* Cleveland, OH: CRC Press, 1976.

Blau, William. *Momentum, Direction, and Divergence.* New York, NY: John Wiley & Sons, 1995.

Bolton, A. Hamilton. *The Elliott Wave Principle, A Critical Appraisal.* Montreal: Bolton, Tremblay & Co., 1960.

Bookstaber, Richard. *The Complete Investment Book.* Glenview, IL: Scott, Foresman, 1985.

Box, G.E.P., and G.M. Jenkins. *Time Series Analysis: Forecasting and Control, 2nd ed.* San Francisco, CA: Holden-Day, 1976.

Briese, Stephen E. "Commitment of Traders as a sentiment index." *Technical Analysis of Stocks & Commodities* (May 1990).

———. "Tracking the big foot." *Futures* (March 1994).

Brower, William. *Inside Edge.* Westport, CT: Inside Edge Systems, (March/April 1996).

Brown, William G.S. "Logarithmic Point & Figure Charting." *Technical Analysis of Stocks & Commodities* (July 1995).

Burke, Gibbons. "Event-based Analysis." *Futures* (April 1995).

Carr, Michael J. "Get out the vote and into stocks." *Futures* (February 1996).

Chande, Tushar S., and Stanley Kroll. *The New Technical Trader.* New York, NY: John Wiley & Sons, 1994.

Chatfield, C. *The Analysis of a Time Series: Theory and Practice.* London: Chapman and Hall, 1975.

Chicago Board of Trade. *CBOT Market Profile.* Chicago, IL: Chicago Board of Trade, 1984.

Church, A.H. *On the Relation of Phyllotaxis to Mechanical Laws.* London: Williams and Newgate, 1904.

Cleeton, Claude. *The Art of Independent Investing.* Englewood Cliffs, NJ: Prentice-Hall, 1976.

Cohen, A.W. *How to Use the Three-Point Reversal Method of Point and Figure Stock Market Trading.* Larchmont, NY: Chartcraft, 1972.

Colby, Robert W., and Thomas A. Meyers. *The Encyclopedia of Technical Market Indicators.* Homewood, IL: Dow Jones-Irwin, 1988.

Commodity Traders Club. *Comparative Performances.* Messena, NY: 1969. (A reprint).

Commodity Trading Manual. Chicago, IL: Chicago Board of Trade.

Commodity Yearbook 1975. New York, NY: Commodity Research Bureau, 1975.

Commodity Yearbook 1987. New York, NY: Commodity Research Bureau, 1987.

Commodity Yearbook 1992. New York, NY: Commodity Research Bureau, 1992.

Commodity Yearbook 1994. New York, NY: Knight-Ridder, 1994.

CompuTrac Manual. Telerate, 1990.

Conners, Laurence A., and Blake E. Hayward. *Investment Secrets of a Hedge Fund Manager.* Chicago, IL: Probus, 1995.

ContiCommodity. *Seasonality in Agricultural Futures Markets.* Chicago, IL: ContiCommodity Services, 1983.

Control Data Corporation. *Control Data 6000 Series Computer Systems Statistical Subroutines Reference Manual.* St. Paul, MN: 1966.

Cootner, Paul (Ed.). *The Random Character of Stock Market Prices.* Cambridge, MA: MIT Press, 1964.

————. "Speculation and Hedging." *Food Research Institute Studies, Vol. VII: 1967 Supplement.* Stanford, CA: Stanford University Press, 1967.

Crabel, Toby. *Day Trading With Short Term Price Patterns and Opening Range Breakout.* Greenville, SC.: Traders Press, 1990.

————. "Opening Range Breakout, Part 4." *Technical Analysis of Stocks & Commodities* (February 1989).

Crim, Elias. "Are You Watching the 'Right' Signals?" *Futures* (June 1985).

CSI Technical Journal. Boca Raton, FL: Commodity Systems Inc., May 1995.

Cycles. Pittsburgh, PA: Foundation for the Study of Cycles, January 1976.

Damodaran, Aswath. *Investment Valuation.* New York, NY: John Wiley & Sons, 1996.

Davis, Jon. *Weather Sensitivity in the Markets.* Smith Barney, October 1994.

Davis, Robert Earl. *Profit and Profitability, 2nd Edition.* West LaFayette, IN: R.E. Davis, 1969.

Davis, R.E., and C.C. Thiel, Jr. *A Computer Analysis of the Moving Average Applied to Commodity Futures Trading.* West Lafayette, IN: Quiatenon Management Co., 1970. (A research report).

DeMark, Thomas R. "Retracing your steps." *Futures* (November 1995).

————. *The New Science of Technical Analysis.* New York, NY: John Wiley & Sons, 1994.

DeVilliers, Victor. *The Point and Figure Method of Anticipating Stock Price Movements.* Trader Press, 1966. (Reprint of 1933 edition).

Dewey, Edward R., and Og Mandino. *Cycles.* New York, NY: Hawthorn Books, 1971.

Donchian, Richard D. "Donchian's 5- and 20-Day Moving Averages." *Commodities Magazine* (December 1974).

Downie, N.M., and R.W. Heath. *Basic Statistical Method, 3rd ed.* New York, NY: Harper & Row, 1970.

Dunn, Dennis. *Consistent Profits in June Live Beef Cattle.* West Lafayette, IN: Dunn & Hargitt, 1972.

Dunnigan, William. *117 Barometers for Forecasting Stock Price.* San Francisco, CA: Dunnigan, 1954.

————. *One Way Formula.* Palo Alto, CA: Dunnigan, 1955.

————. *Select Studies in Speculation.* San Francisco, CA: Dunnigan, 1954. (Includes "Gain in Grains" and "The Thrust Method in Stocks").

Earp, Richard B. "Correlating Taylor and Polous." *Commodities Magazine* (September 1973).

Edwards, Robert D., and John Magee. *Technical Analysis of Stock Trends.* Springfield, MA: John Magee, 1948.

Ehlers, John F. "How to Use Maximum Entropy." *Technical Analysis of Stocks & Commodities* (November 1987).

————. *MESA and Trading Market Cycles.* New York, NY: John Wiley & Sons, 1992.

————. "Moving Averages, Part 1." *Technical Analysis of Stocks & Commodities,* 1988.

————. "Moving Averages, Part 2." *Technical Analysis of Stocks & Commodities,* 1988.

————. "Optimizing RSI with Cycles." *Technical Analysis of Stocks & Commodities* (February 1986).

————."Trading Channels." *Technical Analysis of Stocks & Commodities* (April 1986).

Elder, Alexander. *Trading for a Living.* New York, NY: John Wiley & Sons, 1993.

Elliott, R.N. *Nature's Law, The Secret of the Universe.* New York, NY: Elliott, 1946.

————. *The Wave Principle.* New York, NY: Elliot, 1938.

Emmett, Tucker J. "Fibonacci Cycles." *Technical Analysis of Stocks & Commodities* (May 1983 and March/April 1984).

Eng, William F. "A Mechanical Trading System." *Technical Analysis of Stocks & Commodities* (July 1986).

———. *The Technical Analysis of Stocks, Options & Futures.* Chicago, IL: Probus, 1988.

Ericsson, Christina. *Forecasting Success.* Westport, CT: Kaufman, 1987.

Etzkorn, Mark. "All in a day's work." *Futures* (January 1995).

Evans, Eric. "Why You Can't Rely on 'Key Reversal Days.' " *Futures* (March 1985).

Fischer, Robert. *Fibonacci Applications and Strategies for Traders.* New York, NY: John Wiley & Sons, 1993.

———. *The Golden Section Compass Seminar.* Hamilton, Bermuda: Fibonacci Trading, 1984.

Fishman, Mark B., Dean S. Barr, and Walter J. Loick. "Artificial Intelligence and Market Analysis. *Technical Analysis of Stocks & Commodities* (Bonus Issue 1993).

Floss, Carl William. *Market Rhythm.* New York, NY: Investors Publishing Co., 1955.

Frost, A.J., and Robert R. Prechter, Jr. *Elliott Wave Principle.* Chappaqua, NY: New Classics Library, 1978.

Fuller, Wayne A. *Introduction to Statistical Time Series.* New York, NY: John Wiley & Sons, 1976.

Fults, John Lee. *Magic Squares.* La Salle, IL: Open Court, 1974.

Furguson, James William. "Martingales." *Technical Analysis of Stocks & Commodities* (February 1990).

———. "Reverse Martingales." *Technical Analysis of Stocks & Commodities* (March 1990).

Gann, William D. *Forecasting Grains By Time Cycles.* Pomeroy, WA: Lambert-Gann, 1976. (Originally 1946).

———. *Forecasting Rules for Cotton.* Pomeroy, WA: Lambert-Gann, 1976.

———. *Forecasting Rules for Grain—Geometric Angles.* Pomeroy, WA: Lambert-Gann, 1976.

———. *How to Make Profits in Commodities.* Pomeroy, WA: Lambert-Gann, 1976. (Originally 1942).

———. *Master Calculator for Weekly Time Periods to Determine the Trend of Stocks and Commodities.* Pomeroy, WA: Lambert-Gann, 1976.

———. *Master Charts.* Pomeroy, WA: Lambert-Gann, 1976.

———. *Mechanical Method and Trend Indicator for Trading in Wheat, Corn, Rye, or Oats.* Pomeroy, WA: Lambert-Gann, 1976. (Originally 1934).

———. *Rules for Trading in Soybeans, Corn, Wheat, Oats and Rye.* Pomeroy, WA: Lambert-Gann, 1976.

———. *Speculation: A Profitable Profession (A Course of Instruction In Grains).* Pomeroy, WA: Lambert-Gann, 1976. (Originally 1955).

———. *The Basis of My Forecasting Method for Grain.* Pomeroy, WA: Lambert-Gann, 1976. (Originally 1935).

———. *45 Years in Wall Street.* Pomeroy, WA: Lambert-Gann, 1949.

Gannsoft Publishing. "Ganntrader I." *Technical Analysis of Stocks & Commodities* (January/February 1984).

Gately, Edward. *Neural Networks for Financial Forecasting.* New York, NY: John Wiley & Sons, 1996.

Gehm, Fred. *Commodity Market Money Management.* New York, NY: John Wiley & Sons, 1983.

———. "Does Pyramiding Make Sense?" *Technical Analysis of Stocks & Commodities* (February 1986).

———. *Quantitative Trading & Money Management* (Revised Edition). Irwin, 1995.

Gies, Joseph, and Frances Gies. *Leonard of Pisa and The New Mathematics of the Middle Ages.* New York, NY: Thomas M. Crowell, 1969.

Gilchrist, Warren. *Statistical Forecasting.* London: Wiley, 1976.

Ginter, G., and J. Richie. "Data Errors and Price Distortions." In Perry J. Kaufman (Ed.), *Technical Analysis in Commodities.* New York, NY: John Wiley & Sons, 1980.

Gotthelf, Edward B. *The Commodex System*. New York, NY: Commodity Futures Forecast, 1970.

Gotthelf, Philip, and Carl Gropper. "Systems Do Work . . . But You Need a Plan." *Commodities Magazine* (April 1977).

Gould, Bruce G. *Dow Jones-Irwin Guide to Commodities Trading*. Homewood, IL: Dow Jones-Irwin, 1973.

Greer, Thomas V., B. Wade Brorsen, and Shi-Miin Liu. "Slippage Costs of a Large Technical Trader." *Technical Analysis of Stocks & Commodities* (January 1992).

Grushcow, J., and C. Smith. *Profits Through Seasonal Trading*. New York, NY: John Wiley & Sons, 1980.

Hadady, R. Earl. *Contrary Opinion*. Pasadena, CA: Hadady, 1983.

———. "Contrary Opinion." *Technical Analysis of Stocks & Commodities* (August 1988).

Hallberg, M.C., and V.I. West. *Patterns of Seasonal Price Variations for Illinois Farm Products,* Circular 861. Urbana, IL: U. of Illinois College of Agriculture, 1967.

Hambridge, Jay. *Dynamic Symmetry, The Greek Vase*. New Haven, CT: Yale University Press, 1931.

———. *Practical Applications of Dynamic Symmetry*. New Haven, CT: Yale University Press, 1938.

Handmaker, David. "Low-Frequency Filters for Seasonal Analysis." In Perry J. Kaufman (Ed.), *Handbook of Futures Markets*. New York, NY: John Wiley & Sons, 1984.

———. "Low-Frequency Filters in Seasonal Analysis." *Journal of Futures Markets,* 1, no. 3 (1981).

———. "Picking Software To Trade Technically." *Commodities* (August 1982).

Hannula, Hans. "Trading Planetary Eclipses." *Technical Analysis of Stocks & Commodities* (April 1992).

Harahus, David. *". . . on Market Speculation . . . ."* Ferndale, MI: Harahus Analysis, 1977.

Haynie, F.M. "Doc." "Stretching the 'profile' to cover 24-hour markets." *Futures* (February 1992).

Haze, Van Court, Jr. *Systems Analysis: A Diagnostic Approach*. New York, NY: Harcourt, Brace & World, 1967.

Hewison, Adam. "The Will Rogers Theory of Point & Figure Trading." *Technical Analysis of Stocks & Commodities* (August 1991).

Hieronymus, Thomas A. *Economics of Futures Trading*. New York, NY: Commodity Research Bureau, 1971.

———. *When to Sell Corn-Soybeans-Oats-Wheat*. (Urbana, IL: University of Illinois College of Agriculture, 1967.

Higgens, James E., and Allan M. Loosigian. "Foreign Exchange Futures." In Perry J. Kaufman (Ed.), *Handbook of Futures Markets*. New York, NY: John Wiley & Sons, 1984.

Hildebrand, F.B. *Introduction to Numerical Analysis*. New York, NY: McGraw-Hill, 1956.

Hill, Holliston. "Using Congestion Area Analysis to Set Up for Big Moves." *Futures* (April 1985).

Hill, John. "Simple vs. complex." *Futures* (March 1996).

Hochheimer, Frank L., and Richard J. Vaughn. *Computerized Trading Techniques 1982*. New York, NY: Merrill Lynch Commodities, 1982.

Holland, John H. *Adaptations in Natural Language and Artificial Systems*. Ann Arbor, MI: University of Michigan Press, 1975.

Hurst, J.M. *The Profit Magic of Stock Transaction Timing*. Englewood Cliffs, NJ: Prentice-Hall, 1970.

Hutson, Jack K. "Elements of Charting." *Technical Analysis of Stocks & Commodities* (March 1986).

———. "Filter Price Data: Moving Averages Versus Exponential Moving Averages." *Technical Analysis of Stocks & Commodities* (May/June 1984).

———. "Good TRIX." *Technical Analysis of Stocks & Commodities* (July 1983).

———. "Using Fourier." *Technical Analysis of Stocks & Commodities* (January 1983).

Hutson, Jack K., and Anthony Warren. "Forecasting with Maximum Entropy." *Technical Analysis of Stocks & Commodities* (December 1984).

Jackson, J.T. *Detecting High Profit Day Trades In The Futures Markets.* Brightwaters, NY: Windsor Books, 1994.

Jiler, William L. "Analysis of the CFTC Commitments of Traders Reports Can Help You Forecast Futures Prices." *1985 CRB Commodity Year Book.* Jersey City, NJ: Commodity Research Bureau, 1985.

———. *Forecasting Commodity Prices with Vertical Line Charts.* New York, NY: Commodity Research Bureau, 1966.

———. *How Charts Are Used in Commodity Price Forecasting.* New York, NY: Commodity Research Publications, 1977.

———. *Volume and Open Interest: A Key to Commodity Price Forecasting.* New York, NY: Commodity Research Bureau, 1967.

Johnson, A. Bruce. "Finding Cycles in Time Series Data." *Technical Analysis of Stocks & Commodities* (August 1990).

Johnson, Charles F. "Stochastic Oscillator Program for the HP-41C(V)." *Technical Analysis of Stocks & Commodities* (September/October 1984).

Jones, Donald. *Applications of the Market Profile.* Chicago, IL: CISCO, 1989.

———. "Locating value with auction market data." *Technical Analysis of Stocks & Commodities* (July 1989).

Kaeppel, Jay. "The January Barometer: Myth and Reality." *Technical Analysis of Stocks & Commodities.* (July 1990).

Kase, Cynthia. "Redefining Volatility and Position Risk." *Technical Analysis of Stocks & Commodities* (October 1993).

Kaufman, Perry J. *Handbook of Futures Markets.* New York, NY: John Wiley & Sons, 1984.

———. "High-Tech Trading." *Futures and Options World* (September 1985).

———. "Market Momentum Re-examined." Unpublished Article, November 1975.

———. "Moving Averages and Trends." In Todd Lofton (Ed.), *Trading Tactics: A Livestock Futures Anthology.* Chicago, IL: Chicago Mercantile Exchange, 1986.

———. "Price Shocks: Reevaluating Risk/Return Expectations." *Futures Industry* (June/July 1995).

———. "Safety-Adjusted Performance Evaluation." *Journal of Futures Markets* (1981).

———. *Smarter Trading.* New York, NY: McGraw-Hill, 1995.

———. "Technical Analysis." In Nancy H. Rothstein (Ed.), *The Handbook of Financial Futures.* New York, NY: McGraw-Hill, 1984.

———. *Technical Analysis in Commodities.* New York, NY: John Wiley & Sons, 1980.

Kaufman, Perry J., and Alberto Vivanti. *Global Equity Investing.* New York, NY: McGraw-Hill, 1997.

Kaufman, Perry J., and Kermit C. Zieg, Jr. "Measuring Market Movement." *Commodities Magazine* (May 1974).

Kaufman, Perry J., Dennis C. Koutras, and Peter Psycharis. "Positioning the Greek Equities Market in International Portfolios." *Nonlinear Analysis, Theory, Methods & Applications,* Vol 30, No. 4, *Proceedings of the 2nd World Congress of Nonlinear Analysts.* Great Britain: Elsevier Science Ltd, 1997.

Kelly, John L., Jr. "Kelly Betting System." *Bell System Technical Journal* (July 1956).

Keltner, Chester W. *How to Make Money in Commodities.* Kansas City, MO: The Keltner Statistical Service, 1960.

Kemeny, John G., and Thomas E. Kurtz. *Basic Programming, 2nd ed.* New York, NY: John Wiley & Sons, 1971.

Kemeny, John G., and J. Laurie Snell. *Finite Markov Chains.* New York, NY: Springer-Verlag, 1976.

Kepka, John F. "Trading with ARIMA Forecasts." *Technical Analysis of Stocks & Commodities* (May 1983).

Klein, Frederick C., and John A. Prestbo. *News and the Market.* Chicago, IL: Henry Regnery Co., 1974.

Knuth, Donald E. *The Art of Computer Programming, Vol. 2: Seminumeric Algorithms.* Reading, MA: Addison-Wesley, 1971.

Koy, Kevin. *Markets 101.* Chicago, IL: MLS Publishing, 1989.

Krausz, Robert. *Fibonacci Trader (Tutorial & Educational Supplement).* Ft. Lauderdale, FL: Fibonacci Trader Corporation, 1998.

Kroll, Stanley. *The Professional Commodity Trader.* New York, NY: Harper & Row, 1974.

Kroll, Stanley, and Irwin Shishko. *The Commodity Futures Market Guide.* New York, NY: Harper & Row, 1973.

Kunz, Kaiser S. *Numerical Analysis.* New York, NY: McGraw-Hill, 1957.

Labys, Walter C. *Dynamic Commodity Models: Specification, Estimation, and Simulation.* Lexington, MA: Lexington Books, 1973.

Lafferty, Patrick E. "End-Point Moving Average." *Technical Analysis of Stocks & Commodities* (October 1995).

Lambert, Donald R. "Commodity Channel Index: Tool for Trading Cyclic Trends." *Commodities,* 1980. Reprinted in *Technical Analysis of Stocks & Commodities* (July 1983).

———. "Exponentially Smoothed Moving Averages." *Technical Analysis of Stocks & Commodities* (September/October 1984).

———. "The Market Directional Indicator." *Technical Analysis of Stocks & Commodities* (November/December 1983).

Lane, George C. "Lane's Stochastics." *Technical Analysis of Stocks & Commodities,* (May/June 1984).

Larson, Arnold. "Measurement of a Random Process in Futures Pricing." *Food Research Institute Studies 1,* no. 3 (Nov 1960).

Lefevre, Edwin. *Reminiscences of a Stock Operator.* Burlington, VT: Books of Wall Street, 1980 (originally published in 1923 by George H. Doran Co., New York).

Lincoln, Thomas H. "Time Series Forecasting: ARMAX." *Technical Analysis of Stocks & Commodities* (September 1991).

Lofton, Todd. "Chartists Corner." *Commodities Magazine* (December 1974). (Two series of articles.)

———. "Moonlight Sonata." *Commodities Magazine* (July 1974).

———. *Trading Tactics: A Livestock Futures Anthology.* Chicago, IL: Chicago Mercantile Exchange, 1986.

Long, Jeanne. "Planetary Support and Resistance on the DJIA." *A Traders Astrological Almanac 1994.* Ft. Lauderdale, FL: Professional Astrology Service, 1994.

Loyo, Luis Ballesca. "Price projections on point and figure charts." *Technical Analysis of Stocks & Commodities* (July 1989).

Luce, R. Duncan, and Howard Raiffa. *Games and Decisions.* New York, NY: John Wiley & Sons, 1957.

Lukac, Louis P., G. Wade Brorsen, and Scott H. Irwin. *Similarity of Computer Guided Technical Trading Systems,* CSFM-124, Working Paper Series, Columbia Futures Center. New York, NY: Columbia University Business School, 1986.

———, ———, and ———. "How to test profitability of technical trading systems." *Futures* (October 1987).

Mackay, Charles. *Extraordinary Popular Delusions and The Madness of Crowds.* New York, NY: Noonday Press (Farrar, Straus and Giroux), 1932.

Macon, Nathaniel. *Numerical Analysis.* New York, NY: John Wiley & Sons, 1963.

Mart, Donald S. *The Master Trading Formula.* Brightwaters, NY: Winsor Books, 1981.

Martin, Francis F. *Computer Modeling and Simulation.* New York, NY: John Wiley & Sons, 1968.

Maxwell, Joseph R., St. *Commodity Futures Trading with Moving Averages.* Santa Clara, CA: Speer, 1974.

McGinley, John. *Technical Trends.* Wilton, CT.

McKallip, Curtis, Jr. "Fundamentals behind technical analysis." *Technical Analysis of Stocks & Commodities* (November 1989).

McKinsey, J.C.C. *Introduction to the Theory of Games.* New York, NY: McGraw-Hill, 1952.

McMillan, Lawrence G. "Put-Call Ratios." *Technical Analysis of Stocks & Commodities* (October 1995).

McNutt, Malcolm. "First-Hour Breakout System." *Technical Analysis of Stocks & Commodities* (July 1994).

Meeus, Jean. *Astronomical Algorithms.* Richmond, VA: Willmann-Bell, Inc. 1991.

———. *Astronomical Formulae for Calculators, Fourth Edition.* Richmond, VA: Willmann-Bell, Inc. 1988.

Mendenhall, William, and James E. Reinmuth. *Statistics for Management and Economics, 2nd ed.* North Scituate, MA: Duxbury Press, 1974.

Merrill, Arthur A. *Behavior of Prices on Wall Street.* Chappaqua, NY: The Analysis Press, 1966.

———. "The Presidential Election Cycle." *Technical Analysis of Stocks & Commodities* (March 1992).

Mills, Frederick Cecil. *Statistical Methods.* New York, NY: Henry Holt & Co., 1924.

Montgomery, Douglas C., and Lynwood A. Johnson. *Forecasting and Time Series.* New York, NY: McGraw-Hill, 1976.

Morney, M.J., "On The Average and Scatter." In James R. Newman (Ed.), *The World of Mathematics, Vol. 3.* New York, NY: Simon & Schuster, 1956.

Murphy, John J. *Intermarket Technical Analysis.* New York, NY: John Wiley & Sons, 1991.

———. *Technical Analysis of the Futures Markets.* New York: New York Institute of Finance, 1986.

Neill, Humphrey. *The Art of Contrary Thinking.* Caldwell, OH: The Caxton Printers, 1960.

Nison, Steve. *Beyond Candlesticks—New Japanese Trading Techniques.*

———. *Japanese Candlestick Charting Techniques.* New York, NY: New York Institute of Finance, 1991.

Noble, Grant. "The best trading indicator—the media." *Technical Analysis of Stocks & Commodities* (October 1989).

Omega TradeStation. *Easy Language Manual.* Boca Raton, FL: Omega Research, 1995.

Oster, Merrill J. "How the Young Millionaires Trade Commodities." *Commodities Magazine* (March and April 1976).

Oster, Merrill J., et al. *How to Multiply Your Money.* Cedar Falls, IA: Investors Publications, 1979.

Pardo, Robert. *Design, Testing and Optimization of Trading Systems.* New York, NY: John Wiley & Sons, 1992.

Parker, Derek, and Julia Paricor. *The Compleat Astrologer.* New York, NY: McGraw-Hill, 1971.

Payne, J.J. "A better way to smooth data." *Technical Analysis of Stocks & Commodities* (October 1989).

Perrine, Jack. "Taurus the Bullish." *Commodities Magazine* (September 1974).

Peters, Edgar. *Chaos and Order in the Capital Markets.* New York, NY: John Wiley & Sons, 1991.

Pisani, Robert. "How market structure helps you analyze price behavior." *Futures* (October 1987).

Polous, E. Michael. "The Moving Average As A Trading Tool." *Commodities Magazine* (September 1973).

Powers, Mark J. *Getting Started in Commodity Futures Trading.* Waterloo, IA: Investors Publications, 1975.

Prechter, Robert R., Jr. "Computerizing Elliott." *Technical Analysis of Stocks & Commodities* (July 1983).

———. "Major sea change II." *Futures* (March 1996).

———. *The Major Works of R.N. Elliott.* Chappaqua, NY: New Classics Library, c. 1980.

Prechter, Robert R., Jr., David Weiss, and David Allman. "Forecasting with the Elliott Wave Principle." In Todd Lofton (Ed.), *Trading Tactics: A Livestock Futures Anthology.* Chicago, IL: Chicago Mercantile Exchange, 1986.

Pring, Martin J. *Technical Analysis Explained.* New York, NY: McGraw-Hill, 1991.

Quong, Gene, and Avrum Soudack. "Volume-Weighted RSI: Money Flow." *Technical Analysis of Stocks & Commodities* (March 1989).

Reiman, Ray. "Handicapping the Grains." *Commodities Magazine* (April 1975).

Rhea, Robert. *Dow Theory.* Binghamton, NY: Vail-Ballou, 1932.

Rockwell, Charles S. "Normal Backwardation, Forecasting, and the Returns to Commodity Futures Traders." *Food Research Institute Studies, Vol. VII: 1967 Supplement.* Stanford, CA: Stanford University Press, 1967.

Rotella, Robert P. *The Elements of Successful Trading.* New York, NY: The New York Institute of Finance, 1992.

Rothstein, Nancy H. *The Handbook of Financial Futures.* New York, NY: McGraw-Hill, 1984.

Ruckdeschel, F.R. *BASIC Scientific Subroutines, Vol. 1.* Peterborough, NH: Byte/McGraw-Hill, 1981.

———. *BASIC Scientific Subroutines, Vol. 2.* Peterborough, NH: Byte/McGraw-Hill, 1983.

Ruggiero, Murray A., Jr. "Artificial trader jumps candlesticks." *Futures* (February 1995).

———. "Build a real neural net." *Futures* (June 1996).

———. "Building the wave." *Futures* (April 1996).

———. "Lighting candlesticks with fuzzy logic." *Futures* (March 1996).

Saitta, Alex. "A Price and Volume-Based System." *Technical Analysis of Stocks & Commodities* (March 1996).

Schabacker, R.W. *Stock Market Theory and Practice.* New York, NY: B.C. Forbes, 1930.

Schirding, Harry. "Stochastic Oscillator." *Technical Analysis of Stocks & Commodities,* (May/June 1984).

Schwager, Jack D. *A Complete Guide to the Futures Markets.* New York, NY: John Wiley & Sons, 1984.

———. "A Trader's Guide to Analyzing the Potato Futures Market." *1981 Commodity Yearbook.* New York, NY: Commodity Research Bureau, 1981.

———. *Market Wizards, Interviews with Top Traders.* New York, NY: New York Institute of Finance, 1989.

———. *Risk and Money Management.* In Perry J. Kaufman (Ed.), *Handbook of Futures Markets.* New York, NY: John Wiley & Sons, 1984.

———. *Schwager on Futures: Fundamental Analysis.* New York, NY: John Wiley & Sons, 1995.

———. *Schwager on Futures: Technical Analysis.* New York, NY: John Wiley & Sons, 1996.

———. *The New Market Wizards.* New York, NY: John Wiley & Sons, 1992.

Seidel, Andrew D., and Philip M. Ginsberg. *Commodities Trading.* Englewood Cliffs, NJ: Prentice-Hall, 1983.

Shaleen, Kenneth H. *Volume and Open Interest.* Chicago, IL: Probus, 1991.

Shaw, John E.B. *A Professional Guide to Commodity Speculation.* West Nyack, NY: Parker Publ., 1972.

Sklarew, Arthur. *Techniques of a Professional Commodity Chart Analyst.* New York, NY: Commodity Research Bureau, 1980.

Smith, Adam. *The Money Game*. New York, NY: Random House, 1967.

Smith, Courtney. *Commodity Spreads*. New York, NY: John Wiley & Sons, 1982.

Springer, Clifford H., Robert E. Herlihy, and Robert I. Beggs. *Advanced Methods and Models*. Homewood, IL: Richard D. Irwin, 1965.

———. *Probabilistic Models*. Homewood IL: Richard D. Irwin, 1968.

Statistical Annual. Chicago, IL: Chicago Board of Trade, 1969–1975 eds.

Steidlmayer, J. Peter. *Steidlmayer on Markets*. New York, NY: Wiley, 1989.

Steidlmayer, J. Peter, and Shera Buyer. *Taking The Data Forward*. Chicago, IL: Market Logic, Inc., 1986.

Steidlmayer, J. Peter, and Kevin Koy. *Markets & Market Logic*. Chicago, IL: The Porcupine Press, 1986.

Steinberg, Jeanette Nofri. "Timing Market Entry and Exit." *Commodities Magazine* (September 1975).

Stigum, Marsha. *Money Market Calculations*. Homewood, IL: Dow Jones-Irwin, 1981.

Strahm, Norman D. "Preference Space Evaluation of Trading System Performance." In Perry J. Kaufman (Ed.), *Handbook of Futures Markets*. New York, NY: John Wiley & Sons, 1984.

Sweeney, John. *Campaign Trading*. New York, NY: John Wiley & Sons, 1997.

———. "Maximum Adverse Excursions for Stops." *Technical Analysis of Stocks & Commodities* (April 1987).

Taylor, George Douglass. *The Taylor Trading Technique*. Los Angeles, CA: Lilly Pub. Co., 1950. (This book has been reprinted by Traders Press, Greenville, SC, 1994.)

Taylor, Robert Joel. "The Major Price Trend Directional Indicator." *Commodities Magazine* (April 1972).

Taylor, William T. "Fourier Spectral Analysis." *Technical Analysis of Stocks & Commodities* (July/August 1984).

Teweles, Richard J., Charles V. Harlow, and Herbert L. Stone. *The Commodity Futures Game: Who Wins? Who Uses? Why?* New York, NY: McGraw-Hill, 1974.

Thiel, Charles, and R.E. Davis. *Point and Figure Commodity Trading: A Computer Evaluation*. West LaFayette, IN: Dunn & Hargitt, 1970.

Thiriea, H., and S. Zionts (Eds.). *Multiple Criteria Decision Making*. Berlin: Springer-Verlag, 1976.

Thompson, Jesse H. "The Livermore System." *Technical Analysis of Stocks & Commodities* (May 1983).

———. "What Textbooks Never Tell You." *Technical Analysis of Stocks & Commodities* (November/December 1983).

Thorp, Edward O. *Beat the Dealer*. New York, NY: Vintage, 1966.

Tippett, L.C. "Sampling and Standard Error." In James R. Newman (Ed.), *The World of Mathematics, Vol. 3*. New York, NY: Simon & Schuster, 1956.

Townsend, Robert. *Up the Organization*. New York, NY: Knopf, 1970.

Trading Strategies. Tucson, AZ: Futures Symposium International, 1984.

Tubbs. *Tubbs' Stock Market Correspondence Lessons*. (Chap. 13, Tape Reading.)

Turner, Dennis, and Stephen H. Blinn. *Trading Silver—Profitably*. New Rochelle, NY: Arlington House, 1975.

Vince, Ralph. *Portfolio Management Formulas*. New York, NY: John Wiley & Sons, 1990.

Von Neumann, John, and Oskar Morgenstern. *Theory of Games and Economic Behavior*. Princeton, NJ: Princeton University Press, 1953. (First published 1943).

Walker, Jeff. "What K-wave?" *Technical Analysis of Stocks & Commodities* (July 1990).

Wall, E. Marshall. "Rolling with the punches." *Futures* (July 1996).

Warren, Anthony. "A Mini Guide to Fourier Spectrum Analysis." *Technical Analysis of Stocks & Commodities* (January 1983).

———. "An Introduction to Maximum Entropy Method (MEM) Technical Analysis." *Technical Analysis of Stocks & Commodities* (February 1984).

———. "Fourier Analysis! In a Nutshell; Faster and Better." *Technical Analysis of Stocks & Commodities* (December 1983).

———. "Optimizing the Maximum Entropy Method." *Technical Analysis of Stocks & Commodities* (March/April 1984).

Warren, Anthony, and Jack K. Hutson. "Finite Impulse Response Filter." *Technical Analysis of Stocks & Commodities* (May 1983).

Warwick, Ben. *Event Trading.* Chicago, IL: Irwin, 1996.

Waters, James J., and Larry Williams. "Measuring Market Momentum." *Commodities Magazine* (October 1972).

Watling, T.F., and J. Morley. *Successful Commodity Futures Trading.* London: Business Books Ltd., 1974.

Watson, Donald S., and Mary A. Holman. *Price Theory and Its Uses, 4th ed.* (Boston, MA: Houghton Mifflin, 1977.

Waxenberg, Howard K. "Technical Analysis of Volume." *Technical Analysis of Stocks & Commodities* (March 1986).

Weiss, Eric. "Applying ARIMA Forecasts." *Technical Analysis of Stocks & Commodities* (May 1983).

———. "ARIMA Forecasting." *Technical Analysis of Stocks & Commodities* (January 1983).

Weymar, F.H. *The Dynamics of the World Cocoa Market.* Cambridge, MA: MIT Press, 1968.

White, Adam. "The Eight-Year Presidential Election Pattern." *Technical Analysis of Stocks & Commodities* (November 1994).

Wilder, J. Welles, Jr. *Chart Trading Workshop 1980.* Greensboro, NC: Trend Research, 1980.

———. *New Concepts in Technical Trading.* Greensboro, NC: Trend Research, 1978.

———. "Selection and Direction." In Perry J. Kaufman (Ed.), *Technical Analysis in Commodities.* New York, NY: John Wiley & Sons, 1980.

Williams, Bill. *Trading Chaos.* New York, NY: John Wiley & Sons, 1995.

Williams, Edward E., and M. Chapman Findlay III. *Investment Analysis.* Englewood Cliffs, NJ: Prentice-Hall, 1974.

Williams, J.D. *The Complete Strategyst.* New York, NY: McGraw-Hill, 1966.

Williams, Larry. "The Ultimate Oscillator." *Technical Analysis of Stocks & Commodities* (August 1985).

Williams, Larry, and Charles Lindsey. *The Trident System.* Thousand Oaks, CA: Lindsey, O'Brien, & Co., 1975. (A report).

Williams, Larry, and Michelle Noseworthy. "How Seasonal Influences Can Help You Trade Commodities." *Commodities Magazine* (October 1976).

Williams, Larry R. *How I Made One Million Dollars . . . Last Year . . . Trading Commodities.* Carmel Valley, CA: Conceptual Management, 1973.

Winski, Joseph N. "A Sure Thing?" *The Dow Jones Commodities Handbook 1977.* Princeton, NJ: Dow-Jones Books, 1977.

Working, Holbrook. "Test of a Theory Concerning Floor Trading on Commodity Exchanges." *Food Research Institute Studies, Vol. VII: 1967 Supplement.* Stanford, CA: Stanford University Press, 1967.

Wyckoff, Richard D. *Stock Market Technique, Number One.* New York, NY: Wyckoff, 1933.

———. *The Richard D. Wyckoff Method of Trading and Investing in Stocks.* Park Ridge, IL: Wyckoff Associates, Inc., 1936. (Originally 1931)

———. *Wall Street Ventures and Adventures Through Forty Years.* New York: NY Harper & Brothers, 1930.

Zieg, Kermit C., Jr., and Perry J. Kaufman. *Point and Figure Commodity Trading Techniques.* Larchmont, NY: Investors Intelligence, 1975.

Index